Martyrdom and Persecution in the Early Church

A Study of a Conflict from the Maccabees to Donatus

By W. H. C. FREND

James Clarke & Co. Ltd

James Clarke & Co. Ltd
PO Box 60
Cambridge
CB1 2NT

www.jamesclarke.co.uk
publishing@jamesclarke.co.uk

First published by Basil Blackwell, 1965
Corrected edition by James Clarke & Co. Ltd, 2008

ISBN: 978 0 227 17229 2

British Library Cataloguing in Publication Data
A catalogue record is available from the British Library

Contents

Preface

The original suggestion for this work came from the late Professor H. Last, Principal of Brasenose, in 1951. Last had for many years been interested in the problem of the Christians in the Roman Empire and in his articles in the *Journal of Roman Studies* and his eminent contribution to the *Reallexikon für Antike und Christentum* had demonstrated the continuity of Roman policy towards foreign cults of which Christianity was originally only one. My first aim was to revise and bring up to date E. G. Hardy's *Christianity and the Roman Government*, an excellent book, still offering a basis for any student to approach the subject even though first published in 1894. Difficulties, however, proved insurmountable. Apart from the mass of recent material which would have to be incorporated in footnotes, Hardy wrote as a Classical scholar in an age dominated by Classical studies, whereas my approach was more that of an historian, tending to attribute as much importance to the attitude of the Christians themselves and the influence of Christian doctrine as sources of conflict, as the outlook of the Roman authorities and the legal system of the Roman Empire. A new outline history, widening Hardy's scope to cover as far as possible all the factors, religious, social and economic, which contributed to the conflict between the Church and the Roman Empire in the first three centuries A.D. was necessary.

In this work I have been encouraged by Mr. G. E. M. de Ste. Croix, Fellow of New College, to whom I am especially indebted for information about voluntary martyrdom in Late Judaism and the primitive Church, and whose article 'Why were the Early Christians Persecuted?', *Past and Present*, 26, November 1963, 6–38, I have been able to use before going to press. I have had the advantage of a year's research through the S. A. Cook Bye-Fellowship at Gonville and Caius College, Cambridge, 1952–53, which enabled me to do some of the spadework before full-time

University and College teaching restricted time available for research and writing. I am grateful also to my colleagues, Rev. Professor C. F. D. Moule and Rev. J. A. Emerton for their help and advice on Chapters ii and iii, to Prof. C. O. Brink for reading the proofs of Chapter iv, and to Mr. G. T. Griffith for reading Chapter v, Dr. Ernst Bammel for help on Chapters vi and vii, and Rev. Professor G. W. H. Lampe for advice on Chapter xiii. Finally, I would like to acknowledge with gratitude the help I have received from Miss M. Webb, Mrs. Moira Milne, Mrs. Rosemary Kelly and Mrs. Pat Rignold for their endless patience in typing a manuscript which appeared in all sorts of forms and at all times. I am also grateful to Mr. Schollick and Blackwells for help and advice in preparing the manuscript for publication, and to my wife for her patience and her aid in reading proofs and compiling an index.

W. H. C. Frend

Gonville and Caius College, Cambridge
28 November 1963

Preface to Reprinted Edition

The reprinted edition by Baker Book House has given me the opportunity to correct a number of misprints and minor errors, most of which were pointed out to me by Mr. G. E. M. de Ste Croix, Fellow of New College, Oxford, whose help I acknowledge gratefully. I have also corrected a mistake on page 354, pointed out to me by Mr. Haddon Willmer, late of Emmanuel College, Cambridge.

W. H. C. Frend

Glasgow University
September 1980

Introduction

The story of the successful Christian revolution against the Roman Empire has often been told. In their hour of triumph in the fourth century Christian writers and preachers looked back to the persecutions as the heroic age of the Church. Few doubted the providential nature of its victory. The 'ten persecutions' had been prefigured in the Bible by the ten plagues of Egypt or by the ten horns of the beast in the Apocalypse, and the Roman emperors and their officials were painted in colours befitting the servants of Antichrist.[1] The confessors, according to the brief description of Sulpicius Severus, *circa* 380, had rushed into battle desiring martyrdom with the same eagerness as clerics of his day engaged in the pursuit of bishoprics.[2] The saga of their deeds, especially in the Great Persecution under Diocletian and Galerius sustained the Eastern Churches through their struggles against Islam. Among the last written remains even of the Church in Nubia were homilies on the legend of St. Mercurius and God's judgment on Julian the Apostate. These littered the floor of the great church at Q'asr Ibrim, silent and deserted since the fourteenth century.[3] In the West, the persecutions formed an essential part in a Providential philosophy of history represented by Lactantius and Paulus Orosius which influenced European political thought throughout the Middle Ages. The triumph of the Church over the Empire in the fourth century guaranteed its victory in later but still barbarous days.

In view of the amount of hagiographical and devotional literature which grew up around the persecutions it would have been astonishing if these had not formed a major theme for research since the Reformation. On the one hand, the question could be asked how far Divine Providence used the sufferings of the Christians to vindicate the truth of the Gospel message, and did not the discomfiture of Satan in one period by the blood of the Church's martyrs point to the discomfiture of the Reformers by the same means? On the other hand, it might be argued that the spread of Christianity in the Roman Empire was explicable on historical grounds to which the rules of critical study could be applied. Were the martyrs as few as H. Dodwell suggested in his pioneer study 'De Paucitate Martyrum' (*Dissertationes Cyprianicae*), Oxford, 1684, Dissertatio xi, or were they as numerous as the recent work of a Jesuit scholar Fr. L. Hertling has claimed?[4] Or does, perhaps, the number of authentic martyrs oscillate between those included in Dom Ruinart's *Acta Primorum Martyrum sincera et selecta*, Amsterdam, 1713, and those selected by Knopf and Krüger in their *Ausgewählte Märtyrerakten*, Tübingen, 1929?

The existence, however, of rival ecclesiastical viewpoints has if anything, spurred on research. Today, Le Nain de Tillemont's massive *Mémoires pour servir de l'histoire ecclesiastiques des six premiers siècles* (16 volumes, 1693–1712) remain a valuable starting-point, especially for work on the Great Persecution. In Mosheim's first volume of *Ecclesiastical History* (Eng. tr. A. Maclaine, Dublin, 1767) the basic reasons for the unpopularity of the Christians in the Roman Empire have been given as they might be given today, 'the abhorrence felt by the Christians for the other religions of the Empire', while 'the simplicity of their worship' made them appear 'as a sort of Atheist, and by the Roman laws those who were chargeable with atheism were declared pests of human society' (pp. 48–9). This is perfectly true. Atheism was the real, damning charge against the Christians. Later in the century, Gibbon's sixteenth chapter of the *Decline and Fall* remains one of the finest summaries of the history of the relations between the primitive Church and the Empire ever written. In the sentence 'The Jews were a people which followed, the Christians a sect which deserted the religion of their fathers', Gibbon puts his finger on the central weakness of the Christian position in the first three centuries.

The growth of the study of the Church as an historical move-ment in the latter part of the nineteenth century caused less advance in this aspect of Church history than in many others. Too much time was spent in attempting to define the exact legal situation of the Christians and the precise nature of the charges levelled against them. Studies became hopelessly bogged down as one source after another was subjected to searching examinations in detail by the disciples and the opponents of Mommsen and Harnack. On the other hand, the school of French Roman Catholic ecclesiastical historians, represented by Aubé, Allard and Batiffol in their zeal to controvert the German Protestants were too often inclined to accept the *Acta Martyrum* as they stood, and thereby to turn Church history into pious romance.

In all these controversies of the past the major limiting factor has been the nature of the evidence. Quite apart from coming to terms with Eusebius, the historian of the early Church has been confronted by two serious obstacles. His study of the whole range of Jewish apocrypha and pseudepigrapha and of the New Testament and sub-apostolic literature has been obstructed by the lack of a firm chronological framework in which to place these works. The chronological footnote it has been necessary to write (see below, p. 72 note 70) regarding for instance, iv Maccabees, is an instructive commentary on the situation. It has been a case of every historian and every commentator for himself. It must, however, be perfectly obvious that on the accurate dating of these documents depends the solution of many of the problems connected with the organization and mission of the primitive Church. If iv Maccabees proved to be a work of an Alexandrian Jew of the second century A.D., rather than of an Antiochene Jew contemporary with Jesus its value as one of the sources of inspiration of Christian *Acta Martyrum* would have to be re-assessed, and so also, the historian's view of the relations between the Jewish and Christian synagogues in the first two centuries. Similar problems are raised by the dating of Revelation, the Pastoral Epistles, i and ii Peter, and the various Jewish or Jewish-Christian apocryphal narratives.

Even more difficult, however, has been a rational assessment of the *Acta Martyrum*. Hundreds of these *Acta* were composed in the fourth and fifth centuries in honour of martyrs the anniversaries of whose deaths were celebrated in the Churches.[5] Each of the great provincial sees had its list of martyrs who were to be honoured by a eucharist and sermon which recorded for edification the circumstances of their deaths.[6] The Martyrology of Carthage contained no less than eighty-six entries, for each of which some record of arrest, trial and execution of the saint would have been compiled. Some of these, such as Augustine's sermons on St.

Perpetua and her companions, Crispina of Thagora, or on the
Forty Martyrs, have survived, and the historian's task is to decide
whether any kernel of truth underlies these stereotyped and florid
discourses. The task is facilitated somewhat by the existence
of the contemporary or near-contemporary *Acta* on which
Eusebius drew, and others acknowledged to be contemporary such as the *Acta Scillitanorum* and *Acta Perpetuae*, or by
Cyprian's letters written during the persecutions of Decius and
Valerian, all of which serve as a check on the later versions of
similar events. Despite the work, however, of H. Delehaye and
the Bollandists[7] in attempting to apply rules for assessment and
categories of verisimilitude to each *Acta Martyrum*, the historian
has still to decide each case for himself. On his verdict for instance,
on the value of the *Acta Crispinae* may depend his attitude on the
question whether the Fourth Edict in the Great Persecution was
ever enforced in the West, or not. Was the proconsul's command
that the hair of the accused be shaved the result of dark imaginings
by an hagiographer, or was it intended as a final warning to
Crispina, designed to shame her into surrender before she compelled the imposition of the death-penalty for refusal to sacrifice
as commanded? In such cases, one has to search for analogies,
weigh up probabilities and make up one's own mind. Similarly,
the *Acts of Trypho* may contain some valuable evidence about the
Decian persecution in Rome despite its gross errors in its narrative
of the reigns of Gordian and Philip with which it opens. Each
source has required and still requires detailed study.

These problems of evidence remain and will continue to make
the study of the persecutions a complicated one. Since the turn
of the century, however, the historian has received constant and
continuous help from the archaeologist. The latter, while not
answering his questions in detail, has added a new dimension to
his research. Christianity came up from below. It influenced in
the main the lower orders of Greco-Roman society, people who
have left little mark on the Classical literature of the time, but
whose remains in the form of cemeteries, burial inscriptions and
buildings, have been discovered by the archaeologists. To the
great finds, like the Dead Sea scrolls, which have contributed to
the establishment of a firm chronology for apocalyptic literature,
one must add the constant accumulation of humbler objects

enabling the historian to trace better the progress of the Christian communities and their penetration of pagan society. The *Antike und Christentum* school on the Continent has made possible a new assessment of the first four centuries of Christian history. The persecutions and the whole field of Church-State relations in this period have become ripe for re-examination.

In this work, while not neglecting the legal and administrative problems raised by the early Christians in the Roman Empire, I have attempted to study the rise of Christianity as a social movement and made full use wherever possible of the evidence of archaeology. The canvas has had to be a wide one. In point of time, the Maccabean revolt against Hellenism whether Syrian or Jewish, was the obvious beginning. Here was the first great revolutionary outbreak against what became the values of the Greco-Roman world. From then on, I have traced the successive phases of the triangular struggle which developed between that world on the one hand, the Jews and Christians who were prepared at a price to work with it, and the irreconcilables on the other. The domination of Western theology by the last-named has been one of the most important events in European history. The psychology of the Two Cities, of the gathered Church with its martyrs and saints, and its hope of Millennial triumph have sustained some of Western Christianity's greatest epics as well as some of its greatest inhumanities and tragedies. For Christian optimism, for the hope of salvation for all, and for the reconciliation of rival political and social systems as differing aspects of the Eternal Word of God, one must turn to Philo and to the Alexandrian School of Christian theology. To strike a balance between these forces against the background of the Roman Imperial scene is the object of 'From the Maccabees to Donatus'.

NOTES

[1] See J. Vogt, 'Die Zählung der Christenverfolgung–im römischen Reich', *La Parola del Passato*, ix, 1954, 5–15.

[2] Sulpicius Severus, *Chronicon* (ed. C. Halm, *CSEL.*, i) ii.32.4, 'quippe certatim gloriosa in certamina ruebatur multoque avidius tum martyria gloriosis mortibus quaerebantur quam nunc episcopatus pravis ambitionibus appetuntur'.

³ Found by Rev. Professor J. M. Plumley and the writer during their excavation of the church at Q'asr Ibrim (Primis) in Nubia. To be published, under the auspices of the Egypt Exploration Society.

⁴ L. Hertling, 'Die Zahl der Märtyrer bis 313', *Gregorianum* xxv, 1944, 103–29. 100,000 executions 'possible'.

⁵ Note Augustine's warning to his flock 'that these Acta should not be placed on the same level as Scripture 'Nec scriptura ista canonica est'. *De Natura et Origine Animae* 1.10 (*CSEL.*, lx, 312).

⁶ A useful work on the Martyrologies is R. Aigren, *L'hagiographie, ses sources, ses méthodes, son histoire*, Paris, 1953, and see also, H. Lietzmann (ed.), *Die drei ältesten Martyrologien* (Kleine Texte für theologische und philologische Vorlesungen und Übungen = Kleine Texte) ii, Bonn, 1911. Lists the *Depositiones* of the Chronograph of 354, the Carthage Martyrology and the Syrian Martyrology. The classic still remains H. Achelis, 'Die Martyrologien, ihre Geschichte und ihr Wert', *Abhandlungen Göttingen*, iii, 1900.

⁷ H. Delehaye, *Les Passions des Martyrs et les Genres littéraires*, Brussels, 1921 (a fundamental study).

Acknowledgments

This study has not involved many serious textual problems and I have generally, therefore, used standard translations of Classical and Patristic texts. I would like to acknowledge with gratitude the following: The syndics of the Cambridge University Press for permission to reproduce N. H. Baynes's translation of the Edict of Galerius and the Edict of Milan; to Messrs. Heinemann for permission to reproduce T. R. Glover's translation of Tertullian's *De Spectaculis*, Chapter 30, and extracts from the correspondence of Dionysius of Alexandria translated by J. E. L. Oulton; and to S.P.C.K. for the use of J. Stevenson's translation of a *libellus* of the Decian persecution and other material printed in *A New Eusebius*.

Abbreviations

i. *Original texts*

CIG.	Corpus Inscriptionum Graecarum, Berlin, 1828–77.
CIJ.	Corpus Inscriptionum Judaicarum (ed. J. B. Frey, Vatican City, 1936 and 1952).
CIL.	Corpus Inscriptionum Latinarum, Berlin, 1862–.
C.J.	Codex Justinianus, ed., P. Krueger, Berlin, 1877.
CSEL.	Corpus Scriptorum ecclesiasticorum latinorum (Vienna, 1866–).
FIRA.	Fontes Iuris Romani ante-Iustiniani (ed. S. Riccobono and others, Florence, 1940, 1941, 1943).
GCS.	Die griechischen christlichen Schriftsteller der ersten Jahrhunderte, Leipzig, Berlin, 1897–.
H.E.	Eusebius, *Historia Ecclesiastica* (Books I–V, ed. Kirsopp Lake; VI–X, ed. J. E. L. Oulton, published in the Loeb Classical Library).
IGLS.	Inscriptions grecques et latines de la Syrie, ed. L. Jalabert and R. Mouterde, Paris, 1929–.
I.G.R.R.	Inscriptiones Graecae ad res romanas pertinentes, Paris, 1891.
ILCV.	Inscriptiones latinae christianae veteres, ed. E. Diehl/J. Moreau, Berlin, 1961.
ILS.	Inscriptiones latinae selectae, ed. H. Dessau, Berlin, 3 vols. 1892–1916.
IRT.	Inscriptions of Roman Tripolitania, ed. J. M. Reynolds and J. Ward Perkins, Rome and London, 1952.
M.A.M.A.	Monumenta antiqua Minoris Asiae, vols i–viii (Publications of the American Society for Archaeological Research), Manchester, 1928–62.
OGI.	Orientis Graecae Inscriptiones selectae, ed. W. Dittenberger, Leipzig, 1903.

Papyri

BGU.   Aegyptische Urkunden aus den staatlichen Museen zu Berlin; griechische Urkunden, Berlin, 1892–1937.

P.Oxy.   The Oxyrhynchus Papyri (ed. B. P. Grenfell, A. S. Hunt and their successors, 1898–).

P.S.I.   Papiri greci e latini (ed. G. Vitelli, M. Norsa and others, Florence, 1912–).

P.G.   Patrologia Graeco-Latina, ed. J.-P. Migne, Paris, 1857–1934.

P.L.   Patrologia Latina, ed. J.-P. Migne, Paris, 1843–1890.

P.O.   Patrologia Orientalis, ed. Graffin-Nau, Paris, 1907–.

SHA.   Scriptores Historiae Augustae, ed. E. Hohl, Leipzig, 1955.

ii. *Modern works and translations*

A.B.   Analecta Bollandiana (publ. Société des Bollandistes,) Brussels, 1882–.

A.B.A.W.   Abhandlungen der preussischen Akademie der Wissenschaften zu Berlin.

Abhandlungen Abhandlungen der königlichen Gesellschaft der *Göttingen* Wissenschaften zu Göttingen, Phil. Hist. Klasse. Göttingen.

A.C.   Antike und Christentum, Münster, 1929–. (Lexikon, 1950–.)

AJA.   American Journal of Archaeology, Baltimore, 1885–.

AJT.   American Journal of Theology, Chicago, 1897–1920.

A-N.C.L.   Ante-Nicene Christian Library, Edinburgh.

BSA.   The Annual of the British School of Archaeology at Athens.

CAH.   Cambridge Ancient History.

CP.   Classical Philology, Chicago, 1906–.

CR.   Classical Review.

CQ.   Classical Quarterly.

CQR.   Church Quarterly Review.

CRAI.   Comptes rendus de l'Académie des Inscriptions, Paris, 1857–.

DACL.	Dictionnaire d'Archéologie chrétienne et de Liturgie (ed. F. Cabrol and H. Leclercq, Paris, 1903–50).
D.C.B.	Dictionary of Christian Biography.
EHR.	English Historical Review.
Göttingen Nachrichten	Nachrichten von der Akademie der Wissenschaften zu Göttingen, 1843–.
HTR.	Harvard Theological Review, New York, 1908–.
I.C.C.	International Critical Commentary, Edinburgh.
JAC.	Jahrbuch für Antike und Christentum, Münster, 1958–.
JBAA.	Journal of the British Archaeological Association.
JBL.	Journal of Biblical Literature, Boston, 1881–.
J.E.	Jewish Encyclopaedia, New York/London, 1901.
JEA.	Journal of Egyptian Archaeology.
JEH.	Journal of Ecclesiastical History.
J.O.A.I.	Jahreshefte des oesterreichischen archaeologischen Institutes in Wien, Vienna, 1898–.
JQR.	Jewish Quarterly Review, Philadelphia, 1888–.
JRS.	Journal of Roman Studies.
JTS.	Journal of Theological Studies.
K.W.	G. Kittel, Theologisches Wörterbuch zum Neuen Testament, Stuttgart, 1933–.
Mélanges	Mélanges d'archéologie et d'histoire de l'Ecole française de Rome, Paris, 1881–.
MGH.	Monumenta Germaniae Historia, Berlin, 1877–.
NTS.	New Testament Studies.
PBSR.	Papers of the British School at Rome.
PW.	Pauly-Wissowa, Realencyclopädie für Altertums-Wissenschaft, Stuttgart, 1894–.
R.B.	Revue Biblique, Paris, 1892–.
R.E.	Realencyclopädie für protestantische Theologie und Kirche, ed. A. Hauck, Leipzig, 1896–1913.
RHE.	Revue d'histoire ecclésiastique, Louvain, 1900–.
R.H.R.	Revue de l'histoire des religions (Annales du Musée Guimet), Paris, 1880–.
R.H.L.R.	Revue de l'histoire et de littérature religieuses, Paris, 1896–1922.
RSR.	Recherches de Science religieuse, Paris, 1910–.

SBAW.   Sitzungsberichte der (königlichen) preussischen Akademie der Wissenschaften, Ph. Hist. Kl., Berlin, 1882–.

SHAW.   Sitzungsberichte der Heidelberger Akademie der Wissenschaften, Ph. Hist. Kl., 1909–.

SJT.   Scottish Journal of Theology, Edinburgh, 1947–.

T.U.   Texte und Untersuchungen zur Geschichte der altchristlichen Literatur, Leipzig, 1882–.

ZATW.   Zeitschrift für die alttestamentliche Wissenschaft, Giessen, 1881–.

ZNTW.   Zeitschrift für die neutestamentliche Wissenschaft, Giessen, 1900–.

Z. für K.G.   Zeitschrift für Kirchengeschichte, Gotha, 1877–.

CHAPTER ONE

The Martyrs of Lyons

IN the summer of 177 there took place at Lyons one of the most terrible dramas in the history of the early Church. The story of the persecution is preserved in Eusebius, *Ecclesiastical History*, Book v, Chs. 1–3, from an account sent to the Churches of Asia and Phrygia by an anonymous survivor of the Gallic community.[1] For simplicity, sincerity and for the sheer horror of the events it describes it is unmatched in the annals of Christian antiquity. The respective outlooks of the three parties to the tragedy, the populace, the provincial administration and the Christians themselves are revealed with uncompromising clearness.

The account, however, is worth attention not only as a story of heroism. A careful study of its detail throws light on some of the sources of the early Christian *Acta Martyrum*. It tells us something also of the character of the south Gallic Church and the beliefs of its members, especially their ideas regarding martyrdom. On the other hand, the writer has left a graphic impression of the motives of the pagan population bent on the destruction of the Christian community. There is evidence too, of the official policy of the Empire towards the Church. The account of the martyrdom at Lyons thus provides a starting-point for the study of the clash of cultures that divided the Ancient World, between the theocracy of the Jews and Christians and the equally universal claims of the Greco-Roman state. In this clash, martyrdom and persecution are the abiding features.

Though the persecution broke out in Lyons, there were Christian communities in both the Gallic cities of Lyons and Vienne. Indeed, it may have been from Vienne that the account of the persecution was written.[2] The two Churches were founded perhaps only shortly beforehand, and their founders may have been among those arrested,[3] but how they were related to each other and organized is uncertain. Here at the outset of our study we are confronted by a problem of detail, typical of the incomplete evidence with which the historian of the early Church is confronted at every turn. Did the two Churches form a single ecclesiastical diocese under one bishop, or were they separate, with Vienne administered by its own bishop?[4] On the whole, the balance of probability is that at this period there was one organization which included both Churches. Pothinus and Irenaeus were both bishops of Lyons,[5] and Eusebius adds this detail about Irenaeus' responsibilities. In enumerating letters from bishops which were being written about A.D. 195 on the Easter controversy, he mentions one from Irenaeus 'καὶ τῶν κατὰ Γαλλίαν δὲ παροικιῶν ἃς 'Ειρηναῖος ἐπεσκόπει, evidently the result of consultation among the various Gallic Churches.[6] This implies that Irenaeus was bishop of a number of communities, and Vienne, a bare twenty miles downstream from Lyons, may have been one of these. But there are objections. Vienne was in Gallia Narbonnensis, and there was intense rivalry between the two cities. A century or so before it had come to civil war between them[7] and in 196–97 Lyons was to be held by Clodius Albinus while Vienne supported Severus. As a contemporary writer points out, the wars between rival cities were a feature of this period.[8] Even if the Christians were untouched by civic patriotism, their liturgical needs might have demanded the presence of a bishop of Vienne. To judge, however, from the text of the letter, Sanctus the deacon was probably in charge of the community there. He is referred to as 'τὸν διάκονον ἀπὸ βιέννης', a title not easy to reconcile with the existence of other clergy, including other deacons, at Vienne.[9] He seems, however, to have been associated very closely with Lyons, and it was apparently at Lyons that he was arrested.[10]

Yet, however one looks at the evidence, there is no doubt that the Gallic Churches were in a rudimentary stage of development. In particular, and there seems to be no point in denying this,[11] Greek influences still predominated. Not only was the letter sent to the Churches in Asia Minor written in Greek, but any statements spoken in Latin were specially noted.[12] A reading of Eusebius and of the names of the martyrs preserved in the Martyrology of Jerome (early fifth-century) and the later, ninth-century Martyrology of Ado shows that the leaders and about half of the forty-eight known martyrs were probably

Asiatics.[13] Pothinus, the aged bishop is likely to have been himself an immigrant,[14] his senior presbyter and famous successor, Irenaeus had been brought up in Smyrna.[15] Attalus, described as a 'pillar of the Church' at Vienne was a Roman citizen from Pergamum.[16] Alexander, another prominent Christian at Lyons was a physician who had emigrated from Phrygia.[17] The name Vettius Epagathus suggests a Greek or Asiatic freedman, and among the more humble Christians, Biblis, Elpis, Ponticus and Alcibiades are names that indicate Greek or Asiatic origins. The spiritual home of the two Churches was Asia Minor, for it was to the Churches of the provinces of Asia and Phrygia more than a thousand miles away that they addressed themselves in their hour of need. Here were 'the brethren who had the same faith and hope of redemption'.[18] Their links with these provinces must have been strong indeed.

There is a further piece of evidence which scholars have tended to overlook. Among the Gallic Christians of this period, there was a considerable non-orthodox element. Irenaeus was not writing his *Adversus Haereses* in *circa* A.D. 185 without reference to his own surroundings. From his description of the followers of the Gnostic teacher Marcus, it is quite clear that this heretic and his followers were active both in Asia Minor and among the Christians in the Rhone valley. 'Such are the words and deeds', he concludes, 'by which in our own district of the Rhone, they have deluded many women, who have their consciences seared as with a hot iron'.[19] On the other hand, Irenaeus shows from personal knowledge that Marcus' doctrines were being propagated in the province of Asia as well. He can recount the detailed story of the fall of the wife of a deacon there, and he speaks of the deacon as though he were an acquaintance.[20]

On the other hand, if the Greek/Asiatic element predominated in the Gallic Churches, and indeed left its mark on their liturgy two centuries later,[21] it was not exclusive. Perhaps, had it been more so, the 'new and strange worship' associated with the Christians might have been less unpopular.[22] We have another well-known statement from Irenaeus, also from *Adversus Haereses*, that he used Celtic to spread the Gospel in Gaul.[23] The success which he and other evangelists gained is shown by the numbers of men and women with Romano-Gallic names among the

Christians. Sanctus, the deacon from Vienne, is the senior among those recorded, and he is stated to have spoken in Latin.[24] Maturus, the convert who suffers with him, also may have been of Romano-Gallic origin. Blandina may have been a native Gaul too, though she is always reported as speaking in Greek. It must be noted, however, that whatever use may have been made of Celtic or Latin for preaching, the Gallic Church at this time does not seem to have thought it worth while to translate the Bible into either language, the only sure way of naturalizing Greek-speaking Christianity in a Latin and Celtic province.

Other facts too, suggest the special, immigrant character of the Gallic Churches at this period, and is consistent with Christianity having been introduced via the trade route from the province of Asia to Marseille and the valley of the Rhone *circa* 150–160.[25] Contemporary pagan writers insist that the main body of Christians in the second and early third centuries were made up of 'illiterates and the dregs of the population', the outcasts from Greco-Roman civilization.[26] So far as Lyons and Vienne are concerned, however, this was not true. The Christians there had their own slaves, and these did not in all cases share the religion of their masters.[27] They included members of the liberal professions, such as physicians and advocates,[28] men who were well known and esteemed in what at this time may have been the greatest city in the western provinces of the Empire. The Gnostic heretics too, at Lyons were far from poor. Irenaeus states that Marcus' disciples were 'finely dressed' and 'rich women', and they could support elaborate and expensive ceremonies. There seems to be no doubt that these Gnostics included a number of leisured and well-provided individuals.[29] The Christians too, show a certain disdain in the course of their account of their sufferings for 'the wild and barbarous tribes' among whom they lived.[30] It looks as though they felt cut off from them through their higher culture as well as by their religion.

The evidence is consistent with the Christians in the Rhone valley representing the beliefs of members of immigrant, originally trading communities, such as were to be found in many of the large centres of the West. The Italian merchants who settled in Cirta in the second century B.C.[31] and perhaps in London in the first century A.D.,[32] or the Syrians in the Rhineland and elsewhere in the fourth century[33] are examples. The Rhone valley had been the scene of interchanges with the eastern Mediterranean peoples from Mycenaean times onwards and thither came merchants from the whole Mediterranean area. The inscription from Marseille referring to the probable martydom of Volusianus, son of Eutyches, and Fortunatus can hardly be later than second century, and this with the account of the Lyons martyrs, is the earliest evidence for Christianity in Gaul.[34] At Lyons and Vienne the foreigners seem to have come mainly from Asia and Phrygia, and like other similar communities they brought their religions with them, among which was Christianity.[35] They had prospered, some of them had learnt Latin[36] and taken firm roots in Lyons; they had begun to be influential—and one way or another they had aroused the deep-seated hatred of the mass of the population.

How the trouble started we do not know. Neither the authors of the massacre nor the immediate pretext are mentioned, and it has been suggested with some degree of likelihood that the real villains may have been the chief citizens of Lugdunum. In 176 (or early in 177) the Emperor and the Senate had co-operated in a measure designed to relieve the richer landowners of the provinces of some of the expenses of gladiatorial games, by allowing them to acquire victims in the form of condemned criminals from the imperial procurators at the cost of six *aurei* per head, or one-tenth of the price of hiring a gladiator 5th Class with proportionate savings for the higher grades.[37] In the proceedings in the Senate-House the *porte-parole* of the Senators was a Gallic nobleman who in the style of later politicians praised the measure as 'a step in the right direction' and made a specific reference to the use in his country of *trinqui*, 'who because of an ancient custom of sacred ritual are eagerly awaited in the cities of the most splendid Gallic provinces'.[38] Who these *trinqui* were is uncertain, but it is difficult not to imagine from what was about to happen that the Christians lay ready to hand to fulfil the latter's sacrificial role. The temptation of the priests of the Council of the Gauls to rid themselves of a largely alien and latently hostile group and at the same time to boost their own popularity and save their pockets may have proved too strong to resist.

At any rate during the early summer of 177, feeling in Lyons gradually seethed up against the Christians.[39] First, they were subjected to a series of social and semi-religious sanctions as though they were polluted persons.[40] The baths and the market places were banned to them, and finally they were excluded from all public places, that is to say, from every locality which was under the protection of the city's tutelary gods whose worship their very presence violated.[41] Then, at a moment when the provincial governor was away from the city, the mob broke loose. Christians were hounded out and attacked openly. They were treated as public enemies, assaulted, beaten and stoned.[42] Finally, they were dragged into the Forum on the orders of the city's magistrates (*duumviri*) and the tribune of the XIII *Cohors Urbana* which formed the garrison of Lyons.[43] They were accused, and after confessing to being Christians, flung into prison to await the governor's return.[44]

The latter, the *legatus pro praetore* of the province of Lugdunensis readily took the line of least resistance. At the first hearings, an influential Christian, Vettius Epagathus, protested and was promptly howled down by those around the governor's tribunal.[45] He was asked whether he himself was a Christian. He confessed, and was committed to prison with the others. Then there began a general search for Christians which included a number from Vienne.[46] How this happened is not at all certain, as Vienne was outside the *legatus'* jurisdiction. On the other hand, at Lyons the *legatus* had jurisdiction over every criminal found in his province regardless of origin. The only obvious explanation is that Sanctus and his companions from Vienne were visiting Lyons at the time.[47] Day by day, new victims, the most zealous members of the two Churches, were arrested.[48] From this, it seems that Trajan's directive to Pliny in 112, that Christians should not be sought out, was no longer being observed fully everywhere.[49]

The governor now ordered a public trial of the Christians, and, it may be assumed at this stage wrote informing the Emperor Marcus Aurelius of what was happening[50] and asking what was to be done about the Roman citizens among them. As Marcus was campaigning on the Danube at the time a considerable delay was likely. While there is no evidence for a sacrifice test being imposed, furious and prolonged efforts were made meantime by the authorities to secure recantations.[51] In addition, a procedure was adopted which was permissible in charges of treason only.[52] Pagan slaves belonging to the prisoners were arrested and tortured in order to secure admissions from them that their masters had also indulged in incest and cannibalism—Thyestian feasts and Oedipean intercourse.[53] With a certain amount of prompting from the soldiers some made the desired statements. Meantime a number, the letter says about ten, of those arrested signified a willingness to recant, but evidently the slaves' admissions were held to implicate them in criminal charges, including murder and vice, and they were not released.[54] The criminal charges were angrily denied by the Christians, but by now the populace was thoroughly aroused. For many of the pagans these revelations confirmed their worst suspicions. Popular rage knew no bounds, and the few moderate-minded individuals who had previously tried to protect their Christian friends felt themselves deceived and let matters take their course.[55]

The examinations went on. Though admission to being a Christian was sufficient to convict, the procedure seems to have been extraordinarily long drawn out. Every artifice, and threat was employed, and horrible tortures were applied in order either to break the will of the Christians, or to kill them without the necessity of passing a judicial sentence.[56] The reason for wishing to avoid this is obscure, but the evidence that the authorities at Lyons wanted to avoid the actual promulgation of sentences is clear enough. Some of the martyrs refused, however, to give as much as their names to their torturers. Of Sanctus it was said 'that he did not even tell his own name, or the race, or the city whence he was, but to all questions answered in Latin, "I am a Christian". This he said for name and city and race and for everything else, and the heathen heard no other sound from him'.[57] To such exasperating behaviour the authorities could do little but apply repeated tortures. In addition, they confined their victims in inhuman conditions in prison, and there in the dank and dark confines thinned out their numbers by maltreatment and strangulation.[58] Among those who perished thus was Bishop Pothinus.[59]

At length, perhaps on 2 June,[60] the date of the commemoration of the martyrs in the Martyrology of Jerome, the first batch of Christians was sent to the amphitheatre. Sanctus, Maturus, Blandina and Attalus were led forth to fight the beasts, the authorities having set aside a special day for the spectacle. Sanctus and Maturus perished. Blandina, terribly tortured though she was, nevertheless survived, the animals refusing to touch her.[61] Suddenly, an unexpected incident brought a respite. It was Attalus' turn. He was, we are told, 'loudly called for'. He was led round the amphitheatre preceded by a placard on which had been inscribed in Latin, 'This is Attalus the Christian'.[62] He was greeted with shouts of execration. This time, however, the populace was to be cheated of their prey. Someone told the governor he was a Roman citizen. To send him to the beasts was therefore illegal.[63] The governor hesitated. Evidently, having already written to the Emperor he decided to await instructions and returned the survivors to prison. It was in this period of respite probably that the echoes of Montanism reached the prisoners from Phrygia: and Irenaeus, who somehow had escaped arrest, was charged with conveying their views to Bishop Eleutherus at Rome.[64]

In due course, Marcus Aurelius' answer arrived. In essentials it represented a continuation of the policy of Trajan sixty years earlier.[65] Those who persisted in confessing to Christianity were to be executed. The Roman citizens among them were to be beheaded, the remainder delivered to the beasts. Those who recanted were to be freed.[66] There was, it appears, no reference to the continued detention of those accused of criminal charges, but on the other hand, there was no explicit castigation of informers. The punishments as well as the procedure suggest that damage to the interests of the state by the activities of the Christians was in the forefront of the Emperor's mind.[67]

By now 1 August was approaching. It had been on this day in 12 B.C. that the huge altar to Rome and Augustus had been set up in front of a magnificent temple on the left bank of the Rhone across the river from Lugdunum. It was here on federal territory outside the boundaries of the city that representatives of the sixty Gallic *civitates* from Belgica, Aquitania and Lugdunensis met annually to celebrate the cult of Rome and Augustus and to discuss their common affairs. There was the amphitheatre in which they watched games and gladiatorial shows,[68] and the heavy cost of these shows made the concession granted by Marcus Aurelius the year before relevant. The imprisoned Christians could be substituted for gladiators, and the writer of the martyrs' letter says that they were.[69]

Meantime the governor opened a new set of hearings mainly for the benefit of the confessors who were Roman citizens. A final effort was made to secure recantations. Those, however, who had confessed from the start remained adamant, and by now their example had influenced the waverers.[70] The majority of these withdrew their recantations. The governor examined them individually in the hope of being able to make some abjure in public, but in nearly all cases he was disappointed.[71] It was at this point that a Phrygian physician named Alexander, who had hitherto escaped the net was arrested. He had come to the hearings and openly encouraged those brought before the governor to stand fast in their confession. Finally, the governor ordered all those who appeared to be Roman citizens to be beheaded and the remainder, including Alexander, to be sent to the beasts. Illegally, but probably to court popularity, he allowed the hated Attalus to be committed to the amphitheatre as well.[72] The terrible scenes described in Eusebius followed. The last to die were the heroic slave, Blandina and the fifteen-year-old youth Ponticus. The bodies of the victims were left unburied, carefully guarded by troops, then burnt, and after six days the remains cast into the Rhone.[73] The survivors were left to write the immortal story to their mother Churches on the other side of the Hellenistic world.

The vivid narrative of the survivors' letter tells us much about the main actors in this tragedy. First, as always in the second and early third centuries, there is popular hatred, the prime mover of anti-Christian outbreaks.[74] The intense fury of the people and their fear that somehow or other the Christians might triumph over their gods, stands out on every page of the confessors' story. Not even the death of the Christians was sufficient. At all costs their claim to immortality must be shown to be vain. This is clearly expressed in a statement put into the mouth of pagans to justify the treatment of the bodies of the victims, 'As they said, "that they might not even have any hope of resurrection",' through their religion.[75] There seems to be little doubt that fear of the violation of the tutelary gods through execrable and revolutionary rites provided the final emotional impulse towards persecution. The condign punishment of the Christians was regarded as a necessary vindication of the gods[76] and indeed, a form of human sacrifice to them.[77] There was a sense of triumph in the fact that the Christian God did not come to their aid. The 'Thyestian feasts' and 'Oedipian intercourse' of which the Christians were accused were associated in the popular mind with conspiratorial oaths and with black magic, abominable to God and man.[78] Few seem to have had any doubt that the Christians were in fact cannibals.[79] Hence, the final punishment, the refusal of burial—for even those guilty of *maiestas* were not generally denied decent burial.[80] Even so, and this heightens the tragedy, popular hatred was tempered by a few flashes of human sympathy for the victims. Of Blandina, for instance, those who watched her first tortures in the amphitheatre are reported to have said 'that never among them had a woman suffered so much for so long'.[81] When it was all over, others could ask, half in pity, 'Where is their god, and what good to them was their worship which they preferred beyond their lives?' Sometimes such thoughts proved to be the first stirrings towards acceptance of the Christian faith. But in Gaul it was to be a long time before this happened.

At this period Romano-Gallic paganism was still intellectually and materially in the ascendant. It was the outward symbol of the deep imprint of classical culture in the Celtic lands. The Roman pantheon found itself grafted easily on to the Celtic religion. After its final outbreak in the year of the Four Emperors (68–69) Druidic nationalism had suffered eclipse.[82] The Druids became socially respectable and were no longer a menace to Rome.[83] Even the civil war of 196–97 provoked no nationalist rising in Gaul.[84] This now belonged to an antiquarian past. The Roman gods had become accepted with the same alacrity as the Latin language, with Roman town-planning, roads, amphitheatres, fora, baths and hypocausts. As Jullian points out, in the 170s, Gallic loyalism to the Emperor's person had expressed itself in a number of centres by religious acts.[85] Everywhere, temples and other public buildings, the themes chosen to decorate Samian ware dinner services, and the inscriptions on coins reminded the people of the values represented by Rome. This civilization had another eighty years to run before the economic crises and barbarian invasions of the mid-third century were to rob it of its attractive power. Gaul of the Antonines had place neither for the rebellious Celticism of the Druids nor for the 'strange new worship' of the Christians. *Roma aeterna* was the inspiration of Romanized chieftain and plebeian alike.

Pollution of the gods, even when this was coupled with conspiracy, may not be the only explanation for the Lyons pogrom. There were pagan cults too, whose rites could be offensive to public order and morals. Among such were those of Isis and of Cybele the Great Mother. In time past the cult of Isis had been banned and Roman citizens forbidden to participate in the Phrygian rites.[86] These now, however, went on unhindered. Indeed, at Lyons the *taurobolium* was being performed '*pro salute*' of the reigning Emperor.[87] More significantly, perhaps, one learns from Irenaeus details of the Gnosticism that had taken a grip among the Lyons Christians, and from this it seems evident that the Gnostics were adept in just that combination of magic, secrecy and orgiastic vice that in 177 so incensed the mob against the Christians. Irenaeus describes Gnostics as 'practising magic, using images, incantations, invocations and every other strange art, including the 'theorems of the mathematicians'.[88] These latter would probably be connected with astrology. His description of a Marcosian ceremony points to immorality as well as magic.[89] Yet it is equally evident that the Gnostics of Lyons did not share the fate of their more orthodox brethren. Irenaeus is clear and decisive on this point. He writes, that 'during the whole time since Christ appeared on earth, only one or two of them have occasionally along with our martyrs borne the reproach of the name and been led forth to death'.[90] The Gnostics, said Irenaeus, have never sent martyrs to God and did not think such bearing of witness was necessary. Such statements could only have sounded foolish, if any prominent Gnostic had suffered in the persecution only ten years before. The Gnostics, however, believed in keeping their secrets from the mass of their fellow men, the unfortunate Hylics, who were predestined to remain earth-bound for all time.[91] Perhaps the Catholics, by stressing the virtue of confessing the Name, and by their obstinate refusal to acknowledge the gods of the community in any way whatsoever, were inviting hostility which they otherwise might have avoided. They were 'atheists' and few attitudes were feared and hated more by the inhabitants of the Ancient World.[92]

Once the mob had seized their victims, the provincial authorities were obliged to intervene. At Lyons the governor needed no prompting. He shared fully the prevailing hatred of the Christians. It remains only to underline some points that emerge from his conduct of proceedings.[93] First, on the question of procedure, it is noteworthy that he did not follow the practice usual in Pliny's time and take steps to send the Roman citizens among the Christians to Rome to stand trial there.[94] A report to the Emperor sufficed, perhaps a symptom of the great increase in the numbers of those who could claim Roman citizenship at this period. Marcus Aurelius supported the govenor's action, and had no comment to make on the manner in which the Christians had been apprehended and tried.[95] Moreover, there was no doubt that Christianity was a crime. It is explicitly stated in the survivors' letter that the confessors faced no other charge while they persisted, though the others who had been imprisoned and then recanted immediately found themselves accused of criminal offences.[96] On the other hand, no issue of dogma was at stake in the minds of the authorities, who showed themselves extremely ignorant about the precise nature of Christian beliefs. The governor himself questioned Bishop Pothinus about the nature of the Christian God, and the reply he received, 'If you are worthy you will know', could hardly have enlightened him.[97] Attalus, too, was asked for the name of his God.[98] It was the general complex of ideas associated in the minds of pagans with the Name that aroused fear and hostility, and this feeling was shared from the Emperor downwards. What happened at the Eucharist? Could a pagan husband trust his Christian wife who insisted on participating?[99] These were real questions agitating people at the time, and Christian secrecy did not aid their cause.

At the same time, there is no record in the *Acta* for the confiscation of property belonging either to individual Christians or to the Church corporately. The persecution was directed purely against individuals, who, so far as can be judged, belonged to the orthodox section only of the Christian community. They and not their God were the objects of hatred. Previously, no one had intervened to prevent the establishment of the Church in early days, and no step would be taken to prevent Irenaeus from succeeding the martyred Pothinus. Once popular anger subsided,

Christian life was able to continue. Irenaeus' *Adversus Haereses* evinces no hostility against his fellow-townsmen, but plenty against the Gnostic heretics. He seems to write with a feeling of security, his work circulated widely, to Carthage and as far afield as Oxyrhynchus.[100] By 195 or so, representative meetings of Gallic Christians were being held apparently without let or hindrance, and Gallic clergy were travelling to Rome in an effort to mediate between Pope Victor and the Asiatic Churches over the Paschal controversy.[101] It seems that licensed pogrom rather than a continuous pressure from the authorities was the lot of the Gallic Churches, and that, though it is dangerous to argue from silence, some respect may have been paid to the property of the community.

It is time to speak about the victims themselves. Their constancy and steadfast devotion were truly amazing. No passage of time, no change of circumstances can dim their glory. Blandina is to be numbered among the world's heroines. Physical torture was accepted as a matter of course, whether inflicted in the squalor of the narrow confines of the prison, or before the shouts of the hostile onlookers in the amphitheatre. 'His limbs were burning, but he continued himself unbending and unyielding, firm in his confession, refreshed and strengthened by the heavenly spring of the water of life which proceeds from the body of Christ.'[102] Thus a survivor spoke of the deacon Sanctus. The other martyrs were of like temper. Even in our own day, so used to scenes of barbarism and refined brutality, the examples of these men and women live on, a memorial to the impact which Christianity made on the civilization of the Roman Empire.

Let us put ourselves in the position of the intelligent pagan citizen of Lyons who watched the trials, and ask why these men and women accepted death so readily. They appeared to gain nothing. Their God did not rescue them. The gods whom they had insulted were vindicated. Outwardly, in the minds of their contemporaries, the pagan cults had triumphed. Was their action then mere defiance, the futile but seductive exhibitionism which Marcus Aurelius attributed to the Christians?[103] Or was there, after all, a deep and long-standing tradition of Christian thought which the martyrs represented and in the context of which their actions may be understood?

The answer which the Christians themselves would give leaves no doubt that they represented a vital tradition in the early Church. One of the most interesting features of the letter is the view of martyrdom it contains. It seems that, even in the Lyons community's rudimentary state of development, the martyrs were already regarded as a class apart. The writer refers three times to the κλῆρος τῶν μαρτύρων.[104] The sense in all these passages is not so much the normal sense of 'inheritance', but of an actual group, a portion, set apart.[105] For instance, Biblis after her intervention on behalf of the brethren is 'added to the κλῆρος of the martyrs', to which she had not previously belonged.[106] In the mind of the writer, though death alone rendered the Christian a 'perfected martyr'—Stephen is called 'ὁ τέλειος μάρτυς'[107]—the act of witnessing itself gave the Christian a qualification for this honour. Thus, he records the division of the Christians into two groups at the outset, the πρωτομάρτυρες, who were ready for immediate combat, and the others 'who did not appear to be ready'.[108] On the other hand, the victims themselves are reported as having a much more severe standard. While they were alive they looked upon themselves as 'humble confessors' only.[109] Though theirs indeed was an 'ὁμολογίαν τῆς μαρτύριας',[110] (confession of witness) it was not yet 'martyrdom'. Their view is set out clearly towards the end of the letter. It reads as follows:

> But if ever any one of us called them martyrs either in a letter or in speech they rebuked him sharply. For they gladly conceded the title of martyrdom to Christ, the faithful and true martyr and first-born from the dead and author of the life of God. And they reminded us of the martyrs who had already passed away, and said 'they are already martyrs, whom Christ vouchsafed to be taken up at their confession, and sealed their witness by their departure, but we are lowly and humble confessors'. And they besought the brethren with tears, begging that earnest prayers might be made for their consecration. The power of martyrdom they actually showed, having great boldness towards the heathen, and they made plain their nobleness by endurance and absence of fear or timidity; but the title of martyr they refused from the brethren, for they were filled with the fear of God. (tr. Kirsopp Lake)[111]

Thus, death alone for the faith made a Christian a martyr. Otherwise he was not 'perfected'. The qualities of a martyr could belong to the confessor, but no one could claim the proud title if, for whatever reason, he was not 'sealed' by death.[112] Witness before the magistrates, conflict with the beasts in the amphitheatre was not enough. The Christian's second sealing could not be complete without the faithful victim's sacrifice by death. But having died 'for the glory of Christ' the martyr had 'fellowship (κοινωνία) for ever with the living God'.[113]

Behind their action lies the whole theology of martyrdom in the early Church. They were seeking by their death to attain to the closest possible imitation of Christ's Passion and death. This was the heart of their attitude. Christ himself suffered in the martyr.[114] Love of Christ and hope of salvation through Christ alone was their inspiration and the essence of their faith. The martyr was 'a true disciple of Christ' (ἔστιν γνήσιος χριστοῦ μαθητής), one who 'follows the Lamb wheresoever he goes', namely to death.[115] The same idea is repeated in Irenaeus some ten years later when he speaks of 'those who are killed on account of the Lord, striving to follow in the footsteps of the Lord's Passion'.[116] Even the stake to which Blandina was tied in the amphitheatre was likened in their eyes to a Cross. The confessors 'saw with their outward eyes in the form of their sister Him who was crucified for them'.[117] But she was already viewing the joys of Paradise.[118] Death was the beginning of true discipleship. That Vettius Epagathus was said by the writer of the letter to 'have been' and 'be a true disciple', did not mean that he survived the persecution, but that he had given his witness and was therefore now enjoying the true discipleship of his Master.[119] This crown was the climax of the Christian's earthly life, a reward which all should 'earnestly desire',[120] but it was a reward to be accepted 'in meekness', not grasped at, and by implication, not provoked,[121]— though the line between Christian 'boldness' (παῤῥησια) praised in Vettius Epagathus and Alexander, and 'provocation' must have been difficult to draw.

There is no evidence that the Christians regarded their quarrel specifically with the authorities, let alone with the Roman Empire. Their witness was against the 'world' (which, of course, was represented for the time being by the pagan Roman Empire), but they saw their acts in eschatological and not political terms. The Devil was their enemy;[122] the Paraclete was their Advocate whose verdict on the world would be the same as that of Jesus had been on the Pharisees (Jn. 16⁸⁻¹¹). He was vindicating through them the cause of God and the witness of Jesus.[123] The Christians represented the Church, whose loyal members they were, as the Virgin Mother witnessing to the truth.[124] The persecution they were suffering was the sure precursor of the time of Antichrist which in turn would usher in the Millennium of the Saints.[125] Meantime, the Devil 'fighting with all his strength'[126] was the active agent of mischief. He was responsible for the attitude of the authorities and the mob, for the atheistic hatred, blasphemies, tortures and recantations which the faithful were forced to witness. The arguments, and kindly words even of judges attempting to save the confessor from death were brushed aside as Satan's weapons.[127] There was no greater triumph than when the waverers returned to the faith, thus despoiling the Devil of his prey.[128] Satan was lord of death, and against him the Christian athlete pitted his might with the crown of immortality as prize.

Many of these ideas were being expressed in other *Acta* of this period. Indeed, they seem to be part and parcel of Christian teaching especially among the Churches in Asia. They bring us face to face with a vital problem which was beginning to confront the Church, and was in the forefront of the Lyons confessors' minds also. This was the question of rigorism. Was, or was not, the strictest penitential and moral discipline a prerequisite for the indwelling of the Holy Spirit in a Christian?[129] Could a milder attitude be justified? The Letter from Lyons is a priceless contribution to this problem because one sees the confessors striving to arrive at their own answer under the harshest of stresses, and attempting to pass on their experience to their fellow Christians far away in Asia and Phrygia.[130]

The question has often been debated as to the extent of Montanist influence among the Lyons Christians at this time.[131] The problem would, however, appear to be more one of parallel religious developments rather than allegiances. As we have seen, there were many links between the Churches in Gaul and those of Asia Minor in those years. Movements among the one might be expected to find an echo in the other. If the letter had been written from Asia Minor at this time, the emphatic references to prophecy as among the Apostolic *charismata*,[132] and the description of Vettius Epagathus, 'the Paraclete of the Christians', 'boiling over with the Spirit', and 'having the Spirit in fuller measure than Zacharias', would certainly suggest Montanist influence.[133] So too would the claim made on behalf of the confessors to be able to forgive sins,[134] and to 'bind and loose',[135] as these were claims explicitly made by the Montanist prophets.[136] Indeed, they follow naturally from the confessors' belief that their way of life and death was the Way. Through their intense imitation of Christ's every step, they felt themselves participants in His gifts of the Spirit. Christ freed men from sin and suffering by His death, and so therefore, might His faithful disciples. Though the letter is not so full of visions and divine interventions that characterize the *Passion of Perpetua and Felicitas*, it is assumed that throughout their ordeal the confessors are under the special guidance of the Spirit.[137] Visions,[138] insensibility to pain[139] and conversations with Christ[140] are among the immediate rewards of confession. One must agree that their language and ideas show close affinities to those of their Montanist brethren in Phrygia.[141]

On the other hand, there is a considerable difference in spirit, and in particular in their attitude towards other members of the Church. This, they stress whenever possible. They are merciful to the fallen among them.[142] Their humanity needs no emphasis. They dislike over-rigorous fasts as those indulged in by Alcibiades, as senseless in themselves, and providing a possible 'example of offence'[143] to others. Alcibiades is rebuked and the inclusion of this incident in their letter is obviously designed to point a moral. To whom? Perhaps the Montanists.

The emphasis of the letter is on forbearance, peace and unity. Its final words are a very strong indication of the confessors' views. 'They ever loved peace: peace they commended to us and with peace they departed to God: for their mother they left behind no sorrow: and for their brethren no strife and war, but glory and peace, concord and love.'[144] The idea of division among those whose only name was 'Christian' was unthinkable. This was no doubt the burden of their final letters to their friends in Phrygia, and to Eleutherus of Rome, which Irenaeus carried. Their contents are described by Eusebius as 'prudent and most orthodox', but they can hardly have been unfriendly to prophecy itself.[145] Irenaeus himself was later to be scathing against those who denied the canonicity of the Fourth Gospel and i Corinthians on the grounds of the commendation of the works of the Spirit found in them.[146]

One other aspect of the confessors' religion has received less attention than it deserves, namely its conservative and even Judaistic character. This is revealed in a curious incident. Time and again the Christians under torture have denied the charges of cannibalism and incest made against them. They claimed indignantly that their religion did not involve these or any other evil actions. The authorities tortured a slave girl named Biblis who had previously shown a willingness to recant. In a sudden burst of strength she cried out, 'How could such men eat children, when they are not allowed to consume the blood even of irrational animals (ἀλόγων ζῴων)?'[147] The statement sounds as though it had been made under the stress of the moment, and is interesting. It suggests that the Christians at Lyons were still observing the strict Apostolic rules concerning food (Acts 15[20 and 29]), and as is well known, these were derived from orthodox Jewish practice.[148] The prohibition against eating ordinary meat had nothing to do with the ban on meats offered to idols, but is connected with the taboo against defilement by contact with the blood remaining in the animal after slaughter. Some of the Lyons community such as Alcibiades, carried the prohibition even further and like some of the extremer Jewish sects ate no meat at all.[149] The writer of the *Acta* does not contradict Biblis's statement, and the question arises, where did the Christians get their meat from? The only possible answer is, from a kosher market established for the Jews,[150] and this in turn indicates fairly close personal relations between the Jews and Christians in the city. At Lyons, however, in contrast to the cities in Asia, the Jews are not mentioned among the Church's enemies.

The link with Judaism may have extended beyond common practices concerning food. It seems that even in 185 the Old Israel was still leaving its mark on Christian habits of thought and expression in Lyons. One finds traces of this in the writings of Irenaeus not long afterward. For instance, he still speaks sometimes of the Church as the 'synagogue', only the true one,[151] and of Christians as those 'who feared God',[152] quite as the Hellenistic Jewish proselytes had been termed for centuries before. He himself shares to the full the Millenarist hopes that still inspired some of his Jewish contemporaries,[153] and when he records that followers of Basilides declared that 'they had ceased to be Jews but had not yet become Christians',[154] one feels that one is still living in a world where Judaism was the norm and Christianity progress beyond that.

This becomes evident if one looks closely at the likely sources of the letter. Clearly, the Fourth Gospel and the Apocalypse were two of the main sources of inspiration to the writer.[155] The Christ of St. John's Gospel is the supreme Witness to the Truth and the martyrs follow Him. Thus, Sanctus is described as 'firm in his confession, refreshed and strengthened by the heavenly spring of the water of life' (Jn. 7[38]),[156] and the martyrs see in the rage of even erstwhile friends the fulfilment of Jn. 16[2] 'The time shall come when whosoever killeth you will think that he doeth God service'.[157] The backsliders are reproached as 'sons of perdition' (Jn. 17[12]).[158] Much else would come naturally to any Christian grounded in the literature of the Apostolic and sub-Apostolic age. There are abundant quotations from Acts, the Pauline Epistles and the Pastoral Epistles. But we are left with some interesting ideas and expressions which are not to be found in the New Testament and seem to be derived from late-Jewish rather than Christian literature. A number of similarities in ideas, style and vocabulary have been established between the letter and the Maccabean works.[159] The most obvious point of contact between the two is the identification of the heroic mother of the Maccabean youths and the slave Blandina. She also is 'a noble mother' who 'encouraged her children' and 'sent them forth triumphant to their living'. Having 'completed her task and endured all the tortures of the children hastened after them'.[160] Like her prototype in ii and iv Maccabees, she dies last of all, encouraging the youngest of those martyrs about whom anything is recorded, to be steadfast.

One can point to other resemblances. Bishop Pothinus finds a parallel in Eleazar[161] and both are described as being 90 years old—perhaps a symbol of venerability rather than actual age?[162] Vettius Epagathus may be modelled on Razis in ii Macc. 14[37ff], the one 'the advocate of the Christians', the other, 'the father of the Jews'; and each surrendering their bodies to voluntary death after defying the tyrant.[163] Then, there are the vivid and uninhibited descriptions of torture and death which characterize both the letter and iv Maccabees. In both, martyrdom is likened to a contest (ἀγών) and the confessors are the athletes.[164] They regain youth and vigour amid tortures,[165] they resist suffering,[166] they defeat the desperate strength of their executioners,[167] and in the end, by 'sealing their witness' by death[168] gain the crown of immortality.[169] The martyrs go to their King, while the Maccabean heroes also go 'to God'.[170] Finally, in both the Lyons letter and iv Maccabees, the theme is that the martyrs are honoured by God in a heavenly abode which no act of their adversaries can prevent. Looking at the evidence as it is, it would be difficult to deny that the writer of the Lyons letter was saturated in Maccabean literature. Indeed, as Othmar Perler has pointed out, iv Maccabees may be considered one of the roots of early Christian enthusiasm for martyrdom and literature concerning martyrs.[171]

The evidence of the Lyons letter does not stand alone. It is part of a saga extending over four centuries of Church history. In both the other contemporary accounts of martyrdom in the reign of Marcus Aurelius, that of Evarestus concerning the death of Polycarp[172] and the *Acta Carpi*, one is confronted by the same literary heritage. In both of these works defiance of the authorities is regarded as a necessary part of the combat against Satan himself.[173] If one looks for details, then Polycarp's 'bright and gentle countenance',[174] his miraculous survival of torture despite his great age,[175] his power of prophecy,[176] his purchase of immortality,[177] and even the cessation of persecution on his death,[178] are points which would occur to writers who were steeped in the story of either the scribe Eleazar or the Maccabean youths. In the *Acta Carpi* Carpus is also characterized as a 'noble athlete'[179] and we find, coupled with more outspoken defiance of the authorities, the same stark determination to give away not one iota of the Law—though it happens to be the Christian Law and not Torah.

In both East and West the Maccabees were regarded from the third century onwards as the prototypes of martyrdom and a source of inspiration to confessors. Christians whose theology differed as much as that of Origen[180] from that of Secundus of Tigisis[181] regarded themselves as the Maccabees' descendants. The

Maccabees appear on both the Carthaginian and Syrian lists of martyrs.[182] They are cited by Cyprian (*Ep.*, 58.6) and in his treatise *ad Fortunatum* as prefigurations of Christian martyrdom and indeed, the number seven of the brethren linked these to the whole apocalyptic progress of the Church to the end of the world.[183] In the fourth century Lucifer of Cagliari speaks of Antiochus as 'persecutor nostrae religionis'[184] so close was the emotional identification between the sufferings of the Maccabees and the Christians of his day. Gregory of Nazianzus asks in 375 what would men who were martyred before Christ's Passion have achieved if they had been persecuted after Christ and had His death on our behalf to imitate?[185] To John Chrysostom also, the Maccabees were 'the forerunners of Christian martyrdom', though the force of the sermons he preached in their honour must be assessed in the light of the political warfare John was waging against the Jews at Antioch at this time.[186] In the epic and legendary martyrdoms of the fourth and later centuries the theme of the pious mother and her seven children refusing the demands of an idolatrous ruler recurs time and again.[187] The saga was one of the vital legacies of late-Judaism to the early Church.[188]

In face of this it is curious that eminent students of martyrdom, such as H. Delehaye[189] and his disciples have always denied any but Christian influence both in the concept of martyrdom in the early Church and in the form which the historical *Acta* took. We know now that the New Israel owed so much in regard to the form of its ideas and institutions to the Old Israel that a development from Jewish origins should not be surprising.

We have already seen that the Church at Lyons retained some links, perhaps tangible links with Hellenistic Judaism, and the use of a Jewish model by the author of the letter along with the New Testament would not be unexpected. This does not mean that the events he described have been exaggerated. Simply, that when he came to write to the Churches in Asia Minor of the sufferings of the Gallic Christians, the type of the Maccabean martyrs came automatically to mind, and he regarded the martyrs of Lyons as the heirs of that tradition, and his recipients in Asia would have been familiar with the idioms he used. Christ indeed had come on earth, had ministered, had suffered and died the true martyr, but the idea of suffering and even death being involved in the act of witnessing to the power and truth of God's Law goes far back in the Jewish religion. If this is accepted, we must look beyond the beginnings of Christianity for the origins of the ideas that inspired the martyrs of Lyons. The story may well start with the Maccabees themselves to whose example they owed so much. Martyrs, however, need persecutors. What took place at Lyons was essentially a pogrom, perhaps carefully prepared by influential plotters, the details of which from start to finish have been meticulously recorded. Here too, the Christians continued the tragic lot of the Jews in the Ancient World. Anti-semitism was endemic in the city states of the Mediterranean for 200 years after the Maccabean revolt. Simmering hatred felt by Greeks for the Jews and their proselytes would burst out now in one place, now in another in savage outbreaks of unbelievable ferocity. The Jew demonstrated that only religious steadfastness saved the people.[190] The Christian learnt the same lesson.

What of the official policy of the Roman authorities towards the Church? 'Recant or die'—where does one look for the explanation of the legal procedure, which Tertullian so rightly claimed, was the opposite to the normal accepted standards of Roman jurisprudence?[191] The traditional arguments centred round the meaning of the 'institutum neronianum', or the practice of the provincial governors' power of 'coercitio' still have their relevance.[192] Yet, more to the point, may be the practices in force against recalcitrant proselytes to Judaism and the passions which Judaism in any shape or form were liable to arouse. The problem which the Christians posed to the Empire was fundamentally the same as that posed by Judaism, namely the reconciliation of the claims of a theocracy with those of a world empire.[193] In the West, the problem continued to dominate history in one way or another for fifteen hundred years, until obscured by the new ecclesiology of the Reformers. Lyons, however, set the stage, for there the claims of the State and the pressure of popular opinion confronted in the starkest terms the claims of Christian confession and witness.

NOTES

[1] Eusebius, *Ecclesiastical History* (= *H.E.*), ed. Kirsopp Lake, v.1.1. The best account of the Church in Gaul at this period is to be found in H. Leclercq's scholarly articles, 'Lyon' and 'Vienne' in the *Dictionnaire d'Archéologie chrétienne et de Liturgie* (= *DACL.*) x.1, 1–81 and xv.2, 3047–9. See also Camille Jullian, *Histoire de la Gaule*, iv, Paris, 1913, 489ff., and Elie Griffe, *La Gaule chrétienne à l'Epoque romaine*, i, Paris, 1947, 12ff. From Eusebius, *H.E.*, v.iii.4 we gather that apart from the account of the martyrdoms the survivors sent letters concerning Montanism to the Christians in Phrygia. For a dating of 175 instead of 177, and that the writer was in fact Irenaeus, see P. Nautin, *Lettres et écrivains chrétiens des iie. et iiie. siècles* (Paris, Les éditions du Cerf, 1961), pp. 54–9 and 62–3. I have not been able to see André Chagny, *Les Martyrs de Lyon de 177*, Lyon and Paris, 1936.

[2] The problem is raised by the writer putting Vienne before Lyons at the beginning of his letter. 'οἱ 'εν βιέννῃ καὶ Λουγδούνῳ τῆς Γαλλίας παροικοῦντες δοῦλοι Χριστοῦ' (Eusebius, *H.E.*, v.1.3.). Eusebius, however, leaves little doubt that Lyons was the more important Church, and the order may be explained by the writer living in Vienne and writing from there (see H. J. Lawlor and J. E. L. Oulton's translation and notes of *Eusebius, The Ecclesiastical History and the Martyrs of Palestine*, ii, London, 1954, 154–5).

[3] This is H. Leclercq's interpretation of *H.E.*, v.1.13 'δι'ὧν μάλιστα συνεστήκει τὰ ἐνθάδε', art. 'Lyon', in *DACL.*, x.1.74 and repeated in xv.2, 3048. The sense may, however, be simply 'through whom particularly the community's affairs were organized'—the natural targets of police repression. On the other hand, Sulpicius Severus, *Chronicon*, ii.32 (ed. Halm, *CSEL.*, i), implies that the persecution took place soon after the foundation of the Churches, though his is a late fourth-century opinion.

[4] The pros. and cons. are set out by Leclercq in art. 'Vienne', *DACL.*, xv.2, 3048. I accept his conclusion, 'Les vraisemblances sont pour l'indistinction'; cf. J. Lebreton and J. Zeiller, *Histoire de l'Eglise*, Paris, 1948, ii, 131.

[5] Eusebius, *H.E.*, v.1.29 and 5,8.

[6] Ibid., v.23.3 and 4.

[7] Tacitus, *Histories*, i.65 (period of Nero-Galba).

[8] Herodian (ed. W. Stavenhagen, Leipzig, 1922), iii.2.7–10.

[9] Eusebius, *H.E.*, v.1.17.

[10] Ibid., v.1.13.

[11] H. Leclercq, loc. cit., 'Lyon', 77, for instance, goes to considerable trouble to try to prove that the Church in Gaul at this time was not the product of Asiatic immigration, 'Nonobstant l'origine exotique de certains, on n'a pas l'ombre d'une raison à apporter quand on soutient que la communauté lyonnaise était le produit d'une émigration collective partie de la côte de l'Asie'.

[12] For instance, in *H.E.*, v.1.20 (Sanctus) ἀπεκρίνατο τῇ'ρωμαικῇ φωνῇ. Also, 1.44 and 1.52.

[13] See H. Quentin, 'La liste des martyrs de Lyon de l'an 177', *Analecta Bollandiana* (= *A.B.*), xxxix, 1921, 113–38. Also H. Achelis, 'Die Martyrologien', *Abhandlungen der Kön. Ges. der Wissenschaft zu Göttingen*, Phil. Hist. Klasse N.F. iii, 1900, 145.

[14] Lawlor and Oulton, *Eusebius*, ii.156, and J. Lebreton and J. Zeiller, *Histoire de l'Eglise*, ii, 129.

[15] Eusebius, *H.E.*, v.20.4; Irenaeus, *Adv. Haereses*, iii.3.4.

[16] Eusebius, *H.E.*, v.1.17.

[17] Ibid., v.1.49.

[18] Ibid., v.1.3.

[19] Irenaeus, *Adv. Haer.*, i.13.7.

[20] Ibid., i.13.5.

[21] For instance, the first evidence for the celebration of the Epiphany in the West comes from Vienne in 360. Ammianus Marcellinus (ed. Rolfe), xxi.2.5.

[22] Eusebius, *H.E.*, v.1.63.

[23] Irenaeus, *Adv. Haer.*, Proemium 3, iii.4.2. and iv.24.2.

[24] Eusebius, *H.E.*, v.1.20.

[25] For the importance of this trade route at this time, M. P. Charlesworth, *Trade Routes of the Roman Empire*, Cambridge, 1926, 201–2 and notes (p. 280).

[26] Origen, *Contra Celsum*, i.27 and iii.55 (ed. Koetschau, Leipzig, 1899). Minucius Felix, *Octavius*, 8–9.

[27] Eusebius, *H.E.*, v.1.14.

[28] Ibid., 1.10 and 49.

[29] Irenaeus, *Adv. Haer.*, i.13.3–4.

[30] Eusebius, *H.E.*, v.1.57.

[31] Sallust, *De Bello Jugurthino* (ed. Ahlberg, Leipzig) 26.

[32] R. G. Collingwood and J. N. L. Myres, *Roman Britain and the Anglo-Saxon Settlements*, Oxford, 1936, pp. 71 and 185; and M. P. Charlesworth, *Trade Routes*, ch. 12 and notes.

[33] Cf. Salvian, *De Gubernatione Dei* (ed. and tr. Sanford, Columbia University Press, 1930), iv.14.

[34] This view agrees with that put forward by A. Fliche, 'A propos des Origines chrétiennes de la Gaule', *Mélanges Lebreton* (RSR., XL, 1951–52), 166.

[35] See A. D. Nock, *Conversion*, Oxford, 1933, ch. vi. *CIL.*, xiii, 2005, 2007 (traders from Asia in Lyons).

[36] Attalus, for instance, Eusebius, *H.E.*, v.1.52, 'ἔφη πρὸς τὸ πλῆθος τῇ 'Ρωμαϊκῇ φωνῇ'.

[37] *CIL.*, ii.6278 = Dessau, *ILS.*, 5163. The bronze plate from Italica in Baetica and the fragmentary inscription of the same *Senatus-consultum* from Sardis in Asia are discussed by J. H. Oliver and R. E. A. Palmer in 'Minutes of an Act of the Roman Senate', *Hesperia*, 24, 1955, 320–49. Though the evidence against the interested parties in the S.C. is purely circumstantial, the theory suggested by the joint authors rings true, except for the fact that neither the S.C. which evidently received a wide publicity nor the revolting use made of it was ever commented upon by Christian writers.

[38] Lines 56–7 of the Italica tablet, 'Ad Gallias sed et[t]rin [quo]s qui in civitatibus splendidissimarum Galliarum veteri more et sacro ritu expectantur' (art. cit., 333). For human sacrifice among the Gauls in the Roman period, H. Last, 'Rome and the Druids', *JRS.*, xxxix, 1949, 1–5, and for the tradition see the abundant literature regarding the Gundestrup cauldron.

[39] The martyrologies of Jerome and Ado (not the earliest martyrologies, therefore) commemorate the death of the martyrs on 2 June. But it does not seem likely that the final scenes were enacted before the celebration of the feast of the Three Gauls on 1 August. 2 June may be the date of the first combats in the amphitheatre or that of the death of Bishop Pothinus in prison.

[40] Eusebius, *H.E.*, v.1.5–6.

[41] Theatres and market-places were often associated with temples in the Romano-Celtic cities, e.g. at Trier and also Verulamium. See S. Loeschke, *Die Erforschung des Tempelbezirkes im Altbachtale zu Trier*, 1, 1928, Plan of site, and A. W. G. Lowther, 'Excavations at Verulamium in 1934', *Antiquaries Journal*, xvii (1937), 28ff.

[42] Eusebius, *H.E.*, v.1.7–8.

[43] *CIL.*, xiii, 1833, 1845, 1852, 1857, 1870.

[44] For similar procedure, cf. *Mart. Pionii* (ed. Knopf and Krüger, 1929), 15.3.

[45] Eusebius, *H.E.*, v.1.10.

[46] Ibid., v.1.14.

[47] This is a difficult legal point. The persecution caught Christians both from Lyons

and Vienne, including most of their clergy. If Sanctus and his companions were not in Lyons at the time, it is difficult to understand how the governor of Lugdunensis came to condemn to death inhabitants of a neighbouring province. See, C. Jullian, *Hist. de la Gaule*, iv. 494, n. 3, and K. Müller, 'Kleine Beiträge zur alten Kirchengeschichte', *Zeitschrift für die neutestamentlische Wissenschaft* (= *ZNTW*.) 23, 1924, 215-16.

[48] Eusebius, *H.E.*, v.1.13.

[49] Note also the reference in Celsus (Origen, *Contra Celsum*, viii.69) to Christians being sought out at this period.

[50] Attalus was tried and condemned before the governor knew his status. He had already written to the Emperor and was awaiting a reply when this was revealed (v.1.44). In view of communications difficulties, the governor must therefore have sent his report at an early stage in the proceedings.

[51] Eusebius, *H.E.*, v.1.17-24.

[52] *Digest* (ed. Mommsen and Krüger), xlviii.4.7.2. 'Servi quoque deferentes audiuntur et quidem dominos suos et liberti patronos.' Cf. art. *Maiestas* by Kübler, *PW.*, xiv, col. 553. Further discussion whether Christians were accused of *maiestas*, see ch. vi.

[53] Eusebius, *H.E.*, v.1.14. For the same accusation against Christians in this period: Theophilus, *Ad Autolycum* iii.4 (Antioch); Justin, *1 Apol.* 26 (Rome); Athenagoras, *Legatio* 3 (probably northern Asia Minor); Minucius Felix, *Octavius*, 9 (Rome); Tertullian, *Apol.* 7 and 8 (Carthage); Tatian. *Oratio* 25 (Asia Minor or Syria).

[54] Eusebius, *H.E.*, v.1.33 and 35.

[55] Ibid., v.1.15. Cf. ii Maccabees, 6²⁹ (abandonment by friends).

[56] Ibid., v.1.17-24, 29-31 and 54. For the triumph felt by provincial magistrates when a Christian recanted, Tertullian, *Apologeticus*, ii.13-17, Origen, *Contra Celsum*, viii.44, Lactantius, *Div. Inst*, v.11.15.

[57] Eusebius, *H.E.*, v.1.20. Compare the attitude of Carpus in *Acta Carpi, Papyli, et Agathonike* (ed. Knopf and Krüger, Tübingen, 1929) 1-3, and Perpetua in *Passio Perpetuae*, 3, 2.

[58] Eusebius, *H.E.*, v.1.27-8. Similar treatment to Perpetua and her companions *Passio Perpetuae*, 3, 3-4. The *Mart. Hier.* lists 19 Lyons martyrs who died in prison.

[59] Eusebius, *H.E.*, v.1.31.

[60] See above, n. 39. Also, C. Jullian, *Hist. de la Gaule*, iv.495, n. 6.

[61] Eusebius, *H.E.*, v.1.36-42.

[62] Ibid., v.1.43-5.

[63] Paulus, *Sententiae*, v.23.16. Th. Mommsen, *Römisches Strafrecht*, Leipzig, 1899, 926-8 (references).

[64] Eusebius, *H.E.*, v.iii.4 and iv.1.

[65] Pliny, *Letters*, x.97. See over, p. 219.

[66] Eusebius, *H.E.*, v.1.47.

[67] The punishments decreed were the same as those for *maiestas* offences, 'His autem in perpetuum aqua et igni interdicebatur; nunc vero, humiliores bestiis obiciuntur vel vivi exuruntur, honestiores capite puniuntur', Paulus, *Sententiae*, v.29.1, and *Instit.*, iv.18.3. See Kübler, art. cit., 553. They were not out of line with those being inflicted on Christians in Asia at this time: Eusebius, *H.E.*, iv.15.9 (Polycarp) and *Acta Carpi*, 21.

[68] The majestic inscription found on the site and showing that the amphitheatre was built *circa* A.D. 17 by Caius Julius Drusus is now in the Gallo-Roman Museum at Lyons.

[69] Eusebius, *H.E.*, v.1.40, and also v.1.53. (τῇ ἐσχάτῃ λοιπὸν ἡμέρᾳ τῶν μονομαχίων).

[70] Ibid., v.1.35 and 45.

[71] Ibid., v.1.48.

[72] Ibid., v.1.51.

[73] Eusebius, *H.E.*, v.1.59-60.

[74] Tertullian, *Apol.*, 40, Eusebius, *H.E.*, iv.15.7 and 26 (Polycarp's martyrdom).

⁷⁵ Eusebius, H.E., v.1.63.

⁷⁶ Ibid., v.1.31. Evident from the sense of ἐτύθη καὶ αὐτή. (H.E., v.1.56) 'and she also was sacrificed', and her comrades 'ἐτύθησαν' (ibid., 40). This seems to fit precisely the requirements concerning the trinqui outlined by the Gallo-Roman senator in Rome a short time before.

⁷⁷ Note, also, the macabre practice of dressing those condemned to the beasts in the amphitheatre at Carthage in clothes of priests of Saturn or priestesses of Ceres. In these cases the 'priest' would sacrifice himself to the god. Passio Perpetuae, 18.2.

⁷⁸ See F. J. Dölger, 'Sacramentum Infanticidii', Antike und Christentum (= A.C.), 4, 1934, 188–228; also, J. P. Waltzing, 'Le crime rituel reproché aux chrétiens du 2me. siècle', Académie royale de Belgique, Classe des Lettres, Bulletin de 1925, 205–39, especially pp. 220–2.

⁷⁹ For the possible use of a foetus or new-born child for magical purposes, to do one's enemies damage, Pap. Mich., vi,423–4 (dated 197) commented on by H. I. Bell, JRS., xxxv, 1945, 140. F. J. Dölger, art. cit., 206ff.

⁸⁰ Ulpian, Bk. ix, De Officio Proconsulis, Dig. xlviii.24.1, 'Corpora eorum qui capite damnantur cognatis ipsorum non neganda sunt. . . .'

⁸¹ Eusebius, H.E., v.1.60.

⁸² The revolt of Vindex and Marice. Their Druidic inspiration, Tacitus, Hist., iv.54 ('Druidae canebant').

⁸³ Gallic gods like Belenus become popular once more in the late second century and they and their Druidic priests provided an occupation for the sons of Gallic nobles until late in the fourth century. Herodian (ed. Stavenhagen), viii.3.8 (Belenus worshipped in Aquileia in 238). Ausonius, Commemoratio Professorum (ed. H. E. G. White), iv.7–10 and x.22–30.

⁸⁴ Jullian, op. cit., 514–15.

⁸⁵ Ibid., 490, n. 3. In Britain one finds the same tendency towards loyalism and pride in their share of Roman civilization. Note the wording of an inscription from Caerwent dated A.D. 152. [Deo M]arti Leno sive Ocelo Vellauno | et Num(ini) Aug(usti) M. | Nonius Romanus ob | Immunitat[em] Colligni D.D. | S.D. Glabrione et Homulo Cos. ILS. 9302.

The association of the Emperor's numen with a local god, the dating by consular years, and the grant of authorization to a collegium are indications of a high degree of mutual trust and affection at this period between governor and governed.

⁸⁶ See over, ch. iv.

⁸⁷ CIL., xiii, 1751–5 (A.D. 160–209).

⁸⁸ Irenaeus, Adv. Haereses, i.24.5.

⁸⁹ Ibid., i.13.3.

⁹⁰ Ibid., iv.33.9.

⁹¹ For instance, Tertullian, Scorpiace 15 (CSEL., xx, 178) and Eusebius, H.E., iv.7.7 (citing Agrippa Castor). See my art., The Gnostic Sects and the Roman Empire, JEH., v.i. 1954, 25ff. at 30–1.

⁹² See below, p. 259.

⁹³ See J. Zeiller, 'Legalité et arbitraire dans les persécutions contre les Chrétiens', A.B., lxvii, 1949, 49–54 (comparison of procedures relating to the Christians under Trajan and Marcus Aurelius).

⁹⁴ Pliny, Letters, x.96.4, 'quia cives Romani erant, adnotavi ad urbem admittendos'.

⁹⁵ For a thorough study of the legal questions involved, see A. N. Sherwin-White, Roman Society and Roman Law in the New Testament (Sarum Lectures 1960–61), Oxford, 1963, 64–70. For the view that the Emperor may have implied a rebuke to the governor for complicating the issue by introducing the factor of criminal charges, P. Allard, Le Christianisme et l'Empire romain, Paris, 1925, 60.

⁹⁶ Eusebius, H.E., v.i.33.

97 Ibid., v.1.31.

98 Ibid., v.i.52. For similar pagan questionings in the West at this period, Minucius Felix, *Octavius*, 18, 'Seek not a name for God. God is His name'. In the East, *Mart. Pionii*, 8ff., 'Pionius and his companions were each asked 'whom do you worship?' and 'what sort of God do you worship?' For Jewish reticence regarding God's name, see C. H. Dodd, *The Bible and the Greeks*, London, 1954, ch. i.

99 Tertullian, *Ad Uxorem*, ii.4–5 (ed. Kroymann, *CSEL.*, lxx), 'Quis ad convivium dominicum illud, quod infamant, sine suspicione dimittet?'.

100 *Pap. Oxy.*, 405 (ed. Grenfell and Hunt. *The Oxyrhynchus Papyri*, iii.10). For Dr. J. A. Robinson's identification of these fragments as belonging to *Adv. Haeres.* iii.9, see *The Oxyrhynchus Papyri*, iv.264. Dating of papyrus was 'early third century'.

101 Eusebius, *H.E.*, v.23.4 and 24.11.

102 Ibid., v.i.21–2.

103 Marcus Aurelius, *Meditations*, xi.3. 'μὴ κατὰ ψιλὴν παράταξιν . . . '. For the sort of mulish defiance which this implied, Josephus, *Antiquities*, xviii.8.4. In general, A. S. L. Farquharson, *The Meditations of Marcus Aurelius*, Oxford, 1944, 859.

104 Eusebius, *H.E.*, v.1.26, 48 and 55. See F. Kattenbusch, 'Der Martyrtitel', *ZNTW.*, 4, 1903, 111–27, at p. 111. Kattenbusch's view that the martyrs formed a definite '*Ordo*' at this time seems to go beyond the evidence. In Hermas' time, 'confessors' and 'martyrs' were not strictly divided (*Simil.* 9.28). Indeed they could hardly be an *Ordo* as they did not become martyrs until they were dead.

105 Lawlor and Oulton, *Eusebius*, ii.155; cf. i Peter 5³ for this meaning, and below, ch. ii, p. 31.

106 Eusebius, *H.E.*, v.1.26; cf. iv.15.33 'ἐν ἀριθμῷ τῶν μαρτύρων' (Polycarp).

107 Ibid., v.2.5.

108 Ibid., v.1.11.

109 Ibid., v.2.3.

110 Ibid., v.1.11.

111 Ibid., v.2.3–4.

112 On the significance of 'sealing', see G. W. H. Lampe, *The Seal of the Spirit*, London, 1951, ch. ii. Cf. also, Eusebius, *H.E.*, iv.15.3. (Polycarp).

113 v.1.41 (Blandina's example).

114 Eusebius, *H.E.*, v.1.23. Of the deacon Sanctus, 'Christ suffering in him manifested great glory, overthrowing the adversary (τὸν ἀντικείμενον), and showing the others how where there is the love of the Father nothing is fearful, nor painful where there is the glory of Christ. Also ibid., 1.42 and 2.2.

115 Ibid., v.1.10 and 2.2; ibid., iv.15.42 (Polycarp); cf. Ignatius, *Ad Romanos*, 4.

116 Irenaeus, *Adv. Haeres*, iii.18.5. 'qui propter domini confessionem occiduntur, conantur vestigia assequi passionis domini'.

117 Eusebius, *H.E.*, v.1.41.

118 Ibid., 1.56; cf. *Acta Carpi*, 39 and 42.

119 Ibid., v.1.10.

120 Ibid., v.1.29.

121 Though the opportunity must be accepted 'μετὰ πάσης προθυμίας' (ibid., 1.11); cf. Hermas, *Simil.*, 9.28.4 'ἔπαθον προθύμως'.

122 *H.E.*, v.1.5; also 1.16, 23, 27, 35, 42, 47 and ii.6. Note the parallels in *Passio Perpetuae*, 10.7, in Cyprian, *Ep.*, 22.1; and in epic *Acta Martyrum* such as *Acta Sancti Saviniani* (*A.B.*, lxxx, 1962, 126). Cf. F. J. Dölger, 'Das Martyrium als Kampf mit dem Teufel', *A.C.*, iii, 1933, 177–88.

123 The Paraclete is here taken as Advocate, rather than 'Comforter' or 'exhorter', see C. K. Barrett, *The Gospel according to St. John*, London, 1955, 385–6. Also, the same author in *JTS.*, N.S.i, 1950, 7–15, for a full treatment of the subject.

[124] *H.E.*, v.1.45.

[125] *H.E.*, v.1.5.; cf. Irenaeus, *Adv. Haer.*, v. 28–9.

[126] *H.E.*, v.1.5, 'παντὶ γὰρ σθένει ἐνέσκηψεν ὁ ἀντικείμενος'.

[127] Cf. *H.E.*, iv.15.18 (Polycarp), *Passio Perpetuae* 6 and *Acta Pionii*, 5.

[128] *H.E.*, v.1.46, and v.2.6.

[129] As claimed by Tertullian, *De Jejunio adversus Psychicos* 8 (*CSEL.*, xx, 283–4).

[130] See the interesting study of this aspect of the Letter, by P. Nautin, *Lettres et Ecrivains*, 32ff.

[131] A full and just appreciation of existing evidence is made by P. de Labriolle, *La Crise montaniste*, Paris, 1913, 220ff. Previous discussion is summarized on p. 221, n. 3.

[132] Eusebius, *H.E.*, v.1.19 and 47.

[133] Ibid., v. I.9. On Zacharias, see H. von Campenhausen, *Aus der Frühzeit des Christentums*. 304.

[134] Ibid., v.1.45–7. The confessors receive back the penitent lapsed into the Church.

[135] Ibid., v.2.5. 'Ἔλυον ἅπαντας, ἐδέσμευον δὲ οὐδένα'.

[136] Ibid., v.18.7. See the useful collection of texts in H. Achelis, *Das Christentum in den ersten drei Jahrhunderten*, Leipzig, 1912, ii. Excursus, 91, pp. 440–1.

[137] Eusebius, *H.E.*, v.3.3, 'οὐ γὰρ ἀνεπίσκεπτοι χάριτος θεοῦ ἦσαν, ἀλλὰ τὸ πνεῦμα τὸ ἅγιον ἦν σύμβουλον αὐτοῖς.'.

[138] Ibid., v.3.2 (Attalus' vision or revelation).

[139] Ibid., v.1.51 and 56. For the same characteristic attributed to confessors in Jewish martyrdoms, iv Maccabees 6⁵ and see over, p. 58. Other texts, H. Achelis, op. cit., 444–5.

[140] Ibid., v.1.56 'καὶ ὁμιλίαν πρὸς χριστόν' (Blandina).

[141] See T. Barns, *Expositor*, 6th Ser. viii, 1903, 44.

[142] Eusebius, *H.E.*, v.1.45–6, v.2.6; cf. Nautin, op. cit., 35.

[143] Ibid., v.3.2. 'καὶ ἄλλοις τύπον σκανδάλου'. See P. de Labriolle, op. cit. 228–9.

[144] Ibid., v.2.7.

[145] Eusebius, *H.E.*, v.3.4. 'καὶ περὶ τούτων εὐλαβῆ καὶ ὀρθοδοξοτάτην ὑποτάττουσιν'. The sense of εὐλαβής is careful but in a good sense. It does not seem that the letter contained anything more definite than an appeal for peace. (εἰρήνης ἕνεκα, ibid.) Montanism was not immediately condemned at Rome (see Tertullian, *Adv. Praxean*, 1).

[146] Irenaeus, *Adv. Haer.*, iii.11.9. The passage is the subject of an able discussion by de Labriolle, op. cit., 230ff.

[147] Eusebius, *H.E.*, v.1.26. 'ἀλόγων ζώων'. For the use of the same term for animals, see in iv Maccabees 14¹⁴.

[148] On this question G. Resch, 'Das Aposteldekret', *Texte und Untersuchungen* (= *T.U.*), N.F. xiii.2, 1905, and A. A. T. Ehrhardt, 'Soziale Fragen in der alten Kirche', *Existenz und Ordnung, Festschrift Erik Wolf*, 1962, 156ff.

[149] Eusebius, *H.E.*, v.3.1–2; cf. *H.E.*, ii.23.5. 'οὐδὲ ἔμψυχον ἔφαγεν', referring to James the Just who observed the conditions of a Nazarite vow (Nums. 6³⁻⁵).

[150] H. Leclercq, art. cit., 77. Also Minucius Felix, *Octavius*, 30.6, 'so far are we from partaking human blood that we do not even allow the blood of edible animals in our food', and Tertullian, *Apol.* 9. *De Monogamia*, S.

[151] Irenaeus, *Adv. Haer.*, iii.6.1.

[152] Ibid., 1.13.4.

[153] Ibid., v.28.3. For similar Jewish hopes at this time, *Contra Celsum*, vii.9, and *Apoc. of Baruch* (ed. Charles), 29.2. For the continued circulation of this Apocalypse in Egypt as late as the fourth century, see *P. Oxy.* 403.

[154] Ibid., i.24.6.

[155] Summed up by H. von Campenhausen, *Die Idee des Martyriums in der alten Kirche*, Göttingen, 1936, 49–50.

[156] Eusebius, H.E., v.1.22.

[157] Ibid., v.1.15.

[158] Ibid., v.1.48.

[159] See the very interesting study by O. Perler, 'Das vierte Makkabäerbuch, Ignatius von Antiochien und die ältesten Martyrerberichte', Rivista di archeologia cristiana, 25, 1949, 47–72. I cannot agree, however, that iv Maccabees was the exclusive source used by the writer of the letter from Lyons. The verbal similarities follow ii Maccabees. On the other hand, the writer of the letter imitates the style and rhetoric of iv Maccabees.

[160] Eusebius, H.E., v.1.55. See ii Maccabees 7^{21-23}, 7^{27-29} and 7^{41}, and iv Maccabees 16^{12}ff.

[161] O. Perler, art. cit., 68.

[162] ii Macc. 6^{24}: Eusebius, H.E., v.1.29, and for Akiba at his martyrdom circa 135, L. Finkelstein, Akiba, New York, 1936, p. 264.

[163] ii Macc. 14^{37-38}; Eusebius, H.E., v.1.10.

[164] iv Macc. 6^{10} and 16^{16}; H.E., v.1.11, 19 and 41; cf. Acta Carpi, 35, γενναῖος ἀθλητής, and for the Latin West, Cyprian, Ep. 58 8 (agonem secularem).

[165] iv Macc. 7^{13} (Eleazar); H.E., v.1.19 (Blandina), and 24 (Sanctus).

[166] iv Macc. 6^{10}; H.E., v.1.19, 24 and 56 and Minucius Felix, Octavius, 37.4. Other examples given by H. Achelis, Das Christentum, ii.444, n. 98. See also Asc. Isaiah (ed. Charles) 5^{14}, and Mart. Akiba (ed. Mischle).

[167] iv Macc. 6^4, 7^4, and 11^{26}; H.E., v.1.18 and 24.

[168] iv Macc. 7^{15}; H.E., v.2.3.

[169] iv Macc. 17^{15}, 12^4; H.E., v.1.36 and 42.

[170] iv Macc. 7^{19}; H.E., v.1.41. Other lexigraphic parallels, O. Perler, art. cit., 64.

[171] O. Perler, op. cit., 64.

[172] See over, p. 270.

[173] Eusebius, H.E., iv.15.40, Acta Carpi, 8 and 17.

[174] H.E., iv.15.13 and 25.

[175] Note also, the proconsul's appeal to Polycarp, 'αἰδεσθητί γάρ σου τήν ἡλικίαν' (H.E., iv.15.18) and Antiochus', 'αἰδοῦμαι γάρ σου τήν ἡλικίαν' in iv Macc. 5.6.

[176] H.E., iv.15.10, 28 and 39.

[177] Ibid., iv.15.33. Another small detail common to both ii and iv Macc. and the martyrdom of Polycarp, is that the initiative in both cases is taken by the victim. Both the youngest of the Maccabees and Polycarp ask their judge 'What are you waiting for?' (ii Macc. 7^{30}, iv Macc. 12, Eusebius, H.E., iv.15.24).

[178] Eusebius, H.E., iv.15.3.

[179] Acta Carpi 35; cf. iv Macc. 6^{10}.

[180] Origen, Exhortation to Martyrdom, 23–7.

[181] Augustine, Breviculus Coll. cum Donatistis, iii.13.25 (P.L., xliii., 639).

[182] H. Lietzmann ed., Die drei ältesten Martyrologien (Kleine Texte, 2), pp. 5 and 13.

[183] Cyprian, Ad Fortunatum (ed. Hartel, CSEL., iii.1, 337–43).

[184] Lucifer of Cagliari, De non Parcendo in Deum delinquentibus, P.L., xiii, 958 B.

[185] Gregory of Nazianzus, Oratio, 15 (P.G., xxxv, 912). In its context this is an interesting example of the continuance of the 'Christians before Christ' theme, an optimistic view of human progress which we find in Justin i Apol. 46 and ii Apol. 13, and among the Alexandrian Christians.

[186] John Chrysostom, Sermo, de Eleazar et septem pueris (P.G., lxiii, 523ff.). See Townshend's analysis of these sermons and other material of the same period in R. H. Charles, Apocrypha and Pseudepigrapha of the Old Testament (= Apocrypha), 1913, ii, 659–60, and M. Simon's important article, 'La polemique antijuive de Saint Chrysostome et le mouvement judaisant d'Antioche', Mélanges Franz Cumont (= Ann. de l'Institut de Philologie et d'Histoire Orientales et Slaves, iv, 1936, 403–21).

[187] For example, *Acta Sanctae Symphorosae* (ed. Ruinart, *Acta Sincera*, Ratisbon, 1859), 23–5, and also the implied comparison between Anastasia and the Maccabean mother in *Acta Sanctae Anastasiae*, published by P. Devos, 'Sainte Anastasie la Vierge et la Source de la Passion', *A.B.*, lxxx, 1962, 42. See also, E. Egli, *Martyrien und Martyrologien ältester Zeit*, Zürich, 1887, 91, for Felicitas of Rome and Symphorosa.

[188] For popular edification too. The mosaic in the church of Madaba in Jordan lists the Maccabean martyrs among the heroes of the Christian faith. See also, J. Jeremias, 'Die Makkabäer-Kirche in Antiochien', *ZNTW.*, 40, 1942, 254.

[189] H. Delehaye, 'Martyr et Confesseur', *A.B.*, xxxix, 1921, 30–64, 'Et pour le dire en passant, nous ne reconnaissons nullement l'influence des idées juives par l'intermédiaire du livre ii des Macchabées et de certaines légendes des prophètes sur les Actes historiques des martyrs' (pp. 45–6); though Delehaye accepts their influence on the epic *Acta* and the fact of their general inspiration to the martyr (*Les Passions des Martyrs*, 314–15). It is an odd position, since many of these Acta dismissed as epics may contain a considerable portion of historical truth.

[190] The theme both of Esther and iii Maccabees.

[191] Tertullian, *Apol.*, 2.1ff.

[192] See over, p. 165.

[192] Note *inter alia*, the excellent work by T. M. Parker, *Christianity and the State in the light of History* (Bampton Lectures, 1954), London, 1955. Also, the views of Marcel Simon, *Rev. Historique*, fasc. 458, 1961, p. 443. 'Car je demeure convaincu que la politique chrétienne des empereurs est, en plus d'une occasion et de divers manières, liée à leur politique juive'.

CHAPTER TWO

Judaism and Martyrdom

IT has sometimes been said that Judaism was itself a religion of martyrdom.[1] The words spoken by Moses to his people on Mount Sinai affirm that the Jew was set apart from the rest of mankind in order to witness to God and to interpret His commands to humanity. 'Ye shall be a kingdom of priests, and a holy nation' (Exodus 19[6]).[2] The whole Jewish people was regarded as a κλῆρος, as in the *Acta* of the Lyons martyrs a 'special group', consecrated to God's service (Deut. 9[29] LXX), a service which included responsibilities and dangers as well as ultimate privileges.[3] Significantly, the writer of i Peter repeats the words of Exodus to his hearers, perhaps at the solemn celebration of the Easter Eucharist,[4] and links them with the command to bear witness to God's excellencies in the face of pagan hostility (i Peter 2[9ff.]). At the moment of the outbreak of the persecution of the Christians by the Emperor Maximin in 235, Origen uses the selfsame text to point to the fact that the Christians were 'the only people to fight for religion', and to 'prefer death rather than deny their religion and live'.[5] In both Dispensations, therefore, the role of the Chosen People and their destiny were one and the same.

The early history of the Jews, as preserved in traditions enshrined in the earlier books of the Old Testament, told of a long struggle against odds, and an even greater one to maintain religious cohesion. The Jew had learnt from the early prophets to scorn the religions of his neighbours, even if these for the time being appeared to be more successful in winning earthly rewards than himself. Habakkuk, for instance, writing perhaps at the turn of the seventh century B.C., contrasted the Israel of God with the hostile and more powerful Gentile nations, to the detriment of the latter.[6] Within a few years Ezekiel and Jeremiah were both exhorting their hearers to accept current disasters at the hands of the heathen and to submit to the Lord, remembering that the Lord was with His people, and that eventually judgment would be

31

executed on their enemies. The Day of Jahwe would be a day of reckoning for the Gentiles but of restoration for Israel, and if Jeremiah looked to the conversion of the Gentiles, Ezekiel saw no hope for them.

At the same time, the Jew was always conscious of having an active role as God's advocate in the midst of an evil and unsympathetic world. 'I will speak of thy testimonies before kings and will not be ashamed.'[7] His mission was not only national, but universal. In the first chapters of Isaiah, the world-wide character of Jahwe's kingdom was stressed, as well as its superiority over all its rivals. 'And it shall come to pass in the last days that the mountains of the Lord's house shall be established in the top of the mountains, and shall be exalted above the hills; and all nations shall flow unto it' (Is. 2[2]). The same expression of triumphant confidence is to be found in Micah (4[1ff.]). Jerusalem itself was to be the centre of this divine kingdom. So, at this comparatively early stage of Jewish history one can point to two tendencies which were to recur time and again in the history of both Judaism and the early Church; on the one hand a narrow and assertive particularism, and on the other, universal claims enforced ultimately by the threat of the Day of the Lord and Judgment to come, at which Jahwe's enemies would receive their reward.

These ideas were further developed in the generation that grew up after the fall of Jerusalem in 587 B.C. In Deutero-Isaiah, written probably 545–539 B.C., we find the idea of a positive witness fraught, however, with suffering for those who performed it. 'Ye are my witnesses, saith the Lord, and my servant whom I have chosen' (Is. 43[10]). They were witnesses to the greatness of God, and declared that besides Him there was no Saviour and no other God.[8] Israel's task was to bring this knowledge of God and His commandments to the Gentiles, so that, as the Prophet continues, 'thou mayest be my salvation to the end of the earth'. Even so, suffering and atonement for sin (Is. 53) went hand in hand with the task of prophetic witness. The Servant, perhaps the idealized people of Israel (cf. Is. 42[1] and 44[1]),[9] was presented as 'oppressed and afflicted', and 'taken from prison and from judgment'. Only thus, would he 'please the Lord and prosper in his land'. Only thus, could he 'bear the sin of the many and make intercession for the transgressors', 'pouring out his soul unto death', and 'atoning for sin' (Is. 53[10-12]). In the end too, God would reward his faithful people and punish backsliders. In the final chapter, the prophet vividly describes the unfaithful Israelites being destroyed in the valley of Hinnom outside Jerusalem (Is. 66[24]).

Even at this period therefore, some of the main characteristics of the later concepts of martyrdom were beginning to take shape. Witness to Jahwe was to be associated with suffering, indeed as Leaney has pointed out, every man called by God, from Moses onwards, was called to suffering and submission to God's will.[10] Suffering in turn was regarded as an atonement for Israel's collective sin; there was also an outline of the concept of the Remnant, the loyal and zealous of Israel, to whom the 'saints' of later Judaism and the Christian martyrs themselves were the heirs, and finally, there was the hope of divine deliverance for the Israelite nation itself and retribution on its enemies.

The two centuries of Persian rule brought little interference with Jewish religion.[11] The Persians pursued an enlightened religious policy towards those whom they conquered, similar in many ways to that of Rome, and like Rome they found the Jews potentially useful allies. The Jewish religion, we are told (Ezra 1[2ff.]), was treated with respect. Moreover, the long and generally calm association with the Persians witnessed important additions to Jewish ideas, which were to find a permanent place in the story of Jewish and Christian martyrdom. First, the relative dualism of Iranian religion reinforced ideas already existing in Judaism of an active spiritual force opposed to Jahwe, a force which could eventually be identified with 'idolatry' either in a cosmic setting or merely as represented by the current enemies of Israel. It has been pointed out, for instance, that the Satan of the Book of Job is a different being from the Devil of the New Testament, or the Antichrist of Christian *Acta Martyrum*.[12] Satan is strictly subordinate to God, and acts against Job with God's permission (Job 2[1ff.]).[13] Not so Belial or Antichrist. As we have seen he fights against the saints 'with all his strength', seeking by any means to overcome them.[14] If his final defeat was always foreshadowed, it would be accomplished only after a long and destructive career (Rev. 20[7ff]). This being, while perhaps ultimately deriving from the figure of Gog of the land of Magog (Ezek. 38-9),[15] resembles Angra Mainyu of Iranian mythology, who is also a direct enemy of God and a tempter of mankind, while the 'unclean spirits' and demons of the late-Jewish/early Christian apocalyptic resemble the Iranian 'daevas'.

Associated with the dualism of God and Antichrist may also be the dualism of Heaven and Hell, with corresponding rewards and punishments. In the Iranian *Gathas* individual souls would be judged at death and at a final universal ordeal by fire they would pass to their eternal lot of weal or woe. There is the description of the park-like Paradise, and in contrast, the seething, burning horror reminiscent of Revelation's lake of fire burning with brimstone (Rev. 19[20]) or the abysses of fire which swallow the unfaithful of Israel in Enoch (90.26).[16] The familiar imagery too, of winged spirits, angels or devils, seems ultimately to be derived from Babylonian and Assyrian mythology to which Persia was an heir.[17]

A second legacy from Iranian religion was the tendency towards periodization of history seen in the light of eschatology. In Zoroastrianism, the world was destined to last 12,000 years, divided into four periods of 3000 years each. In the first, Ahura Mazda, the Lord of Wisdom, brought forth his creatures in a spiritual state, and Angra Mainyu fled into darkness. In the second period, Ahura Mazda created the material world, and Angra Mainyu his demons. These latter triumph in the third period, but the human race is saved by the coming of a Saviour (Saoshyant), who ushers in the final period. This lasts until the Day of Judgment, when there would be a general resurrection of the dead, the final defeat of Angra Mainyu, and his destruction along with the material world in one vast conflagration.[18] For a people who already believed in a Day of the Lord when judgment would be executed on their enemies, the precision of Zoroastrianism must have exercised a powerful appeal. From now on, the overthrow of some devilish figure modelled on Angra Mainyu, interwoven with the Babylonian myth of a battle between the supreme God and the dragon of Chaos, penetrates Jewish thought, and is continued in early Christian apocalyptic. It is also not surprising that 'prophecies of Zoroaster' continued to find their way into the apocryphal literature of both Judaism and the early Church.[19]

In retrospect, the Persian period seemed like a golden age. In Isaiah, Ezra and ii Chronicles, Cyrus is hailed as the anointed of the Lord, to whom all kingdoms on earth had been granted.[20] A great number of Jews stayed behind in Persia even after the ending of the captivity in 538 B.C. Babylon remained the greatest centre of Jewry outside Jerusalem, and down to the end of the second century A.D.—for a period of no less than seven centuries— the Jews looked upon the Persians as their friends.[21] Jewish poets and apocalyptists later tended to believe that final deliverance from their idolatrous enemies would come through the agency of victorious armies from the East.[22] When Rome was at war with Parthia/Sassanid Persia, Jewish sympathies were almost invariably with the latter.

The few events recorded in the fifth century were, however, unlikely to give coherence to these incipient aspirations. Nehemiah's governorship *circa* 445–433 B.C., leading to the restoration of the walls of Jerusalem and the establishment of the Temple-cult as the official cult for Jews in the Persian Empire,[23] represented an era of good-will and religious security. The Jewish people became a self-contained theocracy centred round the temple-state at Jerusalem, governed by an aristocracy of priestly families. In *circa* 397 B.C. the priest-scribe Ezra, a descendant of Zadok, high-priest of Solomon, secured further concessions from Artaxerxes. To an observer Judah could hardly have looked very different from other priest-kingdoms in Syria, like that, for instance, of the powerful Ba'al Marcod situated around Berytus. The temple-rulers were able, however, to strengthen the traditional policy of keeping Judaism free from foreign contacts (Neh. 13) and of enforcing obedience to the age-old covenant of Israel. Submission to the Law was from henceforth the decisive token of membership of the Jewish nation.[24]

Perhaps, at the beginning of the fourth century,[25] though possibly earlier, something occurred which struck the imagination of contemporaries and seemed to presage dire events. There seems to have been a series of droughts, and forest fires, followed by an exceptionally destructive plague of locusts. This gave rise, in the mouth of the prophet Joel, to a piece of apocalyptic writing in the style of later eschatologists. The locusts were real locusts, but the havoc they caused moved the prophet to see them as an advancing army of destruction, presaging the Day of the Lord. So, in that time, there would 'be wonders in the heavens and in the earth, blood, and fire, and pillars of smoke' (Joel 2³⁰). The Iranian imagery had become accepted, and with it, prophetic utterances which were to be echoed over the centuries by Jew and Christian alike. In that day, 'I will pour out my spirit upon all flesh, ... your old men shall dream dreams and your young men shall see visions' (Joel 2²⁸). Then the heathen would be condemned and Jerusalem delivered from oppression. Bliss would follow. 'The mountains shall drop down new wine, and the hills shall flow with milk' (3¹⁸). Even in a period of religious peace apocalyptic stirrings were evidently only just below the surface. Joel's prophecies were to inspire the Christians from the earliest moments of the mission, the Apostles at Pentecost (Acts 2¹⁷), and thereafter Cerinthus, (Eusebius *H.E.*, 3.28.5) Papias (ibid., 3.39.12), Irenaeus (*Adv. Haer.*, iv.33.15) and the writer of the *Passio Perpetuae* (c.1), for all of whom salvation depended on millennial eschatology.[26]

How it was that even at this time Jews were 'being sold unto Grecians' (Joel 3⁶) we do not know. Some sixty years later, however, the conquests of Alexander the Great brought about a decisive change in the fortunes of Israel. As a result, Jew and Greek eventually became as much neighbours and adversaries as Jew and Philistine had been in the era of Saul and David. Hellenism, if not a proselytizing creed, was an all-pervading influence. Language, laws, a system of government, the Polis and its institutions spread in the wake of the victorious Macedonian armies. After the death of Alexander in 323 B.C., Israel found herself once more perched uneasily on the frontiers of two great empires and coveted by the successor dynasties of both the Seleucids and the Ptolemies as a valuable outpost.

Under the Ptolemaic domination, however, which lasted throughout the third century B.C., there was again little if any interference with the Jewish way of life.[27] Two points, however, are worth notice. First, there appear the earliest glimmerings of anti-Semitism showing itself in Alexandria, probably arising from Egyptian dislike of the celebration of the Passover. In self-defence the Egyptians began to claim that the Exodus was in fact an expulsion of undesirable and disease-ridden foreigners.[28] Secondly, the problems of adapting themselves to Greek surroundings began to force itself on the Jews in the city of Alexandria. While the production of the Septuagint was probably designed in the main to meet the needs of Jews who were losing the use of Hebrew, Judaism also acquired a means of pushing her religion beyond its national limits. The 'light to lighten the Gentiles' became a possibility.[29]

As against this, the Jews were themselves becoming increasingly subject to the Hellenistic influence. Their own territory was restricted to the province of Judaea. All around them Greek cities grew up, on the coast as at Gaza, Sidon and Joppa, inland at Sepphoris, Gadara and Lydda, and across the Jordan at Jerash,[30] to mention a few of the best-known examples. The effects on the Jewish way of life were noticeable. As early as *circa* 300 B.C., the traveller Hecataeus of Abdera recorded in a well-known passage that, like other races, 'the Jews had greatly altered the ordinances of their forefathers', as a result of the contact with Hellenism.[31] Indeed, for the next century or so they were even in danger of becoming a minority in their own country. Not surprisingly, representatives of the prophetic tradition reacted violently to this situation. It seems plausible to date the later chapters of Zechariah to this period,[32] and in this work Hellas is already being singled out as the enemy of the Temple-State (Zech. 9^{12-17}). Once again, the faithful were comforted with the vision of the destruction of the heathen in the Day of the Lord (Zech. $14^{1 ff.}$). The prophecy of the deliverance of Judah by the lowly King riding into Jerusalem on an ass was to be vividly recalled three centuries later.

The prophetic tradition, however, was only one of the various competing traditions within Judaism. Outside the frontiers of Palestine, Jew and Greek do not seem to have met in the first instance as enemies. Indeed, if we are to believe Josephus, Greek writers of the third century B.C. characterized the Jews as a 'philosophical race', to be compared with Indian fakirs—not the last time this comparison was to be used in describing the religious zeal of Jews or Christians. Their religion and ethic, however, commanded respect.[33] Alexander the Great paid a friendly visit to the Temple and sacrificed there according to the directions of the High Priest.[34] The early Seleucids favoured the Jews as a power in spreading Greco-Asiatic civilization in Asia Minor and particularly in Lydia and Phrygia.[35] Two thousand families were settled in those provinces by Antiochus III, as 'well-disposed guardians of our possessions',[36] and the Jews, using the Greek language, certainly felt more in common with their Greek neighbours in the Seleucid foundations than with the rural native population. It was only under the pressure of later events that hostility developed between the two groups of settlers, and their common interests in the face of a surrounding barbarian world fell into the background.

Towards the end of the third century, one can detect a slight quickening in the pace of Palestinian opposition to Hellenization. In earlier phases of Jewish history any increase in the attractions of heathen cultures among Jews evoked equally strong anti-foreign reactions. Now, the same thing occurred. Some scholars would place the emergence of a definite body of the *hasidim*, the 'strict' or 'pious' ones, to this period. These Jews were determined to resist encroachment of Hellenization and maintain the old order.[37] They were 'mighty men of Israel who willingly offered themselves for the Law' (i Macc. 2[42]). Something of their outlook may be preserved in Ben Sira's protest against the attitude of those of his readers who are becoming ashamed 'of the Law of the Most High and the statute' (Ecclus. 42[2]), his demand for the 'nationalization' of Jewish learning focussed on Jerusalem (34[1ff.]) and his hope that God would 'exterminate the heathen enemy' (ibid., 36[8-9]). But the Ptolemies were, in general, not unpopular, and so long as they ruled, the threat of conflict between the old and new ways of life remained dormant. Nor did the Seleucid victory at Panium (Banias) in 198 B.C. bring any immediate change. Josephus preserves texts which show that the Jews even helped to eject the Egyptian garrison in Jerusalem and that, in return, the victorious Antiochus III solemnly reaffirmed the privileges which the Jews had enjoyed under the Ptolemies. 'All Jews may enjoy their traditional way of life', he stated (*Antiquities*, xii.3.142). This attitude was reciprocated by a considerable number of his Jewish subjects, represented perhaps by the writer of Ecclesiastes who appears to be critical of the Ptolemies but favourable to their Seleucid rivals.[38] Unfortunately, Antiochus overreached himself, and his attempt to extend his empire in Asia Minor was decisively beaten by the Romans in 190 B.C. at Magnesia. When he died three years later, trying to enrich himself by plundering a shrine of Baal, there was a heavy indemnity to be paid off, and the chronic lack of funds which was to afflict his successors had repercussions on their religious policy.

The storm, however, which was to shatter Seleucid dominion in Palestine arose from causes for which Antiochus' successors were not immediately responsible. In Jerusalem, the only Jewish centre of any size, many of the aristocratic families, including some of the priestly families, were moving rapidly towards acceptance of Hellenistic standards.[39] In this they were simply following the pattern of similarly placed families in other Temple-States within the Seleucid Empire. The writer of i Maccabees, probably the official history of the Hasmonean dynasty, *circa* 135 B.C.[40] states that in the reign of Seleucus IV (187–175 B.C.) Jerusalem had its gymnasium, heathen sacrifices were being performed, and that circumcision was tending to die out (i Macc. 1[11-14]). This latter fact is confirmed in Jubilees 15[33-34] (*circa* 160–150 B.C.?)[41] whose writer complains also that the traditional priestly calendar was no longer being observed (Jub. 23[19]). The writer of ii Maccabees (Alexandria? *circa* 120 B.C.)[42] adds that the ephebate, and Greek fashions derived from it were also being accepted by the rising generation (ii Maccabees 4[12-14]). The Hellenizers were, in fact, establishing Jerusalem as a new *polis*, complete with *Boulé* and *Demos* and linked to the Seleucid capital at Antioch.[43] The Mosaic law was fast ceasing to be the law of the Jewish capital city.[44]

These moves, however, were encountering increasing opposition. Whatever might be done in Jerusalem, the Jewish countryside remained firmly attached to tradition. Here, in the villages and hamlets where the mass of the Palestinian Jews lived, Hellenization had made little progress. It was essentially an urban influence. Beyond the city walls, Aramaic was the spoken language.[45] The linguistic barrier denoted a cultural barrier—not for the last time in Jewish and early Christian history. The priestly families at Jerusalem were prepared to come to terms with 'idolatrous' influences, just as the wealthy Christian clergy in Carthage were to do on the eve of the Great Persecution. In both cases, they were thwarted by a rigorist minority in the capital, backed overwhelmingly by a conservative-minded rural population. In Christian North Africa as in Jewish Palestine righteousness had become associated with poverty, and the peasant responded

to the double appeal of 'humbling the mighty' and strict obedience to the teaching of God. In the reign of Seleucus IV, the
traditionalists found a champion in the person of the High Priest,
Onias III, who could claim descent from Zadok.

The long struggle for power between Seleucus IV and his
rival, the future Antiochus IV, had had apparently little effect on
Jewish relations with their overlords. This situation, however,
was to be changed abruptly when Antiochus became king in
175 B.C. The events of the next dozen years were to have a far-
reaching effect on the development of both Judaism and the early
Church.[46]

Shrewd but vain, statesmanlike, yet volatile, theatrical and
obstinate, Antiochus appears to have aimed at welding together
his heterogeneous dominions into a semblance of unity based on
adhesion to a common culture.[47] There is no reason to believe
that he felt any particular animosity against the Jews when he took
over the government. Lack of money,[48] due largely to the need
of making continued payments to Rome as the result of his
father's disastrous defeat, together with a lively appreciation of
Rome's power, based on his experience as a hostage there, formed
the background of his actions. The Temple of Jerusalem was by
no means the only religious sanctuary that he ransacked.[49] If
vanity dictated the appearance of the title Θεὸς Ἐπιφανὴς (= 'God
manifest') on his coins from 169 B.C.,[50] it is fair to add that he was
only expressing what most of his subjects already believed, and
what his rival in Alexandria had no hesitation in proclaiming
(e.g. on the Rosetta stone, dated 196 B.C.) His ultimate objective
was probably to identify each of the provincial gods with the
deity of his House, Zeus Ouranios. This did not, as Bickermann
points out, involve any actual change in the Jerusalem temple.
Jahwe was merely given a name, not a Greek one, be it noted,
but a Syrian one.[51] In Samaria where Torah was also observed,
Mount Gerizim became the site of a temple for the new worship
without any trouble.[52]

Two factors, however, which did not operate to the same
extent elsewhere were to confront Antiochus with the embittered
hostility of a large section of Jewry. In the first place, there was
an organized opposition to Hellenization already in existence, and
secondly, Antiochus' policies embroiled him in the complicated

rivalries of high priestly families who combined the religious and secular government of the state. The result was religious war.[53]

Antiochus' first step seems to have been to put up the office of high priest to the highest bidder. Onias' brother Jason (Jeshua) was as pro-Hellene as he himself was conservative, and offered the immense sum of 360 talents plus an annuity of 80 talents for it. He also asked permission to fit out a gymnasium, extend the ephebate and organize a privileged corporation 'the Antiochenes', under royal protection. (ii Macc. 4[8-9] and i Macc. 1[13].)[54] He was accepted. A presentation of 300 drachmas was sent to the quinquenial festival of Heracles at Tyre (ii Macc. 4[19]) and Onias was packed off an exile to Antioch (ii Macc. 4[33]). Unfortunately, this was not enough. Jason found himself the victim of the same intrigue that he had used against his brother. Another Hellenist, Menelaus, ousted Jason (ii Macc. 4[24]), who was forced to flee to the wilderness east of Jordan. Then, at the instigation of the new priest, Onias was murdered, 171/170 B.C. The roll of martyrs for the Law had been opened (ii Macc. 4[34]).

Such was the situation in 170 B.C. In the winter of that year war broke out between Antiochus and the Ptolemaic kingdom. Antiochus was obliged by his father's treaty with Rome not to attack a friend or ally or Rome, such as Egypt was, but the Egyptians played into his hands and declared war. Antiochus had evidently laid plans for just such an occasion. He was amazingly successful. He took Pelusium, and by the summer of 169 B.C.[55] was in Memphis. On his way back to Syria (Oct./Nov. 169)[56] he plundered the temple at Jerusalem to the tune of 1800 talents— a vast sum, the equivalent of two years' indemnity to Rome (i Macc. 1[20]). Next year, Antiochus invaded Egypt again. This time he allowed himself actually to be crowned king of Memphis.[57] The siege of Alexandria followed, but then, at the moment of complete triumph came the overthrow of his plans. The Senate's emissary Popilius arrived, and the famous incident took place in which Antiochus was solemnly warned off Egypt. Meantime, things had not been going well in Judaea. There had always been a pro-Egyptian party among the people,[58] and one can reasonably suppose that it was from this source that the rumour of the king's death came. Jason returned from his exile, and Menelaus was forced to beat a retreat into the newly established Citadel (Akra).

Jason, however, was himself forced out, this time by a popular rising. Antiochus, hearing that Judaea had risen, returned post-haste determined to punish the rebellious city of Jerusalem. His troops forced an entry: there was considerable loss of life, and Antiochus in exasperation proceeded to slight the town walls and reduce its status to the level of a 'village' dependent on the Seleucid-garrisoned Citadel.[59]

Up to this point Antiochus had dealt with the Jews no more harshly than was to be expected. The inhabitants had shown themselves unreliable, and at the same time, their state lay on a vitally important line of communication. What took place now, however, went far beyond political measures of retaliation. Antiochus seems to have had two aims. That the unification of his realm, no doubt in the face of the renewed Roman threat, was one, is clear from one of the few recorded statements of the king's objective, recorded in i Macc. 1⁴. 'He wrote to his whole kingdom that all should be one people.' The idea of a general decree sounds fantastic; its existence had become part of folk-lore half a century later. We may, however, accept the view that specific orders were issued by Antiochus. The second object was to draw the teeth of the xenophobe Torah which Antiochus realized was the backbone of Jewish resistance. That this view was not uncommon among Hellenistic rulers is clear from the 'decree' of 'king Xerxes'[60] arraigning the Jews for 'having had laws diverse from all people and neither keep they the king's laws: therefore it is not for the king's profit to suffer them' (Esther 3⁸). So far as one can reconstruct Antiochus' actual orders during the winter of 168/7, it seems that burnt offerings in the Temple were to cease, and sacrifices were to be made of forbidden animals.[61] Copies of the Law were destroyed, Sabbath observance and circumcision were forbidden on pain of death, and in December 167 an altar (perhaps a statue as well) set up in the courtyard of the Temple—the famous 'abomination of desolation', and swine's flesh offered on it.[62]

Outside Jerusalem, in the villages, Syro-Greek temples and altars were also erected and Jews were obliged to participate in their rites.[63] Jahwe was down-graded to the rank of a local Baal,[64] just as his city had lost its privileged status and reverted to the rank of a village. The aim of these measures as stated in both i and ii Maccabees was 'so that they (the Jews) should forget the Law and change the ordinances', or more directly, 'that the Jews should leave the law of their fathers and live not after the law of God', (i Macc. 1^{49} and ii Macc. 6^1). But it was only the Jews of Judaea who were singled out for this treatment. So far as we know, the Jews in other parts of the Seleucid dominions were not molested,[65] and as already mentioned, the Samaritans gladly accepted the royal policies.[66]

The inhabitants of the Temple-state of Jerusalem, however, faced the loss of everything that had hitherto marked them off from their fellows. One cannot seek to minimize either the effect or the intention of the decrees. 'It was unlawful for a man to profess himself to be a Jew' (ii Macc. 6^{1-8}). Therefore, recant or die. The Palestinian Jew faced the same alternatives as those that confronted the Christian two or three centuries later on virtually the same issue. 'The name of God was blasphemed' (ii Macc. 8^4), a phrase which was to evoke righteous suffering by Jew and Christian alike. The era of persecutions had begun. Later on, the Jew was to be presented with the same political and religious issues in the reign of Caligula and Hadrian. The Christian was confronted with analogous tests under Decius and Diocletian. Not to have met the challenge would have meant that the prophets, and indeed the whole previous tradition of Israel, had spoken in vain. In the event, Antiochus unleashed the first religious war in the history of mankind.[67]

Antiochus had underestimated the strength of the opposition. The pattern of events, often to be repeated in Jewish and early Christian history, developed. In 167 B.C. it was not a case of the Jewish people united in rebellion against the Seleucid idolaters. The conflict was more in the nature of a civil war, and the decision for or against obedience to the king's commands was placed on the individual. This in itself had important results, for henceforth individual salvation or damnation was to take its place in Judaism alongside the traditional concept of the salvation of the People.

The authorities found a good deal of collaboration among the well-to-do and the cultured, including the spiritual leaders of the people, but outside Jerusalem, among the mass of craftsmen, petty traders and peasants, there was bitter opposition. Five hundred years later, the officials of the Tetrarchy were to find the same balance of acquiescence and resistance in Egypt and North Africa during the Great Persecution. In each case, the inspiration of the resistance was both cultural and religious, the 'foreign ways' of the big town being resented by a rural population which was also open to exploitation and oppression by urban tax-collectors and landlords. 'Whoever is zealous for the Law, and maintaineth the Covenant, let him come after me.' Thus Mattathias (i Macc. 2^{27}). The first act of rebellion, the overthrow of a heathen altar and murder of an apostate Jew at Modin was to be the symbol of the conflict between an exclusive monotheist cult and the universal appeal of Classical civilization for centuries to come.[68]

Three main developments which arose from the revolt were later to influence the Christian attitude towards the Roman Empire. First, was the idea of martyrdom, namely personal witness to the truth of the Law against the forces of heathenism, involving the suffering and even death of the witness. Secondly, derived from this, was the hope of personal resurrection (cf. Daniel 12^{2}) and vengeance on apostates and persecuting powers hereafter, and thirdly, the transfer of the secular struggle to a cosmic level, with the opposition viewed less as human oppressors than as representatives of demonic powers. All the tendencies towards righteous suffering, ultimate salvation and judgment on the enemies of Israel became accentuated and personalized as the struggle proceeded. A generation or so after the success of the revolt, Jason of Cyrene recorded the story of the scribe Eleazar, and of a valiant Jewish mother and her seven sons, who staunchly resisted all attempts to force them into acts of idolatry. The narrative preserved by his epitomist in ii Maccabees 6–8 teaches the rightness of resisting a heathen oppressor to the death, and significantly represents the views of the Jews of the Dispersion living side by side with their heathen neighbours. It is not an isolated pamphlet. The writer of Esther, perhaps *circa* 130 B.C.,[69] and a century later, iii and iv Maccabees[70] proclaimed the same message. It was to bode ill for peaceful relations between representatives of rival religions and cultural outlooks in the Hellenistic East under Roman administration.[71]

Eleazar is described as one of the foremost and most venerable of the scribes. Like others, he was required to eat pork which had been sacrificed at the monthly celebration of the king's birthday.

The authorities hoped to make the most of his renunciation of the prescriptions of Judaism (ii Maccabees 6^{18-31}). But rejecting persuasions and blandishments the old man refused to comply (6^{23}); he was tortured and eventually put to death. The same fate awaited the mother and her sons. They are said to have been actually brought to the king and his *amici*, and ordered to do the same. Despite persuasions and threats they remained steadfast, preferring to die after excruciating tortures rather than submit. The mother perished last of all after watching the martyrdom of her sons.

Important conclusions may be drawn from this first Acts of the Martyrs.[72] First of all, of course, no deviations from the prescription of Torah were permissible, particularly if these could be interpreted as giving even a tacit assent to idolatry. Death must be suffered unhesitatingly and the heathen ruler defied (cf. ii Macc. 6^{29} and ^{39}). Two centuries later, the Rabbi Eleazar ben Arak was to write, 'Be watchful in the study of the Torah and know what answer to give to the unbeliever, and let not one word in the Torah be forgotten by thee, and know before whom thou toilest and who is *Ba'al berithka*'.[73] And, as so often, one finds the Jewish tradition carried into the early Church, and in particular among the rigorist element. During, or soon after, the Great Persecution, the writer of the *Acta Saturnini* warned his hearers against the changing of even 'one jot or tittle of Christ's Law', and of the serious nature of this offence.[74]

Secondly, the martyr was regarded as representative of the people of Israel and 'an example of nobility and a memorial of virtue, not only to the young but also to the great body of his nation' (6^{31}). Eleazar's aim was to set that example (6^{24-28}), 'to die willingly and nobly a glorious death for the reverend and holy laws'. Persecution had been the result of sin, and suffering was its expiation. 'We suffer because of our sins' (ii Macc. 7^{32}), affirmed one of the Hebrew young men. The victim was personally innocent, but died as a vicarious sacrifice on behalf of his people (7^{37}), to stay the wrath of the Almighty (7^{38}): but—and here the story is linked up to the unending theme of Jewish Scripture— God disciplined and corrected even in His most severe punishments. The cup of sin—meaning primarily disobedience to His Law—was never allowed to overflow. Thus, in the next verse we read the words 'And though the living Lord be angry with us for a little while for our chastening and correction, yet shall he be at one again with his servants'. Reconciliation would follow sacrifice. The lesson had already been stated by the author (ii Macc. 6[12-18]). In this connection as well, the story anticipates the Christian *Acta*.[75] Persecution ceases after the sacrifice has been made.

A third and most important point concerns eschatology. The martyr was the agent for the preparation of the Age to come. Reconciliation between God and His people through the 'hastening of God's mercy' would be speeded by his sacrifice.[76] Martyrdom was believed to wipe off a fixed amount of transgression, and reconciliation would take place at a point in time when the cup had been emptied sufficiently. Though the emphasis is, as always, on the Jewish nation,[77] benefit would also come to the individual. The act of martyrdom was the means of his own entry into eternal life, and the sign that his persecutors would not escape God's judgment (ii Macc. 7[14]). For the victorious victim both resurrection and immortality were promised.[78] This is plainly expressed by the speech made by the Mother to her children (ii Macc. 7[22-23]). 'I neither gave you breath nor life, neither was it I who formed the members of every one of you. But doubtless the Creator of the world, who formed the generation of man and found out the beginning of all things, will also of his own mercy give you breath and life again as ye now regard not your own selves for his laws' sake.' Previously, one of the youths addressed Antiochus, 'Thou like a fury takest us out of our present life, but the king of the world shall raise us up who have died for his laws, unto everlasting life' (ii Macc. 7[9]). The king 'who has been the author of all mischief against the Hebrews shall not escape the hand of God' (ii Macc. 7[31]).[79] The 'wrath of God' would fall upon him. He would not rise to life (ii Macc. 7[14]). Once more, we find anticipated the recurrent theme of Christian historiography particularly in the West. The disease which attacked Antiochus (ii Macc. 9[5]) was regarded as an act of God, like that which smote the Emperor Galerius in the spring of 311.[80] In both cases, the righteous victims were avenged by God; death-bed repentance by the persecutor was in vain.

Finally, the sacrifice was willing and unresisting. 'What

wouldst thou ask or learn of us' said one of the youths to Antiochus, 'we are ready to die rather than transgress the laws of our
fathers' (ii Macc. 7³). Eleazar 'steps forward at once to the instrument of torture' (ibid., 6²⁹). There was no appeal to arms; God's
vengeance on the martyr's tormentors was sufficient retribution.
A similar lesson is taught in i Maccabees in connection with the
massacre of the pious Jewish refugees who refused to fight to save
their lives on the Sabbath (though on any other day they would
have fought). 'Let us die in all innocency: heaven and earth shall
testify for us that ye put us to death wrongfully' (i Macc. 2³⁷).
Like them, the Christian martyrs Polycarp, Justin, Pionius and
many others, went uncomplainingly to their fate. Even suicide
in this cause would be justified.[81] Moreover, the reaction of the
Seleucid authorities, namely to regard such an attitude as 'sheer
madness' (ii Macc. 6²⁹) finds its counterpart in that of the Roman
authorities in the second and third centuries A.D.[82] These characteristics of the *Acta Martyrum* of the early Church are also
found in the Passion narratives. For both the pious Jew and his
Christian descendant the emphasis lay on suffering rather than on
armed opposition. Only so long as the religious issue was in the
balance did the *Hasidim* lend militant support to the Maccabees.[83]

I and ii Maccabees had been preceded a generation earlier by
Daniel. The seer of age-old Israelite tradition provided the
pseudonymous cover for what 'may be regarded as the manifesto
of the *Hasidim*'[84] at the height of the war. The main lesson which
the latter wished to teach was identical with that of the narrative
of Eleazar and his companions, namely that martyrdom was to be
preferred to idolatry, even if the act of idolatry involved violation
of only the least of God's commandments. Thus, the seer's
friends affirm, 'If our God whom we serve is able to deliver us,
he will deliver us from ... thy hand, O king, but if not, be it
known to thee O king, that we will not serve thy gods ...'
(Dan. 3¹⁷⁻¹⁸). Their confidence rested on the belief that only
Jahwe was the true and living God and that His power was
irresistible. Other gods were merely helpless idols of wood and
stone devoid of feeling and knowledge (Dan. 5²³). Associated with
this, one finds clearly outlined a philosophy of history which went
beyond previous Jewish hopes. God's omnipotence was portrayed
in terms of the restoration of Israel as the final act of a vast and

fantastic historical drama, an eloquent and lasting testimony to the passions aroused among pious Jews by Antiochus' measures.

In the 'dream' of Daniel 7, four beasts symbolize four successive world-powers, the Babylonian, the (unhistorical) Median, the Persian and finally the Greek.[85] The first three were represented by a fearsome mythological beast, but the seer had reserved to the last the full measure of brutality and ferocity.[86] The reign of Antiochus IV seemed indeed to witness the triumph of demonic evil. But this empire also would be overthrown, and Israel, personified as the 'Son of Man' would come into its own. 'All peoples, nations and languages would serve him. His dominion was everlasting dominion, which would not pass away.' This was the eternal 'fifth empire' whose greatness would be given 'to the people of the saints of the most high',[87] who would 'possess it for ever, even for ever and ever' (7^{18}). The tyrant Antiochus would be 'broken without hand', (8^{25}). Victory would come suddenly by supernatural means, and it would be final. The dominion of the saints would have no end (7^{27}). The challenge to idolatry, represented by the Seleucids, was direct and complete. The same prophecies could also inspire opposition to any other idolatrous world empire, that of Rome included.

In this vision, one finds for the first time militant apocalypticism accompanying the struggle of adherents of a revolutionary creed opposed to a world empire.[88] The sequence of defeat at the hands of overwhelming power, followed by final and glorious victory becomes from now onwards part of the saga of all oppressed humanity. So do the martyrs, the individual fallen in the heroic struggle. They would be rewarded in the world to come ($12^{1ff.}$). It was an appeal too, directed to the common people to whom the overthrow of the mighty, especially if they appeared to be traitors as well, was welcome indeed.

In the final chapters of Daniel, the lesson was driven home to the Jews living and suffering at the time. The pollution of the sanctuary and the apostasy of part of the people were recorded (11^{31-32}) and so too, the deaths of the righteous, which it is implied are accepted by God as part of the price of disobedience (11^{33}). Antiochus himself is seen not merely as an hostile ruler, but as a contrary power to God. 'He shall speak marvellous things against the God of gods' (11^{36}). He was cast for a supernatural, demonic role, the first Antichrist. In the writer's view, the struggle between Judaism and Hellenism becomes part of a cosmic drama, at the end of which the victims would arise from the dust of the earth and shine as 'stars in the heavens'. (12³). Their opponents, the Hellenizers and apostates, in contrast, would 'awake ... to shame and everlasting contempt'. Judgment would reward each according to his merits. In face of this profound confidence in God's justice and omnipotence, recourse to an armed resistance, such as that of Judas Maccabaeus, was 'a little help' (11³⁴) only.

The importance of this outlook for later Jewish and early Christian thought needs no emphasis. Reward and punishment after death were fundamental to the Christian martyr's hope. Salvation followed for those 'who called upon the Name of God'.[89] Shameful and painful death would not otherwise have been so readily faced. The contrast between the pre- and post-Maccabean attitudes towards retribution after death is dramatic. Though in the mysterious Is. 26¹⁹ we find a clear reference to the belief in resurrection of the body,[90] the 'long home' to which most individuals were believed to be destined (Eccles. 12⁵) was the underworld of Sheol. This was the 'land of darkness and the shadow of death' (Job 10²¹⁻²²) and its inhabitants, the dead 'know not anything, neither have they any more a reward, for the memory of them is forgotten'. So wrote the author of Ecclesiastes (Eccles. 9⁵)[91] perhaps half a century or so before Daniel, and he drew on a long tradition.[92] It was Daniel, however, that prevailed.[93] If God could deliver the living from the power of the heathen, could he not also deliver those fallen in heroic combat? In the generation after the Maccabean revolt we find the writer of ii Maccabees reflecting that, 'if he (Judas Maccabaeus) had not expected that the fallen would rise again, it would have been silly and idle to pray for dead men' (ii Macc. 12⁴⁴).

In the same period, the great panorama of history unfolded in Enoch 85–90 shows the throne of Judgment set up in Palestine, 'and all that had perished and were scattered', i.e. all faithful Israelites, would become dwellers in New Jerusalem, while 'blinded sheep', i.e. apostates, would be committed to fiery destruction. In the course of the next century the Pharisees generalized and developed this doctrine of individual resurrection until it became basic to Palestinian Judaism.[94] In parts of the

Dispersion, however, notably in Alexandria and Antioch, the emphasis came to be placed on the immortality not of the resurrected body, but of the soul. Behind the subtle differences in teaching between ii and iv Maccabees, and behind the well-loved passage from Wisdom, (3¹ᶠᶠ)'The souls of the righteous are in the hands of God',[95] lay the beginnings of a cleavage of outlook between the majority of the Dispersion Jews and the majority of their Palestinian brethren. But meantime, death for the Law was accepted as inherent in the status of 'saints of the most high'; in both Palestine and the Dispersion it was regarded as meriting the highest reward hereafter. It was an obligation and a challenge to Jew and Christian alike.

It is not intended to follow the history of the Hasmoneans further,[96] except in so far as events illustrate some of the more lasting features in the Jewish psychology of martyrdom and persecution which were relevant to the Christian outlook. Four points may be made. First, that in both Palestine and the Dispersion the generation of war and revolution which lasted 167–142 B.C. intensified existing divisions between Jew and Gentile. Death for religion's sake and exultant triumph over the heathen became permanent factors in the Jewish heritage. 'Condemn we him to a shameful death; so shall we make examination of his words.' Thus did the Alexandrian Wisd. 2²⁰ sum up the heathen hostility in which the Dispersion Jew was living.[97] Secondly, derived perhaps from this situation, there developed within Judaism a theology of righteous suffering, centred on the alleged experiences of patriarchal and prophetic heroes. This explained and justified to the Jews their role both as a struggling nation and as a fanatical minority scattered about the Greco-Roman world. This theme also played a large part in the development of the Christian outlook in parallel circumstances. Thirdly, however, differences of history and culture which separated Palestinian and Dispersion Jews contributed towards the development of divergent interpretations of this theology, and consequently, to contrasting attitudes towards Greco-Roman society. Fourthly, these differences contain the germs of what at first sight seems a puzzling difference of approach by Western and Eastern Christians to the same issue.

We shall meet the first problem again when we discuss the situation in the Hellenistic East to which Rome was the heir at the moment of Christianity's emergence as a missionary religion in the decade A.D. 35-45. Here, it suffices to refer to the work already done by W. R. Farmer in demonstrating the continuous influence of the Maccabean outlook both in its pacifist and revolutionary forms through the Hasmonean and into the Roman era.[98] As Farmer suggests, 'There was no fundamental change in the relationship of Jewish nationalism to the Torah from Antiochus Epiphanes to Titus'.[99] Among the people, the naming of genera- tion after generation of children after the great revolutionary heroes, Simon, Judas and Jonathan,[100] and the yearly Feast of Dedication, kept the nationalist tradition alive,[101] while educated leaders were no longer of the stamp of Jason and Menelaus, but nationalists like Philo and Josephus.[102]

The testimony of these two writers on the great part which voluntary suffering and death played in Jewish thought at this time is impressive. Both were aristocrats and pro-Roman at heart, and although devout Jews, irrevocably caught up in the crises which beset their people, they remained intelligent and critical observers of the latter's feelings. The Jews living in Judaea 'are men, physically strong, of great courage and spirit', Philo remarks, 'who are willing to die in defence of their national customs and laws in a spirit which some opponents might call barbaric, but which in reality is free and noble',[103]—and he was no mean representative of this attitude himself.[104] As he said, 'a glorious death met in the defence of the Law is a kind of life'.[105] He is quite clear that by A.D. 40 even the most pro-Roman aristocrat would be horror-struck at the suggestion of even the Emperor attempting to impose a breach of God's Law on the Jewish people. King Agrippa had a stroke when Caligula told him of his plan to set up a statue of Zeus in the Temple at Jerusalem.[106] The loyalty which Agrippa felt for the Augustan house, and his gratitude for past favours were outweighed by the sense of disaster which Caligula's plan evoked. He could not acquiesce and remain alive. Indeed, he asked at the end of a long and piteous letter to the Emperor who was also his friend, 'to be got rid of at once'.[107] The reaction of Agrippa's prospective subjects is also vividly described by Philo, who was at Rome at this moment in connection with disasters which had befallen the Jews in Alexan- dria in 38 at the hands of the Greek inhabitants. He leaves no doubt that feelings akin to suicidal hysteria were gripping his fellow-countrymen. The Jewish deputation who met Petronius, the legate of Syria, at Ptolemais in the late spring of 40 solemnly requested that they and all the vast crowd that accompanied them should be killed 'in order that we may not live to see an evil worse than death'.[108] Petronius in his dispatch to the Emperor suggested that the Jews, 'despairing of their traditions and despising life would ravage their fields or set fire to their cornlands in the hills and on the plains'—wholesale destruction rather than submit.[109] This was no idle threat, as the Galilean peasants were to show in 67/68. Caligula, who had 'puffed himself up in that he not only said, but believed himself to be a god' invited the same reaction as Antiochus IV.[110]

Josephus gives a similar account of these incidents. The Jews, he says, knew that armed revolt stood no chance of success. 'We will not make war with Caesar,' their leaders admitted to Petronius in reply to a question, 'but we will die before we see our laws transgressed'.[111] Then, an extraordinary incident took place which Josephus describes. 'They threw themselves down and stretched out their throats and said they were ready to be slain.'[112] At Tiberias similar events occurred, with thousands of Jews 'demanding to be killed rather than countenance a breach of the law of their forefathers'.[113]

Josephus, too, is a valuable witness for the various attitudes towards pagan society and its representatives found among Jews a generation later. Though he wrote the account of the *Jewish Wars* in 75 with the deliberate aim of showing that the revolt was the work of a fanatical minority aided by the crass stupidity and ill-will of the Roman administration, he was a fair-minded if interested contemporary observer. He was sympathetic to the world-renouncing Jewish sects on the one hand, but an admirer of the Roman Empire on the other. He was linked by descent to the royal house of Hasmoneans, he was a Pharisee believing passionately in Judaism, but was not impervious to the cultural achievements of Hellenism.[114] Above all, he was interested in giving an account of events rather than an analysis of ideas, and thus what he says incidentally about the outlook of his fellow Jews is of great interest.

How far did the hopes of a Messianic deliverance of Israel

hastened by the willing deaths of its people provide the inspiration of practical conduct? Like Philo, Josephus also leaves no doubt that in the last resort the Jew was prepared to die for his faith, and that he had been brought up with this obligation in mind. He tells his opponent Apion in 95 (*Contra Apionem*, I, 8), 'For it becomes natural to all Jews immediately and from their very birth to esteem those books (of the Law) above all else to contain divine precepts, and to persist in them, and if occasion be, to die for them'. His words are corroborated by his younger contemporary Tacitus, writing *circa* A.D. 115, who records that the Jews believed that those who died in battle or as a punishment (i.e. by a pagan ruler) were eternal.[115] Josephus connects this attitude with the fact that his people had received their laws through Moses from God; and that such conduct was to be expected of citizens of a Theocracy. The Jews were under permanent discipline in their daily life, restricted by divine ordinances, and for that reason, he adds, 'men ought not to wonder at us if we are more courageous in dying for our laws than all other men are'.[116]

This accepted, there remained considerable differences as to when death on behalf of the Law was to be undergone. Josephus shows that opinions varied from Zealot advocacy of permanent warfare against Rome to acceptance by some religious leaders of Roman domination as a guarantee of religious freedom.[117] He himself, though he had been rebel commander in Galilee in 66–67, came to hate the extremists at Jerusalem as 'atheists'.[118] His picture of the 'young men' taking up arms against the better judgment of their elders after the incident at Caesarea in 66 and regardless of formal sectarian allegiance is typical of violent nationalism of all time.[119]

He leaves the impression that in 66 the driving force of the extremists was both religious and social—as in the Seleucid period. First and foremost, idolatry was the enemy. Rome was hated only because she stood in the way of the Jew's direct relationship to God. At least, this would seem to be the interpretation one should put on the words of Eleazar, the Zealot commander of the Jewish forces in Masada 70–73, 'We have resolved for a long time to be subject neither to the Romans nor to anybody else, but to God alone, for He alone is the true and just master of men'.[120] A similar harshly particularist attitude was displayed by his

namesake, Eleazar the scribe, four years before, when he offered
the Roman commander at Fort Antonia the alternative of
circumcision as a Jew or death.[121] The same treatment, it seems,
was reserved by Zealots (and Essenes) for any Gentile who might
be overheard discussing religion.[122] Interesting too, is the incident
which took place at the end of the rebellion. The surviving
defenders of Masada, after three years of siege, refused utterly to
call Caesar lord, and went willingly to their deaths instead.
'Everyone was amazed', says Josephus, 'at their courage, whether
we ought to call it madness or boldness in their opinions. For
when every sort of torment and torture that could be contrived
was applied to their bodies they could not get one of them to
comply so far as to confess or seem to confess that Caesar was
their lord. They persevered in their opinion in spite of all the
distress they suffered, as if they received these torments and the
fire itself with bodies insensible to pain, and with a soul that in
like manner rejoiced under them.'[123] Seventy-five years earlier,
fanatical young men cut down Herod's Golden Eagle over the
gate of the Temple, thus deliberately courting death. They did
so, they said, believing 'that they would enjoy greater happiness
after they were dead'.[124] Whatever may have been the precise
meaning of immortality or of Torah in the minds of the victims,
here is a phenomenon unknown elsewhere in the Classical world.
The preference, however, for torture and death rather than accept
Caesar as lord is, as we have seen, precisely the spirit that animated
the martyrs of Lyons. Surely one does not have to look further
for the parentage of the more fanatical of the Christian martyrs.

Behind this bitter attitude Josephus suggests that there may also
have been social grievances. The Zealots and the *sicarii* were intent
in enforcing social justice as well as puritanical Judaism. At the
outbreak of the revolt in 66 they went about, he tells us, 'burning
the moneylenders' bonds and hindering the recovery of debts'[125]
with the express object of stirring up 'insurrection against the
wealthy'. The African Circumcellions three centuries later
embodied the same duality of purpose.[126] Meanwhile, at Qumran,
the Covenanters themselves 'the Congregation of the Poor',[127]
believed that they were destined to 'be delivered from all the
snares (of the Pit?) and enter on all the delights (of the earth?)'.
As in the previous age, revolt against idolatry was combined with

poverty and obedience to God's will as an essential part of the armour of the righteous.

Josephus also shows how in contrast to Zealotry the all-important tradition of passive resistance by righteous men continued from the Maccabean period. He himself has no doubt that this was the true way of dealing with heathen oppression. He reports the horror caused among Jews at the massacre of the Roman garrison of Antonia on a Sabbath day.[128] He comments on the callous disregard of prescriptions of the Law by the Zealots,[129] and conversely, he records in detail instances of obedience to the death to God's word. In 63 B.C. when, after a three months' siege, Pompey finally took the Temple he found the priests in their place carrying on the routine of sacrifice. They died at their posts. 'Yet could not', he says 'those who offered the sacrifices be compelled to run away, neither by the fear they were in for their lives, nor by the number that were already slain, thinking it better to suffer whatever came upon them at their very altars than omit anything that their laws required of them.'[130] The Christian who allowed himself to be arrested and gave thanks to God for the pagan magistrate's sentence of execution stands in a clearly marked line of descent.

Passive resistance, however, was not intended to be pointless suffering. There are few more vivid descriptions of the fate in store for the persecutors of the righteous than that preserved in ch. 10 of the *Assumption of Moses* (probably first half of first century A.D.).

> And thou, O Israel, wilt be happy
> And thou wilt mount upon the neck [and wings] of the eagle.
> And the days [of thy mourning] will be ended
> And God will exalt thee
> And He will cause thee to approach the heaven of the stars,
> And he will establish thy habitation among them.
> And thou wilt behold from on high and will see thine enemies in Ge[henna]
> And thou wilt recognize them and rejoice
> And thou wilt give thanks and confess thy Creator.[131]

> (Ch. 10)

The writer had immediately before put into the mouth of the Levite 'Taxo' the quietist advice: 'Let us fast for a space of three days and on the fourth let us go into the cave which is in the field, and let us die rather than transgress the command of the Lord of Lords, the God of our fathers, for our blood will be avenged before the Lord.'[132] Few Jews, at least in Palestine in the century either side of the birth of Jesus, would have denied that the destiny of Israel was ultimately to 'destroy the ungodly nations', and that the Messiah would 'possess the nations of the heathen to serve him beneath his yoke'.[133] Martyrdom was simply one stage in a predetermined scheme of history ending with Israel's salvation.[134]

So deep was the sense of obligation to uphold Torah in all circumstances, 'to sanctify the Holy Name' even to death, that in the period after the fall of Jerusalem in 70, Rabbis set to work to try to define more closely the situation when death was a necessity. Their object was to discourage fanatical voluntary martyrdom which could damage the nation.[135] Their arguments led to the same sort of conflict as that which developed between the laxer and more rigorous party among the Christians a century or so later over these issues. Thus Rabbi Akiba proposed a rule that 'while most of the commandments may be violated to save one's life, three groups of laws must be preserved at all costs and all times. They are those which forbid idol-worship, murder and infringement of chastity'.[136] It will be noted that these formed the *tria capitula*, breach of which Tertullian pointed out against Callistus *circa* 220, could only be forgiven by God Himself.[137] Affront against these must lead the Christian to martyrdom. On the whole, Akiba's views agreed with those of his contemporaries, though Rabbi Ishmael would have allowed sacrifice to idols provided that not more than ten Jews were eyewitnesses.[138] This casuistry, however, roused vigorous opposition. 'Far be it from us that we should follow Rabbi Ishmael's opinion', some cried.[139] Rabbi Nehemiah believed that the atonement gained by chastisement outweighed any disadvantages.[140] At a synod held at Lydda during the Second Jewish War (132–135), the assembled Rabbis decided that all negative commandments in Scripture except the capital sins of adultery, idolatry and murder, could be transgressed in order to save life.[141] Once, however, any *public* breach of the Law had been demanded martyrdom must be accepted. God could not be mocked by the heathen, and then 'a man should rejoice at chastisement more than at prosperity, for chastisements bring forgiveness of his transgressions'.[142] God's Law must continue to be taught despite Roman prohibitions, and with the failure of the second Jewish revolt Akiba passed on to martyrdom reciting the Shema. As one of his companions stated, commenting on Deut. 6[5], obedience and love of God could be interpreted as a willingness to die for Him. 'To love God with all thy soul was to love Him to the pressing out of thy soul',[143] that is until death.

It is not surprising that these ideals, permeating every walk of Jewish society, should have had a profound effect on traditional religious teaching in the Greco-Roman period.[144] The figure of the prophet, always on the side of the Law, proclaiming God's Law against all odds and warning the Israelite kings against compromises with heathendom, was becoming merged with that of the martyr. Already in Nehemiah (Neh. 9[26]) the slaying of the prophets who witnessed against disobedient Israel had been lamented, and as time went on the roll of the victims was increased in folk-lore and literary tradition. Isaiah, Zechariah and even Moses were added to Daniel and the 'Three Holy Children', as victims of ungodly rulers and their accomplices. While their miraculous deliverance or ultimate ascent to blissful salvation demonstrated the power of God over death, their suffering was a constant reminder of the need of atoning sacrifices by the people. 'Every wise man is a ransom for the fool', Philo asserted in discussing the meaning of Abel's sacrifice.[145] In iv Maccabees (6[29] and 17[22]) the flowing of the martyr's blood was represented as expiation for sin and a guarantee that God would avenge the death of His servant. Through them, the preacher argued, the nation gained peace (18[4]); an argument familiar to the second-century Christian and used by Evarestus regarding Polycarp's martyrdom.[146]

This was a strong tradition, and it was to influence the Christian theology of righteous suffering even after the end of the persecution. In late-Judaism, it may best be summed up in the words of the 'Maccabean' mother in her final speech in iv Macc. 18[11-18].

The boys' father, she said, 'read to us of Abel who was slain by Cain, and of Isaac who was offered as a burnt offering, and of Joseph in the prison. And he spake to us of Phineas, the zealous priest, and he taught you the song of Ananias, Azarias, and Misael in the fire. And he glorified also Daniel in the den of lions and blessed him, and he called to your minds the saying of Isaiah, "Yea even though ye pass through the fire, the flame shall not hurt you". He sang to us the works of David the Psalmist, "Many are the afflictions of the Just".'

So the young Jew at Antioch would be told from his earliest years that suffering was the inevitable outcome of his role in the present world, and edified by the example of the prophets and seers of Israel. He also had a part to play in a process which was to last eternally. Nearly four centuries later, the Donatist Petilian of Constantine was to recite a similar catena of evidence to prove the hostility of the world to the Church, and uphold the Donatist claim to be the righteous sufferer and therefore the true Christian.[147]

In Palestine at the time of our Lord this same vigorous tradition was combined with messianic and eschatological hopes.[148] The Jewish portions of the Ascension of Isaiah, and the Assumption of Moses, together with the conflation of texts from ii Chronicles and Zechariah which convert Zechariah into a famous martyr[149] are examples of this type of literature. The general view was that the great prophets had been persecuted and put to death by their own people. 'O Jerusalem, Jerusalem that killest the prophets . . .' (Lk. 13[34]) and Stephen's angry question, 'Which of the prophets have not your fathers persecuted?' (Acts 7[52]) illustrate the popular teaching of the day. The blame in both these instances is laid not on heathen rulers but on the wicked of Israel.

The sufferings of the prophets therefore, and the signs and wonders that accompanied them, such as the darkening of the heavens and the contact of the victim with the world beyond, were accepted as foreshadowings of the approaching End and the establishment of the blessed messianic kingdom.[150] As an example, the development of the Elijah saga shows how, what may have originally been a prophetic call to repentance had come in late-Judaism to be connected also with witness and suffering in the Last Days. In Malachi 3[23] and 4[5-6] the return of Elijah was prophesied; he would be sent 'before the great and dreadful day of the Lord'. He would denounce wickedness, but there is no hint that he would suffer as well. In Sirach, however, this element is present, for Elijah is 'ordained for reproofs in these times to pacify the wrath of God's judgment', and after this, 'to restore the tribes

of Judah' (48[10]). His role of atonement and restoration had therefore become similar to that of the Maccabean youths, with the
same aim and the same means of its fulfilment. In the Testaments
of the Twelve Patriarchs, Elijah was 'the high priest of the last
age',[151] and in Jewish apocalyptic roughly contemporary with
Jesus he was associated with Moses and Enoch as the prophet who
returns, suffers, is put to death and rises again. These themes form
the background to the Transfiguration,[152] they were embodied in
Revelation (11[3ff.]) and played their part in the vivid eschatology
of the primitive Church.[153] Thus Tertullian states that Elijah and
Enoch were destined to die 'so that they might extinguish Antichrist with their blood'.[154] For both Christian and Jew the theme
was suffering, deliverance and victory.

Thus, in post-Maccabean times the Jews in Palestine and the
Dispersion accepted and taught the permanent glory of victorious
suffering by the great prophetic heroes of Judaism.[155] The difference of emphasis, however, between the Dispersion and Palestinian accounts is of interest and was to have far-reaching repercussions on Christian thought. In the Dispersion the Jew formed
part of an embattled minority, for whom the righteous victim
was a stirring example of heroism and the representative of his
own situation. The persecutor was the heathen ruler, and defection among his own leaders was rare enough for tales of transgressions committed by them hardly to seem relevant. In Palestine,
however, the Jew was faced by a corrupt and vengeful tyranny
drawn from his own race, and after 63 B.C. by the overlordship
of a victorious idolatrous power which, if more tolerant than the
Seleucids, was stronger and in the last resort more ruthless. As in
the time of Antiochus IV he found himself threatened on two
fronts, by the Hellenizing and Romanizing ways of Herod and
his supporters,[156] and especially after the fall of Archelaus and the
establishment of the procurators in A.D. 6, by the Romans themselves. The noble example of suffering was not enough. It had
to be justified by hopes of vengeance and the promise of the early
fulfilment of this by a rapidly approaching End.

In Palestine, therefore, one can trace the emergence in the
century after Pompey's capture of Jerusalem of a Hebrew and
Aramaic literature of stern protest directed against both the
Hasmonean rulers and the Roman overlords.[157] Some Pharisaic

and Essene writers drew on the Maccabean and Danielic traditions of anti-Hellenism and apocalyptic. In their fanaticism they
conjured up pictures of the Armageddon in which the extermina-
tion of the idolatrous enemies of Israel was imagined down to the
last administrative detail. [158] The resulting Millennium was to be
attained on earth under the guidance of a divinely directed, but
human, Messiah, a great leader, an idealized Judas Maccabaeus.[159]
It was a revolutionary as well as a religious force. Meanwhile, the
more pacifist, Hasidean tradition, though often perverted, never
died. It was represented also among the different and often rival
movements[160] of the Essenes, the Pharisees and perhaps the
followers of John the Baptist,[161] but all these had in common
a rejection of idolatry, a puritanical interpretation of Torah
and an expectation of an approaching messianic deliverance of
Israel from the Romans. In this Pharisee and Zealot were at
one.[162]

If, as seems most likely, the Dead Sea Covenanters were
Essenes,[163] then one may perhaps look into the minds of a
Palestinian group who combined intense pietism and zeal for
Torah with equally intense militancy towards idolatry, and
towards Rome as its representative.[164] The sect saw itself as an
holy community, 'the sons of Zadok', and elect of Israel, who
had retreated into the desert 'to separate themselves from the
abode of perverse men who walk in the way of wickedness'.[165]
There they would enter into the covenant of the last days, which
included active preparation for the final cosmic and military
struggles in which Belial and all his hosts would be destroyed. The
whole life of the community was marked by its eschatological
expectations. Theirs was the 'assembly of the upright', to quote
the Psalmist (111[1]), called together to praise God, and await the
deliverance of Israel. Like the African Christians of Tertullian's
day, they interpreted all history and lived their daily lives in the
confident expectation that they would themselves hear the Last
Trump.[166] It seems quite evident, to quote F. M. Cross, that the
Covenanters were the 'bearers and in no small part the producers
of the apocalyptic tradition of Judaism'.[167] The library at Qumran
contained an extraordinarily rich and extensive apocalyptic
literature. Danielic literature, such as the Prayer of Nabonidus,
Testaments literature, pseudo-Mosaic and Jeremianic works and

cycles of Enoch are all represented. These texts leave little room for doubt that a whole range of apocalyptic and priestly literature may be placed within a single Palestinian tradition. Most important is the fact that this tradition seems to have contributed to the emergence of a similar outlook in the early Church. To quote Cross again, 'the direct use of Essene and proto-Essene materials in Christian compositions and indeed, the publication of Christian compilations of Essene and proto-Essene sources can now be documented impressively'.[168] The literary forms featured in Qumran apocalyptic, the earthquakes, storms, disgorging of the abyss and the breaking out of evil from the gates of Sheol, remained living literary forms in the Jewish-Christian community. They contributed to the theology of martyrdom which dominated the North African, and thence the Western Church.

One other fact may be mentioned. Who exactly was the Wicked Priest or how the Teacher of Righteousness met his end, we may not yet know.[169] There was, however, a bitter struggle between the two, and the Teacher's enemy was denounced as one 'who rejected the Law in the midst of their whole congreg(ation)'.[170] From this and the reference to 'the House of Absolom and men of their party' who 'kept silence at the chastisement of the teacher of righteousness'[171], we are confronted once more with the idea of a false congregation within Israel in opposition to the community of the Elect. One is reminded of Balak 'casting a stumbling-block before the children of Israel', in the Seer of the Apocalypse's letter to the Church of Pergamum (Rev. 2[14]). This theme was also to persist in Western Christianity. In the late fourth century we find the same beliefs, backed by a similar reading of current events into the interpretation of the Old Testament, among the Donatist Church of the Martyrs. As Tyconius, circa 380, asserted, there had always been a 'Church of Judas', opposed to the 'Church of Peter'. Two altars and Christ divided.[172] These views were not those of an isolated scholar, but are reflected in a cruder and more combative form by Petilian of Constantine twenty years later.[173] How ideas, prevalent in Palestine in the first century B.C., came to have so great an effect on North African Christian thought it is impossible to say. There are many curious links between the religious thought and even the Church architecture of the two areas which need explanation.

Finally, resulting from the rejection of obedience to an idolatrous or renegade ruler, there developed an attitude towards kingship itself which was also to have a long history. 'As the heaven is higher than the earth, so is the priesthood of God higher than the earthly kingdom, unless it fall away from the Lord and is dominated by the earthly kingdom.' This passage, from the Testament of Judah 21[4] seems to fit exactly the situation in which the Covenanters found themselves;[174] but the idea behind it, that the prophet and priest were intrinsically superior to the king, became enshrined in the Christian political thought of the West from Tertullian onwards for a thousand years or more.[175]

It would, of course, be wrong to imagine Jewish-Palestine as existing in an Aramaic vacuum and wholly devoid of Greek influences.[176] The large number of Greek loan-words in use in Palestine in the first centuries A.D., and the preservation of over 2000 in the Talmud argue for some cross-fertilization of cultures.[177] Greek philosophy, however, seems to have been studied in Jerusalem mainly for apologetic purposes, and personal relations between the Jews and the Greek settlers in Palestine would appear inter alia from the Marcan account of Jesus' ministry to have been minimal.[178] The material from the Caves adds to the impression that revolutionary apocalypticism was particularly strong in Palestine in the time of our Lord, and that Aramaic was its main vehicle of communication.

In contrast to the intense and uncompromising theology of the Palestinian Elect, the Greek-speaking Jew of the Dispersion was continually being forced to think in terms intelligible to his pagan neighbours. It was difficult, if not impossible in this period, to insulate himself from current philosophical and political ideas. If he spoke Greek, he had to think Greek as well. What he could do, however, was to restate the essentials of the Jewish faith in terms congenial to his environment.[179] He could claim that this faith was older beyond comparison, and therefore truer, than paganism in any form, and that throughout history the Divine Wisdom which guided and enlightened him had caused his nation to prosper and its enemies to fall. Furthermore, that while accepting the Platonic and Stoic virtues as real virtues, he could claim that they needed completion and fulfilment through the observance of Torah. Thus, even iv Maccabees, hateful diatribe against Hellenism though it is, and written by a Jew 'trained in the Law and the Prophets' (18[10]), opens with the words, 'Philosophical in the highest degree is the question which I propose to discuss, namely, whether Inspired Reason is the supreme ruler over the passions'.[180] The Maccabean youths were, on this showing, the true exemplars of the Stoic virtues (5[23-24]). The ideal preached by the Stoics was right, but the driving force needed to make it effective was Torah. The secret of the heroes' courage had been their education, and the constancy of their mother was due to her faith in God's providence. At the beginning of Philo's *Legatio* we find similar considerations. The Jews were a 'truly reasonable people', enjoying a special relationship to God and mediating His favours to man. They alone 'saw God'.[181]

Thus, though the virtue of martyrdom was preached, and the example of the Jewish heroes praised to the skies, the attitude towards pagan culture differed from that of Palestinian Jewry. However bitter the strife and however destructive the pogrom, the ideals of Hellenism were not destined for the final conflagration. They too, were the product of the Divine Reason that pervaded nature. The Hellenistic Jew, secure in Torah, saw himself as the guide and illuminator of mankind, not its destroyer. While both the Book of Wisdom and the Jewish Sibyllines contain elements of apocalyptic these are not the dominant theme, as they appear to be in Palestine. In the Dispersion, the Jew tends to claim to be the true philosopher, in the Hellenistic sense, however much he hated his Hellenistic neighbour. The Law of Moses was in harmony with the Law of Nature. The heathen legislators, Josephus tells us, had 'an imperfect knowledge of the true nature of God',[182] but they had some perception.

Such views affected profoundly the attitude of Jewish thinkers in the Dispersion towards the society they lived in, and towards its rulers. They were intelligent enough to realize that only the Empire could guarantee peace, and if war broke out they would be among the first to suffer. It was better to convert rather than to fight the representatives of idolatry. This was particularly the case of the Jews in Alexandria. In an interesting passage in the *Legatio*, Philo shows how, in his interpretation of events, the victory of Augustus at Actium put an end to the state of war and chaos in the

world which was threatening the existence of the human race,
and opened a new era for mankind.

> European and Asian nations from the ends of the earth had risen
> up and were engaged in grim warfare, fighting with armies and
> fleets on every land and sea, so that almost the whole human race
> would have been destroyed in internecine conflicts and disappeared
> completely, had it not been for one man, one *Princeps*, Augustus,
> who deserves the title of 'Averter of Evil'.[183]

Here was a direct anticipation of the arguments of Origen[184] and
Eusebius,[185] who sought to demonstrate the providential nature of
Jesus' birth by reference to the peace and unity brought to the
world by Augustus. To Philo the Augustan monarchy in this
respect reflected the monarchy of God, though it was not itself
the ideal state aimed at by the Divine Logos.[186] That had still to
come. However, we are far from Danielic conceptions of the
world empire and its ruler, far from the spirit of revolution which
the same 'Averter of Evil' aroused in Galilee when he imposed the
census in A.D. 6,[187] and far even from the pointed questions put by
the scribes and Pharisees to Jesus about the duty of paying tribute
to his successor.

If one looks ahead, to Justin Martyr,[188] Melito of Sardes,[189]
and Athenagoras,[190] one can recognize at once in this passage the
germ of the Greek Apologists' ideal of the ultimate harmony of
interest between Church and Empire. Polytheism, and polyarchy
leading to the internecine clash of interests between states and
cities which was the counterpart of polytheism, were the enemies of
both. From Philo through Origen to Eusebius runs a continuous
tradition of political thought. Indeed, it is not entirely pointless
to compare Philo's description of the ruler inspired by Wisdom
and Eusebius' representation of Constantine as 'crowned with the
virtues inherent in God'.[191] Persecutions and martyrdoms were
indeed to be accepted and endured, but these were less ideals in
themselves than part of the cost of mankind's progressive advance
through acceptance of Truth towards his final goal of 'his Father's
House'.[192] 'Live according to nature', but that could only be
accomplished if the spirit advanced along the road marked out
by the 'leading philosophy' of Torah.[193] The Therapeutae[194]
as described by Philo were actively pursuing this aim through

lives dedicated to worship and moral excellence. They point the
way to the ascetic philosophies of Clement and Origen—not the
martyr ideal of Tertullian.

Our study of martyrdom in Judaism has brought us to significant results. No other people in the Ancient World has left so
full a record of so long a history, let alone of their religious and
political thought as the Jews, and none show such consistency in
purpose. Deutero-Isaiah and the prophetic tradition which both
precedes and follows it represent the Jews as the martyr people,
suffering not merely for their own sins but bearing mankind's as
well. The crisis of the reign of Antiochus Epiphanes had put this
ideal to the test and the result had been an even more explicit sense
of mission. From that moment begin to flow the currents of
thought which were to influence deeply the ideas of martyrdom
in the early Church. Without Maccabees and without Daniel a
Christian theology of martyrdom would scarcely have been
thinkable. Without the apocalyptic of the Palestinian Essenes, it
could hardly have sustained the necessary fanaticism to overcome
the universal hostility of the Roman Empire. Without the Dispersion, and in particular, the Alexandrian interpretation and
allegorization of this apocalyptic, the ultimate reconciliation of
Church and Empire would have been impossible.

One final point remains. Are these Jewish ideals alone responsible for the Christian hope? Is one justified none the less, in
attributing some influence towards shaping the Christian viewpoint to the contemporary Hellenistic world?[195] To be sure, the
Hellenistic period saw a growing emphasis on the value of self-
sacrifice for a cause, either philosophic or national. Josephus
exaggerated when he claimed that no Greek philosopher would
ever die for his philosophy.[196] Even in the midst of quietist
resignation typical of much of second-century paganism, Celsus
asserted 'If you happen to be a worshipper of God and someone
commands you either to act blasphemously or to say some other
disgraceful thing, you ought not to put any trust in him at all.
Rather than this you must remain firm in the face of all tortures
and endure death rather than say or even think anything profane
about God'.[197] This is a striking statement and one which evidently
took Origen by surprise. But it is not unique. The Stoics were
also prepared to suffer and if necessary die for their beliefs in

defiance of what they esteemed to be tyranny.[198] Both the demands of patriotism—*Dulce et decorum est pro patria mori*—and those of philosophic truth exemplified by the heroism of Socrates and Empedocles had passed into the folk-memory of the Ancient World. In Alexandria, Clement's Fourth Book of *Stromata* devoted mainly to a discussion of martyrdom, is filled with examples of heroism taken from pagan history.[199] Even Tertullian quoted Socrates with approval.[200] In addition, Epictetus' accounts of his heroes' trials before Nero or Domitian record how these are called upon to be 'God's witness' against the tyrants, and here, at any rate, religion and patriotism are united as in Jewish *Acta*.[201] That political defiance committed in full knowledge of the results in the name of patriotism was given divine sanction, is also evident from the Alexandrine 'Acts of the Pagan Martyrs'.[202] Sweat broke out on the forehead of a statue of Serapis during the trial of Hermaiscus, allegedly in Trajan's reign, and there followed scenes of terror and confusion—as in the Jewish accounts of the deaths of the prophets.[203] This adds up to a formidable catalogue, and there can be no doubt that the bearing of pagan heroes at least confirmed Christian confessors in their attitude. Pagan heroism was one of the factors which moulded the Alexandrian exemplarist view of martyrdom.

At the same time, much of the self-sacrifice was on behalf of avowedly political causes. 'Come Romans', shouts the Alexandrian, Appian, 'and see a unique spectacle, an Alexandrian gymnasiarch and ambassador led to execution.'[204] He was prepared to die for the glory of Alexandria, but there was no transcending religious motive 'calling on the Name of God', such as we find in the story of Eleazar and in Christian *Acta*. There was no idea of expiatory sacrifice and atonement, nor even in general terms of bringing divine relief to the community as a whole. There is also no parallel in Greco-Roman history to the scenes of mass hysteria which gripped Palestinian Jewry in A.D. 40. Perhaps the nearest approach would be the suicidal madness of the Carthaginians after their defeat at Himera in 480 B.C., or at the tragic close of the Third Punic War. It seems as though expiatory sacrifice through the willing death of individuals belongs at this period to the Semitic rather than the Greco-Roman world. The latter had no equivalent of the blood sacrifice of *Molk*, one of the common factors between the religions of Syria and Palestine and Punic North Africa.

There is no doubt that if one considers martyrdom in terms of witness to God's mighty works, and the martyr as His agent, Christians looked back almost exclusively to Jewish prototypes. In the Roman catacombs, the stories of God's deliverance of the righteous from death such as Daniel in the Lion's Den, The Three Holy Children, and Jonah and the Whale, play an enormous part in the repertory of Christian artists from the mid-second to the mid-fourth century. It is interesting and perhaps significant that in the late third-century/early fourth-century catacomb on the Via Latina, only three of the great number of pictorial scenes can be definitely attributed to the New Testament, and where scenes and symbols drawn from pagan mythology have been used, these have already been assimilated into Judaism.[205] The remainder are inspired by the Old Testament. At the other extremity of the Christian world, at Dura, the paintings in the Christian church show a comparable cycle of pictorial representation on the theme of salvation such as their rivals and near-neighbours were painting on the walls of their synagogue.[206] In the early fourth century, the painting in the Christian mausoleum at Bagawat, in the oasis of Kufra, is devoted, curiously enough, to the martyrdom of Isaiah.[207] Time and again, in the Christian art and literature of the first three centuries we find the inspiration of the supposed deaths or miraculous deliverances of the Hebrew prophets.[208] Pagan mythology may sometimes play a supporting role, but what inspired the Christian to go to his death was the tradition of Hebrew righteous suffering and trust in God's readiness to deliver His servants from the assaults of idolatry.

Yet for all this, martyrdom in Judaism remained something of a *Hamlet* without the Prince. However much the Jew might regard the Law as 'pre-existent', and 'the breath of the power of God',[209] his sufferings on its behalf were in hope and anticipation only. The Law remained God-created and majestic, but impersonal, and for deep-thinking minds an 'occasion for sin' rather than a means of salvation. Death on the Law's behalf tended in practice to be regarded in negative terms, as atoning for wrong done rather than as positive witness that a New Age had broken on humanity. It was a 'good work' in the Pharisaic sense. Moreover, despite the individual glory attributed to the heroes who died in battle against idolatry, what the Jew really wanted was less individual salvation as such than a personal share in the golden future for the Jewish nation as the prophets had depicted it.[210] Martyrdom for him, as for his Greco-Roman contemporaries was in the last resort an expression of nationalism.

Thus, it needed the life and death of Jesus to give a transcendent and universal application to the notion which had evolved in Judaism. Christianity as a religion which knew no boundaries of language or class, and which avoided the 'general fussiness of the Jews',[211] could extend unequivocally the hope of individual blessedness for those who had borne witness to the reality of Christ's conquest of death. The early Christian fixed his eyes beyond this world in which he was a mere 'sojourner'. The Jew believed that Judaism would be the universal religion of mankind, and that all nations would ultimately be gathered in under the Law. The Christian saw that this was impossible under the Old Dispensation. The claims of Judaism as a national religion clashed with its claims to be the religion of mankind. The Christian, living, suffering and dying a witness to the Living Christ, believed that he was fulfilling the hopes which had inspired Old Israel since Maccabean times.

NOTES

[1] E. Lohmeyer, 'Die Idee des Martyriums im Judentum und Urchristentum', *Zeitschr. für systematische Theologie*, v, 1927, 222–49 and W. Bousset-H. Gressmann, *Die Religion des Judentums*, Tübingen, 1926, p. 374. See also the full collection of references to martyrdom in late Jewish literature made by E. Stauffer, *New Testament Theology*, Appendix i, pp. 331–4 (Eng. tr. by J. Marsh, London, 1955), Part I of Stauffer's article, 'Märtyrertheologie und Täuferbewegung' in *Zeitschr. für Kirchengeschichte*, iii Folge, 3, 1933, 545–609, and A. R. C. Leaney, 'The Eschatological Significance of Suffering in the O.T. and the Dead Sea Scrolls'. *SJT.*, 16, 1963, 286–96.

[2] Cf. Numbers 16³.

[3] For κλῆρος = heritage, Eph. 1¹¹. In general, Arndt and Gingrich, *Lexicon*, 436.

[4] F. L. Cross, *I Peter: a Paschal Liturgy*, London, 1954. The precision of this view has, however, been challenged by C. F. D. Moule, 'The Nature and Purpose of I Peter', *NTS.*, iii, 1956–57, 1–11.

[5] Origen, *Exhortation to Martyrdom* (ed. and tr. J. E. L. Oulton and H. Chadwick, *Alexandrian Christianity*, London, 1954), 5.

[6] Hab. 1⁴⁻¹³. Also, Pss. 9⁵ and ¹⁷, 58¹⁰ and 68². Cf. W. D. Davies, *Paul and Rabbinic Judaism*, London, 1948, 59–60.

[7] Ps. 119[46].

[8] The LXX contains the more positive command to witness, and individuals are called 'μάρτυρες τοῦ θεοῦ', e.g. Is. 43[10] (LXX), 'Γενεσθέ μοι μάρτυρες, καὶ ἐγὼ μάρτυς λέγει κύριος ὁ θεὸς . . . '. Also, 44[8] 'μάρτυρες ὑμεῖς 'εστε, εἰ 'εστι θεὸς πλῆν 'εμοῦ.' and 55[4], ''Ιδού, μαρτύριον 'εν ἔθνεσιν ἔδωκα αὐτόν'.

[9] A. Lods, Les Prophètes d'Israël, Paris, 1935, 275–80. For a survey of learned opinion to 1950, but emphasizing that the Servant may be a future individual, H. H. Rowley, The Servant of the Lord, London, 1952, Lecture ii. Certainly, in the LXX version of the first song the identification between Servant and Israel seems to be close. Thus, Is. 44[1] (LXX), 'But now hear, Jacob my servant, and Israel whom I have chosen'.

[10] A. R. C. Leaney, art. cit., 286–7.

[11] Indeed, in 419 B.C. Darius II instructed his satrap in Egypt to tell the Jews at Elephantine that they were to eat unleavened bread during the feast of Mazzot. See A. E. Cowley, Aramaic Papyri of the Fifth Century B.C., Oxford, 1923, 62ff.

[12] C. N. Seddon, 'Zoroastrianism and its Influence', Modern Churchman, 31, 1941–42, 507ff., especially pp. 514–15.

[13] See G. B. Caird's chapter 'The Great Accuser' in Principalities and Powers, Oxford, 1956, 31ff. See W. Bousset's Antichrist, Göttingen, 1895, 101ff. for their identity.

[14] Eusebius, H.E., v.1.5 (martyrdoms at Lyons).

[15] H. H. Rowley, The Relevance of Apocalyptic (London, 2nd ed., 1947), 33–4.

[16] R. C. Zaehner, The Dawn and Twilight of Zoroastrianism, London, 1961, 57–8, for a careful assessment of the influence of this aspect of Iranian religion on Judaism.

[17] S. H. Hooke, The Siege Perilous, London, 1956, ch. ix, 124ff.

[18] W. O. E. Osterley and T. H. Robinson, Hebrew Religion, London, 1935 ed., 344ff., and Jews and Judaism during the Greek Period, London, 1941, 88ff.; cf. the fiery destruction of Beliar, Test. Judah 25[3], and the 'beast', Rev. 19[20].

[19] Justin, 1 Apol. 44, and Clement, Stromata (ed. Stählin-Früchtel, Berlin, 1960), 1.15.69.6. Apocalypses of Zoroaster and Zostrianes were found in the Sethite library at Nag-Hammadi. See C. H. Puech, 'Les nouveaux écrits gnostiques découverts en Haute-Egypte', Coptic Studies in Honour of Walter Ewing Crum, Byzantine Institute, Boston, 1950, p. 108–10. See below, p. 238.

[20] This extremely favourable assessment of a heathen monarch was to have its effect in preventing complete hostility between the Church and the Roman Empire. It would be possible for a Christian to justify an appeal, for instance, to the good offices of Aurelian or Constantine and expect a just decision.

[21] Note the prophecy of Rabbi Simeon ben Yohai (second century A.D.) quoted by A. H. Silver, 'If you see the horse of a Persian tied to a post in the land of Israel, expect the footsteps of the Messiah', A History of Messianic Speculation in Israel, New York, 1927, 28; also, R. Wischnitzer, The Messianic Theme in the Paintings of Dura Europos, Chicago, 1948, 12–13.

[22] iii Sibyll. 286ff. (ed. Charles, Apoc. and Pseudepig., II). iv Sibyll., 138ff. Aid to Jews in A.D. 70 from across the Persian frontier, Dio Cassius 65.4.3; cf. Rev. 16[12]ff. See R. H. Charles, The Ascension of Isaiah (London, 1900), p. lxiff. and A. H. Silver, loc. cit., for useful summaries of the evidence.

[23] On the Nehemiah-Ezra period, see M. Noth, The History of Israel (Eng. tr., London, 1959), pp. 322ff., and A. Alt, Kleine Schriften zur Geschichte des Volkes Israel, München, 1953, ii.331ff., on the constitutional status of Judah at this period.

[24] M. Noth, op. cit., 331.

[25] The dating of Joel is very difficult. S. L. Brown, art. in Gore's A New Commentary on Holy Scripture, London, 1943 ed., 564, suggests the first half of the fourth century, though G. H. Box, Judaism in the Greek Period, Oxford, 1932, argues cogently for the period of Alexander the Great, 84–5. At the other end of the scale, A. S. Kappelrud

points to the influence of Jeremiah on Joel's ideas, and considers that the original prophecies date as early as King Jehoiakim's time (609–598 B.C.) though they were not reduced to writing until the fourth/third century B.C.—*Joel Studies*, Uppsala Universitets Årsskrift, 1948. 4, 190–2. J. M. Myers in his summary of the evidence, 'Some considerations bearing on the Date of Joel', *ZATW.*, 74.2, 1962, 177ff., comes down on the side of an early date and suggests that Joel 'does unmistakably reflect conditions in Palestine somewhere around 520 B.C.'.

[26] It is interesting and may be significant that Jewish apocalypses of the Christian era do not seem to have made any such direct use of Joel's prophecies.

[27] On this period, V. Tcherikover, *Hellenistic Civilization and the Jews* (tr. S. Appelbaum, Philadelphia, 1959), ch. iii.

[28] Cited by Josephus, *Contra Apionem*, 1.28–30. The dating of this and similar tales is a matter of conjecture. Third/second century B.C. seems the most likely period for their circulation as anti-Jewish propaganda. See I. Heinemann, 'Antisemitismus', *PW.* Suppl., v.28.

[29] G. F. Moore, *Judaism*, 1.288. There may have been some demand for this enterprise among Alexandrian Greeks, curious to know more about the strange 'Jewish philosophy', though it is difficult to conceive of this weighty and expensive series of rolls being much read outside the synagogue.

[30] In general, Tcherikover, loc. cit., and W. O. E. Osterley, *Jews and Judaism*, 18. For the history of Greek settlement in Galilee, A. Alt, 'Hellenistische Städte und Domänen in Galiläa', *Kleine Schriften*, ii, 384–95. For foundation of Sepphoris not earlier than the turn of second/third century B.C., L. Waterman, *Preliminary Report of the University of Michigan Excavations at Sepphoris in 1931* (Ann Arbor, 1937).

[31] 'πολλὰ τῶν πατρίων τοῖς Ἰουδαίοις νομίμων ἐκινήθη', cited from S. Reinach, *Textes d'auteurs Grecs et Romains relatifs au Judaisme*, Paris, 1895, 19ff. Hecataeus, according to Josephus, *Contra Apionem*, 1.22.191, also added that the Jews were prepared to 'face tortures and death in the most terrible form rather than repudiate the faith of their forefathers'. On Hecataeus and the authenticity of this and other citations in Josephus, H. Levy, 'Hekataios von Abdera περὶ Ἰουδαίων', *ZNTW.*, 31, 1932, 117–32.

[32] I have followed G. H. Box, op. cit., 8.

[33] *Contra Apionem* (ed. Thackeray), 1.22–23, especially 1.22 (179), citing the Peripatetic, Klearchos of Soloi.

[34] Josephus (ed. Niese) *Antiquities*, XI.8.5(336). Contrast this view of Alexander with that expressed in i Macc. 1²⁻⁶, a neat example of the Hellenistic-Jewish *versus* the Palestinian-Jewish interpretation of events.

[35] W. M. Ramsay, 'Studies in the Roman Province Galatia', vi, *JRS.*, xiv, 1924, 173. In general, the same author's *Cities of St. Paul*, 169ff.

[36] Josephus, *Antiquities*, xii.3.(149–53).

[37] The date, suggested by W. Foerster, 'Der Ursprung des Pharisäismus', *ZNTW.*, 34, 1935, 41; cf. Tcherikover, op. cit., 125. J. Coppens, 'Les Psaumes des *Hasidim*', *Mélanges Bibliques redigés en l'honneur de André Robert*, (Paris, 1958, 222), claims that the *Hasidim* were originally not a distinct social class or profession, but 'un corps moral dans un Israël où beaucoup avaient abandonné ou negligeaient la Loi du Seigneur'.

[38] See Ernest Barker, *Alexander to Constantine*, Oxford, 1956, 138–9. Dating: one example of a fragment of Ecclesiastes has been found in Qumran, Cave iv (4QQohᵃ) which dates from *circa* 175–150 B.C. As the manuscript shows some development the original can hardly be much later than the turn of the third century B.C. F. M. Cross, *The Ancient Library at Qumran and Modern Biblical Studies*, London, 1958, 121–2.

[39] See Josephus, *Antiquities*, xii.5.1 (240).

[40] Ed. Tedesche and Zeitlin, p. 27. An alternative of 110–100 B.C. is suggested by F. M. Abel, *Les Livres des Maccabées*, Paris, 1949, xliii.

[41] Dated to 'about the middle of second century B.C.' by H. H. Rowley, *Jewish Apocalyptic and the Dead Sea Scrolls*, University of London, Athlone Press, 1957, 11; cf. R. H. Charles, *Apocrypha*, ii.6, but L. Finkelstein, *HTR.*, 36, 1943, 19ff. prefers a just pre-Maccabaean date (175-167 B.C.) on the grounds that it 'contains no reference whatever to the persecution'.

[42] Dating, F. M. Abel, op. cit., xliii, and see also, J. Moffatt's note in Charles's *Apocrypha and Pseudepigrapha of the Old Testament* (= *Apocrypha*), I, Oxford, 1913, 128-9; E. Lohse, *Märtyrer und Gottesknecht*, Göttingen, 1955 (*Forschungen zur Religion und Literatur des A.T. und N.T.*, N.F., 46), 66, n. 2 dates the work to about the time of Christ's birth, but this seems too late, as does Zeitlin-Tedesche's (*The Second Book of the Maccabees*, New York, 1954, 27-30) suggestion of *circa* A.D. 40.

[43] ii Macc. 4[40ff.]; Tcherikover, op. cit., 162-3.

[44] Josephus, *Antiquities*, xii.5.1.(241).

[45] The Scrolls show that Aramaic may already have been contributing to the literary heritage of Palestinian Judaism. For the language problem, especially in Galilee, see M. Black, *An Aramaic Approach to the Gospels and Acts*, OUP., 1954, 13-14. Despite the Hellenization of names there is reason to believe that even in Jerusalem Aramaic was spoken widely.

[46] For the events of the crisis of the Maccabean revolution, see first and foremost, E. Bickermann, *Der Gott der Makkabäer*, Berlin, 1937. Also, J. C. Dancy, *I Maccabees, A Commentary*, Oxford, 1954; and E. Bevan, *Jerusalem under the High Priests*, London, ed. 1952 and *CAH.*, viii, pp. 498ff. and 713ff., F. M. Abel, *Les Livres des Maccabées*, Paris, 1949. W. Tarn, *Hellenistic Civilization*, 2nd ed., London, 1930, ch. VI.; M. Noth, *The History of Israel*, Part iv, ch. 1.

[47] Tarn's view, *Hellenistic Civilization*, 186.

[48] E. Bickermann, op. cit., 66.

[49] For instance, his claim for a 'dowry' from the temple of Atagartis at Bambyce; and he was killed in a vain attack on the temple of Namaia near the Parthian border. He was also accused of robbing temples during his Egyptian campaign of 168 (Bickermann, op. cit., 18).

[50] Dancy, op. cit., 56.

[51] E. Bickermann, op. cit., 112. 'Baal-Shamin = Zeus Olympios'. See also O. Eissfeldt's study, 'Ba'alsamem und Jahwe', *ZATW.*, N.F. 16, 1939, 1-31.

[52] Josephus, *Antiquities*, xii.v.263.

[53] One feels that the religous aspect (cf. ii Macc. 6[2]) has been underestimated by Bickermann. Antiochus' actions must be seen against the background of 'heathen assault' by which all Israel's history was coloured. The hatreds which the Law of Moses aroused at the time are clearly shown in i Macc. 1[61] and Josephus, *Antiquities*, xii.5.4. (256).

[54] Bickermann, op. cit., 59ff.

[55] I have used Dancy's chronology, op. cit., 63ff. Cf. also, Bickermann, op. cit., 13-14.

[56] Dating, Dancy op. cit., 65; Bickermann, 67.

[57] Dancy, op. cit., 69.

[58] Referred to by Polybius, v.86.10, 'the common people in Coele-Syria usually tend to favour the Ptolemies; cf. Jerome, *Comment. in Danielem*, xi.21 (*P.L.*, xxv, 566).

[59] Bickermann, op. cit., 69-71.

[60] See also the slightly different version quoted by Josephus, *Antiquities*, xi.6.6 (Whiston).

[61] Macc. 1[45]. For discussion of the decrees, Bickermann, op. cit., 121ff.; Dancy, op. cit., 73-4; L. B. Paton, *I.C.C.*, *Esther*, 203.

[62] Josephus, *Antiquities*, xii.5.4. (253) See Bickermann, op. cit., ch. iv: For the possible interpretation of the altar as 'the abomination of the Madman (Antiochus)', H. H. Rowley, *ZATW.*, N.F. 9, 1932, 264-5.

[63] ii Macc., 6[7].

[64] Bickermann, op. cit., 109: 'Denn der singuläre Gott Abrahams, Isaaks und Jakobs wurde dadurch zu einem der vielen arabischsyrischen Götzen degradiert'.

[65] e.g. in Antioch itself. Bickermann, op. cit., 121–2. The situation deteriorated for the Jews in the Greek cities on the borders of Judaea once the Maccabean rebellion got under way, ii Macc. 6[8], and 12[1].

[66] ii Macc. 6[2]. Josephus, Antiquities, xii.258–63.

[67] For a study of the events between B.C. 167–142, Tcherikover, ch. vi, and Noth, op. cit., 365ff.

[68] As it had been in other revolutionary assertions of Israel's exclusive loyalty to Jahwe. See Judges 6[25] and ii Kings 10[18]ff. Modin was a large village 17 miles north-west of Jerusalem. For a summary of the effect of the Maccabean revolution, see S. W. Baron, A Social and Religious History of the Jews, 2nd ed., New York, 1952, 230.

[69] Dating: It was 'written in the period of worldliness and self-complacency that followed the attainment of national independence in 135 B.C.', L. B. Paton, I.C.C., Esther, 62.

[70] The dating of this important document is very obscure. Hadas (III and IV Maccabees, New York, 1953, p. 96) suggests circa A.D. 40 on the reasonable ground that the title assigned to Apollonius (4.9) of 'governor of Syria, Phoenicia and Cilicia' would make sense to his hearers only when Syria and Cilicia were in fact associated for administrative purposes, i.e. between A.D. 20–54, and this dating is accepted by Perler, art. cit., 47–8. Dupont-Sommer, however, 'Le Quatrième Livre des Macchabés', Bibl. des Hautes Etudes, 274, 1939, 83–5, suggests an early second-century date. This seems too late, and a date some time in the first half of the first century more realistic, perhaps before the reign of Caligula as Townshend suggests, (Charles, Apocrypha, ii.654). The author would appear to be an Antiochene Jew (Hadas, 113), rather than an Alexandrian as suggested by Pfeiffer (History of New Testament Times, New York, 1949, 215). For the independence of iv Macc. from ii Macc. and the fluctuating popular traditions which gave rise to it, see J. Downing, 'Jesus and Martyrdom', JTS., N.S. xiv, Oct. 1963, 281.

[71] Note the outbreak of anti-Jewish feeling on the periphery of the revolt, at Jamnia and Joppa, ii Macc. 12[1] and Ptolemais, ii Macc. 6[8], where a decree (ψήφισμα) apparently ordering the persecution of the Jews (κατὰ τῶν 'Ιουδαίων ἄγειν) was promulgated.

[72] Note the important study by J. Downing op. cit., 282ff., which I was able to consult while this chapter was still in manuscript.

[73] Pirke Aboth, 2.18. Cited from W. D. Davies, Paul and Rabbinic Judaism, 261. Charles's text, Apochrypha, ii, 697 reads 'Epicurean' for 'unbeliever'.

[74] Acta Saturnini, 18, P.L. viii, 701.

[75] See, for instance, Eusebius, H.E., iv.15.32. Polycarp is designated as a 'whole burnt offering acceptable to Almighty God'. Persecution also, ceased after his death. See below, p. 288–9.

[76] Also, iii Macc. 3[8] and 6[18]. In general, H. L. Strack and P. Billerbeck, Kommentar zum N.T. aus Talmud und Midrasch, 1922, ii, 275; and A. T. Hanson, The Wrath of the Lamb, London, 1957, 42–3.

[77] Note in this connection Caiaphas' utterance recorded in John 11[50]—Jesus' death 'for the (Jewish) nation'.

[78] In this case immortality = reuniting of body and soul in a more glorious guise hereafter, not only the immortality of the soul as taught in iv Macc. 14[5], 16[13] and 18[23].

[79] Cf. i Macc. 2[62], 6[11], ii Macc. 3[28], 4[38], 5[9], 13[8], Wisd. 3[10].

[80] Lactantius, De Mort. Persec. 33.1. (ed. Moreau, 383–4). Cancer of the bowels seems to have been regarded as the most fitting punishment of persecuting rulers. See also, Josephus' description of Herod's end, Antiquities, xvii.6.5; cf. S. Perowne, Life and Times of Herod the Great, 1956, 185.

[81] ii Macc. 6[20]. Eleazar 'advances of his own accord to the instrument of torture'. Note also the attitude of the mother in iv Maccabees 17[1] who cast herself on to the fire 'so that no man should touch her body', and of Razis, ii Macc. 14[42].

[82] Below, p. 218, 289, and 411.

[83] W. O. E. Oesterley and T. H. Robinson, History of Israel, ii, 239.

[84] R. H. Pfeiffer, Religion in the Old Testament (Eng. tr. C. C. Forman, London, 1961), 218.

[85] For a discussion on the origins and development of this concept as far as Daniel, M. Noth, 'Das Geschichtsverständnis der alttestamentlichen Apokalyptik', Gesammelte Studien zum Alten Testament, München, 1957, 248–73, and H. H. Rowley, Darius the Mede and the Four World Empires in the Book of Daniel, Cardiff, 1935.

[86] M. Noth, art. cit., 269–70 convincingly rejects the idea that the representations of the earlier empires are in descending order of wickedness. This would also run counter to the usually more friendly view of the Persians held by the Jews.

[87] On the exact meaning of this term, whether it refers to the heavenly hosts, or simply to Israel itself, see M. Noth, Gesammelte Studien, 274–90. It does seem, however, that whatever the original meaning, the term very quickly became synonymous with 'God's People, Israel', and that the victorious 'saints' in 7[18] became identified with the 'saints' who triumph after defeat in 7[21] and 7[22]. The kingdom of the Saints would therefore be an earthly one.

[88] For this aspect see, N. Cohn, The Pursuit of the Millennium, London, 1957, 3–4; also J. W. Swain, 'The Theory of the Four Monarchies: Opposition History under the Roman Empire', Classical Philology (= CP.), 35, 1940, 1–21, in an important article, emphasizing the oriental, probably Persian, origin of the theory, and also pointing to its adoption by some Greek historians in Asia Minor in the last two centuries B.C. See below, ch.V, p.146, n.4.

[89] Note the importance of the invocation for persecuted Jew and persecuted Christian alike, ii Macc. 8[2] etc. (thirteen other times), iii Macc. 1[27] and 5[6]. Acts 2[21] and 7[59] (Stephen).

[90] No date can unquestionably be assigned to this passage. It may even be as late as the third century B.C. A. Causse, Israël et la Vision de l'Humanité, Strasbourg, 1924, 106.

[91] Also Eccles. 3[18–22], where the writer questions whether the spirit or vital breath of man is any different from that of the beasts.

[92] Represented by Isaiah 38[18] ('they that go down into the pit cannot hope for thy truth') Pss. 86[13], 88[4–6], 146[4], Is. 14[3–21], and even the prayer at the end of Ecclus. (Ecclus. 51).

[93] See G. F. Moore's chapter on 'Retribution after Death', Judaism in the first centuries of the Christian era, Cambridge (Mass.), 1927–30, ii, 287ff.

[94] Note for instance, Jn. 11[24]. The hope was on the resurrection of the body, as Mary Magdalene shows clearly in her utterances at the Tomb. Jn. 20[1–18]. It is also implied in Mt. 10[28].

[95] See also, Wisd. 3[1–16] for the blessedness of those who had suffered for righteousness' sake.

[96] The reader is referred to A. H. M. Jones, The Herods of Judaea, Oxford, 1938, E. Bevan, Jerusalem under the High Priests, chapter ix in CAH., ix, and Ch. Guignebert, The Jewish World in the Time of Jesus (Eng. Tr., S. H. Hooke, London, 1939).

[97] iii Macc. 4[11]: Jews imprisoned in the hippodrome at Schedia near Alexandria in preparation to being destroyed by beasts. Note also the story of Razis, ii Macc., 14[38–42].

[98] W. R. Farmer, Maccabees, Zealots and Josephus, Columbia University Press, 1956, especially pp. 56 onwards. Note also how the writer of the Assumption of Moses, probably a Palestinian living in the first century A.D., attributes the same sort of 'heathenish influences' and impieties indifferently to the Seleucid and Herodian eras (Assumption of Moses, ed. Charles, Apocrypha, ii.407ff.).

[99] W. R. Farmer, Maccabees, 82.

[100] W. R. Farmer, *JTS.*, N.S. iii, 1952, 62 n. 1.

[101] i Macc. 4[36-59]. W. R. Farmer, op. cit., p. 132ff.

[102] Or, even Caiaphas.

[103] Philo, *Legatio* (ed. E. M. Smallwood, Leiden, 1961), 215. Cf. ibid., 117.

[104] For the view that Philo betrays evidence of being secretly opposed to Roman rule as a whole, despite belonging to a family dependent for its prosperity on imperial favour, E. R. Goodenough, *An Introduction to Philo Judaeus*, New Haven, Yale Univ. Press, 1940, 69ff. Criticized by A. Momigliano in *JRS.*, XXXIV, 1944, 164.

[105] *Legatio*, 192.

[106] Philo, *Legatio*, 266.

[107] Ibid., 329.

[108] Ibid., 233.

[109] Ibid., 249; cf. Josephus, *Antiquities*, xiv.4.4 (70) Jews burning down their own homes after Pompey's capture of Jerusalem, and numbers committed suicide.

[110] *Legatio*, 162; cf. ibid., 346 'ἵνα Διὸς 'Επιφανοῦς Νέου χρηματίзη Γάιου'.

[111] *Antiquities*, xviii.8.3.

[112] *Antiquities*, xviii.8.3.

[113] Ibid., xviii.8.5; cf. *Wars*, iii.7.34. Note R. Hengel, *Die Zeloten*, Leiden/Köln, 1961, 268-70 on religious suicide among the Jews.

[114] See W. R. Farmer's valuable note on Josephus' deliberate obscuring of the connections between the Maccabees and the Jewish resistance to Rome, *JTS.*, N.S. iii, 1952, 62 n. 1.

[115] Tacitus, *Histories*, v.5.6; cf. Dio Cassius, lxv.6.3 who records that the Jews were prepared to die with the Temple in 70 rather than survive its destruction, and 'leaped joyfully into the flames'.

[116] Josephus, *Contra Apionem*, ii.33; cf. ii.16(165), and Philo, *Legatio*, 210.

[117] Note also the many examples of the latter attitude assembled by H. Loewe, *Render unto Caesar*, Cambridge, 1938, pp. 21-32.

[118] Josephus, *Wars*, v.13.6 (566).

[119] Ibid., ii.14.8.

[120] Josephus, *Wars*, vii.8.6; cf. vii.10.1. See M. Hengel, *Die Zeloten*, 288ff. and the coins of the period representing 'Jerusalem the Holy' as a reverse type. The situation has been illustrated in awesome detail by the excavation of Masada. See Y. Yadin, 'Masada: Herod's Fortress Palace and the Zealots' Last Stand', *Illustrated London News*, Archaeological Section, 2204, 31 Oct. 1964. For the rebels' coins, ibid., Fig. 2.

[121] Ibid., ii.17.10.

[122] Hippolytus, *Elenchos* (ed. Wendland), ix.18; cf. M. Black, 'The Essenes in Hippolytus and Josephus', *Dodd Studies*, 172-5.

[123] Josephus, *Wars*, vii.10.1; cf. ibid. 8.6 and 7 and iii.7.33. M. Hengel, op. cit. 266.

[124] Josephus, *Wars*, i.33.3 (648-653); cf. *Antiquities*, xvii.6.2, and for similar sentiments by a Christian confessor, Eusebius, *H.E.*, iv.15.6 (Germanicus).

[125] Ibid., ii.17.6; cf. ibid., iv.3.2, Zealots 'robbing their fellow-countrymen', and in Jerusalem 'thirsting after the blood of valiant men, and men of good families' ibid., iv.6.1. Note C. Roth's interesting short contribution 'The Perpetual Pattern of Revolution', *The Listener*, 1960, 465-6, and E. Meyer, *Ursprung und Anfänge des Christentums*, Berlin, 1924, iii.74, n. 4. For the burden of taxation on the Palestinian Jews at this time, Ch. Guignebert, op. cit., 39-40, and E. Fromm, *The Dogma of Christ*, 1963, 16.

[126] See the author's *The Donatist Church*, 171-5.

[127] *Fragment of Comment.* on Ps. 37, col. i.l.11. Cf. Ps. 74[19]. See *Palestine Exploration Quarterly*, lxxxvi, 1954, 69-75, and A. Dupont Sommer, *The Essene Writings of Qumran*, 1961, 271. A slightly different version in T. Gaster, *Scriptures of the Dead Sea Sect*, 243.

[128] Josephus, *Wars*, ii.17.10 (end).

[129] Ibid., iv.5–6.

[130] *Antiquities*, xiv.4.3.(67); cf. *Wars*,vii.8.10.(153)—Essenes 'smiling at their very pains' and laughing at their torturers. For similar Christian attitudes, *Acta Carpi*, 38 (reign of Marcus Aurelius).

[131] *Assumption of Moses* (ed. Charles) 10. See also, Rowley's discussion in *The Relevance of Apocalyptic*, 91–5 and 134–41.

[132] Ibid., 9.6. Note also Enoch 47[2], the Righteous who pray that Judgment shall come speedily so that their blood may be avenged, and cf., of course, Rev. 6[10] for the continuance of this hope in the early Church. See Hengel, op. cit., 272–3.

[133] *Psalms of Solomon* (ed. Gray), 17,32.

[134] The point is made very clearly by J. Licht, 'Taxo or the Apocalyptic doctrine of Vengeance'. *The Journal of Jewish Studies*, xii.3 and 4, 1961, 95–105.

[135] See J. H. Greenstone, art. *Martyrdom* (Restriction of), *J.E.* viii. Quotes Babylonian Talmud (ed. Epstein, Soncino Press, 1935) *Yoma* 85b based on Levit. 18[5], 'live through the laws but do not die through them'. Also, H. Loewe, op. cit., 26–8.

[136] L. Finkelstein, *Akiba*, 261. See also, G. C. Montefiore and H. Loewe, *A Rabbinic Anthology*, London, 1938, 495–6.

[137] Tertullian, *De Pudicitia*, 19; cf. 12, 'compensatio autem revocabilis non est, nisi denique revocabitur iteratione moechiae utique et sanguinis et idololatriae' (ed. Reifferscheid and Wissowa, *CSEL.*, xx, 242). Cf. Acts 15[28].

[138] Babylonian Talmud, *Sanhedrin*, ii.74a. The important point was that the transgression should not be made in public (*b'parrhesia*) in which case it would be tantamount to blasphemy, and not even the least deviation from Torah could be accepted. (Cf. Eleazar's attitude in ii Macc. 6[22] and iv Macc. 5[20].) Discussed by Montefiore and Loewe, op. cit., 495.

[139] See J. Katz, *Exclusiveness and Tolerance*, Scripta Judaica iii, Oxford, 1961, 83–4.

[140] 'Beloved are chastisements, for just as sacrifices atone, so do chastisements atone', *Mechilta Bahodesh*, 10 (ed. Winter and Wünsche), cf. also *Sanhedrin* 47a(end), 'Those who are executed by a Jewish tribunal have no atonement, but those executed by the Government (i.e. as martyrs) have atonement'.

[141] B. Talmud, *Sanhedrin*, 74a. See J. W. Hunkin, *JTS.*, xxvii, 1926, 272–83.

[142] R. Akiba in *Mechilta Bahodesh* 10. See the important evidence on this theme assembled by W. D. Davies, *Paul and Rabbinic Judaism*, London, 1948, 263ff.

[143] Rabbi ben Azzai, *Sifre Deut.*, 6.5.32, cited from W. D. Davies, op. cit., 265. Also, Akiba in *Berakoth* 61b.

[144] See the excellent study by H. A. Fischel, 'Martyr and Prophet', *JQR.*, 37 (1946–47), 265–80 and 363–86.

[145] *De Sacrificio Abel* (ed. Colson and Whittaker), 1.37.121. ὅτι πᾶς σοφὸς λύτρον ἐστὶ τοῦ φαύλου.

[146] Eusebius, *H.E.*, iv.15.3.

[147] Augustine, *Contra Litteras Petiliani*, ii.92.202 (below, p. 554).

[148] See, Ch. Guignebert, *The Jewish World*, ch. iv, especially pp. 133–8.

[149] Mt. 23[35], perhaps a conflation of ii Chron. 24[20–21] and Zech. i. Discussed by A. Michel, *Le Maître de Justice*, Avignon, 1954, 287–92, and S. H. Blank, 'The Death of Zechariah in Rabbinic Literature', *Hebrew Union College Annual*, xii–xiii, 1937–38, 327–46, who also draws attention to the passage in Lam. 2[20] and the Targumist's reference of this slaying of 'the priest and the prophet' to Zechariah (p. 327).

[150] The parallel between the victorious Christian witness who prophesies, converses with the Lord, and is immune from the pain inflicted by his torturers, and his Jewish counterpart is evident. Compare *Ascens. Is.*, 5.14 and *Mart. Polyc.* (ap. Eusebius, *H.E.*, iv.15–17, 28 and 30) and *Acta* of the Lyons martyrs (ibid., v.1.56). Other examples, H. A. Fischel, art. cit., 373ff., and see above, ch. I, note 166.

151 Test. Reub., 6, Judah, 21, Levi, 2.8.18. See J. Jeremias, art. "Ηλ[ε]ιας', Kittel, *Wörterbuch*, ii, 930–46, at 934.

152 Mt. 11¹⁴, 17¹¹⁻¹² and Mk. 9¹²⁻¹³, Jeremias, art. cit., 940–1.

153 Jeremias, art. cit., 941–2. J. considers that the two prophets in this passage are Moses and Elijah. Though his theory of a lost 'Apocalypse of Elijah' embedded in Rev. 11¹⁻¹² is hard to establish, it seems clear that the martyrdom of Elijah on his return to preach repentance in preparation for the approaching New Age was widely accepted, and that Jesus' ministry fitted into that pattern of ideas. See J. Jeremias, art. cit., 942, and for criticism, J. A. T. Robinson, 'Elijah, John and Jesus', *NTS.*, iv, 1958, 263–81 (published also in *Twelve New Testament Studies*, London, 1962, 28–52, n. 39).

154 Tertullian, *De Anima*, 50, 'morituri (Enoch and Elijah) reservantur, ut Antichristum sanguine suo extinguant'. Also, *Apocalypse of Peter* (ed. M. R. James, *The Apocryphal New Testament*, 511–12).

155 Ch. Guignebert, loc. cit. Note too, the veneration of the 'tombs of the Maccabees' in the first century A.D. iv Macc. 17⁸, and 'of the prophets', Mt. 23²⁹, as a permanent reminder of their role and as cult centres.

156 Note the parallel, cited by W. R. Farmer, op. cit., 57, between ii Macc. 4¹¹⁻¹⁹ and Josephus, *Antiquities*, xv.8.1 on the importation of Greek ways by Jason and the introduction of similar customs by Herod. The visual evidence of Herod's Classicizing tendencies can be seen with profit in K. Macleish, art. in *Life*, 31 July 1961.

157 Apart from the Scrolls literature, a good illustration of the antipathy felt for the Hasmoneans by pious Jews in Palestine is to be found in ch. 6 of the *Assumption of Moses*, and in the *Psalms of Solomon*.

158 *The Battle Scroll* (ed. Dupont-Sommer, *The Essene Writings*, Oxford, 1961, 164ff.). For its direction against the Romans, ibid., 167.

159 Cf. i Enoch, 37–70, and for the first century A.D. ii Baruch 72. In Christianity, Rev. 19.

160 E. Meyer, *Ursprung und Anfänge*, ii.283.

161 See J. A. T. Robinson, 'The Baptism of John and the Qumran Community', *HTR.*, 50, 1957, 175ff.

162 On the relations between the two groups at this period see W. D. Davies, *Christian Origins and Judaism*, London, 1962, ch. ii, 'Apocalyptic and Pharisaism'.

163 The case is argued cogently, and in my view decisively, by A. Dupont-Sommer, op. cit., ch. ii, and F. M. Cross, *The Ancient Library at Qumran*, London, 1958, ch. v. For a careful analysis of the evidence for various points of view, Millar Burrows, *More Light on the Dead Sea Scrolls*, London, 1958, Part V. Note also the views of Chaim Rabin, *Qumran Studies*, Oxford, 1957, p. 21, who considers that at least in so far as their admission ceremonies were concerned, the sect had more in common with Pharisee than Essene procedure.

164 For the end of the community during Vespasian's campaign of 68, R. de Vaux, *L'Archéologie et les Manuscripts de la Mer morte*, Schweich Lectures, 1959 (London, 1961), 33, and art., *R.B.*, lxi, 1954, 234. For identification of the 'Kittim' with the Romans, G. Vermès, *Discovery in the Judaean Desert*, New York, 1956, 83–4.

165 *Manual of Discipline*, ed. Dupont-Sommer, op. cit., p. 83; cf. i. Macc. 1⁵⁶.

166 Though as Millar Burrows points out, there was far more unfulfilled promise in their interpretations of the prophets among the Qumran Covenanters than among the early Christians. (Millar Burrows 'Prophecy and Prophets at Qumran', ch. xv in *Israel's Prophetic Heritage* = James Muilenburg Festsch., London, 1962).

167 F. M. Cross, op. cit., 147; cf. M. Black, *The Scrolls and Christian Origins*, 129ff.

168 F. M. Cross, op. cit., 147–8; see p. 148 n. 1 for references. Also, A. R. C. Leaney, art. cit., 293.

169 See the abundant discussion in Millar Burrows, *More Light on the Dead Sea Scrolls*, ch. 28.

[170] 1 Qp. Hab. 5.9–12. Discussed by Millar Burrows, *The Dead Sea Scrolls*, London, 1956, 365ff.

[171] 1 Qp. Hab. 5.12, cited from Millar Burrows, op. cit., 367.

[172] Tyconius, *Comment. in Apocalypsim* (apud Beatus of Libana, ed. Florez, Madrid, 1709, p. 184). Also, Jerome, *Ep.*, 14.9. and cf. the author's *Donatist Church*, 317ff.

[173] Augustine, *Contra Litteras Petiliani*, ii.92.202. To Tertullian, God himself was a zealot, *De Pudicitia* 2!

[174] As W. D. Davies points out, *Christian Origins and Judaism*, 115, of the two Messiahs postulated by the Covenanters, the priestly Messiah of the stock of Aaron takes precedence over the political Messiah of Israel.

[175] See the author's 'The Roman Empire in the eyes of the Western Schismatics during the Fourth Century A.D.', *Miscellanea Historiae Ecclesiasticae*, Louvain, 1961, 9ff.

[176] For examples, W. L. Knox, *Some Hellenistic Elements in Primitive Christianity* (Schweich Lectures, 1922), ch. i.

[177] I owe this information to Professor A. Wasserstein, Department of Classics, the University of Leicester.

[178] See S. Liebermann, *Hellenism in Jewish Palestine*, New York, 1950, 100ff. and J. Bonsirven, *Le Judaisme palestinienne au temps de Jésus-Christ*, Paris, 1935, ii. 261ff. for a collection of taboos and prohibitions in force among the Palestinian Jews to insulate themselves from Greek influences at this period.

[179] As indicated in the Alexandrian *Letter of Aristeas*, 121, 122, and also in fragments of Aristobulus (mid-second century B.C.). See R. H. Pfeiffer, *History of New Testament Times*, New York, 1949, 213ff.

[180] iv Macc. 1.1.

[181] Philo, *Legatio* 3–4; cf. *De Abraham* 90.

[182] *Contra Apionem*, ii.36.

[183] *Legatio*, 144; cf. *De Spec. Legibus* (ed. Colson) iv. 178.

[184] *Contra Celsum*, ii.30.

[185] *Demonstratio Evangelica*, vii.2.

[186] H. A. Wolfson, *Philo*, Harvard, 1948, ii.424.

[187] Josephus, *Wars*, ii.8.1.(117).

[188] 1 *Apol.* 16 and 46.

[189] ap. Eusebius, *H.E.*, iv.26.8.

[190] Athenagoras, *Legatio*, 37.

[191] Philo, *De Spec. Leg.* iv.32.164: 'παράσημον ἡγεμονίας ἀνεπιλήπτου πρὸς ἀρχέτυπον τὴν τοῦ θεοῦ βασιλείαν ἀπεικονισθείσης'. Eusebius, *Tricennalian Oration* 5.1; cf. E. Peterson, *Der Monotheismus als politisches Problem*, Leipzig, 1935, 29ff., and Wolfson, *Philo*, ii.381ff.

[192] For humanity's goal, Philo, *Quis Rerum Divinarum Heres*, 70.

[193] Philo, *Migrat. Abraham*, 128. See, H. Windisch, *Taufe und Sünde im ältesten Christentum*, Tübingen, 1908, 61–71.

[194] Philo, *De Vita Contempletiva*, 1ff.

[195] Notably the view of J. Geffcken, 'Die christlichen Martyrien', *Hermes*, 45, 1910, 481–505, who considers (op. cit. 496) Epictetus one of the main sources of the idea of martyrdom. Opposed by M. Delehaye, *Sanctus, Essai sur le culte des Saints dans l'Antiquité*, Brussels, 1927, 96.

[196] *Contra Apionem*, 1.8.

[197] Origen, *Contra Celsum*, viii.66.

[198] As Geffcken, of course, points out, op. cit., p. 494. 'Sokrates war der erste Märtyrer', and the Stoics Thrasea Paetus, Helvidius Priscus and Rubellius Plautus were others. For the Stoic's emphasis on the practical application of his principles, Seneca, *Epist. Morales* (ed. R. M. Grummere) 24,15.

[199] *Stromata* (ed. Stählin-Früchtel), iv.8.48ff. and iv.8.56. Clement's ref. to Timotheus of Pergamum's work, 'περὶ τῆς τῶν φιλοσόφων ἀνδρείας', is typical. See also, *Acta Pionii*, 17 and *Acta Apollonii*, 19.41. In general, A. Harnack, 'Sokrates und die alte Kirche', *Reden und Aufsätze*, Giessen, 1904, i.27–48, and E. Benz, 'Christus und Sokrates in der alten Kirche', *ZNTW.*, 43, 1950/51, 195–224.

[200] *Apol.* 14.

[201] Epictetus, *Dissert.* (ed. W. A. Oldfather), 1.29.47, 'ὡς μάρτυς ὑπὸ τοῦ θεοῦ κεκλημένος'.

[202] Ed. H. Musurillo, *Acts of the Pagan Martyrs*, Oxford, 1954.

[203] Ibid., pp. 48 and 163.

[204] *Acta Appiani* (ed. E. Musurillo, op. cit. 69). For recognition of the difference of spirit behind patriotic death and martyrdom, Eusebius, *H.E.*, v. Praef. 2.

[205] See E. R. Goodenough 'Catacomb Art', *JBL.*, lxxxi, 1962, 113–42, especially conclusions, and A. Ferrua, *Le Pitture della nuova catacomba di Via Latina*, Rome (Pontifico Instituto di Arch. crist.) 1960 (reviewed by J. M. C. Toynbee, *JRS*, lii, 1962, 256–7).

[206] The Jewish preoccupation with the salvation theme in the synagogue paintings is closely analysed by Miss R. Wischnitzer. *The Messianic Theme in the Paintings at Dura Europos.* In the church David and Goliath provided the Christian with his assurance of victory over the mighty (M. Rostovtzeff, *Dura Europos and its Art*, Oxford, 1938, 132).

[207] A. Grabar, *Martyrium, Recherches sur le Culte des reliques et l'Art chrétien antique*, Paris, 1946, ii.20–1.

[208] For Isaiah, Hebs. 11[37], Justin, *Dial.* 120.4–5. Tertullian, *De Patientia*, 14 and *Scorpiace* 8, Origen, *Ad Africanum*, Ep. 9.1. Ambrose, *Comment on Ps*, 118. Moses: his martyrdom, Origen, *Comment. in Matth.* 10.18 (ed. E. Klostermann, p. 24); cf. also Jude 9 for the incident of Michael and Satan struggling for Moses' body. For a fifth century text, Sozomen, *Hist. Eccl.* ix.17. (tale of the discovery of 'Zechariah's tomb' near Eleutheropolis).

[209] Wisd. 7[25]. Also, *Pirke Aboth* 1.2. The Law as a prime factor in the stability of the cosmos, citing R. Simon the Just, *circa* 300 B.C.; cf. Baruch 4[1], and Ecclesiasticus 24[23] (Wisdom = Law).

[210] G. F. Moore, *Judaism*, ii.312.

[211] *Letter to Diognetus*, 4.6.

CHAPTER THREE

Martyrdom in the New Testament Period

'THERE is nothing, *apart from Christ*, that is original in the teaching of the New Testament. The writers use ideas current among the Jews of the time.'[1] And, with this all-important qualification, this statement, applied by its author to the eschatology of the New Testament, could hold good concerning martyrdom. Suffering and tribulation (θλῖψις) belonged to the very nature of the primitive Church.[2] The Christian, like the Jew, was expected to confess and if need be to suffer for the Name. 'Whosoever shall confess me before men, him will I confess before my Father which is in Heaven. But whosoever shall deny me before men, him will I deny before my Father which is in Heaven.' (Mt. 10[32-33].) In this passage of Scripture Christianity follows current Jewish tradition. Death was to be preferred to the breach of the new Covenant implied in denial of the Name just as it had been of the Old, and he who persevered would be rewarded at the Day of Judgment. The plain word of Scripture was the Christian martyr's source of inspiration.[3] To endure 'the great persecution that is coming', Hermas urged (*circa* 120?) was to be blessed, but to deny was to court rejection by the Lord Himself.[4] It is hardly accidental that St. Luke associates denial with 'blasphemy against the Holy Ghost' (Lk. 12[10]).

In addition, the Christian was called upon not merely to suffer, but to undertake a life of positive witness. For with Jesus, the final era of world history had dawned. The day of the Lord was already 'at hand' (Mt. 4[17]), not in the far distant future. The Christian was required to live, like 'men who were awaiting their master' (Lk. 12[36]),[4a] and their sufferings derived their meaning because they afforded the proof of the speedy return of the Bridegroom and the end of the Age. The seal of baptism made him the participant in Jesus' own destiny, and a witness to His conquest of sin and death. These were aspirations which only a Christian could share, but they must be understood against a background of current Jewish beliefs about vicarious and expiatory sacrifice, reward and Judgment.[5] Jesus could be claimed as the last of the prophets who had died to expiate Israel's sin. The blending of the old and new ideas provides the clue to understanding the Christian view of martyrdom; to cite T. W. Manson, 'The change of meaning of the word (martyr) took place in the early Church, but preparation for it had begun much earlier, and it can be traced in the Old Testament and in the extra-canonical Jewish writings.'[6] As in so much of the doctrine and practice of the primitive Church, the Christian view of the martyr's role prolongs but also supersedes Judaism.

Despite a homeland permeated with nationalist fervour,[7] and fanatical orthodoxy,[8] despite the hopes of the Jewish people, and perhaps indeed of some of His own disciples, Jesus rejected the current idea of a warrior messiah overthrowing the idolatrous occupying power by force, and chose for Himself the way of the Cross.[9] With the important qualifications derived from Trypho's discussion with Justin at Ephesus *circa* 137,[10] and the possible application of the Suffering Servant *motif* to the Teacher of Righteousness,[11] there is no evidence in contemporary Judaism for a suffering messiah of the Davidic line, taking its inspiration from the great Servant passage in Deutero-Isaiah.[12] Indeed, these passages seem not to have been applied by the Jews to the messiah at all. Origen quotes an interesting discussion which he had with some Jews on the subject. He himself had referred Is. 52^{13}–53^8 to Jesus, but the Jews had claimed that the prophecies referred 'to the whole people as though of a single individual, since they were scattered in the Dispersion and smitten', though as a result of this scattering many proselytes were made.[13] The Targum also diverts the element of humiliation, suffering and death from the person of the Servant-Messiah and transfers it to Israel or to the heathen nations.[14] Thus Is. 53^5, 'But he was wounded for our transgressions, he was bruised for our iniquities', becomes 'But he will build up the Holy Place, which has been polluted for our sins and delivered to the enemy for our iniquities'. On the other hand, even if we are prepared to reject direct identification in a number of New Testament passages between Jesus and the Servant,[15] the cumulative effect of the evidence found in the New Testament and sub-Apostolic works such as the Didache and i Clement is compelling.[16] Jesus seems to have had the example of the Servant as well as the persecuted prophet[17] in mind, and He seems consciously to have chosen both these roles in order to fulfil His redemptive mission to mankind. While He Himself may not have claimed that any particular Old Testament texts connected with suffering were being fulfilled by Him, there is no doubt that the primitive Church accepted the Servant passages in LXX as pre-figuring His ordeal. Paul at Thessalonica had no hesitation in telling his audience that 'it behoved the Christ to suffer' (Acts 17[3]). Jesus' blood was the blood 'poured out for many' (Mk. 14[24], Mt. 26[28] = Is. 53[12]) and for His Name the Christian's would be shed also (Mk. 10[30]).

The atoning and vicarious nature of Jesus' sacrifice provides the main link between the Christian and Jewish outlook towards martyrdom. The themes of 'ransom', 'atonement' and 'sacrifice' recur continuously in the Synoptic Gospels, their writers being bent on showing how Jesus summed up this whole long tradition of His People by His sacrifice and death. Discussing the significance of Mk. 10[45] C. K. Barrett[18] has argued that its background was to be found in Daniel 7 rather than Isaiah 53. But in Mark the Son of Man was no longer a conquering figure of Daniel's prophecies, but a martyr, sacrificing himself as a 'ransom for many', 'an expression' as Barrett suggests, 'of the fact that God will surely accept the atoning sacrifice of the martyrs, and because of them deliver his people'. In this respect the Marcan Jesus may be compared with Eleazar in iv Maccabees.[19] The figure also of the 'ransom' was by no means new. The delivery from Egypt had been interpreted as a 'ransom', but this was now to be accomplished by sacrifice and not by might such as that employed against Egypt. Moreover, Jesus' sacrifice had universal application. It was no longer restricted to the house of Israel (as some of the disciples hoped even after three years with Him, Lk. 24[21] and Acts 1[7]), but extended to the whole new Christian race, open to all who repented and received baptism. The field was 'the world'. In the Lukan text 12[50] Jesus' baptism and death were equated, the one preparing the way for the other. The direct connection of this text with Christian martyrdom is pointed out by Tertullian[20] and in a striking phrase by Polycarp in his prayer at his own martyrdom.[21] The immensity of the struggle against Evil demanded correspondingly immense sacrifices. Salvation was through water and blood (1 Jn. 5⁶), through which the Christian took upon himself association with Jesus' own lot. Jesus Himself knew that 'he must suffer many things' and 'be killed'. The cup, symbolizing in contemporary thought the bitterness of death (cf. Mt. 20²², Mk. 10³⁸, Ascension of Isaiah 5¹³), must not be allowed to pass from Him. Just as both ii and iv Maccabees portray the suffering and the sacrifice of innocent victims as a means of atonement for the sins of Israel, so the New Covenant must be sealed in the innocent blood of a sacrificial victim. Without the Cross there could be no Christian Church.

Moreover, Jesus embodied the prophetic tradition of Israel, claiming to interpret the Law without reference to tradition, rejecting religious scrupulosity, dispensing men from Sabbath observance and contrasting his yoke with that of Torah (Mt. 11²⁹). It is not therefore surprising to find Him relating His sufferings to those of prophets in a previous age and the first generations of Christians interpreting them accordingly. Thus, in the words of the writer of the Epistle of Barnabas (5.11), 'So then the Son of God came in the flesh for this reason, that he might complete (or, "sum up") the total of the sins of those who persecuted his prophets to death. For this cause he endured'.²² This is how Jesus' sufferings and death appeared to a Christian community about a century after the Crucifixion, but the Gospels also tell the same story. References to the sufferings of Elijah (Mk. 9¹³ and Mt. 17¹²), the parable of the Wicked Husbandman, and perhaps too, the presence of Moses and Elijah at the Transfiguration may have been designed to leave no doubt as to what was expected of the Son of Man.²³ To his immediate followers, Jesus summed up in His ministry and death the whole process of righteous suffering which the pious Jew regarded as characteristic of the history of the human race from the beginning of time, 'From the blood of Abel to the blood of Zechariah the son of Barachiah' (Mt. 23²⁹⁻³⁶). But to the Christian the slaughter of the prophets would be followed by that of Christ. The prophets, by their sufferings at the hands of the Jewish nation, had been witnesses of God's mercy and Judgment, and to the death and resurrection of Israel under the Old Covenant.²⁴ Jesus, last and greatest of the prophets,²⁵ was witness to the same things under the New.

Jesus' sufferings would be continued in the lives of His followers. They were to be the prophets of the new era. 'Blessed are ye when men shall revile you and persecute you, and say all manner of evil against you for my sake, . . . for so persecuted they the prophets' (Mt. 5[11-12]). They must be prepared quite literally to take up the Cross (Mk. 8[34], Mt. 16[29] and Lk. 9[23]). If they claimed to live by the Spirit, to be the saints to whom the faith once and for all had been delivered (Jude 3), by the Spirit must they walk (Lk. 6[46]) and take the consequences. The Gospels warn continuously that the lot of the disciples would be cast in persecution in imitation of Jesus' own fate (Mk. 13[9-13], Mt. 24[9-13], Lk. 21[12-19]). Peter and James were the first examples. As the servant was not above his Lord, so must the disciples suffer like Jesus Himself and the prophets before Him. The warning is summed up in the Fourth Gospel, 'If they persecuted me, so will they persecute you' (Jn. 15[20]). There would be no reward on earth for the Christian except suffering and death;[26] but beyond, the faithful, rising first, and escorting him on the last trump[27] would share in Christ's glory, as 'imitators of ourselves and the Lord' Paul assures the Thessalonians (1 Thess. 1[6]).

Some writers have also seen in the Passion narratives stories similar to those related about the late-Jewish heroes. 'St. Luke's portrait in the Passion story, we are told, is that of the suffering but faithful servant of God, we may even say, the martyr'.[28] Indeed, both Origen and Cyprian draw the parallel of Christ's death with that of a martyr.[29] Other critics have pointed to parallels in Jewish martyrdoms of the time in some of the incidents recounted in the trial of Jesus.[30] Thus, it has been claimed that the silence in the face of His accusers corresponds to the silence of the accused before Antiochus in ii and iv Maccabees (ii Macc. 7[2 and 11], iv Macc. 6[1], 10[23]). Antiochus is astonished at the bearing of the accused (ii Macc. 7[12]; iv Macc. 8[4]) just as Pilate is astonished at the bearing of Jesus (Mk. 15[5]). The mockery of Jesus by false witnesses is echoed in the Ascension of Isaiah (5[1]), and in this work too, the martyr prophesies a vision just as Jesus prophesies one when standing before the High Priest (Mk. 14[62], Ascension of Isaiah 5[8]). Mighty works accompany His death as those of the prophets before Him.

These are interesting parallels, but it is difficult to know what significance ought to be attached to them. Though the trial of Jesus seems to diverge from what is known about Jewish religious trials of this period the most cursory reading of the Synoptic narratives suggests that these are not the work of copyists using existing Jewish *Acta*. The accounts in Mark and Luke are not indeed reconcilable in all their details. There is telescoping in the one, and elaboration, derived from Luke's independent sources, in the other.[31] The theme, however, of the story so nobly and simply told in Mark of the gradual abandonment of the Lord, first by the leaders of His nation, then by His disciples, then by the people, and finally the sense of the withdrawal of His Father's presence, surely speaks for itself.[32] Moreover, the actual details, such as the blundering attempts of the witnesses to remember Jesus' statements of three years before, and the legal precision of Caiaphas' method aimed at pinning the capital charge of blasphemy on the accused, have a ring of actuality.[33] The hearing before Pilate too, fits the Roman framework remarkably well.[34] Pilate's raised *tribunal*, the accusations duly made by *delatores* of seditious actions, and Pilate's own questions can be related to Roman criminal procedure *extra ordinem* of the time. The existence of the Jewish parallels, however, suggests a similarity of mental climate and literary tradition in which the Jewish martyrologist and the Christian evangelist were working. The Passion Narratives provide some further evidence for the continuity among the early Christians of the traditional Jewish belief that the prophet-martyr was the acceptable sacrifice to God on behalf of sinful Israel.

In Acts and the Pauline epistles the expiatory character of the Christian's afflictions continues to be present[35] with the additional factor however, of the implications of the new age in world history. Persecution was no longer something to be regretted or avoided, but to be expected as part of the age in which the Christian was living, and to be accepted with rejoicing. In the early chapters of Acts, the disciples rejoice at the onset of Herod Agrippa's persecution in 44, and earlier that they have been actually found worthy to suffer for the name (Acts 5[41], cf. 9[16]). Stephen's speech sums up this development. To him, Jesus' death marked the culmination of prophetic suffering in the age-long encounter between righteousness and backsliding and hardness of heart.

'Which of the prophets did your fathers not persecute?' he asks (Acts 7[52]). As imitator of his Lord he prays for his enemies' forgiveness (Acts 7[60])[36] and is granted a vision of His glory in his final moments (Acts 7[56]). Like in Ezekiel's vision,[37] the Son of Man 'stands' at the right hand of God. Stephen is both prophet and martyr. This was the vision which was to set the seal on the martyr's life in the next two centuries; for the martyr now knows that Jesus had conquered death, and had the assurance of his own salvation.[38] Not for nothing was Stephen termed 'the perfect martyr' in the tradition of the second-century Church.[39]

Quite rightly, scholars have pointed to the great significance of the final verses in the account of Stephen's martyrdom.[40] As he begins his address to the Sanhedrin, his face is already 'that of an angel' (Acts 6[15]). He was therefore manifesting the glory of God in the form reserved for the Righteous who participated in Judgment:[41] at the end, he was under the direct inspiration of the Holy Spirit. He not only had a vision of the world beyond, but provided proof of the outpouring of the spirit which traditionally was to be the sign of the end of the existing age.[42]

It is natural to look to Paul for a further statement of this same outlook. Paul passionately believed that suffering, beatings and death were the symbol of his own right to be called an apostle (ii Cor. 4[11], 6[9] and 11[23]). Only through afflictions did one attain the kingdom of God. This was the message he and Barnabas preached on the first missionary journey (Acts 14[22]) and which he had emphasized to his converts at Thessalonica (I Thess. 3[4]). His personal sufferings at the hands of enemies were true service to Christ. In dramatic passages in Philippians he ruminates on whether it was better to die and be with Christ at once or complete his missionary work (Phil. 1[20-24]). Epaphroditus who nearly died in Christ's service also receives high praise (Phil. 4[18]).

Paul faced a problem which was perplexing his converts. Jesus' sacrifice had been efficacious for all mankind, and in Roms. 3[25] he uses the symbol of the expiatory sacrifice found in Levit. 16[14] LXX, the ίλαστήριον, whose blood flows out in expiation of sin. This is what in the opinion of the writer of iv Maccabees (17[21-22]), the Maccabean heroes had accomplished for the Old Israel, and this is what Jesus had now accomplished for both Jew and Gentile (Roms. 3[23-25]).[43] On the other hand, if this were so, why did the

Christian have to suffer at all? Paul's answer reflects Jewish apocalyptic thinking. As we know, Jews of the Pharisaic tradition in which Paul was reared envisaged a predetermined period of natural disaster, war, confusion and persecution before the arrival of the End. In the Markan apocalypse, the Christian is presented with the same picture, but with the proviso that this terrible period in world history had been shortened by Jesus, though not abolished. 'And except the Lord had shortened those days, no flesh would have been saved' (Mk. 13²⁰).⁴⁴ This is also Paul's standpoint. The suffering of Christians had no further expiatory value.⁴⁵ That had already been fulfilled by Jesus, but they completed what still remained of afflictions before the Second Coming.⁴⁶ In addition, they were the guarantee of a share in Christ's suffering and consequently his future glory (Roms. 6³⁻¹¹). To Paul, as to most of his Hellenistic-Jewish contemporaries, the souls of the martyrs were destined to eternal bliss.

Thus, persecution, he tells the Thessalonians (i Thess. 2¹⁶) was the means of 'filling up their sins', and to the Colossians (Col. 1²⁴) he wrote 'I rejoice in my suffering, for your sake, and fill up on my part that which is lacking of the afflictions of Christ in my flesh for his body's sake, which is the Church'.⁴⁷ He certainly believed that his own suffering would hasten that time, and in this too one can discern a link with the writer of the Maccabean saga, here in ii Macc. 7⁹. But Paul also believed that the End would not come before the Gospel had been preached to the uttermost parts of the globe. Hence, his own fantastic missionary journeys, and hence, the explicit statement of Luke in Acts 1⁸. In Paul's mind suffering for the faith and the task of witnessing to it were equally urgent and inextricably interwoven.⁴⁸ The duty and consequences of witness involved the title of martyr itself.

Up to this point, we have been on traditional ground. Atoning sacrifice, tribulations preceding the End, the connection between suffering and the prophet's role, and the futility of forceful resistance to the executioner were common ground between many orthodox Jews and Christians. Jesus' death and resurrection, however, had brought the End much closer. At first, the Apostles qualify for their office because they were witnesses to these events (Acts 1²², 2³² and Gal. 1¹²). Then the witness was extended to all Christians, for all were involved in the resulting destruction of the demonic powers which had hitherto enslaved the world. With the overthrow, however, of their lord, death itself, the era of the Spirit had opened. The Christian shared in a cosmic struggle rapidly approaching its climax. By the end of the first century A.D. the suffering for which he had been warned in the Gospels and the witness which the approaching End demanded had become synonymous in the term 'martyrdom'.

With this in mind, we must turn briefly to the word 'martyr'. The words μάρτυς, μαρτυρία, μαρτυρεῖν occur frequently in the New Testament, and have been the subject of lengthy and learned discussion. If, as we have suggested in the last chapter, there is little reason to accept a pagan philosophical origin for the Christian usage, except as part of a general climate of opinion, there remains some scope for disagreement as to how the term acquired its special sense of dying after confessing the faith.[49] Scholars have been divided into two broad streams of opinion. On the one hand, Delehaye,[50] Campenhausen[51] and Strathmann[52] have emphasized the originality of the Christian sense, and tended perhaps to play down the debt to Judaism. On the other hand, Fischel,[53] Surkau[54] and Perler[55] have attempted to trace out the continuity of the Christian with the Jewish view of martyrdom shown particularly in the *Acta Martyrum* of the two faiths.

From a purely semantic point of view, the school of Delehaye has a good deal of justification.[56] Apart from the reading, in the Alexandrian manuscript of iv Macc. 12[16], [57] and Rev. 11[3] (assuming that this is originally a Jewish source),[58] the term was apparently not used by Jewish writers to describe the act of those who died for Torah. Such heroes later became known simply as 'qedoshim'—people set apart, the equivalent of the Christian 'saint'.[59] 'Martyria', however, is used in connection with witness to the nature and work of Jahwe which led to suffering, as in LXX Is. 43–44, and also in connection with the prophets 'witnessing against' sinful Israel and taking the consequence of their acts.[60] It would seem that the Christian use of the term must be partly a continuation of these Hellenistic-Jewish usages. Thus, in the Fourth Gospel Jesus witnesses concerning His Father before Nicodemus (Jn. 3[11]) and the Jews in general (Jn. 5[31 ff.]), and He suffers and dies on account of that witness. Again, μαρτυρία χριστοῦ (Rev. 1[2]) meaning the preaching of the Christian missionary, has a prophetic sense as it had in Judaism. Death as a witness to the resurrection automatically made the sufferer a prophet, and this duty descended on all baptized believers. Prophecy, however, was no longer for the few as in Judaism. The Holy Spirit was on all Christians inspiring their witness, while Antichrist united Jew and Gentile in common hatred of the 'new race'.

In the New Testament μάρτυς is used by the Synoptics in the general and legal senses as a witness (e.g. Mk. 14⁵⁶, ⁵⁹, ⁶³; Lk. 22⁷¹). From this, as we have seen, one can become a witness to the facts of Christ's life, especially to His resurrection (Lk. 24⁴⁸ and Acts 1⁸). A few chapters later in Acts (Acts 4³³) we are told that 'with great power, the apostles gave their witness to the resurrection of Jesus Christ'. As yet, no penalty is attached, and we have not reached the stage when Antipas' proclamation of Christ's resurrection and his own death for so doing, are summed up in the single term of 'martyr'. Indeed, in Acts 22²⁰, Paul describes Stephen as a martyr, not specifically because he died, but because he confessed the death of Christ, and his death in the process was merely a proof of the sincerity of his witness.[61] It is clear too, that when in i Cor. 15⁴ and 15, Paul points out that if there had been no resurrection the apostles would be ψευδομάρτυρες τοῦ θεοῦ he is thinking of the martyr as primarily a witness to the power of God shown by the fact of the Resurrection—as in LXX usages.[62]

Even so, the distinction between witnessing and suffering on account of that witness was becoming a fine one, and it could only be a matter of time before actual persecution would equate them. By the time i Tim. 6¹³ was written (perhaps A.D. 65–68) Christ's own witness and 'good confession before Pilate' was already linking inseparably the ideas of confession and ultimate death. The reward would be 'the crown of righteousness' (ii Tim. 4⁸).[63] A few years later, perhaps, in i Peter, the 'imitator of Christ', imbued by the Holy Spirit, both witnesses as to Christ's sufferings and the resulting glories (i Peter 1¹¹). He must be himself prepared to perish as Christ had been in order to become a participant in the glory to come (i Peter 5¹ff.).[64] The word κοινωνός which defined this witness-suffering relationship of the Christian to Christ was to have a long history in the martyr-literature of Asia Minor.[65] One can understand how it was that lesser suffering did not qualify for 'martyrdom', as the martyrs of Lyons were quick to point out, and mere verbal witness to Christ was insufficient to secure the Christian this title of honour.

It is, of course, in the Johannine literature that the term μάρτυς/ μαρτυρία moves quickest towards its final Christian sense.[66] John, indeed, uses these words in the ordinary sense on a number of occasions (e.g. Jn. 8[17] or iii Jn. 12) but in numerous other passages μαρτυρία has the sense of positive, missionary witness by Jesus or his disciples.[67] Jesus himself is a witness to the Father (Jn. 3[11] and [32-33]), and He passes on what He has received from the Father (Jn. 5[30ff.]). 'I am come into the world that I should bear witness unto the truth' (Jn. 18[37]) and the truth is 'that God is life eternal and that this life is in his Son' (i Jn. 5[11]). He 'who believed on the Son hath the witness in him' (i Jn. 5[10]). Finally, Jesus gave his witness on the Cross in order that 'ye also may believe' (Jn. 19[35]) and the evangelist emphasizes that the witness was sealed in 'water and blood'. In this Gospel the shedding of innocent blood is connected not only with atonement and the fate of the prophet but with positive witness. A double strand binds the Christian to the Cross.

When Jesus had ascended, the witness would continue through the Spirit. Here, the really important role of the Spirit in 're-proving the world in respect of sin and of righteousness and judgment' (Jn. 16[8]) is to be stressed.[68] The Paraclete will bear witness concerning Jesus (Jn. 15[26]). He would speak through the mouths of the Christians in their hour of peril before the 'governors and kings', His function as Advocate of the cause of God is regarded as the same both by the Synoptics (Mk. 13[11], Mt. 10[19]) and by John (Jn. 15[26]). Just as in the previous age he had spoken through the prophets to a hostile world, so now he bears witness before the persecuting powers, speaking through the confessor. The ultimate justification of the Christian martyr lay in these verses.

Closely linked with these same ideas were those of final judgment and the vindication of the righteous; in this too, we see the Christian drawing upon, but also giving new meaning to contemporary Jewish thought. To the Christian, the Second Coming would include the proclamation of Jesus as supreme and universal Judge. It was He who would come on the world's last day in a burning fire. Paul comforts the Thessalonians in their hour of persecution with a tremendous vision of future judgment and vengeance (ii Thess. 1⁶⁻¹⁰). As one writer has described,[69] he has put together a 'brilliant mosaic' of Old Testament prophesies foretelling the Day of the Lord, and applying them to the Second Coming. Jesus would come with fire, as Jahwe had promised (Is. 66¹⁵). He would pour out indignation on the nations that did not acknowledge him (Jer. 10²⁵). He would come with his saints (Ps. 89⁷) and he would be glorified in His day like Jahwe (Is. 2¹¹ and ¹⁷). Thus, the enemies of the Church would pay the full penalty for their persecution of the righteous. The 'sheep and goats' theme adumbrated in Daniel (Dan. 12²⁻³) continued in Enoch 90, and in Mt. 24 is repeated here. There was no need for the Christian to take up arms against the Roman Empire. It would be done for him in due time, and the destruction of the enemy would be eternal. Meanwhile, the Christian was to be both imitator and witness for his Lord and accept the hatred of the world.

Two New Testament books, Hebrews[70] and Revelation,[71] both written towards the end of the first century in environments in which persecution had been experienced, sum up the two components of the primitive Christian view of martyrdom. Each was imbued by the eschatological situation and strongly influenced the thought of the early Church. In Hebrews, the suffering and death of Christians is associated directly with the expiatory nature of Christ's death and those of the prophets. Christ died, we are told at the outset (1³) ʻκαθαρισμὸν τῶν ἁμαρτιῶν ποιησάμενος': there could be no forgiveness without the shedding of sacrificial blood (9²² and 10¹⁹). Christ, the great athlete, had overthrown Satan, the enemy both of God and man, but the means had been his own sacrifice. Christ was the victim of all victims, the supreme example of faith, whose resurrection had set the seal on his high priestly office. Jesus followed the long succession of those who had witnessed to the truth by faith. Through faith Daniel had 'stopped the mouths of lions' (11³³), because of his faith Isaiah had been 'stoned and sawn asunder' (11³⁷). Jesus, the 'perfecter of faith' endured the cross 'for the joy that was set before him', and the faithful Christians were called upon to tread the same path, 'to run with patience the race that was set before them' and to 'resist unto blood, striving against sin' (12⁴). The terminology of the games, reminiscent of Maccabees, was long to remain the terminology of the *Acta Martyrum*. The triumph of the Christian over Satan, lord of death, inspired his ultimate defiance against the authorities. Apostasy, 'treading under foot the Son of God' (10²⁹) was the most disgraceful of crimes.

In Revelation, this defiance was motivated by similar needs differently expressed. The seer writes with the consciousness that the final blow has been struck against the present Age, that the 'time is already at hand' (1⁴). He himself has suffered exile as the result of having witnessed to Christ (1⁹) and Christ is Himself the 'faithful witness', the 'first-born of the dead' (1⁵). As an exile, he shares the fate of the saints who had already borne witness (6⁹, 12¹⁷ and 20⁴), and he regards the keeping of the commandments and witnessing as one and the same thing (12¹⁷). Furthermore, witness leads straight to death. John sees 'the souls of them that had been slain for the word of God' (6⁹). Antipas had not been deterred from his witness by fear of death (2¹³). His victory, like that of other Christians, had been gained 'because of the blood of the Lamb', and 'because of the word of their testimony they loved not their life, even unto death' (12¹¹).⁷² Here μαρτυρία is used in the technical sense of being a blood-witness, the sense it was to retain from now onwards. Like the Jewish heroes of the previous age, the Christian heroes 'had not worshipped the Beast'. Witness involved defiance of the idolatrous powers (20⁴), after which would follow the resurrection of those who had maintained their witness to the end, and their reign with Christ would last for a thousand years. Then, in the familiar, yet ever terrible words comes the vision of the vengeance for which the martyrs cry out (6¹⁰), of the Last Judgment in which the martyrs would participate as judges, and of the casting of the idolaters into the lake of brimstone 'which is the second death' (21⁸). Thus suffering, witness, judgment, ultimate triumph are welded into the single theme of martyrdom. The unity of Christian martyrdom and Apocalyptic is complete. This martyr-idea which profoundly influenced the first three centuries of Christian history, was given its final meaning in the tense and exalted Apocalyptic of the Asian Churches.⁷³

Are we justified then, in regarding Christianity as a 'revolutionary movement',⁷⁴ and Christians consciously engaged in a political struggle with the paganism of the Roman Empire? Certainly, if Rev. 17–18 stood alone, we should have no hesitation. Not only is the city of Rome condemned in horrific terms, but every aspect of the material world that 'waxed rich by the power of her wantonness' (18³), such as the client rulers, the merchants and shipowners of the Mediterranean. Moreover, we cannot exclude witness against the Roman authorities in the person of Pontius Pilate (1 Tim. 6¹³) from the witness of martyrdom. But does it also follow that the *militia Christi* was, to quote Ehrhardt, 'an active and bloody service in the political field'?[75] The evidence gives us some indications, but no clear-cut answer. As W. L. Knox has written, 'the attitude of the New Testament writers towards the Roman Empire presents a curious picture, varying as it does, from quite remarkable enthusiasm to a violent hostility'.[76] Indeed, it seems that the Christians in this period continued to express the same shades of political opinion as their Jewish contemporaries in Palestine and the Dispersion.[77]

Part of the difficulty arises from apparent contradictions in Jesus' own teaching and actions at different moments in His career. Politically, it seems that He did not deny completely the strongly Maccabean tradition of His native Galilee. As a boy of 13 or 14 He would have seen His homeland engulfed in the futile Zealot revolt under Judas in A.D. 7. Zealotry is always in the background in all four Gospels, and that He came to terms with it is suggested by the presence of one or more Zealots among His disciples.[78] At the beginning of His ministry in Galilee, popular hopes about His political ambitions seem to have run high. Mark's account of the feeding of the 5000 suggests that at that moment Jesus saw His people as a nation without a leader (cf. Numbers 27¹⁶⁻¹⁷ for the sheep and the shepherd simile), and He hesitated.[79] 'He had compassion on them.' His interests certainly lay with the Aramaic-speaking countryside rather than with the Greek cities.[80] His audiences were rural and the idioms He used drawn from the countryside also. He visited the villages of Caesarea Philippi (Mk. 8²⁷) but not the Greek city of Caesarea itself. The Syro-Phenician woman (i.e. a member of the Hellenized settler community) incurred a sharp retort when her identity was disclosed (Mk. 7²⁷). The Synoptists indicate no great feeling of attachment for the local Hellenistic rulers (Lk. 13³² and 22²⁵) and less for the Greek colonizers of Palestine (Mt. 8[34]).[81] St. John suggests that there was a revolutionary tendency in His move-ment. 'They would come and take Him by force, to make Him a king' (Jn. 6[15]),[82] but Jesus' reaction was to withdraw into the mountains alone. He refused to rule others 'as the Gentiles do' (Mt. 4[8-10], Lk. 4[5-8], Mk. 10[42-44]). His entry into Jerusalem, on the other hand, in fulfilment of the prophecy of Zechariah (9[9]) accompanied by hosannas, palm-branches and the spreading of clothes in His paths recalled the secular triumphs of Israelite kings (ii Kings 9[13]) and liberators from pagan yoke (i Macc. 13[51]).[83] In John's account Jesus is hailed as 'King of Israel' (Jn. 12[13]). The cleansing of the Temple at the same time was a forceful affront to the ruling pro-Roman hierarchy of the Sadducees.[84] In the final phase, some of the disciples were carrying arms (Lk. 22[35]) which they were prepared to use (Lk. 22[50], Jn. 18[10]).

It must be conceded too, that the Temptations were real enough, and at the outset of His Ministry Jesus faced up to the real choice whether to free His land physically from pagan Roman domination, just as the Maccabees had freed Palestine from pagan Seleucid domination and which Bar Kochba would attempt to emulate a century later. 'All the kingdoms of the earth' means military and political authority, a repetition of the conquering ways of the Old Israel.[85] Jesus' own thoughts on the subject may perhaps be found in Mk. 8[36], 'What shall it profit a man if he shall gain the whole world, and lose his own soul?' Yet, in the last week of His life we find Him torn between the conflicting instructions of telling His disciples to go and buy swords (Lk. 22[36]) and admonishing them that he who took the sword would perish by the sword (Mt. 26[51]). To have taken up arms would have been an act of disobedience to God and homage to Satan. His kingdom was 'not of this world' (Jn. 18[36]). The tension between what some of the disciples, even at the Last Supper, and the multitudes expected of Him, and the way which He Himself had chosen is one of the most compelling themes in the Gospel story. It is a moving and terrible irony that Jesus Himself was crucified by the Roman authorities as a royal pretender,[86] 'the king of the Jews' in Zealot style, while Barabbas 'guilty of insurrection' obtained his liberty.[87]

The dilemma which Jesus faced, and which was to face the

early Church, is epitomized in the story of the tribute-money. To have urged refusal would, of course, have delighted not only the Zealots, but every nationalist-minded Jew in Palestine. The Census itself, on which the tribute was assessed, was regarded as against God's will,[88] and to have counselled payment with the current *denarius* of Tiberius could have shocked the scrupulous as a counsel of idolatry. The coin depicted on the reverse side, an image of Zeus seated, which the donor would have to handle as he paid. Yet, Jesus advised payment, and on grounds in accord with Rabbinic teaching. 'If the heart be true to God, the purse may belong to Caesar without offence to God.' God has the primacy, but even if not very much would in the last resort be left to Caesar, Jesus accepts *de facto* civil government as a good in itself.[89] His attitude in this respect was almost precisely that of the moderate rabbis of the day.[90]

On social questions, too, one must be careful not to exaggerate the revolutionary character of Jesus' teaching. To be sure, St. Luke thought it appropriate to put the *Magnificat* into the mouth of the Virgin, and the theme of the overthrow of the rich and unjust rulers belongs to Jewish prophetic and apocalyptic writing.[91] Poverty and strict observance of the Law went together, and this tradition was one which we would expect the early Church to continue as the new and purified Israel. At Nazareth, Jesus opened His ministry with an address on Is. 61[1] (Lk. 4[16ff.]). He also had come to proclaim release to the captives, restore the sight to the blind, liberty to the oppressed and the acceptable year of the Lord. This could have been interpreted as more than moral exhortation. He certainly saw wealth as perilous (Mk. 10[24-27], Lk. 8[14]) but He did not refuse dinner with a ruler of a synagogue, presumably a wealthy man (Lk. 14[1]). At the same time, though Jesus criticizes the obvious abuses of contemporary society, including the inexorable severity of the courts of justice (Mt. 5[25]) and the pride and hypocrisy of the Jewish leaders (Mk. 12[38-40], Mt. 6[2, 15 and 16], 23, Lk. 13[14-17]), He never advocates radical changes in the existing system. Obligations to do forced labour (*angareia*) are to be faced cheerfully (Mt. 5[41]). The Temple Tax is to be paid (Mt. 17[18]). Matthew is not criticized for being a tax-gatherer nor are Roman centurions and soldiers for their calling. The Christian is counselled to a policy of non-resistance, and submission to wrongs suffered in the present world. Jesus Himself 'going about doing good' within existing society provides the example which His disciples must follow.[92] It was by dying that He drew all men unto Him (Jn. 12[32]).

One encounters the same problems when one considers the attitude of Paul. Broadly speaking, the apostle stands on the side of his younger contemporary Rabbi Hananiah[93] against the latter's radical opponents in accepting the civil government as a good in itself, and for the same reason, namely, affording protection against the coming of Antichrist and resulting chaos (ii Thess. 2[3]). It is the same standpoint that inspires the loyalist passages in Tertullian's Apology (*Apol.* 32.1) 150 years later, and it has Old Testament support in Jerem. 29[7] and Ezra 6[10]. Anarchy was a real fear, and there is no need to whittle away his injunction to the Romans in 57.[94] The powers that be (and this means 'earthly powers') were of God, their authority was derived from Him, obedience was their due. As Irenaeus pointed out *circa* 185, it was wrong to interpret the powers as 'angelical powers or invisible rulers', and he implies that this was what Gnostics had been doing.[95] There was no need to imitate them. Tribute and taxes therefore were to be paid (Roms. 13[7]).[96] Here too, Paul had Rabbinic authority on his side, not to speak of Philo.[97] 'Even an inspector of cisterns is appointed in Heaven', the Babylonian Rabbi Hanan ben Raba was to say in the third century.[98] Christians should obey the authorities, moreover, not for fear of punishment but because of a positive obligation to obey ministers appointed by God for the welfare of humanity. The same view is stated in the Pastorals. Titus 3[1] reproduces Roms. 13[1]. In i Tim. 2[2] the exhortation to a quiet life is coupled with the reminder of the Christian's duty to pray for the Empire. Strikingly, the writer of i Peter tells the Christian to be 'subject to every ordinance of man for the Lord's sake' (i Peter 2[13-14, 17]), and his instruction that he should 'fear God' and 'honour the king' are all the more significant coming as they do during an outburst of persecution, and from a source independent of Paul.

Even so, the State remains on a lower plane. Here, the early chapters of Acts are significant. 'We must obey God rather than men' (Acts 5[29]) and assuredly, Peter goes on to connect the acceptance of limited obedience only to the secular powers with the demands of Christian witness (Acts 5³²). Civil responsibilities must be fitted to the requirements of the eschatological age, and, if necessary, abandoned. Moreover, some (though not all) persecution was persecution at the hands of authorities representing the Roman State.[99] Both Pilate and Caiaphas were seen as agents of usurping cosmic powers.[100]

The obligations of Christian discipleship were paramount. The State, it would seem, was to be obeyed in so far as it was not *actively* idolatrous, for idolatry in the eyes of Christian and Jew alike, was the enemy against whom 'the armour of God' (Eph. 6¹¹) was put on. This was the ally of 'the world-rulers of this darkness'. Thus far, secular and cosmic adversaries were united against Christ and his followers. In addition, Paul's letters to the Thessalonians show that when roused by the tidings of actual persecution, apocalyptic, with all the hatred for the surrounding world that it implied, was never far below the surface. The bitterness with which he attacks *Pax et Securitas*, the programme of the early Principate, is startling (i Thess. 5³). The detail in which he describes the various manifestations of secular evil which would herald the Parousia, shows that he had brooded deeply on the subject (ii Thess. 2⁶ᶠᶠ·). The final reckoning with Antichrist was at hand. And, there is no doubt that the 'eternal destruction' foreseen by him as a manifestation of divine vengeance (2 Thess. 1⁹) was to engulf the Greco-Roman world, the living example of idolatry. Certainly, ordinary provincials were expected to be caught in sudden destruction (1 Thess. 5³), and were not pitied. Moreover, 'the night was far spent' (Roms. 13¹²).[101] In these passages, the Christian represents the ultimate extreme of contemporary Jewish thought.

Nor is it possible to ignore the social implications of first-century Christian eschatology. Abandonment of civil and home life could and did follow, as Paul shows in his letters to the Thessalonians (i Thess. 4¹¹ and ii Thess. 2² and 3¹¹). Concern for the poor could be transformed into active hostility to the existing social order. The Christians regarded themselves as 'saints' (*quadosh*),[102] separate from the world and at the same time brothers to one another (i Thess. 5²⁷),[103] whose religion was not a creed, but the only way of life (*berith*) possible in the short space that remained to the existing age.[104]

At the same time, when it came to the test of practical situations, the Christian of the New Testament period was far from being a revolutionary.[105] Paul himself was proud of his Roman citizenship, ready to assert it at all times, and touchy on the subject of social affronts. He moved freely among the best circles of eastern Mediterranean society; civil and religious leaders at Ephesus (Acts 19^{32}) and Corinth (Acts 18^8), were his friends. He was far from being at home among the Lycaonian speaking crowds at Lystra (Acts 14$^{11-19}$). He was obviously relieved that the 'barbarous people' of Malta treated him and the ship's company kindly (Acts 28^2). The Pauline congregations may not have contained 'many wise, mighty nor noble' (i Cor. 1^{26}), but there were plenty who had social pretensions and, more to the point, their own slaves, and houses large enough for congregations to meet (Roms. 16 and i Cor. 16^{19}). In his letter to Philemon, Paul does not ask the latter to free the runaway Onesimus, but to treat him kindly, as a Christian brother (Phil. 12–16). His right to exact his legal due is not questioned,[106] and yet the reminder that Christ died for him too, put earthly slavery in a new perspective. These are the ideas which one would expect of a provincial middle-class and mainly urban group, for whom 'the quiet and tranquil life in all piety and gravity' (i Tim. 2$^{1-3}$) was the acceptable life in the remaining time.

One is confronted therefore with a very real contrast between violent and revolutionary theories and conservatism in practice. It was to be a dilemma which was to face all eschatologically-minded Christian communities in the Roman Empire. The Donatists in the early fifth century after a century of denunciation of 'kings' (i.e. the Emperors) as persecutors and emissaries of Satan would declare that 'no force was to be used for the sake of God'.[107] Persecution was to be accepted. The Lord Christ instituted not a form of slaying, but of dying only.[108]

The transition from the loyalism of the Pauline Epistles to the attitude expressed in Revelation can be followed coherently on a theoretical plane. We see it as part of the world view which interpreted all events in terms of the approaching End and saw salvation in terms of individual counsels of perfection. The Church was merely the 'community of the interval'. Famines and wars which might engulf their neighbours could be regarded dispassionately as signs of the rule of Antichrist, and hence of the last hour (i Jn. 2[18]).[109] However, what gives Revelation its peculiar fascination and horror is the writer's belief that the interval was nearly over and that the Day of Judgment was actually at hand. The number of the Elect had almost been completed (6[11]). The martyrdom of the Church was ending (18[20-24]). Therefore, why dissemble? The vengeance demanded by the martyrs (6[10]) would soon fall on the Beast (the Emperor) and those who worshipped him. Babylon (Rome) 'drunk with the blood of saints' (17[6]), would receive her due. She would be destroyed because she had 'deceived the nations through sorcery' and taken upon herself the responsibility for the deaths of the prophets and saints throughout the Empire. The cult of Christ confronted the cult of Caesar which the Christians refused to honour (13[16]), and were martyred as a result.[110] The throne of Satan (2[13]) was set over against the throne of God. Here, the Messiah was a warrior (19[1ff.]) and his mission had the same anti-Roman character as the Messiah of the Jewish Sibyllines. It was the Essene tradition to which something had been added.

The Christian, however, would not have regarded even this as a call to arms. Why should he? 'In the world ye shall have tribulation, but be of good cheer, for lo, I have overcome the world' (Jn. 16[33]). His weapon was faith, not force (i Jn. 5[4]). There was no need of Sicarii, nor of a military leader if 'in a twinkling of an eye' the Old Order was to give way to the New and the Christian be 'caught up in the clouds' (i Thess. 4[17]). 'The last enemy' was not Rome, but death itself.[111] To speak, then, of Christian revolution is misleading, unless the term is used in a figurative sense only. In the Interim before the Second Coming, the Christian was called upon to suffer rather than to inflict suffering. His citizenship was truly in heaven.[112] There could therefore be no head-on clash with the secular authorities on the lines of the successive Jewish revolts of 66, 115 and 132. He was a member of the new, redeemed community of Israel, and through Baptism and Eucharist was united for all time with the Risen Master. If set apart from the world, he was also its light, its salt and its soul.[113] Possessed of and guided by the Holy Spirit, his obligation was to bear witness to the message of the Gospel, of Christ's overthrow of sin and its consequence, Death, and to the new age which this portended. If this involved him in the hatred of the world, that was to be expected and was a cause of rejoicing. He would be avenged, but not by the warrior's sword. The Jew might accept death rather than deny the Law. The Christian gave thanks that he had been offered the chance of martyrdom.

NOTES

[1] C. Ryder Smith, *The Bible Doctrine of the Hereafter*, London, 1958, 219.

[2] Jn. 10[33], Acts 14[22] and 1 Thess. 3[4].

[3] Note for instance, Cyprian, Ep., 38.2 (*CSEL.*, iii.ii, 581) on the influence of reading Scripture as inspiring Christians to martyrdom, 'evangelium Christi legere unde martyres fiunt'.

[4a] cf. *Didache*, 16.1.

[4] Hermas, *Vis.*, ii.2.7–8; 'μακάριοι ὑμεῖς ὅσοι ὑπομένετε τὴν θλῖψιν τὴν ἐρχομένην τὴν μεγάλην . . .'. Cf. Eusebius *H.E.*, v.1.48, apostates 'blaspheming the way'.

[5] See J. Downing, 'Jesus and Martyrdom', *JTS*. N.S. xiv.2, 284.

[6] The view of T. W. Manson, 'Martyrs and Martyrdom', *Bull. of John Ryland's Library*, 39, 1957, 463–84, at 464–5.

[7] For a summary of nationalism in Galilee in the first century A.D., L. E. Elliot Binns, *Galilean Christianity*, London (Studies in Biblical Theology 16), 1956, 19–20.

[8] Josephus, *Antiquities*, xvii.10.5, xviii.8.3 and xx.6.1; cf. xx.2.4 (Eleazar of Galilee). In the Maccabean period Galilee had been largely pagan; probably thanks to synagogues established by the Pharisees it had become progressively more Jewish and developed a fanatical cast of religion. The founder of the sect which started rebellion against Rome was, according to Josephus, a Galilean, *Wars*, ii.8.1, 117. For the Roman view of Galilee, Tacitus, *Annales*, xii.5.4 and Lk. 13[1].

[9] Jesus' 'standing denial of current hopes and beliefs' is emphasized also by T. W. Manson in his challenging *The Servant-Messiah: A Study of the Public Ministry of Jesus*, Cambridge, 1953, 50ff.

[10] Justin, *Dialogue with Trypho*, 89 and 90.

[11] See Wm. H. Brownlee, 'Messianic Motifs of Qumran and the New Testament', *NTS.*, iii, 1956–57, 23–30.

[12] E. Lohse, *Märtyrer und Gottesknecht*, 105. V. Taylor, *Jesus and His Sacrifice*, London, 1937, 113. Also Strack-Billerbeck, op. cit., ii, 282–3.

[13] Origen, *Contra Celsum* (ed. and tr. H. Chadwick) 1.54–5. Written *circa* 248. In *Ep. ad Africanum*, 9.2 he claims that the Jews suppressed passages in Scripture which reflected discredit on their rulers.

[14] Cited from T. W. Manson, *Jesus the Messiah* (Cunningham Lectures), London, 1945, 168–9.

[15] As M. D. Hooker, *Jesus the Servant*, London, 1959, 96.

[16] Note the application of the term 'ὁ παῖς μου' reserved for Jacob in Is. 44[1] (LXX) to Jesus in Didache 9[3], i Clement 59[2], and the earliest account of Polycarp's martyrdom, Eusebius, *H.E.*, iv.15.33.

[17] Cf. Jn. 4[44].

[18] C. K. Barrett, 'The Background of Mark 10[45]', *New Testament Essays. Studies in Memory of T. W. Manson* (ed. A. J. B. Higgins), Manchester, 1959, 12–15, especially p. 14.

[19] iv Macc. 6[27] and 18[4]. See R. H. Lightfoot, *The Gospel Message of St. Mark*, Oxford, 1950, 65, and J. Downing, loc. cit.

[20] Tertullian, *De Baptismo*, 16 (*CSEL*., xx, 214) 'nos faceret aqua vocatos, sanguine electos'; cf. Origen, *Exhort. ad Mart.*, 28.

[21] Cf. Eusebius, *H.E.*, iv.15.33. 'τοῦ λαβεῖν μέρος ἐν ἀριθμῷ τῶν μαρτύρων ἐν τῷ ποτηρίῳ τοῦ χριστοῦ σου εἰς ἀνάστασιν ζωῆς αἰωνίου.

[22] See also Irenaeus' view, *circa* 185, *Adv. Haer.* iv.33.9. 'Thus the Church [passes through an experience] similar to that of the ancient prophets.'

[23] A. Nygren, *Christ and His Church* (Eng. tr., A. Carlsten, London, 1957), ch. iii. 'The heavenly voice speaks the words of Isaiah 42[1], confirming that the Transfigured Christ was none other than the Suffering Servant of the Lord, who will soon move on to the Cross and Resurrection.' For the association of the Transfiguration and the Parousia in the primitive Church, see G. H. Boobyer, *St. Mark and the Transfiguration Story*, Edinburgh, 1942, 30–40.

[24] T. W. Manson, *Martyrs and Martyrdom*, 474.

[25] Cf. Lk. 13[33]. Downing, art. cit., 285.

[26] There is an interesting *Logion* quoted by Origen, 'He that is near me is near the fire, he that is far from me is far from the Kingdom'. Fire in this context is eschatological fire, the furnace of suffering. It was the only way to the Kingdom of God. Origen, *In Jerem. Homil. lat.* xx.3.1. See J. Jeremias, *The Unknown Sayings of Jesus*, 54.

[27] 1 Thess. 4[16-17]; cf. iv Esdras 7[28] for contemporaneous Jewish hopes; discussed by Jeremias, op. cit., 66–7.

[28] R. H. Lightfoot, *History and Interpretation in the Gospels*, 1934, 176. See also, D. W. Riddle, *The Martyrs*, ch. viii, and Downing, art. cit., 289.

[29] Origen, *Comment in Johann*, vi.54 (ed. Preuschen, iv.162, ll. 14ff.) 'λοιπαὶ δὲ καὶ συγγενεῖς ταύτῃ τῇ θυσίᾳ θυσίαι αἱ ἐκχύσεις εἶναι μοι φαίνονται τοῦ τῶν γενναίων μαρτύρων αἵματος.' Cyprian, *Ep.*, 38.2 (*CSEL*., iii.ii., 580).

[30] H. W. Surkau, *Martyrien in jüdischer und frühchristlicher Zeit*, 82ff.

[31] See M. Black, 'The Arrest and Trial of Jesus', *Manson Essays*, 19–33.

[32] See R. H. Lightfoot, *The Gospel Message of St. Mark*, 55.

[33] See E. Stauffer, *Jesus and His Story* (Eng. tr., London, 1960), pp. 102–3. H. Lietzmann, 'Der Prozess Jesu', *SBAW.*, 1930, 310ff., and T. A. Burkill, 'The Trial of Jesus', *Vigiliae Christianae*, xii, 1958, 1ff. Finally, the series of studies on the Trial of Jesus by Paul Winter (P. Winter, *On the Trial of Jesus, Studia Judaica, Forschungen zur Wissenschaft des Judentums*, Berlin, 1961).

[34] A. N. Sherwin White, *Roman Society and Roman Law in the New Testament*, 24–5.

[35] For instance, in the long sequence of woes suffered by apostles outlined in i Cor. 4[6-13].

[36] Note James of Jerusalem's similar action at his martyrdom in 62, Eusebius, *H.E.*, ii.23.

[37] Ezek. 1[ff].; cf. E. M. Sidebottom, *The Christ of the Fourth Gospel in the Light of First-century Thought*, London, 1961, 76.

[38] Similarly, *Acta Carpi* 39, 'εἶδον τὴν δόξαν τοῦ κυρίου', K. Holl, 'Die Vorstellung vom Märtyrer', *Gesammelte Aufsätze zur Kirchengeschichte* II, Der Osten, 71.

[39] 'Στέφανος ὁ τέλειος μάρτυς' (Lyons), Eusebius, *H.E.*, v.2.5; cf. H. W. Surkau, *Martyrien*, 117ff.

[40] H. W. Surkau, op. cit., 114, H. von Campenhausen, op. cit., 146, and K. Holl, loc. cit.

[41] Enoch, 38[4]; cf. *Book of the Secrets of Enoch* (ed., Morfill and Charles), 66.7, 'and they shall be seven times brighter than the sun'.

[42] K. Holl, op. cit., 71.

43 For the use of this term in both Christian and pagan contexts in the first century A.D., see A. Deissmann, 'Ἱλαστήριος und ἱλαστήριον', ZNTW., iv, 1903, 193ff. See also A. D. Nock, St. Paul, 1938, 47, R. H. Pfeiffer, History of New Testament Times, 220–1 and C. H. Dodd, The Bible and the Greeks, 82–95.

44 E. Lohse, Märtyrer und Gottesknecht, 193ff., and C. H. Dodd, 'The Fall of Jerusalem and the Abomination of Desolation', JRS., xxxvii, 1947, 47ff.

45 E. Lohse, Märtyrer und Gottesknecht, 199. 'Das Leiden, selbst das Sterben, das die Juenger Jesu auf sich zu nehmen haben, hat keine selbstaendige in sich ruhende Bedeutung, sondern es ist eine unausbleibliche Folge, die sich aus dem eschatologischen Geschehen, das mit dem Kommen des Christus angebrochen ist, ergibt.'

46 Also Origen's view, Exhort. ad Mart. 37, and Comment. in Johann. vi.54.

47 See, E. Best, One Body in Christ, London, 1955, 130–6.

48 i Cor. 4^9-13.

49 It is not possible to agree with Geffcken, art. cit., Hermes, 1910, 496, that 'the word μάρτυς has a purely philosophical origin', any more than one can support von Campenhausen's claim for an exclusively Christian origin (op. cit., 1).

50 H. Delehaye, Sanctus, Essai sur le culte des saints dans l'antiquité (Subsidia Hagiographica 17), Brussels, 1927, 95ff., especially p. 103, and art. 'Martyr et Confesseur', A.B., xxxix, 1921, 20–49.

51 H. von Campenhausen, Die Idee des Martyriums in der alten Kirche, Leipzig, 1936, ch. 1.

52 H. Strathmann, art., 'μάρτυς, μαρτυρία', in Kittel's Wörterbuch, Vol. iv, 477–519, at 491. Cf. N. Brox, Zeuge und Märtyrer, Munich, 1961, 114–25.

53 H. A. Fischel, 'Prophet and Martyr', JQR., 37 (1946–47), 265–80, 363–86.

54 H. W. Surkau, Martyrien, 139.

55 O. Perler, 'Das vierte Makkabäerbuch', 64ff.

56 For useful summaries of the discussion since Delehaye, see H. Lietzmann, art. Martys, in PW. Suppl. xiv, 1930, col. 2044ff. and B. de Gaiffier, 'Reflexions sur l'Origine du Culte des Martyrs', Maison Dieu, 52, Brussels, 1959, 19ff.

57 M. Hadas, op. cit. 208, 'τῆς τῶν ἀδελφῶν μου μαρτυρίας' (instead of ἀριστείας) Strathmann, op. cit., 485 n. 24, considers this passage 'eine aus späterem kirchl. Empfinden zu verstehende Variante sein'.

58 'καὶ δώσω τοῖς δυσὶ μάρτυσί μου καὶ προφητεύσουσιν . . . '. See R. H. Charles, I.C.C., Revelation, i, 270–1 for discussion suggesting a Jewish pre-70 origin for this passage. Witness, prophecy and suffering are all implied if the two prophets are Moses and Elijah (Charles, loc. cit., 280–2), especially as it is stated that 'when they completed their witness' they would die at the hands of demonic power (117). Also, H. Lietzmann, art. 'Martys', PW. Suppl., xiv, col. 2044ff.

59 J. Katz, Exclusiveness and Tolerance, 82, n. 1.

60 Nehemiah 9^26 LXX.

61 H. Strathmann, op. cit., 498. 'Stephanus heisst nicht μάρτυς weil er stirbt, sondern er stirbt weil er Zeuge Christi ist.'

62 See H. Delehaye, Sanctus, 77, arguing against K. Holl, op. cit., 70; and H. Lietzmann, op. cit., 2045.

63 Cf. Test. Isaiah, 9.12–13. 'The righteous do not receive their crowns until the return of Christ.'

64 For discussion of i Pet. 5^1 see F. L. Cross, 1 Peter: A Paschal Liturgy, 47, and also G. Boobyer, 'The Indebtedness of 2 Peter to 1 Peter', Manson Essays, 43.

65 Mart. Lyons, H.E., v.1.42, and for the Montanist usage of the term, see over, p. 292. In the Great Persecution, Bishop Peter of Alexandria calls himself 'κοινωνός of Christ's sufferings'. C. Schmidt, 'Fragmente einer Schrift des Märtyrerbischofs Petrus von Alexandrien'. T.U., N.F. V, 4b, 1901, p. 7. For the κοινωνία of the Spirit as the bond of

union in the Church, E. E. Aubrey, 'The Holy Spirit in Relation to the Religious Community', *JTS.*, xl, 1940, 1ff.

⁶⁶ H. Strathmann, op. cit., 502 ff.

⁶⁷ H. Lietzmann, art. cit., 2044 and H. Stathmann, op. cit., 505.

⁶⁸ See H. B. Swete's valuable analysis in *The Holy Spirit in the New Testament*, London, 1931, 156ff., and C. K. Barrett, *St. John*, 403-9.

⁶⁹ B. Piault, *What is the Trinity?*, London, 1959, 59.

⁷⁰ This date of Hebrews ('not later than about 85') is accepted from J. Moffatt, *I.C.C.*, *Hebrews*, xxii. For its possible [direct] connections with James and 1 Clement, B.W.Bacon in *JBL.*, 19, 1900, 12-22. For an earlier date, *circa* 70 and suggested authorship of Apollos. see C. Spicq, *L'Epitre aux Hébreux*, Etudes Bibliques, Paris, 1952-53, Vol. i, pp. 210-19.

⁷¹ I have used R. H. Charles *I.C.C. Revelation*, and accept the Domitianic date (cf. Charles, loc. cit., xci ff.).

⁷² An important text—because the words 'καὶ διὰ τὸν λόγον τῆς μαρτυρίαϛε αὐτῶν, καὶ οὐκ ἠγάπησαν τὴν ψυχὴν αὐτῶν ἄχρι θανάτου' indicate victory gained through their own blood-witness. We are surely more than 'on the threshold' of the early Church's meaning of 'martyrdom'—Strathmann, loc. cit., 508.

⁷³ As opposed to H. Delehaye's view, *Sanctus*, 79, 'Le Nouveau Testament ne nous fournit donc aucun exemple certain du mot μάρτυϛ ou de ses dérivés employés dans les sens restraint et précis de martyr qu'il a fini par prendre dans le langage chrétien'.

⁷⁴ See A. A. T. Ehrhardt, *Politische Metaphysik von Solon bis Augustin*, Tübingen, 1959, ii, 15ff.

⁷⁵ Ibid., 13.

⁷⁶ W. L. Knox, 'Church and State in the New Testament', *JRS.*, xxxix, 1949, 23.

⁷⁷ Cf. ibid., 29.

⁷⁸ O. Cullmann, *The State in the New Testament*, London, 1957, ch. i, an illuminating, but one-sided view of Jesus' political outlook. Should be contrasted with C. J. Cadoux' more balanced *The Early Church and the World*, Edinburgh, 1925, p. 34ff.

⁷⁹ Mk. 6³⁴. See H. W. Montefiore, 'Revolt in the Desert' (Mk. 6³⁶ff.)', *NTS.*, 8, 1961-62, 135-41.

⁸⁰ See, E. A. Judge, *The Social Patterns of the Christian Groups in the First Century*, London, 1959, 15.

⁸¹ A. Deissmann, *Light from the Ancient East* (Eng. tr., London, 1927), 248.

⁸² E. A. Judge, op. cit., 62. Judas the Zealot had proclaimed himself king, Josephus, *Antiquities*, xvii, 10.5.

⁸³ See, C. H. Turner, commentary on Mk. 11⁷ in *A New Commentary on Holy Scripture*, ii, The New Testament (ed. C. Gore, 1943 ed.), 93. W. R. Farmer, 'The Palm Branches in John 12¹³', *JTS.*, N.S. iii.i, 1952, 62-6.

⁸⁴ E. Meyer, *Ursprung und Anfänge*, ii, 451.

⁸⁵ See J. A. T. Robinson's study, 'The Temptations', *Theology*, l (1947), 43-8 (= pp. 53-60 in *Twelve New Testament Studies*).

⁸⁶ On the significance of the crown of thorns as a caricature of the radiate crown symbolizing the divine ruler on coins of the period, H. St. J. Hart, *JTS.*, N.S. iii, 1952, 66ff.

⁸⁷ O. Cullmann, op. cit., 43. T. A. Burkill, *The Trial of Jesus*, 15ff. and S. G. F. Brandon, 'Further Quest for the Historical Jesus', *Modern Churchman*, N.S. v, 1961, 212ff.

⁸⁸ Josephus, *Wars*, ii.8.1. (Judas the Gaulonite's revolt). See M. Dibelius, 'Rom und die Christen im ersten Jahrhundert', *Sitzber. der Heidelberger Akad. der Wissenschaften*, Phil. Hist. Kl., 1941/42, 1ff. (= *SHAW*.). Interestingly, one of the acts of the rebels in 66 was to substitute a new shekel with the legend 'Jerusalem the Holy' for the *denarius*. Above, ch. II, note 120.

⁸⁹ Even though Jesus' answer could be used to suggest that He had not advised payment Lk. 23²). See, H. Loewe, *Render unto Caesar*, 38ff.

[90] See S. E. Johnson, *The Gospel according to St. Mark*, London, 1960, 199.

[91] In practice, the 'rich' so far as concerns Galilee were probably Sadducaean landlords.

[92] C. J. Cadoux, *The Early Church and the World*, 47ff. Contrast with A. A. T. Ehrhardt, op. cit., 20.

[93] *Pirke Aboth* (ed. Charles), iii.2. Rabbi Hananiah, Prefect of the Priests says, 'Do thou pray for the welfare of the Empire, because were it not for the fear it inspires, every man would swallow his neighbour alive'. For the dating of this statement to the period before the outbreak of the war of 66, C. Roth, 'The Debate on the Loyal Sacrifices', *HTR.*, 53, 1960, 96. The parallel is an apt one, because Hananiah like Paul himself was influenced at times by Zealotry (ibid., 96).

[94] See also, C. D. Morrison, *The Powers that Be. Earthly Rulers and Demonic Powers in Romans xiii.1–7* (S.C.M. Press, Studies in Biblical Theology, No. 29), London, 1960, ch. iii.

[95] Irenaeus, *Adv. Haer.*, v.24.1—a very important passage.

[96] A. A. T. Ehrhardt, op. cit., 23; cf. H. Loewe, op. cit., 32, M. Dibelius, op. cit., 7.

[97] Philo (ed. Colson), *In Flaccum*, 12.49.

[98] Babylonian Talmud (ed. Epstein, 1935), *Bab. B.* 91b.

[99] Often the persecutors of the Christians were local Jews. See over, p. 155, and E. Bammel, 'Ein Beitrag zur paulinischen Staatsanschaung', *Theol. Literaturzeitung*, xi, 1960, 838–40.

[100] O. Cullmann, *Christus und die Zeit*, Zürich, 1946, 173.

[101] i Cor. 7$^{29-31}$ and A. N. Wilder's comment on this statement of Pauline ethics in 'Kerygma, Eschatology and Social Ethics', *Studies in Honour of C. H. Dodd*, 524.

[102] Phil. 1^1; i Cor. 16^1 and 15.

[103] Acts 28^{14}.

[104] 1 Thess. 5^2; cf. i Cor. 7$^{29-31}$.

[105] See, E. A. Judge's excellent study of the social constituency of the Christian groups at this time, op. cit., 57ff.

[106] Contrasting A. A. T. Ehrhardt's view, op. cit., 18, see Th. Preiss, *Vie en Christ*, Neuchâtel, 1951, ch. iii.

[107] Augustine, *Contra Gaudentium*, 1.35.45.

[108] Augustine, *Contra Litteras Petiliani*, ii.87.192, and 88.194.

[109] W. Bousset, *Antichrist*, 129ff. for references.

[110] See K. Scott, *The Imperial Cult under the Flavians*, Stuttgart, 1936, 130–3; and O. Schütz, *Die Offenbarung des Johannes*, 1933, 48–50, for discussion of these texts.

[111] See *Apoc. Baruch.* (ed. Charles, *Apocrypha* ii, 470ff.) 40.1 for Jewish hope of the material overthrow of 'the last leader of that time', i.e. Rome.

[112] Phil. 3^{20}; cf. Heb. 13^{14}, 'οὐ γὰρ ἔχομεν ὧδε μένουσαν πόλιν, ἀλλὰ τὴν μέλλουσαν ἐπιζητοῦμεν'.

[113] *Letter to Diognetus*, 6.

CHAPTER FOUR

Rome and Foreign Cults[1]

THE logic of Christian eschatology, inherited and developed from Judaism, was bound ultimately to bring the primitive Church into conflict with the Roman authorities. Though the Christians might claim repeatedly that their kingdom was 'not of this world', the influence of the Danielic view of world-history was too strong to be ignored.[2] Too many Christians of the first generations after the Crucifixion saw Rome as the embodiment of 'idolatry', and the power of the Empire as the power of Anti-Christ. Its overthrow would presage a Millennium anticipated in earthly terms and the martyr's death would contribute to this end. The question is not so much why were the Christians persecuted, but how it was that they escaped the rigours meted out to the Jews in 115–117 and 132–135. The answer may be clearer when we have looked at the problem from the Roman point of view. What were the religious ideas on which Roman policy was based? How far did toleration of the religions of conquered or client peoples extend? How much religious loyalty was expected of provincials, especially in the Greek-speaking provinces where Jewish (and Christian) influence was strongest? In this chapter we move over the familiar ground of Rome's policy towards foreign cults until the moment when Augustus steps into the shoes of the fallen Ptolemaic and Seleucid dynasties, and the 'imperator felix' becomes θεός.

Developments leading up to the establishment of the Imperial cult may be briefly told. The Roman Republic was famed for 'religio'. Both foreign observers and citizens testify to the pride felt by the Roman governing classes for their devotion towards their ancestral religion. To Polybius, writing in Rome in *circa* 150 B.C., religious devotion was the one outstanding mark of superiority which Rome possessed over the Greeks of his day. 'But the quality in which the Roman commonwealth is most distinctly superior', he writes, 'is, in my opinion, the nature of their religious convictions. I believe that it is the very thing which among other peoples is an object of reproach, I mean superstition (δεισιδαιμονία), which maintains the cohesion of the Roman State.'[3] The contrast between the disintegration of Hellenistic religion and the strength of the Roman attachment to traditional beliefs was striking enough for comment. So too in Polybius' view, was the contrast between Roman probity and Greek corruption.[4] Polybius was echoed a century later in a statement which Cicero put into the mouth of the Stoic, Balbus. 'Moreover, if we care to compare our national characteristics with those of foreign peoples, we shall find that, while in all other respects we are only the equal or inferiors of others, yet in the sense of religion, that is, reverence for the gods we are far superior' (*De Natura Deorum*, ii.3.8). Sallust (*Jugurtha*, 14.19) and later, Horace (*Odes* iii.6.5) were to repeat the same sentiments. To Vergil (*Aeneid* vi.791-807), Augustus ruled *because* he honoured the gods.

The emphasis lay on Cicero's final phrase, 'religione id est cultu deorum multo superiores'. There could be scepticism about particular gods and particular rites, but *religio*, representing the truths behind them, was inviolable. The gods in their totality were the guardians of Rome. Failure to give them their proper due, embodied in rites handed down from time immemorial, could bring disaster to Rome and her achievement. Thus Livy records how in 397 B.C., during the war against Veii, the Delphic oracle informed the embassy from Rome that a condition of success was the restoration of traditional cults in the old style.[5] During the same war, Livy put into the mouth of Camillus the warning to the Roman people 'that all went well so long as we obeyed the gods, and ill when we spurned them'.[6] When disaster did befall, as in the time of the great pestilence of 463 B.C., the remedy was a general sacrifice to the Roman gods by the whole people.[7] There were long-standing precedents for the action of the Emperor Decius in 250.

Religio was regarded in the nature of a contract. The word *pax* in *pax deorum* implied a treaty relationship. Right worship and due respect ensured that the gods did their work of protecting the Roman people. If the sacred chickens were thrown into the sea, it was not surprising that the battle was lost. There was little scope or need for intellectual justification for the existence of the gods.

It is interesting that Cicero's Balbus, despite his Stoicism, applauds the views of Cotta, a religious sceptic who was none the less Pontifex Maximus, in rejecting the arguments of Epicurean and Stoic philosophers for the existence of gods, as being subject to logical suspicion and therefore unacceptable as a basis of religious conduct.[8] Instead, the only basis Cotta can accept was that of tradition, the *mos maiorum*—and that was to be accepted without question.[9] Indeed, whether one looks at a surviving passage of Ennius,[10] or to the arguments of Symmachus in the Altar of Victory controversy six centuries later, the *mos maiorum* forms the continuous background to the Roman attitude towards religion. It included a whole nexus of ideas and practices, through which government, human relations, morality and justice were maintained. 'If we reject devotion towards the gods, good faith and all associations of human life and the best of virtues, justice, may also disappear.'[11] Religion and the preservation of the Roman state were intimately connected. If the Pontifex Maximus after 103 B.C. became a temporary and political appointment, the holder of the office while in power '*iudex et arbiter habetur rerum divinarum humanarumque*'.[12] Constantine did not ask for more.

Roman religion was therefore less a matter of personal devotion than of national cult.[13] Rome judged the religion of others from the same standpoint. 'Every people, Laelius, has its religion, and we have ours.'[14] A *religio* was *licita* for a particular group on the basis of tribe or nationality and traditional practices, coupled with the proviso that its rites were not offensive to the Roman people or their gods. But, for Roman citizens, loyalty to the national religion precluded participation in the rites of others, unless these had been specifically sanctioned by the Senate. Thus, Cicero's well-known passage, '*Separatim nemo habessit deos neve novos neve advenas nisi publice adscitos*'. Privately, people should worship those gods whose worship they had received from their ancestors.[15] The practice by a Roman citizen of an *externa religio* which had not been accepted could be an insult to the gods and an affront to the greatness of the Roman people. Just as a man would not be a citizen of two states so he could not accept two religions.[16] Not for nothing were *maiestas* and *sacrilegium* linked in the minds of Roman lawyers,[17] and the participation of individuals in a *religio externa* condemned. Christianity was certainly among the latter.

Opinions might differ whether it was a harmful *superstitio* or not. In itself, it called for no more special treatment at the outset than any other foreign cult in the city of Rome.

The problem before the senators and Roman provincial officials was how far harmonization between the Roman deities and those of conquered or allied peoples could be carried. At what point did *religio externa* become *religio prava*? Indeed, this way of looking at religious problems continued from Republic to Empire and persisted in official documents even after nearly a century of official Christianity.[18] In practice, the distinction was often finely drawn. Thus, in the Celtic provinces it was quite possible to find Roman equivalents even for Teutates and Tanaris, while the Druids and their rites were extirpated.[19] In Africa we find that Baal-Hammon was acceptable under the name of Saturn and housed in classical-looking temples, while the human sacrifice connected with his worship in Punic sanctuaries was suppressed. Harmonization, however, was generally taken a long way. In Rome itself many of the Greek deities had been assimilated, probably as part of the Etruscan legacy during the fifth century B.C., and so too had some of the gods and goddesses of the Italic tribes, including Mars and Diana. By about 300 B.C. Aesculapius had been introduced from Epidaurus and his cult of healing esconced on an island in the Tiber. At first, these 'di novensides', or 'newly settled' deities may perhaps have been distinguished from the older 'di indigetes', i.e. Roman indigenous deities, but before long the distinction lost any practical effect.[20] In the crisis of the second Punic War, however, these gods were seen to be unable of their own power to stem Hannibal's onslaught. People began to abandon them in earnest. In Livy's words 'And now not only in secret, and within the walls of private houses were Roman rites abandoned, but in public places also, and in the Forum and on the Capitoline, there was a crowd of women who were following the custom of the fathers neither in their sacrifices nor in prayers to the gods'.[21] This was in 213 B.C., and not surprisingly in the subsequent crisis caused by Hasdrubal's arrival in Italy in 205–204 B.C., the Senate took the drastic step of introducing the cult and black stone fetish of the Phrygian Great Mother Cybele into the city. It was the first time that a native cult from outside of Greece or Italy had been introduced. The battle of the Metaurus was won.

Hasdrubal was slain and Hannibal defeated. By 191 B.C. Cybele had her sanctuary on the Palatine.

There was, however, an important qualification. The annual ceremonies in her honour were drastically curtailed.[22] Down to the reign of Claudius, Roman citizens were forbidden to take part in the disorderly processions and dances by Phrygian priests and their initiates.[23] Instead, there were the more sedate *Megalesia* and *Ludi Megaleses*.[24] Though it was essential from the point of view of the efficacy of the rites that the ceremonies should be conducted as prescribed, and by Phrygian priests,[25] the Roman population must not be allowed to get out of hand. Religion must continue to be controlled by and serve the ruling aristocracy through the Senate.

This aim was from now onward, however, to be continuously challenged by events. The victorious wars and resulting political expansion of the Republic during the second century B.C. brought about an enormous increase in the population of the city of Rome. On the one hand, the city attracted impoverished country-folk from the land and ex-soldiers, and on the other, an increasing tide of immigrants from all over the Mediterranean. Many of these foreigners brought their gods with them. The process is quite clearly described by Livy writing in Augustus' reign. 'So much worship, and a great part of that foreign, penetrated the city, that both gods and men kept suddenly springing into existence . . . '.[26] The number of the *plebs* was increased by the agricultural population who had been driven into the city from fear and poverty, their fields being left untilled owing to the continuous wars. An inscription from Puteoli, though dated rather later, A.D. 79, gives an illustration of a god accompanying a group of Asiatic immigrants. 'The god Helios Sarapetos (i.e. Baal of Sarapt, located between Tyre and Sidon) came on ship from Tyre to Puteoli. Elim brought him according to command' (i.e. through a dream).[27] Two hundred years earlier, Isis was already established in Rome and she was only one of the host of oriental deities which flooded into the city in the second and first centuries B.C.

The problem of the foreign cults is, however, hardly intelligible without our bearing in mind the social implications of the great immigration. One result of this was that the lower classes in Rome became largely Greek-speaking. The immigrants tended to settle down in great blocs, Asiatics on the Aventine, Jews and Phrygians across the Tiber in Trastevere and Africans on the Caelian. Here they formed their societies for worship and self-help, and these *collegia* attracted the adhesion of native Romans.[28] Rome became a vast melting-pot, whose denizens thought 'panem et circenses' not as a phrase but as a grim necessity of life. Neither the immigrants, nor their societies nor their gods were welcome to the ruling houses. In 65 B.C. there was a serious effort to purge the city of immigrants, but in vain. The use to which Clodius put the artisans' *collegia* a few years later was not forgotten, and among Caesar's measures of reconstruction in the city of Rome between 48–44 B.C. was their vigorous control.[29] Only *bona fide* associations of traders and licensed religious groups, such, significantly, as Jewish synagogues were permitted.[30] It is interesting that *collegia* with specifically religious aims were claiming attention, for the Senate always feared that religious disorder could easily be transformed into social revolution. The Sicilian peasants revolt of 134 B.C. had been led by the servant of a Syrian goddess under the influence of religious frenzy, and his followers had bound themselves with solemn oaths and sacrifices.[31] As late as the reign of Commodus the Bucolic revolt in the Nile Delta was led by a priest and cannibalism in the name of religion was practised by the insurgents.[32] Illegal *collegia* and clandestine rites were deeply rooted associations in the minds of the authorities.

The proof of the persistence of these fears in the early years of Augustus' reign is shown by Livy's long and detailed account of the Bacchanal conspiracy of 186 B.C. (xxxix.8–19).[33] The affair took place nearly 150 years before, but the ideas he expresses are those of his own day. The Bacchanalia were of Greek origin. They began, we are told, with a small association of women. The rites caught on, and under the leadership of a Campanian priestess degenerated into large-scale nocturnal orgies and even into secret murders and poisonings. Nobles were implicated, and eventually the scandal came out into the open. The Consul, Spurius Postumius Albinus, was asked by the Senate to investigate the affair *extra ordinem*.[34] His speech shows the fear for the safety of the State mingled with horror at the acts themselves which gripped the senators. The Bacchanalia were regarded primarily as a vast 'conspiracy' (*coniuratio*), whose aims included the firing of the city and seizing control of the state, and whose leaders were drawn from the Roman *plebs*. The immediate safety of the senators and their families was considered to be in danger. An enormous number of people were involved, described by Livy in words which are reminiscent of a similar panic in A.D. 64.[35] 'Multitudinem ingentem, alterum iam prope populum esse.' Rome was gripped by panic. Postumius' opening words to the Senate showed how greatly the uncontrolled practice of foreign cults was feared, and the reasons.

> 'Never for any assembly', he began, 'has this formal prayer to the gods been not only so suitable, but even so necessary, a prayer which reminds us that these are the gods whom our forefathers had appointed to be worshipped, to be venerated, to receive our prayers, not those gods who drive our enthralled minds with vile and alien rites . . . to every crime and every lust.'[36] 'Nothing', he went on, 'is more deceptive in appearance than a false religion (*prava religio*). When the authority of the gods is put forward as a defence for crime, there steals upon the mind the fear that lest in punishing human misdeeds we may violate something of divine law that became mixed up with them'[37] (tr. E. T. Sage).

Nothing endangered religion more than 'where sacrifices were performed not by native, but by foreign ritual'.[38] Nocturnal rites, orgies and secret murders, these were the signs of 'prava religio'. Such actions, the 'flagitia' accompanying the rites, endangered the community through the likelihood of black magic, they polluted the Roman gods and rendered the culprits liable to condign punishment.[39] A similar view was to be taken of the Christians by the Roman authorities of the generation of Tacitus and Pliny—theirs was also 'prava religio', accompanied by 'flagitia'.

Hence the reaction of the Senate is of considerable interest. Measures of defence and repression against the Bacchanals were taken through Senatorial decrees (*senatus consulta*). These were dispatched throughout the Italian provinces, and that addressed to the Taurani, a federated state of Bruttium, in the form of a bronze tablet, has survived to substantiate the general tenor of Livy's account.[40] If one may take the repression of the Christian community in Rome by Nero in 64 as a parallel, then the dispatch of a senatorial decree proscribing Christianity in Rome to some of the provinces cannot be ruled out of account entirely, though the political and social circumstances behind the two crises were wholly different.[41]

The actual measures taken against the Bacchanals are also worth notice. Though more than 7000 individuals were eventually involved,[42] and (probably like the Christians in 64) 'more were killed than were thrown into prison',[43] the cult was not abolished altogether. Ancient Bacchic altars were spared. 'If any person considered such worship to be ordained by tradition (*sollemne*) or to be necessary', he could apply for permission to hold a ceremony to the city praetor, who would consult the senate on the matter.[44] But only five persons might be present at a sacrifice, and there must be no common chest or priest. The question seems to have been handled pragmatically by a mixture of decree and police regulation. Here was an admittedly ancient cult, and therefore offence to gods by its neglect might be incurred if it was abolished altogether; at the same time, its rites were offensive and destructive to social order. Therefore, their practice must be rendered harmless and confined to the narrowest limits. In 64, however, the Christians had no such claim to antiquity. Tacitus explained to his readers,[45] that they originated in Palestine in the reign of Tiberius, their leader had been executed by Pontius Pilate—and they were also noxious.

The Bacchanals survived the blow. They might remain the by-word for a dangerous and disorderly cult in both the Roman and Greek worlds for another two centuries,[46] and their repression by the Senate was praised by Cicero, but they did not die out. By A.D. 79 the rites had become 'respectable' enough to be the subject of wall-paintings at Pompeii, and in the second century A.D. the cult provided a popular theme on mosaics[47] of the houses of the wealthy. They had received treatment which if most severe, was not regarded as exceptional.[48] For over two hundred years, between 150 B.C. and A.D. 69 the cult of Isis was the subject of a bewildering series of conflicting decisions.[49] In Sulla's time there was a *collegium* of Isiac *pastophori*, but as the Bacchanals before them, the cult became suspected of providing a cloak for immoralities, and came under the adverse notice of the Senate. In 58 B.C. it was excluded from the Capitol by the consuls of the year,[50] and other severer measures followed in 53, 50 and 48. But in 42 B.C. amidst the anarchy of the civil wars a temple of Isis was built by the triumvirs; and from now on, the cult though not formally recognized, was tolerated in Rome. Augustus, however, once more ordered its removal from the *pomerium*; its adherents were expelled from Rome by senatorial decree in A.D. 19 on moral grounds, in the same order as that expelling the Jews,[51] but it never lost its popularity especially among women.[52] By Nero's reign there must have been a shrine to the goddess on the Capitol. By the early third century it had become completely naturalized. The story of Isis in Rome is thus the story of the gradual penetration and acceptance of a foreign cult despite opposition and despite periodic repression including the execution of its priests as criminals.

Other groups suffered similarly. The Chaldaean soothsayers and horoscopists (*mathematici*) were the object of malevolent suspicion throughout the period of the Empire, whether in the reign of Tiberius or Valentinian I. They were expelled by senatorial decree in Tiberius' reign, and on five other occasions in the first century A.D. their expulsion was ordered. They too survived. Yet by the mid-second century Chaldaean oracles were highly regarded, and the Chaldaeans themselves were being quoted by Celsus as 'a race endowed with the highest inspiration from the beginning', and an example of the veracity of pagan prophecy.[53] The Druids in both Britain and Gaul were crushed with similar severity. In their case the objections were that their rites were abhorrent and that they encouraged anti-Roman sentiment. Thus, Pliny the Elder—'it cannot be estimated what a debt is owed to the Romans who have done away with these monstrous rites (in Gaul and Britain), in which it was counted the height of religion to kill a man and a most healthful thing to eat him'.[54] Strabo adds that 'they (the Druids) committed acts that are contrary to what is permitted among us and that in consequence the Romans stopped their sacrifices and divinations.[55] Christians were not the only sectaries who incurred the suspicion of cannibalism, and therefore brought down on themselves the wrath of the authorities.

The same policy may be traced with regard to the penetration of Hellenistic philosophies in the capital. The religious practices of Rome were never to develop far beyond what had been suitable for an agricultural people. As a guide to personal life they ceased to hold either the educated classes or the population as a whole.

If it had not been for the over-riding force of ancestral tradition the Roman gods might have passed into oblivion through neglect as Varro thought in the years before the Principate.[56] Their place, as is well known, had been taken by Stoicism and Epicureanism.[57]

Again, the test of acceptability appears to have been not the teaching itself but its effect on morality. To be sure, 'arguments against the gods' were regarded as '*mala consuetudo*', in the sense of being bad manners and a mark of barbarism,[58] but when the Epicureans were expelled from Rome in 175 B.C. it was on the grounds that their teaching encouraged illicit pleasures.[59] Stoicism, it need hardly be stated, became something in the nature of the religion of the Roman upper classes. It dominates the outlook of many of their best minds from the time of Scipio Africanus Minor to that of Marcus Aurelius.[60] The brushes between the Stoics and Domitian were on political grounds—once more, the practical effect of their teaching on the attitude of leading citizens towards the government. Rome had no Socrates, and no *cause célèbre* against 'atheism'. Indeed, the abstract term 'atheus' never became properly acclimatized into Latin.[61]

To sum up, Roman religion like the religion of the peoples Rome conquered was one of acts based on ancestral usage. The complex of ideas defined in such phrases as 'disciplina publica', 'mores nostri', or 'leges veteres', formed a barrier against the foreign cults, and equally against Judaism and Christianity. Except in dire emergencies, acceptance by the Senate took a long time, and even then, the cult might not be recognized within the *pomerium* of the city of Rome. Until recognition was granted conversion to a foreign cult by a Roman citizen which involved neglect of the traditional Roman cult could be punishable, but was not often so. There seems little reason to doubt that the formal grounds for the execution of Acilius Glabrio and Flavius Clemens by Domitian in 95 was suspected conversion to some form of Judaism. That the prohibition could be extended to the wives of Roman nobles is demonstrated both by the punishment of women involved in the Bacchanalian affair, and in A.D. 57 by the case of Pomponia Graecina. In this case, the charge was adhesion to 'foreign religion', and the description of the suspicious symptoms suggests Judaism.[62] Christianity, therefore, when it appeared on the scene in Rome, perhaps a decade before the trial of Pomponia Graecina, cannot be regarded as having presented the authorities with a problem for which there were no precedents.

To the traditional policy of wariness towards foreign cults and associations must now be added factors resulting from the religious change brought about by Augustan principate. It would seem that what came to be the divinization of the Emperor was the result of the intermingling of Greek ideas of kingship with the existing Roman identification of high office-holders with the protecting gods of the city.[63] One may point, for instance, to the customary identification of a victorious general during his Triumph with Jupiter, to the sacred character and personal inviolability of the Tribune, to the super-human concepts connected with an official's *auctoritas*,[64] and the tendency of leaders from Sulla onwards to claim for themselves something more than ordinary human qualities. To these influences were added the profound awe felt in the Greek cities at the unexampled rise of Roman power. Two years after Flamininus' triumph in 197 B.C. the 'goddess Rome' was being worshipped in Smyrna; and other cities of Asia followed suit.[65] At the end of the Republican period many of the Greeks were prepared to attribute divine powers as restorers of peace and harmony to the world, hitherto reserved for the successors of Alexander, to successful and flamboyant Roman generals.[66] When in 48 Caesar built a Caesareum at Alexandria dedicated to the worship of his own divinity and followed this up in the next year with one at Antioch he was merely accepting a role which had long been known in these areas.[67]

Meantime, matters had begun to move in the same direction in Rome itself. Caesar's toying with the title *rex* and the appearance of his head on the coinage, circled with the bay-wreath of Apollo and wearing the insignia of the Pontifex Maximus, suggest pretensions similar to those of the Hellenistic kings he had perhaps envied and admired during his stay in the East.[68] The events following his murder showed how threadbare the Republican tradition had become. The dead Caesar was accorded the title of *Divus*, the month of July was dedicated to him, and the Senate voted his *Consecratio*. His worship was associated with that of *Dea Roma*, and his genius was admitted to the Pantheon. It is difficult not to see in these measures a decisive break with the past, and the preparation for the institution of the Imperial cult under Caesar's adopted heir, his grand-nephew, Octavian.

Both aspects of the renewal of Roman religion under Augustus were to have an effect on the future attitude of Rome towards Christianity. First, Roman religion became associated finally with the imperial mission of Rome, with the peace and order that she brought, and the eternity of her sway.[69] The Augustan age was looked upon almost as a Messianic age, the fulfilment in material terms of the secular hopes of mankind.[70] Against the obvious benefits brought by Augustus, what were the claims of the Zealot Leader crucified in 33 outside the walls of Jerusalem?[71] Secondly, in the Greek-speaking provinces the Imperial cult, both in its form and the vocabulary associated with its organization and practice, could become the rallying point to all who hated Judaism in shape or form, and in their hearts had 'no king but Caesar'.

The myth of Actium, as Syme has shown,[72] was religious as well as national. On the one side stood Rome and all the protecting gods of Italy, on the other, the bestial divinities of the Nile. If the Roman people were to be strong and confident in their future, honour must be done to the gods of Rome. Their dignified and reverent worship was the moral buttress of Rome's continuing power. The qualities of *virtus* and *pietas* could not be dissociated. Thus there begins a period of self-assertiveness in Roman paganism, patriotic as well as religious. It was not that there was active proselytization on behalf of the Roman gods, but these became the symbols of Empire, of the culture and language of Rome. Augustus himself was both superstitious and a statesman, and he actively furthered the revival of the ancestral Roman cults. He set an example which other emperors were to follow.[73] Livy's description (before 20 B.C.) of him as 'templorum omnium conditor aut restitutor' (iv.20.7), is borne out in fact. Eighty-two temples were restored or rebuilt. The Arval Brotherhood was resuscitated, the Secular Games held. 'By the enactment of new laws I restored many traditions of our ancestors which were passing out of use', wrote Augustus of his policy.[74] On Lepidus' death in 13 B.C., he assumed the office of Pontifex Maximus. And as if to show the practical import of these ideas, adultery was converted from a private offence into a public crime.[75] *Romanitas* and stern moral principles were to be associated for the next three centuries—as both Decius and Diocletian were to demonstrate.

Meantime, a wave of relief and gratitude had been sweeping over the Greco-Roman world. For twenty years the Mediterranean from Italy eastwards had been the prey to continuous insecurity. The civil wars between Caesar and Pompey had been followed by Caesar's murder, and yet more war and threat of war. Vergil's lament in I Georgic written *circa* 33 B.C., 'For here, right and wrong are confounded. So many wars the world over; so many forms of wrong. No worthy honour is left to the plough; the husbandmen have been marched away. Our lands lie waste and the crooked pruning hooks have become stiff swords.'[76] He expressed the views of many. Then, with Actium, all was decided. The temple of Janus was closed for the first time in 29 B.C.[77] People saw Augustus as bringing order where disorder had previously reigned: as Zeus had overthrown the Titans. From 28 B.C. onwards the theme of *Pax* associated with Augustus appears on the coins of Alexandria and some Greek cities[78] representing the restoration of harmony between the gods and humanity. In 30 B.C., the Proconsul of Asia, Paullus Fabius Maximus, gave the Greek cities of his province the advice that there could be no better day with which to begin the year than Augustus' birthday (23 September), and in their decrees which accepted the Julian calendar and recorded the acceptance of this view, they thanked Providence (πρόνοια) for producing Augustus as the bringer of peace and as the ruler who cared constantly for the welfare of all his subjects.[79] On the Cyrene inscription, Augustus himself takes up this cue, declaring that 'it will be plain to all who inhabit the provinces how much care I and the Senate take that none of our subjects suffer wrong or extortion'.[80] The *Providentia Augusti* guaranteed justice and peace to the provincials and the eternity of Rome itself.

What of the role of Augustus himself?[81] One looks for the clue in the profoundly conservative character of the man and in the fact that the principate was not intended as a complete break from what had gone before. Thus, to quote his own opinion of his office, 'I refused to accept the award of any form of office which was not in accordance with the institutions of our ancestors'.[82] This applied with no little force to matters of religion. The terse epigrammatic comment by Suetonius reads, 'He treated with great respect such foreign rites as were ancient, and well established, but held the rest in contempt'.[83] In this case, the foreign rites included Judaism which he treated with marked favour both in Rome and the East, but it would hardly have extended to an off-shoot suspected of incendiarism and worse. For anything outlandish or dangerous, Dio Cassius provides confirmation to Suetonius' statement. 'Those who attempt to distort our religion with strange rites you should abhor and punish not merely for the sake of the gods (for if a man despises these he will not pay honour to any other being), but because such men by bringing in new divinities in the place of old, persuade many to adopt foreign practices from which spring up conspiracies, factions and cabals which are not profitable to a monarchy. Do not therefore permit anyone to be an atheist or a sorcerer.'[84] Even though written in the reign of Alexander Severus (222–235), these sentences, put into the mouth of Maecenas, may reflect the outlook of Augustus' court, for the similarity to Livy's views regarding the Bacchanals is striking. In the minds of both writers, *externa religio* involved the suspicion of black magic and conspiracy against the state. It was therefore not to be tolerated until exhaustively tested—and Christianity had no black stone of Cybele to offer.

Augustus' own position in the religion of his subjects was the result not of megalomania such as drove Antiochus IV and Caligula to claim divine honours, but of a personal pre-eminence which resulted in a combination of titles being bestowed on him by grateful subjects.[85] Again, to quote the *Res Gestae*,

> I received the title of Augustus by decree of the Senate, and the door-posts of my house were officially covered with laurels: a civic crown was put over my door, and a golden shield was placed in the new Senate-House with an inscription recording that it was a gift to me from the Senate and the Roman people in recognition of my valour, my clemency, my justice and fulfilment of duty (*pietas*). After that I took precedence over all others in dignity, but I enjoyed no greater power than those who were my colleagues in the magistracy'[86] (E. Barker's translation, *Alexander to Constantine*, 229).

Augustus himself refused to be anything other than 'princeps senatus'. He was not *dictator* and rejected the regal title of *dominus*.

He allowed his hand to be forced. But as Dio pointed out, the title Augustus raised its holder to something higher than an ordinary being.[87] The word belonged to the sacred language of the priests,[88] and in practice Augustus was surrounded with such abundance of religious honour 'that many people thought there was nothing left for the worship of the heavenly gods'.[89] Moreover, the libation of wine offered to his genius at all private and public functions suggested the closest association between the guiding spirit of the ruler and the world of gods. The same impression was given by the appearance of the bay-leaves of Apollo on his head on his coinage, as it had previously been on that of Caesar's.[90] Though he did not regard himself as Apollo incarnate, or descended from the god, he believed that he was under Apollo's special protection.[91]

This 'special relationship' with the gods symbolized for citizen and subject alike in the cult of the Emperor's genius, was to be of immense importance for the relations between the Empire and the Christians. In a veiled form, as Miss L. R. Taylor points out,[92] it was a worship of the Emperor himself, for the genius was rather more than the 'guardian spirit': it could be regarded as something in the nature of the essence, the energizing and life-giving power, the divine force which would secure the future of the Imperial House. For instance, on the coins of Augustus struck before 27 one can see on the obverse Octavian's portrait, on the reverse, a phallic figure with inscription *Imp. Caes.*[93] The chief festival of the cult was naturally the Emperor's birthday, and victims were offered to it on this day. However, it was at least partially rooted in native Roman precedent for it was customary to make a bloodless sacrifice to the Genius of a household—unmixed wine, such as was poured in the libation to the Emperor, incense and flowers. In the new cult the sacrifice of an ox, proper for sacrifice to Jupiter and most of the gods was offered. The libation to the Imperial genius became the token of loyalty to the Imperial house and perhaps even more important than this, the formula of veracity in official matters.[94] If challenged, however, Christians were unable to take this oath.[95] The Jews could and did offer prayer and sacrifice in the Temple on behalf of Augustus and his successors. This was accepted, and its refusal in 66 was regarded as the sign of their open revolt against Rome.[96] After the fall of

Jerusalem the Christians had no obvious centre at which to perform any similar act of collective loyalty, even if they had been
acknowledged as a friendly national cult and encouraged to do so.
In fact, their outlook in this regard, among others, approximated
more to that of the Essenes who refused any religious acknowledgment of Caesar than to orthodox Jews. Though in the third
century Origen (*Contra Celsum*, viii.75) spoke of a service of
prayer rendered by Christians to the Empire, there was never
an attempt to meet the customary requirements of loyalty.

The cult of the Imperial genius, provided a bridge between the
Roman concept of the dignity and authority of Augustus and the
Hellenistic concept of the divine kingship. It united the hitherto
mutually dissenting halves of the Classical world. Moreover, the
confederations of cities which grew up in the major provinces in
both halves of the Empire to do honour to the Imperial genius
provided a religious basis of loyalty to the Empire from which the
Christians excluded themselves.

In the provinces, including Italy itself, the subtle distinctions
between 'divine genius' and 'deity' were, however, blurred from
the outset. In Egypt, of course, which Augustus regarded as his
private domain, the Emperor was a god as the Pharaohs and
Ptolemies had been before him. Immediately after the fall of
Alexandria (1 August 30 B.C.) he was being invoked in declarations
made by artisans, such as temple lamplighters at Oxyrhynchos, as
'god from god' (θεοῦ ἐκ θεοῦ)[97] and identified with Zeus
Eleutheros Sebastos.[98] An inscription from the temple at Sokno-
poe Nesos (Fayum) set up in 25–24 B.C. hails him in the same
terms.[99] In Asia Minor and Syria, the same thing was happening.
As early as 33 B.C. the oath of fidelity taken by the Paphlagonians
at Gangra promising to be faithful to Caesar-Augustus and his
family was by 'Zeus, Terra, Sol and all the goddesses' and by
Augustus himself.[100] All over the Greek world altars were being
erected to Augustus.[101] In the great decree of the province of
Asia which adopted the Julian calendar in his honour he is
also referred to as 'the god whose birthday was the beginning of
the good news (τῶν εὐαγγελίων)[102] for the world that has come to
men through him'. 'Good fortune' regarding 'salvation' began for
the Greeks of Asia on his birthday. The language of the decree—
in the use of words such as *evangelion* and *soteria*—anticipates the

language of the Gospels preached in those same cities half a century or so later.[103] Though the similarities were accidental, they could not have passed unnoticed, as the gleaming white marble and splendid carving of this and other inscriptions in honour of Augustus were there for all to read on the walls of the agora of the main cities of Asia.[104] In addition, first Nicomedia, capital of Bithynia, then Ephesus and Pergamum sought for and were granted permission to dedicate sacred precincts to *dea Roma*, to Caesar his father, whom he named the hero Julius, 'and to consecrate precincts to himself'.[105] Finally, the provincial councils of Galatia and Asia established a cult of Augustus. The statue of the Emperor was later set up in the precincts of the temple of the tutelary deity of the province—'Diana of the Ephesians', and henceforth Imperial and provincial deities were to be united in a single worship.[106]

In Syria, the restoration of 'peace with honour' on the Parthian frontier after 20 B.C., brought forth further paeans of praise. In the West, honour to Augustus took a more restrained form but an 'ara pacis' was probably erected in the capital city of each province, in imitation of that at Rome, and the enthusiasm for the successes of the reign was echoed on the provincial coinage. Though Dio Cassius, commenting on the establishment of the Imperial cult in Asia Minor, claims that no one dared to do like-wise in Rome and Italy, a closer look at some of the Italian provincial inscriptions suggests that few of those who honoured the altars of the 'pater patriae', imagined that they were doing other than honouring a god.[107]

In the Greek-speaking provinces, however, enthusiasm for Augustus the 'divine father of his country' was to have more far-reaching effects. Rome and the Hellenistic world had at last found a basis for a genuine association. But, at the same time, the Imperial cult brought Rome face to face with the internecine religious struggles of the Greek East. The pride and self-confidence of the Augustan messianism was to be challenged by an equally strong messianism derived from among her subject peoples. The pragmatic, rule of thumb methods adequate to control noxious foreign cults in the capital were to find themselves tested to the uttermost by new and unfamiliar situations in the religious life of the eastern provinces of Augustus' empire.

NOTES

[1] See the useful summary in E. G. Hardy *Christianity and the Roman Government* (ed. 1925), ch. i; also, W. Warde Fowler, *The Religious Experience of the Roman People*, London, 1911, Lecture iv, F. Altheim, *History of Roman Religion* (tr. H. Mattingly, 1938), pp. 309ff., and S. L. Guterman, *Religious Toleration and Persecution in Ancient Rome*, London, 1951.

[2] For instance, Hippolytus, *De Antichristo*, 19, 28 and *Comment. in Danielem*, ii, 12, and even Eusebius, *Demonstr. Evangel.*, xv, frag. 1 (ed. Heikel, 494); cf. Irenaeus, *Adv. Haer.*, 5.26.

[3] Polybius viewed religion as a force for inculcating civic virtues and public discipline, vi.56.6–12. See F. Walbank's *Commentary on Polybius*, I, Oxford, 1957, 741–2.

[4] Polybius, ibid., 'A Greek statesman if entrusted with a single talent though surrounded by ten checking-clerks, as many seals and twice as many witnesses yet cannot be induced to keep faith.'

[5] Livy v.16.11.

[6] Ibid., v.51.5, 'invenietis omnia prospera evenisse sequentibus deos, adversa spernentibus'.

[7] Ibid., iii.7.7–8; cf. iv.30.11, the aediles were told to see that no god except Roman was worshipped and that worship should be in the ancestral manner.

[8] See *De Nat. Deorum* ii.168.

[9] *De Nat. Deorum*, iii.6, 'a te enim philosopho rationem accipere debeo religionis, maioribus autem nostris etiam nulla ratione reddita credere'. See the brief but trenchant study in J. Vogt's 'Zur Religiosität der Christenverfolger in römischen Reich', *Sitzungsber. der Heidelberger Akad. der Wissenschaften*, Phil. Hist. Klasse, Abh., 1, 1962, 7ff.

[10] *Annales*, frag. 467, ed. E. H. Warmington, p. 174, 'moribus antiquis stat res Romana virisque'.

[11] Cicero, *De Nat. Deorum*, 1.2.4; cf. *De Legibus*, ii.2.

[12] Festus, cited from C. G. Bruns, *Fontes Iuris Romani Antiqui* (7th ed., Tübingen, 1909), Part ii.20; cf., ibid., ii.14, 'judex, vindexque contumaciae privatorum magistuumque'.

[13] S. L. Guterman, op. cit., 26, 'Citizenship and religion had similar bases', and G. E. M. de Ste Croix, 'Why were the early Christians persecuted?', *Past and Present*, 26, November 1963, p. 30. 'For Cicero's spiritual descendants of the early Principate Roman religion was part of the very stuff of Roman life and Roman greatness.' In many ways, Cicero's attitude provides the key to the Roman authorities' attitude towards the Christians.

[14] Cicero, *Pro Flacco*, 28.69.

[15] *De Legibus*, ii.8.19. Also, Livy, xxv.1.12. 'Neu quis in publico sacrove loco novo aut externo ritu sacrificaret.'

[16] *Pro Balbo*, 11.28.

[17] *Digest*, xlviii.4.1, 'Proximum sacrilegio crimen est, quod majestatis dicitur'. See below, ch. VI, p. 167.

[18] Donatism was condemned, for instance, by Honorius in January 412 on the grounds that it was 'prava religio'. *Cod. Theod.* (ed. Mommsen and Meyer, 1905), xvi.5.52 'a prava religione revocabit'.

[19] With the Druids one finds two degrees of prohibition. Under Augustus participation in the cult was banned to Roman citizens, and under Claudius the worship was proscribed completely. Suetonius, *Vita Divi Claudii*, 25.5.

[20] See Varro, *De Lingua latina* (ed. R. G. Kent), v.74, on the 'di novensides'.

[21] Livy, xxv.i.7 (F. G. Moore's translation). Cf. on this section W. W. Hyde, *From Paganism to Christianity in the Roman Empire*, Philadelphia, 1946, 24–5.

[22] Note the parallel of the rites of Ceres at Rome, by which women 'initienturque eo ritu Cereri, quo Romae initientur', i.e. only with rites in use in Rome—Cicero, *De Legibus*, ii.37.

[23] For Claudius' liberalizing measure, Hübner, art. 'Collegium', *P.W.*, iv.1, 1901, 396.

[24] Cicero's view, *De harusp. resp.*, 12.24, these Games were 'maxime casti, solemnes, religiosi'. But considerable prejudice against Romans participating in the rites of Cybele remained.

[25] See A. D. Nock, 'The Roman Army and the Religious Year', *HTR.*, xlv, 1952, 245. When Roman citizens were allowed to take up priesthoods in the cult, the traditional Greek titles, such as *dendrophori* or archigallus were retained (*CIL.*, vi.29691 and 2183).

[26] Livy, xxv.i.6. Livy is referring to the situation in Rome in 213 B.C., but his words had relevance to his own period.

[27] Cited from A. D. Nock, *Conversion*, 68.

[28] See the excellent description in G. la Piana's art. 'Foreign Groups in Rome during the first centuries of the Empire', *HTR.*, xx, 1927, 183–403, esp. 205ff.

[29] 'Cuncta collegia praeter antiquitus constituta distraxit'—Suetonius, *Vita Divi Julii*, 42.3. In general, Hübner, art. 'Collegium', 403ff., and Piana, art. cit., 240ff. For a *collegium* that was licensed and allowed to meet under the term of the Lex Julia, *CIL.*, vi.4416. (*collegium symphoniacorum*).

[30] Josephus, *Antiquities*, xiv, 10. (214).

[31] 'Syrus quidam nomine Eunus . . . . fanatico furore simulato, dum Syriae deae comes (or *comas*) iactat ad libertatem et arma servos quasi numinum imperio concitavit.' Florus, *Epitome*, ii.17.4. See the analysis of the background to this revolt, P. Green, 'The First Sicilian Slave War', *Past and Present*, 22, 1961, pp. 10–30, and W. G. C. Forrest's and T. C. W. Stenton's *critique*, ibid. 87–91.

[32] Dio Cassius, lxxii. 4.

[33] F. Altheim, *History of Roman Religion*, 293–4 and 314ff., and A. H. McDonald, 'Rome and the Italian Confederation', *JRS.*, xxxiv, 1944, 26ff. (n. 116 on p. 26 for further bibliography). Also G. Tarditi, 'La Questione dei Baccanali a Roma nel 186 A.C.', *La Parola del Passato*, ix, 1954, 265–87.

[34] Livy, xxxix.14.6. 'Quaestionem deinde de Bacchanalibus sacrisque nocturnis extra ordinem consulibus mandant.'

[35] See ch. VI, below, p. 162.

[36] Livy, xxxix.15.3.

[37] Ibid., 16.6.

[38] Ibid., 16.9.

[39] The participants in the discussion written up by Cicero in *De Legibus* pick on the nocturnal character of the Bacchanal rites as being a sound reason for suppressing them. *De Legibus*, ii.36–37. Also, ibid., ii.9 21 (Twelve Tables), and ii.10.25 (foreign rites causing 'confusionem religionum').

[40] See E. Fraenkel, 'Senatus Consultum de Bacchanalibus', *Hermes*, 67, 1932, 369–96.

[41] See over, ch. VI, p. 166. In 186 B.C. the Italian confederation headed by Rome was suffering strain from various forms of social unrest of which the Bacchanal affair seemed the most obvious. The Senate interpreted this as a sign of mass unrest, claimed that Rome was threatened by a *coniuratio*, and acted accordingly (McDonald, op. cit., 33). In 64 the crisis had been provoked by one event in the capital, namely the fire, and there was no need to spread the repercussions outside. For the suggestion that Christianity was also prohibited in 64 by a *senatus-consultum*, see the brief and suggestive article by J. Zeiller, 'Nouvelles remarques sur les persécutions contre les chrétiens'. *S.T.*, 125, 1946 (= Miscellanea Giovanni Mercati, v), p. 3.

[42] Livy, xxxix.17.6.

[43] Ibid., 18.5. 'Plures necati quam in vincula coniecti sunt',—probably as with the Christians in 64.

[44] Ibid., 18.8.

[45] *Annales*, xv.44.1.

[46] In Alexandria in Ptolemaic times members of the cult had to register (*BGU.*, iv, 1211 = Hunt and Edgar, *Select Papyri*, ii.208). But an interesting Oxyrhynchus papyrus (No. 2476) from the archives of the Oxyrhynchus senate shows that in Augustus' reign Dionysiac artists were being granted favours and privileges, which were confirmed by Claudius, Hadrian, Alexander Severus and Diocletian (*Pap. Oxy.*, xxvii, 1962, 164ff.). Local bands of Dionysiac artists combined as a single world-wide group of entertainers probably under imperial patronage in the second century A.D. In general, M. P. Nilsson, 'Bacchic Mysteries of the Roman Age', *HTR.*, 46, 1953, 175ff.

[47] For instance in the splendid second/third century 'villa Dionysus' at Knossos, Crete (report to be published by M. Gough); also at Corinth (S. S. Weinberg, *Corinth*, i.5, Princeton, 115) same date, and Antioch (D. Levi, *Antioch Mosaic Pavements*, 69).

[48] In the discussion on nocturnal rites in *De Legibus* cited above, note 39, Marcus points to Greek laws abolishing nocturnal rites and banishing alien gods from the State, like Sabazius.

[49] See S. Dill's account, *Roman Society from Nero to Marcus Aurelius*, 563ff.

[50] G. la Piana, art. cit. 291, points out that this suppression coincides with the suppression of *collegia* after the riots of Clodius. At Pompeii, the *collegia Isiaca* had a political role in the city's affairs. *CIL.*, iv.787; cf. ibid., 1011. Here *collegia* were synonymous with turbulence and faction. Tacitus, *Ann.*, xiv.17.

[51] Josephus, *Antiquities*, xviii.3.4. Paulina, a Roman matron, allowed herself to be seduced in a temple of Isis by a lover, who with the collusion of a priest, was disguised as the god Anubis; cf. Tacitus, *Annales*, ii.85. The case was debated in the Senate, and the decision taken there.

[52] For an account of Roman women's devotion to the goddess in the second century A.D., Juvenal, *Sat.*, vi.526ff., and *CIL.*, vi.3.17985, line 6 (epitaph of Flavius Agricola) and the cult's popularity even in the early fifth century A.D., Rutilius Namatianus, *De Reditu Suo*, 371ff.

[53] Origen, *Contra Celsum*, vi.80; cf. Juvenal, *Sat.*, vi.553, 'Chaldaeis sed maior erit fiducia'.

[54] *Nat. Hist.*, xxx.12.13. Suetonius, *Vita Claudii* 25.5 'Druidarum religionem apud Gallos dirae immanitatis'. Tacitus, *Annales*, xiv.30.3, 'saeva superstitio'; cf. H. Last, 'The Study of the "Persecutions"', *JRS.*, xxvii.1, 1937, 88, showing the relevance of these acts of suppression for the study of the Persecutions.

[55] Strabo (ed. H. C. Jones), iv.4.5 (= *c.* 198). For the recovery of social prestige among Druids and those who claimed to be their descendants, see above, ch. I, p. 10.

[56] Varro, cited by Augustine, *De Civitate Dei*, vi.2; cf. ibid., vi.10 (worship 'belonging to custom rather than reality'). Also, Juvenal, *Satires*, ii (ed. S. G. Owen), 149–53 for complete contempt for traditional beliefs.

[57] F. Altheim, op. cit., 334ff.

[58] Cicero, *De Nat. Deorum*, ii.67.168; cf. i.23.62.

[59] Cited from W. Hyde, op. cit., 29, n. 38, quoting Athenaeus.

[60] See E. Barker, *Alexander to Constantine*, Part III.

[61] Cicero and some Christian writers use it with reference to Diagoras of Melos but it is not until Arnobius *Adv. Nat.* v.30 in the late third century that the term is latinised. Tacitus does not use it with reference to the Christians,

[62] Tacitus, *Annales*, xiii.32. The 'morositas' of which she was accused was a failing constantly attributed to Jews by Roman aristocrats. See, Rutilius Namatianus in the early fifth century, *De Reditu suo*, 389–90. 'Radix stultitiae: cui frigida sabbata cordi / Sed cor frigidius religione sua.'

[63] The literature on this subject is vast. The following remain the most useful for the student of the conflict between Rome and Christianity: E. Kornemann, 'Zur Geschichte

des antiken Herrschenkulte', *Klio*, i, 1902, 52–143 (fundamental as a starting point), L. R. Taylor, *The Divinity of the Roman Emperor*, 1931, A. D. Nock, 'Early Gentile Christianity' (in *Essays on the Trinity*, ed. A. E. J. Rawlinson, 1927), A. Deissmann, *Light from the Ancient East* (Eng. tr., L. R. M. Strachan, 1927), 338ff., and Wm. Ensslin, 'Gottkaiser und Kaiser von Gottes Gnaden', *Sitzungsber. der bayerischen Akademie der Wissenschaften* (Phil. Hist. Klasse), 1943, fasc. 6.

[64] See M. Grant, *From Imperium to Auctoritas*, Cambridge, 1946, 443ff.

[65] Tacitus, *Ann.*, iv.56; cf. Livy, xliii.6 (Alabanda, 170 B.C.). In general, C. M. Bowra, 'Melinno's Hymn to Rome', *JRS.*, xlvii, 1957, 21ff., Ensslin, op. cit., 18–21.

[66] For the association of the cult of Dea Roma in the East with hopes of peace and harmony, S. Weinstock, 'Pax and the "Ara Pacis"', *JRS.*, l, 1960, 44–58, especially n. 65–8.

[67] J. Ward-Perkins, *PBSR.*, xxvi, 1958, 177–9 draws attention to the specialized form of architecture going back to the reign of Ptolemy III and Berenice, connected with the cult of the divine king, which Caesar copied. For the existence of the Caesareum at Alexandria in A.D. 40, Philo, *Legatio* (ed. E. M. Smallwood, 1961), 151. Caesar hailed as θεός, *CIG.*, 2957 (Ephesus).

[68] E. A. Sydenham, *The Coinage of the Roman Republic* (Oxford, 1952), Nos. 1055–75 (44 B.C.). Note also, Cassius Dio's report (xliii.45.3) that he accepted decrees of the Senate which placed his bust in the temple of Quirinus under the inscription 'Deo invicto', and another which allowed his statue to be set up on the Capitol beside the former kings of Rome; and Suetonius' judgment, *Caes.* 76.1, 'sed et ampliora etiam humano fastigio decerni sibi passus est'.

[69] Tiberius inspired the hope of 'perpetuae securitatis aeternitatisque Romani imperii'— Velleius Paterculus (ed. R. Ellis), ii.103.4.

[70] Note the same author's view, *Historiae Romanae*, ii.89. 'There was nothing which men might pray for to heaven, and nothing which heaven could grant to men—nothing desire could conceive or fortune bestow—which Augustus . . . did not realize for the commonwealth, the people of Rome, and the world' (tr. E. Barker, *Alexander to Constantine*, 230).

[71] For the theme of the rival messianism of Augustus and Christ, see in particular, E. Stauffer, *Christ and the Caesars* (Eng. tr., 1955), chs. vi–vii.

[72] R. Syme, *The Roman Revolution*, Oxford, 1939, p. 448ff. See Vergil, *Aeneid*, viii.675ff. (emblems on the Roman shield).

[73] e.g. Antoninus Pius, *CIL.*, vi, 1001, the Emperor honoured 'ob insignem (eius) erga / caerimonias publicas curam ac religionem'; cf. A. D. Nock, 'The Augustan Restoration', *CR.*, 39, 1925, 60–7.

[74] *Res Gestae* (ed. and tr. E. G. Hardy, Oxford, 1923), ch. 8.

[75] *Lex Julia de adulteriis coercendis*. Augustus established a *Quaestio perpetua* before which cases of adultery (i.e. illicit intercourse with a *mater familiae*) were tried. Also, Suetonius, *Vita Divi Augusti*, 34.1.

[76] *Georgics* (ed. H. F. Fairclough), i.505–8; cf. Tacitus, *Annales*, 1.1, 'qui (Augustus) cuncta discordiis civilibus fessa nomine principis sub imperium accepit'.

[77] Livy, i.19.3, Dio Cassius, li.20.4.

[78] M. Grant, *From Imperium to Auctoritas*, 281 (Pella) and S. Weinstock, 'Pax and the "Ara Pacis"', *JRS.*, l, 1960, 47. See Th. Mommsen, 'Die Einführung des asianischen Kalenders', *Ges. Schriften*, v, 518–28.

[79] *OGI.*, 458, lines 42–52 and note by A. H. M. Jones, 'L. Volcaecius Tullus, Proconsul of Asia,' *CR.*, N.S. v, 1955, 244–5.

[80] Fifth Edict (between 1 January and 1 July 4 B.C.). From F. de Visscher, *Les Edits d'Auguste découverts à Cyrène*, Louvain, 1940, 22–3 (lines 79–82).

[81] See A. H. M. Jones's art., 'The *Imperium* of Augustus', *JRS.*, xli, 1951, 112–19 and H. Last's discussion of A. Magdelain, *Auctoritas Principis*, in *JRS.*, xl, 1950, 118–23.

[82] *Res Gestae*, ch. 6 (Hardy, op. cit., 46–9).

[83] *Vita Divi Augusti*, 93.

[84] Dio Cassius, lii, 36.1–3.

[85] In the early third century African Christians accounted it to Augustus' credit that he had refused to be addressed as *Dominus*, Tertullian, *Apol.* 34; and cf. Orosius, vi.22.4.

[86] *Res Gestae*, 34 (Hardy, op. cit., 159–61).

[87] Dio Cassius, liii.18.2; cf. ibid., 16.8. 'What Augustus accepted in his life involved not indeed divinity, but a more than human status', so, A. D. Nock, 'Severi and Augustales', *Mélanges Bidez*, 627–38, at p. 638.

[88] Ovid, *Fasti*, 1.609. 'Sancta vocant augusta patres.' Also, Suetonius, op. cit., 7.

[89] Tacitus, *Annales*, 1.10.5.

[90] See H. Mattingly's appendix to M. Rostovtzeff's art. 'Commodus-Hercules in Britain', *JRS.*, xiii, 1923, 104ff.

[91] Vergil (*Aeneid*, viii, 704) speaks of Apollo as 'the god of Actium' who gave the victory to Augustus. For a discussion on the connection between Augustus' special veneration of Apollo and the institution of the Imperial cult, see P. Lambrechts, 'La politique apollinienne d'Auguste et le culte imperial', *Nouvelle Clio*, v, 1953, 65–81.

[92] L. R. Taylor, op. cit., 193.

[93] The same idea is expressed in the boyish but impersonal features of Augustan statues and such as the colossal statue in the Vatican. See M. Grant, op. cit., 356ff. The statue from Herculaneum now in Naples Museum shows Augustus also carrying a thunderbolt, demonstrating his association with Jupiter.

[94] For instance, *Pap. Oxy.* 6, 2472. 'We swear by the genius of the Emperor Caesar Trajan Hadrian Augustus that we have soundly and truthfully presented the foregoing account', A.D. 119—the account of the proceeds of a tax. Or, in association with gods to whom one owed deliverance from peril. *P.S.I.*, xii, 1261 (Caracalla); or, in confirmation of a declaration that oil put on public sale in the marketplace at Oxyrhynchus would be of fine quality and that there would be no fraud (*Pap. Oxy.* 1455, dated A.D. 275). It is difficult to see how anyone refusing to take this oath could conduct normal business.

[95] See for instance, Eusebius, *H.E.*, iv.15.21 (Polycarp) or Tertullian, *Apol.* 32.2, and Celsus (Origen, *Contra Celsum*, viii.67). See ch. IX, p. 257.

[96] Josephus, *Wars*, ii.197 and 409. Cf. Philo, *Legatio*, 155–8 (Jewish loyalty to Augustus) and see, E. M. Smallwood's comments on the passage in her ed., pp. 233–42.

[97] *Pap. Oxy.* xii, 1453, l.11 (Grenfell and Hunt, xii, 166–70).

[98] *Corpus Papyrorum Rainerii* (ed. Wessely, Vienna, 1895), 224. See H. I. Bell, *Cults and Creeds in Roman Egypt*, Liverpool, 1956, 56, who cites other examples.

[99] F. Krebs, 'Aegyptische Priester unter römischer Herrschaft', *Zeitschrift f. Aegyptische Sprache*, xxxi, 1893, 33.

[100] *OGI.*, 532.

[101] A. B. and A. E. Raubitschek, 'Arae Augusti', *Hesperia*, 28, 1959, 65–85 for a full list of these altars.

[102] *OGI.*, 458, line 41. On the meaning of the term εὐαγγέλιον in relation to the Imperial cult in first century A.D., in Asia see J. Schniewind, *Evangelion*, iii, 1931, ch. x.

[103] Lines 49–50, 'διὸ τύχηι ἀγαθῆι καὶ σωτηρίαι δεδόχθαι'. For this and many other parallels between the language of the Imperial cult and that of Hellenistic Christianity, A. Deissmann, op. cit., 338ff.

[104] The single panel of the copy of *OGI.*, 458 which I found at Apamea (Dinar) in September 1954 was in perfect condition, cut as clearly as if it had been hewn yesterday.

[105] Dio Cassius, li.20.6–8; cf. Tacitus *Annales*, iv.37.3 (Pergamum).

[106] Dio Cassius, ibid.; cf. J. Keil *J.Ö.A.I.*, 27, 1930 (*Beiblatt*, 1, 59). At Athens a statue of Augustus was set up on the Acropolis perhaps in A.D. 4. *I.G.R.R.*, ii², 3253. It is worth

remembering perhaps, that once it had been started it was difficult and indeed dangerous for a Greek city to neglect the Imperial cult, as the citizens of Cyzicus discovered in the reign of Tiberius. Tacitus, *Annales*, iv.36.2.

[107] Dio Cassius, 51.20.8; cf. Suetonius, *Vita Divi Augusti*, 52; L. R. Taylor, op. cit., 181–205.

CHAPTER FIVE

The Legacy of the Hellenistic East to A.D. 41

THE institution of the Imperial cult in the Roman provinces may or may not have been intended as a master-stroke of Augustan policy. Its enthusiastic acceptance, however, particularly in the Hellenistic East, contributed towards bringing about far-reaching changes in Rome's relations with the various subject peoples in the eastern Mediterranean, and not least with the Greeks and Jews.

In the last century of the Republic the Greek cities had caused Rome considerable trouble. The legacy of the asylum given by the Seleucids to Hannibal was a long one, breeding prejudice and suspicion on both sides. Attalus' bequest of his kingdom to Rome in 133 B.C. had been the signal for Aristonicus' revolt. In the Mithradatic war of 88–84 B.C. the support which Mithradates received from the oligarchies of Pergamum and Tralles and many others, and the massacre of Roman citizens which ensued were long remembered.[1] These acts branded the Asiatic Greeks in Roman eyes, as fickle, dissolute, untruthful and malicious.[2] Cicero's defence of the corrupt and grasping governor of Asia, L. Valerius Flaccus, fully expresses the contempt which members of the Roman governing class felt for them. Though Cicero is an advocate and could be expected to exaggerate in his client's favour, he would hardly have used this approach if the jury had been philhellenes. He knew he was not antagonizing the wealthy Romans whom he was addressing.

In return, Greeks in Asia kept up a subtle barrage of polemic against a power whose strength they feared but whose culture they despised. Probably during the Mithradatic war an oracle which eventually found its way into the Jewish iii Sibylline expressed the hatred felt by some Greek for his Italian overlords.[3] 'O Rome pampered off-spring of Latium, drunken with successful

127

suitors'; she would be taken by the scruff of her neck and thrown about like a ball by victorious Asia. She would have to repay ten-thousandfold what she had extorted from the province by her hideous violence.[4]

Unfortunately, these predictions did not come true, but the defeat of Mithradates did not quench ill-feeling. *Der geistige Widerstand gegen Rom*, was a fact in the Greek world of the first century B.C.: and the rhetorician Timagenes could say sourly, even when living in Rome, that the only reason why he did not like fires at Rome was because he knew that what was rebuilt would be an improvement on what had been burnt.[5] Only with the battle of Actium and the peace which Augustus' triumph brought about, did permanent reconciliation begin. Even then, as we know from the record of intrigues by Romans in Cyrene in Augustus' reign 'framing' local Greeks on capital charges, this development was often painfully slow.[6]

It is against a background of mutual distrust that the contrasting Greek and Roman attitudes towards the Jews must be understood. Without delving deeply into the basic problems of Hellenistic political thought,[7] it may be said that there appear to be three main factors which influenced Greek relations with the Jews in the half-century either side of the birth of Christ. First, despite the cosmopolitan tendencies in Greek thought which followed the campaigns of Alexander the Great, the Greeks of the Seleucid and Ptolemaic kingdoms remained, in practice, wedded to their city states, and the close-knit religious and political ideology which these engendered. Ehrhardt has rightly pointed out how the idealized concept of the Greek Polis grounded in a personified Nomos clashed with that of the unalterable Law given by God to His Chosen People, Israel.[8] Even intellectual dissent from the religious premises on which the institutions of the Polis rested could be regarded as dangerous. 'Atheism' had a rather wider connotation than the parallel Latin 'sacrilege' or 'impiety'. It included intellectual belief or otherwise in the gods, not necessarily connected with specific acts of impiety; and it seems clear that it involved not merely lack of respect for the 'usual gods', i.e. of one's own city, but of gods in general.[9]

The great 'atheists' of the Hellenistic world were thinkers who would hardly have dreamt of robbing temples, yet unlike Socrates they were not heroes even among intellectuals. Diagoras of Melos, Protagoras of Abdera and Theodorus of Cyrene went down to history as men who 'cut at the root of all the fear and reverence by which mankind is governed'.[10] Plutarch would dissuade his friends from any discussion of religious matters and saw in the resultant 'atheism' an 'abyss' which 'lies at our feet if we resolve each of the gods into a passion, or a force or a virtue'[11]—a development to which his Roman contemporary, beholding current coin types featuring Virtus, Pietas, Securitas, etc., would have raised few objections. It was a matter for rejoicing that atheists were expelled from their cities and their works burnt in the market-places.

Secondly, the Greek rulers of the successor kingdoms of Alexander's empire inherited the religious bond which tradition-ally linked king and regional or tribal deity in the eyes of their subjects. The great sanctuary of Nimrod Dagh erected by the kings of Commagene in the first century B.C. represents each ruler in the dynasty with the countenance of a god. Gods and divine rulers faced each other across the majestic stairway which led to the royal shrine from the plains below.[12] In kingdoms such as this, 'Soter', 'Epiphanes' and 'Euergetes' were simply titles which emphasized the divine relationship between ruler and people.

Finally, wherever they settled, the Greeks tended to regard themselves as urban outposts against the barbarian world.[13] They did not generally assimilate the surrounding native popula-tions to their culture. Town versus countryside is a recurring theme in the social history of the Ancient World, and not without cause. In Asia Minor, the Phrygians, Lycaonians and even the immigrant Celtic Galatians maintained for centuries their gods, traditions and languages, and resisted Hellenization.[14] Of the Phrygians, the fifth-century Church historian, Socrates, states in a well-known passage, with reference to the predominance of Novatianism in Phrygia and Paphlagonia, that even in his day 'the sports of the circus and theatrical exhibitions were not in much esteem among them'.[15] The Greek cities of Asia with their fine walls, public buildings, temples and agora stood as isolated in the barbarian countryside on which they depended for their food, as the cities of the early Industrial Revolution stood in the European landscape.

The Jews offended against all these canons. In the Dispersion, they spoke Greek, were in the great majority town-dwellers, and at least in Alexandria, despised the rural Egyptians as barbarians.[16] They were often wealthy and influential in the communities in which they had settled. The chief synagogue at Antioch was, for instance, described as 'of great magnificence',[17] and similar comments could be made of other big Jewish communities. But they remained settlers, πάροικοι, a people apart,[18] with their own customs and religion which admitted little intermingling with their Greek neighbours. As late as the third century A.D. Philostratus complained 'these people (the Jews) cannot share with the rest of mankind in the pleasures of the table, nor join in their libations or prayers or sacrifices. They are separated from us by a greater gulf than are Susa, Bactria or more distant, India'.[19] The Jews would have agreed. Theirs was a 'theocracy', not an oligarchy or democracy.[20] The synagogue, with its school and charities provided a focus for the activities of the community, parallel to but alien from the institutions of the *polis*. In the larger cities the Jews formed a πολίτευμα, which generally denotes a 'corporation formed by members of a race or community domiciled in a foreign state'.[21] In Alexandria the Jewish *politeuma* had its own record office[22] and courts, to a large extent independent of the Greek authorities. Strabo hardly exaggerates when he says that the Jewish community there was virtually autonomous.[23]

Not, however, content with the status of privileged foreigners, the Jews claimed the same rights as the Greek citizens, while insisting on religious privileges which robbed citizenship of its meaning. 'Why', asked the outraged Apion at the end of the first century A.D. 'do the Jews claim to be citizens of Alexandria when they will not worship the same gods as we?'[24] Not only did they refuse these deities recognition as gods, but from the mid-second century B.C. onwards the Hellenistic Jews poured out a constant stream of anti-pagan propaganda. They despised their Greek neighbours as unclean idol-worshippers, as immoral as their gods, and claimed that whatever good there was in their philosophy had been plagiarized from Moses. Naturally, claims to divine honours by local rulers were rejected as decisively as they had been in the Maccabean Wars. The Letter of Aristeas, Psalm 115, the Book of Wisdom, Esther, Pseudo-Justin's *Hortatio ad Graecos*, and the

Third Book of the Sibyllines are all examples of Jewish apologetic work directed against the Greeks at this period.

This constant political warfare was combined with active proselytism. The frontiers between Judaism and Hellenism in the Dispersion were never static. While sometimes it is possible to see Jewish and Hellenistic forms of worship finding common ground in, for instance, the widespread cult of Zeus Hypsistos,[25] and also in the more limited cult of Sabazios,[26] one senses that these are somewhat exceptional. Jewish proselytism had become proverbial by New Testament times (Mt. 23[15]). The Hellenistic Jew regarded himself as 'to all mortals a guide to life', and he acted in this belief.[27] Thus, of the Jews in Antioch, Josephus, after saying that the Jews enjoyed equal privileges (ἐξ ἴσου τῆς πόλεως) with the Greeks, goes on, 'They also made proselytes of a great many of the Greeks continuously, and thereby in a sort of way brought them to be a portion of their own body'.[28] In Alexandria, the Jews offered a 'friendly welcome' to interested Greeks,[29] and wherever he went in Asia Minor Paul found his most attentive hearers from among the outer fringe of proselytes and semi-proselytes which were the feature of synagogue life there (Acts 13[43-44]).

In the propaganda war the Jews had the advantage. Before the establishment of the Imperial cult, Greek religion had tended to become a culture and tradition without moral and ethical depth. Capricious Fortune, or Tyche was the supreme goddess, and Uncertainty was something to be delivered from, rather than to die for. Cicero writing in 59 B.C. in defence of Flaccus, asserted that the Greeks in Asia 'had never revered the religion and faith of tradition', and were 'ignorant of the strength, authority and weightiness of everything of this nature'.[30] As against this, the Jews alone of the ancients possessed a religion, ethic and theory of history which could be found in a single book, the LXX, accessible to all.[31] They had a world view of events, based on the continual handing on of a tradition which extended back to the creation of the world. Anyone could see that the Hebrew prophets were real people who lived in remote but nevertheless historical times.[32] And, in an age when the claim of antiquity to be the equivalent of truth was strong,[33] the Jews could present to the world a monotheism and high religious ethic and history which their chronicles proved were far older than Homer (*Contra Apionem*, ii.16). The *Antiquities* of Josephus is itself a demonstration of how strong an appeal this literary form exerted. It was to be equally prominent in the chronicle-literature of the early Church.

Against this, the Greeks could pick holes in individual aspects of Judaism. They could point to the immoralities of the Patriarchs, the outlandish names of the prophets, that, literally translated, Jerusalem (*Hierosylema*) was named from the success of the Jews in robbing temples, and to the obviously forced nature of Jewish allegorization of the LXX.[34] But this was not enough. As Nock has pointed out, the normal pagan might well feel that there was something to be said for Jewish customs maintained with such determination against all opposition. Sabbath observance, fasting, abstinence from some foods and the lighting of lamps were observed far outside the limits of Judaism.[35] The dedication of a *proseuche* in Alexandria in 102/01 B.C. to the nameless 'great god who hears prayer' may have been the work of one of these interested pagans.[36] By the middle of the first century B.C. Judaism seems to have established a sort of religious and ethical superiority. Instead of succumbing to Christianity, Hellenism might have succumbed to this had it not been for the stumbling-block of the Law.

As it was, there were many cases, Josephus admits, where there was only a temporary flirtation with Judaism. Many Alexandrian Greeks we are told 'did not persevere',[37] but others did, and the demands of Judaism, symbolized by circumcision, the proselyte bath, and finally the offering in the Temple, signified a complete rejection of the convert's previous culture. The formal but searching questions put to him by the Rabbi emphasized his breach with the past. Tacitus' epigrammatic 'contemnere deos, exuere patriam, parentes, liberos, fratres vilia habere',[38] had been eroding the Hellenistic world for the previous two centuries.

For the Jews were ubiquitous. When King Agrippa addressed the Jews in Jerusalem in 66 and sought to dissuade them from revolting against Rome, he warned them that they would be endangering not only their own lives, but those of their fellow Jews spread throughout the Roman world. 'There is not', said he, in words put into his mouth by Josephus, 'a community in the entire world which does not have a portion of our people.'[39]

Some 150 sites in the Mediterranean have provided literary or archaeological evidence for the existence of a Jewish community.[40] There were multitudinous Jews in Rome, Alexandria, Damascus, Antioch, Caesarea, Cartagena, Volubilis,[41] and beyond the frontiers of the Empire, Babylon[42] was the largest centre of Jewry outside Jerusalem. The well-known claims by Philo that there were Jewish colonies in all the mainland provinces in the eastern Mediterranean, and in the islands, Euboea, Cyprus and Crete, 'to say nothing about the regions beyond the Euphrates',[43] are amply borne out by other sources. The million Jews claimed by the same author for Egypt and Cyrenaica in A.D. 40 may have been an exaggeration, but it is difficult to refute, and the estimated total of one-seventh of the Mediterranean population of the Empire at this time may be taken as possible.[44] The Dispersion Jews could constitute a threat to the very existence of the Greek cities and their way of life. Thus, the proselyte was a traitor in a very real sense of the term. As the incidents in Damascus in 66 showed, the existence of proselytes and Jewish sympathizers among most of the families of the Hellenized leaders in the city, prevented them taking action against the Jews there on the outbreak of the Jewish War in Palestine.[45]

None the less, the movement on the fringes of the two rival cultures was not all one way. If the Jews had the better of the intellectual argument and ethical example, the Greeks could point to superior standards of civilization, achievements in the fields of arts and sciences,[46] and a tradition worth maintaining in face of rural barbarism. In particular, the practice of self-government gave them an innate feeling that despite all, they were superior to barbarian, Persian and Jew. 'The Jews', wrote Celsus (Origen, Contra Celsum iv.31) 'were runaway slaves who escaped from Egypt and they have never been of any prominence or significance whatever.' This assertion provided the Greek with a reasonable defence of his civilization and a means of counter-attraction. We have seen already how the gradual conversion of many of the wealthier Jerusalem Jews to Hellenism was one of the chief causes of the Maccabaean revolt. In Asia Minor in the first century A.D. the gradual falling away from the Law by many Jews is indicated by evidence for the abandonment of circumcision and the substitution of the proselyte bath as the means of entry into Judaism.[47]

This seems to have been widespread and the case of Timothy does not appear to have been exceptional. At Tanais in the Bosphorus there is evidence for the acceptance of pagan priesthoods by Jews.[48] All sorts of semi-Jewish religious sects, like the Hypsistarii (or worshippers of the Most High) in Cappadocia, or the Sabbatistai in Cilicia, existed.[49] That these backslidings were bitterly resented is shown by the recorded request of the Jewish leaders in iii Maccabees to Ptolemy that apostates should be handed over to them for punishment. The fate dealt out to 10,000 of these was a merciless one (iii Macc. 7[10]).

All these factors contributed to maintain a state of tension between the two cultures wherever they came into contact. To many Greeks the Dispersion itself was an offence, and as the writer of iii *Sibylline* ruefully remarked, 'Every country shall be filled with thee and every sea, and every one shall be incensed by thy customs' (lines 271–2). Right through the late Classical period the most persistent accusation against the Jews was 'hostility towards the rest of mankind'. The so-called decree of Xerxes ordering the destruction of the Jewish nation, which finds a place in Esther 3[13] LXX, gives as the reason for this act that the Jews were an 'ill-disposed people mixed up with all the tribes throughout the world, opposed in their laws to every other nation, and continually neglecting the commands of the kings'. In iii Maccabees Jewish 'enmity against all nations' was also the pretext for action against them.[50] The Jews were regarded as irreconcilable enemies of the rest of humanity, and this charge, the *odium generis humani*, was to be passed on to the Christians. So, if in the eyes of the Jews the Greeks were unclean, and where they were in a minority, as at Jamnia in Palestine, to be denied religious rights and treated as hostile strangers,[51] to the Greeks the Jews were enemies, and for good measure, 'atheists', 'donkey worshippers', 'lazy', 'sacrilegious' and 'treacherous'.[52] A petty incident like the beating of Sosthenes before Gallio's tribunal could lead to a massacre (Acts 18[17]). It was no accident that Philo and his companions on their embassy to Caligula's court in 39/40 feared that if the Emperor gave way to their enemies, 'what city would refrain from attacking the Jews, living in it? What synagogue would remain unmolested?' (*Legatio*, 371).[53] Indeed, from the Maccabean wars onwards Greek-Jewish relations were characterized by endemic hostility breaking out now in one place, now in another, in pogroms, riots, demonstrations and massacres.

The evidence for these scenes of violence comes mainly from Josephus and Philo, but there are hints elsewhere, such as in iii Maccabees and Esther. Josephus refers to a whole series of Greek cities during the first century B.C. where the authorities had sought to molest the Jews or to curtail their religious privileges. Ephesus, Miletus, Laodicea, Tralles, Halicarnassos in Asia Minor, and the merchant-city of Delos are among those specifically mentioned.[54] In Augustus' reign the Greeks of Asia and Libya are again accused of wanting to do the Jews mischief.[55] Antioch and Alexandria were cities where the trouble seems to have been endemic,[56] and we hear of incidents between Jew and Greek in Damascus,[57] and the Palestinian cities of Jamnia,[58] Caesarea,[59] Scythopolis,[60] Ptolemais[61] and Ascalon.[62] Philo's description of the Alexandrian pogrom of 38 is a classic.[63] The speed at which the conflagration of 66 spread throughout Palestine and Syria and that of A.D. 115–117 spread round the eastern Mediterranean provinces from Mesopotamia to Cyprus and Cyrenaica shows that there was plenty of inflammable material in these provinces. To this situation of communal bitterness the new and more formidable sect of Judaism was the heir.

One of these horrible affairs may be mentioned in more detail, because it shows clearly the problem the presence of Jews and proselytes presented to the local authorities, and also the attitude of the Romans at this time. In A.D. 67 Antioch was the scene of bitter ill-feeling against the Jews on account of the outbreak of the war in Palestine.[64] An apostate Jew, named Antiochus, accused his fellow countrymen, including his own father who was Ethnarch, before the city authorities of conspiring to set Antioch on fire. In one night the whole town was to be consumed, and Antiochus produced some 'conspirators' in the persons of foreign Jews who happened to be in the city at the time. There was apparently just enough evidence to lend colour to his story. The mob immediately demanded that the prisoners should be burnt alive, and the authorities complied. The unhappy Jews, presumably innocent of the charge, were burnt in the amphitheatre. Then the mob set on other Jews, and Antiochus, after doing sacrifice himself, persuaded the city authorities to order a sacrifice test 'because they would by that means discover who they were that plotted against them, since they would not do so; and when the people of Antioch tried the experiment, some few complied, but those that would not do so, were slain'. This was followed by the abrogation of the Jewish privilege of resting on the Sabbath. As if this was not enough, when there was a real fire in the agora shortly afterwards, people were only too ready to believe more of Antiochus' accusations against the Jews. Even those who had been well disposed before were now prepared to vent hatred on them. The massacres were only stopped by Roman intervention, and a subsequent inquiry by Cnaeus Collegas, the legate, established the complete innocence of the Jewish accused.

This story has a number of points of interest. The year 67 saw the fortunes of the Jews in Palestine evenly balanced, a situation which would tend to embitter any existing tenseness in Antioch. It is evident, too, that Jewish prophesyings about the signs which would presage the end of the existing age had struck home and were readily believed. In Antioch, Jews were associated with conflagrations, and this may have been the case in Rome only three years before.[65] As in the persecution of the Christians at Lyons, there were a number of pagan well-wishers who were prepared to stand up to popular clamour until they were convinced by new evidence that the case against the accused was a fair one. Significant, however, is the differing attitude of the Greek and Roman authorities respectively. The Greeks seized on the incident to do what their fellows had tried to do in city after city in Asia Minor, namely to curtail the special privileges enjoyed by the Jews. Now super-loyalists themselves, they asserted that the Jews by their rebellion had forfeited their special status and therefore must sacrifice just as the Greeks were bound to do (ὥσπερ νόμος ἐστὶ τοῖς ᾿Ελλησιν). 'Sacrifice or die.' The choice was soon to have a familiar ring in these same cities.

The Romans, despite the fact that they were engaged in a tremendous struggle with the Jews in Palestine, intervened not only to restore order, but to see that a modicum of justice was granted to the Jewish community. There is no trace of the vindictive attitude displayed by the magistrates of Antioch. Finally, it is clear that the sacrifice test was employed to establish the fact of Judaism. Nearly fifty years later, Pliny's advisers in Bithynia urged the same course and for the same reasons, against the Christians. Supplication with incense to the Emperor's statue and the recitation of prayer to the gods were 'things (which so it was said) those who are really Christians cannot be made to do'. Implicit in both situations was the charge of atheism, and this, when combined with offences which touched the fears and interests of the mob spelt death to Jews and Christians alike in the Hellenistic East.

The contrast between this phrenetic loathing which separated Jew from Greek and the comparatively tolerant official Roman attitude towards the Jews may be further demonstrated by an incident which took place at the end of the siege of Jerusalem. Josephus has narrated one terrible incident after another showing the fantastic lengths to which the ferocity of the fighting was carried,[66] until the Romans at last forced their standards into the remains of the Temple, and acclaimed Titus 'imperator' there. The speech which Titus is then alleged to have made to the Jewish leaders, who had at last surrendered, is full of interest.[67]

We are told that he first 'charged his soldiers to restrain their rage and leave their javelins alone'—there was to be no indiscriminate massacre—such as often took place even after a short victorious siege, like that of Maiden Castle in A.D. 43/44.[68] He then spoke to the Jews in cold and studied terms. They were wholly responsible for the miseries which had now befallen their country. They had behaved like madmen, and they had brought their people, city and 'holy house' to destruction. They had been constantly in rebellion against Rome for the previous century, and yet they had received 'nothing but kindness from the Romans'. The latter had safeguarded for the Jews their land, their autonomy and their ancestral customs. They had allowed them to send tribute to Jerusalem. The Romans had warned them of the consequences of rebellion, but in vain. Even after their treacherous rising, however, Titus was prepared to be merciful. He concluded, 'If you throw down your arms and deliver up your bodies to me, I grant you your lives, and I will act as a mild master of a family; what cannot be healed will be punished. The rest I will preserve for my own use'.

The difference of outlook is striking. At Alexandria and Antioch petty incidents could result in massacres. Titus after three years of the grimmest warfare solemnly assured the rebel leaders that their lives would be spared. Moreover, Rome was to continue to protect the Jews in the practice of their religion despite Greek opposition until the crisis of Hadrian's reign, and then, after this disastrous interlude, resume toleration permanently. Two factors contributed towards maintaining a policy which was later to have repercussions on Rome's handling of Christianity. First, Romans and Jews came into contact originally as allies against the ruling Seleucid overlords of Syria, and secondly, in Rome itself Judaism was never strong enough to be a threat to the life of the city as it was among the scattered Greek communities in the eastern Mediterranean. Judaism was simply one of the multifarious national cults in the city brought thither by foreign immigrants.

The facts of both situations are well known and require only brief mention here. It was in 161 B.C. that Judas Maccabaeus sent an embassy to the Senate to make a treaty of friendship directed against the Seleucids. (i Macc. 8²³).[69] Rome's policy, designed to prevent any one of the Hellenistic kingdoms becoming too powerful, found the Jews an admirable partner. In 139 B.C. Roman friendship was extended to the Jews of the Dispersion (i Macc. 15²²) and the alliance continued to be demonstrated on both sides. Jewish contingents fought for Rome in the Mithradatic War, and in Egypt they fought for the Romans in the Egyptian wars of 55 and 47 B.C.,[70] thus exacerbating enmity with the Greek settlers. Despite Pompey's capture of Jerusalem in 63 B.C., and despite the personal antipathy felt towards them by influential Roman senators such as Flaccus and Cicero, official relations continued good in the last decades of the Republic. In the civil wars between Caesar and Pompey the Palestinian Jews fought valiantly on Caesar's side. As a reward the alliance between them and the Roman people was formally renewed in 46 B.C. and tribute paid to their loyalty.[71] It was again renewed in 42.[72] Finally, in Herod, Rome found an able and trusty if revoltingly cruel ally. So long as strong parties in the Greek cities were hostile to Roman rule, Roman friendship with the Jews was a political necessity.

This fact goes far to explain the remarkable series of rescripts dating to the decade 50–40 B.C., preserved by Josephus, in which Jewish privileges were safeguarded by successive Roman administrations in the teeth of local Greek hostility. Indeed, the tendency of the Romans to favour the Jews at the expense of the Greeks is clearly shown in a rescript of the praetor Caius Julius(?) to the Parians on behalf of the Jews in Delos.[73] In this case, the Jews were described as 'friends and allies' (φίλοι καὶ σύμμαχοι), they were allowed to live according to their customs and the payment of subscriptions 'for common suppers and holy festivals' which the Parians had tried to prevent, were authorized. On the other hand, other θίασοι (synonymous with Bacchanals) were expressly forbidden to meet, and the praetor invoked Caesar's authority in making this order. At about the same time, an embassy from Hyrcanus to Dolabella, the proconsul of Asia, resulted in an unequivocal statement of the privileges of the Jews which were regarded as traditional.[74] 'I do therefore grant them', the decree runs, 'freedom from going into the army, as the former prefects have done, and permit them to use the customs of their fore-fathers, in assembling together for sacred and religious purposes, as their law requires and for collecting oblations necessary for sacrifices, and my will is that you write this to the several cities under your jurisdiction'. These rescripts provided a firm founda-tion for their privileged status in the Empire. They were con-firmed explicitly several times in the case of Jews who were Roman citizens[75]—but not, it appears, for proselytes. These still remained under the law of their own city. Here, the story of Pomponia Graecina is significant.

In Augustus' reign a further crop of rescripts are recorded, protecting the Jews from various injustices and abuse to which their Greek neighbours in the cities of Asia and Cyrenaica were subjecting them. Robbery of Jewish sacred books and money was made punishable as sacrilege.[76]

Even in Palestine, as we have seen, the personal relations between members of the Roman forces and the Jews were not uniformly bad. The story of the centurion in St. Luke's Gospel speaks for itself. Here was a Roman officer of whom the local Jews said 'he loved our nation, and has himself built our synagogue for us', and Jesus' comment was 'Never have I heard such faith, nay, not in Israel' (Lk. 7[9]). The treatment of the unfortunate swineherds from the Greek city of Gadara was different. Indeed, running through the Gospels, and the writings of Philo and

Josephus is the feeling that the Romans, if harsh and exacting masters, were also to be respected for their impartiality and justice. The same could not be said of the Hellenistic rulers and their subjects.

In Rome itself there was a large Jewish community that tended to group itself in an area across the river near the Vatican hill.[77] Immigration had begun, like that of other Mediterranean groups, during the second century B.C., but the community grew very slowly until the autumn of 61 when Pompey returned in triumph from his eastern conquests, bringing a train of captives. According to Philo (Legatio, 23.155) the nucleus of the Jewish community was formed chiefly by enslaved prisoners of war, and perhaps these have left their mark for posterity in the four inscriptions recording the existence of a Συναγωγὴ τῶν 'Εβρέων', forming part of the Jewish colony on the Monteverde.[78] But as Cicero's speech in defence of Flaccus shows, there were many Jews in Rome at this time who were not captives, and the community was prosperous as well as numerous. In 4 B.C., it is recorded that no less than 8000 Jewish residents in Rome greeted the deputation of fifty Jews from Palestine who were coming to the capital with a petition demanding the deposition of Archelaus.[79]

In the city, the Jews were treated as an allied nation and so far as their religious observances were concerned were left much to their own devices. In the same decree of Caius Julius(?) to the Parians, already cited, the praetor draws attention to the fact that 'even at Rome itself' the Jews were allowed 'to live according to their own customs, and to contribute money to common meals and sacred rites'.[80] They were regarded as a separate nation with their own laws and cult, and so long as they did not violate the jurisdiction of the city's gods there was no reason for the authorities to interfere. In return, the attitude of the Roman Jews was loyal, and a group who dedicated a synagogue in Augustus' reign evidently felt no scruples about calling themselves 'Augustesi'.[81] The Emperor in his turn demonstrated good-will towards the Jews by sending gifts to the Jerusalem Temple, and commanding that a burnt offering be made there daily for ever at his expense, in token of his respect to the supreme God of the Jews.[82] Little wonder that the deaths of both Julius Caesar and himself were bitterly lamented by the Roman Jews.

Throughout the Republican period and in the first decades of the Empire clashes between the Roman authorities and the Jews seem to have been very few, and were due to specific offences. Thus, in 139 B.C., we hear of the *praetor peregrinus* Cn. Cornelius Scipio Hispanus,[83] expelling Jews on the ground that 'they were tainting Roman manners with the worship of Jupiter Sabazios'. The men concerned may have been members of the embassy of Simon Maccabaeus who had come to Rome that year, but are more likely to have been residents. The identification of Jahwe with the Anatolian Sabazios is interesting, for Rome was not the only place where the two deities were identified.[84] Secondly, this is the first indication that Jewish proselytism would not be accepted and that those who indulged might be punished. But this seems to have been an isolated incident in a century and a half of normal relations.[85] As the Chaldaeans were also attacked at the same time on the grounds that they might be selling their foreign lore, it would appear that this was merely another example of perennial fears of the influence of 'foreign magic' and manners in Republican Rome.[86]

In the Augustan period the Jews had begun to attract some notice among literary and aristocratic circles in the capital: Aristius Fuscus tells Horace that he cannot discuss private affairs with him as it was the 'thirtieth Sabbath', and he did not want to upset the 'circumcised Jews',[87] and Horace laughs at the Jews for their superstition in believing in 'miracles' like those performed in the Temple of Gnatia where incense was believed to liquefy without being fired.[88] It was, however, out of their contacts with the Roman upper classes that the peace between Roman and Jew was broken. In A.D. 19 Josephus records that a noble Roman lady named Fulvia, the wife of the senator Saturninus, had become a proselyte, and found herself victimized by unscrupulous immigrant Jews.[89] These persuaded her to part with a sum of money and costly fabrics for the Temple of Jerusalem. Somehow or other this incident became connected in the minds of the authorities with some particularly vicious conduct by priests of Isis. So, Jews and Isis-worshippers found themselves the victims of an impartial justice directed against cults whose representatives misbehaved. Tacitus states that 'action was taken to expel Egyptian and Jewish rites', and that the Senate decreed that four thousand of the freedman class (*libertini generis*) who were tainted with this superstition and whose age was suitable, should be transported to Sardinia to suppress bandits there—and if they perished through the bad climate, the loss would not be severe.[90] Suetonius adds the detail that the followers of 'this superstition' (he does not say, whether Jewish or Egyptian) were forced to burn vestments and religious paraphernalia as well.[91] Tacitus says in addition, that others were ordered to leave Italy by a certain day if they had not in the meantime abandoned their profane rites.

The interest of these accounts is first, that the Jews were treated on a par with any other foreign religion—in this case Egyptian worshippers of Isis. There is no special outcry of 'sacrilege', such as would certainly have been raised in a Greek city. Secondly, deportation seems to be the normal punishment for members of a recalcitrant community, and the case of Priscilla and Aquila under Claudius (Acts 18[2]) therefore had its precedent. Further, the repression did not last long. Probably after the fall of Sejanus in October 31, the Jews were restored to their previous rights in Rome.

Even so, the situation was beginning to change. In Sejanus the Jews had been confronted by a determined and powerful enemy imbued with a fanaticism like that found in the Hellenistic world.[92] This was to be repeated in the person of Caligula a few years later. Underlying the apparent goodwill which the Jews enjoyed there had for long existed a current of hostility against them. Cicero's denunciation of them during his defence of Flaccus could not have been wholly isolated: 'Even while Jerusalem was standing, and the Jews were at peace with us, the practice of their sacred rites was at variance with the glory of our empire, the dignity of our name, and the customs of our ancestors.'[93] This is an interesting statement for even allowing for its *ex parte* character, it shows that under pressure, the Roman ruling class might be expected to come to the same conclusions about the Jews as their Greek counterparts.

Meantime, in Palestine the ten-year rule of another unsympathetic administrator, the procurator Pontius Pilate,[94] showed that there too the old friendship was beginning to wear thin. Jewish nationalist pressure against 'idolatry' had begun to assert itself. Despite official goodwill, the time was not far off when an exasperated Roman soldier would be throwing the Scrolls from a village synagogue into the fire.[95] The Jews were regarded as at heart revolutionary,[96] and Rome was finding it as difficult to conciliate them as the Seleucids had in their day. By 33 the fear of a national Jewish uprising under a king of the Jews had become a reality. This deep-seated anxiety was echoed by Philo in 39/40, when he pointed to the vast numbers and extent of the Jewish nation and put into the mouths of Petronius' Council the impossibility of the military situation 'if these vast hordes' should rise against Rome.[97] The shift of Roman interest and sentiment away from the Jews was already taking place in the reign of Tiberius.

This process was to be assisted by the series of incidents in Egypt and Palestine between A.D. 38 and 41. These demonstrated both the incompatibility of Romano-Jewish friendship with the Imperial cult, and the fact that in the East Rome's interests lay ultimately with the Greek settlers rather than with their Jewish enemies. It was characteristic that trouble should start in Alexandria. There, as Josephus states, Jews and Greeks had been on bad terms for as long as could be remembered.[98] The Jews had always been numerous in the city, and by 38 they occupied two entire quarters, while there were Jewish families scattered about in other parts.[99] To instinctive dislikes were added economic and political grievances. The Jews were to some extent rivals of the Greeks in commerce, some were engaged in profitable tax-farming,[100] and their loyalty to the Romans had been rewarded by the confirmation of existing privileges and the grant of their own senate (γερουσία).[101] But they did not possess Alexandrian citizenship, which the Greeks kept jealously for themselves; and among these Greeks was an extremist group who equated anti-Semitism and anti-Romanism, and were prepared to go to all lengths to satisfy their hatreds.[102] Indeed, Alexandria represented in an extreme form a situation which had been arising all over the Hellenistic East, where in the previous century Jews and Romans found themselves in alliance against a partially dispossessed ruling aristocracy of Greeks or Hellenized natives.

In the summer of 38, the extremists were in power and had their chance of making trouble. King Agrippa chose to travel via Alexandria to take up his new kingdom in northern Palestine which Caligula had granted him nearly eighteen months earlier. His arrival in the city was the signal for enthusiastic demonstrations by the Jews.[103] The Greeks, however, replied by dressing up a well-known local idiot in mock-royal state and escorting him through the town to the shouts of 'Marin, Marin'—the Syrian for 'King'.[104] They then proceeded to demand that the Emperor's images should be placed in the synagogues,[105] just as Caligula himself was to order in Palestine fifteen months later. The prefect, Aulus Avillius Flaccus, caught in a web of intrigue, and fearing for his own safety was prepared to make a bargain with them.[106] An edict was published declaring the Jews 'aliens and intruders',[107] and a pogrom broke out, the description of which in all its horrible details has been left to us by Philo.[108]

Though Flaccus was arrested and banished in the autumn of 38, the Jews do not seem to have secured much redress. A year later, both they and the Greeks sent an embassy to Caligula, which Philo describes in his *Legatio*. When the Emperor eventually deigned to grant them an audience, probably in the early summer of 40, he spared no pains to show his contempt and hostility towards the Jews. The *volte-face* was a terrible blow, for the Alexandrian Jews had hitherto been punctiliously[109] and probably sincerely loyal to the Imperial House, and now felt the ground cut away from under them. The second and more formal interview held in the gardens of Lamia on the Esquiline, sometime after 31 August when Caligula had received his ovation, was represented by Philo as a farce.[110] It is difficult to see that the Jews accomplished anything.

Meantime, affairs in Palestine were also going badly for the Jews.[111] During the winter of 39/40 the Jews in Jamnia destroyed an altar which the Greek minority had erected, with the express purpose, according to Philo, of annoying the Jews.[112] The news of the incident reached Caligula and he instructed that as a punishment a colossal gilded statue of himself should be made and erected in the Temple. Caligula's exaggeration of the Imperial cult in his own favour, and his hostility to the Jews for not respecting it, entailed a major shift in Roman policy in the Mediterranean, for these resembled the acts of a Seleucid king more than Roman tradition. The violence of the Jewish reaction showed what the results of such a shift might be. Fortunately, the old friendship between the Roman and Jewish reigning houses was just strong enough for Agrippa to avert the crisis by persuading Caligula to rescind his order. On 24 January 41 he was assassinated.

The Alexandrian Jews on hearing the news of Caligula's death rose against the Greeks,[113] calling in their compatriots from the rest of Egypt and Syria as allies. Order, however, was restored by the Prefect of Egypt. The stage was set for a settlement. First, Claudius dispatched an edict restoring to the Jews the rights they possessed before 37, including religious liberty, but making no reference to their claims to Alexandrian citizenship.[114] Both sides then sent embassies to Rome. Nominally, the delegates were congratulating Claudius on his accession. In fact, it was a trial of strength between Jew and Greek, with perhaps severe penalties for the loser. Claudius, as revealed in the letter which he sent to Alexandria towards the end of 41,[115] was rigorously fair. Both sides were heard. Claudius' decision deals first with a number of administrative matters, and mentions his own rejection of divine honours, which must have cheered the Jews, and so too, his decision that the creation of an Alexandrian Senate must depend on the Prefect's decision—and this was to wait 160 years![116]

Then, the Emperor comes to the main issue. 'As to the question which of you were responsible for the riot and feud (or rather, if the truth must be told) the war ("τῆς δὲ πρὸς 'Ιουδαίους ταραχῆς καὶ στάσεως μάλλον δ' εἰ χρὴ τὸ ἀληθὲς εἰπεῖν τοῦ πολέμου") against the Jews, I was unwilling to commit myself to a decided judgment.'[117] 'But,' he goes on, 'I tell you plainly that if you do not desist from this baneful and obstinate mutual hostility, I shall perforce be compelled to show what a benevolent prince can be when turned to just indignation.' Then, he turns to the Jews. He refers to them as 'profiting by what they possess and enjoying bounteous wealth in a city not their own'. However, their privileges and customs, confirmed by Augustus, would also be confirmed now, but they were not to behave as though they lived in a separate city from the Alexandrians, sending two distinct embassies to him. At this point, the Emperor suddenly shows his feelings. The Jews 'are not to introduce or invite other Jews who sail down to Alexandria from Syria or Egypt, thus compelling me to conceive the greater suspicion; otherwise, I will by all means take vengeance on them ("καθάπερ κοινήν τεινα (*sic*) τῆς οἰκου-μένης νόσον ἐξεγείροντας") as fomenting a general plague for the whole world'.[118] 'The general plague'. This could mean a disorder.[119] The Emperor's suspicion that the Jews could be a menace to the whole Roman world was apparent, and out-weighed all sentiments based on previous friendship. The Greek oligarchies could be a nuisance, but the Jews were seen as a chal-lenge and a possible enemy. So too, were the Christians to be in their turn.[120] The effect of the Imperial cult and Rome's involve-ment in the affairs of the Hellenistic world had reached its logical conclusion. Whatever he might intend, Claudius was 'god' as well as emperor in the provinces.[121] It was now the 'Greco-Roman world', with no secure place for the Jewish theocracy. This was the moment at which the Christian Church enters the stage of history. For its future relations with the Roman Empire it could scarcely have been a worse one.

NOTES

[1] Cicero (ed. L. Lord) *Pro Flacco* 25.61. On the 'Asiatic Vespers', M. Cary, *History of Rome*, 333. In general, H. Guite, 'Cicero's attitude to the Greeks', *Greece and Rome*, 2nd. ser. ix.2, 1962, 142–159.

[2] Ibid., 24.57–8. Note also Sallust's caustic, 'Neque litteras Graecas didici, parum placebat eas discere, quippe quae ad virtutem doctoribus nihil profuerant', *Jugurtha* 85.32. and *Livy*, ix.18.6, reproaching the 'levissimi ex Graecis "for praising Parthians at the expense of Romans" '.

[3] *Orac. Sibyll.* (ed. Geffcken), iii.350–62. Dating and identification, J. Geffcken, 'Komposi-tion und Entstehungszeit der Oracula Sibyllina', *T.U.*, N.F. viii, 1902, 8–9.

[4] Note, F. Cumont's dictum, 'L'Asie vaincue par les armes étrangères, continua à lutter pour la suprématie à coups d'oracles', in 'La Fin du monde selon les mages occidentaux', *R.H.R.*, 103, 193, 172. For the later Empire, see Lactantius, *Instit.* vii.15.11.

[5] Timagenes, in F. Jacoby, *F. Gr. Hist.* IIA. no. 88, T. 8 (*ap.* Seneca, *epp.* 91.13). Note also the activities of the philosopher Aristion at the siege of Athens in 87 B.C. See H. Fuchs, *Der geistige Widerstand gegen Rom*, Leipzig, 1938, p. 14.

[6] F. de Visscher. *Les Edits d'Auguste découverts à Cyrène*, 76, referring to Edict No. 1, lines 10ff. See H. Last's comment in *JRS.*, xxxv, 1945, 93.

[7] For a fundamental study of the religious concepts implicit in the Polis, A. A. T. Ehrhardt, *Politische Metaphysik von Solon bis Augustin*, Tübingen, 1959, especially chs. 1–3.

[8] A. A. T. Ehrhardt, op. cit., ch. iii, Excursus.

[9] For instance, Clement, *Strom.* vii.1.4 (ed. and tr. Oulton and Chadwick). 'An atheist is one who does not believe in the existence of God.' Also, Josephus, *Contra Apionem*, ii.38, '(Socrates) neither betrayed his city to the enemy, nor was he guilty of sacrilege with regard to the temples, but on this account, that he swore certain new oaths ... was condemned to drink poison'. *Sacrilegium* is, on the other hand, defined by Cicero (*De*

Legibus ii, 16.40–1). 'Sacrilego poena est, neque ei soli, qui sacrum abstulerit sed etiam ei, quo sacro commendatum', in either case, material acts rather than thoughts; see also, Apuleius, *Metam.*, ix.14, 'deos destruere', art. Pfaff, 'Sacrilegium' in *PW*, and A. B. Drachmann, *Atheism in Pagan Antiquity*, Gyldendal, 1922.

[10] Minucius Felix, *Octavius*, 8, 2–3, Athenagoras, *Legatio* 4 (who narrates, however, that Diagoras chopped up a statue of Heracles to boil his turnips). Cf. A. Harnack, 'Der Vorwurf des Atheismus in der antiken Welt', *T.U.*, N.F. xiii. 4, 1905, 11. In contrast, Socrates is represented on mosaics and gems with other philosophers. On the Apamea mosaic he is seated in a place of honour in the centre. (See G. M. A. Richter, 'Engraved Gems in Cambridge', *Coll. Latomus*, 44, 1960, 671 and Pl. XLV.)

[11] Plutarch, *Amatorius*, 13.756 A, D; cited from T. R. Glover, *The Conflict of Religions*, 76.

[12] The ruler, Antiochus I, was styled 'βασιλεύς [μέ]γας, θεὸς δίκαιος[ἐπι]φανής'; cf. M. Rostovtzeff, 'Dura and the Problem of Parthian Art', *Yale Class. Studies*, v. 1935, 175, and A. D. Nock, *Harvard Studies in Classical Philology*, 41, 1930, 27. Recent excavations by Theresa Goell are to be published.

[13] Note *inter alia* the examples of Greek contempt for the peoples of Asia Minor among whom they had settled (*Pro Flacco*, 27.65–6).

[14] Note W. M. Calder's remarks on the strict relationship of the Phrygian language, as shown by inscriptions, with the boundaries of the Phrygian province, *M.A.M.A.*, vii, pp. ix–xvi. For discussion of the traditional material, see K. Holl, 'Das Fortleben der Volksprachen in Klein-Asien in der nachchristlichen Zeit', *Hermes* xliii, 1908, 240–54.

[15] Socrates, *Ecc. Hist.*, iv.28 (see below, p. 291).

[16] Philo, *Legatio*, 166, 'Αἰγύπτιοι, πονηρὰ σπέρματα'.'

[17] Josephus, *Wars*, vii.3.3 (45).

[18] Josephus, *Antiq.*, 10.23(259) (Sardes) 'οἱ κατοικοῦντες ἡμῶν ἐν τῇ πόλει ἀπαρχῆς Ἰουδαῖοι πολῖται'. (On πολῖται, see R. Marcus's note, Josephus, *Jewish Antiquities*, vii, 587). Roman traders in the Akmonia area are called οἱ κατοικοῦντες Ῥωμαῖοι, *CIG.*, 3874. For the casual nature of παροικεσία, note the reference to villagers from Busiris 'παροικοῦσι ταῖς πυραμίσι'. (*OGI.*, 666, line 12).

[19] Philostratus, *Vita Apollonii* (ed. F. C. Conybeare), v.33.

[20] Josephus, *Contra Apionem*, ii.17.

[21] H. S. Jones's definition in *JRS.*, xvi, 1926, 27. See the exhaustive studies by E. Ziebarth in *PW.*, xxi.2.1401–2 and W. Ruppel, 'Politeuma', *Philologus*, lxxxii, 1926–27, 268–312 and 433–54. For politeuma = politeia, see the Boulé Papyrus (*P.S.I.*, 1160), 1.5, 'ἐλασσῶσι καὶ τὸ π[ο]λίτευμα τῶν Αχεξανδρείων' (ed. H. Musurillo, *The Acts of the Pagan Martyrs*, p. 1).

[22] *BGU.*, iv, 1151, 7–8 'διὰ τοῦ τῶν Ἰουδαίων ἀρχείου' (13 B.C.). For a thorough description of the economic and social position occupied by the Jews of Alexandria, see V. A. Tcherikover and A. Fuks *Corpus Papyrorum Judaicarum*, Harvard, 1957, i, 48–93.

[23] Cited by Josephus, *Antiquities*, xiv.7.2 (117). See E. M. Smallwood (ed.) *Legatio ad Gaium* (Leiden, 1961), 5–6 and E. R. Goodenough, *The Jurisprudence of the Jewish Courts in Egypt*, 1929, 15–18.

[24] Josephus, *Contra Apionem*, ii.6.1, and for the same reproach against Christians, Tertullian, *Apol.*, 24.1, 'nec Romani habemur, qui non Romanorum deum colimus'.

[25] C. H. Roberts, T. C. Skeat and A. D. Nock, 'The Guild of Zeus Hypsistos', *HTR.*, 29, 1936, 39ff. There is an interesting example of this apparent syncretism from a statue base found at Chersonesos in Crete (Heracleon Museum, Catalogue No. 231) τερτυλα Θεῷ | ὑψίστῳ | εὐχης accompanied, however, by an eagle with outstretched wings; surely in this case, Zeus.

[26] W. O. E. Oesterley, 'The Cult of Sabazios', *The Labyrinth*, 1935, 115–58; cf. F. Cumont, *CRAI.*, 1906, 63ff.

[27] iii Sybill. 195; cf. Roms. 2[19] on Jewish claims in the first century A.D.

[28] Josephus, *Wars*, vii.3.3(45). Proselytes in Rome, H. Leon, *The Jews of Ancient Rome*, Philadelphia, 1960, 254–6.

[29] Josephus, *Contra Apionem* ii.29.

[30] Cicero, *Pro Flacco*, iv. 9–10.

[31] Though in fact not often read outside Jewish and proselyte circles.

[32] One of Josephus' main arguments against Apion in *Contra Apionem*, i, especially 1.7–8.

[33] Note Cicero, *De Legibus*, ii.16.40, 'Et profecto ita est, ut id habendum sit antiquissimum et deo proximum, quod sit optimum'.

[34] Josephus, *Contra Apionem* 1.34(311); cf. ii.2(27) (Sabbath = Sabbo or the Egyptian for a bubo of the groin!) for other dialectic defences against Judaism.

[35] Josephus, *Contra Apionem* ii.39 (282–3).

[36] *OGI.*, 742, 'θεῶι [με]γάλωι ἐ[πηκό]ωι . . .', A. D. Nock, *Conversion*, 61–2.

[37] Josephus, *Contra Apionem*, ii.10(123).

[38] Tacitus, *Hist.*, v.5.3.

[39] Josephus, *Wars*, ii.16.4(398); cf. ibid., vii.3.3(43).

[40] A. Deissmann, *St. Paul*, 41. Since he wrote in the early years of this century many more traces of Jewish communities in the Mediterranean lands have been found, particularly at Ostia and Stobi. See also W. M. Ramsay, *Cities and Bishoprics*, chs. xv and xvi, and arts. in *Expositor*, 1902, 1904 and 1906.

[41] Africa. P. Monceaux, 'Les Colonies juives dans l'Afrique romaine'. *Rev. des Etudes juives*, 44, 1902, 1ff. (still the best statement).

[42] Josephus, *Antiquities*, xv.2.2(14).

[43] Philo, *Legatio*, 282.

[44] In *Flaccum*, 43; cf. A. Harnack, *Mission*, 5–6. Is the Jewish rejection of the practice of exposing infants sufficient in itself to explain the high birth-rate?

[45] Josephus, *Wars*, ii.20.2(559–61).

[46] Josephus, *Contra Apionem*, 1.22(161–2).

[47] iv Sibyll. 165—converts having bath of purification only. For outright apostacy, see *CIG.*, 9897 (Smyrna) οἱ πότε 'Ιουδαῖοι. Comparative laxity of Phrygian Jews in the first century A.D., W. M. Ramsay, *Cities and Bishoprics*, 675. Apostacies in Alexandria shown by the polemic against backsliders in Wisd., 1–5.

[48] See A. D. Nock, *Conversion*, 63–4.

[49] See H. Leclercq's art. in *DACL.*, vi.2, 2945–6.

[50] iii Macc. 7⁵. See above, ch. II, p. 42.

[51] Philo, *Legatio*, 200, the Greeks there were, 'τινες ἀλλόφυλοι παρεισφθαρέντες ἀπὸ τῶν πλησιοχώρων . . .'. Note too, the behaviour of the Jews to their neighbours when they gained the upper hand (Esther 9¹ff·).

[52] Cf. Apollonius Molon cited by Josephus, *Contra Apionem*, ii.14.

[53] Cf. *In Flaccum*, 47.

[54] Josephus, *Antiquities*, xiv.10.214, 241, 242, 245, 258, 264.

[55] Ibid., xvi.6.1(160–1).

[56] Josephus, *Wars*, ii.18.7 (Alexandria).

[57] Ibid., ii.18.1—riots and massacres in the towns of Palestine and Phoenicia in 66.

[58] Philo, *Legatio*, 200.

[59] Josephus, *Wars*, ii.13.7 and 14.4. (Whiston ed.)

[60] Ibid., ii.18.4.

[61] Ibid., ii.18.5.

[62] Ibid., ii.18.5, Philo, *Legatio*, 205.

[63] *In Flaccum*, 45ff.

[64] Josephus, *Wars*, vii.3.3–4. For a second, somewhat similar affair at Alexandria at this time, Josephus, ibid., ii.17.7–8, though here the legionaries showed themselves less impartial than at Antioch.

[65] On the association of Jews and Christians with conflagrations at this period see the learned but somewhat perverse article by L. Herrmann, 'Quels chrétiens ont incendié Rome?', Rev. Belge de Philologie, 27.2, 1949, 637ff.

[66] Josephus, Wars, v.11.1 (Whiston).

[67] Josephus, Wars, vi.6.2 (327ff.).

[68] For the Maiden Castle massacre, see R. E. M. Wheeler, Maiden Castle, Dorset (Reports of the Research Committee of the Society of Antiquaries of London, No. xii), Oxford, 1943, 61–2.

[69] Also, Josephus, Antiquities, xii.10.6(416–19). Literature to 1939 is cited by R. Marcus in Appendix J to his edition of Antiquities xii–xiv (Vol. vii of the Loeb edition of Josephus, Antiquities). There seems to be no good reason to doubt the existence of this early treaty, though some scholars have been sceptical. See, E. Bevan, CAH., viii, 519.

[70] Josephus, Antiquities, xiii.10.4(284–7) and ibid., xiv.6.2(99). See, H. I. Bell, 'Juden und Griechen im römischen Alexandreia' Beiheft zum Alten Orient, Heft, 9, Leipzig, 1926, 9–10 and 50.

[71] Josephus, Antiquities, xiv.10(211–12).

[72] Josephus, Antiquities, xiv.10.9(217).

[73] Discussed by J. Juster, along with the other rescripts cited by Josephus, Les Juifs sous l'Empire romain 1.132ff. Josephus, Antiquities, xiv.10.8(213–16). The praetor's name is uncertain. For the discovery of a Jewish synagogue at Delos, dating to the first century B.C., with inscriptions dedicated to θεῷ 'υψίστῳ, see A. Plassart, 'La Synagogue juive de Delos', Mel. Holleaux, 1913, 201–15. One of the dedicants actually came from Paros (No. 4, p. 206), and whatever the precise constitutional position, the links between the Jews in Paros and those in Delos seem to have been very close.

[74] Josephus, ibid., xiv.10.12(226).

[75] Josephus, Antiquities, xiv.10.228, 232, 234, 235, and 237.

[76] Josephus, Antiquities, xvi.6(160–73).

[77] The standard work is now H. J. Leon, The Jews of Ancient Rome, Philadelphia, 1960 —very detailed, if inclined to be uncritically favourable to the Jews. See also, G. La Piana, 'Foreign Groups in Rome during the First Centuries of the Empire', HTR., 20, 1927, especially pp. 341–93.

[78] Details in Leon, op. cit., 147.

[79] Josephus, Antiquities, xvii.11.1(300–1) and Wars, ii.6.1(80). Leon, op. cit., 135, suggests a Jewish population in Rome of about 40,000 at this time.

[80] Josephus, Antiquities, xiv.10(214) 'τοῦτο ποιεῖν αὐτῶν μηδ' 'εν 'Ρώμη κεκωλυμένων.'

[81] Six inscriptions mentioning this synagogue have been found. Leon, op. cit., 142, considers it to have been named in honour of Augustus who may even have been patron to the community. Some inscriptions from the Ostia synagogue begin, 'Pro Salute Aug . . . '.

[82] Philo, Legatio, 157–8.

[83] T. R. S. Broughton, The Magistrates of the Roman Republic, New York, 1951, 1.482 (references), and on the significance of the events of 139 B.C., H. Last, 'The Study of the "Persecutions" ', 86–7.

[84] Note L. Herrmann's view (Nouvelle Clio 1953, 64) that there was a real apprehension at this time of oriental influences traducing the national religion. The rites of Sabazios were suspect at this time on moral grounds—Cicero, De Legibus, ii.37.

[85] See W. O. E. Oesterley, 'The Cult of Sabazios', The Labyrinth, 1935, 115–58.

[86] Valerius Maximus, i.3.3, 'ne peregrinam scientiam venditarent'.

[87] Horace, Satires, 1.9.67–72. 'curtis Iudaeis'—slightly contemptuous.

[88] Horace, Satires, 1.4.140–3. 'Let the Jew Apella believe that. I won't.'

[89] Josephus, Antiquities, xviii.3.5 (81–4.)

[90] Tacitus, Annales, ii.85.4.

[91] Suetonius, *Tiberius*, 36. It is interesting, though perhaps a coincidence that in vi Satire Juvenal discusses Judaism immediately after the worship of Isis in Rome (vi.529–47).

[92] Philo, *Legatio*, 159–60.

[93] Cicero, *Pro Flacco*, 28.69.

[94] Philo, *Legatio*, 38, 299–305.

[95] Josephus, *Antiquities*, xx.4(113–17). *Wars*, ii.12(228–31). Cf. E. M. Smallwood, 'Some Comments on Tacitus, *Annales*, xii.54', *Latomus*, 18, 1959, 561.

[96] Note the words put into Titus' mouth by Josephus, *Wars*, vi.6.2. 'You (Jews) who have from the first since Pompey reduced you by force, never ceased from revolution.'

[97] Philo, *Legatio*, 214–15.

[98] Josephus, *Wars*, ii.18.7. See U. Wilcken, 'Zum alexandrinischen Antisemitismus', *Abh. Kön. Sachs. Gesellschaft der Wissenschaften*, lvii, 1909, 783–839.

[99] Philo, *In Flaccum*, viii.55. See H. I. Bell, *Jews and Christians in Egypt*, Oxford, 1924, 10ff.

[100] U. Wilcken, *Griechische Ostraka aus Aegypten und Nubien*, Leipzig and Berlin, 1899, i, 523–4 (ostraka of second century B.C.).

[101] On this question, H. I. Bell, loc. cit., 1, and E. M. Smallwood, ed. *Legatio*, 6.

[102] As shown by the Alexandrian, *Acts of the Pagan Martyrs*, *Acta Alexandrinorum* (ed. H. Musurillo, Oxford, 1954) especially, Texts V–Vʙ (Pp. 18–31).

[103] For the sequence of events see E. M. Smallwood, op. cit., 14ff.

[104] *In Flaccum*, vi.36–40.

[105] *In Flaccum*, 41 'ἀνεβόησαν ἀφ' ἑνὸς συνθήματος εἰκόνας ἐν ταῖς προσευχαῖς ἀνατιθέναι'.

[106] See E. M. Smallwood, loc. cit., 15–17. H. I. Bell, *Jews and Christians*.

[107] *In Flaccum*, vii.54. 'τίθησι πρόγραμμα, δι' οὗ ξένους καὶ επήλυδας ἡμᾶς ἀπεκάλει'.

[108] *In Flaccum*, vii.44ff.

[109] Note Philo's emphasis on the Jewish veneration (ὁρμητήρια) for the Augustan house (*In Flaccum*, vii.49) and the fact that Jewish workshops were closed as a sign of mourning for Drusilla (died 10 June 38), ibid., viii.56.

[110] Philo, *Legatio*, 351ff.

[111] The chronology of the Palestinian incidents has been ably worked out by Miss Smallwood in her 'The Chronology of Gaius' attempt to desecrate the Temple', *Latomus*, xvi, 1957, 3–17. Also op. cit., 31ff.

[112] *Legatio*, 200.

[113] Josephus, *Antiquities*, xix.5.2(278).

[114] Ibid., xix.5.2(280–5).

[115] Published there in November 41. See for the text and detailed commentary, H. I. Bell, *Jews and Christians*, 21ff. Also, the valuable art. H. S. Jones, 'Claudius and the Jewish Question at Alexandria', *JRS.*, xvi, 1926, 17–35.

[116] The Alexandrians did not get their Senate until 202.

[117] *Letter*, lines 73ff. Bell, op. cit., 25.

[118] *Letter*, lines 96–100. Bell, op. cit., 25.

[119] Philo uses νόσος in this sense, *Legatio*, 145. For detailed discussion, Smallwood, op. cit., 228–9. In any event, Claudius was no philosemite (see Tcherikover and Fuks, op. cit., 73–4).

[120] Cf. Acts 17⁶ and 24⁵.

[121] His refusal of divine honours was nullified by his own officials in Egypt, who called upon the inhabitants to reverence 'τὴν μεγαλειότητα τοῦ θεοῦ ἡμῶν καίσαρος'. For the temple dedicated to Claudius in distant Camalodunum, Tacitus, *Ann.*, xiv.31, and one dedicated to 'Claudius, the god', in Cys in Caria (*Bull. Corresp. Hell.*, xi, 1887, 307). In general, H. I. Bell, op. cit., 5–8.

CHAPTER SIX

The Church and the World to A.D. 70

IN 41 the Christian Church was hardly a cloud on the horizon
of the Greco-Roman East. But for a number of extraordinary
circumstances, it might have lingered on in the obscurity of
Galilee as it was later believed that Jesus' relatives had done.[1]
Immediately after the Crucifixion it seems that Peter and the
other disciples returned to Galilee in response to Jesus' words
recorded in Mk. 14[28] and the command of the angel, Mk. 16[7].
There, however, Peter may well have had the vision narrated in
Jn. 21, and as a sequel, the disciples went back to Jerusalem and
awaited the Lord's return there.

This step was to be of the greatest importance, and in some
ways it was unexpected. While one Jewish tradition represented
in the Prophets and continued in ii Macc. 2[17-18] looked forward
to the final gathering of Israel in Jerusalem to await the Day of
the Lord,[2] another at this moment almost as powerful, had
pointed to the wilderness as the place of this event. This tradition
is represented in the preaching of John the Baptist as recorded in
all four Gospels (Mt. 3[2], Mk. 1[3], Lk. 3[4-6], Jn. 1[23]) and in the
Scrolls,[3] and it was to persist for another two centuries among
the more eschatologically-minded Christians.[4] Its literal acceptance, however, would soon have spelt ruin to those who obeyed
it. By A.D. 70 Qumran had been abandoned and its adherents
lost to sight, until they were resurrected by the archaeologist's
spade nearly 1900 years later. Not so, the disciples in Jerusalem.
There, they were at the centre of the Jewish world where they
could truly 'go out after the lost sheep of the house of Israel', and
if they so willed, the lost sheep of the Dispersion.

It was the presence of the latter in Jerusalem during the Passover
that launched the Christian mission. The experience of Pentecost
was followed by the formation of an organized congregation and
by the emergence of the Seven. All these bore Greek names and
one, Nicolaus, was a proselyte. This immediately represented a

151

challenge to the Jewish authorities at Jerusalem. It is clear that the latter had no serious objection to the disciples forming their own synagogue, particularly as, we are told, 'they were assiduous in the Temple' (Acts 2⁴⁶), that is, they were not as heterodox even as the Essenes at this stage. But the attraction of Hellenistic Jews resident in Jerusalem to the new body complicated matters. Among these Jews there was already a tendency to question the usefulness of the ceremonial observances prescribed by the Law. Stephen's onslaught on the whole conservative outlook of official Judaism caused tumult among his fellow Hellenistic Jews (Acts 6⁹)⁵ and roused the Temple authorities to action. It also embarrassed the Jerusalem Christians, for up to this time these had tended to emphasize those elements in Jesus' teaching which united them with their fellow Jews. Stephen demonstrated that the Sanhedrin may have been right after all. The Law had failed to achieve its object: Jesus had repudiated it. The building of Solomon's temple was a denial of the true nature of God.⁶ The Jews had murdered the prophets, and now had murdered Jesus, the greatest of them all. Acceptance of Jesus as Messiah involved a complete break with the existing rulers of Israel. This was too much. The pro-Jerusalem elements among the resident Dispersion Jews found themselves on the same side as the conservative Sadducaic priesthood; always on the watch for outbreaks of religious enthusiasm. Stephen was lynched. The first Christian martyr had given his witness. The date is *circa* A.D. 37.

The effect of Stephen's martyrdom, however, was not what his enemies expected. His followers among the Hellenistic Jews fled from Jerusalem, but began to evangelize farther afield. In the south, Philip preached around Gaza and the frontiers of Egypt. In the north, Christians made the Word known in Samaria, Antioch and even Cyprus (Acts 11¹⁹). Though the original disciples had not been molested, they too began to move out of the city, particularly as news of the success of the Gospel message in Samaria reached them (Acts 8¹⁴ᶠᶠ·). In this also Peter took the lead, first in Samaria and then in the coast towns. His baptism of the centurion Cornelius (Acts 10) was a momentous step. Official Judaism was challenged from now on not merely regarding Jesus' claims to be Messiah, but whether under the new covenant a man might be admitted to the Way without submitting himself to the food laws and circumcision. At Caesarea, Christianity was in full contact with the pagan world. Soon it spread to Damascus and Antioch, where perhaps the Christians formed their own synagogue, that of the χριστιανοί.[7] There was now no question of not 'going into the way of the Gentiles' (Mt. 10⁵).[8] Finally, Stephen's death raised questions in the minds of men like Saul the Pharisee who were already wondering whether the Law was the final answer to sinful man's quest for reconciliation with God. His 'threatenings and slaughters' against the Christians ended abruptly on the road to Damascus.

Paul's inner struggle expressed something of the inner struggles of Judaism itself at this very time. How could its claims to universality be reconciled with the narrower concept of the religion of Israel? Did the Messiah imply earthly deliverance from Rome? Above all, was Torah the complete Way of the Lord? Some, like Paul's contemporary Philo, suppressed their doubts by adopting Stoic and Platonic ideals and then by means of free allegorical interpretation of the LXX absorbing these into a renewed and purified Judaism. Adam became synonymous with Reason as the foundation of human activity,[9] Sarah and Hagar the equivalent of 'virtue'[10] and 'sound education'.[11] But Philo was head and shoulders above his contemporaries, and his influence outside Alexandria is uncertain. To minds like Paul's, a more direct approach was necessary. Sarah and Hagar were not personifications of the means of virtuous living, but 'the two covenants',[12] one from Mount Sinai, betokening bondage, the other of Jerusalem, symbolizing freedom, and her children, the 'children of promise'. The autobiographical chapters of Romans show Paul struggling with the problem of Torah. If there were no Law, there would be no sin. The Law could not save mankind from sin. 'I had not known sin but for the Law. For I had not known lust except for the Law had said "thou shalt not covet". I was alive without the Law once, but when the commandment came sin revived and I died' (Roms. 7⁹). The Law 'ordained to life I found to be death' (Roms. 7¹⁰). The Law therefore could bring salvation neither to him nor to Israel nor the Gentile world. Man's last hope had gone unless some new intervention by God came to the rescue.[13] The crisis came at the very moment when he had been sent by the Sanhedrin on special mission to arrest

Christians in Damascus. It was probably a sudden, blinding intuition that the condemned criminal was in reality the Anointed One of God, and that henceforth he must preach him. This involved a complete change of outlook, for the old bottles of the Law would not hold the new wine of Christ Crucified.

Others, equally sincere, thought differently. Many believed that the first necessity for the coming of God's kingdom was the cleansing of Israel and the expulsion of the Roman idolator. The Dead Sea community, to whom Christianity may owe something of its organization and liturgy at this period,[14] continued to believe in a Warrior Messiah of the House of David who would do this work. As we have seen,[15] they abominated the Romans. To such men abatement of the Law in favour of idolators, such as Roman centurions, would be abhorrent. They shared the views of the Zealots on the inevitability of war with Rome, and these, if the hints dropped by Paul about his own early 'zeal' in the cause of the Law may be trusted, were not favourable to the Christians. These men, to whom the Day of the Lord was to see the literal overthrow of idolatry, would add their weight to the forces of conservatism, orthodoxy and privilege that had opposed Jesus' teaching.

Thus Christianity came at a moment when the internal stresses affecting Judaism were already acute. These it exacerbated by offering the Jew a solution from which, however, he recoiled.[16] The Cross was too great a scandal. The blasphemy of the new teaching must therefore be repressed. The tradition preserved in the Synoptics is of trials to be faced before 'Sanhedrins and synagogues', at which grave hour the Christian was promised the aid of the Holy Spirit (Mt. 10[17-20]). The 'governors and kings' too, may be interpreted as local Jewish officials and rulers, and not necessarily the Roman authorities. Persecution in the first three decades after the Crucifixion was fratricidal clash between rival groups of Jews, and this element continued to be represented strongly until at least the end of the second century. The Roman authorities were only indirectly concerned. So long as public order was maintained the Jews could dispute about the Law to their hearts' content (Acts 19[15]). Not until 64, when the conflagration at Rome forced Nero to find his scapegoat among those whom popular opinion associated with the fiery extinction of the world, does the Empire take cognisance of the new religion that had arisen in Palestine.⌐

At first, it seemed that the battle-ground between Jew and Christian would continue to be Palestine. Arrived from Alexandria in 41, Herod Agrippa had gone out of his way to show himself to be a zealous upholder of the Law. He made Jerusalem his centre, and 'not a day passed without his offering prescribed sacrifices'.[17] It was probably intolerance born of excessive zeal that led him to turn on the Christians early in 44. 'He killed James the brother of John with the sword. And when he saw it pleased the Jews he proceeded further to take Peter also' (Acts 12[2-3]). Peter's miraculous escape was due partly to the fact that it was Easter, and action was being delayed until the end of the feast. Once more, the conservative forces in Jerusalem had taken the lead against the Christians.

But the persecution was not pressed home. Peter left Jerusalem and Herod Agrippa died soon after. James, Jesus' brother, who, if one interprets Acts 12[17] aright, was already leader of the Jerusalem Christians, won a respite. The Roman procurators took over again and for a while Jewish extremism faded. For the next eighteen years James governed the Church from Jerusalem as its undisputed ruler.[18] Though we hear in the early 'fifties of another persecution in Judaea (i Thess. 2[14-16]) which roused Paul to Messianic expectations,[19] the Christian community prospered. 'Thou seest brother how many thousands of Jews there are which believe and all are zealous for the law' (Acts 21[20]), so James' own sanhedrin told St. Paul in 58. The emphasis was, however, on 'zealous for the Law', and James was worried at reports that St. Paul was preaching abandonment of Jewish traditions as part of Christian teaching. He was on the side of the conservatives on this issue. The *modus vivendi* achieved at Jerusalem was on the basis of common acceptance of the Law, albeit in a modified form in the case of Gentiles (Acts 21[25]). James himself had achieved the title in popular speech of 'the Righteous'[20]—no less than the Essene Teacher of Righteousness in a previous age and perhaps for similar reasons. His ultimate aim, and that of Peter also, seems to have been not to establish a Christian community as a rival alongside the existing Jewish community, but to make Jewry as a whole the community of Jesus. This aim, however, was

frustrated by conditions in the Hellenistic world, by the personality of Paul, and finally by the catastrophe of the Jewish revolt
of 66.

Paul had been preaching a different message. With the converted Levite, Barnabas, he was bringing to the movement a new
enthusiasm coupled with a change of objective which made the
Dispersion and not 'the cities of Israel' the main target of the
Christian mission. The time had now come for the prophecy of
Is. 49⁶, 'I will give thee a light to lighten the Gentiles' to be
fulfilled (cf. Acts 26¹⁸). The 'mystery which had been hid from
all ages and generations but hath now been manifested to his
saints' (Col. 1²⁶). This was the announcement which Paul was to
take from one end of the Mediterranean world to the other. It
was nothing less than a claim that the Resurrection had restored
the primitive natural order of harmony between God and creation
broken by the Fall. Before the Existing Age closed the Gentiles
would be gathered in under the yoke of the new Covenant.
Wisely, the Apostolic Council of 49 decided there was to be one
mission for the Jews and one for the Gentiles. The reaction of
Jews and Gentiles towards the latter ultimately set the Roman
authorities the problem of how to treat Christianity.

The missions which Paul and his friends were to carry out
between 45 and 65 might be described as proseletysing missions
on a vast scale. What the Pharisees sometimes attempted and the
followers of John the Baptist at Ephesus had shown the way
(Acts 19¹ff.), Paul and his friends actually achieved. Paul's and
Barnabas' own travels through some of the roughest country in
Asia Minor are almost matched by the work of men like Epaphras
who penetrated as far as Colossae (Honi), Laodicea and Hierapolis,
towns on the headwaters of the Maeander, to found churches.
(Col. 4¹²⁻¹³.)

But while their ambitions may have been to convert the
Gentiles, their approach to this task was beset by insurmountable
obstacles of character and upbringing.[21] It is difficult to imagine
two more typical Jews than Paul and Barnabas, Barnabas the
Levite from Cyprus, Paul the former trusted apostle of the
Sanhedrin who had been chosen as an agent between Jerusalem
and the Dispersion. Paul's knowledge of the literature of those
whom he was seeking to influence probably came from antholo-

gies. He had been educated not in the Greek university of Tarsus, but by Gamaliel in Jerusalem (Acts 22³). He gloried in his status as 'an Israelite, of the seed of Abraham, of the tribe of Benjamin' (Roms. 11¹), and the reaction of pagan hearers was what one would expect. 'These men who are Jews disturb our city and proclaim (καταγγέλουσιν) customs which are not lawful for us to receive or practice being Romans' (Acts 16²¹) at Philippi,[22] or simply, as at Athens, 'What rubbish are these men talking?' (Acts 17¹⁸).[23] In these circumstances a direct appeal to pagans[24] to 'abandon idols' and 'serve the living God' was calculated to fall on deaf ears.

In practice, the Pauline mission was directed very largely towards the Hellenistic Jews and the outer circle of Gentile proselytes. Except at Athens, the synagogue and not the agora was the centre of Paul's activities. The appeal was to 'children of the stock of Abraham and whosoever among you feareth God, to you is the word of salvation sent' (Acts 13²⁶). At Thessalonica, he goes to the synagogue 'as was his wont'—after five years of preaching (Acts 17²). At Corinth (Acts 18⁴) and at Ephesus (18¹⁹) he 'reasons with Jews and Greeks' in the synagogue. At Philippi, where there evidently was no synagogue, he sought out 'the place of prayer' (οὗ ἐνομίζομεν προσευχὴν εἶναι) used by the local Jews (Acts 16¹³). His success was among Greeks who were already 'devout' (Acts 17⁴). Those mentioned in Acts as people with whom he came into contact were also Jews or proselytes, such as Lydia, Priscilla and Aquila, Crispus, or Justus. Andronicus and Junias are 'of note among the apostles' because they are fellow Jews of the tribe of Benjamin (Roms. 16⁷). Apart perhaps from Titus and Trophimos of Ephesus, it is difficult to find any avowed ex-pagan in Paul's circle. When he declared at Corinth that 'henceforth he would go unto the Gentiles' (Acts 18⁷), the extent of his move was across the street from the synagogue 'to the house of Justus, one who worshipped God', i.e. a proselyte. It was not very far. As his opponents asserted, he was a mover of sedition among the Jews throughout the world (Acts 24⁵).[25]

One must not, however, lose sight of the indirect and incidental effect which Paul's preaching on the ordinary inhabitants of the towns of Asia Minor who happened to hear him. The story of his and Barnabas' reception at Lystra speaks for itself,[26] and there is just possibly a kernel of truth in the story of Thekla of Iconium.[27] *Acta Pauli et Theclae* were circulating in Asia and N. Africa by the end of the second century. But, as Ramsay has pointed out, all the elements in the tale, from Thekla first overhearing Paul's discussion in a neighbouring house, her vow of chastity, her encounter with Alexander the rich young man in charge of the new style Roman games at Iconium, the accusation of sacrilege against her when she resisted him, and her salvation thanks to the intervention of Queen Tryphenia, all have an authentic ring.[28] Later on, the hostility of Demetrius and his colleagues at Ephesus would not have been so pronounced if Paul's teaching had not caused at least a temporary decline in the worship of Artemis (Acts, 19[26]).

Nevertheless, the temples and the provincial cults play only an incidental part in Acts. The synagogue was the centre of the tense controversy which raged for or against the new teaching. On the Pauline missionary journeys the course of events was nearly always the same. The Apostles would arrive at a town and go to the synagogue where they would enjoy a first, favourable hearing. Then trouble would start. Jews from neighbouring centres, as Antioch and Iconium in the case of Lystra (Acts 14[19]), or local Jews as at Thessalonica (Acts 17[5-7]), would stir up opposition.[29] The Apostles would be assaulted, 'left for dead' or imprisoned and sent on their way at the first opportunity. The account of the preaching of the Gospel at Beroea may be quoted as a typical example (Acts 17[10-15]). Only at Corinth and Ephesus was Paul able to make a prolonged stay. And, whereas pagan opposition came mainly from individuals who were worried about their living, like the employers of the young woman with a spirit of divination at Philippi (Acts 16[19]) or the silversmiths at Ephesus (Acts 19[27]), the Jews saw in Paul a deadly enemy, the leader of a heretical sect striking a treacherous blow at Judaism.

Jewish fears were justified on the deep-felt emotional grounds that 'this is the man that teacheth all everywhere against the people, the law and this place (the Temple)' (Acts 22[28]). Their tactics were those used successfully against Jesus, namely to implicate the Apostle in a charge of treason and so have the death-sentence pronounced against him and executed by the Imperial authorities.[30] The rousing of the rabble at Thessalonica

(Acts 17[6-7]) and the more formal charges before Festus at Caesarea (Acts 25[8]) are of a piece.[31] Ominously enough for the Christians, they were not without echo among the provincials in general. At Philippi aggrieved pagans and aggrieved Jews found themselves united in the plea that Paul and his companions were preaching ideas which were incompatible with loyalty to the Roman Empire (Acts 16[21]).[32] At Thessalonica the claims of Christ were already being compared with those of Caesar (Acts 17[7]).[33] Local magistrates rent off the apostles' clothes in horror at the impieties preached by them and ordered their beating on the spot (Acts 16[22]). It was not the last time that the similarity of religious terms used in Emperor-worship with those used in the worship of Christ in Asia were to render the loyalty of Christians suspect. For the time being, however, the Roman provincial governors were glad to steer clear of internecine Jewish quarrels, and the dispute about Jesus and the resurrection was regarded as one of these (Acts 25[19]).

So far then, there was no clash between the Church and the Roman Empire. Acts, though probably not a contemporary document, shows the Roman authorities consistently in a favourable light, and in no way obstructing the spread of the Christian mission.[34] We read of Paul's discomfiture of Elymas the sorcerer at Paphos probably in 46, and there is no doubt about the governor, Sergius Paulus' friendliness towards the Apostle and his preaching (Acts 13[12]).[35] At Corinth five or six years later, in 52/53, Annius Gallio, Seneca's brother and Proconsul of Achaea, showed not the least desire to listen to the Jewish attack on Paul. He drove his accusers from the tribunal (Acts 18[17]).[36] Previously, at Philippi, Paul received an apology from the magistrates for imprisonment and ill-treatment (Acts 17[38-40]). At Ephesus, between 53 and 56, Paul was on good terms with the chief religious and civil officials of the province of Asia and they saved him from risking his life at the hands of the mob (Acts 19[31]), an interesting fact in view of the part these same authorities were to play against the Christians in the next century. Then, when we come to Paul's trial at Jerusalem, both the military commander, Claudius Lysias, and the procurator Felix took the view that Paul's preaching of the Way was not an offence, and only Felix's greed prevented him from being acquitted there and then.[37] Both

Festus and Agrippa regarded Paul as innocent, and Acts closes with the authorities in Rome itself permitting the apostle to live 'two whole years in his own hired house preaching the Kingdom of God and teaching boldly the things of Jesus Christ without let or hindrance' (ἀκωλύτως). For his part, within the limit already discussed, Paul was loyal to the civil power and he was proud of his title of Roman citizen.

What caused the sudden crisis of 64? We know very little about the Christian community in Rome at this period. From Acts 2[10] we hear of proselytes from Rome being present in Jerusalem on the first Pentecost, and it is as reasonable a surmise as any that the Church was founded by them on their return or by a similar group of pilgrims. If one could be sure that Roms. 16 was an integral part of the Epistle, it would afford us an interesting picture of how the Roman Church was built up by Christian immigrants from other parts of the Empire—and this is what one would expect. Then, there is the much discussed scrap of evidence[38] in Suetonius' life of Claudius written *circa* A.D. 115. (*Claudius* 25.4.)[39] 'Since the Jews constantly made disturbances at the instigation of Chrestus, he (Claudius) expelled them from Rome.'

It is noticeable that Suetonius speaks of an 'expulsion' (*Roma expulit*) of the Jews, while Dio Cassius (LX.6.6) believed the action was confined to 'meetings' (of the synagogues?). Moreover, Dio suggests that these events took place in 41, whereas Suetonius records the incident along with others connected with the Emperor's dealings with subject or foreign peoples, without indication of date. However, Paulus Orosius,[40] quoting an unknown source, records events for the year 49 which correspond more or less with the account of Priscilla and Aquila's arrival in Corinth given in Acts (18[2]). It may be, even, that we are dealing with two separate events, in the first instance Claudius enforcing regulations against unlicensed *collegia*, in the second, proceeding to a more general measure of expulsion following riots. We are confronted, too, with similar difficulties when it comes to interpreting these texts. Suetonius states that the troubles which led to the expulsion of Jews from the capital were stirred up by Chrestus, 'Chresto impulsore'. Is this a distant echo of the first conflicts between the new and old Israel in Rome?[41] In the West, we know that by the end of the second century Jesus was habitually referred to as 'Chrestus' instead of 'Christus'.[42] As against this, however, Chrestus was a common name among Asiatic immigrants[43] and Acts 18[2] speaks of 'Jews' (not Christians) being affected by Claudius' actions. All in all, it looks as though we are dealing with measures similar to those carried out by Tiberius in 19 or by Sejanus in 30/31, and that these hit Christian-Jews like Priscilla and Aquila as well as others. Of Chrestus himself we must plead *non liquet*, and there is nothing in this incident to suggest that the authorities in Rome were turning against the Christians as such.

Nor is there any information in the next decade that could throw further light on the subject. Paul's letter to the Romans, written probably in 57, shows that so far as his information went, the church there was flourishing. It seems to have been largely of the Jewish-Christian type.[44] Paul thanks God, 'that your faith is proclaimed throughout the whole world' (Roms. 1[8]), he looks forward to his own visit (1[11]), and he does not allude to any stresses which the community might be suffering. The storm of 49–50 had soon passed. When he does land in Italy, probably in 60, Paul is met by Christians in the port of Puteoli (Acts 28[14]). In Rome, however, his first recorded contacts are with 'those that were the chief of the Jews' (28[17]), and they appear to be singularly ill-informed about the Church. All they know, or pretend to know, is that Christianity was 'a sect (αἵρεσις) that is everywhere spoken against' (28[22]). How this could be the case, if there had been active Christian mission in Rome inspired by one as outspoken as St. Peter, is hard to understand. Perhaps there may be some truth in the tradition preserved in the *Apocritus* of Macarius Magnes (early fourth-century?) of a short mission of Peter lasting a few months, ending with his martyrdom, i.e. between 63–64.[45]

Certain, however, is it that in the next two years Paul preached in Rome and evidently he converted a number of Imperial freedmen (Phil. 4[22]). Among these early converts may have been members of the household of Narcissus, Claudius' powerful freedman (Roms. 16[11]). There is no evidence of hostility to the New Israel on the part of the authorities, while the Old Israel in Rome was distinctly in favour.[46]

Such was the position on 19 July 64.[47] The conflagration which broke out and burnt for six days and seven nights[48] gutted three entire quarters of the city. Thousands were made homeless.

Immediately a rumour began to grow that the Emperor himself was responsible.[49] His grandiose—and if one considers that he himself had started to cut the Corinth Canal in 61,[50] not always unconstructive—building schemes were well known. He may, indeed, have hoped to clear and re-plan an area of the city to his own liking and extend the Palatine. What happened next is well known, but the background is a matter of speculation. Tacitus writing in *circa* 115, some fifty years after the event, did not think that the Christians were guilty of setting fire to the city, but he had no love for them. Theirs was a 'deadly superstition' (*exitiabilis superstitio*), which deserved repression even though their fate turned out to be unreasonably cruel.

Three things emerge from this account. First, that the main reproach levelled by the populace against the Christians,[51] that of 'odium generis humani' was the same as that often applied by Classical authors to the Jews. It involved not so much the desire to do personal damage but to turn one's back on obligations to one's fellow men,[52] and it was regarded as a characteristic Jewish fault. Thus, in the *Histories*, Tacitus describes the Jews as 'apud ipsos, fides obstinata, misericordia in promptu, sed adversus omnes alios, hostile odium'.[53] In his masterly study of Tacitus' reference to the Christians, Harald Fuchs[54] has drawn attention to a passage in Diodore Siculus' account of the siege of Jerusalem by Antiochus VII in 135 B.C. The advisers of the Syrian king urged him to wipe out the Jews. Their hostile attitude to the rest of mankind was due to the tradition of Moses, whence they derived their μισάνθρωπα καὶ παράνομα ἔθη.[55] So it was, in Tacitus' view, with the Christians. And, perhaps, as Beaujeu suggests,[56] *genus humanum* may be identified with the Empire itself. Secondly, the use of the phrase 'ingens multitudo' to describe the numbers of those involved is interesting. Tacitus may have had Livy's account of the Bacchanal conspiracy in mind, which as we have seen,[57] is described in almost identical terms. Moreover, the Christian 'flagitia' are accepted by Tacitus[58] as acts typical of the 'nocturnal rites' of an 'exitiabilis superstitio'. These 'flagitia' could include incendiarism as had those of the Bacchanals (cf. Livy, xxxix.14.10). Thirdly, the punishment, including both the *molesta tunica* as well as combat against beasts was both cruel and theatrical. While both penalties could be prescribed in cases of incendiarism,[59] there was also an obvious element of primitive human sacrifice such as that contained in the macabre acting of the legends of Acteon.[60] One hundred and fifty years later, Tertullian records how he had seen someone burned alive dressed up as Hercules.[61] As in the Bacchanal conspiracy, the aim of the authorities was both to appease the gods and to strike terror. Both Tacitus and Livy regarded 'wrong religion' as dangerous to the State, and the Christians, like the Bacchanals, exemplified one such religion. So far as one can tell, there was no sacrifice test, and no attempt to secure recantation from the victims. We are told simply that 'they confessed'[62] (to Christianity?) and were then punished.

When one turns to the brief reference to the Christians in Suetonius' *Nero* (16.2) one finds the repression tucked away among Nero's miscellaneous police acts (*coercita*) of which the author approved. In his view, the Christians were guilty of magic as well as of introducing a new and dangerous religion, but there is no reference to the fire at Rome, though (ch.38) Suetonius devotes a whole section to this event.[63] Perhaps Suetonius' reference is an echo of the statement of Cicero's a hundred and fifty years before, that new religions could not be accepted unless duly authorized (*De Legibus*, ii.8). The handling of the Christians by the police had much the same basis as the treatment of the Chaldaeans and professional astrologers.[64] The scale of punishment was comparable in its severity.[65] To Suetonius, as to his friend Pliny, Christianity represented a *superstitio*, a *superstitio nova et malefica* in the one case, and *superstitio prava et immodica* in the other; both terms are redolent of ill-starred magic, perpetrated by a foreign revolutionary secret society.[66]

The foregoing places the action against the Christians in 64 within the framework of the action by the authorities against cults which they considered harmful. In the eyes of members of the Senatorial aristocracy fifty years after the event Nero's action represented the crushing of a conspiracy fomented by a new type of Jewish sectary accompanied by nocturnal rites and black magic abominable to the gods and dangerous to the safety of the city. The situation was therefore dealt with along lines similar to those used against the Bacchanals, against Catilina, and from time to time in moments of panic against Chaldaeans and others. There was a single savage act of repression directed at guilty individuals. But as i Clement shows, a generation later, the worship itself was not proscribed nor was the organization of the Church destroyed.

Two further indications from Christian sources support the view that the Christians in Rome were being identified at this time with Jewish sectaries. First, in the earliest account of the persecution in i Clement, written probably between A.D. 95–100, we are told that it was 'through jealousy and envy (διὰ ζῆλον καὶ φθόνον) that the most righteous pillars of the Church were persecuted and contended even unto death' (i Clement 5.2).[67] Clement has just been describing the dire effect of envy and jealousy in the Israelite community down through the ages, and it was to drive home his conclusion that he 'ceases from the examples of old time' to speak of his own day. It looks from the context as though 'envy and jealousy' were symptoms of internal conflict among a Jewish community, especially as Clement time and again draws his readers' attention to fratricidal struggles in Jewish history, such as Cain and Abel, Jacob and Esau, Joseph and his brethren.[68] In this case, the warring brothers could be the Old Israel and the New (cf. Acts 13[45]). In any event, these are not the terms used in connection with conflict with an outside, pagan, body. For instance, Paul charges his opponents that they were preaching καὶ διὰ φθόνον καὶ διὰ ἔριν (Phil. 1[15]) in order to make difficulties for him. A persecution is called in the New Testament and in i Clement a θλῖψις (Mt. 13[21], Mk. 4[17], i Cl. 57[4]) or a διωγμός (Mk. 4[17], 10[30] and Acts 8[1]). One may perhaps draw the same conclusion from the use of the term in St. Mark's Gospel (15[10]) where the Jewish high priests are described as delivering up Our Lord 'through envy' (διὰ φθόνον). Secondly, the Christians in Rome at the time (circa 120) when Hermas was writing still considered themselves as a 'synagogue' (Mand. 11.9), a term also used in James 2[2]. Perhaps, one may take the accounts of the affair of 64 given by Clement and Tacitus as consistent with each other.

On this reading of the evidence, the persecution represented a triumph for the orthodox Jews, who were able, through influence at Court, to shift the odium of the outbreak on to the hated schismatics, the Christian synagogue. This they hoped to destroy at a single tremendous blow.[69] In the persons of Poppaea Sabina and the actor Tigellinus they had the ear of the Emperor,[70] and they succeeded in so far as a great number of Christians were killed, including the leaders, Peter and Paul.[71]

Finally, how did the Neronian persecution affect the legal position of the Christians? Ever since the discussion centred round Th. Mommsen's famous article in the *Historische Zeitschrift* of 1890,[72] scholars have been sharply divided, often along national and denominational boundaries. As Sherwin-White has pointed out, two main lines of argument have developed though with a degree of overlapping and variety.[73] First, the majority of the French and Belgians, and in general Roman Catholic church-historians have held until recently that after Nero's persecution, Christianity was forbidden by a General Law.[74] Subsequent persecutions of the Name took place largely in virtue of this; and the 'institutum Neronianum' recorded by Tertullian (*ad Nationes*, 1.7 and *Apol.*, 5) was this particular edict which had never been revoked.[75] J. Zeiller, for instance, pointed out that some general prohibition must have existed for Pliny to have taken the action he did against Christians, and that prohibition must go back to the time of Nero. (*L'Empire romain et l'Eglise*, 1928, 31). In his subsequent study,[76] he modified this position to the extent of interpreting 'institutum' in the sense of 'something customary', rather than synonymous with 'lex'. This may be nearer the truth, especially when one recalls the long-standing Roman prejudice against the cult of Bacchus, and others such as Isis-worship or the Druids whose worship was in some way considered noxious.

On the other hand, the majority of English and German scholars,[77] and lay researchers generally,[78] have stressed the administrative and police character of the repression. Some, like Max Conrat,[79] have gone further and emphasized that the Christians were punished as individuals, and then only for offences against the law, such as treason, incendiarism, incest and black magic. All this school of thought, however, seem to have envisaged direct police action, or investigation leading to the arrest and punishment of the guilty without the ordinary forms of trial, by virtue of the power of *coercitio* which was vested in senior magistrates in the provinces. The wide extent of these powers is well illustrated by a passage from Pliny, quoted by Sherwin-White in his study of the legal aspects of the persecutions,[80] 'esse enim se provinciales et ad omne proconsulum imperium metu cogi'.[81] The fear was designed to inspire a wide variety of malefactors whose specific crimes fell outside the older criminal code of the *leges publicae*, and were known therefore as *crimina extra ordinem*.

It must be admitted, however, that if the analogy between the punishment of the Christians and the Bacchanals can be sustained, then one might have expected the issue of a *senatus-consultum* 'De Christianis' after the executions. In 19 the Senate had decreed against Jews and Isis-worshippers in Rome; why not now, against the Christians? Apart from the fact, however, that no inscription relating to any such decree has ever been found, and no pagan or Christian writer living in the first two centuries alludes to it, there are several reasons for doubting its existence. First, the persecution was confined to Rome. It was not extended to the provinces,[82] and it was not re-opened on the outbreak of the Jewish War in 66. Secondly, the existence of such a *senatus-consultum* could hardly have escaped the knowledge of the experienced administrative lawyer, Pliny the Younger, and it would have formed an excellent basis for his report to Trajan concerning the Christians in Bithynia. Similarly, it could have formed the starting-point for the Christian Apologies of the second century. Then again, there was evidently no attempt to confiscate the Church's property which could have been expected under the terms of an edict, and finally, an edict presupposes a certain degree of importance for its subject, which it is doubtful whether the Christians at this stage could claim. What one sees in Nero's action is a brutal application of police administration, Suetonius' *coercita*, a single catastrophe for the Church, but not the beginning of a policy launched by an edict. It was a century and a quarter before Christians were systematically harried again in Rome, and the reign of Decius before the whole Church in the city was involved in persecution.

Though one cannot rule out the bare possibility of a *senatus-consultum*, Nero's suicide and his subsequent *damnatio memoria* by the Senate would have voided his legislative acts. When carefully analysed the 'institutum Neronianum' tends to subside to the level of a 'usage'. It is doubtful if Tertullian intended more than to tar the persecutors of the Christians in Carthage with the Neronian brush.

It would be dangerous, however, to minimize the long-term effects of the affair. It put the Church on the wrong side of the State, and so, as Sherwin-White has suggested,[83] afforded a precedent to which appeal could be made by any who sought to damage its interests. This fact must lead to some modification of the *coercitio* theory, for as the same author has shown,[84] the mode of operation against the Christians was not police action on its own initiative, but private delation, followed by a *cognitio* undertaken by a magistrate in the presence of both parties. During the second century trials of Christians were always initiated through this method, and without a *delator* the case could be automatically quashed.[85] There must also, as Zeiller argues, have been some basis of accusation which even informers could have evoked in order to win a hearing from a magistrate, and so render Christians liable to 'coercion'. Mommsen's theory of 'national apostasy'[86] does not fit the situation in the provinces, though popular opinion in the Greek cities was quick to point out the incompatibilities between Christian teaching and the duties of loyal subjects of Rome. We seem, therefore, to be back with Callewaert and Zeiller and the 'General Law' school, especially as there is nothing to show that in Bithynia, for instance, Christians were bent on defying the Roman authorities. Pliny, as well as sources as varied as 1 Peter, Hegesippus and the Palestinian Rabbis, agree that when denounced to the Roman authorities, Christians were liable to punishment, even death.

However, when one looks for some crime which could always be invoked against the Christians, difficulties arise. The most likely charge would be *maiestas*, to which, insult to the gods *sacrilegium* or *impietas*, was closely allied.[87] Both are translated by Dio as ἀσέβεια, and this term was used as a reproach, if not as a technical charge against both Jewish proselytes and Christians.[88] Moreover, as Momigliano has pointed out with reference to the Neronian persecution, the concept of *maiestas* could be extended to stirring up civil strife, such as might result from indignant rejection by the populace of the claim that Christ (not Caesar) was Lord, or simply *vis* (public violence).[89] By the end of the second century in the Latin-speaking provinces both *sacrilegium* and *maiestas* were being urged against the Christians,[90] though one cannot be quite sure whether Tertullian is using the terms in a technical sense when he speaks of Christians '*sacrilegii et maiestatis rei*'.[91]

This, however, hardly meets the situation at the time of the Neronian persecution and during most of the next century. First, in the provinces, refusal by non-citizens to participate in the Imperial cult was not treasonable in itself,[92] and neither Pliny nor Trajan nor any of their contemporaries suggested that it was. Secondly, from Nerva to Septimius Severus there was a tendency to restrict the scope of the *maiestas* procedure and in particular, to discourage the delation of individuals on this charge.[93] *Maiestas*, too, involved a formal trial, and down to 177 there is no evidence from existing trials of Christians for this accusation or the procedure connected with it. The most probable solution may be simpler. *Salus publica suprema lex esto*.[94] Roman magistrates in the provinces had a good idea that *prava religio* was connected with illegal oaths and conspiratorial conduct. They were baffled by the apparent contradictions in the conduct of the Christians, men and women claiming at one moment to be good citizens who paid their taxes and led exemplary lives, and the next, displaying utter contempt for the established worship of the gods and flagrant disobedience to the commands of the representative of Rome.[95] When this was combined with membership of an illegal organization punishment was inevitably severe. The mental processes of Pliny in 112 and Vigellius Saturninus at Carthage in 180 seem to have been just these.[96]

One other factor must be taken into account. It is not possible to treat Christianity in the first century as an isolated problem, a *nova superstitio*, without reference to its Jewish parentage. If one aspect of St. Luke's account of the Pauline mission is the tolerance and good-will of the authorities towards the Christians, the other is that Paul represented true Pharisaism (Acts 23[6]), that the Church was 'the hope of Israel', nay, Israel itself (Acts 24[14ff.]). The Christian claim to be Israel was a vital element in the situation. Persecution of the Christians cannot be divorced from Rome's policy towards Judaism. In the study of the persecutions the Jews, Christians, and authorities have an equal partnership in the drama. The Jews also were regarded as 'obstinate', obstinate indeed to the point of death rather than transgress even their dietary laws.[97] Yet no one doubted their right to their religion. The Christians, however, claimed to be the true Jews,[98] the true Vine (Jn. 15¹), but at the same time did not obey Jewish ceremonial law. It was the rejection of their claim both by the orthodox Jews and by the authorities that led to their precarious situation. There did not need to be a general edict against them, for it was accepted that a man must be subject to some law, and if he was not subject to Jewish law, then he must be subject to that of his own city. If not, he was suspect as an enemy of the gods and thus of the community in which he lived.[99] In such circumstances, denunciation to the authorities by personal enemies, including orthodox Jews, was always a danger for the Christian. Once denounced, and persisting in his outlook, he was at the mercy of the magistrate's *coercitio*. His basic problem was the same as that of the Jewish proselyte, namely lack of recognized status in society; to this anomalous situation it was easy to add 'flagitia'. It was a peril which Christians understood and indeed accepted. As Hermas was to explain, 'the elect', if they did not choose to obey the laws of the ruler of this world, must be prepared to leave his city, if required.[100]

Church and State had clashed at a critical moment. One sequel of the events of 64 was a marked change for the worse in Rome's dealings with the Jews. Up to this moment Nero's policy towards the Jews had been friendly, but in 65 he appointed Gessius Florus procurator of Judaea. Josephus tells us that Florus received his appointment through Poppaea,[101] and therefore ought to have been pro-Jewish. In fact, he was precisely the opposite, the one utterly and unashamedly anti-semitic governor Josephus mentions. And, he adds significantly, that his brutalities were 'as though he had been sent on purpose to show his crimes to everybody'.[102] The hint is unmistakable; there was a violent reaction in Nero's attitude, for reasons we can only guess. One year of Florus' rule, sufficed to provoke revolution in Palestine. In 66 Jewish and Greek hatreds, coupled with official injustice, forced Rome finally to accept the legacy of the Seleucids.

The Jewish War was another turning point in the affairs of the primitive Church.[103] Up to now, acceptance of Jesus as Messiah could be reconciled with zeal for the Law, and hopes of national restoration. 'Lord, wilt thou at this time restore again the kingdom to Israel?'[104] This, the final question of the disciples, after three years of companionship with the Master, is a revealing one. To these followers of Jesus at any rate, the Kingdom was to be of this world, and the Gentiles as such would have little place within it. Twenty years later, Jewish Christians could still interpret faith in Jesus' Messiahship as in no way contradictory to their loyalty to their ancestral religion. Jesus was 'Lord', recognized among the Aramaic-speaking (or -thinking) Christians as the Lord (*Maran*).[105] He was not worshipped 'as God' as He would be in the Hellenistic churches in the next century.[106] Paul might comment bitterly to the Galatians that his opponents 'compel you to be circumcised only that they may not be persecuted for the Cross of Christ' (Gal. 6[12]), but James could counter by pointing to the position which the Church had gained in Jerusalem. For all Paul's missionary success, James was head of the Church and Jerusalem was its centre.[107] When in 58 Paul went up to Jerusalem accompanied by some of his Gentile converts, he was himself obliged to take the stringent test of Jewish orthodoxy provided by the Nazarite vow (Acts 21[26]). Whatever he might preach to Gentiles, he himself, though a Christian, was expected to keep the Law (Acts 21[24]). In this period the authority of the Jerusalem Church was unchallenged in the life and counsels of the Church as a whole.

This situation depended, however, on events in Palestine. In the decade preceding the revolt feelings between Jews on the one hand, Greek settlers and Roman authorities on the other, gradually worsened, until Florus' clumsy intervention in a street brawl between the Jewish and Greek inhabitants of his capital city, Caesarea, goaded the Jews into revolt.[108] In these years the role of the 'moderate' Jew became increasingly difficult. The Church might maintain the apocalyptic tradition of the Essenes and their allies, but Jesus' example had been against 'taking up the sword'. The binding conspiracy to ambush Paul on his way to Jerusalem[109] and the violent scenes accompanying his arrest [110] indicate the quickening pace of fanaticism for the Law. In 62 an interregnum caused by the departure of the procurator Felix and the arrival of his successor gave the Sadducees and the Sanhedrin their chance to challenge the Church in the name of Jewish orthodoxy. Despite his immense reputation for personal sanctity according to the strictest Jewish standards James was murdered by the same combination of Jewish authorities and Jerusalem mob that had proved fatal to his Brother.[111] Another Zadok had been destroyed. Characteristically, his last recorded thoughts were of Israel.[112]

The Church indeed recovered momentarily. Another kinsman of the Lord, Symeon, was elected without opposition in his place.[113] The respite did not last long. We have no evidence of the counsels of hope and desperation which must have wracked the Christians in Jerusalem during the first years of the war.[114] We cannot, however, say simply that 'the Jerusalem Church fell together with the Jewish nation in the catastrophe of A.D. 70',[115] for the two surviving traditions we have are that the Jerusalem Christians fled to Pella some 60 miles north-east of the city, across the Jordan,[116] and the Church at Jerusalem was reconstituted after the war. Pella, however, was a Greek city, and whatever may be the difficulties in interpreting this tradition precisely, it suggests that the Christians took up an indecisive attitude to the war. It was this attitude, rather than the defeat of the revolt, that proved fatal to them. Neutrals who evaded danger could not claim to be the New Israel in the midst of those who had fought and died for the cause of Jewry. The Essenes persisted with a constancy which aroused the admiration of their bitterest enemies.[117] The Christians survived, but they were never to regain in their own homeland the position which James had won for them. Jerusalem ceased to be the directing centre of the Christian mission.

NOTES

[1] Eusebius, *H.E.*, iii.20.2–5.

[2] Represented in the primitive Church by Jn. 11[52].

[3] *Manual of Discipline* 8.12b.–16 (cited from Th. Gaster, *The Scriptures of the Dead Sea Sect*, London, 1957, 65); cf. O. Cullmann, 'The Significance of the Qumran texts', *JBL.*, 74, 1955, 218ff. and J. A. T. Robinson, 'The Baptism of John and the Q'mran Community, *HTR.*, 50, 1957, 177–8.

[4] As the Montanists with their hope of New Jerusalem descending at the village of Pepuza, or the Syrian Christians described by Tertullian, *Adv. Marcionem*, iii.24.

[5] Perhaps to be identified with the 'Synagogue of the Freedmen' founded by Theodotus, the freedmen of the Roman family of the Vetteni, commemorated on a first-century A.D. inscription found on Mt. Ophel, commented on by G. E. Wright, *Biblical Archaeology*, Philadelphia/London, 1957, 237.

[6] This also seems to have been the view of Jewish extremists at the siege of Jerusalem in 70; cf. Josephus, *Wars*, v.458 (Niese) ʽκαὶ νάου[ἀπολουμένου]ἀμείνω τούτου τῷ θεῷ

τὸν κόσμον εἶναι'. This may be another instance of Christianity embodying, at this stage, elements of extreme puritan and eschatological thought among the Jews. O. Cullmann's suggestion that 'the Hellenists were in contact with the kind of Judaism we find in the Q'mran text', may also be relevant (*JBL.*, lxxiv, 1955, 223), though as Black argues (*The Scrolls and Christian origins*, 75–77), the link with Qumran would surely be through the 'Hebraists', i.e. the local Aramaic-speaking Jews. One thing that the Qumran sectaries were not, was Greek-speaking! In Egypt, however, the Essenes may have been Greek-speaking and thus provide some grounds for the view that the 'anti-cultic' outlook of *Barnabas* 'may reflect a Greek-speaking Essenic school tradition' (R. A. Kraft, Dissertation, 'The Epistle of Barnabas. Its Quotations and their Sources'. Noted in *HTR.*, 54.4, October 1961, 300).

[7] E. J. Bickerman's view, 'The Name of Christians', *HTR.*, 42, 1949, 115–16. They 'belonged to Christ', hence the *-anus* ending in the Greek: cf. καισαριανοί (*Caesaris servi*). Ibid., 118–19.

[8] See E. Meyer, *Ursprung und Anfänge*, iii.150. Meyer places Peter's mission after the persecution of 44. Ibid., 155.

[9] Philo, *Legum allegor.*, ii.19 (ed. Cohn, 1.94).

[10] Philo, *Quis Rerum Divinarum Heres sit*, 258 (Cohn-Wendland, iii.59)

[11] Philo, *De Congressu Eruditionis Gratia*, 24 (Cohn-Wendland, iii.77), ἀρετὴ Σάρρα πρὸς παιδείαν Ἄγαρ'.

[12] Gal. 4²⁵⁻²⁶.

[13] W. L. Knox, *St. Paul and the Church of the Gentiles*, Cambridge, 1938, 91ff.; also H. J. Schoeps, *Paul. The Theology of the Apostle in the Light of Jewish Religious History* (Eng. tr. 1961). Reviewed by E. Bammel, 'Paul and Judaism', *Modern Churchman*, N.S. vi, 1963, 279–85.

[14] See the essay by B. Reicke on 'The Constitution of the Primitive Church in the light of Jewish Documents', in *The Scrolls and the New Testament*, ed. K. Stendahl, London, 1958, 143ff.

[15] Above, ch. II. I have accepted Dupont-Sommer's view (*The Essene Writings*, 167) that the *Kittim* referred to in the *War* Scroll are the Romans. Perhaps another straw in this particular wind is provided by the discovery at Masada of a document dealing with the liturgy of Sabbath sacrifice and utilizing the Qumran calendar (reported in *Newsweek*, 10 February 1964).

[16] Justin, *Dialogue with Trypho* (ed. A. Luykn Williams), 89.2.

[17] Josephus, *Antiquities*, 19.6.1(293). Nazirites 'were to have their heads shorn', (ibid., 294) and he appointed a new High Priest in the person of Simon son of Boethus (ibid., 297).

[18] Cf. E. Bammel, 'Judenverfolgung und Naherwartung zur Eschatologie des Ersten Thessalonicherbriefs', *Zeitschrift für Theologie und Kirche*, 56, 1959, 294–315.

[19] For the dating of James' primacy nearer 49 than 44, T. W. Manson, *Studies in the Gospels and Epistles*, Manchester, 1962, 195–6. A good sketch of the role of James at Jerusalem may be found in W. Telfer, *The Office of a Bishop*, London, 1962, ch. i.

[20] Eusebius, *H.E.*, ii.23.4. On his other title 'Oblias', see H. J. Schoeps, *Theologie und Geschichte des Judenchristentums*, 1949, p. 124.

[21] See A. D. Nock's interesting survey of Paul's early upbringing: *St. Paul*, ch. ii, and E. Meyer, op. cit., iii.312ff.

[22] Note the suggestion made by A. Deissmann, *Light from the Ancient East*, p. 97, that the Athenians supposed that Paul was trying to introduce them to a new kind of mystery cult with a male and female deity, Jesus and Anastasis.

[23] On the force of καταγγέλουσιν, A. Deissmann, loc. cit., and Arndt and Gingrich, *Lexikon*, 410.

[24] 1 Thess. 1⁹; cf. Acts 14¹⁵ and 17²⁹.

[25] See A. Deissmann, *St. Paul* (Eng. tr., L. R. M. Strachan, 1912), 210–12.

[26] See A. D. Nock, op. cit., 92ff.

[27] Tertullian, *De Baptismo* 17 (ed. Lupton, p. 48), gives the evidence for the *Acta* having been fabricated by a presbyter of the province of Asia 'quasi titulo Pauli de suo cumulans'. They would appear to date to 160–170, and are, of course, interesting as an example of an incident redounding to the honour of both Paul and confessorship having passed into legend at this time.

[28] W. M. Ramsay, *The Church in the Roman Empire*, Ch. xvi.

[29] The responsibility for persecution in this period is placed firmly on the Jews, 1 Thess. 2¹⁵, The Jews 'ἐκδιωξάντων ἡμᾶς . . . κωλυόντων ἡμᾶς τοῖς ἔθνεσιν λαλῆσαι ἵνα σωθῶσιν'.

[30] Lk. 23², Jn. 19¹²; cf. Acts 17⁶, and 18¹³.

[31] See G. B. Caird, *The Apostolic Age*, London, 1955, 160–2.

[32] See the discussion on the significance of the archaic-sounding complaint in A. N. Sherwin-White, *Roman Society and Roman Law in the New Testament*, Sarum Lectures, 1960–61, Oxford, 1963, 78–83.

[33] 'βασιλέα λέγοντες ἕτερον εἶναι, 'Ιησοῦν.' Cf. K. M. Setton, 'The Christian Attitude towards the Emperor in the Fourth Century', *Columbia University Studies in History, Economics, etc.*, 482, 1941, 21. The statement is significant in view of the attitude of the Thessalonian Christians towards the State shown in Paul's two letters to the Church there.

[34] See W. M. Ramsay, *St. Paul, Traveller*, 281, and S. B. Easton, *Early Christianity*, S.P.C.K., 1955, 41–55.

[35] The family were great landowners on the Phrygian-Pisidian border. See W. M. Ramsay, 'Studies in the Roman Province of Galatia', *JRS.*, xvi (1926), 202ff., and B. Lewick, *Anatolian Studies*, viii (1958), 222.

[36] Dating, Kirsopp Lake, *The Beginnings of Christianity*, v.460–4, and T. W. Manson, 'The Letters to the Thessalonians' = ch. 14 in *Studies in the Gospels and Epistles*, Manchester, 1962, 265.

[37] On the legal aspects of Paul's trials in Palestine, L. Wenger, 'Erste Berührungen des Christentums mit dem römischen Rechte', *S.T.*, 125, 1946 (*Misc. G. Mercati*, v), 584–93, and A. N. Sherwin-White, op. cit., 48ff.

[38] For the latest summary of the evidence, with bibliography, E. Bammel, *Judenverfolgung und Naherwartung*, pp. 295–7, and the important study by H. Janne, 'Impulsore Chresto', *Annuaire de l'Institut de Philosophie el d'Histoire orientales* (*Mélanges Bidez*), 1934, 531–53. Janne, however, dates the affair to 41, connecting it with Claudius' reply to the Jewish embassy from Alexandria in that year (op. cit., 548). This does not seem, however, to fit the facts presented in Acts 18¹⁻² where, as Janne, admits (p. 548), it is difficult to ignore the word προσφάτως in connection with Aquila's and Priscilla's arrival in Corinth.

[39] 'Iudaeos impulsore Chresto, assidue tumultuantes, Roma expulit.'

[40] *Historia adversus Paganos* (ed. C. Zangemeister, *CSEL.*, v, 451), vii.6.15–16.

[41] As assumed for instance, by M. Gough, *The Early Christians*, 1960, 41, and argued in detail by H. Leon, *The Jews of Ancient Rome*, 25ff., and Janne, art. cit., 540.

[42] Tertullian, *Apol.*, 3.5, *Ad. Nat.*, 1.3; cf. Lactantius, *Instit.*, iv.7.5. Similarly, the Lebaba inscription (Marcionite, 318/9), south-east of Damascus, see A. Harnack, *SBAW.*, 1915, 746ff. and *OGI.*, 608.

[43] The writer has seen inscriptions dedicated by persons named Chrestus in places as far apart as Istanbul and Brindisi. For Rome, note the Aelia Chreste inscription from the catacomb of Callistus, *ILCV.*, 2504. A Chrestus was bishop of Syracuse in the early years of the fourth century, Eusebius, *H.E.*, x.5.21.

[44] P. Styger, *Juden und Christen im alten Rom*, Berlin, 1934, 19ff., based on an examination of Paul's letter to the Romans. See also, W. Telfer's chapter, 'The Church of Rome' in *The Office of a Bishop*, and his comment, p. 49, 'We may therefore conclude that

Roman Christian traditions were well moulded to the pattern of the Judaeo-Christian synagogue before there was any admission of uncircumcised Gentiles into the Roman Church'.

45 Macarius Magnes, *Apocritus* (ed. T. W. Crafer), iii.22; cf. A. Harnack, 'Porphyrius gegen die Christen', *ABAW.*, 1916, Bruchstück 26, p. 56. Rejected by K. Heussi, *Die römische Petrustradition in kritischer Sicht*, Tübingen, 1955, 47. See also, O. Cullmann, *Petrus*, 114, K. Aland's 'final reply' to Heussi in the *Historische Zeitschrift*, Heft, 191/3, December 1960, 585–7, and M. Guarducci, *The Tomb of St. Peter* (Eng. tr., J. McLellan, 1960), 9–12.

46 Josephus, *Antiquities*, xx.8.11 (Whiston).

47 Tacitus, *Ann.*, xv.38–44. For an English translation and comments, see J. Stevenson, *A New Eusebius*, 2–6. On the Neronian persecution, see L. H. Canfield, 'The Early Persecutions of the Christians', *Columbia University Studies in History*, 55, 1913, part i, ch. ii, and part ii, ch. ii (quotes earlier sources), H. Fuchs, 'Tacitus über die Christen', *Vigiliae Christianae*, 1950, 65–93, M. Dibelius, *Rom und die Christen*, A. Momigliano, *CAH.*, x.726ff. and 887–8, J. Beaujeu, 'L'Incendie de Rome en 64 et les Chrétiens', *Latomus*, xix, 1960, 65–80 and 291–311, and J. B. Bauer, 'Tacitus und die Christen', *Gymnasium*, 64, 1957, 497–503. Also, among the earlier works, E. G. Hardy, *Christianity and the Roman Government* (London, 1894, reprinted 1925). Ch. iv, and A. Manaresi, *L'Impero romano e il Cristianesimo*, Torino, 1914, 50–7.

48 Suetonius, *Nero*, 38.4 'per sex dies septemque noctes'. J. Beaujeu, loc. cit., 66 and 69, on the extent of the disaster.

49 Tacitus, *Annales*, xv.44, 'quin iussum incendium crederetur'.

50 Dio Cassius, lxiii.16.

51 For the relation between the charge of incendiarism and the reproach of *odium generis humani*, E. Cuq, 'De la nature des crimes imputés aux chrétiens', *Mél. de l'Ecole française à Rome*, vi, 1886, 115ff. It does not seem, however, that *odium* could have been a legal charge.

52 Note Cicero, *De Officiis*, 1.29, 'Sunt etiam qui aut studio rei familiaris tuendae, aut odio quodam hominum suum se negotium agere dicant nec facere cuiquam videantur injuriam. Qui altero genere injustitiae vacant, in alterum incurrant. Deserunt enim vitae societatem, quia nihil conferunt in eam studii, nihil operae, nihil facultatum'. Also, *Tusc.*, iv.11.25, 'odium . . . in hominum universum genus'.

53 Tacitus, *Histories*, v.5.1: 'apud ipsos fides obstinata, misericordia in promptu, sed adversus omnes alios, hostile odium'. Philostratus wrote in the same vein in the early third century A.D., *Life of Apollonius* (ed. Conybeare), v.33, on the specific grounds of their social and religious exclusiveness: see above, ch. V, p. 130. Also, Josephus, *Contra Apionem*, ii.14, and ibid., ii.15 for his claim that in reality the Jewish Law disposed its followers to a 'general love for mankind'.

54 H. Fuchs, 'Tacitus über den Christen', *Vigiliae Christianae*, 1950, 65–93, especially pp. 82–8. Also, W. Nestle, 'Odium generis humani' (zu Tacitus, Ann. xv.44), *Klio*, 21, 1927, 92ff. and J. B. Bauer, art. cit., *Gymnasium*, 1957, 501–2, on the same subject.

55 Diodore (ed. Dindorf, ii.531), 34.1.3; cf. Josephus, *Contra Apionem*, ii.14.

56 J. Beaujeu, loc. cit., 296–7, discussing Tacitus, *Hist.*, 1.30.5 'consensus generi humani'.

57 See above, p. 110. Note also that magicians (*magi*) were 'humani generis inimici credendi sunt', *C.J.*, ix.18.7, under Constantius, A.D. 358.

58 These were reckoned against the Christians as 'sontes et novissima exempla meritos'; cf. Fuchs, art. cit., p. 86. For an accusation of 'incest accompanied by magical rites', Tacitus, *Annales*, xvi.8.

59 *Digest*, xlvii.9.9, and 9.12. H. Last, 'Christenverfolgungen', 1211, considers that the Christians were in fact punished as incendiaries, which would also be implied in Tacitus' reference to the *crimen incendii*.

[60] Theatrical murder in the amphitheatre at the Emperor's command is again instanced in the reign of Commodus, when the latter had cripples dressed up to represent giant Anguipedes as the Evil Power in the religion of Mithras, and killed them (*SHA.*, Commodus, 9.15). i Clement's comparison of the Christian women to 'Danaids' and 'Dirkae', seems less likely to be connected with their punishment, as with his aim of praising their example of endurance as 'true Danaids and Dirkae' (see M. Dibelius, *Rom und die Christen*, 24).

[61] Tertullian, *Apol.*, 15.5.

[62] Or simply, 'made declarations'—Bauer, op. cit., 501. For some intentional vagueness on the part of Tacitus, see F. W. Clayton, 'Tacitus and Nero's Persecution of the Christians', *CQ.*, 41.3 and 4, 1947, 81–5.

[63] M. Dibelius in *Forschungen und Fortschritte*, xviii (1942), 189, seeks, mistakenly in my view, to deny any connection between the Fire and the Neronian persecution. See also, A. Momigliano, *CAH.*, x, 887.

[64] H. Last, 'The Study of the "Persecutions"', *JRS.*, xxvii, 1937, 80ff., and art. 'Christenverfolgungen', II (juristisch), *A.C.*, ii, 1208–28, at 1209. Also, E. Cuq, art cit., 123–9.

[65] Paulus, *Sententiae* 5.20 and *C.J.*, ix.18.3; cf. M. Conrat, *Die Christenverfolgungen im römischen Reiche vom Standpunkte des Juristen*, Leipzig, 1897, 68ff., and E. Cuq, art. cit., 131ff.

[66] Isis-worship is termed by Suetonius 'varia (or *vana*) superstitio'. Suetonius, *Vita Domitiani*, 1.2, and as already cited, the Bacchanals: 'prava religio', Livy, xxxix.16.7.

[67] L. H. Canfield, op. cit., 44ff. connects the persecution with Jewish 'envy', but denies connection with the fire at Rome.

[68] i Clem. iv, especially para. 7 where Clement writes, 'ὁράτε, ἀδελφοί, ζῆλος καὶ φθόνος ἀδελφοκτονίαν κατειργάσατο'.

[69] L. H. Canfield, loc. cit., P. Styger, *Juden und Christen*, 41ff., A. Manaresi, *Il Cristianesimo*, 54–5; opposed by H. Leon, *The Jews of Ancient Rome*, 28. In the *Acts of John* Roman Jews are recorded as deflecting a persecution by Domitian on to the Christians! This, however, appears to be a late work (M. R. James, *The Apocryphal New Testament*, 228).

[70] Josephus, θεοσεβὴς γὰρ ἦν (*Antiquities*, xx.8.11.195) referring to Poppaea seems clear enough, but the implication that she was a 'semi-proselyte' has been challenged, in my view unsuccessfully, by Miss E. M. Smallwood in a note in *JTS.*, N.S. 10, 1959, 329–35.

[71] We have no idea of the number of victims, but the *Martyrlogium Hieronym.* (ed. Duchesne-de Rossi, *Acta Sanctorum*, Bruxelles, 1894) commemorates on 29 June, Peter and Paul and '977 other saints' who died at Rome in 64, but this figure has no corroboration.

[72] Th. Mommsen, 'Der Religionsfrevel nach römischen Recht', *Historische Zeitschrift*, N.F. xxviii, 1890, 389–429.

[73] Discussed in the extremely able article by A. N. Sherwin-White, 'Early Persecutions and Roman Law Again', *JTS.*, N.S. iii, 1952, 199–213, and by J. Beaujeu, loc. cit., 297ff., who curiously makes no mention of Sherwin-White among the voluminous contributions which he cites.

[74] Note particularly for this view, the series of articles by C. Callewaert, 'Les premiers chrétiens, furent-ils persecutés par edits généraux ou par mesures de police?', *Rev. d'Histoire Ecclesiastique*, ii, 1901, 771–97, iii, 1902, 5–15, 324–48, and 601–14, and contributions by J. Zeiller, in Vol. i of the *Histoire de l'Eglise* (ed. A. Fliche and V. Martin), 1946, pp. 292–7, and H. Leclercq in art. 'Droit persécuteur' in *DACL.*, iv; also J. Guérin, 'Etude sur le fondement juridique des pérsecutions dirigées contre les chrétiens' in *Nouvelle Revue Historique du Droit Français et Etranger*, xix, 1895, pp. 601ff. and 713ff.

[75] Cf. Sulpicius Severus, *Chron.*, ii.29.3, alleging the execution of Peter and Paul after 'the publication of laws' against Christianity.

[76] 'Institutum Neronianum', *Rev. d'Histoire Ecclesiastique*, 55, 1955, 393–400.

[77] For instance, Th. Mommsen, *Der Religionsfrevel*, 398ff., E. G. Hardy, *Christianity and the Roman Government*, pp. 62ff., and H. Lietzmann, *Geschichte*, ii.157ff.

[78] A. Manaresi, *Il Cristianesimo*, 105, L. Dieu, 'Les Persécutions aux premiers deux Siècles. Une loi fantôme', *Rev. d'Hist. Eccles.*, 38, 1942, 5ff. H. Grégoire, *Les Persécutions dans l'Empire Romain*, Brussels, 1951, 24ff. L. H. Canfield, op. cit., 69, Paolo Bressi, *Cristianesimo e Impero Romano*, Rome, 1944, 36ff.

[79] M. Conrat, *Die Christenverfolgungen*, 17ff. 26 and 53ff.

[80] A. N. Sherwin-White, art. cit., 203.

[81] Pliny, Ep. iii.9.15. Also, Tacitus, *Ann.*, vi.11, 'ut saevitia coerceret et quod civium audacia turbidum, nisi vim metuat', and Cicero, *De Legibus*, iii.6, 'magistratus nec obedientem et noxium civem multa vinculis verberibusve coherecto, ni par maiorve potestas populusve prohibessit'. (See below, note 96.)

[82] There was no persecution in North Africa, for instance, before 180 (Tertullian, *Ad Scapulam* 3), and Melito of Sardes writes as though persecution in the Sardes area of Asia was a rarity in his lifetime (Eusebius, *H.E.*, iv.26).

[83] A. N. Sherwin-White, art. cit., 209.

[84] Ibid., 205, and *Roman Society and Roman Law*, 48–9.

[85] See, Athenagoras, *Legatio*, 1. Tertullian, *Ad Scapulam* 2, and note the statement attributed to the Proconsul Valerius Pudens (*circa* 166), 'Pudens etiam missum ad se christianum in elogio concussione eius intellecta dimisit, scisso eodem elogio, *sine accusatore negans se auditurum hominem secundum mandatum*' (Tertullian, *Ad Scapulam*, 4.4, CSEL., lxxvi, 14).

[86] art. cit., 407, and cf. M. Conrat, *Die Christenverfolgungen*, 23.

[87] *Digest*, xlviii.4.1. For a thorough discussion of the various crimes Christians might have been accused of, E. Le Blant, 'Sur les bases des poursuites dirigés contre les chrétiens', *Mémoires de l'Acad. des Inscriptions et Belles Lettres*, 1886, 358ff.

[88] Dio Cassius, 66.19.1 and 68.1.2 (ἀσέβεια = maiestas); cf. Kubler, art. 'Maiestas' in *P.W.*, xiv.553. The punishment was death. Christians, however, were often scourged only. Lucian, *De Morte Peregrini*, 14.

[89] A. Momigliano, *CAH.*, x.888.

[90] Tertullian, *Apol.*, 15.7 and 24.5, *Ad Scapulam* 2.4 (CSEL., lxxvi), Octavius, *Minucius Felix* (ed. G. H. Rendall), 12.4.

[91] Tertullian, *Apol.*, 10.1. Th. Mommsen, *Römisches Strafrecht*, 569–70.

[92] Th. Mommsen, op. cit., 568ff. and H. Last, *Christenverfolgungen*, ii.1216–17.

[93] Spartian, *Vita Hadriani*, 18.4. 'Maiestatis crimina non admisit' (but Christians did not go scot-free!); Capitolinus, *Vita Antonini Pii*, 7.2. 'Quadruplatores extincti sunt' (i.e. informers who claimed a quarter of their victim's estate) and in *Vita Pertinacis*, 6.8. 'Quaestionem maiestatis penitus tulit cum iureiurando, revocavit etiam eos, qui deportati fuerant crimine maiestatis', and as if to emphasize the peculiarity of Domitian's policy, see Dio Cassius, 66.19.1 on Titus' contemptuous attitude towards charges of *maiestas*.

[94] Cicero, *De Legibus*, iii.3.8.

[95] There is one passage in the *Acta Carpi*, where the governor invokes the Imperial command as a means of getting Carpus and his companions to sacrifice. This may be a later emendation, or merely a spontaneous threat by the exasperated official. But as Mommsen points out (op. cit., 571), when it was a matter of swearing an oath, this would be taken 'by the Imperial genius' and the Roman gods.

[96] For the heinous character of *contumacia*, Cicero, *De Legibus*, iii.3.6, 'Justa imperia sunto, isque civis modeste et sine recusato parento. Magistratus nec obedientem et noxium civem multa vinculis verberibusve coherceto'. The anger of the Proconsul of Africa against the Scillitans on account of their obstinacy is shown by his statement, 'Though time was given them to return to Roman tradition, yet they remained obstinate in their will. Therefore, I condemn them to death by the sword'. A similar attitude was

adopted by the governor of Palestine during the Great Persecution. Eusebius, *Mart. Palest.*, iv.2. For criticism of Sherwin-White's emphasis on *contumacia* as 'the core of the official objection' to Christianity, see G. E. M. de Ste Croix, 'Why were the Early Christians persecuted?' *Past and Present*, 26, November 1963, 18–19, and subsequent debate between these two scholars, ibid., 27, 1964.

[97] Tacitus, *Histories*, ii.4, and v.5.13, and Josephus, *Wars*, ii.8.10. Cf. Julian, Ch.20.

[98] See Gal. 6[16]. Rev. 2[9], Ignatius, Philad. 6, and Justin, *Dialogue*, 123.7–8.

[99] A good example of this is provided by Thrasea Paetus quoted by Tacitus,*Annal.*, xvi.22, 'Quin et illa obiectabat, principio anni vitare Thraseam sollemne ius iurandam; nuncupationibus votorum non adesse, quamvis quindecemvirali sacerdotio praeditum; numquam pro salute principis aut caelesti voce immolavisse'. Only born Jews could be 'peregrini dedicitii nullius civitatis cives'.

[100] Hermas, *Simil.*, 1.3.

[101] *Antiquities*, xx.11.1.

[102] Ibid. My attention to these references has been called by Mr. C. E. Stevens of Magdalen College, Oxford.

[103] See S. G. F. Brandon's brilliant, *The Fall of Jerusalem and the Christian Church*, London, 1951, for many of whose insights I am indebted.

[104] Acts 1[6]. See Brandon, op. cit., 85.

[105] Rev. 22[20], *Didache*, 10.6.

[106] ii Clement, 1.1. 'Brethren, we must think of Jesus Christ as God . . . ' and also Pliny, *Letters*, x.96. For an interesting contribution on the LXX background of 'Kurios Christos' in Lamentations 4, J. Daniélou, 'Kurios Christos', *Mélanges Lebreton* (*RSR.*, 39, 1952, 338–52).

[107] Indicated by the contributions which the Pauline churches made to Jerusalem, Roms. 15[26-27]. On Paul's relations with James, T. W. Manson, 'The Problem of the Epistle to Galatians' = ch. 9 in *Studies in the Gospels and Epistles*, Manchester, 1962, especially 179ff. and for the tradition of James' personal pre-eminence as wearing the *Petalon* of the High Priest, Epiphanius, *Panarion*, 30.16.7 and 78.14.

[108] Josephus, *Wars*, ii.15.3 (Whiston).

[109] Acts 23[12ff.].

[110] Ibid., 21[30ff.].

[111] Josephus, *Antiquities*, xx.9.1., Eusebius, citing Hegesippus writing *circa* 170, *H.E.*, ii.23.4–18; cf. Lietzmann, *Geschichte*, i.185, and Telfer, op. cit., 14–16.

[112] Eusebius, *H.E.*, ii.23.16.

[113] Eusebius, *H.E.*, iv.22.4. The fact of kinship with Jesus was a vital qualification.

[114] Perhaps the apocalyptic pamphlet embedded in the Ethiopic *Ascension of Isaiah* may be dated to this period, in which the flight of believers in Jesus 'from desert to desert', awaiting His coming is justified. There is no reference to armed resistance to Belial.

[115] Brandon, op. cit., 180.

[116] Eusebius, *H.E.*, iii.5.3, Epiphanius, *Panarion*, 29.7.7. I am inclined to accept the dating of 68 for this event on the basis of Lk. 21[20]. See B. J. Kidd, *History of the Church*, 1.48. The civil war in Jerusalem in the winter of 67/8 leading to the triumph of the extremists would surely be the occasion for the flight of the Christians. For a contrary view, Brandon, op. cit., 170ff., and for the date 69/70, A. A. T. Ehrhardt, *Studia Theologica*, ix.2, 1955, 94.

[117] Josephus, *Wars*, ii.8.10. John the Essene commanded in north-west Judaea, ibid., iii.2.1.

CHAPTER SEVEN

Old Israel and New, 70–135

THERE is an interesting passage in Sulpicius Severus'
Chronicle which has sometimes been thought to have been
inspired from a lost book of Tacitus, to the effect that, after
the burning of the Temple,[1] the Emperor Titus turned over in his
mind the possibility of destroying both Judaism and Christianity.
*Quippe has religiones, licet contrarias sibi, isdem tamen ab auctoribus
profectas Christianos ex Judaeis extitisse, radice sublatam stirpem facile
perituram.* The terseness of the style is reminiscent of Tacitus, but
the content can hardly be so. By no stretch of imagination would
an author writing in the first years of the second century have
placed Christianity and Judaism on level terms. Tacitus in his
famous description of the Neronian persecution had to inform
his readers of the recent origins of the Christians before dilating
on their crimes. The Jews needed no such introduction. Nevertheless, the statement expresses remarkably accurately the relationship between Judaism and Christianity in the period between the
two great Jewish wars. 'Contrarias sibi, isdem tamen ab auctoribus
profectas', is reflected at every step in the sub-apostolic period.
The contest between the Old Israel and the New took precedence
over that between Christ and Caesar.

The fall of Jerusalem left a permanent mark on the development
of the Church. First and foremost, it meant a violent shift of
centre, in which the Church was gradually to lose Palestine, the
homeland of Jesus and his disciples, and with Palestine Aramaic-
speaking Judaism, including the opportunity of spreading eastwards beyond the Roman Empire into Persia and to the second
great centre of Jewry at Babylon. The tendency even in Palestine
was for the Church to become Hellenized, and hence, divorced
from national Jewish tradition.[2] In return, it gathered strength in
the large towns of the Dispersion, particularly in Antioch and the
coast of Asia Minor where there was a Jewish and proselyte
population. The language of its Scripture, liturgy and mission was

to be for the next century and a half almost exclusively Greek. Christianity thus became a 'Western' faith, and for the Romans another problem in the Greek-speaking lands of the Mediterranean.

From the scattered evidence of the Rabbinic sources, we can trace how, in the thirty or forty years after the fall of Jerusalem, the Christians in Palestine faded into a despised and dwindling heretical sect of Nazoreans.[3] Bishop Symeon and his successors at Jerusalem were no match for Rabbi Johanan ben Zakhai, Gamaliel II, Akiba and other leaders of the reforming movement within Judaism which emerged in the 'eighties and 'nineties. The synod of Jamnia in *circa* 90, confirmed their authority. While Gamaliel II was accepted as 'nasi' or 'universal patriarch' of the Jews by the Roman authorities,[4] the house of David sank into rustic obscurity.[5] The Jewish canon of Scripture was drawn up so as to exclude the Gospels and about the same time the sentence was added by Rabbi Samuel the Lesser to the traditional malediction of separatists, 'Let the Christian (*notzrim*) and the heretics (*minim*) perish as in a moment. Let them be wiped out of the book of life and with the righteous let them not be written'.[6] This petition was not intended as empty words. Gamaliel ordered the Benedictions to be recited three times a day.[7] It effectively excluded Christians from synagogue worship. From the Jewish point of view the separation was now complete.[8]

Nevertheless, the removal of the leadership from Jerusalem did not diminish acceptance of Jewish values, arguments and forms of worship in the Church. The sacrificial system and the Temple itself might be no more. What the Christians had foreseen the Zealots had now achieved.[9] It would be no longer possible for the Old and New Israels to find unity in Jerusalem. But another century was to pass before all recognizable links with the parent religion in the Greek-speaking world were to be severed. Christians might repudiate 'Jewish myths' (Tit. 1[14]), circumcision[10] and 'the fussiness and pride of the Jews',[11] but their way of thinking and life continued to resemble Judaism. Thus, Casey has wisely commented in his study of early Gnosticism, 'However much philosophy may have softened the blow, conversion to Christianity involved submission to the Jewish way of conceiving the origin of the universe and much of the history of mankind'.[12]

This is quite true. In the later books of the New Testament and the writings of the Apostolic Fathers we are still in what may best be described as a Judaeo-Christian world, even though the stage has moved from Palestine to Syria, Egypt and Asia Minor.[13] But in the Dispersion too, Christians, like the orthodox Jews, claimed to be the Way,[14] and they argued with their Jewish opponents in Rabbinical style over detailed questions of ceremonial observance.[15] Should one fast on Mondays and Thursdays, or on Wednesdays and Fridays?[16] Was the Jewish or the Christian interpretation of Leviticus 11 (food prescriptions) and Isaiah 7[14] the correct one?[17] Was the Crucifixion the true Passover? The Christian rite of baptism, down to the detailed prescriptions about the use of running water and women loosening their hair, seems to be derived from current Jewish proselyte baptism.[18] The outward forms of Christian organization and, it would seem, many features of the Christian liturgy, were recognizably those of the Hellenistic synagogue.[19] Jews and Christians might mutually insult each other as 'hypocrites',[20] 'heretics'[21] and 'atheists',[22] but the vital issue at stake was still which synagogue[23] represented Israel.[24]

The struggle in the period 70–135 was fought out with great bitterness both in Palestine and the Dispersion. In the former, orthodox Judaism was victorious, but in the latter the Christians held their own and began to gain ground. There was now, however, an interested third party, whose representatives were also convinced of the divine sanction for their mission to mankind.[25] The Roman authorities were no longer bystanders as they had been in Gallio's time. The events in Rome in 64 and in Judaea in 66–73 had changed this. The Jewish War was aptly described by Josephus in *circa* 75 as the 'greatest of all those not only that have been in our times but in a manner, of those that were ever heard of'.[26] So far as contemporary public opinion was concerned Josephus was right. The capture of Jerusalem was regarded as a great feat of arms, legitimizing the title of Vespasian to be celebrated and remembered throughout the Empire. The coinage of the time provides the proof. As Hart points out,[27] it is 'in all metals—not only gold and silver, it is on the poor man's brass, the money of the people, even to the little *quadrans* with its emblematic palm tree'. The whole Empire must concentrate on the one theme '*IUDAEA CAPTA*'. Nor was the struggle over. The perennial hostility between Jew and Greek burst out in a Jewish revolt in Cyrenaica in 73, as a result of which Vespasian had the second great centre of Jewish worship, the temple at Leontopolis, destroyed, as a possible focus for future revolt.[28] In 115–117, the Jewish rising engulfed most of the Hellenistic world, and the final terrible outburst in Palestine 132–135, justified all Rome's latent fears of Judaism. One of her main preoccupations in the Hellenistic east became the curbing of Judaism and its ramifications. One of the ramifications was Christianity.

For the time being, however, Christianity was a minor problem. Classical authors, representing the Roman and provincial upper classes speak of Judaism and conversion to Judaism,[29] but it is hard to find specific references to Christianity, despite the effort which has been expended in the search for new evidence. It is interesting that the only time when Roman authorities are recorded as taking the initiative against the Christians, was the reputed inquisition of Jesus' family's descendants about the character of 'the Christ and his kingdom' in the reign of Domitian.[30] They suspected the practical application of apocalyptic hopes, as well they might. Even in Asia Minor, where the Church was strongest, Christianity was one of the lesser problems which confronted Pliny in his investigations into provincial mismanagement in 112–113. In Antioch and in Palestine there were isolated conflicts between the authorities and the Christians, but none in Alexandria nor the remainder of the Hellenistic world. The total recorded 'incidents' in the whole Empire for two generations may be counted on the fingers of one hand.

Thus, the historian of persecutions and martyrdom is faced with a conflict of evidence. On the one hand, there is relative lack of notice taken by the authorities of the Christians. They exist, and if Hermas' evidence means anything, by the early second century the community in Rome was well organized, active and faced with all the problems of lapse, schism, apostasy and self-indulgent contact with pagan society that the Church as a whole hardly found itself involved in until a century later.[31] But the authorities, after careful consideration, treated the Christians with indulgence. Denunciation and anonymous pamphlets against them were regarded as 'a very bad precedent', and 'out of keeping

with the spirit of our age'—so Trajan to Pliny.[32] Christians were
not subjected to the rapine and massacre that befell their Jewish
neighbours in the great uprising of 115–117 and in the Second
Jewish War, 132–135.

Yet in contrast, and almost as if in defiance of the indulgence
of the Roman authorities, the sub-apostolic age marks the long
climax of the first wave of Christian apocalyptic,[33] and in these
yearnings Rome was cast in the role of the Second Babylon, the
capital of corruption, the persecuting enemy.[34] The Emperor
himself was represented as Beliar, 'the matricide' (Nero)[35] or 'the
Beast' (Domitian).[36] The Christians saw themselves as the People
chosen to prepare the way for the Millennium by their suffering
and by martyrdom to earn its enjoyment hereafter. They vied
with the orthodox Jews in their descriptions of the Age to Come
and the fiery fate in store for their enemies; and the Greco-Roman
world was the enemy.

Many congregations must have been kept at fever pitch by
such hopes and expectations. Writings as different in origin and
viewpoint as the Christian recension of the Ascension of Isaiah,
the Didache, the Epistle of Barnabas and the sermon known as
ii Clement all assume that the interregnum in which Christians
were living was fast coming to a close.[37] 'Let grace come and the
world pass away. Hosannah to the God of David' (Didache 10.6).
This was the theme,[38] and it was often accompanied by lurid
expectation of horrors such as those portrayed in the Apocalypse
of Peter, or fantastic descriptions of the material joys of Paradise.[39]
Thus writes Papias of Hierapolis *circa* 130 in a lost work cited
by Irenaeus:

> The days will come in which the vines will grow each having ten
> thousand branches, and in each branch ten thousand twigs, and in
> each [true] twig ten thousand shoots, and in each one of the shoots ten
> thousand clusters, and on every one of the clusters ten thousand
> grapes, and every grape when pressed will give twenty five measures
> of wine. And when any of the saints shall lay hold of a [holy] cluster,
> another shall cry 'I am a better cluster, take me and bless the Lord
> through me'.[40] (Tr. Roberts and Donaldson, *A.N.C.L.*, slightly
> altered.)

In emphasizing the reality of this fervent anti-world and anti-
Greco-Roman movement in the Church at this period, one must

not ignore the existence of more moderate voices. In the Pastorals, for instance, Christians were advised against raising charges against themselves, and persecution was regarded as a misfortune. In i Peter, charges, if they were of a criminal nature were to be avoided, but persecution 'for the Name' was to be accepted gladly as a sign that Judgment was about to begin (i Peter 4[16]). In i Clement there was praise for the discipline of the Roman legionaries (who would have been the agents of any persecution) and indeed for the whole Imperial chain of command,[41] and this would have sounded curious to the apocalyptist. So too, would the beautiful prayer on behalf of earthly rulers with which Clement's letter ends.[42] To these may be added the apparently more restrained attitude of the writer of the 'Unknown Gospel' (early second century) towards the State.[43] The story of the tribute penny has been modified, and the question of the scribes made more general than in the Synoptics. 'Should we give to the kings what pertaineth to their rule? (Should we give) or not?' No doubt Jesus returned the same answer as in Mt. 22[21], but now there was less question of Interim ethics and more of a general obligation to obey the civil authorities.

There were even those who were beginning to doubt the approach of the Parousia. 'The fathers had fallen asleep and all things continue as they were from the beginning of creation.' ii Peter 3[3ff.] sharply rebukes such individuals, as 'mockers, who walk according to their own lusts'. Such voices would become increasingly common during the second century. They were the forerunners of those Apologists who sought to find common ground between the Church and the Empire, and of the Catholics who sought to moderate the zeal of the voluntary martyr. Further along this same road was the Alexandrian school of Gnostics who, towards the end of the reign of Hadrian,[44] were beginning to raise their voice against martyrdom itself. For the time being, however, these voices of reason were muffled by the ecstatic cries of those who saw the 'throne of the Lamb' opposed to Satan's throne (Rev. 2[13]). In the resulting cosmic struggle the martyrdom of the saints at the hands of the Roman authorities would ensure the victory of Christ.

Not unreasonably, educated Romans and provincials who came into contact with Christians regarded them either as mad or as dangerous sectaries.[45] The fact that such contact was happily rare involves the historian of the period working on two levels, that of prophecy and eschatology when he is concerned with Christian writings, and that of human activity and events when he turns to the Classical authors. Only seldom, such as on the arrest of Ignatius of Antioch *circa* 107 or during Pliny's investigations in Bithynia in 112–113 do these levels coincide. For the rest, Jerusalem and Babylon move on different planes.

The one continuing theme throughout this period is Jewish-Christian hostility, the *contrarias sibi* aspect of their relationship. Occasionally, this involved intervention by the Roman authorities, as suggested perhaps in Revelation, and in the trial of Bishop Symeon ben Clopas before the Roman governor of Jerusalem in *circa* 107. At other times, the Jews would take direct action, expressed perhaps in the term 'blasphemies' attributed to the 'synagogue of Satan' at Smyrna (Rev. 2⁹). The Jewish tactics did not vary from those employed in the previous generation, namely the denunciation of Christians as dangers to the State, accompanied by a constant harrying of their daily lives. For readers of Matthew's Gospel this situation presaged the end of the world.[46] A greater readiness to witness for the Name and die the martyr's death before it was too late was the result.

Palestine provides the first direct evidence of denunciations and ample proof of the reactions produced among the Christians to these and other hostile acts. In *circa* 95 Gamaliel accompanied by two colleagues from Jamnia paid a prolonged visit to Rome, probably with a view to convincing Domitian of the loyalty of their people in face of threatening persecution.[47] One consequence of this visit was to strengthen the Jamnia assembly's claim to represent Israel at the expense of rivals, including Christianity. Gamaliel's life's work was regarded as determination 'that factions should not increase in Israel', and he may even have assisted personally in controverting Palestinian Christians.[48] In 107(?), Eusebius records on the authority of Hegesippus (*flor.* 150–170) that Symeon ben Clopas, a younger cousin of Jesus and now aged bishop of Jerusalem, was accused by 'certain heretics', and 'tortured in various manners for being a Christian', eventually being martyred.[49] Significantly, having regard to Roman anxieties on this score, the accusers added the fact that he 'was descended from David', that is, a possible Pretender, as well as a

Christian. The Roman governor, Atticus, even though he commanded him to be crucified, was evidently amazed at the old man's constancy. Hegesippus claims further that the accusers were themselves of 'royal Jewish lineage', which would leave no doubt that the inspiration of the charge against Symeon came from Jewish enemies in Jerusalem.[50] He was not the only victim. In the same period, Rabbi Eliezer of Lydda also was accused before the governor (*hegemon*) of Christianity.[51] Fortunately in his case, the governor ridiculed him, 'Will an old man such as you busy yourself about these vanities?' he asked, and then released him.

These are early cases of Christianity being treated as an offence, and they appear to be the direct outcome of Jewish hostility. So deep was the cleavage between Jews and Christians in Palestine becoming that Jews would refuse the healing offices of Christians and preferred to perish rather than allow a Christian to help them.[52] Akiba consigned to perdition all Jews who so much as read Christian books.[53] Rabbi Tarpon was said to have declared that he would prefer to flee to a heathen temple rather than a sectarian meeting-house.[54] The Christians were hated and despised worse than the pagans who had the excuse of ignorance.[55] They openly flouted God's law.[56]

Christian sources confirm these impressions. Perhaps some of the bitterness of Matthew's Gospel,[57] such as the terrible denunciation of the Jewish leaders in Mt. 23 and the awful picture of wars and disaster drawn in the next chapter are to be explained by reference to these tribulations. Houses were divided, Christians were being haled before the justices, the love of many was waxing cold (24[12]). There was tribulation and mutual hatred. The faithful were exhorted to endure to the end, and comforted, as the Pauline Christians had been, by the hope that present suffering would shorten even the brief interval to the end of the Age (Mt. 24[21–23] and 28[20]). In the Fourth Gospel, the Jewish people are depicted in unrelieved black. 'Ye are of your father the Devil' (Jn. 8[44]). They were the unbelieving and perverted nation, the constant foe of Jesus and his disciples, and determined on his death despite Pilate's opposition.[58] It has been well pointed out that the controversies in which Jesus engages may reproduce the theological debates of Church and synagogue at the end of the first century. The penalty for acknowledging Jesus was cursing and expulsion from the synagogues.[59] In the Gospel of Thomas (*circa* 100–140?) the Aramaic tradition embedded in it presents the Jews as 'men who did not understand Jesus', and therefore opposed him (Logion 44). An angry silence walled off the two communities.[60] We hear of Christians in some of the larger Palestinian centres such as Capernaum, Sepphoris, Tiberias and Jerusalem, but Palestine as a whole remained loyal to Judaism.[61]

Defeat in Palestine was, however, compensated by success in the Dispersion. By the end of the first century, the Church had begun the long process of absorbing the great majority of the 'devout' and semi-proselytes. This was the justification for Eusebius' statement at the beginning of Book iv of the *Ecclesiastical History*, that whereas the situation of Judaism went from bad to worse, that of the Church steadily improved.[62] During the second century the term for Jewish proselyte θεοσεβής became interchangeable with χριστιανός in Antioch,[63] while at the other geographical extreme of the Dispersion, at Lyons, Christians were known by the other term used for converts to Judaism, φοβουμένοι.[64] How would this have sounded in the ears of Jews, say at Miletus, where 'θεοσεβεῖς' and ''Ιουδαῖοι had once been regarded by the authorities as one and the same?[65] Some indication of this process may be found perhaps in the first chapter of i Peter. This shows the Church in existence in the Asian provinces of Pontus, Bithynia and Cappadocia whither Paul had never penetrated. The latter itself appears to be addressed to communities who had a previous acquaintance with the language and hope of Israel, and had been 'begotten again unto a lively hope by the resurrection of Jesus Christ from the dead' (i Peter 1[3]).

More than that, the Church was making its appeal to the born pagan, men and women who had not previously been in contact with the synagogue. An echo of this tendency may be preserved in Epictetus' complaint about this time, 'Why do you act the part of a Jew when you are a Greek?'[66] The personal story of Justin, told by himself, is an interesting example of one such conversion *circa* 130.[67] Justin was born probably of Greek settler family in Neapolis in Palestine. He apparently never considered solving his religious problems by becoming a Jew, but he tried his luck for a good many years with all the main philosophic schools. The Stoics he rejected, because of their lack of interest in God, the

Pythagoreans because of their insistence on an acquaintance with music and numbers as essential steps to that knowledge. He nearly settled with the Platonists until his encounter with an ancient Christian on the sea-shore (near Ephesus?) and the sight of Christian martyrs finally converted him to Christ.[68] He became a Christian philosopher, combining the mantle, the solitary and ascetic life of the pagan convert to philosophy with trust in salvation through Christ. And like his pagan contemporary he used the ease of communication to wander abroad and preach his message. From Ephesus he travelled to Rome, established a primitive school for Christians, and he was martyred there *circa* 165. We see in Justin an example of the dissatisfied Greek mind, muddled, but unattracted either by current philosophy or Judaism, and therefore turning to Christianity. He represents an attitude of unexpressed revolt against his times and perhaps it is no accident that he eventually found the Cynics his nearest and deadliest rivals.

The steady spread of Christianity in the Greek-speaking East during the last part of the first and the early second century is evident when we turn to the individual provinces. For Bithynia there is the independent testimony of Pliny who describes in his report to Trajan on the Christians in the eastern part of the province, how some had abandoned the new religion 20 years previously (i.e. around 92).[69] On the Black Sea coast at Sinope, there must have been a Christian community in *circa* 85, for Marcion's father was bishop of it. Farther south, in the province of Asia, it has been plausibly suggested that the Seven Churches addressed by the seer in Revelation 2–3 were missionary centres.[70] Phrygia, as Papias shows, had Christian communities by the middle of the second century.[71] In the islands a start towards the evangelization of Crete was undertaken by Titus.[72] In Syria, Ignatius' correspondence shows that Christianity had spread beyond Antioch into the province.[73] In Egypt, perhaps by the reign of Hadrian, St. John's Gospel was circulating among communities in the Nile valley in Greek,[74] and so, too, was the mysterious 'Unknown Gospel'[75] composed of Johannine and Synoptic material mingled with accounts of Jesus from independent and yet non-Gnostic traditions. Asia Minor and Egypt, two of the main centres of the Dispersion, replaced Palestine as the main sources of Christian missionary endeavour and doctrinal speculation. Christianity became irrevocably bound up with Rome's policy in the Hellenistic world.

In the West progress was slower. However, there may have been Christian families in Pompeii and Herculaneum before 79.[76] At Rome itself, leaders of the Greek-speaking communities in the capital were beginning to step into the place left by the decline of Christianity in Jerusalem.[77]

The Church's advance was, however, sharply contested by the Jews of the Dispersion. These now appear in Christian sources in the guise both of persecutors and heretics. The Nicolaitans of Revelation,[78] the Docetists of Ignatius' correspondence,[79] and the Cerinthians[80] all seem to be Jewish or Judaeo-Christian heretics active in the province of Asia at the turn of the first century. More significant than any dialectic obstruction, however, was the open and intensive rivalry between the two Synagogues, competing for the conversion of the pagan world before the end of the existing Age took place.

Far from retiring into its shell after 70, the next fifty years sees Hellenistic Judaism make one final bid for victory over both paganism and Christianity.[81] Indeed, what strikes the historian is the equality of resource, propaganda and attractive power at the disposal of the contestants. In wealth and position the Jewish communities had the advantage. It is evident that benefactors like Claudius Tiberius Polycharmus, who left a synagogue and indeed an entire cult area complete with elaborate buildings, to the Jewish community at Stobi in northern Macedonia, may not have been altogether exceptional.[82] Descendants of the Phrygian royal house seem to have been among the benefactors of the synagogue at Akhmonia in Phrygia,[83] the rich guild of purple-dyers at Hierapolis was headed by a Roman citizen, Publius Aelius Glycon,[84] and in Egypt a papyrus dating to A.D. 113 records the large payment of 1536 drachmae (128 dr. a month) 'by the rulers of the Jews for the synagogue of the Thebans' at Arsinoë, for water supplies.[85] They and others like them were wealthy and influential communities. The Jews in the Empire could boast their Josephus and even Tiberius Claudius Alexander, both high in Imperial favour and of world-wide renown.[86]

When one compares this with what little we know of the Christian communities of the day a difference is evident. Polycarp's Church at Smyrna, *circa* 110, was a tightly knit and well-organized group, containing some individuals who were wealthy enough to undertake hospitality and charity,[87] and sufficiently literate to understand and no doubt read the Christian Scriptures, now in process of being committed to writing. Hermas' Church in Rome was similarly placed.[88] Elsewhere, the churches must have had their patrons, like Phoebe at the port of Cenchraea, 'who hath been a succourer of many' (Rom. 16[2]), but no one pretended that the Christian synagogues were wealthy places. Though the conversion of 'whole houses', including family and slaves, must have preserved a social balance within the Church, the general impression left on contemporaries was of squalor as well as disrepute.[89] Slaves made up a sizeable part of the community.[90] If one may judge from Polycarp's letter to the Philippians the Church at Smyrna tended also to be inward-looking, concerned with perfecting its own morality in preparation for the End, blameless 'before the Gentiles' rather than striving to convert them.[91]

On this score as well, the Dispersion Jews showed themselves to better advantage. They were intensely keen to propagate their religion, hawking proselytism and groceries from door to door[92] and influencing those around them long after they ceased to be politically dangerous.[93] In *circa* 128 Juvenal wrote his account of the gradual conversion of a family to Judaism in a process extending over two generations. It was slow, but thorough, and in the end complete.[94] In these proselytes, the Jews had their firmest allies in the struggle against the Church. They, after all, had everything to lose by the latter's victory, and Justin records that those whom he came across preserved a double portion of hatred for Christians.[95]

In other ways Jewish propaganda was intelligent and took full account of the mood of the day. In the capital they had succeeded in adapting their religion to some aspects of the prevailing mystery cults. The Seven-branched candlestick appears on sarcophagi otherwise given over to Dionysiac symbols.[96] In Carthage[97] and Alexandria[98] they continued to gain adherents among pagans until the turn of the third century;[99] and as trump card, Jewish magic and associated powers of exorcism and healing retained a high repute.[100]

These efforts were supported by skilful argument. As Seneca had pointed out, the Jews 'knew the cause of their rites, whilst the greater part of the people know not why they perform theirs'.[100a] The iv and v Sibyllines, written probably around 80 and 130 respectively, show that the major Jewish appeal to pagans was still that theirs was a universal faith for mankind, a lofty monotheism teaching an equally lofty ethic. In the Flavian period, many Jews in Asia were not sorry to see the end of the Temple and the sacrificial system. The writer of iv Sibyllines attributed the disaster of 70 to the Jews themselves, and regarded the destruction of the Temple as God's condemnation of Jewish folly and godlessness.[101] Josephus himself had come to the same conclusion through his personal experience of the conduct of the war by the rebel leaders.[102] These Jews spoke instead of a 'sacrifice of prayers',[103] of the restoration of spiritual worship without buildings made with hands, inaugurated by the prophets.[104] With these liberal views went an appeal to 'sensible men' in the provinces. 'Discern rightly, distinguish between piety and impiety, keep oneself from evil.' That was the ideal of just men, and what better guide was there than Torah?[105] 'For I suppose it will thence become evident that the laws we have given us are disposed after the best manner for the advancement of piety, for mutual communion with one another, for a general love of mankind, as also for justice and for sustaining labours with fortitude, and for contempt of death.'[106] Josephus' answer to Apion *circa* 90, dedicated to the rich freedman Epaphroditus, fairly expressed the propaganda appeal which Judaism was making to educated provincials. The Dispersion had given the Jews the means of spreading God's truth universally, and not unnaturally, they emphasized their traditional claim to be the future 'guide of life to all mortals'.[107]

There was also the war of nerves. Josephus might tell Apion that the Alexandrian Greeks would receive 'a warm welcome' from their Jewish brethren if they cared to join them,[108] but there was the prospect of an even warmer one hereafter if they did not. Jewish writings of the period between the two Jewish wars were marked by the most intense hatred for Rome and all her works. There was even a certain tenderness towards 'poor Corinth'[109] and even 'poor Egypt',[110] a solidarity, that is, even with the pagan inhabitants of the Greek cities, but Rome herself was treated without mercy. In both v Sibyllines and iv Ezra the saga of the four empires was recalled, with Rome as the fourth and most iniquitous, soon to be destroyed. The Roman eagle would be struck down, 'and the whole earth freed from thy [Rome's] violence would be refreshed again'.[111] The author of iv Ezra looked for the coming of the Messianic kingdom in Domitian's day.[112] He was not alone. In the Apoc. of Baruch, and those verses of iii Sibyllines which may perhaps be attributed to the period after the Fall of Jerusalem, Rome and Antichrist seem to be equated, and Rome's overthrow was prophesied at the hands of a messianic war-leader (Apoc. of Baruch, 40.3). The great earthquakes in Cyprus in 76 and the eruption of Vesuvius in 79 encouraged the writer of iv Sibylline to hope that this was a sign of an equally violent end of the Roman world. 'God shall burn the whole earth, and consume the whole race of men. He shall burn everything up and there shall remain sooty dust'.[113] Both he and the writer of v Sibylline looked forward with glee to the destruction of Rome, her armies crushed by Parthian enemies from the East, led by Nero redivivus.[114] This appeal was relevant in Asia in the last quarter of the first century.[115] The Jews of Asia combined their lofty sounding universalism with a direct appeal to the old Hellenistic tradition of hostility to Rome. They yielded not a whit to the Christians in apocalyptic fervour. The two rival religions were appealing to the same latent discontents among the Eastern provincials.

All the advantages, however, of wealth, lawful status, a coherent religious sense and revolutionary appeal to dissatisfied provincials, were nullified by one fact. Judaism remained a national cult, protected indeed by its claim to antiquity, but repellant to most non-Jews. So reasonable a man as Trypho must open his discussion with Justin, at Ephesus, circa 137, with the admonition (Dialogue, 8.4) 'If you are willing therefore to listen also to me, first be circumcised, then as is commanded by the Law, keep the Sabbath Feasts and God's New Moons, and in short, do all the things written in the Law, and then perhaps you will find mercy from God'. How distasteful such advice would sound to the individual who had rejected idolatry and the mystery cults is evident from the early chapters of the Letter to Diognetus.[116] It was not only the oppressive ceremonial law that had to be

accepted. The Jew seems even at that time to have been distinguished by his dress, [117] his food, his dwelling in a separate quarter
of the town,[118] distinctions which the Christians explicitly
rejected.[119] Though some eminent individuals, like Aquila of
Pontus[120] and Theodotion were prepared to pay the price, this
was too high for most people. Christianity provided the alternative, and the new religion was conscious of gradually winning
the struggle.[121]

These deadly rivalries resulted in constant strife between Jew
and Christian. In the province of Asia, persecution of the Christians by the Jews seems at times to have been severe, and it was
supported by fierce polemic against the person and work of
Jesus Christ. The 'evil teachers' and disobedient windbags among
the circumcised in Titus (Titus 1[10–11]) become in Revelation,
persecutors, and agents of persecution, to be denounced in
memorable and terrible terms. While the debate with 'false
Jews'[122] was continuous, the threat of imprisonment and death at
their hands was never far absent.[123]

On three occasions during his discussion with Trypho at
Ephesus, Justin accuses the Jews of having chosen 'selected men
from Jerusalem' and sending them out into all parts of the earth
saying 'that a godless sect, namely the Christians, had appeared
and recounting what all who know us not are wont to say against
us'. So, adds Justin, 'that you are not only the cause of iniquity for
yourselves, but in fact for all others'.[124] The reference to Jerusalem
suggests the existence of a longstanding tradition persisting down
to the time, *circa* 160, when Justin wrote up the account of his
debate and which he repeated as well-known facts. The same
reproach was made by Origen,[125] and Eusebius preserves a
further interesting piece of corroborative testimony. He claims
that 'we found in the writings of former days (ἐν τοῖς τῶν παλαιῶν
συγγράμμασιν) that the Jewish authorities in Jerusalem sent round
apostles to the Jews everywhere announcing the emergence of a
new heresy hostile to God, and that these apostles, armed with
written authority, confuted the Christians everywhere'.[126] This
is practically the same as Justin's account, and like it, must in its
original form go back to the period before the fall of Jerusalem.

From a third source, the debate between the Jew and the
Christian preserved in Celsus, and dating perhaps to the first half

of the second century (certainly no later than 160), we can gain some idea of the character of the Jewish propaganda about Jesus. Jesus was born, they said, in a village, the illegitimate child of a peasant woman and soldier named Panthera.[127] The woman was divorced by her husband who was a carpenter, for adultery. Jesus himself emigrated to Egypt, hired himself out as a labourer there, and after picking up some Egyptian magic, returned to his own country and full of conceit because of his powers proclaimed himself God. His so-called miracles were unauthenticated, his prophesies were proved false and in the end he was not helped by the Father, nor could he help himself.[128] His disciples had taken his body and pretended that he had risen again and was Son of God.[129] The emphasis of this critique lay on the fraudulent nature of Jesus' claims. The Christians were regarded as having been deceived and had abandoned the true teaching of Israel for the sake of 'an imposter justly punished for his misdeeds'.[130] 'Where is your master, whose follower you were? He has deceived you, this Nazarene has hardened your hearts, and perverted you from the tradition of your fathers.' Thus speaks the Pharisee whom John is related to have met in the Temple after the Crucifixion in the opening lines of the Egyptian Gnostic, *Apocryphon Joannis*,[131] and the setting of the scene by the Temple suggests an early tradition. But all the time, Christianity was regarded by these Jews as a heresy within the context of Judaism, and the vigour of the Jews of the Dispersion in the generation which followed the fall of Jerusalem boded ill for the Christians.

To the tensions engendered by daily conflict with the Jews were added the effects of the conscious policy of Romanization (or Hellenization) pursued by the Flavians and their successors in the provinces. This contributed to bring Christianity into direct conflict with the predominant pagan order, as we can trace from the 'seventies onwards.[132] Vespasian made a considerable effort to ensure the allegiance and contentment of the cities of the province of Asia, and in return, many of these conferred the title of Benefactor upon him.[133] As a mark of this, a handsome temple to the Augusti was built at Ephesus, and it seems likely that the establishment of the neocorate, the priesthood directly connected with the Imperial cult began in this reign.[134] Moreover, the spread of civilized ways of life throughout the provinces was accompanied by the development of intimate relations between the provincial authorities and the representatives of the traditional native cults. Ramsay quotes the instance of Vespasian including the great *hieron* of Comana on the military road towards the Persian frontier though it lay off its natural line.[135] Under Domitian, the process of associating native religions and the Imperial cult gathered pace. In the medium-sized Phrygian town of Laodicea a temple was built in 83 in honour of the Emperor's victories in Germany, and the festival of Zeus came to be celebrated on the same day as that of Domitian. In Ephesus dedications to Artemis were also associated with those to the Emperor,[136] and in the precincts of the great temple to Diana stood a colossal statue, three times life size, of the Emperor.[137] At Pergamum stood the Temple of Augustus and altar of Victory—the Satan's throne of Rev. 2[13] in all probability.[138] Romanization had brought the cults of the native and Greek cities into strictest alliance with that of the Emperor, and in Asia the process reached a climax during Domitian's reign.[139] There was nothing consciously anti-Christian in this. Similar processes were going on in other provinces, in Britain for instance.[140] The result was, however, intensified apocalyptic fervour among the Christians in the province, who now saw visible evidence of the increasing influence of idolatry, added to the hostility encountered from 'the synagogue of Satan'. The Second Beast which arose from the sea may well represent the Imperial priesthood in Asia (Rev. 13).[141] This combination of evils contributed to Christian hostility towards Rome, regarded as the centre of idolatry, and as a corollary, to the fanatical desire for martyrdom found among many Christians.

We turn finally to the characteristic expression of this outlook found in the works of Hermas and Ignatius, the latter meditating on the meaning of martyrdom during his long journey as a prisoner on the way from Antioch to Rome *circa* 107, but Hermas, as a prophet writing in Rome *circa* 100–130, without apparent reference to any known persecution. Indeed, his work is a striking illustration of how small was the contact between the eschatological hopes of a Christian community and events at this time. Despite his allusions to the Sibyl of Cumae, Arcadia, the countryside outside Rome, and his characterization of the Church as a Tower, like the Pythagorean 'Tower of Zeus', Hermas is thoroughly Judaeo-Christian.[142] His association of Wisdom-Holy Spirit, his limited dualism and his apocalyptic imagery are derived directly from post-Maccabean Jewish models, and not surprisingly, some critics have gone so far as to recognize him as a convert from immigrant Essenism in Rome.[143] In any event, the Shepherd sheds light on ideas circulating among Christians drawn from among the petit-bourgeoisie in Rome, and surprising these are.

Hermas has no doubt about the hostile relations between the People of God and the world, and the exclusive nature of the former. Indeed, the Babylon-Jerusalem concept of Revelation is formalized into that of the two permanently opposed cities.[144] The Christian had his city in heaven, whose law (νόμος) was that of the Son of God,[145] and whose governor was the archangel Michael.[146] The Church was the people of God, organized as a synagogue on earth, but represented ideally as a tower built from material taken from twelve mountains—a clear allegory of the twelve tribes of Israel[147]—whose members had received the seal of baptism.[148] Hermas' simile for the Church on earth was a vast willow tree, whose branches were given to the elect as protection against the Devil and the Kosmos over which he ruled.[149] This 'earthly city' had a law of its own. It was described as foreign to the Christian, being 'under the power of another'. Its ruler could reasonably say to the servant of God, 'Either use my law, or go out of my country',[150] and the Christian should gladly accept his expulsion. So, adds Hermas, 'you may go out from his city and depart to your own city, and follow your own law, suffering no harm'.[151]

This remarkable passage, indicating a conscious opposition to the life and civilization of the Roman world, may explain much of the stubborn will to martyrdom, the *obstinatio*, of the Christian in this period. For people brought up to hear 'frightful words such as a man cannot bear', uttered against heathen and apostates,[152] and to associate the Imperial power with a devouring monster,[153] little sense of loyalty to the Empire could have been possible. The heathen, who included the Christian's earthly rulers, 'would be burnt, because they did not know their creator'.[154] The apocalyptic vision involved destruction of entire peoples and nations.

Yet even amid all the threats against the enemies of the Church, there are glimmerings of more hopeful and realistic views regarding the role of Christians in the world. Hermas had meditated on the problem of wealth. On the one hand, he anticipates the outlook of the Africans Tertullian and Cyprian, who condemned wealth and good living as symbols of apostasy, and he can write, 'When tribulation comes on account of their riches and because of business they deny the Lord',[155] and castigate 'those who become rich and in honour among the heathen'.[156] But, even so, he refuses to condemn wealth out of hand. The rich might be 'poor in the sight of the Lord',[157] but charitable work on behalf of the materially poor was also pleasing to Him. Indeed, rich and poor both work together to complete the work of prayer to God.[158] Just as when he considers the problem of sin and repentance,[159] he is reluctant to take away all hope from those whom on general grounds he feels belong to the adversary. Like other Christians in the second and early third centuries he is torn between a sympathy for his fellow men and the demands of the approaching End which he both welcomed and feared.

Hermas anticipated tribulation.[160] Persecution of the elect was part of the natural order of events. There would be 'Stripes, imprisonments, great afflictions, crucifixions, wild beasts for the sake of the Name'.[161] These were the signs that 'would accompany the end of the world', which 'must be destroyed by blood and fire'.[162] The elect would be 'tried in the fire'[163] and having passed through it 'would be chosen by God for eternal life'.[164] The martyrs represented the highest station within the ranks of the elect, on 'the right side of the holiness',[165] superior to himself, prophet though he was. 'As many as ever suffered for the name are glorious before God', he declares elsewhere, 'and the sins of these have been taken away because they have suffered for the name of the son of God'.[166] These were glorious before God. Here, too, Hermas anticipates the North African tradition exemplified by Tertullian.[167] Martyrdom was thus the sovereign atonement for sin. His picture of eternal reward resembles that portrayed in Daniel, the emphasis being on suffering bringing its own vindication through forgiveness of sin. This was the aspect of martyrdom which the Western Church was to continue to stress in the third and fourth centuries. However, the positive New Testament ideas of witnessing to the truth and the martyr's imitation of the Passion of Christ are absent. With Hermas we seem to return to the older, pre-Christian tradition of Jewish martyrdom, with the Roman emperors in the role of the Seleucids. His legacy lasted long in Western Christendom, and, significantly, the Church at Lyons regarded the Shepherd as Scripture.[168]

Similar ideas are present in the Epistle of Barnabas[169] where the State is accepted to be an instrument of Satan. Christians were told (c. 2) that 'the worker of evil himself was in power', and that the final trial was at hand (c. 4).[170] We find the same message in the Hellenistic-Christian sermon which has been preserved under the title of ii Clement (*circa* 120–150). Here too, the brethren are urged to have no fear of the world, but to leave it. 'Let the lambs have no fear of the wolves after their death.'[171] Service to the world would bring only eternal punishment. The day of Judgment was already approaching 'and the whole earth shall be as lead melting in the fire'.[172] Once more, as in Hermas, the unrighteous 'enjoyed wealth'[173] and the servants of God 'endured tortures'.[174] Denial of the Lord would bring 'terrible torture in unquenchable fire'.[175] Suffering at the hands of the authorities was not regarded as accidental. ii Clement sees it as part of a pattern of events in which the people of God, 'awaiting the kingdom of God from hour to hour'[176] and gathered into a Church which had pre-existed from all time, opposed the worldly powers.[177] In their own age these were characterized by the Roman Empire.

Against this background of exaltation, hostility to pagan society and hope of speedy deliverance, the phenomenon of Ignatius of Antioch can best be studied. In the seven genuine letters[178] written to the Churches in Asia Minor through which he passed on his way to Rome, *circa* 107–108,[179] and to the Roman community itself, he exhibits the theology of martyrdom of the primitive Church at its most intense. Ignatius is the first Christian martyr (apart from Paul) who has left us evidence of his state of mind as he went on the long journey under guard which led from Antioch, through the Greek cities of western Asia Minor to Troas and then by the Via Egnatia to Rome. He had been condemned, probably as a Roman citizen, to fight the beasts in the amphitheatre at Rome.[180] His letters display a state of exaltation bordering on mania, but his example of voluntary martyrdom had its forerunners among the Jews, and was to be followed in the second century by Christians like Agathonike,[181] Lucius of Rome,[182] and Quintus who deliberately courted death at the hands of the authorities.[183] His outlook was to be praised by Irenaeus (*Adv. Haer.*, v.28.4). Why did Ignatius do this? His letter to the Christians in Rome (*Roms.* 4) speaks for itself.

> 'I am writing to all the Churches', he says, 'and I give injunctions to all men, that I am dying willingly for God's sake, if you do not hinder it. I beseech you, be not "an unseasonable kindness" to me. Suffer me to be eaten by the beasts, through whom I can attain to God. I am God's wheat, and I am ground by the teeth of wild beasts that I may be found pure bread of Christ. Rather entice the wild beasts that they may become my tomb, and leave no trace of my body, that when I fall asleep I be not burdensome to any. Then shall I be truly a disciple of Jesus Christ, when the world shall not even see my body. Beseech Christ on my behalf, that I may be found a sacrifice through these instruments' (tr. Kirsopp Lake).

Like the Maccabees in the tradition of the Antiochene-Jewish iv Macc. he regards his death in sacrificial terms,[184] and as 'sweet' and as a 'grace'.[185] True discipleship was also equated with death as a witness to the death and resurrection of Jesus and as a symbol of the bonds which bound disciple to Master. Ignatius' religion may be summed up by the words 'ἐν χριστῷ', and the quotations from John and Paul testify to the mystical inspiration of his thought.[186] 'My soul is devoted to the Cross, which is an offence to unbelievers, but to us salvation and eternal life' (*Ephes.*, 18.1). 'It is better to die in Christ Jesus than to be king over the ends of the earth', he tells the Romans (*Roms.*, 6.1). Here, he echoes the famous Pauline 'For to me to live is Christ and to die is gain' (Phil. 1^{21}), and like Paul 'sharing in His sufferings' in the same epistle (Phil. 3^{10}), Ignatius urged the need of direct imitation of the Passion of Christ.[187] 'Suffer me to follow the example of the Passion of my God', he writes (*Roms.*, 6.3), and this objective was to be urged also by Ignatius' contemporary, Polycarp, in his letter to the Philippians (8.2). He regards his bonds and sufferings as powerful means of exhortation (*Trall.*, 12.2). The Christian was enjoined to be literally nailed to the Cross with Jesus. For the reward of being eternally with his Master, he must die at the hands of the authorities also (*Magnes.*, 1).[188]

Primarily, therefore, Ignatius regarded martyrdom as a sacrifice.[189] Though he rejected and hated Judaism,[190] he finds his own inspiration in the Hebrew prophets 'who lived according to Jesus Christ. Therefore they were also persecuted, being inspired by his grace, to convince the disobedient that there is one God, who manifested himself through Jesus Christ, his Son' (*Magnes.*, 8.2). Though the thought is that of the New Testament, the terminology Ignatius uses to express the sacrificial element in martyrdom is Jewish through and through, evidence perhaps for the continuing closeness of relations between Church and Synagogue at Antioch.[191] As Perler has pointed out in his study of iv Maccabees,[192] Ignatius uses the rare word ἀντίψυχον (ransom). This also is found twice in iv Maccabees[193] but no less than four times in his letters in the sense of the substitutionary atoning sacrifice, the Pauline ἱλαστήριον. Thus, to the Ephesians, 'May my soul be given for yours, and for them whom you sent in the honour of God to Smyrna'.[194] To the Church at Smyrna, 'May my spirit be in substitution for your life'.[195] Ignatius takes up the theme of innocent, expiatory suffering as the means of overthrowing Satan in the Last Times. The imitation of the Passion thus becomes the imitation of Jesus' own sacrifice on the model of that performed for Israel by the 'Maccabean' martyrs.

Martyrdom, however, had yet another object, namely, the vindication of the reality of Christ's earthly ministry, and the liturgy and way of life practised in His service by the Church. Ignatius' opponents appear to have been Jewish (or Judaizing) Docetists who regarded Jesus' ministry as akin to the theophanies in the Old Testament, and appealed to it to justify their beliefs.[196] Ignatius replied with an integrated theology designed to show how the high priestly significance of episcopal office, the right celebration of the Eucharist and Christian conduct, even his own sufferings all depended on a belief in the reality of Jesus' earthly ministry. 'For if it is merely in semblance' he writes to the Church of Smyrna, 'that these things were done by our Lord, I am also a prisoner in semblance. And why have I given myself up to death, to fire, to the sword, to wild beasts? Because near the sword is near to God;[197] with the wild beasts is with God; in the name of Jesus Christ alone am I enduring all things, that I may suffer with him, and the perfect man himself gives me strength' (4.2). The

Docetists, he went on to complain, 'who had strange opinions about the grace of Jesus Christ' (6.2) also 'abstained from Eucharist and prayer because they do not confess that the Eucharist is the flesh of our Saviour Jesus Christ' (7.1) and for the same reason cared nothing for the widows, orphans and those in distress (6.2). Here was the first explicit association of martyrdom with orthodox Christology. To Ignatius, as to Justin[198] and Irenaeus, it was impossible for one who did not accept the reality of the Incarnation to die a blood-witness to Christ.[199] Neither Docetist nor Gnostic could be a man of martyrdom.

It is interesting that one on his way to certain death should make so few comments on the authorities who had condemned him. Apart from the grim joke about the ten leopards, meaning his guards who probably were drawn from the *cohors pardalariensis* (*Roms.* 4.3), there is no direct reference to the Empire and its servants. Ignatius, however, saw the situation in the same terms as other Christian apocalyptic writers. These were the last times.[200] Satan must be overthrown by worship in the Christian community and by personal martyrdom.[201] The world, which in Ignatius' mind was connected with sorcery, black magic and unbelief, had been disrupted by Christ's coming.[202] Its inhabitants, which meant the overwhelming majority of Ignatius' fellow provincials, were committed to 'death', just as the Christians were destined to 'life'. One does not have to look beyond these ideas for a justification of non-cooperation with the Imperial authorities. The writings of Ignatius and Hermas between them explain why Christianity was never tolerated explicitly until it had achieved victory.

Ignatius alludes to 'those who have preceded me from Syria to Rome to the glory of God',[203] which indicates that his martyrdom was not an isolated case. He also gives the name of two deacons, Philo and Rheus Agathopous who 'have renounced this life' and were being sent on their way after him.[204] Yet, in the same letter, that to the Philadelphians, he tells his readers that 'the Church which is in Antioch in Syria' is in peace,[205] and that there was free movement between the communities of Antioch and Philadelphia. As Polycarp shows, at the same time, there was also free movement between those of Smyrna and Philippi. It is a curious picture, arrests and martyrdoms on the one hand, peace and security among the churches and comparative freedom for Christian clergy on the other. In Ignatius' letters there is more concern about Jewish heretics than the attitude of the provincial authorities. Christianity was an offence, but repression was not systematic. Why?

NOTES

[1] Sulpicius Severus, *Chronicon* (ed. Halm, *CSEL.*, i.85) ii.30.6. For discussion of the possible relationship to Tacitus, E. Schürer, *Geschichte*, 1.530, n. 115. Also W. M. Ramsay, *The Church in the Roman Empire*, 230ff. (in favour), and H. W. Montefiore, 'Sulpicius Severus and Titus' Council of War', *Historia*, xi, 1962, p. 156ff. (against). In general, M. Simon, *Verus Israel*, 87ff.

[2] See W. Telfer, 'Was Hegesippus a Jew?' *HTR.*, 53, 1960, 146. Christians seem to have been most numerous in Greek colonist centres such as Tiberias and Scythopolis in the early Roman Empire.

[3] Christians as Nazoreans in Jewish apologetic: (a) *Apocryphon Joannis* (ed. W. Till, *T.U.*, lx, p. 78) an interesting reference, as in this instance the term is used regarding Christians in Palestine, where the scene of the *Apocryphon* is set. (b) Tertullian, *Adv. Marcionem*, iv.8. 'Nos Iudaei Nazorenos appellant'. (c) Epiphanius, *Panarion*, xxix.9.2 (ed. K. Holl, *GCS.*, 332. Valuable notes). (d) Jerome, *In Isaiah*, ii.5.19 (*P.L.*, 24, 86A). 'Et ter per singulos dies in omnibus synagogis sub nomine Nazarenorum anathemitizent vocabulum Christianum.' For a discussion on how far this name could have been associated in the minds of contemporaries with the puritan Nazirites (cf. Mt. 2²³), see M. H. Black, *The Scrolls*, 81–3.

[4] Babylonian Talmud (ed. J. Schachter, Soncino Press, 1935), *Sanhedrin*, 11b. See W. H. Bacher, art. 'Gamaliel II', *J.E.*, v.560ff., and A. A. T. Ehrhardt, 'The Birth of the Synagogue and Rabbi Akiba', *Studia Theologica*, ix.2, 1955, 96ff.

[5] Eusebius, *H.E.*, iii.20.3. In contrast, on the comparative wealth of the leading Palestinian rabbis at this time, E. Bammel, art. πτωχός, *K.W.*, vi.899.

[6] *Berakoth*, 29a. It is stated that Samuel discussed the matter at Jamnia, though not specifically with reference to the synod. The petition itself was found in the Cairo Geniza and published by S. Schechter, *JQR.*, x, 1898, 654ff. See also, James Parkes, *The Conflict of the Church and the Synagogue*, London, 1934, 77, M. Simon, *Verus Israel*, 235, and E. J. Bickerman, 'The Civic Prayer for Jerusalem', *HTR*, 55, 1962, 171.

[7] W. H. Bacher, art. cit., 561; cf. Justin, *Dialogue*, 96.2, and also, Epiphanius, *Panarion*, xxix.9.2, on Christians being cursed in synagogues three times a day in fourth-century Palestine.

[8] T. G. Jalland places the decisive schism between Judaism and the Church between 90 and 135, *The Origin and Evolution of the Christian Church*, London, 1948, 79.

[9] Josephus, *Wars*, v.11.2. Attention is drawn to C. H. Dodd, 'The Fall of Jerusalem and "the Abomination of Desolation"', *JRS.*, xxxvii, 1947, 47–54. Did Lk. 21²¹ imply that Christians were to secede from the already doomed population in Jerusalem, or was the flight something in the nature of a demonstration, like that of Mattathias and his sons recorded in i Macc. 2²⁸?

[10] Justin, *Dialogue*, 16.2; 47.2.

[11] *Letter to Diognetus*, 4.6. Dating would appear to be between 120–150. The dependence on Jewish apologetic against paganism (c. 2) and the absence of Euhemerism characteristic of later apologetic, the detailed comparison between Christians and Jews (c. 3, 4), as is to be found in the *Apology of Aristides*, and the relatively simple Christology point in this direction. (See discussion in H. G. Meecham, *The Epistle to Diognetus*, Manchester University Press, 1949, 18–19); cf. Ignatius, *Trall.* (ed. Kirsopp Lake), 8.1, 'old fables' of the Jews, rejected by Christians, and *Magnes.*, 8.1.

[12] R. P. Casey, 'Gnosis, Gnosticism and the New Testament', *The Background of the New Testament and its Eschatology, Studies in Honour of C. H. Dodd*, Cambridge, 1956, 56.

[13] See the excellent work by J. Daniélou, *Théologie du Judéo-Christianisme*, Desclée, Paris, 1958, particularly ch. i.

[14] Jewish sources: ii Enoch, 30.15, viii Sibylline, 399–400, Manual of Discipline, iii.13–iv.26, compare with Didache 1.1, Barnabas 18.1, and i Clement, 35.5. Discussion and literature, J. P. Audet, *La Didache, Instructions des Apôtres* (Etudes Bibliques), Paris, 1958, 254ff.

[15] See A. Lukyn Williams, *Adversus Judaeos*, 11ff. (quotes examples).

[16] Didache, 8.1; cf. J. P. Audet, op. cit., 368–71.

[17] Justin, *Dialogue with Trypho*, 66–7, and Barnabas, 10.

[18] Didache, 7,1–2 (running water) and Hippolytus (ed. Easton, p. 45), *Apostolic Tradition*, c. 21; cf. J. Jeremias, *Infant Baptism in the first four Centuries* (Eng. tr., London, 1959), pp. 29–37.

[19] Note T. G. Jalland's useful account of *The Origin and Evolution of the Christian Church*, especially chs. iv and v, C. W. Dugmore, *The Influence of the Synagogue upon the Divine Office*, Oxford, 1944, especially 65–7, and Gerh. Loeschke, *Jüdisches und Heidnisches im christlichen Kult*, Bonn, 1906; for the Christians in Bithynia, C. J. Kraemer, 'Pliny and the Early Christian Service', *CP.*, 29, 1934, 293–300, and C. C. Coulter, ibid., 35, 1940, 60–3.

[20] *Hypocrites*: Mt. 23 and Didache 8.1. Christian reproaches against Jews, cf. J. P. Audet, op. cit., 368.

[21] *Heretics*: Hegesippus (ap. Eusebius, *H.E.*, iii.32.2) and conversely, *Berakoth*, 29a, and above, p. 185.

[22] *Atheists*: Ignatius, *Trall.*, 10.1 (Christians to Jews). Justin, *Dialogue with Trypho*, 17.1 (vice versa). Christians appear to have been regarded like the Samaritans who sent up false signals on the Feast of Rosh Ha-Shanah. See E. Danby, *Mishnah*, 189, Rosh Ha-Shanah 2.2.

[23] Church as a synagogue, Hermas, *Mand.*, 11.9. For the end of the century, Irenaeus, *Adv. Haer.*, iii.6.1, and in fourth century, Epiphanius, *Panarion*, 30.18 (Judaeo-Christians), and from the Marcionite chapel at Deir-Ali near Damascus, *OGI.*, 608, 318/19 A.D.

[24] Cf. Justin, *Dialogue*, 123.7.

[25] See M. Charlesworth's article, '*Providentia and Aeternitas*', *HTR.*, 29, 1936 and on Domitian's outlook, below, p. 213.

[26] Josephus, *Wars*, Preface, c. 10.

[27] H. St. J. Hart, 'Judaea and Rome, The Official Commentary', *JTS.*, N. S. iii, 1952, 172–98, at 184. K. Christ, 'Antike Siegesprägungen', 3 (Iudaea Capta), *Gymnasium*, 64, 1957, 317.

[28] Josephus, *Wars*, vii.10.4.

[29] Dio Cassius, 67.14, Seneca (cited in Augustine, *De Civitate Dei*, vi.11), Epictetus, *Dissert.* ii.9.21; Juvenal, *Satires*, xiv. 96ff., and J. Bernays's commentary on this passage in his 'Die Gottesfürchtigen bei Juvenal', in *Commentarii philologii in honorem Th. Mommseni*, 1877, 563–9. J. Juster, *Les Juifs*, 275–85 for other refs.

[30] Eusebius, *H.E.*, iii.20.4.

[31] Especially, *Simil.*, viii. 8, 9 and 10, *Vis.*, 3.6, *Mand.*, 10.1.4.

[32] Trajan to Pliny, Pliny *Ep.*, x.97; cf. art. by W. Weber, '. . . nec nostri saeculi est', *Festg. f. Karl Müller*, Tübingen, 1922, 24–45.

[33] See W. Bauer, 'Chiliasmus', *A.C.*, ii.1073–8, H. Leclercq, 'Millénarisme', *DACL.*, xi.1, especially cols. 1183–5, and D. W. Riddle, *The Martyrs*, 139ff.

[34] Rev. 18, i Peter 5[13]; cf. Apoc. of Peter (ed. James, 518) and Ascension of Isaiah v for similar expressions.

[35] Ascens. Isaiah 4.2, 'descendet Beliar . . . in specie hominis regis iniquitatis matricidae'; cf. v Sibyll., 143, for an identical Jewish view.

[36] Rev. 17[8].

[37] Provisionally, one places the Didache and the Christian element in the Ascension in Antioch *circa* 100, both no doubt drawing on earlier traditions. For the Didache, see J. P. Audet's exhaustive study, op. cit., 212–19. ii Clement and Barnabas seem more likely to be Egyptian in origin.

[38] See M. Simon's interesting study of the Jewish and Christian hopes in these years and the parallel between the Christian expectation of the Parousia and the Jews of the restoration of the Temple, *Mélanges Goguel*, Paris/Neuchâtel, 1950, 247–57.

[39] The Apocalypse of Peter: *textual problems* see, M. R. James, *The Apocryphal New Testament*, 505ff., and *P.O.*, xviii, 482ff.

Dating: Perhaps Trajanic, see, A. Harnack, 'Bruchstücke des Evangeliums und der Apokalypse des Petrus', *T.U.*, ix.2, 1893, 51.

Influence on Christian thought, particularly in North Africa and Egypt, A. Rutherford, *Ante-Nicene Library*, ix, 1897, 141–7.

In general, J. Daniélou, *Théologie du Judéo-Christianisme*, 35–6.

[40] Irenaeus, *Adv. Haer.*, v.33.3–4; cf. Eusebius, *H.E.*, iii.39.4, and for similar views propagated by the Judaeo-Christian Gnostic, Cerinthus, *circa* 100, ibid., iii.28.5. These ideas may have been influenced by current Jewish speculations such as those found in the Apoc. of Baruch, 29.5.

[41] i Clement, 37.

[42] i Clement, 60.4–61.

[43] P. Egerton, 2.1.48, ed. H. I. Bell and T. C. Skeat, *Fragments of an Unknown Gospel*, London, 1935, 28. *Dating*: 'the original composition can hardly be later than the early years of the second century', ibid., 30.

See in general, the useful collection of first- and second-century texts discussed by E. Barnikol, 'Römer 13, Der nichtpaulinische Ursprung der absoluten Obrigkeitsbejahung vom Römer 13[1-7]', *T.U.*, 77, 1961, 65–133. It is not necessary for our purpose to discuss B's general thesis, that the command to obey earthly rulers is non-Pauline; it was well enough known to Christians in the second century and was a powerful influence towards Christian obedience to the Empire and its authorities in secular matters.

[44] See over, ch. viii. Eusebius, *Chron.* (Helm, p. 201) places the emergence of Basilides late in the reign of Hadrian, just before Bar Kochba's rising.

[45] Indicated in the attitude of Pliny (*Ep.*, x.96) and perhaps in the passage relating to the Galileans in Epictetus, *Dissert.*, iv.7.6. For the previous generation of Roman officials, Festus in Acts 26[4], see, M. Dibelius, *Rom und die Christen*, 40.

[46] See for instance, G. Bornkamm, 'Enderwartung und Kirche in Matthäusevangelium', *Studies in Honour of C. H. Dodd*, 222ff., at 230–1.

[47] Below, p. 215.

[48] W. H. Bacher, art. cit., 560.

[49] Eusebius, *H.E.*, iii.32.2–4. *Chronicon sub anno Abraham*, (221 Olympiad) = A.D. 106/07. The entry immediately precedes the record of Ignatius' arrest and execution (ed. Helm, 194). Miss E. M. Smallwood identifies this Atticus with Tib. Claudius Atticus Herodes and places his governorship of Judaea as early as 99/100–102/03. *JRS.*, lii, 1962, 132–3.

[50] Eusebius, citing Hegesippus, H.E., iii.32, 4–6.

[51] The charge was *min* or 'heresy', but R. Eliezer admitted that he had been influenced by a disciple of 'Jeshu the Nazarene' whom he had met in Sepphoris, *Aboda Zara* 16b–17a. See H. Travers Herford, *Christianity in Talmud and Midrash*, London, 1903, 137–9, and A. Schlatter, *Die Kirche Jerusalems*, 70–130, Gütersloh, 1915, p. 10ff.

[52] *Tosefta Chullim*, ii.22–3. Story of Rabbi Eleazar ben Dama, cf. M. Simon, *Verus Israel*, 219.

[53] Cited from Foakes Jackson and Kirsopp Lake, *Beginnings of Christianity*, 1.1.319.

[54] Ibid.

[55] *Tosefta shabb.*, 13.5; cf. M. Simon, *Verus Israel*, 237.

[56] Christians as Sabbath-breakers, Schlatter, op. cit., p. 20. The Gospel of Thomas rejects the notion of merit in fasting, prayer and almsgiving, and in the observance of any laws of the clean and unclean.

[57] The compilation of this Gospel in the form we have, is assumed to be somewhere *circa* A.D. 80, and that it was intended for an audience whose background was Palestinian. For a Phoenician location see G. D. Kilpatrick, *The Origins of the Gospel according to St. Matthew*, ch. vii, and F. V. Filson, *A Commentary on the Gospel according to St. Matthew*, London, 1960, 15.

[58] For the gradual 'promotion' of Pilate from harsh and despotic governor to quasi-saint in the period 70–150, and the deliberate anti-Jewish intention of the process, see P. Winter, *On the Trial of Jesus*, Brill, Leiden, 1961, 55–61, and 175–83.

[59] Jn. 9²², 12⁴⁵ and 16². See E. L. Allen, 'The Jewish Christian Church in the Fourth Gospel, *JBL.*, lxxiv.2, 1955, 88–92.

[60] No dealings with *minim*. *Tosefta Chullim*, ii.20 and 21, and Justin, *Dialogue*, 38.1. For the persistence of this situation in the mid-fourth century, see *Vita Sancti Epiphanii*, 6 (P.G., 41, 29D), 'πῶς σύ, Ἰουδαῖος ὤν, ἐπερωτᾶς χριστιανὸν μαθεῖν τίς 'εἰμι; ὅτι βδέλυγμα οἱ Ἰουδαῖοι τοῖς χριστιανοῖς, καὶ οἱ χριστιανοὶ τοῖς Ἰουδαίοις'.

[61] For the decline of Christianity in Galilee in the fourth century, Epiphanius, *Panarion*, xxx.11.9, who also indicates, however, the emergence of Christians into the open under Constantine (ibid., xxx.5.6–8).

[62] Eusebius, H.E., iv.2.1.

[63] Theophlus of Antioch, *Ad Autolycum*, iii.4 (P.G., vi.1125), 'στομάτων ἀθέων ψευδῶς συκοφαντούντων ἡμᾶς, τοὺς θεοσεβεῖς καὶ χριστιανοὺς καλουμένους'. Also Eusebius, H.E., vii.10.3 (Dionysius of Alexandria).

[64] Irenaeus, *Adv. Haer.*, 1.13.4.

[65] For a description of the Miletus inscription designating a special block of seats in the theatre as the 'τόπος Ἑιουδέων τῶν καὶ θεοσσεβίον', A. Deissmann, *Light from the Ancient East*, Appendix viii, 451–2.

[66] Epictetus, *Dissert.*, ii.9.20.

[67] Justin, *Dialogue*, 2–7.

[68] Justin, ii *Apol.*, 12.

[69] Pliny, *Ep.*, x.96.3.

[70] W. M. Ramsay, *The Letters to the Seven Churches of Asia*, London, 1906, p. 191ff.

[71] Eusebius, H.E., iii.39.9.

[72] Titus, 1⁵.

[73] Ignatius, *Ephes.*, 21.2; cf. Acts 15⁴⁰.

[74] C. H. Roberts, *An Unpublished Fragment of the Fourth Gospel in the John Rylands Library*, Manchester, 1935, 13ff.

[75] H. I. Bell and T. C. Skeat, *Fragments of an Unknown Gospel*, London, The British Museum, 1935, 30ff.

[76] See A. Maiuri, 'La croce di Ercolano', *Rend. della Pont. Accad. romana di arch.* Ser. 3, xv, 1939, 193–218, E. L. Sukenik, 'The earliest records of Christianity, *AJA.*, ci, 1947, 364.

For Pompeii, M. della Corte, 'I cristiani a Pompeii', *Rend. R. Accad. di Arch. Lettere e Bella Arti della Soc. Reale di Napoli*, 1939, 19, 179, and *Rend. della Pont. Accad. di Arch.* Ser. 3, xii, 1936, 397–400. On the Rotas-Sator square, found at Pompeii, H. Last, *J.T.S.*, N.S. iii, 1952, 92ff., and L. Herrmann, 'Quels chrétiens ont incendié Rome?' *Rev. Belge de Philologie*, 27.2, 1949, 645–8.

[77] A strong and influential contingent of Roman Christians would be found among the freedmen of the great aristocratic houses. Apart from the formal evidence of Phil. 4[22], the names of Clement's aides, Claudius Ephebus and Valerius Vito (i Clem. 65.1) shows that there were leaders drawn from their ranks.

[78] See W. M. Ramsay, 'The Letter to the Church in Thyateira', *Expositor*, 1906, 45ff. Later, the Nicolaitans seem to have formed their own separate Church in Asia Minor, see F. Miltner, publishing a fourth-century inscription from Haymana referring to an 'επίσκοπος τῆς 'εκ(κ)λησίης τῆς Νικολᾶει', *Türk Tarih*, 3, 1936, 97–8.

[79] Einar Molland, 'The Heretics combatted by Ignatius of Antioch', *J.E.H.*, v.i, 1954, 1–6.

[80] Eusebius, *H.E.*, iii.28.

[81] See S. Grayzel, 'Christian-Jewish Relations in the first Millenium', in *Essays on Anti-Semitism* (ed. Pinson), New York, 1946, p. 85.

[82] Now in the National Museum, Belgrade. See A. Marmorstein, 'The Synagogue of Tiberius Claudius Polycharmus at Stobi', *JQR.*, N.S. 27, 1937, 373–84, and E. Kitzinger, 'A Survey of the Town of Stobi', *Dumbarton Oaks Papers*, iii, 1946, 141ff. The top of the stone is broken off and the dating could be either A.D. 79 or 165, according to whether the calculation was made by the era of Actium or that of Macedonia. Another rich synagogue which seems to have existed in the mid-first century A.D. is that of Ostia (Phase 1). See, M. F. Squarciapino, 'La sinagoga recentemente scoperta ad Ostia', *Rend. di Pontif. Acad. Roman. di Arch.*, 34, 1961–62, 128ff. Boarding-houses connected with synagogues, *CIJ.*, 1404.

[83] W. M. Ramsay, *Cities and Bishoprics*, ii, 650ff., and by the same author, 'The Date of St. Polycarp's Martyrdom', *JÖAI.*, xxvii, 1931, 256 (Beiblatt).

[84] E. Schürer, *Geschichte des jüdischen Volkes*, iii.18 and 91–6 (other examples).

[85] Pap. Lond. 1177, 11. 57–63 = *Corp. Pap. Jud.*, No. 432.

[86] On Tiberius' career and views and relations to Judaism in the crisis years 66–70, see E. G. Turner, art. *JRS.*, xliv, 1954, 54ff.

[87] Polycarp, *Ep. ad Phillip.* (ed. Kirsopp Lake), 6 and 10.

[88] Hermas, *Simil.*, ix.27.2. 'Bishops and hospitable men who at all times received the servants of God into their houses . . . and ceaselessly sheltered the destitute. . . . '

[89] e.g. Origen, *Contra Celsum*, iii.52 and 55 (Phoenicia?) and Minucius Felix, *Octavius* 8.4 (Rome).

[90] For slaves making up part of the Roman Christian community, Hippolytus, *Apost. Tradition*, 16, and slaves in Polycarp's Church at Smyrna, Ignatius, *Ad Polyc.*, 4.3.

[91] Polycarp, *Ep. ad Philipp.*, 10.2; cf. Phil. 3[7] for the technical use of ἄμεμπτος. For the hint of lack even of solidarity among individual Christian communities in Asia, Ignatius, *Philad.*, 11.

[92] Juvenal, *Satires* (ed. Owen), vi.543–5.

[93] For Carthage, circa 190–200, Tertullian, *Ad Nationes*, 1.13; cf. Josephus, *Contra Apionem*, ii.39.

[94] Juvenal, *Satires*, xiv.96–104.

[95] Justin, *Dialogue*, 122.2.

[96] F. Cumont, 'Un fragment de Sarcophage Judéo-päien', *Rev. archéologique*, 1916, ii.1–6.

[97] Tertullian, *Adv. Judaeos*, 1.

[98] Origen, *Comment. in Math.*, 16 (P.G., 13, col. 1621). 'Est autem videre eos usque nunc. . . .'

[99] Commodian, *Instructiones*, 1.28 (*CSEL.*, xv.31) for the fourth century or even later.

[100] Josephus, *Antiquities*, viii.2.5. Pap. Paris, 1231 and Pap. W. (Leemans), p. 145, lines 22ff., Origen, *Contra Celsum*, iv.33. For use of Christ's name for similar purposes Justin, *Dial.*, 85.2. See in general, W. L. Knox, *St. Paul and the Church of the Gentiles*, 44.

[100a] Cited from Augustine, *De civitate Dei*, vi.11.

[101] iv Sibyll. (ed. Charles) 117–18.

[102] Josephus, *Wars*, vii.1.

[103] Justin, *Dialogue*, 117.2.

[104] iv Sibyll. 24ff. For analogous Christian propaganda, Barnabas 2–3.

[105] Josephus, *Contra Apionem*, ii.29.282. An important reference because this type of Jewish approach is confirmed by Seneca (ap. Augustine, *De Civitate Dei*, vi.11).

[106] Josephus, *Contra Apionem*, ii.15 (Whiston).

[107] iii Sibyll. 195; Josephus, *Contra Apionem*, ii.40.

[108] Josephus, *Contra Apionem*, ii.29. Both this work and Philo's *On the Contemplative Life*, and *That Every Virtuous Man is free* were addressed to Gentiles.

[109] v Sibyll. 214.

[110] Ibid., 112, and 179ff.

[111] iv Ezra (ed. Charles) 11.46; cf. J. W. Swain, *CP.*, 35, 1940, 16, n. 40.

[112] H. H. Rowley, *The Relevance of Apocalyptic*, 70 and 102. Also E. Kautzsch, *Apok. und Pseudepigraph. des Alten Testaments*, Tübingen, 1900, ii.352ff. for a date shortly after 90, and detailed discussion.

[113] iv Sibyll. (ed. Charles), iv.178.

[114] iv Sibyll. 119–24, and 138ff.; v Sibyll. 137–74, 363ff.; see A. Kurfess, 'Zum V Buch der Oracula Sibyllina', *Rheinisches Museum*, 99, 1956, 225–41, especially 232.

[115] For an Asiatic false Nero in the reign of Titus who secured support in Asia and asylum in Parthia, Dio Cassius, lxvi, 19; and for Nero's well-deserved popularity among Greek-speaking provincials and their reluctance to accept his death, M. P. Charlesworth, 'Nero: some Aspects', *JRS.*, xl, 1950, 69ff., especially 72–6; and hence, the Jewish and Christian view, both ultimately anti-Roman and anti-Greek which accepted *Nero redivivus*, but only in the role of anti-Christ.

[116] *Letter to Diognetus*, iv and v.

[117] Veiling of Jewish women in Carthage—Tertullian, *De Corona*, 4.

[118] Jewish quarters in Alexandria and Edfu, Tcherikover and Fuks, *Corpus Pap. Iud.*, Section ix, 108–9.

[119] For instance, note the Jewish-Christian controversy over the Jewish dietary laws, Barnabas 10, and Tertullian *Apol.*, 21–2. There were many Christians, however, who ate *mazzot* on the Jewish Passover, and also abstained from meat (cf. Minucius Felix, *Octavius*, 30.6). In general, Tertullian, *Apol.*, 42.1. Christians 'eat the same food, wear the same dress, use the same furniture and have all the same necessities of life (as pagans in Carthage). We are not Brahmins or Indian fakirs'. He may, however, have been exaggerating.

[120] See F. C. Burkitt, 'Aquila', *JQR.*, x, 1898, 207ff. His contempt for the Christians, *Chron. Paschale* (Olymp. 227 = A.D. 132), *P.G.*, 92, 617B.

[121] For instance, ii Clement 2.3, Christians becoming aware that they were more numerous than the Jews.

[122] Ignatius, *Philad.*, 6.

[123] Rev. 2⁹⁻¹⁰ and 3⁹. For other evidence of hatred, Justin, *Dial.*, 16.4, 47.4, 95.4 and 135.6 (cursings in the synagogues of Asia).

[124] Justin, *Dialogue*, 17.1, and 47.4, compare 96, 108.2 and 117.3. Against this view, J. Parkes, op. cit., 80; but Justin's reference to 'the allegations of the ignorant' would seem to point to slanders against the Christians. The ordinary provincials would hardly be interested in reports confined to Jesus' claim to be Messiah, but would listen to stories about black magic and cannibalism, as indeed, we know they did. (Eusebius, *H.E.*, v.1.15.)

[125] Origen, *Contra Celsum*, vi.27; cf. ibid., iv.32.

[126] Eusebius, *In Isaiah*, xviii.1 (*P.G.*, 24, col. 213A).

[127] For Panthera as the name of a soldier from Sidon in Phoenicia in the beginning of first century A.D., A. Deissmann, op. cit., 68 and Fig. 5. An additional source of the Jewish-Christian debate at this period might be the discussion between Timothy and Aquila which centres round Jesus' claim to be Messiah. But until this can be dated and the whole problem of the *Testimonies* re-assessed, Celsus and Justin remain our prime sources.

[128] Origen, *Contra Celsum*, 1.27, 29, 32 and 41.

[129] Justin, *Dialogue*, 108.2; cf. for the end of the century in Carthage, Tertullian, *Apol.*, 21, 22.

[130] Origen, *Contra Celsum*, ii.4 and 9.

[131] *Apocryphon Ioannis* (ed. W. Till), *T.U.*, lx, 78.

[132] For the correlation between Romanization and tension with the Christians, see in particular R. Schütz, *Die Offenbarung des Johannes und Kaiser Domitian*, Göttingen, 1933, 19ff.

[133] D. Magie, *Roman Rule in Asia Minor*, 572 and 1431.

[134] J. Keil, *J.Ö.A.I.*, xxvii, 1930 (Beiblatt), i. 59, and xxxviii, 1931 (Beiblatt), 3ff., Abb. 36–40, Tafel iii. D. Magie, op. cit., 1432; also, P. Touilleux, *L'Apocalypse et les cultes de Domitien et de Cybèle*, Paris, 1935, pp. 80–5.

[135] W. M. Ramsay, *The Social Basis of Roman Power in Asia Minor*, Aberdeen, 1941, 108.

[136] J. Keil, *J.Ö.A.I.*, xxviii, 1931 (Beiblatt) 43. Also M. McCrum and A. G. Woodhead, *Documents of the Flavian Emperors*, Cambridge, 1961, No. 142. Also, 144 (Lyrboton Kome).

[137] J. Keil, *J.Ö.A.I.*, xxvii, 1930 (Beiblatt), 55 and Abb. 40 and Taf. iii.

[138] W. M. Ramsay, *Letters to the Seven Churches*, 293–4.

[139] J. Keil, *Wiener Numis. Zeitschrift*, xii, 1919, 115–20, points out that the Temple to Domitian at Ephesus was the first divine honour to be paid there to any emperor by the Koinon.

[140] Tacitus, *Agricola*, 21. For Agricola's construction of the forum at Verulamium, *JRS.*, xlvi, 1956, 146–7, and also the vast, Italian-style villa built *circa* 70 at Fishbourne (Sussex), see B. Cunliffe, 'Excavations at Fishbourne, 1962', *The Antiquaries Journal*, 43.i, 1963, 1–15.

[141] P. Touilleux, op. cit., p. 85.

[142] J. P. Audet, 'Affinités littéraires et doctrinales du Manuel de Discipline, ii, *Revue Biblique*, 60, 1953, 41–82. See also, W. J. Wilson, 'The Career of the Prophet Hermas', *HTR.*, 20, 1927, 21–62, R. Joly, 'Judaisme, Christianisme et Hellénisme dans le Pasteur d'Hermas', *Nouvelle Clio*, 1953, 394–406, M. Dibelius, *Der Hirt des Hermas* (Handbuch zum N. T. Ergänzungsband, Die Apostolischen Väter iv), Tübingen, 1923, 415–644, and L. W. Barnard, 'Hermas and Judaism' (Fourth Internat. Conference on Patristic Studies), to be published in *T.U.*

[143] J. P. Audet., op. cit., 82, retaining, moreover, 'des attaches personelles au judaïsme' (p. 58).

[144] See A. A. T. Ehrhardt, op. cit., ii.52.

[145] *Simil.*, viii.3.2; cf. A. A. T. Ehrhardt, op. cit., ii.50.

[146] *Simil.*, viii.3.3.

[147] *Simil.*, ix.17, though allegorized in turn, as 'the twelve nations which inhabit the whole world'.

[148] Ibid., ix.17.4.

[149] *Simil.*, viii.3.2.

[150] *Simil.*, i.3.

[151] Ibid., i.6.

[152] *Vision*, i.3.3 and i.4.2; cf. D. W. Riddle, *The Martyrs*, 142ff. The apostates are regarded as the worst offenders, and worthy of double punishment, *Simil.*, ix.28.8, and

ix. 8.18, as in the Alexandrine Jewish *iii Maccabees,* and also in the 'Apocalypse of Peter' (ed. M. R. James, *The Apocryphal N.T.,* 516, Gr. 34). For N. T. Times, above, pp. 79 and 91.

153 *Vis.,* iv.1.9 and 10. The Lord, in contrast, is called 'the great King', ibid., iii.9.18; cf. W. J. Wilson, art. cit., 30, and E. Buonaiuti, *Geschichte des Christentums* (Berne, 1948), i.181.

154 *Simil.,* iv.4. For a similar contemporary Jewish expectation iv Sibyll. 678. M. Dibelius, op. cit., 485.

155 *Vis.,* iii.6.5; cf. Tertullian, *De Cultu Feminarum,* ii.9, Cyprian, *De Lapsis,* 12.

156 *Simil.,* viii.9.1; cf. viii.9.4.

157 *Simil.,* ii.5; cf. 9.20.

158 Ibid., 2.7.

159 *Mand.,* iv.2–4, *Vis.,* iv.2.

160 *Vis.,* ii.3.4.

161 *Vis.,* ii.1; cf. *Simil.,* viii.3.7, and *Vis.,* iv.3.6. On whether the Name is 'of God' or 'of the Lord', Audet, op. cit., 48–9.

162 *Vis.,* iv.3.3.

163 *Vis.,* iv.3.4.

164 *Vis.,* iv.3.5.

165 *Vis.,* iii.2.1; cf. ibid., iii.1.9, and Apoc. of Peter (James, 512).

166 *Simil.,* ix.28.3, and 5.

167 Tertullian, *Apol.,* 50.16.

168 Irenaeus, *Adv. Haer.,* iv.20.2.

169 *Dating:* probably the end of the first century A.D.—A. L. Williams, 'The Date of the Epistle of Barnabas', *JTS.,* xxxiii, 1934, 237–46.

170 For the view that 'Barnabas' may have been drawing on some Jewish apocalypse dating to *circa* 70 in this chapter, see P. Pringent, *L'Epître de Barnabé i–xvi et ses sources,* Etudes Bibliques, Paris, 1961, 150–2.

171 ii Clement, 5.4.

172 Ibid., 16.3.

173 Ibid., 6.1–6.

174 Ibid., 17.7.

175 Ibid., 17.7.

176 Ibid., 12.1.

177 Ibid., 14 and 16.

178 On this, the fundamental work is still J. B. Lightfoot, *The Apostolic Fathers,* ii, S. Ignatius. See also, D. W. Bauer, *Die Briefe des Ignatius von Antiochia und der Polykarpbrief* (Handbuch zum N.T., Ergänzungsband, Tübingen, 1920) and Kirsopp Lake's brief but pertinent remarks in his introduction to the Ignatian *Letters, Apostolic Fathers* i, 166ff.

179 Eusebius, *Chron.,* sub anno 108 (Helm, 194). Ignatius' own description and purpose of his journey, *Ephes.* 1.2. Rules governing despatch of prisoners to Rome, Bauer, op. cit., 197.

180 On his name, see D. W. Bauer, op. cit., 189, particularly its significance for a martyr.

181 *Acta Carpi* (ed. Knopf and Krüger), 42.

182 Justin, 2 *Apol.,* 2.15.

183 Eusebius, *H.E.,* iv.15.7.

184 *Roms.,* 2.2, 'ὡς, 'ἔτι θυσιαστήριον. . . .'.

185 *Roms.,* 6.1 and 4.1; cf. iv Macc. 9¹⁻⁹ and 11.

186 See J. Weiss, *History of Primitive Christianity* (Eng. tr.) ii, 766–773.

187 See R. M. Grant, 'Hermeneutics and Tradition in Ignatius of Antioch', *Archivo di Filosofia,* 1–2, 1963, 183–201, at 199.

188 Note also, the implications of Ignatius' surname, θεοφόρος (*Ephes.,* 1), that as confessor he was particularly closely associated with God, who would be the inspiration of his every act. (Bauer, op. cit., 191.)

[189] *Ephes.*, 1.1 and following, also 10.3 and *Magnes.*, 5.2. The point stressed by H. von Campenhausen, op. cit., 73, and by G. Jouassard, 'Aux Origines du Culte des Martyrs dans le Christianisme', *RSR.*, 39, 1952, 363.

[190] *Magnes.*, 8.1, 10.3, *Philadelphians*, 6.

[191] Cf. J. Daniélou, *Théologie du Judéo-Christianisme*, 50–3, and R. M. Grant, loc. cit., 200.

[192] O. Perler, *Das vierte Makkabäerbuch*, 47ff.

[193] iv Macc. 6^{27-29} and 17^{20-22}.

[194] Ignatius, *Ephes.*, 21^1; cf. iv Macc. 6^{29}, 17^{21}.

[195] Ignatius, *Smyrn*, 10. 2.

[196] Einar Molland, 'The Heretics combatted by Ignatius of Antioch', *JEH.*, v.1, 1954, 6.

[197] Note the *Gospel of Thomas*, Logion 82, 'He who is near me is near the fire', a phrase which is also quoted by Origen (*Hom. in Jeremiah*, 20.3, P.G., 13, 531D–532A)—another example of the early tradition embodied in *Thomas*, a tradition inspired by hopes of martyrdom.

[198] Justin, *1 Apol.*, 66.

[199] Irenaeus, *Adv. Haer.*, iv.33.9.

[200] Ignatius, *Ephes.*, 11.1.

[201] Ibid., 13.1.

[202] Ibid., 19.

[203] *Roms.*, 10.2.

[204] *Philad.*, 11.1 and *Smyrn.*, 10.1.

[205] *Philad.*, 10.1, and *Smyrn.*, 11.2.

CHAPTER EIGHT

Lord Caesar or Lord Christ, 70–138?

TO answer this question we must now consider how Christianity presented itself to the Roman authorities in this period. How is one to fit the evidence for the Domitianic repression, the Pliny-Trajan correspondence, and the temperate policy of Hadrian into the incomplete and confusing picture provided by contemporary sources? Eusebius says that there were 'partial attacks in various provinces', but no open persecution. There were plots 'even contrived by the local authorities' and martyrdoms resulted. Christians, clearly, were not popular.[1] Can we say more? If we are right, however, in regarding Christianity in the half-century that followed the fall of Jerusalem as both behaving and appearing like a rival to Judaism, we should start this enquiry with the relations between the Jews and the Roman governing class.[2] We have seen that the capture of Jerusalem was itself hailed as a great feat of arms, and we have seen, too, how the attitude of many Jews in the Dispersion, towards Rome had become one of unrelenting hostility. Many Christians, for slightly different reasons, had also followed this lead. As regards the Jews, this antipathy was beginning to be reciprocated in full measure from the Roman side. What had previously been suspicion, tinged with a certain amount of contempt and hostility by individuals, becomes a widespread and deep-seated fear from which Christians were also to suffer.

Despite the efforts of pro-Roman Jews such as Josephus, despite Titus' obvious inclinations towards conciliation,[3] relations between the Jews and the majority of educated Romans went from bad to worse.[4] Among Latin authors, writing between 70 and 130, Martial,[5] Quintilian,[6] Tacitus,[7] Suetonius,[8] and Juvenal[9] are united in their common scorn and odium for the Jews, their customs and their proselytes. Quintilian,[10] despite his friendship with Domitilla and Flavius Clemens did not conceal his contempt for Moses as founder of 'Judaicae superstitionis', dangerous to the rest of mankind. Tacitus saw the Jews as a contemptible and perverse people, haters of the human race and abandoned by the gods. At the same time, he feared them, pointing out to his readers that there were people 'who feared life more than death'.[11] There was an awareness that conversion to Judaism meant conversion to a way of life completely alien to that of Greco-Roman civilization. To become a proselyte was 'exuere patriam'.[12] It entailed rejection of all previous family ties, and, incidentally, contributions to the Jewish war-chest.

The views of the Roman governing class were edging towards those of the anti-Semite nationalists in the larger Greek cities. The process had taken two centuries or more, but as the Greco-Roman world became united in common loyalty to the Imperial idea, so it stood increasingly on its guard against the rival ideology presented by Judaism and by Christianity. The 'ultras' of Alexandria might continue to grumble that Trajan's Concilium was filled with 'godless Jews',[13] but their anti-Semitism was no longer out of step with the ideas of the rest of the Greco-Roman world. The wit who scrawled 'Sodoma' and 'Gomora' on a house in Pompeii, presumably occupied by Jews, may have expressed popular reaction to the latter's persistent fire and brimstone talk.[14] There was fear, too, fear justified by the terrible events of 115-117, of a general Jewish uprising, and an attempt to establish a Jewish kingdom as the rival to the Empire. Jewish prophecies of world domination were remembered and were recorded in the first decades of the second century by Tacitus and Suetonius. Some vast Jewish inspired revolt was in the air.[15]

As for the Christians, the passage of Hegesippus that 'Domitian like Herod was afraid of the coming of the Christ',[16] and suspected the 'house of David', showed how these fears could be extended to them.

Nevertheless, the reigns of Vespasian and Titus were uneventful. So, too, was the early part of Domitian's reign, though in Asia Minor it would appear from i Peter that Christians were being increasingly subjected to criminal charges and were unpopular, perhaps as 'proseletysing busy-bodies'.[17] We hear, too, that Timothy 'had been set at liberty' (Heb. 13[23]), though the circumstances of his arrest are unknown.[18]

Towards the end of Domitian's reign, however, one reading of the evidence provided by Revelation, together with an inscription suggests the possibility of anti-Christian outbreaks in Asia following on natural disaster, thus anticipating the pattern of events in the next century. The livelihood of the Greek cities always tended to be precarious, and probably in 92/93 there was a serious famine in Pisidian Antioch. The governor appealed for a spirit of fair dealing and humanity towards the sufferers. Grain was not to be sold beyond one sesterce per *modius* (instead of two sesterces, which profiteers were charging).[19] About the same time Dio Chrysostom refers to a famine at Prusa in the north of the province.[20] Revelation shows that prices of up to 4 sesterces (one denarius) a modius were not unknown (Rev. 6[6]) and indicates the existence of boycotts and trade sanctions directed against the Christians in the towns (Rev. 13[16-17]). These were accompanied by the banishment of some of the leading Christians to penal settlements in the Aegean Islands, and the execution of others, such as Antipas (Rev. 2[13]). In contrast, the Christians of Asia regarded natural disasters, including famine, as presaging the Last Days, and thus to be welcomed. The strident advance of the Four Horsemen has become part of the legend of the Church. In the Jewish or Christian Apocalypse of Abraham famine was an apocalyptic symbol, the Fourth Plague which would precede the overthrow of the great in this world.[21] Behind this prophetic imagery lay the reality of the triangular struggle which was building up between Christians, pagans and Jews in the towns of Asia towards the end of the first century. This was an area where religious strife had been traditional, and sudden natural disasters not infrequent.

This was one aspect of the 'Domitianic persecution' alluded to by Melito of Sardes[22] and Tertullian.[23] Other causes of tension were more directly due to the policy of the Emperor himself. First, financial stringency seems to have led him to take energetic steps to garner as much of the proceeds of the 2 drachma contributions from the Jews for the benefit of the treasury.[24] Secondly, his profound hostility towards any form of religious unorthodoxy resulted in the punishment of any prominent citizen who lapsed too blatantly into an 'external religion'.

The Jews were no longer a 'nation', whatever protection might be granted to the Jewish religion on the grounds of its antiquity.

The 2 drachma formerly payable annually by all Jews over the age of twenty in the Temple were appropriated by the victorious Jupiter Capitolinus.[25] The authorities possessed a strong financial inducement to define the limits of Judaism, and this process was carried on brutally under Domitian. Suetonius tells us that there were many 'who lived like Jews',[26] people who roused the contempt of the Stoic Epictetus.[27] Christians fell into this class. They claimed to be Israel (cf. Hebs. 11[40]), but disregarded the ceremonial law and were disowned by those whose orthodoxy as Jews could not be doubted. Thus, they had no claim to the rights and privileges conceded to the latter. The effect of Domitian's measures and incidentally, their repeal by Nerva was to increase the legal distinctions between Jews and Christians in the eyes of the authorities to the disadvantage of the Christians, for these were now deprived of their one claim to legality.[28]

Domitian was not the man to tolerate religious deviations. When one discounts the senatorial prejudices of Tacitus and Suetonius, the Emperor stands out as a shrewd but jealous-minded ruler, a strong upholder of public right and the state religion,[29] whose prejudices and fears for his own safety increased with age. Evidence from different sources points in this direction. It is interesting, for instance, that in the cases of adultery by Vestal Virgins, overlooked in his father's and brother's reigns, Domitian ordered dire punishment. In 83 the lovers were exiled, but in a similar case in 90 the unfortunate offender was ordered to be beaten to death by rods. The Vestals themselves were allowed to choose their own form of death in the first instance, but the Chief Vestal, Cornelia, was immured in the traditional manner in the second.[30] This was perhaps not merely horrid ritual, but in the Emperor's mind the only means of averting the danger to the *aeternitas* of Rome incurred by her act.[31] Similarly, after a business-like and militarily successful opening to the reign, we can trace growing megalomania from *circa* 86 onwards when Domitian appears to have persuaded himself that he was 'Deus et dominus', and ordered his courtiers and poets to greet him as such.[32] In 89 Martial speaks of 'edictum domini deique nostri'.[33] It was under Domitian that the practices of taking an oath by the Emperor's genius, of offering libation and incense before his statue, and addressing him as *Dominus* grew up. These were retained by

Trajan and later emperors, despite the open condemnation of Domitian's memory.[34] It is clear that the Emperor's fantasy was moving him along the same road as Caligula and Nero, with the inevitable possibility of clash with Jewry and its offshoots. It is clear, too, that it was not altogether contrary to prevailing tendencies in official thought.

The assumption of these honorific titles had its counterpart in suspicion of all who might be expected to doubt the Emperor's divinity. Between 89 and 93 republican-minded politicians, like Helvidius Priscus, and Junius Rusticus,[35] and philosophers such as Epictetus,[36] Artemidorus[37] and Apollonius of Tyana,[38] felt the hand of tyranny through exile, imprisonment or execution.[39] The fear and suspicion which reigned in the capital in the last years of the reign may be summed up in two lines of Juvenal:

> Tempora saevitiae, claras quibus abstulit urbi
> Inlustresque animas impune et vindice nullo.
>
> (*Satires*, iv, 151–2)

There is no reason to suppose Christians would be subjected to special treatment. It is against this background of general terror and suspicion that the action of Domitian against members of his family accused of 'atheism' must be assessed.

The historian has to rely on Xiphilinus' epitome of Dio Cassius for the most informative account of the events of 95.[40] It is related that in this year Domitian had his cousin Flavius Clemens arrested, along with his wife, Domitilla, and also the consul for the year 91, Acilius Glabrio. Against Flavius Clemens and Domitilla 'were brought the charges of atheism (ἀθεότητος) for which also many others were condemned, who had drifted (ἐξοκέλλοντες) into the practices of the Jews'. Of these some were put to death, others deprived of their property. Domitilla was only banished 'to Pandataria'.[41] Suetonius[42] says nothing about the charge of atheism, but adds the detail that Clemens' fate was 'sudden on a very slight suspicion' that he was conspiring against the Emperor, and mentioning also as though to suggest that the charge was very unlikely, that he was 'a man of the most contemptible laziness'.[43]

It is not easy to see a persecution of the Christians in this narrative. Suetonius, hostile to Christianity and contemporary with the events, does not associate Glabrio's and Clemens's fall with the new religion. Glabrio was accused with other senators and ex-consuls as a revolutionary (*quasi molitor rerum novarum*), but not as 'superstitiosus', which could be expected if there was a religious background to this accusation.[44] Tacitus congratulates Agricola on the happy moment of his death, missing 'the massacre of so many men of consular rank, and the exiling of most noble women',[45] also without hint of any religious issue. Pliny takes the same line.[46] This was a case of unnatural slaughter of kinsfolk.

It seems evident, however, that Domitian's lust for self-importance entailed stricter control over acceptance of foreign religions by Roman citizens, especially when this might detract from respect to be paid to his own majesty.[47] The authorities' readiness to accept the Jews' right to their own customs was not to extend to converts and imitators.[48] This policy had been implicit for years, and was clearly accepted in the provinces, as Acts 16[20–21] and 18[13] show. Clemens' and Domitilla's cases, like that forty years before of Pomponia Graecina,[49] illustrate its application to the higher reaches of the Roman aristocracy also.[50] Here, if one accepts the Alexandrian *Acta Hermaisci* as reflecting scandalous rumours about Jewish influence among the latter *circa* A.D. 100, there may have been grounds for action.[51] But the sudden and violent application of the principle was a shock to the Jews themselves. Rabbi Gamaliel hastened from Palestine to Rome in the winter of 95, presumably with the idea of averting persecution, and incidentally, bringing home to audiences he is said to have addressed the real distinction between Jews and pseudo-Jews (Christians).[52] For the former he was perhaps too alarmist. None the less, conversion to Judaism by a Roman citizen might from now onwards involve a charge of atheism, and this fact, still recorded over a century later when Dio Cassius wrote his history, could not do the Christians any good.

Two other fragments of evidence remain to be considered. First, the opening passage of i Clement, the letter addressed by the Roman Church to the Church of Corinth, perhaps *circa* 97–100, begins, 'Owing to the sudden and repeated misfortunes and calamities (συμφορὰς καὶ περιπτώσεις) which have befallen us, we think that we have been too long delayed in turning our attention to the matters disputed among you, beloved. . . . ' The alternative reading περιστάσεις in the Codex Constantino-politanus ('hindrances') is possible,[53] and in any event, it is not clear why, if the writer wanted to speak of 'persecutions', he did not speak of the διωγμός or θλῖψις, especially as he used θλῖψις in the sense of affliction resulting from persecution in ch. 57.4.[54] The remainder of the letter gives no hint that anything had been amiss with the Christians at Rome. Praise for the Roman legion-aries as examples of discipline (ch. 37) would have read like misplaced humour if in fact the Church in Rome had just been suffering repressive measures; and the casual reference to the three messengers sent by the Church to Corinth as 'having lived among us without blame from youth to old age'[55] suggests a stable community. One must agree with Merill's conclusion that all the writer intended to say was that he meant to write long ago, but various troubles had prevented him from doing so.[56] As the schism was still continuing and bringing discredit on the Christian Church in a city which had the closest ties with Rome (ch.47.7), some explanation for the delay in writing was to be expected.

The second piece of evidence has come from de Rossi's excava-tions of the *Coemeterium Domitillae* on the Ardeatine Way in the 1860s and 1870s. There is no doubt that this catacomb was constructed on Domitilla's land for her freedmen, and she herself is named on an inscription 'neptis Vespasiani'.[57] Moreover, Christian remains were found, which de Rossi thought referred to Domitilla herself.[58] Unfortunately, archaeology was in its infancy at the time. Many hazards were not realized. For instance, in contrast to usual archaeological stratification, the latest material from a catacomb would be on the lowest level, representing the latest extension of the galleries. Applying shrewd common sense and an accurate measure, Styger rapidly demonstrated how all catacombs started with a passage some 6 ft. 6 in. high, and were extended downwards gallery by gallery in course of time so as to avoid crossing into a neighbouring property.[59] The deepest and most complicated catacombs were thus the latest, and the fourth century was the period of maximum use. These conclu-sions did away with the previously held view that catacombs were ordinarily secret meeting places for Christians, and it caused drastic revision of hitherto accepted canons of dating. It is now evident that Christian burials in the *Coemeterium Domitillae* do not start until the mid-second century at the earliest.[60] Though members of the families of Glabrio and Domitilla had become Christian by the mid-third century,[61] the archaeological evidence does not lead one to suppose that in Domitian's reign they accepted beliefs which had barely begun to influence their slaves and freedmen. Moreover, it was unlikely that the *area* granted by Domitilla for the use of her freedmen should also house her own body.[62]

In Rome, therefore, the persecution of Domitian does not appear to have amounted to very much. We may, if we allow maximum weight to the testimony of the author Bruttius[63] quoted by Eusebius in his *Chronicle*, believe that in Domitilla's case 'Jewish customs' meant Christianity,[64] but it is harder to accept this for Clemens. The compilers of the Roman Martyrology in the fourth century evidently did not see fit to include his name, and there *faute de mieux* one must leave him. In 97 Nerva recalled the surviving victims of Domitian's repression.[65] Dio states that no one was allowed to bring accusations of impiety or *maiestas*, or for adopting Jewish ways of life. Nerva's copper coinage proclaimed with the words FISCI IUDAICI CALUMNIA SUBLATA that abuses connected with the collection of Jewish tribute, such as the taxing of non-Jews, had been suppressed.[66] Few mourned Domitian or wished to vindicate his acts.[67]

Meantime, the scene shifts once more from Rome to Asia Minor. In the first part of Trajan's reign the cities of Pontus-Bithynia on the southern shore of the Black Sea had fallen into serious financial and administrative difficulties. The province had been inefficiently governed by men whose annual terms of office had too often merely whetted an appetite for gain. The elected councils of the cities had mismanaged their affairs. There was corruption, public buildings had been started at great expense and left half finished.[68] Contractors had been fraudulent and architects incompetent. Some cities faced bankruptcy as the result. There was underlying political and social instability—all this despite the great potential wealth of the province.[69] Pliny, whom Trajan sent out to the province in the summer of 111 as *legatus pro praetore* directly responsible to him, had considerable legal and financial experience and, above all, he was an honest man. In addition, he possessed a fair share of moral courage, and had a love of the detailed administrative problem. His previous career had included a number of important administrative posts in Rome.[70] In addition, he had defended two governors of Bithynia, probably in 104 and 106 and so had some idea of conditions in the province.[71] He had no experience as a provincial governor, and was averse to taking decisions on his own. The fact, however, that he remitted so many petty administrative matters for his chief's decision has left us a full picture of the problems of a Roman province in this period and not least that posed by the Christians.

Pliny does not appear to have come across Christians in any numbers until he had passed Amisus and reached Amastris in the eastern part of the province in the autumn of 112.[72] The hearings probably took place in Amastris whose coinage shows her to have been the 'metropolis' of the province, where the provincial council and priest of the Imperial cult would be situated. Only two letters out of 104 covering his mission concern the Christians (x.96 and 97). The texts are well known.[73] Pliny's letter shows that there were two main phases in the affair. At the outset, he was met with a number of denunciations against individuals, both citizens and non-citizens, on the grounds that they were Christians (*ad me tamquam Christiani deferebantur*). He did not initiate action himself. He explains to Trajan that he had never been present at any trials of Christians and that he did not know whether the mere profession of Christianity was a crime or whether only the crimes associated therewith were punishable. Was it the '*nomen*' itself or the '*scelera*' connected with it? He investigated, however, following the procedure of a *cognitio*, whereby the defendant who pleaded guilty could be condemned on his own confession without calling witnesses.[74] All pleaded guilty, and having persevered in their confession after the question had been put three times, the non-citizens were haled off to execution. Pliny observed that 'for whatever the nature of their creed might be, I could at least feel no doubt their contumacy and inflexible obstinacy deserved chastisement' (*pertinaciam certe et inflexibilem obstinationem*).[75] The Roman citizens among them he sent to Rome for trial, 'for similar madness'.[76]

Then complications began to arise. 'These accusations spread (as is usually the case) from the mere fact that the matter was being investigated, and several forms of mischief (*crimina*) came to light.' A large number of people were accused in an anonymous pamphlet. Some of these were apparently innocent, others admitted that they had once been Christians but had given this up in some cases three, in others as much as twenty, years before. Pliny applied the sacrifice-test, probably in the form of an individual *supplicatio*, through a libation of incense and wine before the Imperial statue, which he had had brought forward with the images of the gods.[77] In addition, he ordered the accused 'to curse Christ'—'none of which acts, it is said, those who are really Christians can be forced into performing'. Those who performed, however, he let go. Now, thoroughly interested, he carried the investigation further. These former Christians claimed that theirs had been a religious cult 'the whole of whose guilt' consisted in the habit of its adherents to meet 'on a certain fixed day before it was light, when they sang in alternate verses a hymn to Christ, as a god, and bound themselves by a solemn oath (*sacramentum*) not to do any wicked deeds, but never to commit fraud, theft or adultery, bear false witness', and other crimes.[78] Even their common meal, which they said consisted of ordinary food, had been suspended on the publication of Pliny's order against associations (*hetaerias*).[79] Further inquiry, assisted by the torture of two female slaves who were styled deaconesses (*ministrae*) confirmed Pliny's impression that this was an extravagant (*immodicam*) and depraved (*pravam*) superstition,[80] intolerable perhaps, but not to be regarded as conspiracy.[81] Numbers of people of all ranks of society in town and countryside alike appeared to be involved.[82] The investigation was therefore adjourned while Trajan's ruling was sought. Meantime, the situation had begun to mend. Temples were being frequented again and there was a general demand for the sacrificial animals once more; and Pliny congratulates himself on the results of his firm and tactful policy.

Trajan's reply upheld Pliny's actions including the form of tests applied, and allowed him discretion, albeit within the framework of the Emperor's general policy of restoring strict law and order to the province. 'It is not possible to lay down any general rule which can be applied as the fixed standard in all cases of this nature.'[83] There was, therefore, no general edict proscribing Christians, and it was not intended to pronounce one. If Christians, however, were denounced, and proved to be such, they were to be punished. But, at the same time, they were to be given the chance of repentance and recantation, 'that is, by worshipping our gods',[84] and they were not to be sought out (conquirendi non sunt). Moreover, anonymous accusations were not to be accepted. These were not consistent with the spirit of the age ('nec nostri saeculi est').

Eighty years later, Tertullian[85] might ridicule the Emperor's decision, but its very illogicality gave the administrators the cue they needed. Christians were not to be treated like common criminals against whom the Emperor's representative must act as a matter of course. But Christianity was not religio licita and if it drew attention to itself then its members were liable to punishment. Otherwise sleeping dogs would be allowed to lie. The Emperor's Utilitas omnium and concern for the 'Salus Generis Humani' required the mild and liberal government of all the provincials, Christians included. It was common prudence too. Three years later, nearly the whole Hellenistic East was engulfed in the great Jewish revolt, but as in 70 and 132 the Christians stood aside.

Their situation, however, was riddled with ambiguities, and attempts to disentangle the contradictory strands lead the student into the same sort of legalistic stalemate already experienced with regard to the Neronian persecution. It is clear, however, that open profession of Christianity had been and continued to be an offence. Trials of Christians had previously taken place. Why? Hardly because the religion had been specifically proscribed, because in that case Pliny would not have needed to consult Trajan at all. Christianity was also something unusual. Pliny writes as though he knew that there were such people as Christians, and that they committed crimes, but otherwise had to learn details as the inquiry proceeded.[86] We may imagine that he arrived at Amisus, found the temples in a bad way, and the blame put on 'the Christians'. He therefore started an investigation into a suspected organization. He was obviously relieved to hear that the food they ate at their common meals was ordinary food, and not some horrible preparation used for magical rites. He did not know a great deal about them, and the deaconesses had not enlightened him. He asked Trajan, therefore, what exactly was the charge against them, how severe should punishment be, should allowance be made for physical weakness or youth, and should recantation be followed by pardon. However, he had no doubt that, whatever may have been the exact legal position, these individuals were potential dangers to the state. More absolute than in Acts fifty years before is the contrast between the claims of Christ and Caesar. We have seen how the religion of Kurios Christos which inspired Ignatius led to defiance of the Empire and to martyrdom. Inevitably, therefore, acceptance of Kurios Caesar by the great majority of Greek-speaking provincials as the embodiment of 'lawful rule' over mankind, demanded ἀνάθεμα χριστῷ.[87] However, *maiestas* does not seem to have been in Pliny's or Trajan's mind, at least explicitly.[88] 'Atheism', or the conflicting demands of the Roman gods and the Christian God, were. We shall hear more of 'dii nostri'.

A possible solution is that Pliny had taken his stand on the fact that the Christians denounced to him belonged to an illegal Judaistic *collegium* or *hetaeria* of conspiratorial inclinations.[89] The combination of crimes might explain the immediate imposition of the death penalty, for open disobedience to his edict against unlicensed *collegia* required stringent penalties. It might also explain the resort to the sacrifice-test, which as we have already seen, was used in the Greek cities for the purpose of establishing beyond doubt Jews and their sympathizers.[90] Throughout the second century it was to be used for the same purpose against the Christians. The *collegium* theory also would account for Pliny's reference to the common meals, which were the hall-marks of a *collegium*,[91] and in the background lurked the fear of secret magic rites which could harm the community. Hence, the requirement of 'cursing Christ', implying the abjuration of a demonic name. His lurid description, too, of the vast numbers of both sexes from town and countryside alike who were tainted '*superstitionis istius contagio*', points in the same direction.[92] *Collegia* had a thoroughly bad name in Bithynia, and there is no doubt that both Pliny and Trajan believed them to be largely responsible for the rotten condition of the province.[93] Altogether, the active Christian *collegium* with its bishops and close-knit organization would appear to Pliny to be typical of the *inlicitos coetus*[94] which it had been his duty to suppress. If he does not refer explicitly to illegal *collegia* in connection with the Christians, he certainly had them in mind as he wrote his dispatch[95] (*quo secundum mandata tua hetaerias esse vetueram*, etc.).

If the situation in Bithynia stood alone, there would be reasonable grounds for accepting this solution, but the question must be asked whether this accounts for arrests of Christians elsewhere. Had Ignatius of Antioch been sent to Rome a few years before on the ground that he, a Roman citizen, was a leader of an illegal *collegium*? Or in the cases of Symeon and Rabbi Eliezer in Palestine, was this the charge against them? It may have been so, for the judge's attitude that the rabbi 'was an old fool to get himself mixed up in this sort of thing', was consistent with the accused belonging to a disreputable organization, against which, however, irony and ridicule were the best weapons. We cannot be completely sure.

Other pieces of evidence, however, from the same part of the world point in this direction. First, in *circa* 165, Lucian of Samosata refers to the head of a Christian community as a θιασάρχης, meaning a 'leader of a cult',[96] and associates the term with those of 'prophet' and 'head of a synagogue' which would suggest, in addition, a Jewish background. Secondly, Celsus opens his attack on the Christians *circa* 178 with the words, 'Societies which are public are allowed by the laws, but secret societies are illegal'.[97] After pointing out that the *agape* 'is more powerful than any oath', he states that 'Christian associations violate the common law' (τὸν κοινὸν νόμον) and therefore by definition were punishable.[98] Finally, in the last years of the century, the burden of Tertullian's impassioned *Apologeticus* was that the Christian 'corpus' was being classed among the 'inlicitas factiones', dangerous to public order, without the slightest justification.[99]

The danger of making concessions to any offshoot from Judaism was made abundantly clear three years later. This time, it was the Jews of the Dispersion who rose.[100] It began apparently in Cyrene in 115, just when the crisis of Trajan's Parthian campaign seemed to be passing. There, the temple of Zeus with its enormous pillars which still excite the tourist's wonder, was elaborately mined and destroyed.[101] A Jew named Andrew (or Lukuas) was hailed as King of the Jews, and gained control.[102] Fighting raged with the utmost ferocity all over the province. Andrew's rule was characterized by a destructive fury which extended even to hacking up the provincial road system[103]—no doubt in the belief that everything 'idolatrous' must be destroyed before the Day of the Lord would dawn. Their reputed eating of their dead enemies and anointing themselves with their blood showed what could be expected from the triumph of Jewry.[104] 'Thyestian feasts' were not perhaps entirely myth. The revolt spread to Alexandria by mid-October 115, where however, the Jews were worsted, and thence to the Delta and among the cities of the Nile valley to the Thebaid.[105] Then, Palestine, Syria, Mesopotamia and Cyprus all had their taste of war against the Gentiles.[106] In the last-named, the Jews destroyed the capital, Salamis, and as in Cyrene proceeded to annihilate the non-Jewish inhabitants. It was not until 117 that the revolt was crushed by forces which Trajan had detached from Mesopotamia. The repression was as merciless as the rising itself. Tens of thousands of Jews were slain. No Jew from henceforth might land on the island of Cyprus.[107] The Rabbinic boast that 'Jews are like wild beasts to the heathen, but like doves before God'[108] had been justified. The Greco-Roman world had been in danger of destruction from the 'Rulers of the East' with whom the Jews were in alliance. Some Christians in Palestine and Syria had prophesied a 'general convulsion of all ungodly kingdoms' at this very moment.[109] These prophesies of Elkesai are the last great Christian apocalyptic revelation, but this time they had, unfortunately, an element of truth. Perhaps, even more significantly, they were remembered sufficiently to survive in book form a century later.[110] Even though the Christians might repudiate orthodox Judaism they still stood too near the Chosen People for any Roman administration to take chances on their behalf.

Under Hadrian, however, it does seem that the Emperor and his advisers made a real distinction in favour of the Christians. In Asia Minor the suppression of the Jews may have been taken as a signal for the populace and the local authorities to make trouble for the Christians. In 123 or 124 the Emperor received a dispatch from Licinius Granianus, Proconsul of Asia, asking advice regarding accusations brought by informers accusing Christians.[111]

If Eusebius' account in the *Ecclesiastical History* is correct, Granianus stated that he thought it was unjust to kill them without accusation or trial, to appease popular clamour.[112] Even though Eusebius adds that the dispatch was 'on behalf of the Christians' (ὑπὲρ χριστιανῶν), and that Justin preserved the Latin text,[113] it does not seem that Granianus did more than ask for the law to be enforced, and those accused to be given a fair trial. As Canfield has urged,[114] it seems that the fuller statement in the *Chronicle* that Granianus 'sent letters to the Emperor, saying that it was very unjust to sacrifice the blood of innocent men to the clamours of the mob, and to make criminals of those who had committed no crime, simply for the name alone and for their belief', is an elaboration by Jerome. It certainly seems doubtful whether Granianus suggested a radical change in Trajan's ruling given only ten years before, which would be implied if the *nomen* was no longer to be grounds for accusation.

Hadrian did not reply at once, but in 124/125, after visiting the province, wrote to Minucius Fundanus, Granianus' successor, who was a friend of Pliny. Like Trajan's rescript in similar circumstances, Hadrian's reply was concerned with meeting the specific points raised by the proconsul. He was determined to prevent people being harassed by informers, and he meant to restore public order. Therefore petitions and popular accusations were not to be recognized. But 'if the inhabitants of the province can clearly sustain this petition against the Christians, so as to give answer even in a court of law, let them pursue this course alone, but let them not have resort to men's petitions and out-cries'. If, however, anyone accused them 'and shows that they are doing anything contrary to the laws, do you pass judgment on them according to the nature of the crime'. But, if the charge was libellous, Fundanus was to 'proceed against that man in accordance with his heinous guilt'.

At first sight, it is difficult to understand why Justin should have attached a copy of the rescript to the end of his *First Apology*, *circa* 150,[115] or that a quarter of a century later Melito of Sardes should remind Marcus Aurelius of its existence,[116] as though it gave full protection to the Christians. It did not. Christians could still be accused, but by due process initiated by an *accusator* or *delator*. 'The courts are open', to echo previous official reaction to clamorous charges against them (Acts 19[38]). Hadrian leaves the whole question of Christianity vague.[117] He does not, however, confirm explicitly that the Name was a crime, and throughout the rescript the emphasis is on actual offences against the law. The accuser must prove 'crimen coherens nomini', rather than 'crimen nominis'. Hence the satisfaction of the Apologists.[118] Even so, after Trajan's rescript membership of the Christian *hetaeria* was a crime if proved, and Hadrian lets this be. None the less, the Christian was now protected against purely vexatious attacks by *indices* (informers) by the full force of the *calumnia* procedure.[119] This would allow the accused, if acquitted in such circumstances, to see his persecutor visited with the same penalty to which he would have been subjected if the charge had been proved.[120] Even the bait of a quarter of the property of the accused was hardly worth an unsuccessful prosecution,[121] and for a Christian to give a fellow-Christian away invited the direst ecclesiastical penalties.[122] In addition, in order to bring a capital charge an accuser would have to visit the provincial capital or else await the governor's assize in the regional capitals. All this would cost time and money, especially as only one man in each province was empowered to pass a death sentence.[123] Usually, his time would be taken up with more pressing matters. To all intents and purposes, the Christian would be free from molestation except in quite extraordinary circumstances.

Thus, in practice, the rescript of Hadrian was the nearest to toleration that the Christians were to attain before the end of Valerian's persecution in 260.[124] Even so, the occasional martyrdom took place, including Telesphorus *circa* 137–138, listed by Eusebius as seventh bishop of Rome,[125] and those which so stirred Justin before his final conversion.[126]

The significance, however, of Hadrian's ruling can be seen when compared to the Emperor's policy towards the Jews which provoked the second great Palestinian war of 132–135. In the first decade of his reign relations with the Jews in Palestine were apparently improving. The vigorous but oppressive Moor, Lusius Quietus, was removed from his post as governor of Judaea. Hadrian considered seriously the re-building of the Temple, and as a preliminary, ordered that the city of Jerusalem itself should be restored. Opposition, however, began to gather.[127] Non-Jews in

Palestine urged delay, and protested that, in any event, the Temple should not be restored on its former site. The Emperor himself became progressively more phil-Hellene after his initiation into the Eleusinian mysteries in 124. Finally, strategic considerations seemed to have decided him against conciliating the Jews. Jerusalem was now the headquarters of *legio* X and a supply point on the eastern frontier. If one takes into account his frontier policy in Britain and Africa, one can well see that he regarded the existence of a loyal population immediately behind the lines as a necessity. Therefore, during his visit to Palestine in the early summer of 130 he decided that the city should be rebuilt, but should be named Aelia Capitolina, and worse still, on the site of the Temple there should be a temple to Jupiter Capitolinus. There were to be 'Greek' settlers with a Roman temple and not Jews.[128] To the latter who considered that the Holy Land belonged to them alone,[129] this was a grave affront.

It is not clear why Hadrian went on to hinder the conduct of Jewish observances, such as the sounding of *Shofar* on New Year's Day or the reading of the Book of Esther, and finally to forbid circumcision.[130] Perhaps he connected the rite with castration for religious purposes performed in Egypt,[131] perhaps it was just another aspect of his phil-Hellenism, and what Dio describes as his 'great strictness, curiosity and meddlesomeness'.[132] But this was the final straw, and after deep-laid preparation extending nearly two years the Jews revolted in 132.[133] The leader, Simon Bar Kôsbā, attempted to assert complete independence from Rome. He assumed ownership of the Imperial estates in areas under his control. His coinage and his orders proclaimed the freedom of Israel.[134] His own title was 'Prince over Israel'.[135] The grape clusters and vine-leaf of the Maccabees and the War of 66–73 were stamped on the Roman imperial denarii and as much of the original designs on these latter, erased.[136] In Palestine he was recognized as Messiah, 'the Son of the Star' (Bar Kochba), by leaders as cautious as Rabbi Akiba and his followers.[137] For the rebels a new period of world history had begun.[138]

It was the revolt of the Maccabees over again, directed against the same threats to Judaism, only this time, the heathen were strong enough to conquer. Once more the claims of pagan and imperial universalism clashed with the demands of Jahwe. The war itself, beginning significantly enough with guerrilla activity, was fought out with unparalleled ferocity. As in Antiochus' time the chief resistance came from the villages, 985 of which were destroyed in 3½ years' fighting.[139] The flourishing countryside of south-east Judaea, probably the main centre of resistance, seems to have been utterly devastated.[140] When Bethar, Bar Kochba's stronghold five miles south of Jerusalem eventually fell in the autumn of 135, Hadrian felt justified in proclaiming himself Imperator II.[141] The statue of a pig was placed on the Bethlehem Gate of Jerusalem.[142]

The Emperor's policy had come to aim at the extirpation of Judaism. The school of Jamnia had supported the war, even if not unanimously, and the penalty for failure had to be paid. Akiba himself was martyred during the war for teaching Torah, which had been declared illegal. The Midrash of the Ten Martyrs mentions a similar fate suffered by Rabbi Ishmael after he had refused to renounce Judaism. Rabbi Hananiah was burnt alive. Nathan, the Babylonian Jewish sage, is reported as commenting, 'The expression in the Decalogue "Those who love me and observe my commandments" applies to the people who live in Palestine and give their lives for the Law. "Why art thou being taken to execution?" Because I circumcised my son. "Why art thou being taken to crucifixion?" Because I read the Torah and ate the mazzot. "Why art thou being beaten with a hundred stripes?" Because I took the *lulab.*'[143] This evidence, taken with Hadrian's other measures[144] against the Jews which precipitated the crisis of A.D. 132 suggests that Rome, when faced by the problems of militant Judaism, reacted in much the same way as had the Seleucid kings three centuries before.[145] Indeed, the continuation in the East of the divine aspects of the Hellenistic monarchs by the Roman Emperors would make this almost inevitable. Religious persecution and trials were not a misfortune reserved for Christians alone.

Indeed, the contrast in treatment is striking. In this period, Judaism was the enemy. The Palestinian Christians had not joined in the revolt. Indeed, we know from Justin Martyr that they and other 'moderates' had been cruelly persecuted by the insurgents,[146] and the letter of Bar Kochba found in a cave at Murabba'at, some 16 miles south-east of Jerusalem, regarding 'Galileans' as potentially hostile may be confirmation of the fact.[147] Of all would-be imitators of the Jews, the Christians were treated the most leniently.[148] There is an interesting passage in Origen, *Contra Celsum*, ii.13, in which the writer in a somewhat obtuse way draws attention to the more favourable treatment accorded to Christians in contrast to unauthorized imitators of Judaism. The Samaritans, he points out, who accept Jewish practices 'are put to death on account of circumcision as Sicarii, on the grounds that they are mutilating themselves contrary to the established laws and are doing what is permitted to the Jews alone'. Mere evidence of the fact was sufficient warrant for a death sentence. The Christians, however, were given a chance to recant even at the last moment by taking an oath and sacrificing. Small comfort, perhaps, but it puts the policy of the second and early-third centuries' Emperors towards the Christians into its proper perspective.

NOTES

[1] *H.E.* iii.33.2, immediately preceding a brief account of Pliny's governorship, derived from Tertullian's Apology—not very sound evidence for events of the period.

[2] The educated pagan was to regard Christianity as 'sub umbraculo insignissimae religionis' (Judaism) at least until 200 (Tertullian, *Apol.* (ed. T. R. Glover), 21.1.), and often believed that Jesus himself was 'someone who had been executed by the Jews' (ibid., 21.3.) I translate 'judicaverunt' as 'executed', rather than 'thought', as per Glover, loc. cit., 103.

[3] Josephus, *Wars*, vi.6.2.

[4] E. G. Hardy, *Christianity and the Roman Government*, 25–6, though, as the case of Fl. Clemens shows, Judaism had not lost its attraction to some members of the Senatorial aristocracy.

[5] Martial, *Epigr.*, vii. 35. Cf. Pliny, *Hist. Nat.*, xiii.4.

[6] Quintilian, *Inst. Or.*, iii.7.21. 'perniciosam caeteris gentem'.

[7] Tacitus, *Histories*, v.8. 'despectissima gens', and 'taeterrima gens'.

[8] Suetonius, *Domitian*, 12. Also, *Claudius*, 25.4—an example of the feeling against the Jews at this period.

[9] Juvenal, *Satires*, xiv, 96–104.

[10] Quintilian, loc. cit., 'qualis est primus Iudaicae superstitionis auctor', cf. F. H Colson. *CR.*, 39, 1925, 166–70. For a full catalogue, J. Juster, *Les Juifs*, 45 n.1.

[11] Tacitus, *Hist.* v.2–13.

[12] Ibid., v.5.5., and 5.2. See discussion of these texts by A. M. A. Hospers Jansen, *Tacitus over de Juden*, Groningen, 1949.

[13] *Acta Hermaisci*, 1.44 (ed. Musurillo, 45). Dating to 113–114, ibid., pp. 167–8.

[14] *CIL.*, iv. 4976; on this and other anti-Jewish and anti-Christian graffiti in Pompeii, L. Herrmann, art. cit., 645–8.

[15] Tacitus, *Histories*, v.13.4; Suetonius, *Vespasian*, iv.5.

[16] Eusebius, *H.E.*, iii.20.1.

[17] 1 Pet. 4[15-16], 'ἤ ὡς ἀλλοτριοεπίσκοπος'. For suggested meanings of this term, cf. E. G. Selwyn, *The First Epistle of Peter*, p. 225. For the suggestion that it might imply that the Christians were regarded as inciters of disaffection, F. W. Beare, *1 Peter* (Blackwell, 1961), 167. On the dating of the Epistle, one cannot help thinking that it refers to a situation similar to that which confronted Pliny in Bithynia in 112 (cf. i Peter 4[15]) especially as Pontus-Bithynia figures prominently among the provinces addressed. It must be admitted that the 'reign of Domitian' is something of an unsatisfactory compromise solution between the 'early' and 'late' schools of thought. See J. Knox, 'Pliny and 1 Peter. A Note on 1 Peter 4[14-16] and 3[15],' *JBL.*, 72, 1953, 187–9.

[18] Note the reference, albeit obscure, to persecution in Ephesus sometime in the Flavian period. Ignatius, *Ephes.*, 12. In general on this phase, W. M. Ramsay, *The Church in the Roman Empire*, 291ff.

[19] W. M. Ramsay, *JRS.*, xiv, 1924, 179ff. No. 6, and 203ff.; cf. M. P. Charlesworth, *The Roman Empire*, 119–20.

[20] Dio Chrysostom (ed. Lamar Crosby), *Oratio*, 46.6 and 10.

[21] Apoc. Abraham 30 (ed. C. H. Box, 1919, p. 83). *Dating*: post A.D. 70, but whether Jewish or Christian in origin, is obscure.

[22] Melito, ap. Eusebius, *H.E.*, iv.26.8.

[23] Tertullian, *Apol.*, 5.4.

[24] Suetonius, *Domitian*, 12. 'Praeter ceteros Iudaicus fiscus acerbissime actus est'.

[25] Literally, εἰς τὸ καπετώλιον, Josephus, *Wars*, vii. 218, Dio Cassius, lxv.7, and *CIL.*, vi.8604, an official called 'procurator ad capitularia Iudaeorum'. In general, J. Juster, *Les Juifs*, 282–6, and M. Ginsberg, 'Fiscus Judaicus', *JQR.*, 1930, 218ff. For the actual payment and collection, *Corp. Pap. Jud.*, p. 115.

[26] Suetonius, *Domitian*, 12, 'ad quem deferebantur qui vel improfessi Judaicam viverant vitam, vel dissimulata origine imposita genti tributa non pependissent'.

[27] Epictetus, *Dissertations*, ii.9.20. 'acting the part of Jews'.

[28] See A. Manaresi, op. cit., 81.

[29] For an interesting glimpse of the kind of conduct Domitian expected from his officials, see the text of his letter to the Procurator of Syria on the proper administration of the public post, *IGLS.*, v.1998.

[30] Suetonius, *Domitian*, 8.4; also Juvenal, *Sat.*, 4.18; and Dio Cassius, lxvii.3.3–4.

[31] M. P. Charlesworth, *Providentia and Aeternitas*, p. 127.

[32] Suetonius, *Domitian*, 4.4, 13.2., Dio Cassius, lxvii.7.

[33] Martial, v.8.1., cf. also 1.30.7. His celebration of *ludi saeculares* in 88 and aspiration to institute a 'new order' point in the same direction. See K. Scott, *Imperial Cult*, 102–12.

[34] M. P. Charlesworth, 'Some observations on the Ruler-Cult, especially in Rome', *HTR.*, 28, 1935, 33. See also, *ILS.*, 9059—a solider in Egypt in the year 94 takes an oath by Jupiter Optimus Maximus, and 'Genium sacratissimi imperatoris Domitiani'.

[36] Suetonius, *Domitian*, 10.4, Tacitus, *Agricola*, 45.

[36] Emigrated to Nicopolis. See art. by C. Robert, 'Epictetos', *P.W.*, vi.1.127.

[37] Pliny, *Ep.*, iii.11. Pliny relates his visit in 94 to Artemidorus, who was living outside Rome, when he was Praetor, at considerable risk to himself.

[38] He was imprisoned and died in Nerva's reign.

[39] Pliny, *Ep.*, iii.11 speaks of the time 'cum philosophi ab urbe summoti'.

[40] Dio Cassius, lxvii.14. See also E. G. Hardy, op. cit., 83ff., L. H. Canfield, op. cit., ch. iii, A. Manaresi, op. cit., 63ff., R. L. P. Milburn, 'The Persecution of Domitian', *C.Q.R.*, 1945 pp. 154–64, and J. Moreau, 'A propos de la Persécution de Domitien', *La Nouvelle-Clio*, v.1953, 121–9.

[41] Eusebius, *H.E.*, iii.18.4, and *Chron. ad ann. Abraham* 2110, (Helm, 192) on the other hand, banishes her to Pontia, and calls her the daughter of a sister of Clemens, instead of a daughter of a sister of Domitian and wife of Clemens. It hardly seems likely that there

were two Flavia Domitillas at this time, and the difficulty is removed if one adopts Styger's view, that Bruttius, the pagan author cited by Eusebius in the *Chronicle*, omitted the word 'uxorem' in his description of Domitilla. This should read 'Flavii Clementis [uxorem] ex sorore neptem'. P. Styger, *Die römischen Katakomben*, Berlin, 1935, 80.

⁴² Suetonius, *Domitian*, 15, 'repente ex tenuissima suspicione'.

⁴³ Ibid., 'Flavium Clementem patruelem suum contemptissimae inertiae'.

⁴⁴ Ibid., 10.2. In view of the pettiness of Domitian's spite and his repute for cunning and violent measures, Glabrio's prowess in dispatching a large lion at the festival of the Juvenalia in 91 may quite possibly have been the real reason for his fall. (Dio Cassius, lxvii.14.3). Note also Commodus' execution of Julius Alexander for a similar feat of arms in the amphitheatre (Dio Cassius, lxxiii.14.1). For a full discussion of the evidence, E. T. Merrill, *Essays in early Christian History*, London, 1924, 155ff.

⁴⁵ Tacitus, *Agricola*, 45.1.

⁴⁶ Pliny, *Panegyricus*, 48.3. 'Ille immanissima belua cum propinquorum sanguinem lambebat'.

⁴⁷ For the practical identification of *impietas* with *maiestas* by Domitian, Pliny. *Paneg.*, 33.3–4, and see M. Hammond's note in *The Antonine Monarchy* (Papers and Monographs of the American Academy in Rome, xix, 1959), 240.

⁴⁸ Juvenal, loc. cit.; Origen, *Contra Celsum*, ii.13 and v.41, and cf. Dio Cassius, lvii.18.5 where the expulsion of the Jews from Rome in 19 is attributed to their proseletyzing activities. This passage, however, is unfortunately only a citation from John of Antioch who may not be quoting Dio *verbatim*. See J. Juster, *Les Juifs*, p. 232, and A. Manaresi, op. cit., 81. 'Proselitismo guidaico e cristianesimo rimanevano sempre illegali'.

⁴⁹ Tacitus, *Annales*, xiii.32.

⁵⁰ Th. Mommsen, *Der Religionfrevel*, 407.

⁵¹ Ed. H. Musurillo, *Acts of the Pagan Martyrs*, 45ff. J. Moreau, art. cit., 123, comments that the Roman aristocrats were punished for living 'à la juive', 'ce qui peut signifier qu'ils sympathisent de près ou de loin avec le christianisme. Tel est, à ce sujet, le dernier mot de la critique'. The view, also, of Milburn, op. cit., 163–4. Manaresi, op. cit., 74, believes in the possibility of aristocratic Christians being involved in a plot against Domitian. His eventual murderer, the freedman Stephanus, was steward to Domitilla.

⁵² For the tradition see art. 'Gamaliel ii' in *The Jewish Encyclopaedia*, v. 560–61; cf. M. Charlesworth, *Ruler Cult*, 34 n. 1.

⁵³ See Kirsopp Lake's brief note, *Apostolic Fathers* i,8 and 9. On chronology, 'it is safest to say that it must be dated between A.D. 75 and 110, but within these limits there is general agreement among critics to regard as most probable the last decade of the first century', ibid., 5.

⁵⁴ See other refs. in Arndt and Gingrich. *Lexicon*, 362.

⁵⁵ i Clement, 63.3.

⁵⁶ E. T. Merrill, op. cit., 160–1.

⁵⁷ *CIL.*, vi.8942; cf. *CIL.*, vi.16246. See the discussion in P. Styger, *Die römischen Katakomben*, Berlin, 1933, 64ff.

⁵⁸ J. B. de Rossi, 'Roma sotterranea', *Bull. di arch. cristiana*, 1865, 34–40; cf. O. Marucchi, 'Roma sotterranea' Nuov. Ser., *Monumenti del cimiterio di Domitilla*, Rome, 1914, 80.

⁵⁹ P. Styger, op. cit., 5ff.

⁶⁰ Ibid., p. 80, and L. Hertling and E. Kirschbaum, *Die römischen Katakomben und ihre Märtyrer*, Eng. tr. J. Costelloe, 1956, pp. 22–9. Also A. M. Schneider, 'Die ältesten Denkmäler der römischen Kirche', *Sitzungsberichte Akad. Wissenschaften*, Göttingen, 1951, *Phil. Hist. Kl.*, 166–98.

⁶¹ This seems a reasonable conclusion from the evidence taken as a whole. See H. Leclercq, art. 'Aristocratiques (classes)', *DACL.*, 1.2. 2845–86 at col. 2854; R. L. P. Milburn, art. cit., 163.

⁶² P. Styger, op. cit., 71–2.

⁶³ L. Bruttius Praesens (?), governor of Galatia under Hadrian (*I.G.R.R.*, iii, 273 = 1487).

⁶⁴ Eusebius, *Chronicon, sub ann.* Abraham, 2110 (= 16th year of Domitian's reign), *H.E.*, iii.18.4. 'Scribit Bruttius plurimos christianorum sub Domitiano fecisse martyrium. Inter quos Flaviam Domitillam, Flavii Clementis consulis [uxorem?] ex sorore neptem, in insulam Pontiam relegatam, quia se christianam esse testata sit' (Helm, 192). cf. L. Canfield, op. cit., 81–2, and H. Leclercq, op. cit., col. 2850–4.

⁶⁵ Dio Cassius, lxviii.2. According to Jerome (*Ep.*, 108.9) Domitilla did not return from exile. John may have returned from Patmos. Jerome, *De Viris Illust.* 9, Eusebius, *H.E.*, iii.8.20 and Clement Alex., *Quis dives salvetur*, 42.

⁶⁶ See H. St. J. Hart, 'Judaea and Rome. The Official Commentary', *JTS.*, N.S.3, 1952, 172–98, at 190.

⁶⁷ Suetonius, *Domitian*, 23, Martial, *Epigr.*, x.72 and Dio Chrysostom, *Oratio*, xlv.1, a violent denunciation of Domitian's calling himself 'Dominus et Deus'.

⁶⁸ Pliny, *Letters*, x (ed. Hardy), 37 and 39. (Nicomedia and Nicaea).

⁶⁹ See the excellent detailed description of the political, social and economic situation in Pontus-Bithynia at this time, given by W. Weber, '. . . nec nostri saeculi est', *Festgabe Karl Müller*, Tübingen, 1922, 24–45, at p. 29ff. Also, D. Magie, *Roman Rule in Asia Minor*, 600ff.

⁷⁰ Outline of his career, M. Schuster, art. *P.W.*, xxi.1, 442–3.

⁷¹ Pliny, *Epp.*, iii.9 and v.20. Canfield, op. cit., 86.

⁷² The literature on this incident is vast. E. T. Merrill's account, op. cit., ch. vii, is as usual, clear and well documented. On the whole, I think that his view that the Christians were being accused of belonging to some forbidden *hetaeria* is correct, though he misses the significance of the Christian connections with Judaism. A. Manaresi, op. cit., 112ff., emphasizes the absence of *maiestas* in Pliny's requisitory against the Christians. E. Schwartz, *Kaiser Constantin und die christliche Kirche*, Leipzig, 1936, 31–4, also stresses the role of the Christians at this period as an 'illegal corporation' suspected of atheism. See, in addition, L. Canfield, op. cit., ch. iv., 100ff. W. M. Ramsay, op. cit., 196ff., E. G. Hardy, op. cit., and H. Last, 'Christenverfolgung ii. (juristisch), *A.C.*, ii, 1218–19.

⁷³ See E. G. Hardy's ed. Pliny, *Letters*, 210–17, or J. Stevenson, *A New Eusebius*, 13–18.

⁷⁴ See E. T. Merrill, op. cit., 185, A. N. Sherwin-White, *Early Persecutions*, 204–5.

⁷⁵ For a similar instance of the workings of an official mind, there is the reply of the Government of Massachusetts to Charles II's inquiry into the hanging of five Quaker leaders in the colony in 1660. 'The Quakers died not because of their crimes how capital soever, but upon their superadded presumptions and incorrigible contempt for authority' (cited from J. A. Williamson, *A Short History of British Expansion*, Macmillan, 1945, i.299).

For Christian 'obstinatio'—Tertullian, *De Spectaculis*, 1, and *Apol.*, 50.15, who, naturally, claims it as a virtue, but note also the advice given to Christians in i Peter 3¹⁵, 'Be prepared always to make a defence to anyone who calls you to account for the hope that is in you, yet do it with gentleness and reverence', i.e. no 'obstinatio' or 'amentia'.

⁷⁶ 'similis amentiae'—another indication of how the will to martyrdom struck educated Romans in this period. Cf. Celsus, ab. Origen. *Contra Celsum*, viii.65.

⁷⁷ 'cum praeeunte me deos appellarent et imagini tuae, quam propter hoc iusseram cum simulacris numinum adferri, ture et vino supplicarent'; cf. Eusebius, *H.E.*, iv.15.20, the proconsul's order to Polycarp at Smyrna, *circa* 167. See also M. P. Charlesworth, art. cit., *HTR.*, 1935, 32.

⁷⁸ i.e. the recitation of the Decalogue.

⁷⁹ 'Quod ipsum facere desisse post edictum meum, quo secundum mandata tua hetaerias esse vetueram.'

⁸⁰ The *ministrae* would have appeared to Pliny as the slaves of the *hetaeria*. They would

have served at the common meals and might be expected to give an account of what went on there. See Merrill, op. cit., 193.

[81] See J. Vogt, 'ein verkehrtes, anmassendes Schwarmgeistertum, damit das Gegenteil von *religio*.—'Zur Religiosität der Christenverfolger in römischen Reich'. *Sitzungsber. der Heidelberger Akad. der Wiss.*, 1962, 1, 1–30 (at p. 12).

[82] 'Multi enim omnis aetatis, omnis ordinis, utrius sexus etiam, vocantur in periculum et vocabuntur. Neque civitates tantum sed vicos etiam atque agros superstitionis ist ius contagio pervagata est. . . . '

[83] For the spirit of Trajan's dealings with Pliny, and how far his replies reflected his own ideas and how far were the routine of a secretariat, A. N. Sherwin-White, 'Trajan's Replies to Pliny: Authorship and Necessity'. *JRS.*, lii, 1962, 114ff.

[84] 'Id est supplicando dis nostris'.

[85] *Apologeticus*, 5. See also, E. T. Merrill, 'Tertullian on Pliny's Persecution of the Christians'. *AJT.*, xxii (1918), 124–35.

[86] His own unquestioning loyalty to the traditional gods of Rome can be demonstrated by the passage at the end of the *Panegyric* (*Paneg.*, 94) 'in fine orationis praesides custodesque imperii divos ego consul pro rebus humanis ac te praecipue, Capitoline Iuppiter precor, ut beneficiis tuis faveas tantisque muneribusque addas perpetuitatem'. His indignation against the obstinate provincials who refused to acknowledge the Roman gods on whom their welfare depended, can be imagined.

[87] For instance, at Smyrna in 165–168, Eusebius, *H.E.*, iv.15.20; cf. Th. Mommsen, *Der Religionsfrevel*, 394–5, and H. Achelis, *Das Christentum*, ii.235.

[88] The tendency in this period was to cut down the scope of *maiestas*; cf. Spartian, *Hadrian*, 18.4. 'Maiestatis crimina non admisit', and further texts, above, p. 176, n.93.

[89] An interesting example of a small *hetaeria* meeting explicitly for religious purposes was found at Dura-Europos. Six families clubbed together as a *hetaeria* to set up a statue to the god Aphlad on the 'twentieth day of Gorpaios', in the year A.D. 54. (*Excavations at Dura-Europos*, Fifth Season, 1931–32, p. 114.)

[90] Above, p. 136. It was a Jew-test, not merely a loyalty test in Asia Minor and Syria. I see no reason to doubt A. Harnack's dictum that in the second century 'jeder angeklagte Christen opfern solle', and that this requirement was often accepted by martyrologists as assuming the existence of edicts (προστάγματα) ordering sacrifice to the gods. (A. Harnack, 'Der Proces des Christen Apollonius' *SBAW.*, 1893, 728, n.8.)

[91] Just previously, Pliny had asked Trajan whether the people of Amisus should be allowed to continue their longstanding custom of eating common meals as part of the functions of a benefit club (*eranum*). Amisus was a 'civitas libera', and this privilege had apparently been specifically preserved in the treaty of alliance between it and Rome. Trajan had replied that this could not be abrogated by administrative action (*Ep.*, x.92) but the fact that Pliny asked shows how seriously unlicensed *collegia* and their functions were being regarded; and indeed, Trajan continues 'in ceteris civitatibus, quae nostro jure obstrictae sunt res huiusmodi prohibenda est'. See A. H. M. Jones, 'Civitates liberae et Immunes', *Anatolian Studies presented to W. H. Buckler*, 114.

[92] This phrase came to be used as so much official jargon applicable to 'wrong religion'. Thus, Constantine's well-known grant to the people of Hispellum of permission to build a temple in honour of the *gens Flavia*, contains the significant proviso, 'ne ae/ dis nostro nomini dedicata cuiusquam con/ tagiose superstitionis fraudibus polluatur' (*CIL.*, xi.5265 = *ILCV.*, 5).

[93] Note particularly Trajan's answer to Pliny on the subject of the fire brigade at Nicomedia (*Ep.*, x.33): 'meminerimus provinciam istam et praecipue eas civitates eiusmodi factionibus esse vexatas, quodcumque nomen ex quacumque causa dederimus eis, qui in id contracti fuerint (collegia quoque), hetaeriae brevi fient'. Hence, Pliny's edict against *collegia* referred to by the Christians some months later. See W. Weber, art. cit., 31, and

compare W. H. Buckler's art. 'Labour Disputes in Asia', in *Anatolian Studies presented to Sir William Ramsay*, 30–3 (strike action by the guild of bakers at Ephesus).

⁹⁴ Pliny, *Ep.*, x.93.

⁹⁵ H. Last, art. cit., *A.C.*, ii, 1219 for objections, and E. G. Hardy, op. cit., 128ff. and E. T. Merrill, op. cit., 198ff. for further information on the probable importance of *collegia* in the minds of the authorities at this period.

⁹⁶ Lucian, *De Morte Peregrini* 11. Peregrinus became successively, 'prophet, cult-leader and head of the synagogue'.

⁹⁷ Origen, *Contra Celsum*, 1.1.

⁹⁸ Note, *Dig.* 1.3.1. 'Papinianus libro primo definitionum. Lex est commune praeceptum, virorum prudentium consultum, delictorum quae sponte vel ignorantia contrahuntur coercitio, communis rei publica sponsio'. See also, Tacitus, *Ann.*, xiv, 17 for the dissolution of *collegia* on Pompeii, which were organized illegally (*quae contra leges instituerunt*). The punishment for membership of an illegal *collegium* was defined in *Dig.*, 48.2.22 as the same as that for seizing public places or temples by force, namely exile for *honestiores* and condemnation to the mines for *humiliores*.

⁹⁹ Tertullian, *Apol.*, 38.1. 'Proinde nec paulo lenius inter licitas factiones sectam istam deputari oportebat, a qua nihil tale committitur quale de inlicitis factionibus timeri solet?'

¹⁰⁰ See the important article summarizing the evidence for the revolt, by Alexander Fuks, 'Aspects of the Jewish Revolt in 115–117, *JRS.*, li, 1961, 98–104, and also H. I. Bell, *Antisemitismus*, 37–42.

¹⁰¹ R. G. Goodchild, *Cyrene*, p. 71, and P. M. Fraser and S. P. Appelbaum, 'Hadrian and Cyrene', *JRS.*, xl, 1950, 83ff.

¹⁰² Dio Cassius, lxviii.32.1, Eusebius, *H.E.*, iv.2.4.

¹⁰³ *L' Année épigraphique*, 1928, 1 and 2; 1929, 9: Orosius, *Historia adv. paganos*, vii.12.6. cf. R. P. Longden, ch. vi in *CAH.*, xi.250–1 and Fuks, loc. cit., 99.

¹⁰⁴ Note the prayer to the gods from Eudaimonis, the mother of the Strategos, Apollonios, that her son shall not be roasted by the Jews, *Corp. Pap. Jud.*, No. 437, Fuks, loc. cit., 101. Xiphilinus in Dio Cassius, lxviii.32.1.

¹⁰⁵ Eusebius, *Chron.*, ad ann. 114 (Helm, 196). 'Verum gentilium pars superat in Alexandria', Orosius, *Hist.*, vii.12.7. Fuks, loc. cit., 99. A Jewish defeat near Memphis after an initial victory, *Corp. Pap. Jud.*, 438 and 439.

¹⁰⁶ Dio Cassius, lxviii.32.3, and Fuks, loc. cit., 103, n. 69.

¹⁰⁷ Ibid. Destruction of Jewish community at Edfu, Tcherikover and Fuks, *Corp. Pap. Jud.*, p. 109, and other examples of repression, ibid., Nos. 445 and 448.

¹⁰⁸ Rabbi Jokhanan (died 279) Midrash Cant., ad Cant. 2⁷; cf. J. Juster, op. cit., 220 n.18.

¹⁰⁹ Hippolytus, *Elenchus*, ix.16.4. (Wendland, 255).

¹¹⁰ Hippolytus, *Elenchus*, ix.13.1. (Wendland, 251).

¹¹¹ Note C. Callewaert, 'Le rescrit d'Hadrien à Minucius Fundanus', *Rev. d'Hist. et de lit. réligieuse*, viii, 1903. L. H. Canfield op. cit., ch. v; E. T. Merrill, op. cit., ch. viii (excellent on the subject of the rescript's authenticity). W. M. Ramsay, *Church in the Roman Empire*, ch. xiv. P. Allard, *Histoire des Persécutions*, Paris, 1885, 240, and *Le Christianisme et L'Empire Romain*, 40–4.

¹¹² Eusebius, *H.E.*, iv.8.6.

¹¹³ 1 *Apol.*, 68.

¹¹⁴ Canfield's analysis of the two incompatible accounts in the *Ecclesiastical History* and the *Chronicle*, and his decision in favour of the former is convincing, op. cit., 104–8; and so, too, his vindication of the authenticity of the correspondence as a whole. For details, op. cit., 193–8, also Ramsay, op. cit., 320–2. Jerome admits, *Chron. Praefatio* (Helm, 6) that he has added in some details to the Roman history in the *Chronicle* ('nonnulla, quae mihi intermissa videbantur, adieci . . . '). Perhaps these are among them! The only point which still seems curious, is that Eusebius calls the Proconsul Serennius Granianus,

when his real name was Licinius Granianus (here, see Callewaert, art. cit., 180, and Merrill, op. cit., 208–9).

[115] Justin, *1 Apol.*, 68.

[116] Melito of Sardes, ap. Eusebius, *H.E.*, iv.26.10.

[117] See particularly, W. M. Ramsay, op. cit., 323.

[118] A. Manaresi, op. cit., 145.

[119] The legal justification of such procedure is given by Gaius, *Digest*, 50.16.2 33, 'per fraudem et frustrationem alios vexare litibus' which would fit the cases Hadrian had in mind. See art. by Hitzig, *P.W.*, iii.1, 1414–21.

[120] Hitzig, art. cit., 1417, though the exact penalties in all cases are not known. The case of the slave who accused Apollonius before the Praefectus Praetorio, Perennis, circa 183, and had his legs broken by order of the latter (Eusebius, *H.E.*, v.21.3) is not a case in point. He was probably executed in accordance with the law against slaves who betrayed their masters, over, p. 315.

[121] Tacitus, *Annales*, iv.20; cf. S. Dill, *Roman Society*, 25.

[122] See for instance, Canon 73 of the Council of Elvira (ed. Hefele, tr. W. R. Clark, p. 168).

[123] In the *Passio Perpetuae*, 6.2 it is specifically stated on the death of the Proconsul. Minucius Timinianus, the procurator Hilarianus 'tunc loco proconsulis M. T. defuncti ius gladii acceperat'. See, A. N. Sherwin-White, *The Early Persecutions and Roman Law*, 212–13.

[124] Hadrian may have had syncretistic leanings, which would have allowed Christianity a place among the religions of the Empire. (Lampridius, *Vita Alex. Severi*, 43.6). Lampridius, however, admits that the story about Hadrian wishing to raise a temple to Christ was hearsay ('quod et Hadrianus cogitasse fertur', ibid.). Lampridius is good evidence for Alexander Severus, but not for a hundred years before. The 'Letter to Servianus' quoted by Vopiscus may be interesting for the third century, but hardly for Hadrian. Fl. Vopiscus, *Vita Saturnini*, 7.8.

[125] Eusebius, *H.E.*, iv.10.1, Irenaeus, *Adv. Haer,*, iii.3. Telesphorus 'qui gloriosissime martyrum fecit'. On other 'martyrs' in Hadrian's reign see P. Allard, *Les Persécutions*, 202ff.

[126] Justin, *2 Apol.* 12.

[127] L. Finkelstein, *Akiba*, 251ff.

[128] Dio Cassius, lxix.12.1.: cf. L. Finkelstein, *Akiba*, 260, and M. Auerbach, 'Zur politischen Geschichte der Juden unter Kaiser Hadrian', *Festschr. zum 50 Jahr, Bestehen des Rabbinerseminars zu Berlin*, Berlin, 1924, 1–40.

[129] Tertullian, *De Resurrectione Carnis*, 26, 'et ipsam terram sanctam Iudaicum proprie solum reputant'. The Jewish view in Carthage seventy years later.

[130] *Dig.*, 48.8.11.1. *SHA.*, Hadrian, 14.2; cf. Auerbach, art. cit., 8, and the important article by E. M. Smallwood 'The Legislation of Hadrian and Antoninus Pius against Circumcision', *Latomus*, 18, 1959, 334–47. There does not, however, seem to be any corroborative evidence that Hadrian also prohibited circumcision among other Semitic peoples and Egyptian priests (Smallwood, op. cit., 339).

[131] J. Juster, *Les Juifs*, 1.256, and E. Schürer, *Geschichte*, 1.677.

[132] Dio Cassius, lxix.5.1. His loyalty, despite all, to purely Roman religious traditions, *SHA.*, Hadrian, 22.10.

[133] Dio Cassius, lxix.12.1.

[134] A contract drawn up in Aramaic found in the Dead Sea area in 1952 is dated 'the third year of the liberty of Israel'. J. T. Milik, *R.B.*, 61, 1954, 183. For the coinage, L. Mildenburg, 'The Eleazar Coinage of the Bar Kochba Rebellion', *Historia Judaica*, xi, April 1949, 77ff. The rebels replaced the palm-tree symbol by which Titus had represented Judaea with their own palm tree and the inscription 'Year One of the Redemption of Israel', with Simon (Nasi Israel) and Eleazar the Priest.

135 The title used in his order concerning treatment of Galileans (neutrals and perhaps Christians (?)) to Yeshua ben Gilgola found in the Dead Sea area in 1952, J. T. Milik, *R.B.*, 60, 1963, 276ff. and F. M. Cross, 'La Lettre de Simon ben Kosba', *R.B.*, 63, 1956, 45–9.

136 L. Mildenburg, art. cit., 101–2. On the light thrown by recent discoveries in the Judaean desert on the scale of the revolt, see the articles by Y. Yadin, 'New archives of the Revolt of Bar Kochba', in *Illustrated London News*, of 4 and 11 November 1961 (the finds made in the Nabal Hever cave).

137 Midrash Rabbah on *Lamentations* ii.2.4. (Eng. tr., 157); L. Finkelstein, *Akiba*, 261; for Jesus as Christian 'Bar Kochba', Justin, *1 Apol.*, 32 citing Is. 11[1] and 51[5] combined with Nums. 24[17].

138 Note, of course, the modern parallels of periodized and apocalyptic historical thought shown in the French Revolutionaries, and Italian Fascists' replacement of the Christian Era by their own.

139 Dio Cassius, lxix.14.1.

140 Y. Yadin, art. cit. In 1961 important finds, including fragments of looted Roman standards, dating to the period of the rebellion were found in caves in the sides of the Wadi Murabbat (*The Times*, 28 March 1961).

141 Dio Cassius, lxix.14.1. Eusebius, *H.E.*, iv.6. on the struggle for Bethar.

142 Jerome, *Chron. ad. ann. Abr.*, 2152 (Helm, 201).

143 Mechilta, *Jethro Bahodesh*, vi (Winter u. Wunsche, 213). See L. Finkelstein, *Aikba*, 270, and S. Zeitlin, *JQR.*, N.S. 36, 1945–6 1–11, on the martyrdoms resulting from the war.

144 Including, of course, the building of a temple to Jupiter Capitolinus on the site of the Temple of Jerusalem, an act not far removed from Antiochus's 'abomination of desolation'.

145 For the repression of the rebellion, M. Noth, *The History of Israel*, 451, and an interesting cameo study of those days, R. Aron, *Jesus, The Hidden Years*, (Eng. tr. 1962), 146.

146 Justin, *1 Apol.*, 31; cf. *Dialogue*, 1.3, and Jerome. *Chron. loc. cit.*

147 Discussed by J. T. Milik, *R.B.*, 60, 1953, 276ff., J. J. Rabinowitz, ibid., 61, 1954, 191–2, and F. M. Cross, ibid., 63, 1956, 47–8.

148 At the same time, the new Aelia Capitolina did not spare the Christian Holy Places. Hadrian covered the site of Calvary and of the Tomb with temples of Jupiter and Venus.

CHAPTER NINE

The False Dawn, 135–165

W ITH the end of the second Jewish War the Christian Church entered on thirty years of precarious quasi-toleration.[1] Its numbers increased, its organization was strengthened and Judaistic apocalyptic, though remaining a powerful influence, began to lose its stranglehold on its thought. The Church was coming out into the world, making its converts among the Greek-speaking provincials, presenting them with a message of personal salvation and illumination, and attempting to convince them through a reasoned approach to religion. We enter on the classic age of the Gnostics and the Apologists. With their emergence, comes a gradual change of the Church's outlook towards secular society. The latter's long continuance, if not its permanence, was becoming increasingly accepted, and this foreshadowed the possibility of a future *modus vivendi* between Church and Empire.

For their part the Roman authorities were content, generally speaking, to let the Church be, and up to *circa* 150 the provincials were usually prepared to do likewise. This was the high-water mark of Roman provincial civilization, which saw the great expansion of Romanized cities from end to end of the Mediterranean and from the Euphrates to the Wall, the progressive conquest of steppe and waste by cultivation and the genuine acceptance of Greco-Roman institutions and culture. One cannot treat the eulogies of the period as mere rhetoric. Wars had in fact so far vanished as to be regarded as legendary affairs of the past.[2] There was security and ease of travel, deserts were being transformed into cultivated land, porticos, gymnasia, temples, libraries and schools did spring up in out-of-the-way provincial towns, and well-being was spread wider than at any time before the seventeenth century. Even for the peasant, prices seem to have been both low and stable.[3]

The Church adapted itself to the prevailing urban culture with permanent effects on its organization. From now on, the bishop was to be bishop of the community in a *civitas*. Even so, the calm which the Church enjoyed was an uneasy one. It depended, as it had in the previous generation, on its relative insignificance, swamped amidst the general prosperity of the age. The time would come when its solidifying organization and proselytizing zeal could not be treated with the same contempt as the awe-inspiring but individualistic threats of Christian prophets. When, *circa* 150 the Greco-Roman world began to awake to the threat which it constituted, toleration came to an end. Already in the reign of Antoninus Pius there was a tendency to blame local calamities on the atheism of the Christians. Under his successor, the storm broke.

The general quiet enjoyed by the Church under Antoninus Pius and in the first years of the reign of Marcus Aurelius did not imply any improvement in its status, only a lenient administration of the existing law. It could hardly be otherwise. Antoninus is characterized both by his contemporaries, and by later tradition as a conservative, religious, and high-minded ruler whose *pietas* was universally acknowledged and applauded.[4] He would never allow, it was said, 'any sacrifice to be delegated unless he was sick'.[5] According to Marcus Aurelius, while he was 'not superstitious in the service of the gods', he 'always stood by the old places and the old ways', and 'he did everything according to Roman usage'.[6] Such a ruler could be expected to promote the widest possible measure of content among his subjects, to repress busybodies and informers,[7] and to remove sense of grievance, but not to give special dispensations to unauthorized and suspect religious groups.

Events prove that this was the case. The outward marks of the fury of the Jewish war were removed as soon as possible. Circumcision was once more permitted to Jews, but if performed on non-Jews was regarded as castration and punishable by the same penalties.[8] Thus the situation pre-130 was restored. Judaism was once more *religio licita*, but restricted to the narrowest national limits. This was to remain official policy, and it excluded the Samaritan and 'the stranger within the gates' from the privileges accorded to the Israelites.[9]

A significant fragment of contemporary evidence shows how

strictly Jewish activities in the eastern provinces were being circumscribed. Justin in his *First Apology*, *circa* 150, remarks[10] that death had been decreed against 'those who read the books of Hystaspes or Sybil or the prophets'. This looks like an attempt to restrict Jewish propaganda and proselytism, for all three categories of book were being used by the Jews in Asia Minor and Alexandria in their ceaseless war against 'idolatry' and to maintain their hopes of the ultimate destruction of Rome by Parthia.[11] But Justin's reaction is equally interesting. Despite his dislike of Judaism he does not praise the Imperial government. Indeed, the solidarity of Christians with Jews on this issue is striking in an age which produced Marcion. It was the 'working of the wicked demons' that had prompted this decree, 'so that they might frighten people away from receiving the knowledge of good things by consulting them, and keep them in slavery to themselves'. And then, he goes on, 'But they did not succeed in this for ever, for we not only boldly consult these books, but also, as you see, offer them for your inspection being sure that what they declare will be welcome to all. For if we only persuade a few, this will be a great gain for us, for as good husbandmen we will receive our reward from our Master'. As good as his word he quotes them (*1 Apol.*, 20) in order to support his claim that the world would end in conflagration.[12] Thus, Justin offers formal defiance to the Roman State while at the same time asking that his Apology should be laid before the Roman Senate.[13] Mild administration would not lead to any abatement of the Christian's claims to the allegiance of the world on a basis wholly at variance with that represented by Antonine Rome. If the law stood in the way, then the law was the inspiration of demons. This was not an isolated claim. It was to be repeated just as forcefully by Origen on the eve of the Decian persecution.[14] By its overthrow of political Judaism in 135, the Roman world had won a respite, but not final victory over the enemy within the gates.

For the Christians, however, it was the policy of Hadrian continued. From Eusebius we learn that Antoninus Pius forbade outbreaks of mob violence against them, and sent rescripts to the citizen bodies of Athens, Larissa and Thessalonica, and perhaps a general order to the cities of Greece forbidding riot and disorder directed against them.[15] But formal charges against individual Christians could still be made, and the roll of martyrs continued to swell.[16]

One document, always disputed, but which could none the less throw light on the official attitude towards irresponsible provincial agitation against Christians may be briefly noted.[17] It is supposed to be an imperial rescript in answer to a petition by the Council of Asia denouncing the Christians as 'atheists' and bringers of evil on the community. If genuine, it would date either to the last months of Antoninus' reign or the first months of his successor's. It was known to Tertullian and it still existed in Eusebius' time, and therefore its fabrication, if fabrication it was, dates from before the end of the second century.[18] Eusebius reproduces it in the *Ecclesiastical History* (iv.13) immediately following the text of Justin's petition to Antoninus Pius and Lucius Verus which prefaces the *First Apology*; and a version also survives in the Paris MS. (Parisinus Regius 450) which includes Justin's two *Apologies*, where it follows the Second Apology, Eusebius further maintains that 'testimony to these events' (i.e. the petition of the Council of Asia and the Emperor's reply) was given by the contemporary Christian leader Melito, Bishop of Sardes, and was also used by him in his own *Apology* to Verus a few years later.[19]

The 'rescript' is far too favourable to the Christians for the liking of most critics. It informs its recipients that the 'gods also take care that such men (i.e. Christians) should not escape notice, for they would be far more likely to punish those who are unwilling to worship them', than the Council would be. By provoking the Christians, and calling them atheists, the latter simply confirmed them in their opinions, and encouraged them to seek death on behalf of their god. Moreover, during the recent earthquakes, the Christians had worshipped their god, whereas the provincials had neglected theirs, and then proceeded to persecute the Christians. The Emperor went on to remind the Council that 'our divine father' had informed many provincial governors that 'they were not to be interfered with' unless they appeared to be plotting against the Roman government. That was also his policy. But he ends with the striking injunction, 'But if any persist in taking action against any one of such persons, on the grounds that he is so, let that one who is accused be released from the charge, even if it appear that he is such, but the accuser shall be liable to penalty'.[20]

This last sentence must rule the document as it stands out of court. Some provincial governors were lenient towards Christians even if these were accused of common law crimes as well,[21] but an injunction automatically to apply the *calumnia* proceedings against any accuser of Christians would make nonsense of Imperial policy hitherto. Moreover, the death penalty, which is implied, could not be inflicted by the provincial magistrates to whom the 'rescript' was addressed and the latter were sometimes made aware of the fact.[22] At the same time, the remainder of the rescript could have a genuine basis. There had been severe earthquakes in the province of Asia circa 152[23] (which the rescript describes vividly as τῶν σεισμῶν τῶν γεγονότων καὶ γινομένων),[24] and outbursts against Christians were to follow natural disasters in Asia Minor for the next century.[25] Contemporaries believed that these resulted specifically from neglect of the gods.[26] 'Atheism', as the martyrdom of Polycarp probably in 165/68 was to show, was the most damning charge against the Christians at this time in the Asiatic cities, while the willingness of the Christians to die for their god was a well-known fact and one commented upon by observers of diverse views and living as far apart as Lucian, Justin, Tertullian, Clement of Alexandria and the populace of Lyons. It was to impress Marcus Aurelius himself, though not necessarily so early in his reign. Its mention is curious, but not incredible in a rescript to a provincial Council, for this, though an official document, could be couched in less formal terms than an edict. Moreover, it is followed by the re-affirmation of Hadrian's policy discouraging private denunciation. At the same time, there is no intention, in this part of the text of restricting the range of action of the authorities. One is tempted to conclude, in some measure of agreement with Ramsay and Harnack, that Antoninus Pius did send a rescript concerning the Christians to the Council of Asia which Melito of Sardes quoted, but that the text preserved in Eusebius is corrupt, and interpolated by Christians to suit their own purposes. In particular, the last sentence is forgery, perhaps the expression of what educated Christians in the late second and third centuries were asking for their creed.[27]

However we treat this document, the decade 140–150 passed easily enough for the Christians even in the nerve centres of religious strife. Thus at Alexandria, there is record of a peaceful discussion between a Jew named Jason and a Jewish-Christian named Papiscus taking place *circa* 140 which survived as something of a *cause célèbre*.[28] Ten years later a young Christian actually obtained a hearing from the Prefect of Egypt, L. Munatius Felix, for a request that he be allowed to castrate himself on religious grounds. The request was refused, but nothing appears to have happened to the young man.[29]

In Asia, too, similar quiet prevailed. By now, Christian communities had become part of the landscape in many cities. They had their 'Father' or bishop, just as the rival Jewish community had theirs, and he had become a well-known figure.[30] Polycarp's career demonstrates this. Allegedly '86 years in the service of Christ', and bishop for half a century or more in Smyrna he could hardly have escaped notice in a part of the world where religion was and remains everybody's business.[31] Moreover, that he had his own slaves,[32] mixed with the local aristocracy and counted members of the Proconsul's staff in his congregation. Such members 'wished to stand well with him'.[33] In the provincial capital at Ephesus Christians went freely about their business. In *circa* 137 Justin, recently converted from Platonism, had a two-day discussion with a Jew named Trypho under the colonnade, probably forming one side of the Agora of the city. It was watched in its final stages by a large crowd.[34] Both men began by declaring their religious allegiances, Trypho in a few words, Justin in the course of a long autobiographical sketch detailed before none too friendly witnesses.[35] It was not the first of such discussions which he had held.[36] Here also, quasi-toleration prevailed, and in a revealing sentence Justin pointed to the contrast between Jewish malevolence and the liberty being accorded to Christians by the authorities. 'You have not the authority to raise your hands against us, because of them that are now supreme', he told Trypho. 'But', he adds, 'as often as you could, you did.'[37]

These instances confirm the picture which Eusebius draws of the Church in the Antonine age. Now it was that 'the Churches like brilliant lamps were shining throughout the world, and the faith in our Saviour the Lord Jesus Christ was flourishing among all mankind'.[38] The Devil, he goes on, debarred from using the weapon of persecution against the Church, resorted to attempts to undermine its faith through the Gnostic heresies.[39] Indeed, the period is dominated by the great Gnostic leaders, Valentinus and Basilides, and by Marcion. They voyage up and down the Mediterranean, writing, preaching, discussing and founding groups and communities without let or hindrance. In Rome, where at the end of the second century Athenaeus claimed with characteristic bombast 'one might see whole peoples dwelling together, Cappadocians, Scythians and men of Pontus',[40] Greek-speaking Christians of every persuasion congregated. The Neronian persecution had passed into history. The mid-second century sees Christian freedmen of the Imperial House and noble families beginning to take over in the Christian interest the burial places put at their disposal by their masters. In the catacombs of Domitilla, Lucina and Priscilla, Christian art makes its first appearance.[41] There must have been relative security. Moreover, the same intellectual and trade movements which linked Asia to the capital now linked the Christian communities together. Of the orthodox, Polycarp, Justin and probably Irenaeus made the journey, while their heretical rivals challenged them through Marcion and Valentinus, Cerdon and Marcellina. There were vivid discussions as Gnostics and orthodox battled for supremacy. In the cemetery on Vatican Hill by 165 a small niche in what may have been a boundary wall had been dedicated to the memory of St. Peter. Rome's claims to primacy were to be founded on the bones of martyr-apostles.[42]

Martyrdom and anti-martyrdom were to find their representatives in the confusion of Christian schools which relaxation of tension and material prosperity produced. However, there was no complete break with the pre-Jewish War legacy. The Jewish-Christian battle of words supplemented by an underhand battle of blows continued. The Jews, as Justin's *Dialogue with Trypho* shows, were always ready to confute the Christian heretic, and, taking full advantage of their opponents' lack of knowledge of Hebrew, were able to point to many weak links in the current Christian argument from prophecy. Meditating over the debate some twenty years later, Justin declared that the Jews could not be saved, and commented bitterly on those who cursed the

Christians in their synagogues.[43] This was the period, too, in which Marcion repudiated the Jewish Scriptures as having any relevance to Christianity, and many Christians accepted his thesis. In Palestine the total failure of the Jewish rising enabled local Christians to launch an appeal to the Jews to turn Christian in order not to become strangers in their own land. It was not very successful.[44]

Nor had Judaistic apocalyptic ceased to influence Christian communities. The Antonine period must have seen the wide circulation of the works of Hermas, of the Apocalypses of Peter and of Eldad and Modad, the latter quoted in ii Clement, as well as the eschatological ii Peter, and indeed ii Clement itself. Justin believed throughout his life that there would not only be the resurrection of flesh, but that 'Jerusalem would be rebuilt in all its splendour', and that 'Christians and the righteous of Old Israel would live with Christ for a thousand years'.[45]

Yet, Millenarism was never Justin's main theme. Indeed, if he had stopped to think, he would have found it difficult to combine with his message that Christianity was the 'true philosophy', towards which the best of mankind, both Jew and Greek, had always been tending. His confusion illustrates how apocalyptic was beginning to lose its appeal, becoming more residual, while enlightened Christian thought moved on to a more reasoned and philosophic plane. By the mid-second century the primitive theology of martyrdom-judgement-Paradise was being seriously challenged by the views of both the Gnostics and their opponents the Greek Apologists.

It has been to R. M. Grant's credit to connect the flowering of Gnosticism in the mid-second century with the shock administered to Jewish (and Jewish-Christian) apocalyptic hopes by the disastrous Second Jewish War.[46] While much of the terminology of the apocalyptic message survived in Gnostic writings and many Gnostic apocalypses existed,[47] some of the bitterness and urgency of this type of writing had been eliminated. The eschatological dualism, for instance, of traditional apocalyptic which could be applied to the current political situation was removed from visible sight to the spheres beyond the world. As for humanity, the frontiers of salvation, even if still pre-determined, were enlarged. Scope was left for inhabitants of the Gentile world to receive the saving message of Gnosticism and be delivered from an existence dominated by the Demiurge and his archons. The mass of 'Hylics', however, were lost. There was little overt sympathy with Greek thought as such. The writer of *The Treatise on the Three Natures* could state that the Greek philosophers 'did not have the possibility of knowing the cause of existing things', and were therefore in error.[48] None the less, it was the current Greek concept of God that the Gnostics taught and not that of apocalyptic Judaism. The Saviour and Illuminator, Christ, also had more in common with accepted heroic teachers of mankind such as Heracles or Osiris, or Seth in Jewish legend, than with the Jesus of the Gospels. His ministry was not a true ministry, and His Incarnation did not amount to a true unity between God and Creation. It was merely a moral and transitory union between a heavenly aeon and the personality of Jesus.[49] Jesus the man might die on the Cross, but not the Divine Logos. His Passion and Resurrection were not therefore realities, and His death could not be understood either as the Atoning Sacrifice (Hebs. 7[27]) or as the Johannine witness to the Father.

These views, which placed the Christian message on the same plane as other messages of Salvation current in the Mediterranean world, challenged the value of martyrdom in three ways. First, as Ignatius of Antioch had been quick to point out against his Docetist opponents, one did not die for a phantom.[50] Being 'in Christ' only had meaning if Christ's life and ministry had really taken place. Secondly, the Gnostic substituted the duty of guarding the Secret of Salvation for the duty of witness and confession to the truth of Christ's Lordship. There was no Gnostic doctrine of the Holy Spirit in the normal sense, for the object of existence was the soul's mystic union with the eternal Logos, not confession prompted by the Spirit.[51] Thirdly, since the End of all things was not by fiery judgment in which martyrs would be avenged, there was little point in refusing the minimum requirements of secular society. Why should not those whose salvation was assured eat meat which had been offered at sacrifices—and in any case was probably the only meat to be had? Understanding one's true nature as a step in a ladder of ascent rather than any cult or ritual, let alone public confession, was the measure of the individual's progress towards redemption.[52]

Perhaps it was no accident that Alexandria should be a major centre of this school, and Basilides who taught there and in the Delta *circa* 130–160 should mark the beginning of half a century of Gnostic domination of Egyptian Christianity.[53] He is interesting because while many aspects of his thought appear to be purely Jewish, he makes a serious effort to solve the difficulties of literal New Testament teaching by the aid of current Platonism. His is the earliest known attempt by a Christian to reconcile the Jewish requirement of righteous suffering as an atoning sacrifice with the Platonic view of Providence. The result was the first major attack on the spiritual value of martyrdom in three hundred years of Jewish and Christian history. He is also the first representative of the Platonic tradition in Christianity, and it is not perhaps to be wondered that his influence continued to be strong in Alexandria and elsewhere in the Greek-Christian world for nearly a century after his death. Clement, on whom he left his imprint, laboured to refute him,[54] so did Irenaeus[55] and Origen.[56] The latter's verdict was, as usual, shrewd and accurate. He inspired, he said, those who accepted Christ but rejected the demands of witness. His theology of suffering derived from both Scripture and Plato, was as important to Christians of his age as that of Marcion on the meaning of Redemption.

Basilides' doctrine of martyrdom arose from his doctrine of Man, and his view of human suffering. Anticipating Valentinus, he believed that man was originally immortal, and that death was the work of the Demiurge, who created the world.[57] The Gnostic, however, had dominion over creation and all corruption. He was already 'as though by his nature beyond the world' (ὡς ἄν ὑπερκόσμιον φύσει οὖσαν), divorced from the flesh and free from its infection.[58] Salvation was the abolition of death, and not its ready acceptance through martydom.

But what of the martyrs? Why did they have to suffer? Was not suffering itself an evil? How could it be reconciled with the providence of God? In what might be a commentary on 1 Peter 4[15], Basilides claimed that even those who suffered not as adulterers or murderers, but as Christians suffered on account of sin, i.e. their souls required purification. This did not mean that the sufferer had necessarily led an evil life. He might be compared to an infant who had committed no actual sin, but nonetheless

possessed the power to commit sin and therefore needed atonement.

'For', says Basilides, 'just as the man who desires to commit adultery
is an adulterer, even if he does not succeed in committing adultery,
and he who wants to do murder is a murderer, even if he is unable to
kill; so also, if I see the man without sin whom I mentioned suffering,
even if he has done nothing wrong, I should say that he is wicked
because of his desire to sin. For I will say anything rather than call
Providence evil[59] (from J. Stevenson, *A New Eusebius*, 83).

The reminiscence of Plato, *Republic*, Book ii, is unmistakable.
'If our commonwealth is to be well-ordered, we must fight to
the last against any member of it being suffered to speak of the
divine, which is good, being responsible for evil.'[60] Yet Basilides
had arrived at his conclusions only after a profound study of
Scripture. This had led to a commentary on the New Testament
extending to twenty-four books[61]—the first such commentary
after Papias' of which record survives. He was on common
ground with his Jewish and Christian predecessors when he
claimed that martyrdom was in essence an atonement for sin, sin
committed in this or a previous life[62] and that it shortened the
period of penance which the imperfect soul must undergo hereafter. But, consistent with his view of Providence, he did not see
such action as victory over the Devil, leading to the material
triumph of the saints. Rather it was an act which benefited an
individual soul struggling upwards on its way to perfection. In
the last resort, it was a means of education without eschatological content. The Gnostic, already perfect, needed no martyrdom. In this we see Basilides as the forerunner of Clement.

There is thus no question in Basilides' mind of the merit of
witness to the facts of Christ's life and death. Indeed, such an
idea would have appalled him. Gnosis was secret revelation,
handed down through a succession of teachers and prophets to
the initiate,[63] and not to be divulged until the last day. That
Basilides was representing a trend of current Gnostic thought is
clear from other sources. In the Apocalypse of the Great Seth,
found at Nag-Hammadi, believers are warned that 'these revelations are not to be disclosed to anyone in the flesh. They must only
be communicated to the brethren who belong to the generation
of life'.[64] Thus, these Gnostics rejected the whole tradition of both

Jewish and Christian martyrdom. In *circa* 160–170 Basilides' followers were being criticized for maintaining that 'there was no harm in eating things offered to idols or in light-heartedly (ἀπαραφυλάκτως) denying their faith in times of persecution'.[65] No wonder they were hated by all other Christians and condemned as cowards, 'atheists' and worse.[66] However, their ideas were contributing towards spreading the Gospel among educated Greek-speaking provincials.[67] 'The gospel of truth is joy'[68] to those who received it, claimed Valentinus, and there can be no doubt that ultimately Gnostic influences facilitated the penetration of Platonic ideas into Christian thought.[69] By the last quarter of the century these were initiating a revolution in the prevailing Christian attitude towards pagan society and pagan values.

Less immediately destructive to the martyr-idea, but ultimately guiding the Church into ways of thought which would render it superfluous except in rare crises was the teaching of the Greek Apologists. Their appearance, at the same time as the Gnostic leaders, from the end of the reign of Hadrian onwards was a further sign of the change which was taking place in Christian thought. The world was going on, despite prophecies of doom. So was pagan society, and its condition in the second-century was flourishing. Christianity must justify its existence to a sceptical public opinion. Thus the Apologists, while maintaining the place of the martyr's struggle in the forefront of the Church's relationship with the world, were also intent on arguing the reasonableness of the Christian faith, its intellectual truth and its ultimate harmony with its earthly surroundings. Created by the same Divine Logos, Jerusalem and Babylon could not be eternally opposed. Christianity was divine revelation, but it was also the true philosophy acceptable to Reason. Its adherents, the Christians, were a 'third race', the representatives of the original religious experience of mankind from which the Jews and Greeks had deviated.[70] They were not a nationality or a tribal entity like the pagan nations.[71] They were true servants of God representing a new stage in man's approach to God and combining this with a new religious and also a new social outlook. They were the Empire's allies, not its enemies.[72] Hence their claim for toleration, indeed, for a privileged status among their fellows.

The Apologists also had to prove the orthodox case against Gnosticism and Marcion. In this debate, too, their emphasis on the creative role of the Divine Logos and the ultimate harmony of the universe with its creator were of prime importance. Against the separation of God from creation, the Apologist preached that all things were made by God through the Logos. Since the Fall there had been a gradual approach stage by stage of man to God, in which the coming of the Incarnate Logos marked the final phase. Against moral dualism and the irrevocable division of mankind into the earthbound (χοικοί), psychics, and spiritual men, and the fatalism that resulted from such divisions, the Apologists claimed that God was apprehendible to all men, and that through free-will any man could become a Christian. Thence he could overcome his evil passions and achieve salvation. These ideas also led away from the ruling sectarian and Pharisaic ethic of the Christian communities towards a more liberal attitude to pagan society. If all men could be saved, the Church must become truly universal. Christians must read history as the continuous unfolding of God's will, in which Christ's birth in the reign of Augustus, and His advice regarding civic duties were relevant. We can see these lines of argument developing in the Antonine period, first with Jewish overtones, derived perhaps from Wisdom literature, and then with Justin's *First Apology* as the fervent plea of a converted Hellene to his fellow provincials for toleration, coupled with a warning against the attractive counterfeit to Christianity provided by Gnosticism. 'We do not hate you, but we wish to convert you', thus Justin (*1 Apol.*, 57.2) to the pagans. While the threat of a fiery end for the unconvinced remained in the background, the positive values of pagan philosophy could also be stressed. The progress of mankind was upward, with the Christians in the lead.

Of the first of the Apologists, Quadratus, writing in Asia in the reign of Hadrian,[73] we may record simply that he was the first who attempted to argue with the heathen instead of mentally abandoning them to the flames or worse.[74] The Apology of Aristides, written perhaps *circa* 145, marks a transition.[75] Its approach to the heathen is eirenic in form though not in content, but it is still entirely in the tradition of Jewish apologetic. Textual links may be noted with the Jewish-Christian tradition of the

Preaching of Peter, and Barnabas.[76] The writer makes the typical Judaistic assertion that the world was made for the Church (as True Israel),[77] it divides humanity into three great groups, according to religion, Greeks (who are subdivided into 'Greeks, Aegyptians and Chaldaeans'), Jews and Christians.[78] He seems to criticize the deification of dead emperors, though he is guarded in his language on this subject,[79]—far less guarded than Justin in his attack on the 'deification' of Hadrian's favourite Antinous.[80] High praise is given to the Jews on account of their monotheism and ethics. God had showed them His power through signs and wonders.[81] But the Christians had gone further along the way of truth, by recognizing Jesus Christ as Son of God Most High 'descending from heaven in the Holy Spirit for the salvation of men'.[82] They combined the good works of the Jews with correct belief about God. They thus alone possessed the whole truth, while the rest of mankind wandered in the darkness, Christianity preserved the world from destruction. On account of the Christians 'there flows the beauty that is in the world' (*Apology of Aristides*, 16).

This is the essence, too, of the plea made by the writer of the *Letter to Diognetus*. The letter uses the same critique of pagan religion derived from Hellenistic-Judaism[83] found in the *Apology of Aristides*, and its claim that the Christians were the 'soul' of the world has its echoes in both Rabbinic and Alexandrian philosophic Judaism, but there is far more effort to make the appeal palatable to Greek-speaking provincials. The truth and excellence of Christian teaching is related to the philosophical thought of the age. Thus, the writer claims, 'Broadly speaking, what the soul is in the body, that Christians are in the world'.[84] This means that the Christians had a clearly defined and constructive role to play in the world, despite the persecutions they were suffering. 'The soul loves the flesh that hates it and the limbs, so the Christians love them that hate them.'[85] It serves as a curb and restraint against the pleasures of the world. 'To so high a rank has God appointed them and it is not right for them to refuse it.'[86] The Christian faith was thus a reasonable one, devoted to the service of mankind, the true revelation of the will of the divine Logos which Christians sought to share with their fellow men.

Justin, however, writing his two Apologies, *circa* 150 and 155 respectively,[87] carries this argument a stage further.[88] His was an outlook not moulded in the first place by Judaism, but by a long study of the current philosophies, and especially Platonism, before he adopted Christianity. It is not surprising that he claimed that Christians were following the lead of Plato, the greatest of the Greek philosophers, in worshipping one God, and rejecting the demons who were masquerading as gods. Human intelligence, endowed with a particle of the Divine Logos, had the power of recognizing and worshipping God. But God could only be truly apprehended through a Person, and that Person Justin identified with Jesus Christ who had been foretold by the prophets of Israel long before the Greek philosophers had propounded their own ideas.[89] But these ideas were not necessarily hostile to Christian revelation. The whole human race partook of Reason, 'and those who live according to reason are Christians, even though they are accounted atheists. Such were Socrates and Heraclitus among the Greeks and those like them; among the barbarians Abraham, Ananiah, Azariah and Mishael, and Elijah and many others'.[90] In his more personal, *Second Apology*, he makes the point even more clearly. 'I prayed and strove with all my might to be found a Christian, not because the teachings of Plato are contrary to those of Christ, but because they are not in all respects like them, as neither are those of others, the Stoics, poets and prose-writers. For each discoursed rightly, seeing that which was akin to Christianity through a share in the seminal divine reason.'[91] Thus Christ is Reason Incarnate and Christianity is the true fulfilment of philosophy, the climax of human endeavour to apprehend God, the light that lighteth every man.

With Justin, we are no longer dealing with the eternal contradiction of Church and World. The outlook of the latter is seen as a distorted and incomplete version of Reason represented by the new race of Christians. The 'demons' were the enemy of all men of good will, pagans and Christians alike. The crude and confused ideas, borrowed now from Stoicism, now from Platonism, now from Scripture, which allowed Justin to identify the Holy Spirit of the last-named with the Logos of each, and all with the Incarnate Christ, did in fact break new ground. Though martyrdom remained in the forefront of his own mind, and he went unflinchingly to his fate, he tends like Philo on the one hand, and the Alexandrian Christians on the other, to regard the martyrs as examples, rather than as essential actors in an eschatological drama.[92] We can see Justin as an orthodox Christian example of the tendencies we have already encountered in a Jewish setting in Philo and his school, and like Philo he regarded the Roman world not as a hostile but as a positive force and one to be obeyed.[93] Indeed, he goes some way towards exonerating the emperors from blame for the persecutions. These could be laid to the door of the demons and their agents the Jews and their proselytes. He saw Church and Empire bound together by the same Providence, and he emphasized that the birth of Christ took place under Roman rule in Judaea. Even the Cross, to Justin, representing the Word 'placed X-wise in the universe',[94] found an expression in the cross-shaped *vexillum* of the Roman legion.[95] As H. Chadwick has pointed out, we are not far from the Constantinian *labarum*. This more hopeful and optimistic view of the Christian's relation with his surroundings was paralleled by his convictions regarding current philosophy.[96] His claim that some of the philosophers were 'Christians before Christ', prepared the way for the more generous assertion of Clement that 'philosophy was the schoolmaster to bring the Greek mind to Christ, as the Law brought the Hebrews',[97] and the school of Christian Platonism at Alexandria. Paradoxically, like the Gnostics whom he hated, his Christianity also implied the illumination and not the destruction of the civilization in which he lived. There was more in common between Justin and Basilides than either would have admitted. Both pointed the way forward to reconciliation between Church and State.

This, however, was to lie far in the future. All the time, even in periods of apparent peace and quiet the peace of the Church hung on a thread. By 150, educated opinion in Rome and the provinces had moved a long way from the time when Tacitus and Suetonius had to explain to their readers who the Christians were. They knew, and they did not like them. The most significant transformation had taken place among the Senatorial aristocracy who in one way or another influenced the minds and policy of the emperors. It is unfortunate that the speech made by Marcus Aurelius' tutor and confidante M. Cornelius Fronto against the Christians has not been preserved, except in a fragmentary paraphrase in ch. 9 of Minucius Felix' *Octavius*. It may, however, reflect opinion in the capital in the decade 150–160, and it gives an astonishing picture of black magic, scandal and Bacchanalianism attributed to the Christians.

> 'On the day appointed', Fronto wrote apparently, 'they gather at a banquet with all their children, sisters, and mothers, people of either sex and every age. There, after full feasting, when the blood is heated, and drink has inflamed the passions of incestuous lust, a dog which has been tied to a lamp is tempted by a morsel thrown beyond the range of his tether to bound forward with a rush. The tale-telling light is upset and extinguished, and in the shameless dark lustful embraces are indiscriminately exchanged; and all alike, if not in act, yet by complicity, are involved in incest, as anything that occurs by the act of individuals results from the common intention'
>
> (tr. G. H. Rendall).

What was believed by Fronto was readily believed by the less educated and enlightened populace in the capital. It can reasonably be claimed that one purpose of Justin's *First Apology* was to try to draw his readers' notice to the distinction between the orthodox Christians who were not scandalous, and the Gnostics who were.[98] Indeed, the readiness of Christians to accuse one another of horrific behaviour lends some credence to the almost universal pagan attacks against them at this time.[99] To these charges, critics in the capital were adding the more or less scurrilous accusations which were habitually attached to the Jews. 'Alaxamenos worships God' scrawled beneath an obscene looking figure representing a crucified donkey on the walls of the Palatine, has provided mute witness as to how some members of the Roman populace regarded the Christians.[100] And, as we know from Tertullian, the charge stuck.[101] Judaistic Bacchanals whose views both affronted the gods and broke up family life might well have represented the opinion of Justin's enemies about 'the third race' during his long stay in the capital.

There, two cases reveal the kind of circumstances in which Christians were being denounced to the authorities. Sometime between 152 and 156[102] a squalid matrimonial quarrel resulted in a certain Ptolemy who had been instrumental in converting the wife of a dissolute Roman to Christianity being denounced by the aggrieved husband as a Christian. The account, preserved by

Justin in his *Second Apology*,[103] is extremely interesting. The scene is Rome. The husband first persuaded a centurion who was a friend of his to cast Ptolemy into prison, and then 'to interrogate him on this sole point; whether he was a Christian'. Ptolemy admitted the fact, was brought before Lollius Urbicus, Prefect of the City,[104] confessed to being a Christian and was executed. A bystander named Lucius protested against the sentence, shouting that Ptolemy was not guilty of any crime such as adultery, murder, brigandage, or theft, but only 'because he is called by the name of Christian'. He found himself subjected to a summary trial on the spot. Neither accused, apparently, was given the usual chance of recantation. Denunciation ended both freedom and life. And, states Justin, this sort of thing was happening up and down the Empire under the provincial governors.

Justin was himself to be the victim of a similar grudge. He was denounced by a personal enemy, the Cynic philosopher Crescens,[105] an anti-Christian whom he had upbraided nearly ten years before in his *Second Apology* and worsted in debate.[106] Crescens did not forget. He tried once unsuccessfully and then used perhaps the despondency caused by the plague in Rome in 165 to denounce his adversary.[107] The text of the account of the trial before the Prefect of the City, the Stoic, Q. Junius Rusticus, has always been regarded as near-contemporary.[108] Rusticus himself a friend of Pliny and Consul as early as 133 was by now an old man,[109] but his influence with Marcus Aurelius was very strong, and his attitude may well reflect the views of the inner circle of the Emperor's friends.[110] Apart from its simplicity, the correct judical style of Rusticus who is always prefaced as ἔπαρχος (*praefectus*) when he speaks, are in its favour. Even casual reading should convince the critic of the verisimilitude of the account, in particular of the little biographical details of Justin's fellow accused. Let us take the following:

> The prefect Rusticus said to Hierax: 'Are you also a Christian?'
> Hierax said: 'Yes, I am a Christian, for I worship and adore the same God.'
> The prefect Rusticus said: 'Did Justin make you Christians?'
> Hierax said: 'I was, and shall ever be, a Christian.'
> A man called Paeon stood up and said: 'I also am a Christian.'
> The prefect Rusticus said: 'Who taught you?'

Paeon said: 'I received from my parents this good confession.'

Euelpistus said:[111] 'I listened indeed gladly to the words of Justin, but I too received Christianity from my parents.'

The prefect Rusticus said: 'Where are your parents?'

Euelpistus said: 'In Cappadocia.'

Rusticus said to Hierax: 'Where are your parents?'

He answered, saying: 'Our true father is Christ, and our mother our faith in Him. My earthly parents are dead, and I was dragged away from Iconium in Phrygia before coming hither.'

The prefect Rusticus said to Liberian: 'And what do you say? Are you a Christian? Are you an unbeliever like the rest?'

Liberian said: 'I also am a Christian; for I am a believer and adore the only true God'[112] (tr. J. Stevenson, op. cit., 29-30).

A forger would hardly fabricate details about Iconium and Cappadocia, though the historian welcomes these as showing the growth of a class of native Greek-speaking Christians in Phrygia and Cappadocia and the links between Asia Minor and Rome.[113]

The story is as clear as that which Justin told concerning Ptolemy. Rusticus opens proceedings with an order of the same type as Pliny to the Christians in Bithynia. 'First of all obey the gods, and make submission to the Princes.' Justin evades the direct issue, and tries to justify the Christian attitude. He uses a question by Rusticus, 'What belief do you mean?' to unfold a line of apologetic which he had used before in *1 Apology*, namely, that Christians were neither atheists nor evil-doers but the worshippers of the One True God in the best way open to mankind. 'We believe in one God, existing from the beginning, Maker and Artificer of the whole creation, seen and unseen: and concerning our Lord Jesus Christ, the Son of God, who has been proclaimed aforetime by the prophets as about to come to the race of men as herald of salvation and master of true disciples'. The quasi-credal statement fortified by argument from prophecy is reminiscent of phrases in *1 Apology*. Thus, God as 'Maker and Artificer' of creation corresponds to 'Father and Fashioner of all things' (*1 Apol.*, 8), and the argument from prophecy is stated by Justin in *1 Apol.*, 23. There can be little doubt that this is really Justin making his own final defence. The Prefect heard him out, but then after establishing that Justin had a definite meeting-place and disciples, brought the case to a head. 'To come to the point then, are you a

Christian?' Justin said, 'Yes, I am a Christian.' His disciples are each given a brief examination. At the conclusion Rusticus again turns to Justin. Did he think that he would ascend to Heaven and be rewarded? Justin did. He also believed that the world would come to a fiery end. The Prefect made a final effort to dissuade him. 'Let us now come to the pressing matter in hand. Agree together and sacrifice to the gods.' Justin refused, 'No one who thinks rightly will turn from piety to impiety.'[114] The Prefect added a last warning of the consequences of disobedience. It was in vain, and the sentence of scourging and beheading fell on them all.

These cases illustrate Roman imperial policy towards the Christians in the Antonine period. While little or no encouragement was given to those who wanted to denounce Christians, and non-Christians were protected from false accusation, Christian communities remained illegal societies. It is interesting that Rusticus put the decisive question after he had established that Justin was the leader of a group which gathered in one particular place.[115] He was therefore conducting an illegal society, and moreover, had refused to perform an act of civic duty to the emperors and the gods who protected the Roman Empire at a moment of peril in the city. One feels the force of Piny's complaint of Christian *contumacia* in the accused's final reply, 'ποίει ὃ θέλεις ἡμεῖς γὰρ χριστιανοί ἐσμεν καὶ εἰδώλοις οὐ θύομεν'. ('Do what you like. For we are Christians and we will not sacrifice to idols.')[116] As to Christian beliefs, educated officials possessing a philosophical training themselves either regarded them as so much moonshine unworthy of the calling of a philosopher, or as actively noxious. This was 'superstitio' opposed to the 'religio' of Rome.[117] Despite all Justin's efforts, there was as yet little sign of a common language between Christians and Greco-Roman society. What was εὐσέβεια to the pagan was ἀσέβεια to the Christian and vice versa.

Rome was the only city in the West where Christians were numerous and well organized enough by 150 to attract notice. As in the previous generation, it was in the Greek-speaking provinces, especially Asia, that tension between the Christians and their neighbours simmered. There, it is impossible to ignore the general statement by the writer of the *Letter to Diognetus* that

'Christians were condemned and persecuted by all men',[118] explicitly confirmed by Justin, who tells us that he himself was finally converted from Platonism to Christianity by the sight of the steadfastness of martyrs.[119] This was in Hadrian's reign and could not have been long after the latter's rescript to Fundanus. Moreover, Justin's broad assertion in the *Dialogue with Trypho*, 'For though we are beheaded and crucified and exposed to all forms of torture, it is plain that we do not forsake the confession of our faith', must be based on more than hearsay.[120] From Athens also, Eusebius has preserved the record of one pogrom in this period which cost Publius, the Christian bishop, his life, and for many years almost eliminated his community.[121] Finally, from Dionysius of Corinth's correspondence, we learn of Christians being sent to work in the mines, and of the Roman Christians sending contributions to them.[122]

The apparent contradiction between the general picture of Christian prosperity and expansion which Eusebius gives, and some clear indications to the contrary especially after 150 is not difficult to understand. In the East as in the Celtic West the Antonine age marked the climax in the growth of a genuine loyalty to the Empire and the person of the emperor. 'Roman' was truly a name 'not of a city, but of a whole race'.[123] The speeches of Aristides of Smyrna simply echoed what countless humbler provincials themselves believed. There is striking evidence for that in the decree of the grateful citizens of Ephesus in honour of Antoninus Pius on his accession, the 'saviour of the whole human race'.[124] In such an environment the Christian sect displayed not merely an indifference to the efforts of fellow provincials to make life easier and more attractive, but nearly all the characteristic faults of the local Jews, accompanied by claims to immunities and privileges to which not even they had ever aspired. Even those who were prepared to disbelieve the popular charges against the Christians regarded their arrogant assertion of a unique God whose ear they possessed, and their demand for special recognition as His true servants as both sacrilegious and insane.[125]

Our sources both pagan and Christian show the Christian community of the Antonine period little changed in outlook from that of the early part of the century. Celsus' 'frogs squatting around a marsh'[126] discussing who was the most sinful among them, suggests small, introspective, sectarian communities. They gloried in the fact that they were 'sojourners' in the present world[127] and awaiting its speedy end, contracted out of civic obligations to it. It was not merely suspicions of black magic and horrid rites nourished by the pre-dawn hour of the Eucharist that enraged their fellow-provincials, but their refusal to take part in the ordinary daily life of the city even in its simplest details. Unlike the Jews, the Christians were not prepared to offer any tangible substitute as a token of loyalty to the Empire for the oath to the Emperor's genius which they refused. The Jewish 'καινῇ καὶ φιλοθέῳ πολιτείᾳ'[128] which the convert was invited to enter had tradition and generations of toleration behind it. Christianity had neither. Its 'newness' was regarded as proof of subversive intent. In the circumstances, it was difficult for Christians to convince an hostile audience that the Empire to which they looked forward was not an earthly one.[129]

Even so, the Christians possessed strong means of attracting their fellows, especially the underprivileged members of Classical society. Their claim to overthrow demons, or in other words free men from the overwhelming power of Fate was one factor.[130] Their steadfastness, in face of torture and shameful deaths and their high moral ethic were others that made them formidable.[131] Even at this stage Churches had their roll of honour of martyrs whose 'birthdays' (natalicia) were celebrated each year.[132] The niche in the Red Wall under St. Peter's with its fragmentary πετF . . . . . may be the earliest material evidence for the cult. In addition, they inherited from Judaism a sense of social obligation which even if it was confined mainly to benefiting their own members, impressed outsiders with their cohesion and inner strength. 'See how they love one another',[133] could be echoed from one end of the Mediterranean to the other. The Roman see in particular sent alms and money to other Churches, to the needy and to confessors condemned to the mines.[134] The egalitarianism of the primitive community seems generally to have been maintained. Slaves, widows and paupers were fed out of the savings of the faithful, and solidarity was often carried to fantastic lengths.[135]

The Christians were strong precisely where contemporary

paganism was weak. In contrast to the resignation and fatalism[136] of so many pagan intellects, theirs was both a liberating and a fighting creed, good news worth dying for.[137] Moreover, though the code of behaviour expected of the individual pagan was honourable and chaste,[138] there was also gross impurity unrestrained by effective moral censorship. The innumerable grave-memorials testifying to the decency and affection of family life must be contrasted with such objects as the *erotica* of the first two centuries found on lamps at Vindonissa and elsewhere,[139] or some of the wall paintings and table-mountings from Pompeii. When Justin wrote of Christianity reforming men's moral characters and 'changing their tyrannical dispositions', including his own, he was probably speaking from experience,[140] and his words are corroborated by Origen in the next century.[141] With tenderness towards the young there was also heartlessness, so well illustrated in the classic letter written by the Egyptian labourer Hilarion to his wife Alis telling her to expose the child she was expecting if it was a girl.[142] The Christians, like the Jews, protested against such cruelties and immoralities in pagan society,[143] and it is not surprising that those most affected by them, sensitive and educated women, should have joined their ranks so eagerly.

It was probably the gradual increase in the numbers of Christians as much as any other single cause that broke the general calm which the Christians had been enjoying. The people of Pontus, for instance, did not take kindly to the fact that their province was 'filled with atheists and Christians'.[144] It is interesting how many of the denunciations of Christians in the period 150–200 were made because one member of a family was converted and thus threatened the cohesion of family life.[145] Nor were the Christians over-scrupulous about the methods they employed to attract people to their faith. 'It was by fear rather than by love of beauty', it was claimed, that they persuaded.[146] And, they preached and debated incessantly.[147] In Asia, the pagans and Jews were threatened by the same enemy, and for the first time for many generations united against him.

This strange alliance dates from after the defeat of 135. It was one of the means by which Israel saved itself from destruction, but at the cost of forfeiting for ever its claim to the universal allegiance of mankind. From now on, the domestic struggle between the Old Israel and the New becomes merged in the general conflict between Church and Empire. In the persecutions which were to wrack Asia in the reign of Marcus Aurelius the Jew was often in the background. For nearly another century he continued to stir up trouble wherever he could.[148] The threat from this combined attack was obvious to the sufferers. 'The Christians', wrote the author of the *Letter to Diognetus* 'are warred upon by the Jews as foreigners (ὡς ἀλλόφυλοι) and persecuted by the Greeks: and those who hate them cannot state the cause of their enmity'.[149] To Justin, 'the Jews regard us with personal enmity (ἐχθρούς) and active hostility (πολεμίους) slaying and injuring us, just as you Gentiles do'.[150] The double-headed attack is confirmed by a third source, namely the *Codex Bezae* version of Acts, probably compiled in Asia *circa* 150–160.[151] In Acts 14⁵, the editor has emphasized collaboration between the two enemies of Christianity by inserting a record of 'a second persecution by Jews and Gentiles against the Apostles' at Lystra. Clearly, such scenes were becoming familiar at this time. It is interesting that in this same edition of Acts, the Roman officials are still given credit for friendly acts towards the Apostles and the greater responsibility both for Jesus' death and the harrying of His followers placed on the Jews.[152]

As the decade 150–160 wore on, Christians gradually concentrated on themselves the hatred of the Greek-speaking world previously reserved for the Jews. The crowd believed the anti-Christian rumours about cannibalism, incest and vice, but more than these was needed to focus the fury of the entire population, aristocrat and pauper alike, together with the authorities, on one sect. After all, no one was to arrest Carpocrates and his followers despite their avowed antinomianism, nor for that matter, the travelling troupes of debauchees, worshippers of the Great Mother, described by Apuleius.[153] The key to the deepening wave of hatred was the accusation of 'atheism',[154]—the old battle cry of Greek provincial against the Jew, and now turned against the Christians. The Christian's failure to give formal acknowledgment of the gods of the community in which he lived, was coupled with anxiety that his presence there could be a source of danger. Age-long fears were aroused in an era when superstition was never far from the surface. And if the worst happened and the gods deserted the Greek cities, their vaunted prosperity would vanish overnight in the smoke of earthquake and the clamour of social revolution.

We have already seen that even if 'sacrilege' or 'atheism' were not specifically mentioned by Pliny in 112, they were certainly in his mind and in the minds of those who denounced the Christians, for otherwise the sacrifice-test he imposed would have had no meaning.[155] In 150[156] and 155[157] Justin refers specifically to Christians being denounced as atheists. It was the cry taken up by Jews and pagans in Asia.[158] Polycarp was 'the teacher of Asia, the destroyer of our gods'.[159] The same charge was echoed in the 'forged decree' of Antoninus Pius. It is repeated in Apologists as different in their outlook towards Greco-Roman civilization as Athenagoras[160] and Tatian.[161] In Alexandria as late as 200 it was still the charge against Christians[162] and Clement turns to its refutation time and again in the books of the *Stromata*. In Carthage 'failure to worship the ancestral gods' marked down the Christians 'above all else' as law-breakers.[163] How fierce could be the prejudice against those suspected of not honouring the gods may be shown in the celebrated Alexander of Abonouteichos' proclamation at the beginning of his sacred mysteries *circa* 165: 'If any godless person either Christian or Epicurean has come to spy on the mysteries, let him depart; let those who believe the god be initiated propitiously'.[164] Alexander was a quack, but his hold on the population of Bithynia in the decade 160–170 was immense. The charge against the Christians stuck.

Atheism and black magic, these provided the fuel to the sporadic outbursts of anti-Christian feeling which broke the peace of the Antonine era. The Christian name could never achieve toleration without total victory. Always underlying periods of relative calm glowed fires of fear and hatred. It needed only a petty incident to set the crowd at Smyrna roaring 'Kill the atheists. Let Polycarp be fetched'.[165]

NOTES

[1] See, Sulpicius Severus, *Chron.*, ii.32: 'Post Adrianum Antonino Pio imperante pax ecclesiis fuit'. Also, Tertullian, *Apol.*, 5, 6–7.

[2] Aristides of Smyrna, *Panegyric on Rome, Orat.*, xxvi. 70 (ed. B. Keil, Berlin, 1898, ii. 111).

[3] Aristides, *Oratio*, xiv. 391 (ed. Jebb, i, p. 223), and ibid. 394 (Jebb. i.225). Note the astounding career of Opramoas, a local worthy of Rhodiapolis in Lycia during the reigns of Hadrian and Pius, celebrated on 55 inscriptions, published by R. Hebeday, *Opramoas, Inschriften vom Heroon zu Rhodiapolis*, Vienna, 1897. See also the still valuable sketch of the period in S. Dill, *Roman Society from Nero to Marcus Aurelius*, Macmillan, 1905, 196ff., and M. Rostovtzeff. *Social and Economic History* (2nd ed., 1957), especially ch. viii, also, Mason Hammond, *The Antonine Monarchy* (Papers and Monographs of the American Academy in Rome, xix, 1959), chs. vi and xiii.

[4] For Marcus Aurelius' character sketch of his father, *Meditations* 1.14, and in general A. S. L. Farquharson, *Marcus Aurelius, His Life and World* (ed. Rees), Oxford, 1952, 79–80.

[5] *SHA.* (ed. Hohl), Julius Capitolinus, *Antoninus Pius*, xi.5.

[6] *Meditations*, 1.13.; cf. W. Hüttl, *Antoninus Pius*, Prague, 1936, 164ff.

[7] Capitolinus, op. cit., 7.2.

[8] *Digest*, xlviii.8.11.1 (Modestinus), and Paulus, *Sententiae* v.22.3–4. See E. M. Smalwood, art. cit. *Latomus*, 1959, 340ff., for discussion of the dating of these measures.

[9] Origen, *Contra Celsum*, ii.13.

[10] *1 Apol.*, 44.

[11] The anti-Roman character of the oracle is obvious from the text recorded in Lactantius, *Div. Inst.*, vii.15.11 (Brandt, p. 632), 'Romanum nomen quo nunc regitur orbis—horret animus dicere, sed dicam, quia futurum est—tolletur e terra et imperium in Asiam revertetur ac rursus oriens dominabitur et occidens serviat'. See H. Leclercq's interesting study of Jewish and Christian use of the Sibyls at this period, art. 'Oracle', *DACL.*, xii.2. at 2225–6. For Christian use of these and other apocryphal words, as 'the writings of Zoroaster', at this period, Clement, *Stromata*, 1.69, and Celsus (ap. Origen, *Contra Celsum*, v.61 and vii.53). For Gnostic use, Porphyry, *Vita Plotini*, 16, and J. Doresse, 'Les Apocalypses de Zoroastre, Zostrien, et de Nicothée', *Coptic Studies presented to W. E. Crum*, 1950, 255ff.

[12] At the turn of the third century, Roman Christians were still using similar threats, Minucius Felix, *Octavius*, 11.

[13] *1 Apol.*, 56.

[14] Origen, *Contra Celsum*, 1.1

[15] Eusebius, *H.E.*, iv.26.10.

[16] The victims of the various outbreaks against the Christians recorded in the *Letter to Diognetus*, 5.11 may date to this period, while Eusebius, *Chron.*, places the martyrdom of Telesphorus (above, Ch. viii, n. 126) to the first year of Pius' reign.

[17] Most authorities dismiss the 'rescript' as a forgery and worthless as evidence (cf. J. B. Lightfoot, *Ignatius*, i, pp. 485ff., P. Winter, *On the Trial of Jesus*, 60, 'a blatant falsification', and the severe summing up of the position by Lawlor and Oulton, *Eusebius*, ii.128–9), but W. M. Ramsay, 'The Date of St. Polycarp's Martyrdom', *J.Ö.A.I.*, 27, 1932, 249ff. suggests historical grounds for thinking there may have been such an exchange between the Emperor and the *Koinon* of Asia, and for a detailed examination of the text leading to the same conclusion, A. Harnack, *T.U.*, xiii.4, 1895, (Summary, pp. 63–4)

[18] Tertullian, *Apol.*, 5.6. The words 'adjecta etiam accusatoribus damnatione, et quidem tetriore' indicate that the final sentence of the 'rescript' which would have made denunciation of Christians practically impossible was known to Tertullian.

[19] Eusebius, *H.E.*, iv.13.8. Unfortunately, the extract from Melito which Eusebius quotes refers only to Hadrian's rescript to Minucius Fundanus. Ibid. iv. 26.5–11.

[20] This is repeated in the course of the third document in the collection contained in the Paris MS., an alleged letter of Marcus Aurelius to the Senate testifying to the aid given by the Christians in his army in securing him victory over the Sarmatians (the story of the 'Thundering Legion'). It is an obvious forgery, since it makes the Emperor order that accusers of Christians should be burnt alive! At the same time this collection of apologetic material must be pre-Constantine to find its way into Eusebius' *History*. The most detailed examination of this text is still that of Harnack, 'Das Regenwunder im Feldzug M. Aurels', *SBAW.*, 1895, 835–82. For the identity of the Egyptian seer whose prayers were claimed to have saved the legion, see J. Cerny, *Ancient Egyptian Religion*, London, 1951, 141.

[21] See, for instance, Eusebius, *H.E.*, v.18.9.

[22] For instance, at Smyrna, in 250, Polemon the *neocoros* explains why it was not possible to punish the confessor Pionius on the spot. "Ἀλλ' αἱ ῥάβδοι ἡμᾶς οὐ προάγουσιν ἵνα 'ἐξουσίαν ἔχωμεν'. (*Mart. Pionii.*, 10.4). Only the Proconsul could inflict the death penalty on Pionius and his companions.

[23] Capitolinus, *Antoninus Pius*, 9.1.; Aristides, *Oratio de sacris sermonibus*, ii (Jebb, 1.317) Hierapolis and Laodicea, where there were Christian communities, had suffered severely, and the town of Dionysopolis had subsequently to be re-founded. W. M. Ramsay, art. cit., 252.

[24] Surely this touch would be too much to expect from a fabricator of the complete document?

[25] Cyprian, *Letter*, 75.10. (Hartel, p. 817).

[26] Origen, *Contra Celsum*, viii.45.

[27] See Justin, *1 Apol.*, 68, and Athenagoras, *Legatio*, 2.

[28] Origen, *Contra Celsum*, iv.52. See A. L. Williams, *Adversus Judaeos*, 28–30, and A. Harnack, *T.U.*, iii, 1883.

[29] Justin, *1 Apol.*, 29—a curious demand in view of legislation directed expressly against the custom. However, in both East and West there is evidence for Christians castrating themselves on religious grounds, Athenagoras, *Legatio*, 33 and 34, Tertullian, *De Res. Carnis*, 61.6, and *De Virg. Vel.*, 10.1, the Gnostic *Acta Joannis*, 53, the third century anon. *De Singularitate Clericorum*, 33, and Eusebius, *H.E.*, vi.8.1. (re Origen). Pagan practice at this time, Lucian, *De Syria Dea*, 15, 20, 22, 25 and 27.

[30] Eusebius, *H.E.*, iv.15.26 re Polycarp. For Jewish 'pater synagogi' *CIJ.*, i, 536 (Stobi) and ibid., 537 (Porto). In general, Juster, *Les Juifs*, 1.448.

[31] Eusebius, *H.E.*, iv.15.20.

[32] Ibid. 15.11 and implied also in 15.30.

[33] Ibid., v.20.4–5 (Florinus).

[34] Justin, *Dial.*, 122.4.

[35] Ibid., 1–7.

[36] Ibid., 50.1.

[37] Justin, *Dial.*, 16.4.

[38] Eusebius, *H.E.*, iv.2.6.

[39] Ibid., 7.2.

[40] Athenaeus, *Deipnosophistae* (ed. Kaibel, 1888) 1.36.

[41] P. Styger, *Römische Katakomben*, 80 (Domitilla), 143–6 (Lucina and Priscilla). The first Christian inscription in Rome, that of L. Paccius Euticus, a freedman, commemorating his friend or relative Glycon, on the Muro Rosso in the Vatican cemetery, probably dates to *circa* 160, see M. Guarducci 'Un inscrizione Greca della Necropoli Vaticana'. *Atti dell' terzio internaz. Congresso di Epigrafia Greca e Romana*, Rome, 1959, 25–8.

[42] J. Toynbee and J. Ward Perkins, *The Shrine of St. Peter's*, Longmans, 1956, 159,

H. Chadwick, 'St. Peter and St. Paul in Rome', *JTS.*, N.S. viii.1, 1957, 31. and M. Guarducci, *The Tomb of St. Peter* (Eng. tr., 1959), 81ff and 132–3.

43 Justin, *Dialogue*, 47.4.

44 'The Rest of the Works of Baruch' (ed. Rendel Harris), Cambridge, 1889, 13.

45 *Dial.*, 31 and 80.5: cf. ii Clement 16.3 (cited above, ch. vii, note 172).

46 R. M. Grant, *Gnosticism and Early Christianity*, Oxford and New York, 1959, 29ff.

47 For instance, the Apocalypse of James, of Peter, and of Seth, all found at Nag-Hammadi.

48 See, F. L. Cross, *The Jung Codex*, London, 1955, 59–60.

49 See the excellent brief accounts of Gnosticism in H. Lietzmann, *Geschichte*, 1, ch. 15, and L. Duchesne, *The Early History of the Church*, i.127ff.

50 Ignatius *Smyrn.* 6. Also, Agrippa Castor, cited by Eusebius, *H.E.*, iv. 7.7, concerning Basilides and his followers.

51 Note A. Ehrhardt's remark, 'The Egyptian Gnostic's concentration on the Risen Logos, on the other hand, made a separate doctrine of the Holy Spirit appear rather superfluous', *HTR.*, 55, 1962, 100.

52 See, for a detailed study of Gnostic texts relating to martyrdom, A. Orbe, 'Los primeros herejes ante la persecucion', (Estudios Valentinianos, v) *Analecta Gregoriana*, 83, 1956, especially 26–33 and 87–101, H. von Campenhausen, *Die Idee des Martyriums*, 93ff. and 109–12 and the author's 'The Gnostic Sects and the Roman Empire', *J.E.H.*, v.1, 1954, 25–37.

53 Eusebius, *Chron.*, Olymp, 228 = A.D. 132 (ed. Helm, p. 201). See also W. Bauer, *Rechtgläubigkeit und Ketzerei im ältesten Christentum*, Tübingen, 1934, 49ff. For the possible link between Alexandrian Gnosticism and Philo, R. McL. Wilson, *The Gnostic Problem*, ch. ii.

54 *Stromata* (ed. Stählin-Früchtel) iv.12.84–88. Clement hated Basilides' concept of the independent existence of Evil, which he denounced as that of an atheist (iv.12.85).

55 Irenaeus, *Adv. Haer.*, 1.24.6; cf. S. Pétrement, *Le Dualisme chez Platon*, Paris, 1947, 192.

56 Origen, *Tract. 38 in Matth.* (ed. Klostermann, 73), 'Basilidis quoque sermones detrahentes iis, qui usque ad mortem certant pro veritate ut confiteantur "coram hominibus" Jesum'.

57 Clement, *Stromata*, iv.89.1–3. 'ἀπ' ἀρχῆς ἀθάνατοί ἐστε καὶ τέκνα ζωῆς ἐστε αἰωνίας . . .

58 Ibid., iv.26.165.3 (Stählin-Früchtel, 321).

59 Clement, *Stromata*, iv.82.2 (Stählin-Früchtel, 284).

60 *Republic* (ed. Cornford, ii.9.379).

61 Eusebius, *H.E.*, iv.7.7.

62 Clement, *Stromata*, iv.83.2.

63 Agrippa Castor, ap. Eusebius, *H.E.*, iv.7.7; cf. Frend, 'Gnostic Sects and the Roman Empire', 31.

64 Cited from H. C. Puech, 'Les nouveaux écrits gnostiques découverts en Haut-Egypte', *Coptic Studies in Honour of Walter Ewing Crum*, Byzantine Institute, Boston, 1950, 108. Cf. also, Irenaeus, *Adv. Haer.*, 1.19.6.

65 Agrippa Castor, loc. cit., and Origen, *Tract. 38 in Matth.* (Klostermann, 73).

66 Clement, *Stromata*, iii.13.92 and iv.16.3. δειλίας σοφίσματα. From Carthage, Tertullian, much more strongly, *Scorpiace*, 7 and Irenaeus, iv.33.9; cf. Eusebius, loc. cit.

67 As accepted by Origen, *Contra Celsum*, iii.12.

68 *The Gospel of Truth* (ed. and tr. R. M. Grant, *Gnosticism, an anthology*, 146).

69 As stated explicitly by Clement in his discussion of the views of Julius Cassianus, whom he regards as the 'founder of Docetism', and whom he criticizes for thinking too much like Plato, even though Cassian was quoting what would now appear to be the Judaeo-Christian *Gospel according to the Egyptians* and/or the *Gospel of Thomas* in support of

encratite teaching, *Stromata*, iii.13.93. Cassian seems to have been a younger contemporary of Valentinus. Discussion and bibliography, N. Walter, 'Der angebliche Chronograph Julius Cassianus', *T.U.*, 77, 1961, 177–92.

[70] See the important passage on this theme in Harnack's *Mission*, 180. Gives abundant references.

[71] Note the apologetic edge to this argument against the current view of the coincidence of religion and nation, see *Contra Celsum*, v.41.

[72] Justin, *1 Apol.*, 12.

[73] Eusebius, *H.E.*, iv.3.1. A second Apology, that of Ariston and Apelles may also have been written *circa* 134, and addressed to Hadrian. Nothing is known of its contents. *Chronicon Paschale*, Olympiad 228 (= A.D. 134) (*P.G.*, 92, 620A).

[74] For the grotesque and horrible fate to which Christian imagination consigned the heathen at this period, Apoc. of Peter, 21ff. (James, *Apoc. N.T.*, 508–10).

[75] Dating, Harnack, *Chronologie*, 1.271ff., For the earlier, Hadrianic, date based on Eusebius, *Chron.*, see D.M. Kay, *Ante-Nicene Fathers*, ix (additional volume), 261.

[76] See, Rendel Harris and J. A. Robinson, *Cambridge Texts and Studies*, 1.1, 1891, 86ff. Also, E. Hennecke, 'Die Apologie des Aristides', *T.U.*, iv.3 1893, and Eng. tr. of both the Greek and Syriac texts by D. M. Kay in vol. ix (additional vol.) of the *Ante-Nicene Christian Library*, pp. 263–79.

[77] *Apology of Aristides*, 1.

[78] Ibid., 2.

[79] Ibid., 7. 'Whatsoever creates must be greater than whatever is created': a cryptic enough phrase, but Setton (*The Christian Attitude towards the Emperor*, 34–5) points out that Athanasius was to use much the same language in an attack on emperor-worship.

[80] Justin, *1 Apol* 29.

[81] Aristides, 14.

[82] Ibid., 15.

[83] *Letter*, 2.

[84] *Letter*, 6.1: cf. Harnack, *Mission*, 193. Note for a parallel Jewish argument, Rabbi Simeon, *circa* A.D. 70, 'On three things the age stands, on the Torah, on the Temple services and on acts of piety' (*Pirke Aboth*, 1.2).

[85] *Letter*, 6.6: cf. Justin, *2 Apol.* 7.

[86] *Letter*, 6.10.

[87] Dating. A. Ehrhardt, 'Justin Martyr's Two Apologies', *J.E.H.*, iv.1, 1953, 1–12.

[88] See H. Chadwick, 'Justin Martyr on Church and State' (Fourth International Conference on Patristic Studies), *T.U.*, to be published.

[89] Justin, *1 Apol.*, 23.

[90] Ibid., 46.

[91] *2 Apol.*, 13.

[92] Note how he uses the martyrs as examples of those in whom the Word dwelt and who throughout history had incurred the hatred of their contemporaries (*2 Apol.* 8 and 10). Yet, no one died for Socrates' views!

[93] Justin, *1 Apol.*, 17—an interesting early use of Mt. 22$^{20-21}$ as a proof of Christian loyalism.

[94] *1 Apol.*, 60.

[95] *1 Apol.*, 55.

[96] H. Chadwick, loc. cit.

[97] Clement, *Stromata*, 1.5.28.

[98] *1 Apol.*, 26.

[99] For instance, *Contra Celsum*, v.63–4, and the interesting attack by Tertullian as a Montanist on the Catholic Christians in Carthage, *circa* 210, 'Apud te agape in caccabis fervet, fides in culinis calet, spes in ferculis iacet. Sed maioris est agape quia per hanc

adulescentes tui cum sororibus dormiunt . . .' (*De Jejunio adv. Psychicos*, 17, *CSEL.*, xx, 296). Also, 'atheism'—Ignatius, *Trall.*, 10.

[100] See H. Leclercq's art. 'Ane', *DACL.*, i, ii, 2043–4, and J. Préaux, 'Deus Christianorum Oenoeketes', *Coll. Latomus*, 44, 1960, 639–54.

[101] Particularly in Carthage at the turn of the third century. See Tertullian, *Ad Nationes*, 1.14 and perhaps Apuleius, *Metam.*, ix.14. An interesting point is that Gnostic angelology includes an archon with the head of an ass. 'Some say that Sabaoth has the shape of an ass others of a pig' (Epiphanius, *Panarion*, xxvi.10.6). For the second-century tradition—*Contra Celsum* vi.30, 'The seventh (angel) has the face of an ass and he is called Thaphaboath or Onoel'. For the more usual, erotic sense of Onon in this period, J. Préaux, art. cit.

[102] *Dating*: A. A. T. Ehrhardt, 'Justin Martyr's Two Apologies', *J.E.H.*, iv.1953, 1ff.

[103] *2 Apol.*, 2.

[104] A large part of the duties of the *Praefectus urbis* would be judicial. Ulpian points out that he was the judge in all criminal cases where the crime had been committed within 100 miles of Rome. 'Omnia omnino crimina praefectura urbis sibi vindicavit, nec tantum ea, quae intra urben admittuntur, verum ea quoque, quae extra urbem intra Italiam.' *Digest*, 1.12.1 preface, referring to the period of Septimius Severus.

[105] Tatian, *Oratio Ad Graecos*, 19.

[106] Eusebius, *H.E.*, iv.16.1. Justin, *2 Apol.*, 3 and 11; cf. P. de Labriolle, *La Réaction païenne* (Paris, 1950 ed.), 62–3.

[107] Suggested by R. M. Grant, *The Sword and the Cross*, 82.

[108] H. I. Delehaye, *Les Passions des Martyrs*, 119–21.

[109] He was *Praefectus urbi*, 163–7. Career, art. Iunius Rusticus, *P.W.* x.1, 1083.

[110] See, A. S. L. Farquharson, *Marcus Aurelius*, 61.

[111] Euelpistus is described as a δοῦλος καίσαρος, a lower grade civil servant who seem to have been recruited largely from among immigrants from Asia Minor.

[112] Ed. Knopf-Krüger, *Ausgewählte Märtyrerakten* (1929), 15–17 (Eng. tr. J. Stevenson, *A New Eusebius*, 29–30). cf. F. C. Burkitt, 'The Oldest Manuscript of Justin's martyrdom', *JTS.*, xi. 1910, 61–6.

[113] The opening paragraph, however, reading: 'In the time of the wicked defenders of idolatry impious decrees were issued in town and country against the pious Christian folk to compel them to offer libations to vain idols. So the saints were seized and brought before the prefect of Rome, by name Rusticus', must obviously be attributed to a later, perhaps post-Constantinian, editor. We know nothing of 'impious decrees' being issued 'in town and country' at this stage.

[114] *Acta Justini*, v.4. Ὁυδεὶς εὖ φρονῶν ἀπὸ εὐσεβείας εἰς ἀσέβειαν μεταπίπτει'.

[115] Ibid., iii.3. This fact would reinforce the prefect's responsibility for judging the case. See *Digest*, 1.12.1.14, 'Divus Severus rescripsit eos etiam, qui illicitum collegium coisse dicuntur, apud praefectum urbi accusandos'.

[116] Ibid., v.7.

[117] Brought out very clearly 50 years later in Caecilius' concluding remarks as reported by Minucius Felix (*Octavius*, 13.5) 'ne aut anilis inducatur superstitio aut omnis religio destruatur'. Cf. Pfaff, art. 'Superstitio', *PW.*, ii.7 (1931), 937–9.

[118] *Letter to Diognetus*, 5.11; cf. Justin, *1 Apol.*, 1 and 4.

[119] *2 Apol.*, 12.

[120] *Dial.*, 110.4.

[121] *H.E.*, iv.23.2.

[122] Ibid., iv.23.

[123] Aristides, *Panegyric*, 63 (Keil, ii.109), cf. *Orat.* xiv.391–4 (Jebb).

[124] Th. Mommsen, 'Der Volksbeschluss der Ephesier zu Ehren des Kaisers Antoninus Pius', *J.Ö.A.I.*, iii, 1900, 1ff. (lines 20–1). See also, similar sentiments expressed on a series

of magnificent inscriptions by the people of the small town of Rhodiapolis in Lycia, R. Heberdey, *Opramoas* (above, note 3).

[125] For instance, Apuleius, *Metam.*, ix.14, 'mentita sacrilega praesumptione dei, quem praedicaret unicum' about a woman who appears to have been a Christian *circa* 165.

[126] *Contra Celsum*, iv.23.

[127] See *Letter to Diognetus*, 5.5.

[128] Philo, *De Spec. Legibus* (ed. Colson) 1.ix.51.

[129] Justin, *1 Apol.*, 11; cf. Theophilus of Antioch, *Ad Autolycum*, 1.11, P.G., 6, 1041A.

[130] Justin, *1 Apol.*, 57. See H. B. Workman, *Persecution*, 125ff.

[131] See Tertullian, ibid., 50.14 and Minucius Felix, *Octavius*, 37.

[132] Eusebius, *H.E.*, iv.15.45 (Smyrna) and cf. ibid. 41, the fear of the local Jews that Polycarp would be 'worshipped' after his death. H. I. Delehaye, *Sanctus*, 125, cites the later *Mart. Polycarpi*, 18 to attest the existence of the cult. For Rome, M. Guarducci, *The Tomb of St. Peter* (Eng. tr.), 87ff and 132–3.

[133] Tertullian, *Apol.*, 39.7.

[134] Dionysius of Corinth (*circa* 170); cf. Eusebius, *H.E.*, iv.23.10.

[135] *Apol. of Aristides*, 13; cf. Justin, *1 Apol.*, 14 and 37. For Jewish parallels, Secrets of Enoch, 51.1 and ii Sibyllines, 75.

[136] The *taedium vitae* expressed on many funerary inscriptions of the time, and in the spirit of resignation permeating Marcus Aurelius. *Meditations*. Note Justin's reference to this spiritual malaise in *1 Apol.*, 57.

[137] See particularly for this period, Justin, *Dial.*, 110.4 and *2 Apol.*, 11–12.

[138] For instance, those inscriptions discussed by G. Charles-Picard from North Africa of this period, '*La Civilisation de l'Afrique romaine*', Paris, 1959, p. 278, from the pagan cemetery under the Vatican. J. M. C. Toynbee and J. Ward-Perkins, op. cit., 36ff., and from Asia in A. Deissmann, *Light from the Ancient East*, 318ff.

[139] S. Loeschke, *Lampen aus Vindonissa*, Zurich, 1919, Tafel viii.

[140] *1 Apol.*, 16; cf. ibid., 14, and *Dial.* 110.2–3.

[141] *Contra Celsum*, 1.9.

[142] Dated 1 B.C., and written from Alexandria. Cited from A. Deissmann, op. cit., 154–7.

[143] *Letter to Diognetus*, 6; cf. Justin, *1 Apol.*, 27.

[144] Lucian, *Alexander*, 25, 'ἀθέων ἐμπεπλῆσθαι καὶ χριστιανῶν τὸν Πόντον'. See H. D. Betz, 'Lukian von Samosata und das Neue Testament', *T.U.*, 76, 1961, 7–8,—a very thorough study.

[145] Justin, *2 Apol.*, 2.4, *Passio Perpetuae*, 3, Tertullian, *Ad Scapulam*, 3.5. In *Acta SS. Agape, Chioniae et Irene* (Knopf and Krüger, 95–100) the women are related to have regarded their husbands as their worst enemies. In general, Tertullian, *Apol.*, 3.4 and *Ad Uxorem*, ii.4 (cf. over, Ch. XI, note 244).

[146] Justin, *2 Apol.*, 9, also, Origen, *Contra Celsum*, iii.50, 52 and 55, and Minucius Felix, *Octavius*, 11.

[147] Origen, *Contra Celsum*, iii.50.

[148] Tertullian, *Scorpiace* 10 (Carthage). Origen, *Contra Celsum*, vi.27, (Alexandria and Caesarea). Jewish contempt for Christianity (*Acta Pionii*, 4.8, Smyrna, 250).

[149] *Letter to Diog.*, 6.

[150] Justin, *1 Apol.*, 31. (P.G., 6.376B).

[151] Though perhaps in Lyons, a suggestion which I owe to Mr. H. R. Creswick, Librarian of the University Library, Cambridge.

[152] Discussed by W. M. Ramsay, *St. Paul the Traveller*, 113–14. In general, see the note in *HTR.*, 54.4, 1961, 299 on E. J. Epp's Dissertation, 'Theological Tendency in the Textual Variants of Codex Bezae Cantabrigiensis', and Epp's art. in *HTR.*, 55.1, Jan. 1962, 51ff. for further references.

153 Apuleius, *Metam.*, viii.24.

154 See G. E. M. de Ste Croix, art. cit., *Past and Present*, 25ff., and my own observations in *J.E.H.*, ix, 1958, 141–58.

155 As Mommsen, *Religionsfrevel*, p. 395, points out, the Bithynian Christians were executed because they refused to sacrifice; cf. A. Harnack, 'Der Vorwurf des Atheismus in den drei ersten Jahrhunderten' (*T.U.*, N. Folge, 13.4, 1905).

156 *1 Apol.*, 6.

157 *2 Apol.*, 3. Crescens' charge that the Christians were 'atheists and impious'.

158 Justin, *Dialogue*, 17.1.

159 Eusebius, *H.E.*, iv.15.26; cf. W. H. C. Frend, *Persecutions, Links between Judaism and the Early Church*, 155–6.

160 Athenagoras, *Legatio* (ed. Schwartz, *T.U.*, iv. 2, 1891) 30,

161 Tatian, *Oratio ad. Graecos* (ed. Schwartz, *T.U.*, iv., 1888), 27.

162 Clement, *Stromata*, ii.1, vii.1.1. and 54.3.

163 Tertullian, *Apol.*, 6.10.

164 Lucian, *Alexander*, 38.

165 Eusebius, *H.E.*, iv.15.6.

CHAPTER TEN

The Years of Crisis, 165–180

THE account of Polycarp's arrest and martyrdom, which Evarestus sent to the Church of Philomelium in southern Phrygia probably *circa* 165–168,[1] showed that the Church in Asia was entering a new period of crisis. Polycarp was not the only victim. Eusebius prefaces the account of his martyrdom by saying that in the joint reigns of Marcus Aurelius and Lucius Verus, 161–169, 'very great persecutions again disturbed Asia' (*H.E.*, iv.15.1). They continued until the end of Marcus Aurelius' reign with their main impact in 164–168 and 176–178, and they had the full weight of public opinion behind them.[2] Educated provincials were at last taking the Church seriously. The spate of Apologetic writing between 175–180 signifies an attempt by Christians to explain their faith to an hostile but literate provincial audience. The Christians were being challenged on their own ground, by Celsus, probably in Caesarea in Palestine, by Autolycus in Antioch and by Lucian of Samosata writing for the Greek world as a whole. Meantime, a crisis was developing within the Church itself. Episcopal organization and institutional development were being confronted by the prophetic movement of the Montanists drawing on the latent apocalypticism of the ordinary Christian in Asia and Phrygia; and this movement was inflamed by hopes of the Last Days which persecution always produced. These were the crisis years, and the fact that the Church survived them augured well for its eventual triumph.

Why Marcus Aurelius should have allowed 'new edicts' in the province of Asia, which enabled Christians to be denounced with rather less risk to the informer than hitherto, must remain a mystery.[3] Like his predecessor he was a devout traditionalist so far as the State religion was concerned. The philosopher saw no contradiction in many gods representing Divine Providence, while the power of those of Rome was taken for granted.[4] Even on a *dies nefastus* he sacrificed at home,[5] and the hecatombs of animals he had slaughtered in honour of the gods after his victories over the Germanic invaders became proverbial.[6] It is not surprising, therefore, to find him ordering relegation to an island for those who introduced new cults without permission and 'disturbed irresponsible mentalities with superstitious fear of supernatural power'.[7] There is no reason to suppose that the measure was aimed at the Christians, but it shows the Emperor's hostility towards religious innovations. Moreover, he disliked Jews[8] and Christians from experience,[9] the one because he regarded them as dangerous and unpleasant people, the other as morbid and misguided exhibitionists. For the Stoic who could accept death and disaster as facts not subject to human change he had no patience with men who provoked their doom and openly despised the gods to whom the Empire owed its security. In this he reflected accurately the temper of educated men of his age.[10]

The influence, too, of his closest advisers Cornelius Fronto and Junius Rusticus was anti-Christian. Both were now old men and hated and feared the revolutionary tendencies they saw in the Christians. Rusticus was Justin's judge in 165, and Fronto's speech against the Christians remained well enough known in the capital to find a place in the Christian-pagan debate of the early third century. Their Stoicism was a religion of duty and authority, and had no place for fanatics who looked forward to their own salvation at the expense of the rest of humanity destroyed in eternal fire. In Asia, however, there may have been local developments which *circa* 165 brought hostility towards the Christians to boiling point. About this time the great plague, which eventually ravaged the whole of the eastern and central provinces of the Empire, began to make its presence felt. From Aristides[11] we know that its effects in the provinces were to be severe, though not 'the major turning point in the history of the Empire' that has sometimes been asserted. In town and countryside the aid of Aesculapius and the cleansing river deities was being besought by the pagans,[12] while in contrast, some Christians would be accepting the situation as an apocalyptic sign. This would provoke a not unjustified outbreak of anger against them and especially 'the destroyers of the gods', their leaders.

The details, however, remain uncertain. All one can say is that after what was remembered as a long period of calm—so long that

Melito of Sardes thought that persecution 'had never happened before'[13] in the province—instructions were received by the authorities and informers went about their evil work.[14] One can detect a growing tendency to whittle away the procedures laid down by Trajan and Hadrian and to have the Christians sought out for punishment. Smyrna in 166–167,[15] Lyons in 177,[16] and Palestine-Phoenicia (?) in 178 on the explicit authority of Celsus,[17] provide examples. Celsus could write of the Christians as open enemies of Greco-Roman society, to be compared with 'male-factors who with good reason undergo the punishments which they suffer for their robberies'.[18] Even' so, as Marcus Aurelius' rescript to the governor of Lyons shows, recantation still carried pardon, unless 'flagitia' had also been alleged against the accused.

There was thus no reversal of Imperial policy under Marcus Aurelius, but a substantial modification of procedures, probably in response to the combined pressure of the Emperor's advisers and public opinion in cities where Christian communities were prominent. The correspondence of Dionysius of Corinth (circa 170) refers to recent persecutions in Athens, Crete and perhaps also in the city of Rome and in Pontus. At Gortyna the capital of Crete, Bishop Philip was congratulated on having borne witness to his church by numerous acts of courage.[18a] If one is justified in placing the death of Polycarp in the period 165–168, the strength of public feeling in Asia is obvious. In Philadelphia, a traditional stronghold for fanatical and apocalyptic Christianity,[19] there had already been a savage outbreak against the Church. A group of eleven Christians had been cruelly tortured and sent down to Smyrna to be dispatched by the beasts in the annual Provincial Games. One of the condemned men, Germanicus, had to drag a reluctant animal towards him before he could be eaten.[20] This incensed the crowd. Polycarp's arrest was demanded. The hunt ended in a farm outside the city.

Evarestus' account of what took place illustrates the situation of Christianity in Asia; respect felt for its leaders being out-weighed by panic hatred for the sect in moments of crisis.[21] Polycarp himself possessed considerable standing in Smyrna. When he was discovered, his guards were considerate, and even reluct-ant to arrest him. He was given time to eat and to pray. On the way back to the city he was met by the irenarch (police chief)

Herod and his father Nicetas, who took him into their carriage and tried to persuade him to save his life. 'But what harm is it to say "Lord Caesar", and to offer sacrifice and be saved?' Polycarp remained silent, and finally said, 'I am not going to do what you counsel me'. Then the pair threatened him and eventually pitched him out on the road near the arena.[22] The Proconsul also tried to save him, and the following famous scene took place.[23]

> The Proconsul asked him if he were Polycarp, and when he admitted it he tried to persuade him to deny, saying: 'Respect your age', and so forth, as they are accustomed to say: 'Swear by the genius of Caesar, repent, say: "Away with the Atheists"'; but Polycarp, with a stern countenance looked on all the crowd in the arena, and waving his hand at them, he groaned and looked up to heaven and said: 'Away with the Atheists'. But when the Governor pressed him and said: 'Take the oath and I will let you go, revile Christ', Polycarp said: 'For eighty and six years have I been his servant, and he has done me no wrong, and how can I blaspheme my King who saved me?' But when he persisted again, and said: 'Swear by the genius of Caesar',[24] he said: 'If you vainly suppose that I will swear by the genius of Caesar, as you say, and pretend that you are ignorant who I am, listen plainly: I am a Christian. And if you wish to learn the doctrine of Christianity fix a day and listen.' The proconsul said: 'Persuade the people.' And Polycarp said: 'You I should have held worthy of discussion, for we have been taught to render honour, as is meet, if it hurt us not, to princes and authorities appointed by God; but as for those, I do not count them worthy that a defence should be made to them.' And the proconsul said: 'I have wild beasts, I will deliver you to them, unless you change your mind.' And he said: 'Call for them, for change of mind from better to worse is a change we may not make; but it is good to change from evil to righteousness.' And he said again to him: 'I will cause you to be consumed by fire, if you despise the beasts, unless you repent.' But Polycarp said: 'You threaten with fire that burns for a time, and is quickly quenched, for you do not know the fire which awaits the wicked in the judgement to come and in everlasting punishment. But why are you waiting? Come, do what you will'[25] (tr. Kirsopp Lake).

The proconsul then had Polycarp's confession proclaimed in formal terms by his herald.[26] This was the signal for the crowd, which included pagans and Jews, to show its feelings. 'They cried out with uncontrollable wrath and a loud shout "This is the teacher of Asia, the destroyer of our gods, who teaches many neither to offer sacrifice nor to worship".' Even if one allows with Parkes that 'the Jews can hardly be considered to have taken the active part in that cry', the remainder of the account shows the Jews co-operating gleefully with the pagans in having a common enemy removed.[27] Thus, when it was impossible to set a lion on Polycarp as the Asiarch 'had closed the sports', the Jews 'were extremely zealous, as is their custom, in preparing wood and faggots'[28] to use for burning Polycarp. Later, when Polycarp was dead, they took the initiative in persuading the Roman governor not to give up the body to the Christians, and in consequence, the centurion had it placed on a pyre where it was consumed.[29] There is no need to discuss whether the Jewish action was 'official' or not.[30] The threat presented by Christianity had been obvious to them for the last hundred years. In Smyrna some old quarrels with the pagans were patched up in a common effort at self-preservation.

The same period, 164-168, saw other martyrdoms in Asia. The proconsulate of Sergius Paulus, probably between 164-166, was remembered by Christians for the martyrdom of Sagaris (probably) in Laodicea.[31] On the coast, at Pergamum, the trial of Papylas and Carpus took place before an unnamed Proconsul who was on circuit in the city.[32] Here, the attitude of the accused was deliberately provocative, and the charge of 'blasphemy against the gods and the emperors' was not undeserved.[33] In vain, the Proconsul argued with them in an attempt to persuade them to save their lives. They refused to sacrifice, and like Polycarp, were condemned to be burnt alive. As Carpus gave thanks for his fate, a woman in the crowd named Agathoniké rushed forward and demanded to share death with him.[34] The bystanders besought her to think of her family, but she was bent on death and was immediately condemned. Then surprisingly enough, the crowd reacted against the sentence. 'This is a harsh judgment and an unjust sentence', they cried.[35] It was a sign that the Christian who was prepared to accept the consequences of his faith had begun to win respect. It was a sign, too, of the spirit abroad among the Christians in Asia, a spirit that was to inspire Montanus' movement a few years later.[36]

Neither Polycarp nor his fellow sufferers had been the victims of the crowd alone. The opposition to Christianity had by now become articulate, and between 165–180, three, if not four, Greek provincial writers set out their reasons for opposition. These had little ˛to do with *flagitia*. Instead, they went to the heart of the problem. How could an atheistic proseletyzing, clannish and potentially disloyal sect be allowed to survive in the Greco-Roman community? The 'third race' must conquer or perish finally.

Lucian's 'Proteus' in the 'Death of Peregrinus' may actually have existed. Athenagoras alludes to what appears to be the same incident as Lucian, namely Peregrinus' ultimate public suicide as the crowning spectacle of the Olympic games in 165.[37] Lucian's pamphlet would therefore date in all probability shortly afterwards. Christianity, however, was merely one episode in Peregrinus' strange life; for he later accepted some form of Egyptian Yoga, flirted with Brahminism, and died as a Cynic. The Christian period came comparatively early, during his exile from his native city of Parium, after strangling his father for whom he thought 60 years on this planet long enough. In Palestine, he fell in with Christians, and became one of their leaders, a prophet and Biblical exegete. 'On this account' he was thrown in prison. Release and escape were impossible. Then to quote Lucian,

Then, as this was impossible, every other form of attention was shown him, not in any casual way but with assiduity; and from the very break of day aged widows and orphan children could be seen waiting near the prison, while their officials even slept inside with him after bribing the guards. Then elaborate meals were brought in, and sacred books of theirs were read aloud, and excellent Peregrinus—for he still went by that name—was called by them 'the new Socrates'.

Indeed, people came even from the cities in Asia, sent by the Christians at their common expense, to succour and defend and encourage the hero. They show incredible speed whenever any such public action is taken; for in no time they lavish their all. So it was then in the case of Peregrinus; much money came to him from them by reason of his imprisonment, and he procured not a little revenue from it. The poor wretches have convinced themselves, first and foremost, that they are going to be immortal and live for all time, in consequence of which they despise death and even willingly give themselves into custody, most of them. Furthermore, their first lawgiver persuaded them that they are all brothers of one another after they have transgressed once for all by denying the Greek gods and by worshipping that crucified sophist himself and living under his laws. Therefore they despise all things indiscriminately and consider them common property, receiving such doctrines traditionally without any definite evidence. So if any charlatan and trickster, able to profit by occasions, come among them, he quickly acquires sudden wealth by imposing upon simple folk[38] (tr. A. M. Harmon, *Lucian*, v, pp. 13–15).

The text is very interesting. Lucian, like other provincials who took trouble to study the Christians, seems to regard them as some sort of Jewish mystery sect.[39] His use of the titles προφήτης and ξυναγωγεύς in a Palestinian environment, and the allusions to Jesus as 'the first lawgiver'[40] (ὁ πρῶτος νομοθέτης), the title used by Josephus when referring to Moses, and the food laws which he asserts were enforced by Christians,[41] strengthen this possibility. We glimpse the compact organization of the Church, with wealth and property enough for its representatives in Asia to send help to a prominent member when imprisoned in Syria, nearly 600 miles away.[42] The confessor also was the object of favour and popular veneration, just as he was to be in North Africa thirty years later. We have further corroboration for the view that atheism was the real charge against the Christians. Their clannishness owed its existence to the fact that 'they had transgressed once and for all by denying the Greek gods, and worshipping the crucified sophist',[43] whom they accept 'without any question'. The reference to the 'once and for all' character of the break with classical culture points to the depth of the imprint left by baptism on the mind of the convert, and his consequent readiness—as in Justin's case—to accept martyrdom. There is the streak of fanaticism which recurs time and again which makes 'most of them even willingly give themselves up' (ἑκόντες αὐτοὺς ἐπιδιδόασιν οἱ πολλοί). The conflict between this attitude and Hellenism was plain enough. But Lucian, like the governor of Syria whom he describes, evidently considered that the Christians could still be treated as 'poor wretches', victims of their 'wondrous lore',[44] too gullible and stupid to be serious menaces. For him, they were absurdities, useful as a means of further discrediting the object of his real attack, namely the Cynics. Both were rabble-rousing frauds and exhibitionists, and if one who had indulged in both fantasies cared to end his life on a blazing pyre, would not sensible men draw the right conclusions?

Lucian's inclusion of the Christian episode in Proteus' life in his general diatribe against the Cynics raises some interesting problems. His hero's migration from Christianity to Cynicism was not so extraordinary. Justin, it will be remembered, had been denounced by the Cynic Crescens, and it is reasonable to see behind this denunciation the professional jealousy of a rival but less successful preacher of reform. Aelius Aristides, towards the end of a long life in *circa* 180, denounced the various enemies of Hellenism. He turned his attention to those who claimed to despise riches in the name of philosophy, who advocated 'having all things in common', and who from the shadow of the porticos surrounding the market-places hurled insults at their superiors, 'very similar in their behaviour to those impious fellows who live in Palestine. It is those indeed who demonstrate their impiety in this obvious way, namely that they do not recognize their superiors'.[45] From the reference to Palestine, it would seem fairly clear that Aristides had the Christians in mind. The latter were sometimes called Galileans, and his description would fit a man like Tatian who hated Hellenism and was known a generation after his death as a Cynic.[46] In the *Acts of Apollonius circa* 185 an intervention by a Cynic philosopher against the Christian confessor is recorded,[47] and Apollonius himself was also known as 'Saccas'.[48]

The evidence for similarity between the two groups is drawn from too wide a range of sources to be brushed aside. Outwardly, some Christian preachers, with their old philosopher's cloak and few worldly goods, must have resembled their rivals. So too did their disciples. If the Cynics filled their ranks 'with Paphlagonian slaves' and 'barbarians from Sinope',[49] so did the Christians. There were slaves and ex-slaves among their clergy,[50] and, more to the point, slaves among their heroes. The names of Blandina, Biblis and Felicitas have been remembered by the Church. Though Christians possessed slaves and did not denounce the institution of slavery as the Cynics may have done, the converted slave of a Christian master was often regarded as a brother or sister, whatever his status in the world. The blow against the established order was no less telling for being masked. The tactics and the message of the two groups of reformers, as Origen saw,[51] often coincided. Both made use of the streets and market-places for harangues and speeches,[52] and the inequalities and superstitions of the age presented an open target for attack. But while the Cynics were a nuisance they were not a danger. They could point to a respectable ancestry in popular folklore. Diogenes and his tub were as well known to schoolboys then as in nineteenth-century Britain.[53] In the last resort cynicism led not so much to outright denial of the gods as to indifference, a point which Justin himself made against Crescens.[54] The Christians, however, presented a more intractable problem. Theirs was a 'barbarian' (non-Greek) message,[55] backed by a world-wide organization. Their ramifications and spirit of self-help made them formidable. In *circa* 178, Celsus, an educated and far-sighted Platonist, probably from Palestine-Phoenicia, took up the challenge they were presenting to the Greco-Roman world.[56]

Celsus is an important witness, for his work does not suggest an exceptional individual and he shares the superstitions and prejudices of his time. Like Lucian, he had observed the Christians, but in addition he had made an extensive study of current Jewish and Christian literature both orthodox and sectarian. He had read parts at least of Matthew and Luke and Hebrews, but not, probably, the Pauline Epistles.[57] He knew of the Preaching of Peter and possibly also of the Gospel of Thomas. He alludes to Genesis, Deuteronomy, Daniel, Jonah, the Psalms and i Enoch—in themselves an interesting collection of Scripture circulating among the Christians with whom he had contact. He was very well informed about Jewish-Christian controversies. He knew something of the internal life of the Church, including some significant facts about the spread of Marcion's communities[58] and the clash between the Gnostics and the 'Great Church'.[59] He was able to point to detailed parallels and contrasts between Mithraism and Gnostic Christianity.[60] Also, he had studied the Christians at work from first hand. He had seen the effect of their message on the minds of the ill-educated, the women and the young.[61] He speaks of 'multitudes of converts',[62] and he realized that despite the fantastic doctrines and absurd predilections of its representatives, the Church was gaining ground. Its effectiveness alarmed him. He recognized its ultimate subversive aim against the established institutions of the Empire. His was a warning to his fellow provincials that the danger could no longer be neglected.

Celsus' objections to Christianity in his *Alethes Logos* were not merely that Christians were members of a secret, illegal organization, though this is the point he makes first, and he returns to it at the climax of his work.[63] His attack covered the whole field of culture, politics and religion. He put into logical and precise form what many educated contemporaries were thinking, and as a deeply religious man himself,[64] he demonstrated an alternative approach to God to that being preached by the Christians. His was the first salvo in the long duel between Neoplatonist and Christian which was to continue for over two centuries, until the Cappadocian Fathers provided Plato with a permanent place within the Church. It was by no means the least damaging.

He believed that there was 'a true doctrine', which confronted 'anyone who ventures to write anything at all about such matters', that this doctrine was of the greatest antiquity and that it was held by pious races such as the Indians and Chaldaeans, by the wise men of the past, notably Plato.[65] It had, however, been perverted and misunderstood by the Jews, and even more so by their corrupt and rebellious offspring, the Christians. As a result the latter were in hopeless error concerning God, Creation, and man's duty as a citizen. Celsus thus used against his opponents the current Christian arguments found both in Paul (Roms. 1) and Justin,[66] and later in Eusebius,[67] that there was an original law of righteousness from which mankind had fallen away with disastrous results, only to be restored by the coming of Christ and the emergence of the race of Christians.

Celsus, however, took exactly the opposite view. There were no 'chosen people' and certainly not the Christians as he knew them. Within creation each race, and even each species, had its part to play.[68] True religion could be understood differently according to differences of nation and city. Each people worshipped its own gods and observed its own laws. Each individual was subject to the Nomos or law of his city or tribe.[69] Just as mankind was divided into a multiplicity of peoples, so the harmony of the natural order demanded the existence of a multitude of deities. These gods were 'satraps' or ministers of God, representing the races of humanity, providing each with its distinctive qualities, and hence, worthy of honour by all thoughtful and religious individuals.[70] Celsus saw the Roman Empire and its gods as a great federation of beings living under a divine providence who guided all creation with equal justice. Man himself enjoyed no special privileges, still less one small part of mankind. 'Why, if God wanted to deliver the human race from evils did He send this (divine) spirit into one corner?'[71] Here Celsus saw the weakness of the Christian claim that attributed a privileged status to one religious group at the expense of the rest of creation.

Indeed, the Christians had abandoned their Law, in their case that of the Jews,[72] an act which put them in opposition to humanity. It was 'impious to abandon the customs which have existed in each locality from the beginning'.[73] The reaction of the Imperial authorities was therefore justified. In a very interesting section Celsus sums up current opinion concerning the significance of the failure of Jewish messianic hopes on the one hand, and current repression of Christianity on the other.

> You will surely not say that if the Romans were convinced by you and were to neglect their customary honours to both gods and men and were to call upon your Most High, or whatever name you prefer, He would come down and fight on their side, and they would have no need for any other defence. In earlier times also the same God made these promises and some far greater than these, so you say, to those who pay regard to him. But see how much help he has been to both them and you. Instead of being masters of the whole world, they have been left no land or home of any kind. While in your case, if anyone does still wander about in secret, yet he is sought out and condemned to death.[74]

So, quite reasonably, the Christians constituted in Celsus' eyes a revolutionary movement, a στάσις, 'a revolt against the community'.[75] The task of winning them back to their former loyalties was an urgent one. He was not the last of the pagan leaders to base his appeal on patriotism, but his, even over this distance of time, remains moving and compelling. It was not possible for a common law, such as Christianity, to unite the peoples of the world.[76] The lesser gods had their uses. They should be given their formal acknowledgement 'so far as this is expedient'.[77] And if we 'should never forsake God', what was wrong in 'propitiating the powers on earth and the rulers and emperors among men since not even they hold their position without the might of the demons. . . . Even if someone tells you to take an oath to an emperor among men, that also is nothing dreadful. For earthly things have been given to him and whatever you receive in this life you receive from him'.[78] Thus, the Christians should 'help the emperor with all their power and so co-operate with him in what is right, and fight for him, and be fellow-soldiers if he presses for this, and fellow-generals with him . . . and accept public office in our country if it is necessary to do this for the sake of the preservation of the laws and of piety'.[79]

Seventy years later, when Origen wrote his reply, Celsus could not have argued convincingly on these lines. By then, Christianity had become much stronger, and it was within the realms of possibility that 'all men may call upon the name of the Lord and may serve him under one yoke' (Zeph. 3[9]).[80] The same Platonic argument by which Celsus defended polytheism and Imperial federation could be used by Origen and Eusebius in the interests of Christian monotheism and the Imperial monarchy. The Platonist attack was effective against sectarian and Judaistic Christianity but failed when outflanked by the Christianized Platonism of the school of Alexandria.

Origen was forced to defend Christianity by sacrificing the views of what he calls the 'simple-minded' who lived by 'mere faith'.[81] In the 170s, however, theirs were still the dominant opinions among Christians. Indeed, one of the most interesting facts emerging from a study of Celsus and Lucian is how extraordinarily primitive in its Christology, angelogy, and ethic the Church of the mid-second-century had remained. Celsus ruthlessly exposed its weaknesses. His attack on the current Christian doctrines of God and of Man added weight to his denunciation of the Christians as disloyal, and his analysis went far to show that the one was the result of the other. The Christians' disloyalty towards the empire was the outcome of arrogance towards their fellow-men, and this in turn followed from their false, Judaistic view of God.

Again, one is struck by the continued association of Christians with Jews in the minds of educated contemporaries. Celsus saw little to choose between Jewish and Christian beliefs. 'Both Jews and Christians worship the same God'[82] he claimed. Their wrangles about Christ 'were no different from that called in the proverb, a fight about the shadow of an ass'.[83] His introduction of the Jew in the early part of the *Alethes Logos*, who picks holes in the Christian case from the Jewish standpoint was a clever if superficial piece of work, because it confronted his readers at once with the intellectual world in which both Jew and Christian moved, and it contrasted this with their own. The weakness of the Christian position could be more effectively demonstrated by reference to similar Jewish claims. Having shown that even on their own assumptions Christian claims were false, Celsus moved on to the argument that even where Christianity was true, it could be traced back to popular legend (for instance, the resurrection was paralleled by the story of Aristeas of Proconnesos[84]) or from accepted philosophical commonplaces. The remainder was rubbish, rejected even by Jews, themselves a perverted and objectionable race.[85] In many ways Celsus was anticipating the Emperor Julian's polemic two centuries later. Both emphasized the distinctively Jewish element in Christianity, and for both, Judaism was a genuine faith of a people, Christianity the subversive counterfeit.[86]

The attack was well conceived and calculated to convince educated provincials for whom it was written. Intervention by God in the Kosmos was incomprehensible to minds brought up in current Stoic and Platonic ideas.[87] Few would have disputed Celsus' view that God 'does not participate in Being',[88] or 'partake in movement.'[89] The idea 'asserted by some Christians and by Jews, the former saying that some God or son of God has come down to earth to judge mankind, the latter saying that he will come, is most shameful and no lengthy argument is required to refute it'.[90] 'Either', argued Celsus, 'God really changes to a mortal body, which is impossible, or He himself does not change, but makes those who see Him think He does so, and leads them astray and tells lies.'[91] 'God leaves His throne'[92]—did He indeed? 'Bringing down fire like a torturer', or acting like 'a cook!'[93] Did not the Christians realize that 'if you changed any one quite insignificant thing on earth you would upset and destroy everything?'[94] And what about this blundering, ignorant, ferocious Being described in Genesis, unable to control the universe or the people who inhabited it?[95] Was this God? The God to whom the soul must move was not a God 'eating the flesh of sheep, drinking gall and vinegar, consuming filth'.[96] No wonder Christians 'would never enter a gathering of intelligent men', but 'babbled about God impiously to arouse the amazement of uneducated people'.[97]

What about the Christians themselves? Their anthropology was utterly false. 'God did not make man in his own image, for God is not like that.' It was therefore futile

> for the race of Jews and Christians to cluster like bats or ants coming out of a nest, or frogs holding council round a marsh, or worms assembling in some filthy corner, disagreeing with one another about which of them are the worse sinners. They say: 'God shows and proclaims everything to us beforehand, and He has even deserted the whole world and the motion of the heavens, and disregarded the vast earth to give attention to us alone; and He sends messengers to us alone and never stops sending them and seeking that we may be with Him for ever'.

Christians were:

> like worms who say: 'There is God first, and we are next after Him in rank since He has made us entirely like God, and all things have been put under us, earth, water, air, and stars; and all things exist for our benefit, and have been appointed to serve us'.[98]

This passage sums up Celsus' case. He appreciated how on the one hand, the Christians could have that complete self-confidence in their own salvation, so that they could say 'Do not ask questions, only believe. Faith will save you. The wisdom in the world is an evil thing and folly good'.[99] On the other hand, he understood the theological basis of their unco-operative arrogance towards their fellow-men. If the world had been made for them, why should they assume the exacting burdens of active citizenship, or fight for what they conceived to be idolatry? Celsus realized, too, that 'the Great Church' whose adherents expressed these doctrines was the real enemy. Marcionites and Gnostics even though Christian in appearance could be played off against each other and against it. He emphasizes the mutual hatred which divided them.[100] Divide and rule would have been better policy for the authorities to have pursued than persecution.

Yet all the time the danger was growing. Celsus' note changed from irony to anger as he described the Christian proselytization among women and slaves, and he speaks from first-hand knowledge.[101] The famous passage in the *Alethes Logos*[102] may be cited:

> In private houses also we see wool-workers, cobblers, laundry-workers, and the most illiterate and bucolic yokels, who would not dare to say anything at all in front of their elders and more intelligent masters. But whenever they get hold of children in private and some stupid women with them, they let out some astounding statements as, for example, that they must not pay any attention to their father and schoolteachers, but must obey them; they say that these talk nonsense and have no understanding, and that in reality they neither know nor are able to do anything good, but are taken up with mere empty chatter. But they alone, they say, know the right way to live, and if the children would believe them, they would become happy and make their home happy as well. And if just as they are speaking they see one of the school-teachers coming, or some intelligent person, or even the father himself, the more cautious of them flee in all directions; but the more reckless urge the children on to rebel. They whisper to them that in the presence of their father and their schoolmasters they do not feel able to explain anything to the children, since they do not want to have anything to do with the silly and obtuse teachers who are totally corrupted and far gone in wickedness and who inflict punishment on the children. But, if they like, they should leave father and their schoolmasters, and go along with the women and little children who are their playfellows to the wool-dresser's shop, or to the cobbler's or the washerwoman's shop, that they may learn perfection. And by saying this they persuade them (trs. H. Chadwick).

The tactics were a mixture of those employed by the Cynic and those of the Jewish apostle. As we saw in the last chapter, the targets were those who did not reap the benefits of classical civilization, namely the women and the poorer, unprivileged provincials in the towns.[103] The Christian message was succeeding where the Jewish had failed. The loser was the accepted social ethos of the Hellenistic world and its adherents.

How far was Celsus dealing with a real danger? Christianity was making progress, but its sectarian outlook and long preparation prior to baptism[104] would be preventing large-scale conversions. However, his arguments concerning the impiety of abandoning ancestral customs were being repeated elsewhere. In the *Clementine Homilies* the pagan speaker Apion, declared 'it is the greatest impiety to abandon the customs of one's ancestors to embrace those of the barbarians'.[105] Clement answered that 'one should not retain ancestral customs at all cost, but keep those which are conformable to piety and reject those which are not', and, he goes on, 'There is a great difference between truth and custom, for truth sincerely sought after finally reveals herself, while custom whatever it may be, whether religion, truth or falsehood, merely asserts itself without allowing for reflection'.[106] Though it was difficult to abandon the ideas of one's ancestors, even when they were absurd, it was necessary. The danger of this attitude to established ways was obvious at the time, and still more obvious in view of the Christian appeal to the underprivileged but not necessarily ignorant. In the next century the villagers of the Imperial estates in southern Phrygia, one of the strongholds of Montanism, were quite capable of representing their case before the Imperial procurator.[107] Literacy was not the prerogative of the city-dweller only.

To Celsus, however, such people would be numbered among the 'uneducated and stupid' whom the Christians aimed to convert, and he admits that they were outside the range of current philosophical argument.[108] This view finds rather startling corroboration in Athenagoras' *Legatio*, composed at this very time. In chapter 11 he writes in support of the value of Christian moral teaching that, in contrast to the ambiguities and confusions of the philosophers and their disciples, 'with us, on the contrary, you will find unlettered people, tradesmen and old women, who though unable to express in words the advantages of our teaching, demonstrate by acts the value of their principles'. Tatian, too, in the same decade 170–180, affirms 'You (pagans) who assert that we gossip among women and children, young girls and old women, and whom you reproach us with because they do not accept you, listen what absurdities there are among the Greeks', which he then recounts at considerable length.[109] And, if one moves on a quarter of a century to Carthage the example of Perpetua shows just how Christianity appealed to the bored and frustrated intelligent woman of the Greco-Roman world. The social consequences for her family and traditional religion were disastrous.[110]

Celsus was justified also in stressing the question of civic duty, for this had now become an issue among the Christians themselves. The 'Great Church' was attracting recruits whose attitude towards their age was the opposite to friendly. So long as the Second Coming was believed to be near, so long would Christians tend to reject civic claims and interpret their beliefs in a way which left little room for family and social life. Tatian and the Montanists both represent the encratite movement which throve on this attitude. It was the product of the fears and exaltation which prolonged repression and frequent acts of hostility had aroused.

When one reads Celsus it is impossible to dismiss Tatian as a curiosity. Though few educated Christians in the Greek-speaking world were to share his utter contempt of pagan society and its culture, the surviving fragments of Hermias[111] demonstrate he was not isolated. His encratism had its followers, even if they, like Bishop Alexander of Jerusalem or Pinytus of Knossos, were more circumspect than he. His was a psychology of rejection. Like his master, Justin, he had been won for Christian monotheism by the simplicity, cultural priority and consistency of Hebrew prophecy contrasted with the endless fruitless quarrels of the philosophical schools.[112] To this was added the purity of Christian moral teaching, their interest in educating the poor, and readiness to suffer for their faith.[113] His conversion showed that not every educated provincial was prepared like Lucian to accept the Greek gods—and laugh about them. Christianity might be 'barbarian' in origin but it was better than this. Where, however, Justin remained fundamentally a friend of the culture he had abandoned, Tatian became an enemy. In a few years, he had moved from initiation into the mysteries to utter rejection of Greek culture as a whole. 'We have renounced your wisdom', he wrote sometime after 172,[114] 'though I was once proficient in it'.[115] 'What noble thing have you produced by your pursuit of philosophy?' he asks his hearers.[116]

The tone of his *Address to the Greeks* is as biting as anything one finds in Tertullian. Sarcastic criticisms, venomous reproach, and the rapid change from argument to personal reminiscence point to the deep feelings of the author. Like Tertullian, he attacks not only the Olympian deities, but the laws, customs and institutions of the cities of the day. The boast of Christianity is simply that it is 'barbarian', and barbarian culture was superior to Greek, both so far as age was concerned, and because the main institutions of the Greeks had been learnt in the first place from barbarians.[117] By the 'Greeks' he meant the ruling classes in the Greek cities for whose way of life he felt nothing but contempt. Hermias[118] and Theophilus of Antioch attacked the inconsistencies of the philosophers and the pretentious futilities of paganism with all the verve of Tatian, but the latter has an unmistakable political animosity which is absent among his other Greek-speaking contemporary apologists. As one who came originally either from beyond the Roman frontier or from the frontier province of Assyria, he could look at the Empire from the outside, and he makes no attempt to hide his dislike based on personal experience. 'The things I set before you I have not learned at second hand. . . . We bid farewell to the arrogance of the Romans, and the idle talk of the Athenians. I embraced our barbaric philosophy. I began to show how this was more ancient than your institutions.'[119] Elsewhere, 'On this account, I reject your legislation also; for there ought to be one common polity for all. But now there are as many different codes as there are states, so that things held disgraceful in some are honourable in others'.[120] Tatian had no place for the Roman world, and no interest in its rulers. So far as his own age was concerned, he was an anarchist, the living embodiment of the revolutionary forces which at that very moment Celsus was attempting to thwart.

Like his Western counterpart, Tertullian, Tatian's rigorism eventually drove him right outside the Church. There, however, he left behind him writers more aware of the realities of the situation than he and readier to come to terms with the Greco-Roman world. The hope which had inspired his master, Justin, of ultimate harmony between Christianity and the Empire was not lost on the next generation of Apologists. Each in their own way Athenagoras, Theophilus of Antioch and Melito of Sardes stressed their loyalty towards the State, and sought belatedly to convince their fellow citizens that Christian prayer and conduct were more efficacious means of protecting the Empire than the *supplicatio* and active service of the conventional sort.

Athenagoras may perhaps be placed better in Asia of the 170s than in Athens,[121] and is a valuable source of information for the reaction of an educated Christian provincial to the continued repression of his faith.[122] He felt deep indignation at the situation in which respectable citizens were wrongly accused of hideous crimes.[123] He shows marked respect for the emperors, addressing them as 'greatest, most humane and most learned', and 'mighty sovereigns'.[124] He stresses his loyalty to the Empire, citing i Tim. 2² as the Christians' aim ('that we may live a quiet and peaceful life') and Roms. 13⁷⁻⁸ as the basis for this attitude.[125] He tries to present, like Justin before him, Christianity as a new and superior philosophy destined to supersede the contradictory teachings of the pagan world. Athenagoras, in particular, attempts to disprove the charge of 'atheism' by equating the monotheism of the Christians with that taught by Plato, Aristotle and the Stoics. 'If Plato is not an atheist when he considers the one uncreated maker of the universe to be God, neither are we atheists when we recognize and affirm him to be God by whose Word all things were created, and by whose Spirit they are held together.'[126]

Even the apologetic against polytheism was set out in a form freer from traditional Judaistic argument, and less repellant to the ears of his hearers. After all, Euhemerus had been a philosopher himself. His theory that the gods were originally men, promoted to deity as Prometheus and Osiris had been, on account of their services to humanity, was of honourable pedigree. This was only what Alexander the Great had told his mother !![127] In contrast to Tatian he valued what he had learnt from his training in philosophy. He believed in the essential harmony of Christian culture and the philosophies of the day, though the Father and Maker of the universe was worshipped truly by Christians alone. There was no justification for the charge of 'atheism', let alone incest and cannibalism. It was only right that the prosperity and mild rule which the empire was enjoying should be extended to the Christians.[128]

Athenagoras' Apology was a simple plea for fair play for the recognition of Christians as loyal subjects, and a defence against the popular charges against them. In Antioch, Bishop Theophilus was attempting the same approach in his three longwinded tomes addressed to Autolycus. It was left, however, to Melito of Sardes to associate Christianity with the prosperity of the Roman

Empire, and urge by implication the greater the freedom given to the Christians the better for all.[129] It is unfortunate that only four fragments of Melito's Apology have survived, three in Eusebius (*H.E.*, iv.26) and one in the *Chronicon Paschale*,[130] as it looks back to St. Luke's Gospel and anticipates the arguments of Origen and Eusebius of Caesarea, that Church and Empire should co-operate. Augustus and Christ were both bringers of peace to a world disturbed by civil war. 'Our philosophy first grew up among the barbarians (Jews?), but its full flower came among your nation in the great reign of your ancestor Augustus, and became an omen for good to your empire, for from that time the power of the Romans became great and splendid.'[131] Only 'bad emperors', like Nero and Domitian, were persecutors. Hadrian and Antoninus had been favourably disposed to the Christians, and like Justin, he alludes to the rescript to Minucius Fundanus. Marcus Aurelius was warned that his prosperity was 'on condition that you guard that philosophy which has grown with the Empire, and which came into existence under Augustus'. To Melito, therefore, while the 'barbarian' origin of Christianity was an admitted fact, the goal was the harmony of Christians with the world-monarchy of Augustus and his successors. Within a few years of each other Christian Apologists had stated contrasting ideals. The outlooks of Tatian and Melito admitted of little compromise, and the rift was making itself felt among the less articulate of the faithful as well.

The last half of Marcus Aurelius' reign was no more free from disturbance for the Christians than the first. Evidence from a number of sources leaves the impression of angry outbreaks now in one place, now in another, of which that at Lyons was the most destructive and terrible. But the storm was centred in the province of Asia. It appears that on 27 October in a year near the end of the reign, Thraseas, bishop of Eumeneia, was martyred in Smyrna,[132] and his fellow-townsmen Gaius and Alexander died at Apamea.[133] These were all anti-Montanist martyrs. The Montanists also claimed that many of their number had been killed.[134] Moreover, the Apologies of this period all refer to persecutions. Tatian, in particular, speaks of the flesh of Christians being consumed in various ways to dispel hopes of bodily resurrection,[135] and in view of the accounts of the martyrdoms at Lyons and of

Polycarp's death this can be accepted as true. The Jews also continued to take an active part in these local outbreaks. Being stoned, and beaten in the synagogues of the Phrygian towns seems to have been so usual that the credentials of Montanus and his companions were called in question when this had not befallen them.[136] The long and bitter denunciation of Israel by Melito of Sardes in his *Homily on the Passion*[137] must be put into the context of these feuds. All in all, there is little evidence of Christians entering into reasonable personal relationships with their opponents in this period.[138] The decade 170-180 was the high water-mark of their unpopularity in the East.

Not for the last time the reaction among Christians to this situation was to be as important as the persecution itself. Thanks to Père Nautin's shrewd analysis of the correspondence published by Eusebius in Books iv to vi of the *Ecclesiastical History*, it is clear that one of the chief preoccupations in the minds of Dionysius of Corinth and the confessors of Lyons was rigorism, both in the form of unreadiness to re-admit the casualties from persecution into the Church, and also excessive demands covering fasting and continence expected of a Christian in face of what was now believed to be the approaching end of the world.[139] Wherever a community suffered persecution the same questions were arising. The long and earnest debates in the darkness of the prison at Lyons may have had their counterparts elsewhere, but in Asia where the repression had been most savage and continuous the outcome was schism. The Montanist movement exactly foreshadows the Novatianist schism after the Decian persecution in the same area, and the Donatists following the Great Persecution in Africa a half-century later.

Already in the 160s we have noted the defiant attitude of some of the Asian confessors.[140] In contrast, one can detect a reaction against voluntary martyrdom in the early recension of the Acts of Polycarp preserved in Eusebius *H.E.*, iv.15. Even if we agree with von Campenhausen and see in the story of the rash and vainglorious Phrygian Quintus, an anti-Montanist addition, the lesson of the Acts is clear.[141] Evarestus was writing under the stress of crisis. He had no time for theological niceties. He wanted to tell the Christians of Philomelium and the world how the great Polycarp had been arrested, tried and gone serenely to his end.[142]

His was the model martyrdom, victim like his Lord had been, of the unholy alliance of pagans and Jews. But, he was also at pains to show that this 'apostolic figure' had not sought this honour. He had placed himself in God's hands, first by withdrawing from the city where anti-Christian feeling was at boiling point, and then though warned in a vision that he would have to die for Christ's sake, making no move to hasten his end.[143] Polycarp, moreover, showed no exaltation, no outpouring of prophecy during the proceedings and his attitude to the proconsul had been firm rather than defiant. His death was not connected in Evarestus' mind with the approach of Antichrist. The devil was 'jealous and envious', and 'resisted the family of God 'but he was not threatening it with his presence.[144] In every way, Polycarp died 'the wonderful martyr, who was in our days an apostolic and prophetic teacher, bishop of the Catholic (or Holy) Church in Smyrna'.[145]

We may contrast this outlook with that of the writer of the Acts of Carpus and his companions. Carpus and Papylas 'hasten to the amphitheatre in order that they may speedily leave the world',[146] and they laugh in defiance at the bystanders when being bound to the stake. 'Why are you laughing?' Carpus is asked. 'I have seen the glory of the Lord and I rejoiced; and I am departing from you at once and I am not an accomplice in your wickedness.[147] Instead, he looked forward to his appearance 'at the true seat of judgment', having endured all things.[148] Carpus, the wandering Christian prophet, and Polycarp the bishop, who never so much as mentions prophets in his surviving letter to the Philippians, represent divergent forces in the Church in Asia at this time. Were divine *charismata* and the power of binding and looseing to be channeled through an hierarchy dispensing regular penitential discipline, or were they to remain the prerogative of the 'friends and companions' of the Lord, His confessors and martyrs? It can hardly be accidental that successive editions of Polycarp's *Acta* were all anti-rigorist, and Quintus, the 'proto-Montanist' became a foil to Polycarp. Unlike Cyprian a century later in Africa, to whom he might be compared, Polycarp's influence on the Church was wholly on the side of hierarchical orthodoxy. The *Acta Cypriani*, on the other hand, became a Donatist pamphlet.[149] The different fortunes of Montanism in

Asia and Donatism in Africa cannot be entirely divorced from the respective influences of the two great bishop-martyrs of the early Church.

Whether Polycarp or Carpus and his companions truly represented Christianity in Asia was soon to be put to the test. In 172,[150] the village of Ardabav, probably Kallataba some fifteen miles up the Hermus valley from Philadelphia,[151] was the scene of astonishing events. To quote an anonymous contemporary, probably a well-educated Phrygian presbyter, writing to a leading anti-Montanist layman, Avircius Marcellus of Hierapolis *circa* 192:[152]

> In Phrygian Mysia there is said to be a village called Ardabav. There they say that a recent convert called Montanus, when Gratus was proconsul of Asia, in the unbounded lust of his soul for leadership gave access to himself to the adversary, became obsessed, and suddenly fell into frenzy and convulsions. He began to be ecstatic and to speak and to talk strangely, prophesying contrary to the custom which belongs to the tradition and succession of the church from the beginning.[153]

This already tells us much. For the Anonymous the issue was clearly 'strange prophecy' as against the 'tradition and succession of the Church'. Prophecy itself was admissable, but not when it was ecstatic, that is, when the prophet was no longer himself and therefore no longer uttering under the control of the ordained clergy.[154] A century later in Africa, martyrs themselves were to be denied their honours if they were 'necdum vindicatus'[155] (i.e. unauthorized). Donatism was the popular response to this situation: now, the Montanist took up the priestly challenge to the prophet.

Insufficient is known about economic and social conditions in rural Phrygia in the mid-second century to push the analogy between Montanism and Donatism to its conclusion. It seems, however, that Montanus himself had been a priest of Cybele,[156] the traditional cult of Phrygia which had its roots far back in the worship of the Hittite Kubaba. Its priests were credited with the gift of prophecy[157] and they enforced a rigorous standard of ritual purity on her worshippers. Those who fell short of this were disciplined by a penitential ritual following confession (*exomologesis*).[158] The whole transaction was duly recorded by an inscription in honour of the deity.[159] This puritanical native cult formed one aspect of the background to Montanism, just as the cruel and demanding cult of Saturn influenced Numidian Donatism.[160] Phrygia and Numidia also contained vast rural areas situated on the high plateaux whither classical language and culture had penetrated only superficially.[161] Phrygia, however, had had a considerable leavening of Jewish colonists, which may account for the spread of Christianity into the countryside so early, and their influence perhaps may also be traced in some of Montanist teaching.

Two other influences are discernible. First there was the continuance of the prophetic tradition within the Church in Asia. Orthodox and Montanists were to dispute who were the real successors of Agabus, Judas, Silas, the daughters of Philip, Ammia the prophetess, and Quadratus.[162] Secondly, there was the immense strength of Johannine teaching. The tradition which placed the resting place of John at Ephesus was a living one, and it sustained the Asian bishops twenty years later in their struggle with Pope Victor in defence of their customs regarding the celebration of Easter.[163] This tradition, however, demanded positive missionary witness, and looked forward to the End painted in the frightening terms of Revelation. Such ideas had upheld the confessors of Lyons, and they were equally to inspire their persecuted contemporaries in Asia.

Montanus' movement was therefore a compound of provincial, in this case Phrygian, rural Christianity, protest against both compromise with the world and the continued institutionalization of the Church,[164] and probably also, fierce reaction against a decade of sporadic repression and persecution. He and his companions, the prophetesses Priscilla and Maximilla,[165] claimed to be possessed by the Paraclete who spoke directly through them.[166] Their message seems to have been purely eschatological, with an ever reiterated stress on the glory of martyrdom and the associated requirement of ritual purity and freedom from the encumbrances of ordinary daily life. The evidence of both the anti-Montanist opposition and surviving Montanist oracles is consistent on all these points. From the Anonymous' second book, we learn that Maximilla prophesied 'universal war' and 'revolutions', and was attacked by orthodox opponents when these did not come to pass.[167] From his third book, he makes clear that prophecy and martyrdom were combined in the Montanist message. 'So when', he says, 'they have been refuted in the whole discussion they take refuge in martyrs, saying that they have many martyrs, and that this is a trustworthy proof of the power of the alleged prophetic spirit among them.'[168] Their followers certainly believed this. The Montanist confessor was an object of popular veneration and (as among the Lyons Christians) formed a category apart.[169] He had the prerogative of forgiving sins and preaching to the people.[170] Two Montanist oracles preserved by Tertullian, *De Fuga*, indicate that martyrdom was the death to which a Christian must aspire. 'Do not look forward to dying in your bed, in child-birth or in the lassitude of fever, but in martyrdom so that He who has suffered for you may be glorified.'[171] Again, 'You are exposed to public shame. So much the better. You are not exposed thus before men, but before God. Do not blush for shame. It is righteousness that displays you before all. Why blush when you are acquiring glory? Your power is born at the moment when men's eyes are fixed upon you.'[172] For the African, and no doubt for the Phrygian Montanist too, the prompting of the Spirit was nearly always towards martyrdom.

The climax of all this hope and suffering would be the descent of New Jerusalem, not in some great metropolitan centre, but a desert place in the Phrygian countryside, near the townships of Tymion and Pepuza.[173] After Maximilla there would be no more prophetesses. The End would come.[174] In preparation for the event, the Montanist organization differed considerably from that of the orthodox Christians, and their ritual was harsher as befitted a community awaiting the End. Below the Patriarch (a borrowing from native Judaism?) came the Koinonos, or Companion of Christ in His Passion by witness and confession.[175] This term had already been hallowed in Rev. 1[9] and reserved in orthodox circles for the bishop-martyr Polycarp. There were Montanist presbyters also, but the diaconate seems to have been supplemented by a ministry of maidens who carried lamps at services and prophesied.[176] Oddly enough for so eschatological a community, they alone seem to have had a full-time financial officer (ἐπίτροπος) who combined worldly and spiritual achievements.[177] Services were punctuated by rigorous acts of penance, and new and exacting fasts, the so-called 'dry fasts' (xerophagies) were introduced in addition to standard abstinences.[178] Though marriage was not forbidden, it was discouraged, sexual continence was preached, and second marriages banned.[179] Behind all these rigours was the aim of preparing Christians for reception of the Holy Spirit, who, as Tertullian was to point out,[180] could not take up his abode in a body filled with impurities.

This prophetic and eschatological faith appealed to latent forces in Christianity at this period. From Celsus we know that Phrygia was by no means the only part of the East where the prophetic tradition had retained its vigour.[181] His description of the Palestinian prophets whom he had seen at work is so precisely like the Montanists, that it has sometimes been thought that it was Montanism that he was describing. At Lyons, as we have seen, it only needed the onset of persecution to bring a Spirit-dominated interpretation of Christianity to the fore. In Athenagoras we find a striking condemnation of second marriages as ʹεὐπρεπής μοιχεία (adultery)ʹ,[182] and acceptance of ecstatic prophecy.[183] Finally, the urge to martyrdom was itself strong. A few years later, in 185, the Proconsul of Asia, Arrius Antoninus, a stern and incorruptible official, was confronted by a group of individuals carrying halters round their necks, and demanding execution. He sent them on their way. If they wanted to commit suicide there were cliffs and precipices they could jump over. The spirit of Christian fanaticism was not easily quenched,[184] and here was the Montanist equivalent of the Donatist Circumcellions two centuries later.

It is interesting that this story has been preserved by Tertullian writing in protest to the persecuting Proconsul of Africa, Scapula, in 212/213. There, Montanism was to find its most fertile field of conquest. Meantime, it spread like wildfire. Rome, Lyons, Syria and Thrace beyond the bounds of Asia Minor,[185] and the capital of Galatia, Ancyra[186] were all affected. But the evils which Montanus and his followers prophesied did not take place, and the death of Marcus Aurelius was followed by another period of religious calm. Eschatological hopes began to fade finally for many influential people in the Church.[187] The bishops and clergy whose position had been threatened, rallied. The prophets were challenged. Fraud and good living were uncovered among them. The prophetesses were harried and persecuted.[188] Gradually the more sober, orthodox, Christianity of the educated Hellenized town congregations gained the upper hand.[189] The story of the discomfiture of the prophets in Ancyra could no doubt be repeated elsewhere.[190] Thyateira remained, however, Montanist until the late third century.[191] Episcopal councils saw to it that the pressure was maintained.

In rural Phrygia, however, Montanism remained a powerful force for six centuries or more.[192] Like Donatism in Numidia it dominated the rural areas, like the Tembris valley in the northern part of the province where Phrygian custom and language long survived,[193] and the Hermas valley in the south. Like the Donatists and also the Novatians, its 'bishops' were not restricted to towns.[194] As early as 200 it was known as 'the Phrygian heresy'.[195] In its continued observance of Easter on 14 Nisan,[196] its insistence on 'monogamia',[197] and use of unleavened bread at Easter,[198] its acceptance of the 'wilderness tradition' for the Parousia, it showed how in a rural backwater of the Roman Empire a blend of Judaism with native prophetic tradition and eschatological hopes could combine to form the living creed of a Church of the Martyrs.

The main outcome of the crisis years 165–180 had been the split between this Church on the one hand, and the Church of the Bishops on the other. As time went on, Montanism took on more and more the character of a revolt, the prophetic and eschatological religion of the native countryside against the Hellenized Christianity of the towns. However, so long as Christianity was confined to one culture and one language, namely Greek, it was possible for one or the other side to gain a decisive victory. In Asia the bishops held the whip hand. With the emergence, however, of the Latin Church with the Martyrs of Scilli in 180, and its rapid acceptance of the rigorist view of the world and its responsibilities towards it, a new situation arose. From now on the two rival interpretations of Christianity were to have entrenched support in the Latin and Greek halves of Christendom.

NOTES

[1] I have accepted the dating of 165–168 of Eusebius, iv.15 and *Chron. Paschale* (sub Olymp., 235) now adopted by von Campenhausen, Telfer and Marrou. See my note on the subject in the Catania University Festschrift in honour of the opening of the Second Ecumenical Council published in *Oikoumene*, 499–506.

[2] Eusebius, *H.E.*, v.1.1.

[3] καινὰ δόγματα, Melito of Sardes, ap. Eusebius, *H.E.*, iv.26.5. Denunciations were still not encouraged. Athenagoras, *Legatio* 3, states that 'informations against us were forbidden', but they happened all too frequently, ibid., 1. M. Sordi, 'I "nuovi decreti" di Marco Aurelio contro i cristiani', *Studi Romani* 9, 1961, 365ff. draws attention to the grouping of the martyrs of the reign into the years 163–7 and 176–8 respectively, and R. M. Grant, 'The Chronology of the Greek Apologists', *Vig. Christ.* ix.1, 1955, 27ff. suggests that the 'new decrees' against the Christians may have been occasioned by the revolt of Avidius Cassius in 175. The Christian (?) writer of Sibylline ix saw in Marcus the 'Beast' of Rev. 13 and Cassius as legitimate ruler. The Emperor was in Asia in 176, and this could have provided an occasion for both Melito's and Athenagoras' works.

[4] *Meditations*, xii.28.

[5] Dio Cassius, 72.34.25.

[6] Ammianus Marcellinus, xxv.4.17.

δι βόες οἱ λευκοὶ μάρκῳ τῷ καίσαρι χαίρειν.

ἄν πάλι νικήσῃς, ἄμμες ἀπωλόμεθα.

[7] *Digest*, xlviii.19.30 (Modestinus). See J. Beaujeu, *La réligion romaine*, 349ff.

[8] Ammianus Marcellinus, xxii.5.5.

[9] *Meditations*, xi.3.

[10] See Celsus, for instance, Origen, *Contra Celsum*, viii.54. Christians 'offering their bodies to be tortured and crucified to no purpose'.

[11] Aristides, *Oratio* 33.6 (Keil, ii.229), 48.38–39, (Keil, ii. 402–3) and 50.9 (Keil, ii.428). See J. F. Gilliam's interesting art. in *AJP.*, lxxxii, 1961, 225–51 on the relative severity of the plague.

[12] *C.I.G.*, 3165, a dedication praising the god of the River Meles near Smyrna for 'deliverance from pestilence and evil', but as Gilliam points out, there is nothing to connect this inscription specifically with the reign of Marcus Aurelius (though the epigraphy would argue against any much later date).

[13] *H.E.*, iv.26.5. 'τὸ γὰρ οὐδεπώποτε γενομένον . . .'

[14] Also in Syria, Theophilus, *Ad. Autolycum*, iii.4.

[15] *H.E.*, iv.15.6.

[16] Ibid., v.i.7–8.

[17] *Contra Celsum*, viii.69.

[18] Ibid., viii.54.

[18a] Eusebius, *H.E.*, iv. 23.5.

[19] Rev. 3⁷⁻¹³. See W. M. Calder, 'Philadelphia and Montanism', *Bull. of John Rylands Library*, vii, 1923, 309–54.

[20] Eusebius, *H.E.*, iv.15.6.

[21] The fundamental study of Polycarp's martyrdom has been made by H. v. Campenhausen, 'Bearbeitungen und Interpolationen des Polykarpmartyriums', in *Sitzungsber. der Heidelberger Akad. der Wiss.*, Ph. Hist. Kl., 1957, 3 Abh. 1–48. v. Campenhausen believes that before the final text of the *Acta*, preserved under the name of Pseudo-Pionius, had been compiled, these had been drastically edited in an anti-Montanist and anti-rigorist sense, in order to portray Polycarp's martyrdom as a model death in accordance with the Gospels. He considers that the account preserved in Eusebius, *H.E.*, iv.15 which lacks the emphatic analogies between Christ's Passion and Polycarp's death is, with some modifica-

tions, the older and more reliable text. I have accepted this view with some reservations, particularly regarding the date of the 'Evangelion Redaktor' which seems to fit a third-century rather than fourth-century situation (see my review of v. Campenhausen, *JTS.*, N.S. ix.2, Oct. 1958, 370–3). For the older view, H. Delehaye, *Les Passions des Martyrs*, 11–59. Detailed and somewhat dramatic account of events, P. Allard, *Les Persécutions*, 296–313.

[22] Eusebius, *H.E.*, iv.15.15.

[23] Ibid., 18–24.

[24] Cf. Theophilus, *Ad Autolycum*, 1.11. 'Why do you not worship the emperor?' (*P.G.*, 6, 1041A).

[25] Eusebius, *H.E.*, iv.15.18–24.

[26] The role of the herald on such occasions is neatly described by Apuleius, *Florid*, 1.9. 'Praeco plerumque contentissime clamitat: enimvero ipse Proconsul moderata voce et sedens loquitur.'

[27] J. Parkes, *Conflict*, 136. At the same time, the taunt of 'teacher' and 'father of the Christians' would come quite naturally to Jewish lips, accustomed to their own rabbis and 'fathers of the Jews'.

[28] Eusebius, *H.E.*, iv.15.29.

[29] Ibid., 15.41. As at Lyons, the Christians would have had a right to claim the bodies of the victims. *Digest*, xlviii.24.1 (Ulpian).

[30] J. Parkes, art., 'The Jewish attitude to Early Christianity', *Jewish Chronicle*, 4 Aug. 1961, p. 17.

[31] Eusebius, *H.E.*, iv.26.3.

[32] The edition used is that of Knopf and Krüger, *Ausgewählte Martyrerakten*, 7–13, for bibliography q.v. The *Acta* are not easy to use. It has been recognized long ago by J. de Guibert (*Rev. des Questions historiques*, 83, 1908, 5ff.), that the scene could be the Decian persecution, for only then are προστάγματα τῶν 'Αυγούστων commanding sacrifice by the provincials known (c.4), but the language of the remainder, together with Agathonike's voluntary martyrdom, fit the situation in Marcus Aurelius' reign better. It may be, as Delehaye has suggested (*Les Passions*, 137–41), that the *Acta* though based on the genuine ὑπομνήματα recorded by Eusebius have been re-edited much later. They are used with this reservation.

[33] *Acta*, c.21.

[34] Ibid., 42.

[35] Ibid., 45.

[36] Note the alleged reaction of the women spectators in the amphitheatre at Iconium to the exposure of Thecla to the beasts, though this may have been on purely ethical grounds at her being denied the customary *subligaculum* at her execution (*Acta Pauli et Theclae*, ed. Lipsius, 1891, 264). For the dating of the *Acta* to the end of the second century, and therefore their relevance to a study bf Christianity in Asia at this period, W. Schneemelcher, *N. T. Apokryphen*, ii. 241., and W. M. Ramsay, *The Church in the Roman Empire*, 398.

[37] Athenagoras, *Legatio*, 26: cf. Tatian, *Oratio ad Graecos*, 25. Dating: A. M. Harmon, *Lucian*, v, 24–5.

[38] Lucian, *De Morte Per.*, 12–13.

[39] In Jebb's opinion 'Lucian did not differentiate between Jew and Christian', 'Lucian', *Essays and Addresses*, Cambridge, 1907, 166.

[40] *Nomothetes* is not a N.T. title, but used in Josephus, *Contra Apionem*, ii.18 and ii.15.154, *Antiquities*, 1.3.6.

[41] *De Morte Per.*, 16.

[42] Ibid., 12, cf. *Didascalia*, 19 (ed. Connolly, 161). 'Ye shall not turn away your eyes from a Christian who for the name of God, and for his faith and love is condemned to the games, or to the beasts or to the mines, but of your labour and the sweat of your brow do

THE YEARS OF CRISIS, 165-180 297

you send to him for nourishment and for a payment to the soldiers that guard him that he may have relief and care be taken of him.' Also Aristides, *Apol.*, 15 and Hermas, *Simil.*, v.3.7 for similar injunctions.

⁴³ *De Morte Per.*, 13. For the educated provincial's view of Christianity as primarily a narrow sect, Celsus (Origen, *Contra Celsum*, iii.9), 'If all men wanted to be Christians, the Christians would no longer want them'.

⁴⁴ τὴν θαυμαστὴν σοφιάν (*De Morte Per.*, 11), cf. H. D. Betz, *Lukian von Samosata*, 12.

⁴⁵ Aristides, *Oratio*, 46 (ed. Dindorf, ii.394ff.). See P. de Labriolle, *La Reaction paienne*, 80ff.

⁴⁶ Hippolytus, *Elenchos*, x.18, κυνικώτερος βίος referring to Tatian.

⁴⁷ *Acta Apollonii* (ed. Knopf and Krüger), 33.

⁴⁸ Ibid., 24.

⁴⁹ Lucian, *The Runaways* (ed. Harmon). See S. Dill, *Roman Society*, 350ff.

⁵⁰ Such as Bishops Pius and Callistus of Rome. See C. J. Cadoux, *The Early Church and the World*, 199–200 and 285–6.

⁵¹ *Contra Celsum*, iii.50. An interesting sidelight on the comparative immunity enjoyed by Christian preachers.

⁵² Ibid.; for the Cynics' use of similar public places for harangues, Dio Chrysostom, *Oratio*, 32.9. S. Dill, op. cit., 349.

⁵³ See references in Dill, loc. cit., and *P.W.*, art. 'Diogenes' (44).

⁵⁴ Justin, *2 Apol.*, 3 (end).

⁵⁵ Cf. *Contra Celsum*, 1.2.

⁵⁶ The internal evidence suggests that he was writing somewhere in the broad area between Alexandria and Antioch (*Contra Celsum*, vii.2 and 9). He knows the religious situation in Phoenicia and Palestine personally and here his work was being read 70 years later. Though the variegated Gnostic sects which he mentions could be found in Rome and perhaps in some of the larger towns in Asia, they seem more like the society which Origen describes in Alexandria during his youth. There one would find also the intensive Jewish-Christian controversy which Celsus utilizes against the Christians, the Judaeo-Christian works which he knows, and also the Logos-theology of Hellenistic-Judaism. Then, as Chadwick has pointed out, the curious description of the Mithraic mystery of the ladder with seven gates corresponding to the seven planets, and his explanation of it by means of musical theories could be related to Alexandrian neo-Pythagorean doctrines of the harmony of the spheres. The patriotism which Celsus displays was not by any means confined to the city of Rome. It was by now the common sentiment of most of the vocal elements among the provincial middle classes in the East. There is nothing positive to suggest an area other than Alexandria-Antioch as the scene of Celsus' work. For literature on Celsus, see H. Chadwick, 'Origen, *Contra Celsum*', pp. xxxv–xl. Origen himself thought that Celsus was an Epicurean (*Contra Celsum*, 1.8), and Theodor Keim (*Celsus' Wahres Wort*, Zurich, 1873, 275–93), would identify him with the Celsus for whom Lucian wrote *Alexander the False Prophet*. But this does not fit the writer of *Alethes Logos*. As Chadwick, op. cit., xxvi, says, Celsus' philosophy is that of an eclectic Platonist, and his affinities are with Middle Platonists, such as Albinus. His identity must remain therefore, unknown.

⁵⁷ See K. J. Neumann, art. 'Kelsos', *R.E.*, 1897, 774.

⁵⁸ *Contra Celsum*, v.54 and 62; cf. vi.52–3; and 74.

⁵⁹ *Contra Celsum*, v.62–3.

⁶⁰ Ibid., vi.22–5.

⁶¹ Ibid., iii.44, 50–5, vi.14.

⁶² Ibid., iii.73.

⁶³ See the brief but excellent summary by E. Barnikol, 'Celsus und Origenes', *T.U.* 77, 1961, 124–7.

⁶⁴ *Contra Celsum*, viii.49 and 63.

65 Ibid., 1.14, and vi.9–10. On the Chaldaeans and Indians, vi.80.

66 See Justin, *1 Apol.*, 23 and 46.

67 Eusebius, *H.E.*, 1.4.15.

68 See *Contra Celsum*, iv.99. 'Accordingly, all things have not been made for man, any more than for the lion, or the eagle, or the dolphin, but so that this world, as God's work, may be made complete and perfect in all its parts', cf. iv.78.

69 *Contra Celsum*, v.25–6; cf. C. Andresen, 'Logos und Nomos', *Arbeiten zur Kirchengeschichte*, 30, Berlin, 1955, 308ff.

70 *Contra Celsum*, viii.35, and v. 32.

71 Ibid., vi.78.

72 Ibid., ii.1 and 4.

73 Ibid., v.25.

74 Ibid., viii.69.

75 Ibid., iii.5. 'στασιάζεν πρὸς τὸ κοινόν'.

76 Ibid., viii.72; as claimed by Tatian, *Oratio ad Graecos*, 28.

77 *Contra Celsum*, viii.62, 63.

78 Ibid., viii.67.

79 Ibid., viii.73.

80 Ibid., viii.72.

81 Ibid., 1.48; cf. 1.42 (end).

82 Ibid., v.59.

83 Ibid., iii.1.

84 Ibid., iii.26; cf; P. de Labriolle, *La Réaction païenne*, 119.

85 *Contra Celsum*, ii *passim*. Also v.33 'I will ask them where they come from, and who is the author of their traditional laws. Nobody, they will say. In fact, they themselves originated from Judaism, and they cannot name any other source for their teacher and chorus-leader. Nevertheless, they rebelled against the Jews': cf. v.41,59 and 61.

86 *Contra Celsum*, v.41. Note also Julian's reproach; the Christians ἀπολιπόντες τὰ πάτρια for the sake of a novel cult,—(*Adversus Christianos*, ed. Neumann, 207); also Porphyry, *Letter to Marcella*, 18. Cf. below, Ch. XV, n. 73.

87 See M. Simon, 'Christianisme antique et pensée païenne: Rencontres et Conflits', *Bull. de la Faculté des Lettres à Strasbourg*, 38, 1960, 314–15.

88 *Contra Celsum*, vi.64.

89 Ibid.

90 Ibid., iv.2.

91 Ibid., iv.18; cf. iv.14.

92 Ibid., iv.5.

93 Ibid., iv.11, and v.14.

94 Ibid., iv.5.

95 Ibid., iv.43.

96 Ibid., vii.13.

97 Ibid., iv.10; cf. iii.52.

98 Ibid., iv.23.

99 Ibid., 1.9; cf. iii.44 and 59.

100 Ibid., v.63.

101 Ibid., iii.52, cf. iii.44. 'Their injunctions are like this. "Let no one educated, no one wise, no one sensible draw near, for these abilities are taught by us to be evils. But as for ignorant, anyone stupid, anyone uneducated, anyone who is a child, let him come boldly".' Also 1.9.

102 Ibid., iii.55.

103 For the importance of the women in converting educated households to Christianity even in the late-fourth-century, Libanius, *Ep.*, 1057 'When men are out of doors

they listen to your plea for the only right course and they come to the altars. But when a man gets home, his wife and her tears and the night plead otherwise, and draw him away from the altars' (cited from B. J. Kidd, *Documents*, ii, no. 102).

[104] Three-year catechumenate, Hippolytus, *Apostolic Tradition*, 17 (ed. Easton, p. 43). At Elvira (A.D. 309) the period was still 2 years. Canon 42. Also the general encratite tradition which discouraged the baptized Christian from marriage would tend to discourage conversions.

[105] *Clementine Homilies* (Ante-Nicene Lib., xvii) iv.7–8. I accept the view that these are of Syrian or perhaps even Judaeo-Christian Palestinian origin.

[106] *Clementine Homilies*, iv.11; cf. Clement, *Protrepticus*, x.89.

[107] See the author's 'A third century Inscription relating to *angareia* in Phrygia', *JRS.*, xlvi, 1956, 56.

[108] *Contra Celsum*, vi.12; cf. Galen, *De Pulsuum Differentiis* (cited from R. Walzer, *Galen on Jews and Christians*, 14).

[109] Tatian, *Oratio ad Graecos*, 33; cf. J. Leipoldt, *Die Frauen*, 157.

[110] See G. Bardy, *La Conversion au Christianisme durant les premiers siècles*, Aubier, 1949, 221ff. Moreover, it was generally recognized that such converts were permanently lost to the old tradition. See the fragment of Porphyry quoted in *De Civitate Dei*, xix.23. The reply of Apollo to an inquirer, 'Forte magis poteris in aqua impressis litteris scribere aut adinflans leves pinnas per aera avis volare, quam pollutae revoces impiae uxoris sensum'.

[111] In *P.G.*, 6, 1169–80. See A. Puech, *Histoire de la Littérature grecque chrétienne*, Paris, 1928–30, ii, 225–6.

[112] *Oratio*, 26, 27 and 29 (ed. E. Schwartz, *T.U.*, iv.1, 1888). See M. Elze, *Tatian und seine Theologie*, Göttingen, 1960, ch. iii.

[113] *Oratio*, 19; cf. 32 on free education for poor Christians. For a similar complaint, Hermias, *Irrisio*, 2.

[114] *Dating*, Elze, op. cit., 42, R. M. Grant, 'The Date of Tatian's Oration'; *HTR.*, 46, 1953, 99–101, prefers *circa* 178.

[115] *Oratio*, 1.

[116] Ibid., 2.

[117] Ibid., 2, cf. 25. Elze, op. cit., 25ff. Tatian, unlike Justin, does not identify 'barbarian' with Jewish, but with all that did not belong to contemporary Hellenized culture.

[118] A. Puech, *Histoire de la Littérature grecque chrétienne*, ii.225–6.

[119] *Oratio*, 35.

[120] Ibid., 28.

[121] See R. A. Knox's note in *Enthusiasm*, Oxford, 1950, 42.

[122] For the dating of Miltiades, Athenagoras, Melito, Apollinaris of Hierapolis, Tatian and Theophilus between 175–85, R. M. Grant, 'The Chronology of the Greek Apologists', *Vigil. Christ.*, ix.1, 1955, 25–33. Miltiades, however, may be slightly earlier. Tertullian, *Adv. Valentinianos*, 5, places him between Justin and Irenaeus. He could therefore be writing any time after 165.

[123] *Legatio*, 1–3.

[124] Ibid., 2.

[125] Ibid., 37. Cf. Theophilus of Antioch, *Ad Autolycum*, 1,11, 'Indeed, I honour the emperor, not worshipping him but praying for him', and Justin already cited, *1 Apol.*, 17.

[126] *Legatio*, 6.

[127] *Legatio*, 28.

[128] Ibid., 37.

[129] A. Puech, *Histoire de la Littérature grecque chrétienne*, ii.191–3.

[130] *Chronicon Paschale* (Olymp., 236) *P.G.*, xcii.632A; Puech, op. cit., 191.

[131] Eusebius, *H.E.*, iv.26.10.

[132] Eusebius, *H.E.*, v.18.13 and 24.4. Dating of 27 October is from the Syrian Martyrology. An alternative date of Thraseas' death, 27 October 165 or earlier, is proposed by Lawlor and Oulton, *Eusebius*, ii.186. This depends on whether one places the outbreak of Montanism *circa* 157 or *circa* 172, because the martyrdom of Thraseas is mentioned by the anti-Montanist author Apollonius as being contemporary with early efforts to suppress the movement (*H.E.*, v.18.13). However, the statement of *H.E.*, v.24.5, that Thraseas' 'sleeps in Smyrna' suggests that he was martyred there. Since Evarestus does not mention him in connection with Polycarp, it would seem that his death occurred after the latter's. If Polycarp's martyrdom were placed 166–167, then Thraseas' death could be placed *circa* 176–177, as the result of the severe local pogroms of this period to which Eusebius (*H.E.*, v.1.1) refers.

[133] *H.E.*, v.16.22. The date must be towards the end of the reign, as the martyrs refused to associate with Montanist confessors.

[134] Ibid., v.16.20.

[135] *Oratio*, 6.

[136] *H.E.*, v.16.12.

[137] Ed. Campbell Bonner, Michigan, 1940, pp. 18–20 and 135ff., especially p. 153.

[138] The tone of Theophilus of Antioch, *Ad Autolycum* is perhaps slight evidence to the contrary, but it stands alone.

[139] P. Nautin, *Lettres et Ecrivains chrétiens*, chs. i and ii. Also, P. de Labriolle, *La Crise Montaniste*, 148–9, and *Acta Pauli* for the same tendency.

[140] Eusebius, *H.E.*, iv.15.6, regarding Germanicus is a good example.

[141] H. von Campenhausen, art. cit., 20, 'eine tendenziöse antimontanistische Interpolation des dritten oder schon des späteren zweiten Jahrhunderts'.

[142] Cf. *H.E.*, iv.15.14. Polycarp a 'venerable and godlike old man'.

[143] *H.E.*, iv.15.10.

[144] Ibid., 15.40.

[145] Ibid, 15.39. For the reading, 'Holy', Lightfoot, *Ignatius*, 1.2, 606.

[146] *Acta Carpi*, 36; cf. *Acta Pionii*, 21.1.

[147] Ibid., 38–9.

[148] Ibid., 41.

[149] See R. Reitzentstein, 'Die Nachrichten über den Tod Cyprians', *Sitzungsber. der Heidelberger Akad. der Wiss.*, Phil. Hist. Kl., 1914, 3, and *Göttingen Nachritchten*, 1914, 85–92.

[150] The most important collection of source material is still N. Bonwetsch, 'Texte zur Geschichte des Montanismus' (Lietzmann's *Kleine Texte*, no. 129, 1941). Also, the collection of Montanist 'Oracles' assembled by P. de Labriolle, *La Crise Montaniste*, 1913, ch. ii.

[151] W. M. Calder, 'Philadelphia and Montanism', *Bull. of John Rylands Library*, vii, 1923, 324.

[152] *Dating*: He wrote thirteen years after the death of Maximilla, which can hardly be placed later than the end of Marcus Aurelius' reign. Avircius Marcellus must have died before 216 when his epitaph was copied for Alexander, Bishop of Hierapolis in the Phrygian Pentapolis (Ramsay, *Cities and Bishoprics*, 722ff.). This leaves a fairly wide bracket, but the end of Commodus' reign when the Church was certainly enjoying peace in Asia seems reasonable.

[153] Eusebius, *H.E.*, v.16.6.7. See Lawlor and Oulton's note, *Eusebius*, ii.171–2 on the 'Anonymous' and the dating of his treatise to Aviricius.

[154] Eusebius, *H.E.*, v.17.1, citing the title of Alcibiades' anti-Montanist tract, 'περὶ τοῦ μὴ δεῖν προφήτην ἐν ἐκστάσει λαλεῖν. For Montanism as a challenge to the hardening of institutional control of the Church in Asia. S. L. Greenslade, *Schism in the Early Church*, 109.

[155] Optatus of Milevis, *De Schismate*, 1.16.

156 The inference from Jerome's statement (*Ep.* 41.4), that Montanus had been 'abscisum et semivirum habuisse', as customary among the priests of Cybele.

157 Strabo, xi.4.7, 'ἐνθουσιῶσι πολλοί καὶ προφητεύουσι. Strabo visited temples in Phrygia, Pontus and Cappadocia.

158 Cited from W. Schepelern, *Der Montanismus und die phrygischen Kulte*, Tübingen, 1929, 98 and 196.

159 W. Schepelern, *Der Montanismus*, 95ff.

160 See the author's *The Donatist Church*, 98ff.

161 Note for instance Socrates' statement giving a fifth-century view. *Eccl. Hist.*, iv.28, that among the Phrygians and Paphlagonians 'neither the sports of the circus nor the theatre were held in much esteem'. For the association of Montanism with native Phrygian language and culture K. Holl, 'Das Fortleben der Volksprachen in Klein-Asien in der nachchristlicher Zeit', *Hermes*, xliii, 1908, 240–54.

162 Eusebius, *H.E.*, v.17.3. See also, H. Bacht, 'Die prophetische Inspiration in der kirchlichen Reflexion der vormontanistischer Zeit', *Rom. Quartalschrift*, Scholastik, Heft 1, 1944, 1–18.

163 Eusebius, *H.E.*, v.24.4.

164 N. Bonwetsch, *Die Geschichte des Montanismus*, Erlangen, 1881, 153–4.

165 The importance of the women in the movement may be understood by the fact that Hippolytus, *Elenchos*, viii.19 appears to give Maximilla and Priscilla precedence over Montanus, and Origen (in *1 Cor xiv. 34*, ed. Cramer, *Catena*, p. 279) mentions them but not Montanus.

166 See the 'Montanist Oracles' collected by de Labriolle, *La Crise Montaniste*, ch. ii, especially nos. 1–3 and 13.

167 Eusebius, *H.E.*, v.16.18.

168 Ibid., 16.20.

169 Ibid., 18.6, a prominent Montanist honoured 'ὡς δὴ μαρτύρων.'

170 Eusebius, *H.E.*, v.18.5 and 7. P. de Labriolle, op. cit., 123–6.

171 Tertullian, *De Fuga*, 9.

172 *De Fuga*, 9. See P. de Labriolle, *La Crise Montaniste*, 50–4.

173 Eusebius, *H.E.*, v.18.2, Epiphanius, *Panarion*, xlviii.14.1. 'τόπον τινὰ ἔρημον'.

174 Epiphanius, *Panarion*, xlviii.2.4. 'μετ''ἐμὲ προφῆτης οὐκέτι ἔσται, ἀλλὰ συντέλεια.'

175 Jerome, *Ep.*, 41.3 refers to the κοινωναι as the rank following the Patriarch of Pepuza in seniority in the Montanist hierarchy. The term is also used in *Cod Just.*, 1.5.20. The controversy over the interpretation of this title (see P. de Labriolle, op. cit., 497ff.) has now been brought to a close by the discovery of the inscription of Bayam Alan Ciftlǧi in which the 'holy Paulinus' is termed[μο]ίστης καὶ κοινωνός. W. M. Calder, *Anatolian Studies*, 1955, 5, p. 37.

176 Epiphanius, *Panarion*, xlix.2.2, Also, Augustine, *De Haeresibus*, 27 (women ministers among the 'Pepuziani and Quintilliani'). A πρωτοδιακόνος is recorded on an inscription from Bekilli, W. M. Calder, *Byzantion*, vi.1931, 421.

177 Theodotus and his trances—Eusebius, *H.E.*, v.16.14. Also, Themiso who claimed to be a confessor and composed a 'catholic epistle', ibid., 18.5.

178 From Eusebius' second anti-Montanist sources, Apollonius, writing *circa* 210, i.e. second-generation Montansim, *H.E.*, v.18.2. Also, Hippolytus, *Elenchos*, viii.19—'dry fasts' and 'radish fasts'.

179 *ILCV.*, 1003 (Carthage).

180 *De Exhort. Castitatis*, 10.

181 *Contra Celsum*, vii.9 (Chadwick, p. 402, cites relevant literature).

182 *Legatio*, 33.

183 Ibid., 7 and 9. The prophet was the flute and the Holy Spirit the flute-player—as the Montanists claimed.

[184] Tertullian, *Ad Scapulam*, 5.1, citing a Greek text. On Arrius Antoninus, see Lampridius, *Commodus*, 7.1. An interesting parallel was provided in Cambridge by young members of the C.N.D. in Nov. 1961. Six of these arrived at the city police station and demanded to be put under arrest. By a coincidence the Senior Proctor was also there, and asked the customary question 'Your name and College, Sir?' This was refused (also in true early Christian style). Then 'the Tutors were sent for'. History does not relate the sequel. From *The Times*, 9 Nov. 1961.

[185] Eusebius, *H.E.*, v.18–19. P. de Labriolle, op. cit., 150ff.

[186] Eusebius, *H.E.*, v.16.3–4

[187] Note the scornful tone of the Anonymous' rejection of Maximilla's prophecies of doom. Eusebius, *H.E.*, v.16.19.

[188] Eusebius, *H.E.*, v.16.17. 'I am driven away like a wolf from the sheep. I am not a wolf. I am word and spirit and power' (Maximilla).

[189] Eusebius, *H.E.*, v.16–19 gives a good summary, drawn from the Anonymous, and Apollonius of Hierapolis writing *circa* 210 of the gradual wearing down of the Montanists in the cities of Asia. Archaeology, however, tells a quite different story for the countryside.

[190] Ibid., v.16.3.

[191] Epiphanius, *Panarion*, li.33.

[192] Jerome, *Ep.*, 41, Epiphanius, *Panarion*, xlviii, and Sozomen, *Hist. Eccl.*, ii.32 for Montanism in the late fourth-century; the sect still existed in the reign of Leo III, *circa* 720, and is referred to by John of Damascus, *Haer.*, xlix, *circa* 750.

[193] Sozomen, *H.E.*, ii.32, 'great numbers of Montanists in Phrygia'. Distribution, W. M. Calder, *Philadelphia and Montanism*.

[194] Montanist and Novatianist village sees, Sozomen, *H.E.*, vii.19.

[195] Clement, *Stromata*, iv.13.93.1, and vii.108. Muratorian Fragment, *circa* 200, the Montanists are called 'Cataphrygum' (ed. H. Lietzmann, *Kleine Texte*, I, 1933, 11); cf. Hippolytus, *Elenchos*, x.25.

[196] Epiphanius, *Panarion*, l, Sozomen, *H.E.*, vii.18.12–14. P. de Labriolle, op. cit., 514–18. Epiphanius means to imply that the 'Quartodecimans' were a branch of Montanists, whose Judaic proclivities they emphasized by keeping the entire Deuteronomic Law (*Panarion*, l.2.1–3).

[197] For explicit Jewish recognition of the virtue of observing a once-married state, *CIJ.*, 541 (Porto) 'Ρουφειναι| μονανδρου| τη φιλοτεκνοων', and see P. Maas, *Theol. Lit. Zeitung.*, 1922, 311 discussing the *Protogamia* inscription from Carthage (*ILCV.*, 1003).

[198] Pseudo-Tertullian, *Adv. Haer.*, 8. Note also the career of Blastus who seems to have been a Roman Montanist, but was also regarded as a 'judaizer'. He was an opponent of the Roman presbyter Gaius and leader of the pro-14 Nisan group among the Roman Christians from Asia (Eusebius, *H.E.*, v.15 and 21), Pseudo-Tertullian, loc. cit. For the tendencies even in the late fourth century for Phrygians and Galatians to keep the Passover, Socrates, *H.E.*, v.21.

CHAPTER ELEVEN

The Turn of the Tide, 180–235

IN the twenty years that followed the death of Marcus Aurelius, the achievement of the primitive Greek-speaking Church reached its climax. Its unitary character, expressed through a common language, and, generally speaking, through common traditions derived from the Hellenistic synagogue, had been proof against the pogroms of Marcus' reign and also against Gnosticism and Montanism. It was not only the great sees such as Rome, Antioch and Corinth which maintained regular contact with one another, but less important centres, such as Knossos or Amastris produced prominent leaders who had something to add to the collective life of the Church.[1] By 180, a Rule of Faith existed and was accepted by 'the great Church' whether in Gaul, Rome, Asia Minor and apparently at Nisibis on the eastern extremity of the Greco-Roman world. Irenaeus could write with some confidence that the tradition of the Church was the same whether Christians dwelt in Germany, Gaul or in his native Asia Minor.[2] Travellers, such as the Palestinian Hegesippus[3] or the Phrygian merchant Avircius Marcellus[4] said the same. If the canon of Scripture had still to undergo some minor modifications, the four Gospels were accepted as the authoritative life of Christ, and the Pauline epistles as an equally authoritative interpretation to the Christian world. The Church in 180 was probably more united than it ever has been before or since.

Moreover, the 'sojourn' of the second-century Christian community was becoming a permanent stay. The bishop, presiding over each of the larger communities, not only contributed to the cohesion of his flock, but in some measure guaranteed the unity of the Church as a whole. The day of the prophet had come and gone. Quite suddenly, within a year or so around A.D. 190, the great bishoprics of the Hellenistic Church emerged into the full light of day. In 189, Demetrius became the first bishop of Alexandria of whom we know anything certain, and he was to rule the see for the next forty-two years. In 190, Serapion began a twenty-year rule at Antioch. In Rome, Popes Victor and Zephyrinus were to span a stretch of twenty-eight years (189–217) between them. But with Victor a new era opened for the Roman Christians. He was an African, and spoke Latin. His handling of the Easter controversy and of the Montanists was to show that the predominance of the Asiatic Christians in the Roman Church was also passing.[5]

Meantime, the Church was expanding. In 180, the ordinary provincial would still have followed Celsus and regarded it as a dangerous sort of Judaistic sect. In 235 the danger remained but the Judaism was less evident. Despite the ceaseless nagging of the Old Israel, Christianity had become one of the main religions of the Roman Empire. 'Everywhere', as Avircius Marcellus stated, 'I found brothers in the faith', and he partook of 'the mixed cup with bread' (l.15) wherever he went.[6] 'Rome to Osrhoene' was a reality in the Christian world,[7] and it became more so in the early decades of the third century as numbers grew, property in the form of buildings and cemeteries increased, and the Church's corporate rights achieved greater respect. With the important exception of the years 202–203 it was called upon to meet no widespread persecution. In North Africa, however, its comparatively sudden emergence in the last two decades of the second century evoked the same bitter reaction that had struck the Church in Asia less than a generation before. While the rest of the Church remained at peace, the African Christians were subjected to a series of ferocious assaults in the period 195–215. But nowhere did respect win popularity. It needed only an ill-disposed provincial governor, or a local disaster for the populace to raise once more the cry of 'Christians to the lion'.[8]

The rivals of Christianity were prospering also. This was the classic age for religious syncretism in the Greco-Roman world. The period of the Severi (193–235) saw devotion to the Imperial cult undiminished either in the capital or the provinces, accompanied by the prosperity of local cults, and the maximum extension of the Mithraic and Pythagorean mysteries. 'Gaul to Osrhoene' applied to them also, and beyond, for the Church could boast no blossoming of support equal to the fifteen Mithraea that flourished at Ostia alone,[9] and no advance to the foggy dampness of the northern frontier, as instanced by the Persian god's shrines at Carrawburgh[10] and Housesteads on the Wall.[11] At Ostia, moreover, the shrines were scattered about every part of the city, and had been built by patricians and freedmen alike.[12] There was no 'Mithraic quarter' like the Jewish and Christian quarter at Dura. The synthesis offered by the cult corresponded to the outlook of the day. The Mithraic shrine was hospitable and it would often contain dedications to other deities; to Serapis, to Cybele, Mercury, Bacchus and Heracles.[13] These also were manifestations of the powers of light. For with peace, ease of communications and progressive standardization of material tastes went standardization of religious life also. As Celsus had written in *circa* 178, 'I therefore think that it makes no difference whether we call Zeus the Most High, or Zen, or Adonai, or Sabaoth, or Ammon like the Egyptians, or Papaeus like the Scythians'.[14] In this Celsus was speaking for the provincials as a whole. Gradually, all the major local deities were becoming merged into aspects of a single divine power, manifested to humanity as the God of Light, with whom the Emperor himself might be associated and whose celestial excellence he must imitate. The Constantinian coin-type SOLI INVICTO COMITI was the outcome of a century of religious development.[15]

In this pattern Christianity was no longer an isolated and barbarian creed. The charges of 'diabolic imitation' levelled by Justin[16] and Tertullian against Mithraism[17] are evidence that both religions promised salvation from the powers of fate and evil by the same methods, namely the sacrifice of a victorious saviour through whose teaching and through whose blood mankind would be saved. Mithras was also 'life to wandering men'.[18] The walls of the Santa Prisca Mithraeum (late second and early third century) at Rome show a painting with a ritual meal of bread and wine in progress,[19] and the congregation sang or recited hymns exalting the prophetic and saving power of the god.[20] Like Jesus, Hermes Trismegistos could also be represented as guide and instructor of the soul,[21] Attis as 'Good Shepherd',[22] while Heracles symbolized the salvation of mankind by the overthrow of evil powers,[23] and the myth of Ulysses the quest of the instructed soul for bliss and immortality.[24]

Religious life in the early third century was moving along

similar paths towards similar ends, but in this encounter Christianity had advantages. First, the Christian Saviour was not just the reality behind a myth, but an historical personage, who 'truly ate and drank', and 'truly suffered under Pontius Pilate'. Christians could claim that Jesus was the true Orpheus, the true Good Shepherd of current portraiture and the true Wise Man in the Ulysses saga.[25] Moreover, as the prosperity of the era waned after 235, the Christian could claim with greater conviction that the pagan gods, even the great provincial deities, were malevolent 'demons', or alternately, useless 'dumb idols' unable to aid their worshippers. Increasingly too, the Christian's willingness to die for his creed, and his uncompromising opposition to the obvious evils of a materialist and uncreative society won support. The Church strengthened its role as focus for much of the latent discontent in the provinces. In this period, perhaps more than in any other, 'the blood of martyrs' was 'seed'.[26]

One instance of this kaleidoscopic religious scene may be recorded. Dura Europos, on the Euphrates frontier, was an area where Christianity was comparatively strong, and where all the evidence was sealed by the fall of the city to the Persians probably in 255/256.[27] Thereafter the site was abandoned, and was a deserted spot when Julian led his army past it in 363.[28] Thus the excavations have revealed a case history of third-century life and thought in the eastern Roman world. We find Judaism established and Christianity beginning to make its presence felt in the community.

The first thing that strikes one is the reality of the Roman gods and the Imperial cult, at least in so far as the garrison and its dependants were concerned. Among documents found in the temple of Artemis Azzanathkona, belonging to the records of the *cohors XX Palmyrenorum* was a fragment of the *Feriale* in use by the garrison between 224/225 and 235.[29] It records the official round of religious ceremonies, and the outstanding importance of the Imperial cult is shown by the proportion of entries relating to it, amounting to no less than 27 out of 41 extant on the papyrus.[30] While the celebration of the various *dies imperii* and ordinary public festivals, such as the *natalis urbis Romae aeternae* on 23 April, or *Mars pater ultor* on 12 May, would be expected, it is almost grotesque to find local troops on the Euphrates commemorating the ancient ceremonies of the Roman people, like the Quinquatria or Neptunalia.[31] But they did so. It was part of the process of self-Romanization as well as 'breaks in the monotonous routine of military life'.[32] 'Men given citizenship were *Romani facti*, and expected to act as such'.[33] The scandal caused by the Ordnance N.C.O. at Lambaesis who refused to wear the customary laurel crown or perform *turificatio* on the occasion of an Imperial donative in 211, on the grounds that he was a Christian,[34] shows what this status demanded.

Observances of the cult of Roman deities included in the *Feriale* did not discourage participation in other, local rites. Senior army officers and their families have left their mark to posterity by their dedications to Jupiter Dolichenus and other even more local deities.[35] The temple of Bel contained the splendid paintings of the tribune Terentius and his standard-bearer, with two rows of members of his cohort offering to three Palmyrene gods.[36] Elsewhere, a graffito shows an officer offering incense to the Palmyrene solar deity Jahribol, and a standard-bearer (without standard) doing likewise.[37]

Such acts typify the brightly varied religious scene which would confront any visitor to Dura in the first half of the third century. Every group and tradition in the city seems to have had its temple. The old Seleucid connection was represented by the aristocratic priesthoods of Zeus and Apollo,[38] and the temple of Artemis-Nanaia.[39] Parthian influence is recognizable in the temple of Aphlad, built in A.D. 54 as the shrine of an association perhaps of a group of foreign immigants.[40] But as one would expect, the sources of religious inspiration were now Syria and Babylon. Temples, even though dedicated to 'Zeus Theos', and 'Adonis', were usually Babylonian in style, built round a central courtyard containing an altar, and enclosed by elaborate precincts and side-chapels housing statues of the god, their oriental appearance modified by the use of Hellenistic-Doric columns.[41] Along with these greater temples were shrines dedicated to oriental gods, such as the Palmyrene Gadde frequented by Palmyrene merchants,[42] or the Syrian Baal-Shamin,[43] and Phoenician Adonis-Eshmoun.[44] Amid this profusion of Semitic worship the cult of Mithras was represented in the Roman quarter of the city.[45] He was a late-comer, the earliest shrine dating to *circa* 168, but this was twice reconstructed and embellished, the work on the second temple, built *circa* 211 being carried out by military labour. By Dura standards it was, however, a poor building and seems to have been used mainly by members of the garrison. The religious life of the city was concentrated in traditional cults, some of which, like that of Nanaia, now associated with the Seleucid Artemis, went back three millennia of time.[46]

There was no sign of decay or declining influence. The ritual dances to the clash of cymbals and squeal of pipes characteristic of the worship of the female divinities aroused the perplexed astonishment of contemporaries.[47] The religious bent in the minds of the people is demonstrated by the varied repertory of gods and goddesses, their shrines, their sacred symbols, and their sacrifices which bulked so largely among the graffiti found during the excavations.[48] The more intense side of popular piety is displayed in the numerous detailed horoscopes—horoscopes which show no little astronomical knowledge—designed to foretell from the conjunction of the stars and planets at the precise hour of an infant's birth, the individual's destiny.[49]

Finally, and perhaps last in importance, came the Jews and Christians. Their cult-buildings were both found in the same quarter, two blocks away from each other, adjacent to the city wall on the south side of Dura, and both had developed in the early third century from private houses. The synagogue[50] in the time of the Severi was an elaborate building. It had a prayer hall, with a forecourt and precincts extending through a block of private houses, the plan being a group of rooms set round a semi-colonnaded court, similar to an ordinary private house. The entrance, however, had been obscurely placed, 'on an alley leading to a neighbouring house instead of a public street'. In the opinion of the excavators, there were 'indications that the Jewish religion was kept isolated and was not popular among the inhabitants of the city, and it is a fact that the workmen who finally blocked the building with the mud brick of the embankment (built during the siege of 256) contemptuously gouged out the eyes from some of the painted figures'.[51] Perhaps the Jews were known to be sympathetic to the Persian cause, and that the Salvation cycle depicted on the walls at this time may have had contemporary meaning.[52] The area round the synagogue may have been a Jewish quarter, but the community was heterogeneous enough to include in the final phase Parthian, as well as Aramaic-speaking and Greek Jews. They seem, too, to have prospered, for a new building far more ornate in style and deocoration superseded the old on the same site in 245.[53] It lasted a bare ten years.

The story of the Christian church is very similar.[54] Originally, it also had been the house of a private citizen and perhaps a distinguished one, to judge from the size, but nearly all the rooms seem to have served the purposes of the Christian community. The church proper extended along the southern side of the house (away from the street) and consisted of two rooms which were later converted into a single rectangular hall, with a raised platform, perhaps the seat of the bishop or presbyter. On the walls were richly painted scenes from the Old and New Testaments—Adam and Eve, the Good Shepherd, the Healing of the Paralytic, Christ walking on the Water, the Women at the Sepulchre. There was a baptistery, a sacristy which opened from the east end of the church, and another large room to the west of the central court, used perhaps as a sort of catechetical school. Graffiti on the walls ask the faithful 'to keep Christ (in your heart) and remember the humble Siseos',[55] and proclaim the existence of 'One God in the heavens'.[56] An inscription dates the construction of the church to 232/233, and as the excavators point out, there seems at this time to have been no effort to conceal the fact of Christian worship. Indeed, one may perhaps imagine scenes such as those described in the *Clementine Recognitions*, perhaps contemporary with the Dura church, in which Peter seated on a chair raised on a platform taught the crowds of inquirers who visited the 'palace of Theophilus' which had been converted by its owner into a church.[57]

The situation in Dura could be reproduced almost anywhere else in the Roman Empire. In Africa, for instance, we find the same tendencies towards syncretism under the aegis of official or national cults, and toward gnosticism and fatalism in private belief.[58] Here, too, Judaism and Christianity are in the background. In Cappodocia there were small Christian communities which possessed recognizably Christian buildings.[59] The great majority of the people, however, were still devoted to ancestral deities. Even in Britain, some of the best examples of dedications to the local deities, like those to Coccidius and the Dii Veteri on the

Wall, date to the early third century. At the Walbrook Mith-raeum, Mithras had as his associates Mercury and Hermes, the gods of the Roman pantheon.[60]

Indeed, dominating the abounding life of sect and cult stood the official religion of the Roman gods, binding together local and regional patriotism into a single loyalty to the Empire. Temples to Jupiter, Juno and Minerva looked down upon the fora of the provincial cities. In Africa the cult of the Severi themselves was celebrated in new monumental temples such as at Leptis,[61] and Cuicul, the latter built as late as 229.[62] To many—if not the great majority—of provincials the continuance of Rome was personified in the Emperor.[63] It was to the *divina providentia* of Commodus, for instance, that the oppressed *coloni* on the Saltus Burunitanus appealed in 183.[64] He represented their guarantee of security and earthly peace. As ruler of the world he was devout mediator between his subjects and the world of gods. He was *Pius Felix* as well as Augustus.[65] The coin types so common in the Severan and post-Severan period, SALUS AUGUSTI or PIETAS AUGUSTI expressed these beliefs. The FELICI-TAS SAECULI, the return of the Golden Age of Saturn, the gift of Jupiter, was the idea which Commodus and successive emperors in the third century hoped to stamp on the minds of their subjects.[66]

The infinite variety of the religious scene was accompanied by conditions which were indirectly to affect the future relations between Church and Empire. The period 180–235 was in the main an era of internal well-being, perhaps more apparent to those who were enjoying it than to modern historians and economists probing into the causes of the economic collapse of the mid-third century. But with the important exception of the gradual but continuous debasement of the currency by Septimius Severus and his successors, the barometer was Set Fair.[67] Where we have direct evidence of prices, as at Dura, life seems to have been reasonably inexpensive (*Report*, iv.140–3). In Egypt, the Severan age was looked upon 50 years later with nostalgia. There and elsewhere, building activity developed an astonishing momentum despite increased taxation. It is in evidence not only in favoured centres like Leptis, but in out of the way places like Caernarvon where an aqueduct was restored,[68] or Choba, a small port west of

Hippo Regius, where municipal baths were erected.[69] Numerous cities were promoted to municipal and colonial status, and more significant, perhaps, prosperous villages outstripped their bounds and petitioned for higher status.[70]

The civil wars of 193–197 between Septimius Severus and his rivals and the bitter inter-city feuds which accompanied them did not leave deep traces. The latter part of Severus' reign and those of his three successors were on the whole peaceful and secure. On the east, south and north, the expeditions of Severus or his lieutenants had either reduced dangers of invasion or established outposts far into the territory of potential enemies.[71] The feeling of security and well-being was recorded not only on triumphal arches which sprang up in a variety of provincial cities but in the writings of none too friendly Christians. Even in Commodus' reign, Irenaeus comments, 'The world has peace, thanks to the Romans. Even we Christians can walk without fear on the roads and travel withersoever we please' (*Adv. Haer.*, iv.30.3), while Tertullian's paeans of praise in *De Anima*, 30[72] and *De Pallio*, 2.7 stand in stark contrast to his deep-felt antagonism to the civilization which surrounded him.[73]

One important result of continued prosperity was the blurring of the contrasts between Romanized and native in the provinces. Roman Africa provides many examples of the process. With the growth of cities the differences between Roman and Berber tended to die out. One can name Dougga, Uchi Maius, Thuburbo Maius, Masculula and many other sites where the colony of veterans merged with the native community in these years. The latter would gain municipal status, the two *Ordines* would be amalgamated, and their union symbolized perhaps by the erection of a triumphal arch or a common dedication at the Capitol.[74] The native landowners entered the ranks of the senatorial nobility. Great sums were left to provide *alimenta* for children or amusements for adults.[75] Lesser men could rise high in the social scale, and like the ex-foreman of Mactar who became a noted citizen of his own town, were proud to leave memory of their achievements for future generations to read.[76] This movement was also a movement towards Romanization by the adoption of Latin language and usages. Never was Roman Africa more prosperous than in the period 175–240.[77]

The constitutional aspect of these developments was the *Constitutio Antoniniana* of 212. It conceded what had been due for a generation, namely the status of Roman citizen to nearly all free men in the Empire, regardless whether they lived technically in town or village.[78] In fiscal terms it meant that many more should now pay the inheritance tax and, more seriously, become liable to city liturgies, and in terms of religion it was to provide the Roman gods with more worshippers.[79] In this, one can see perhaps the counterpart of Caracalla's dream of uniting all his subjects under the protection of one divinity represented by the Egyptian Serapis.[80] The *Constitutio Antoniniana* may well have been a sudden, vainglorious act, which the Emperor thought worthy of his self-styled role as the new Alexander.[81] In its religious aspect, however, it was of fundamental importance to the Church. Caracalla announced that he was showing his gratitude to the gods of the State for their protection in an hour of danger (the alleged conspiracy of Geta) by bringing them new worshippers on a scale worthy of the divine majesty. The aim was to be a general *supplicatio* of thanks to the immortal gods. Naturally, the new citizens were bound if not to worship, at least to respect these same tutelary gods, and their earthly representative the Roman Emperor.

Participation in the Imperial cult had not been forced on the provincials. So far as concerned the Christians, it had been used as a test to prove or disprove an accused individual's adherence to the Christian sect, and hence his membership of a noxious and illegal organization. Now, however, there was a change of emphasis. Something which was natural to the Roman legionaries and auxiliaries could be required from the population as a whole. Citizenship carried duties as well as rights, including religious duties.[82] Refusal could be construed as treason. A call to sacrifice by all might not happen more than once in a lifetime, but when it did, in 250, the Christians were confronted with a demand they could not escape. The loyalism which would offer prayers for the Emperor's *Salus* was found at variance with an attitude which treated his *Genius* as a demon.[83] The *Constitutio Antoniniana* made general persecution possible.

These new dangers for the Christians were already discernible as a result of the Romanization which had been taking place in the provinces in the previous generation. At Carthage, Tertullian was fully aware, when he wrote his *Apology* in 197, that Christians could find themselves regarded as outside the pale of civilized Roman society. 'Nec Romani habemur, qui non Romanorum deum colimus' (*Apol.*, 24.5). If he had attended any trials of African Christians in the previous decade or so he would have seen that he was correct.

Perhaps on 4 July 180,[84] the Proconsul of Africa, Vigellius Saturninus, ordered the execution at Madaura of a group of native Christians, Namphamo, Miggin, Lucitas and Sanae, in circumstances which are not recorded. According to Tertullian, he was the first Roman administrator in Africa who had taken active measures against the Christians.[85] His victims were remembered long after he had passed into oblivion.[86] A fortnight later, on 17 July, he was in Carthage,[87] and there in his council chamber condemned to death a group of twelve Christians from Scilli (probably near Carthage) for refusal to sacrifice to the gods. From their names, the victims, seven men and five women, seem also to have been drawn from the native, non-citizen element of the population. As at the trial of Justin and his companions in Rome fifteen years before, the hearing consisted mainly of a dialogue between the judge and the spokesman for the accused. Only towards the end of the brief proceedings were the minor characters interrogated. All affirmed their faith, asserted they were law-abiding subjects, but refused a month's grace which was offered them for reconsidering their decision. They went to their deaths with *Deo Gratias* on their lips. There has never been any reason for challenging the authenticity of the *Acta*.

The Proconsul's interrogation contains a feature which is not explicitly found in previous official interrogations of Christians. Throughout the proceedings he shows that there was a clear connection in his mind between the act of swearing by the 'genius of our lord the emperor', and the 'mos Romanorum' to which he tried to persuade the Christians to return. This formed the basis of his own religious outlook.[88] 'Crimen majestatis' in the form both of 'laesae Romanae religionis', and 'titulum laesae augustioris maiestatis',[89] were being added to the previous religious and disciplinary accusations. The accused were well aware of the implications of the Proconsul's cross-examination. Once they had failed to make good their plea that by living exemplary lives they were doing honour to the Emperor, they came out into the open. 'Speratus dixit. Ego imperium huius saeculi non cognosco ... quia cognosco dominum meum, regem regum, et imperatorem omnium gentium.'[90] There was no compromise here. Moreover the reward for rejecting the 'mos Romanorum' was immediate entry into Paradise. 'Hodie martyres in caelis sumus.'[91] This was to be the rallying-cry of African Christians against the Imperial authorities for the next two centuries. The religion of the Book allowed no other conclusion.

There was no immediate sequel to these martyrdoms in Commodus' reign. Indeed, the Proconsuls of Africa seem to have been notably lenient towards the Christians. Tertullian cites two incidents of officials who went out of their way to help Christians who had been denounced to them. Thus, circa 190, at Thysdrus (el-Djem) Cincius Severus secretly informed some believers who had been denounced to him, of a form of words which he would accept as a means of avoiding passing sentence on them.[92] His successor, Vespronius Candidus refused to judge a Christian whom a fanatical mob had haled before him.[93]

In Asia Minor, too, the death of Marcus Aurelius was succeeded by an era of peace. The Anonymous added to the discomfiture of the Montanists by pointing out that since Maximilla had died (circa 179?) thirteen years previously 'there had been in the world neither local nor universal war, but rather, by the mercy of God, continuing peace even for Christians'.[94] It may be in this period that the curious incident took place at Ephesus, when the Proconsul, Aemilius Frontinus actually released a robber, when he claimed that he was a Christian, much to the local Church's disgust.[95] This, however, did not deter those who sought martyrdom, but incidents similar to that in which the Proconsul Arrius Antoninus was involved in 185, were evidently few and far between.

The same comparative peace seems to have descended on the Christian communities in other parts of the Roman world. The horrors of Lyons were not repeated, and Irenaeus was to enjoy an episcopal office for nearly a quarter of a century (178– circa 200). As Eusebius described the period as a whole,

In the reign of Commodus our treatment was changed to a milder one, and by the grace of God peace came on the churches throughout the whole world. The word of salvation began to lead every soul of every race of men to the pious worship of the God of the universe, so that now many of those who at Rome were famous for wealth and family turned to their own salvation with all their house and with all their kin.[96]

Rome provides most information about the improved lot of the Christians at this period. It must seem strange at first sight, that the bloodthirsty individual who fought no less than 735 combats with the beasts in the amphitheatre,[97] and believed himself to be a god,[98] should have shown the slightest pity for the Christians. But apart from the trial of a well-known figure at Rome, Apollonius, the senator (?) before the Praetorian Prefect Tigidius Perennis between 183–185, there is little evidence for repression. Some Christians, including the future Pope Callistus, were sent to the mines in Sardinia, but that was all.[99]

Eusebius gives a brief account of the martyrdom of Apollonius, based on material he found in the collection of *Acta Martyrum* which he drew upon. He states that the devil, angered at the Church's progress, stirred up an accuser (probably one of Apollonius' slaves) to act as informer, and denounced him as a Christian.[100] The trial was held in Rome before the *Praefectus Praetorio* himself, instead of the more usual *Praefectus Urbi*, an indication perhaps of the importance attached to the case. Perennis promptly ordered the legs of the informer to be broken, a surprising, but not altogether unusual penalty for a slave who informed against his master,[101] but he did not quash the case. Instead, he invited Apollonius to give up his Christian beliefs and swear by the *Tyche* of the Emperor Commodus (ch. 3). Apollonius refused, declaring, however, that Christians prayed for the Emperor (ch. 9). Perennis gave him a day to consider his position (ch. 10), and then 'after three days' held a public hearing 'before a large number of senators, counsellors and philosophers' (ch. 11).[102] Another warning from Perennis to heed the 'sentence of the Senate' was followed by a lengthy speech (chs. 14–42) by Apollonius.[103] At the end of it, a peremptory invitation to recant, and this time to do sacrifice was refused (chs. 43–4) and Perennis regretfully condemned the accused to death (ch. 45), 'because', comments Eusebius, 'an ancient law obtaining among them (the Senate) that there should be no other issue for the case of those who once appeared before the court and did not change their opinion'.[104] Apollonius was beheaded (ch. 47).

The *Acta* were something of a *crux interpretis* at the turn of the century, when first F. C. Conybeare brought out an English translation of the fifth century Armenian text of the Greek original in the *Guardian* of 21 June 1893, and then in 1895, the Bollandists published a Greek text identified from Paris Codex graec. no. 1219.[105] In turn, Harnack,[106] Seeberg,[107] Hardy,[108] Hilgenfeld,[109] Mommsen,[110] Harnack's pupil Klette,[111] Geffcken[112] and the Belgian Callewaert,[113] published commentaries on the complicated historical and legal questions which the *Acta* raised. More recently, J. Zeiller[114] has revived the discussion by claiming the *Acta* as material support for his thesis that an explicit law forbidding the practice of Christianity existed at this time, and that Apollonius was a victim of it.

Out of the microscopic investigations to which the *Acta* have been subjected a number of points emerge. First, there seems to be little doubt that the document to which Eusebius refers (*H.E.*, v.21) is the Greek version of the *Acta Apollonii* from which the Armenian translation was made, and further, that a different version of the same *Acta* was used by Jerome in his account of Apollonius in *De Viris Illustribus* (ch. 42).[115] Secondly, there is also no reason to doubt the essential truth of the narrative. As Klette has shown, the details of the procedure are correct on points of law, and the trial unfolds on the same lines as other trials of Christians in this period.[116] Perennis, though determined to pursue the matter to the end, is also fair-minded, convinced of the soundness of his own philosophical position, and anxious to get Apollonius to change his mind. His attitude is precisely that of the Proconsul of Asia at the trial of Polycarp,[117] the Prefect Rusticus at that of Justin,[118] or the magistrates who condemned Pionius and his friends at Smyrna during the Decian persecution.[119] Apollonius' defence, too, emphasizing the truly reasonable nature of Christianity,[120] the inanity of pagan animal worship,[121] the assimilation of the Divine Logos to Jesus Christ,[122] the Christian's calm readiness for death, buttressed by the noble examples of philosophers of the past,[123] and his acceptance of Divine Judgment[124] are typical of late second-century Greek apologetics. The arguments so precisely and logically presented could have been those of Justin or Athenagoras. They fully justify Eusebius' description of Apollonius' speech as an ἀπολογία and Jerome's use of the term 'insigne volumen' for it. Moreover, the vivid detail of the intervention of the Cynic (ch. 33) would be surprising, though not, of course, impossible to find in a fabricated document, but as it stands, it is evidence for the public character of the hearing, as claimed by the writer of the *Acta* (ch. 11). While a case can be made out that the historian is confronted with an anonymous Apology inserted into the *Acta* of the trial,[125] it is difficult not to agree with Zeiller that the existing *Acta* seem to be 'un texte de fort bon aloi'.[126]

Thirdly, the 'decree of the Senate that there should be no Christians' (ch. 23) may conceivably be the same as the 'vetus decretum' referred to by Tertullian, *Adv. Nationes*, 1.7, by virtue of which the Senate's approval was necessary before a new religion could be introduced into the city, and was now invoked against Christianity. It could, however, also be a curt definition of the procedure enforced against accused Christians since Trajan's time, namely public recantation or short shrift.[127] In either event, Perennis' reference of Apollonius' case to the Senate between the two hearings for an opinion would not have been impossible, since the latter was traditionally concerned with the ordering of religion within the city of Rome. The fate of Apollonius was the same as other individual Christians denounced for their faith at this period. Once the case had been opened there was little chance of going back, and once sacrifice to the gods had been formally refused all Perennis could do was to grant Apollonius a merciful end, which he conceded.

Perennis had been reluctant to apply the full rigour of the law. In 185/186 another case was brought before the *Praefectus Urbi*, Fuscianus.[128] The slave Callistus was denounced as a Christian by local Jews whose synagogue worship he had disturbed during a feud over debts which they allegedly owed him. His master, Carpophorus, himself a Christian, interceded with Fuscianus. 'Don't believe him: he's not a Christian but merely seeks death'. He was guilty of embezzling his master's money, and wanted a martyr's glory instead of facing his just deserts. Fuscianus believed

Carpophorus, dismissed the case, and ordered Callistus to be scourged and deported to Sardinia. The scathing account of his later career given by his rival for the see of Rome, Hippolytus, throws light on some cross-currents at the Imperial court which were now operating in favour of the Christians. From Hippolytus and from the epitomizer of Dio Cassius, Xiphilinus, we hear of the activities of Commodus' mistress, Marcia, who 'greatly favoured the Christians and rendered them many kindnesses, inasmuch as she was able to do everything with Commodus'.[129] After 130 years the Christians now had their Poppaea. One of those who benefited was Callistus.

Evidently Marcia persuaded Commodus to send a rescript to the procurator in charge of the Imperial estates in Sardinia, which included the mines, recalling a number of Christians condemned to work there.[130] It was the first time there had been authoritative intervention to quash the operation of the law once this had been enforced. The list drawn up by Pope Victor was of confessors alone. Callistus, who had been deported for criminal offences, had been omitted. Hyacinthos, an aged eunuch priest whom Marcia used as envoy to the procurator, added his name, and he was included in the party who returned to Rome. Victor then moved him to Anzio on a monthly pension, and there he remained until Victor's successor, Zephyrinus found good use for him.[131]

Christian influence at Court was not confined to Marcia. In general terms, Irenaeus refers to 'Christians in the Imperial palace' who prospered (*Adv. Haer.*, iv.30.1), and we hear of two other Christian Greek-speaking freedmen in Commodus' service, Carpophorus who had been Callistus' master, and Proxenes, who was to hold a number of increasingly important Court offices under the Severi, entered the Court (*ordinatus in castrense*) at this time.[132] These are the first named highly placed freedmen officials who continued to represent Christianity at the Courts of the third-century emperors down to Diocletian.

Of the aristocratic families whose conversion Eusebius mentions we know little precise. As Piana has stated, there is no evidence that men of the new or old senatorial aristocracy became Christians in any numbers before Constantine, but during the whole of the second century conversions of aristocratic women were numerous.[133] Their adhesion was eagerly sought because of the assistance they could offer to the poor, and for securing burial places for the Christian community. In fact, it seems that during the reigns of Marcus and Commodus the catacomb of the Caecilii, the Afro-Roman senatorial family, was enlarged, and probably became used exclusively by Christians.[134] This catacomb was to form the nucleus of the Cemetery of Callistus. In addition, not long after 200 Christian tombs began to make their appearance in the cemetery underlying San Sebastiano on the Appian Way.[135]

Finally, the last of Galen's references to the Christians shows the beginnings of a change of mood among the governing classes of the Empire towards the new faith. It is taken from a lost Arabic summary of Plato's *Republic*, written *circa* 180. He says

> 'Most people are unable to follow any demonstrative argument consecutively; hence they need parables, and benefit from them' —and he (Galen) understands by parables tales of rewards and punishments in a future life— 'just as now we see the people called Christians drawing their faith from parables [and miracles]. and yet sometimes acting in the same way [as those who philosophize]. For their contempt of death [and of its sequel] is patent to us every day, and likewise their restraint in cohabitation. For they include not only men but also women who refrain from cohabiting all through their lives; and they also number individuals who, in self-discipline and self-control in matters of food and drink, and in their keen pursuit of justice, have attained a pitch not inferior to that of genuine philosophers.'[136]

Taken in conjunction with the emergence of the great bishoprics at this time, the reign of Commodus marks an important stage in the growth of the influence of the Church and its assimilation with surrounding society. In Rome particularly, the Christians were gaining in both power and respect when on 31 December 192 Commodus was murdered.

The civil wars which followed Commodus' death had no immediate effect on the Christians' position. None of the leading personalities in the Church seem to have been molested. In the West, the Christians prided themselves on having been consistently loyal to Severus,[137] but there now is little doubt that in the East they and the Jews held a position powerful enough to influence the fortunes of the Emperor and his rivals. This factor may well have contributed to Severus' otherwise inexplicable edict of 202 which forbade conversion either to Judaism or to Christianity.[138] In the first round of the conflicts which marked the years 193–197, the civil war between Severus and Niger from mid-193 to the late autumn of 194, both Jews and Christians supported Severus, while the Samaritans rallied to Niger.[139] The latter's hatred for the Jews was notorious,[140] while in Byzantium, which held out for Niger until 196, the Christians gave his commander Caecilius Capella enough trouble during the siege for the fact to be reported and well remembered in Carthage nearly twenty years later.[141] Shechem, the Samaritan city, therefore was punished by the victorious Severus,[142] and it may be that the significant if in practice dubious, extension of privileges to the Jews enabling them to take their place on city councils without compromising their religion was granted at this time.[143]

The East was quiescent in the civil war between Severus and Albinus (196–197) which was fought out in Gaul, but when Severus again moved East and was involved in a war with Parthia in 198–199, the Jews rose, as they had against Trajan in similar circumstances eighty years before. Once more, they demonstrated their fundamental disloyalty to the Roman Empire and preference for Parthia. Severus' pacification of Palestine in 200–201 would form the natural background to an edict attempting like his predecessors to confine Judaism to the narrowest national bounds.

But why were the Christians included?[144] The tendency to treat both as representatives of the same culture discernible in Celsus and Galen may provide one reason, but another may perhaps be found in the extraordinary outbreak of apocalyptic exultation which broke out in Asia and Syria around the year 200, and left its trace on Hippolytus of Rome's *Commentary on Daniel*[145] and Tertullian's *Adv. Marcionem*.[146] Discipline in Severus' army could hardly have been improved by his soldiers declaring that New Jerusalem was descending every morning in the deserts they were traversing on their way to besiege Hatra. The siege was unsuccessful. Five hundred miles away, in Pontus, a leader of the Church there was prophesying the immediate end of the world. And, as a cursory reading of Hippolytus shows, such sentiments were not accompanied by affection for the 'Fourth Empire', the

Iron Kingdom which Rome was deemed to represent.[147] Then again, popular hatred of the Christians of the East in the previous quarter of a century, had by now spread to the Latin-speaking provinces, particularly Severus' own North Africa. There seem to have been sporadic outbreaks against the Christians all through the years 195–200[148] and again in 208 and 212/213.[149] These factors, to which might conceivably be added the Emperor's devotion to the cult of Serapis, might account for the edict of 202.[150]

Severus' edict, as might be expected, had more effect on the Christians than on the Jews. So far as concerned the Jews it soon became a dead letter. In the *Life* of Caracalla in the *Scriptores*, there is a record of one of the young prince's friends having been beaten 'because of his Jewish religion',[151] but Eusebius mentions a Domnus of Antioch who was converted from Christianity to Judaism 'during the time of persecution',[152] presumably to avoid the consequences of being a Christian. Dio Cassius, too, writing *circa* 225 speaks of the Jews of his day as having 'increased to enormous proportions, despite being often punished and repressed, to the extent that they have won for themselves religious liberty'—an interesting text if Dio also had the Bithynian Christians of this period in mind.[153]

The Severan persecution was the first co-ordinated world-wide move against the Christians.[154] While it affected only the relatively small class of Christian converts and was confined to the major centres, it provided a precedent for later official actions. Perhaps because of the relatively high social standing of some of the victims, it produced a profound impression on the Christians themselves. Carthage, Alexandria, Rome, Corinth and Antioch all witnessed burnings, beatings and beheadings, and perhaps what repelled the Christians more than anything, the judical consignment of high-born women converts to the *lupanaria*.[155] At Antioch, government measures included the imprisonment of the future bishop Asclepiades.[156] Elsewhere, steps were more drastic. At Carthage, the persecution has been immortalized by the *Acts of Perpetua and Felicitas* who perished in the amphitheatre at Carthage either on 2 or 7 March 203. This first-hand narrative shows vividly the utter disruption to family life and tradition that a conversion to Christianity could cause. The disgrace which

Perpetua's father felt she had brought on him is only too obvious,[157] and so also the contempt which the procurator Hilarianus displayed towards him for having produced such a daughter.[158] The mob also was bitterly hostile, even demanding additional punishments for the martyrs in the arena before they faced the beasts.

In Alexandria, Clement writes as though the 'roastings, impalings and beheadings' which he witnessed were not uncommon experiences.[159] The victims included Origen's father, Leonides, and Origen himself would have followed his example if his mother had not intervened effectively by hiding his clothes. As it was, he saw some of his friends and contemporaries go to their death. They included Plutarch, the brother of Heraclas the future bishop of Alexandria, Serenus, Hero and Heracleides, and Herais, all pupils of the Catechetical School of which Clement was then head. Eusebius records that of these converts,[160] Heracleides was only a catechumen and that the others had been lately baptized, and he provides evidence in the account of the death of Potamiaena and her mother Marcella of the appalling punishments meted out to the Christians by the local governors.[161] In the face of mob violence and refinements of torture Origen looked back forty years later to the Severan persecution as the crowning glory of the Alexandrian Church.

> 'This was when', he writes in the *Fourth Homily on Jeremiah*, 'one really was a believer, when one used to go to martyrdom with courage in the Church, when returning from the cemeteries whither we had accompanied the bodies of the martyrs, we came back to our meetings, and the whole church would be assembled there, unbreakable. Then the catechumens were catechized in the midst of the martyrdoms, and in turn these catechumens overcame tortures and confessed the living God without fear. It was then that we saw prodigies. Then too, the faithful were few in numbers but were really faithful, advancing along the straight and narrow path leading to life.'[162]
>
> Now, he says regretfully, Christians were numerous, and things were different.

In Rome too, the mob manifested its hatred for the Christians. 'Rid the earth of such-like. They are not fit to live', they shouted.[163] Perhaps among their victims was the virgin,

Caecilia.[164] As at Smyrna forty years before, Jews and pagans united in common action.[165] Hippolytus, perhaps an eyewitness of the events, denounced their agreement in word and deed directed against the Christians.[166] In another angry passage in his *Commentary on Daniel*, he pointed to the existing persecution of the saints as foreshadowing future (apocalyptic) strife. The blood of the righteous was being shed in town and countryside, men were being burnt alive and thrown to the beasts, children killed on the streets and left to be eaten by dogs, women and virgins shamefully treated, cemeteries robbed and destroyed, and the bones of the dead scattered.[167] All this suggests official action directed against both Christian lives and property, perhaps a local extension beyond the limit of the original intention of the edict.

In Corinth also there seem to have been denunciations, in which the Christians were accused of anti-government sentiments. Another text of Hippolytus, which found its way into Palladius' *Lausiac History* tells the story of a noble Christian woman who was denounced to the magistrates as 'one who had blasphemed both the times and the emperors and spoken ill of the idols'.[168] The magistrate failed to seduce her, had her consigned to a brothel and she was eventually martyred. The charge in this case is clearly treason plus *sacrilegium*. The *Felicitas Saeculi* which the confessor apparently denounced was one of the slogans of the dynasty and features among the coin types for the year 203. The lavish imperial bounty portrayed on the coin was all part of the Severan Golden Age.[169] To this Christian at any rate, a change of religion expressed innate protest against the established order. Her example was to be followed by many in the course of the century. It is remarkable that her contemporaries Tertullian and Hippolytus who not only spoke, but wrote against the 'happy times' did not suffer a like fate.

Apart from the years 202–203, and the situation which had developed between the Christians and pagans in Carthage, the reigns of Septimius Severus and his son Caracalla (211–217) were tolerant. This fact was recognized by Tertullian himself, who reminded the Proconsul Scapula in 212 that 'even Severus, Antoninus' father, treated the Christians with favour; for he had fetched to Court the Christian Proculus, surnamed Torpaion, the steward of Evodia, who had once cured him by the use of (holy) oil', and his success guaranteed him a lasting place at the Imperial palace.[170] He also employed a Christian nurse for Caracalla,[171] and, adds Tertullian, 'Men and women of the highest rank whom Severus knew full well were Christians, were not only authorized to continue to practise their religion without any hindrance, but on several occasions even to give public witness of the favour they were enjoying, rescuing them from the hands of an enraged mob'.[172] This may be exaggerated, but the relative security and prosperity which the Church in Rome was enjoying can be shown in the intense liveliness of the intellectual disputes at this period, which are known to history as the Monarchian Controversies.

When Zephyrinus died in 217, his successor Callistus took a step which also demonstrated the growing power of the Church in society especially among women.[173] He decided that the Church might accept as lawful and binding marriages contracted by Roman women of free birth with freedmen or slaves. This was liable to put the Church formally at variance with civil law which in this case represented deeply rooted tradition.[174] It would have confirmed the view that Christians were potential revolutionaries, but at the moment it produced no noticeable pagan reaction. It can be interpreted as a sign of strength, both of the Roman Christians and of their bishop. In the East also, Christian leaders were in favour. Origen's visit to the governor of the province of Arabia at the latter's special request took place in the years 211–214—a small but significant straw in the wind.[175]

One other important test of the growing security enjoyed by the Church was the development of Church property. The reign of Severus provides an important piece of information. A passage in Hippolytus' *Elenchos* ('Refutation') records that when Pope Zephyrinus (199–217) assumed office he recalled the deacon Callistus from Anzio to assist him reorganize the clergy, and 'to put him in charge of the cemetery'.[176] This had been up to now on the property of the Acilii on the Via Salaria. Callistus moved it to the catacomb of the Caecilii on the Via Appia near those of Domitilla, Lucina, Priscilla and the Praetextati, where the Christians already had a firm foothold.[177] It became known as the catacomb of Callistus, where the Roman bishops were buried, though he himself was not buried there. The importance of this move was that from now on the Christians in Rome were no longer completely dependent on the goodwill of rich families who allowed them burial on their property. There was henceforth a cemetery belonging to the bishops of Rome and administered by them. Thus the Church in Rome could aspire to secure and hold property legally. The situation at Rome was not isolated. By 212 the Christian cemeteries (*areae*) near Carthage had become the objective of pagan attack.[178]

This is not the place to discuss in detail the precise legal means by which the Church was able to acquire these rights. It seems evident, however, both that they had existed for a long time and that they were not acquired by subterfuge. This would include the pretence that a Church was a 'collegium tenuiorum', and entitled to benefit from *Senatus-consultum* and successive Imperial re- scripts which permitted such *collegia* to accept contributions for the purpose of assuring their members a decent burial.[179] In this case, property could have been acquired by Christians, not as belonging to the Church in a particular city, but as individuals who were members of a *collegium tenuiorum*. This theory, once accepted by the majority of Church historians, comes up against insuperable objections.[180] First, the size of the membership of the Church—perhaps as many as 40,000 in Rome by the middle of the third century—alone would rule out any such possibility, even if the Christians had divided themselves into numerous smaller groups for the purpose. The funerary *collegia* were pre-eminently small groups, but 200 Christian groups masquerading as burial societies with 200 members apiece would very soon have attracted attention. Moreover, Christians met once a week, not once a month as allowed to the *collegia tenuiorum*. Again, the *collegia* were designed for the poor, and though the majority of the Christians were drawn from the lower classes in the towns, there were by now numerous wealthier individuals among them. Finally, Christianity was strongest in the East where there is no evidence for the existence of these *collegia tenuiorum*, while there is evidence for Christian churches, for instance at Dura and in Cappadocia. It is quite evident from expressions used by authorities as different as Ignatius of Antioch[181] and Lucian of Samosata[182] that the Churches possessed common funds. As Bovini points out, the *collegia tenuiorum* theory propounded by de Rossi does not do justice to the strong centralizing tendencies operating in the

Church at the time. Gnostic sects could form 'burial clubs', but not an episcopally-governed 'great church'.[183]

A more likely solution might be, that in the early period (say, up to the middle of the second century) the Church continued to benefit in this respect from its association with Judaism. As Philo and Josephus recorded, Caesar deliberately exempted Jewish *collegia* from restraints placed upon others,[184] and this of course included Jewish cemeteries and catacombs. There is some evidence that at Carthage, Jews and Christians were buried side by side in the cemetery at Q'mart;[185] and at Milan, Jewish and Christian burial inscriptions have been found intermingled in the same area.[186] Use of the Jewish cemetery would account for the complete lack of identifiable Christian sepulchral remains except in Rome before *circa* 250. In Rome, however, the emergence of cemeteries belonging to the Church itself might be regarded as the normal development of the *de facto* toleration which it was enjoying. If the Christians could meet to hold services, they could also acquire buildings in which to hold them,[187] and cemeteries in which to bury their dead. In Edessa they certainly possessed a building for worship in 200, for it was washed away in a flood the next year.[188] The criterion whether a *collegium* was *licitum* or not, was, as Bovini has argued, less a matter of defect of form than relationship to the State, and in Rome in the Severan period, the existence of Christianity was an acknowledged fact, even if every effort was made to restrict the numbers of Christians.[189] In Alexandria also, it is impossible to think of the catechetical school as a clandestine organization, holding its property through some legal chicane.[190] 'Christianos esse passus est', would seem to account for the situation in Rome and, indeed, nearly everywhere else in the Roman Empire.

These words of Lampridius amply sum up the period following Septimius Severus' death. However glaring the shortcomings of the emperors themselves, their court attracted for a generation a succession of distinguished intellects who were acutely interested in religious questions. Septimius Severus' wife, Julia Domna (died 217) was a Syrian, the daughter of the priest king of Emesa. She and her niece, Julia Mammaea, especially the latter, may have felt some sympathy towards a religion which was in some respects akin to their own. In Domna's circle too, had been Galen in his old age, whose ideas seem to have had a real attraction for the Aristotelian school of Roman Christians, to whom the manhood of Christ and His moral development was all-important.[191] But any sympathies Galen may have had for the Christians would probably have been counterbalanced by Ulpian, who *circa* 215 had set about codifying the various rescripts condemning the practice of Christianity[192]—and could hardly be counted as a friend of the new religion.

Another factor must be considered, namely the influence of these Syrian princesses on the Imperial cult as a whole. Commodus had already elevated this to well-nigh grotesque proportions. There was to be little diminution under the Afro-Syrian emperors.[193] Severus himself wished to exalt and ensure his own position by divine consecration, and on his magnificent arch at Leptis Magna erected in 203 he appears with Julia Domna as Serapis and Isis. The Isis was to be the predominant partner in religious matters. Her title, 'mater castrorum' once awarded to Faustina II as Marcus Aurelius' faithful consort on his campaigns, became expanded into 'mater castrorum et senatus et patriae', the divinized patron of the Empire, and 'mother of gods'.[194] Not for nothing did she bear on her coinage the sceptre of divine majesty and the phoenix on the globe, the symbol of eternity. Her son Caracalla styled himself 'Lord', or 'Ruler of the world', the reflection of the divine power and light that governed the universe.[195] Though the latter might eventually be interpreted as the God of the Christians, at this stage he was Serapis or 'the immortal god' of Rome.

The one surviving product of Julia Domna's circle, Philostratus' *Life of Apollonius of Tyana*, warns the historian not to exaggerate the pro-Christian elements in the policy of the Severi. The *Life* was based supposedly on a diary left by Damis, one of his disciples, and despite its length and relative triviality, has some traits found in another example of Greek-Syrian writing, namely the Christian Gospels. Apollonius of Tyana, as we have seen, was a real person, and a member of the philosophic opposition to Domitian. He was a brave and outspoken individual, and it is true that Philostratus does not attempt to portray him as a god. But the reader would soon gather than he was more than human. His mother was a virgin who was the recipient of an annunciation of the honour which was to be conferred on her.[196] His childhood and youth show promise of marvels. He travels to India and then to Rome. He is the master of the languages of mankind, aspires to be a religious leader, he works miracles and he addresses multitudes wherever he goes. He is consulted 'by kings as a counsellor of virtue.'[197] De Labriolle has drawn attention to the parallelism between Apollonius' healing of a young woman (*Life*, iv.45) and St. Luke's account of the raising of Jairus' daughter (Lk. 8[40 ff.]).[198] There is also a version of the Parable of the Sower, and Apollonius' missionary journeys bear a resemblance to those of Paul. His preaching includes forbearance towards the fallen and sinners. He is brought before the Imperial judgment seat, not merely that of a procurator, and he disappears from view amid the singing of a heavenly choir.[199] After death he inspires an oracle to refute those who doubted that the soul was immortal.[200]

These similarities suggest that Philostratus may have known the Christian Scriptures and used them.[201] They also show what was expected of a saviour and example to mankind, but those qualities did not include the humility of Christ. On this point the critique of Celsus and Apollonius of Tyana would have been at one. The real interest of Julia and her court is shown perhaps to lie in 'the mysterious East', in Hinduism and the wisdom of the Brahmins. Apollonius is said to have been a fervent admirer of their practices.[202] We learn more about them, and therefore about the intellectual contacts between the Roman and the Indian worlds from Philostratus than from almost any other Greco-Roman author.[203] One can understand the attraction exercised by religious movements from the East, even by Manichaeism[204], on the Empire of the third century, but there was still a long way to go before a Galilean saviour would be acceptable. In the Great Persecution, Apollonius of Tyana did service on the anti-Christian side.[205]

Meantime, in the summer of 222, the bishop of Rome, Callistus, seems to have come to an untimely end at the hands of a Roman mob, perhaps with his presbyters Calepodius and Asterius who are associated with him as martyrs,[206] but their fate was exceptional. If any credence can be lent to Lampridius' account of Elagabalus' reign, the Christians were regarded as akin to the Jews and Samaritans, whose existence was accepted by all.[207]

The thirteen years' reign of Alexander Severus (222–235) that followed Elagabalus' demise (11 March 222) has been looked upon as a sort of golden age of the pre-Constantinian Church. So far as the Emperor himself and his all-powerful mother, Julia Mammaea, were concerned, this is probably true. The evidence from both pagan and Christian tradition is consistent. Lampridius' long biography of Severus Alexander contains six references to the latter's partiality towards the Christians.[208] Though it need not be emphasized that Lampridius' biography is merely the description of a fourth-century pagan senator's Ideal Prince on which has been stamped the label 'Alexander Severus', there may be an element of truth in them.[209] It would not be surprising if a young Syrian priest-king showed interest in both Judaism and Christianity. Only a decade before, in *circa* 213, the royal house of Osrhoene under King Abhgar IX (179–214) had been converted from their ancestral worship of the heavenly deities to Christianity.[210] In the same part of the world, the religion of Bardaisan[211] and Julius Africanus[212] mingled Persian dualism, magic and orthodox Christianity in one faith. Maybe, Alexander Severus ordered the erection of a statue of Christ along with those of Apollonius of Tyana, Abraham and Orpheus, no doubt as benefactors of the human race, in his private chapel.[213] He may also have expressed his admiration for the organization of the Jewish and Christian communities,[214] and perhaps sided with the Christians in Rome against the restauranteurs in a dispute over the ownership of a piece of former Imperial property.[215] There is nothing inherently improbable in these traditions, especially as the Dura excavations suggest that Christianity was being practised progressively more openly as his reign advanced.[216]

The Christian sources, which are varied and may be based on contemporary material, tell the same story more emphatically. The friendly relations between Alexander and Julius Africanus are well attested, not least by a papyrus fragment which points to the latter as the architect of the new Imperial library which was constructed in the Pantheon, *circa* 227.[217] The climate of opinion must have changed considerably for Hippolytus to dedicate his work 'On the Resurrection' to Mammaea; but the most important piece of evidence comes from Eusebius.[218] He relates that the Empress Mammaea was 'an uncommonly religious woman', high praise indeed from Eusebius, and that she laid great store on seeing Origen and 'testing that understanding of divine things which was the wonder of all',[219] When she was staying in Antioch, therefore, she summoned him to Court and provided him with a military escort.[220] Origen is related to have remained there discussing religious matters some time before returning home.

The incident probably took place *circa* 232, when preparations for the Persian campaign of that year would have brought Alexander and his mother to Antioch, and when Origen, now an exile in Caesarea, would have found this journey easy.[221] Its importance is not to be underestimated. It implied recognition, albeit through the personality and teaching of Origen, of Christianity as one of the accepted religions of the Roman world. People were interested in Christianity (like Gregory Thaumaturgus as a boy)[222] even if they never became Christians. It could never again be ignored. A *modus vivendi* between Church and Greco-Roman society had become more probable. The Severan dynasty marks the turn of the tide in the history of the Church.

Not surprisingly, evidence drawn from many parts of the Roman Empire points to progress by the Church in these years. In the West, Tertullian throws down his challenge to the pagan world in a well-known passage in the *Ad Nationes*.[223] 'Day by day, you groan over the ever-increasing number of Christians. Your constant cry is that the state is beset by us, that the Christians are in your fields, your camps, and in your blocks of houses (*insulas*). You grieve over it as a calamity, that every age, in short, every rank is passing over from you to us'. '*Fiunt non nascuntur Christiani*'.[224] Tertullian himself was a convert, perhaps at one time a Stoic lawyer, drawn probably to Christianity by the ethical standards, idealism, and readiness to die for belief displayed by the Carthaginian Christians. This had been enough to conquer doubts about Judgment and bodily Resurrection.[225] Others may have thought likewise. In Rome, the situation was similar, with the Christians obviously gaining ground, and pagans filled with foreboding. To such men the Christians had become a '*latebrosa et lucifuga natio*'—a vast invisible empire conspiring against the state.[226] Thus, Caecilius in the *Octavius*: 'Already—for ill weeds grow apace—decay of morals grows from day to day, and throughout the wide world the abominations of this impious conspiracy multiply'.[227] His Christian friend, Octavius, admitted the accuracy of his statement. 'Nor need we plume ourselves upon our numbers; to ourselves we seem many; but to God we are very few.'[228] In Alexandria, we find first Pantaenus (died *circa* 180), and then Clement making a real effort to convert educated Greeks to Christianity, and they were not unsuccessful. The names of some of these converts who included Heraclas, Demetrius' successor as bishop of Alexandria have survived,[229] but their influence on the Church was away from traditional rejection of the world and what the world offered. No one before Clement would have answered the question 'Can a rich man be saved?' so uncompromisingly in the affirmative.[230] And, if Christ's teaching on riches could be allegorized away, so might be that on martyrdom. The world in awakening from error, as Tertullian described it in 207, would also be making its impact on traditional Christian ways of thought.[231]

The causes of the sudden expansion of Christianity in the West are obscure. As individuals, Tertullian and Minucius Felix both give the impression that sheer disgust at the immorality and senseless cruelty of the age were influences. There is a note of real outraged indignation in the passage where Minucius Felix describes the scenes he had witnessed in the name of religion.

> Examine into their attendant rites, how ridiculous, how pitiable even they appear! Men running about naked in mid-winter; others marching about in felt caps, or parading old shields; drumming on skins, and dragging their gods to beg from street to street. Some temples may only be entered once a year, some never visited at all. There are rites which a man may not attend, others which may be held only in the absence of women; others where the mere presence of a slave is an outrage needing expiation.[232]

The same feeling of repulsion may be found in Tertullian's momentary self-revelation of his previous convictions in *Apologeticus*, 15.

> We have seen Jove's brother, too, hauling out the corpses of gladiators, hammer in hand. And all the details of it, who could inquire into them? If they overturn the honour of deity, if they blot out every trace of majesty, it simply means the sheer contempt felt by those who do these things, and by those for whom they do them.[233]

This would explain scattered individual conversions, like that of Justin's seventy years before or Tatian's a generation previously, but something more needs to be said about the obvious swing to Christianity which was taking place in Carthage and some other African towns in Tertullian's day. Some element of cultural protest cannot be ruled out. Standardization seems to have been the effect of Roman policy in the latter part of the second century, and in Africa it was resented. Charles-Picard has pointed to the gradual romanization of the cult of Saturn.[234] From the time of Marcus Aurelius, dedications to the Emperor were being made in the temples of the national god.[235] The cruel, but none the less traditional rites associated with his worship were prohibited under pain of death.[236] At the same time the groups of *Kohanim* which had hitherto preserved the lively Punic tradition in African religion were tending to disappear, and the old Punic ceremonies were being increasingly celebrated by the lower classes alone.[237]

In 189–190 there seems to have been an outright revolt inspired by the prophets of Caelestis who were finding themselves superseded in favour of an official romanized Sibyl.[238] This may not add up to very much, but when one considers that Tertullian wrote the *De Pallio* in protest against what he considered the abandonment of Carthaginian peculiarities in dress and custom in favour of Roman,[239] it may well be that the drift towards Christianity in the 190s was in part an outlet for suppressed but outraged Carthaginian feeling. The heavy, uninspired copies of Roman models which typify African plastic art in the time of the Severi were hardly enough to satisfy those who still spoke the Punic language and hankered after its religion and culture. Christianity, a powerful Semitic religion with more than a few reminiscences of both local Rabbinic Judaism and African Saturn-worship provided many with a ready-made answer.[240]

The dramatic increase in the numbers and influence of Christians may have been accepted by the Court, but it was not accepted by the majority of the Greco-Roman governing class, nor by the urban populace as a whole. The Maecenas speech which condemned 'foreign religion' and 'magic' might refer to the time of Augustus, but it was edited by Dio Cassius in the 220s, and the advice no doubt was regarded as relevant for his own day.[241]

It is interesting that Dio Cassius who haled from Bithynia, one of the most Christianized provinces of Asia Minor, never refers to Christians by name. There is evidence from his *History* that he loathed the Jews also. Other senior administrators shared his hostility. One of these, Aelius Serenianus, who had been a member of Alexander Severus' *Concilium*, was responsible for initiating persecution in the neighbouring province of Pontus in 236.[242] Ulpian and the Proconsul Scapula were not exceptional. Their views were shared by the legionary commander of Legio III at Lambaesis, and the governor of Mauretania.[243] Tertullian refers to the ill-will of the proconsuls of Africa, Vigellius Saturninus and Caecilius Capella, and of the governor of Cappadocia, Cl. Lucius Hieronymianus, the last due to conversions within his household.[244] He also refers to the massive ill-will of the Carthaginian magistrates, and this is paralleled by Clement's evidence for Alexandria. There, Christians were being condemned as 'those guilty of a sin against life',[245] a charge or reproach which suggests atheism and consequent damage to the community. For Rome the *Octavius* contains a classic re-statement by a member of the Senatorial class of grievances against the Christians in the West, such as Celsus had done for the East a quarter of a century or more ago. Thus Caecilius to his Christian friend Octavius,

> Fellows who gather together illiterates from the dregs of the populace and credulous women with the instability natural to their sex, and so organize a rabble of profane conspirators, leagued together by meetings at night and ritual fasts and unnatural repasts, not for any sacred service but for piacular rites, a secret tribe that shuns the light, silent in the open, but talkative in hid corners; they despise temples as if they were tombs; they spit upon the gods; they jeer at our sacred rites; pitiable themselves, they pity (save the mark) our priests; they despise titles and robes of honour, going themselves half-naked![246] (tr. G. H. Rendall)

In *circa* 200, the governor of Syria was about to hunt down Christians who, on the inspiration of their bishop, had gone out into the wilderness in the expectation of meeting the *Parousia*, but he was dissuaded by his wife who was a Christian![247] In the event, the Christians were always liable to sudden, short-lived acts of persecution according to the whim of individual governors. The fact that people of such different views as Natalius,

Alexander bishop of Jerusalem, Praxeas, and Theodotus of Byzantium could all claim the title of 'confessor' shows that the peace of the Severan epoch was by no means complete.

Lower down the social scale, the popular attitude was still one of amused or amazed contempt, especially in the West. Tertullian's journalistic sense picked out snatches of gossip heard in Carthage, 'Christ was some man whom the Jews had condemned',[248] or 'A good man, this Seius Gaius, only that he is a Christian', or 'I am surprised that that wise man, Lucius Titius, has suddenly become a Christian', and the final insult, 'the fast set —they have become Christians'.[249] Nor had the old hostility died out among the populace.[250] Christians shared with murderers and informers the lowest depths of unpopularity.[251] Not a few in other Mediterranean parts of the Roman world would still have agreed that the Christians were responsible for every type of natural disaster from earthquake to lack of rain.[252] The best place for the believer was still the lion's belly.[253]

Behind this agitation stood the Jews. It is interesting how the Jews in Carthage and seemingly in Rome too, played precisely the same part against the Christians as their co-religionists had in Asia thirty or forty years before. Asia and North Africa have the same evolution separated, however, by a generation. Tertullian's outburst 'synagogae Judaeorum fontes persecutionum' (*Scorpiace*, 11) cannot be dismissed as mere rhetorical flourish. A decade before, in his *Adv. Nationes* he had singled the Jews out as the most formidable enemies of his new faith, the 'seminarium' for Christian shame,[254] and he described how a renegade Jew had represented the Christians in hateful travesty as donkey-worshippers.[255] The Jews, in Carthage as in the East, were happy to use the Christians as scapegoats for traditional libels against themselves. Public debates between Jews and Christians seem also not to have been rare in Carthage, and after one of these Tertullian, disgusted at the inept defence of Christianity in an argument with a proselyte, sat down to write the *Adversus Judaeos*.[256] In the East, where personal relations between the members of the two religions seem to have been more tolerable, Origen lamented that the Jews concentrated their efforts not against the pagans but against the Christians, whom they regarded with implacable enmity,[257] and to judge from his description of the authority of the Jewish patriarch, 'no less great than royalty', they had the means of making that enmity felt.[258]

It was the army, however, which eventually took action to bring the period of comparative toleration to an end. Alexander Severus was far from being the paragon of virtue described by Lampridius,[259] though as the text of his edict concerning the *aurum coronarium* shows, he (or his advisers) did deliberately claim Trajan and Marcus Aurelius as 'ancestors'.[260] He was weak, kindly, vacillating and perpetually under his mother's influence.[261] In the last years of his reign the military situation on the frontiers deteriorated. The victorious Sassanid revolution of 226 revived Persian claims to the empire of Darius. The whole of Asia Minor, Egypt and Syria was at stake. Perhaps Alexander Severus' Persian campaign of 232–233 was a partial success. At least he won a breathing space to turn to dangers threatening from elsewhere. In 234 came the opening moves of the tremendous Germanic onslaught on the Danube and Rhine defences which were to dominate the next half-century. The Emperor set up his headquarters at Mainz, but he hoped to buy off the Alemanni. The troops took this for cowardice, and the Pannonians declared their leader Maximin emperor.[262] In mid-March 235 Alexander was deserted by his own troops and killed. His mother shared his fate. According to Eusebius, the new reign opened with the slaughter of Christian servants and office-holders in Alexander's court.[263] As the contemporary historian, Herodian, commented, Maximin regarded members of his predecessor's court as 'secret enemies'.[264] The age of peace and toleration for the Christians was over.

NOTES

[1] Eusebius, *H.E.*, iv.23.

[2] *Adv. Haer.*, 1.10.

[3] *H.E.*, iv.22.1.

[4] See H. Strathmann and Th. Klauser, 'Aberkios', *A.C.*, 1, 12–17, lines 10–14 of inscription, and W. M. Calder's note suggesting that the last word in line 11 should read συνομήμους instead of συνομηγύρους, *JRS.*, xxix, 1939, 2–4.

[5] See G. la Piana, 'The Roman Church at the end of the Second Century', *HTR.*, 18, 1925, 201–77, especially 222ff.

[6] Aberkios inscription, line 11, Calder, loc. cit.

[7] Eusebius, *H.E.*, v.23.4.

[8] Tertullian, *Apol.*, 40.2; cf. the cry 'delatores ad leonem', Lampridius, *SHA.*, *Commodus*, 18.10.

[9] G. Becatti, *Scavi di Ostia*, ii, *i Mitrei*, Rome, 1954, 133–5.

[10] I. A. Richmond and J. P. Gillam, 'The Temple of Mithras at Carrawburgh', *Archaelogia Aeliana*, 29, (4th Ser.), 1951, 1–92.

[11] R. C. Bosanquet, *Archaeologia Aeliana*, 2nd Ser. 25, 1904, 255–63, Also Rudchester, see note in *JRS.*, xliv, 1954, 88, and excavation report by J. P. Gillam and colleagues, *Arch. Ael.*, 32 (4th Ser.) 1954, 176–219.

[12] G. Becatti, op. cit., 137.

[13] See, M. J. Vermaseren, *Corpus Inscriptionum et Monumentorum Religionis Mithraicae*, i.1956 for complete series, and J. M. C. Toynbee, *Art in Roman Britain*, London, 1962, 128–9, 132–3 and 137–8 for a description of the Walbrook Mithraeum finds.

[14] *Contra Celsum*, v.41.

[15] See A. D. Nock, 'The Emperor's Divine *Comes*', *JRS.*, xxxvii, 1947, 102–16.

[16] Justin, *1 Apol.*, 66.

[17] Tertullian, *De Corona*, 15 and *De Baptismo*, 5; cf. *De Jejunio*, 16, directed against the fasts in the cult of Isis and Cybele.

[18] 'Hominibus bitam bagis' (= *vitam vagis*) from Walbrook. J. M. C. Toynbee, op. cit., 128–9.

[19] Not yet published. Illustrated and reported in *The Times*, 29 Dec. 1954. One dedication appears to date to 19 Nov. 202.

[20] Ibid. Note the words, 'Viros servasti (Mithras) eternali sanguine fuso|in viro ut nascent omnia magna Mithra|,'from a wall-painting in the Mithraeum.

[21] See J. Carcopino's discussion of the Urbanilla mosaic from a third-century tomb at Lambiridi in southern Numidia, *Aspects Mystiques de la Rome païenne*, pl. iv.

[22] Hippolytus, *Elenchos*, v.9.

[23] See M. Simon's *Hercule et le Christianisme*, Strasbourg, 1955, for a study of the parallels between the figure of Hercules and that of Jesus in Roman religious life in the late second and third centuries, especially chs. ii and iii.

[24] Instanced by the Ulysses painting in the Catacomb of the Aurelii, illustrated by C. Cecchelli, *Monumenti cristiano-eretici di Roma*, Rome, 1944, 100 (Plate).

[25] Note Th. Klauser's remarks in his *Studien zur Enstehungsgeschichte der christlichen Kunst*, iv, *J.A.C.*, iv.1961, 144, and cf. Clement of Alexandria's opening paragraph of his *Protreptikos*.

[26] Tertullian, *Apol.*, 50.14.

[27] See, M. Rostovtzeff, *Dura-Europos and its Art*, Oxford, 1938. The city formed part of the province of Syria. It may not have fallen until 260 after the Roman defeat at Edessa (pp. 29–30).

[28] Ammianus Marcellinus, xxiii.5.8 and xxiv.1.5.

[29] R. O. Fink, A. S. Hoey and W. F. Snyder, 'The Feriale Duranum', *Yale Classical Studies*, vii, 1940, 22–3. Discussed by A. D. Nock, 'The Roman Army and the Roman Religious Year', *HTR.*, 45, Oct. 1952, 187ff.

[30] A. S. Hoey, 'The Feriale Duranum', 173.

[31] Ibid., 165ff. An interesting point because, as Tertullian makes clear in *De Idololatria*, 19, junior ranks 'etiam caligata vel inferior quaeque cui non sit necessitas immolationum', did not have to sacrifice to the gods. They were obviously ready to do so.

[32] Ibid., 172.

[33] A. D. Nock, art. cit., 204.

[34] Tertullian, *De Corona Militis*, 1 (ed. Kroymann, 153–4). The soldier was a 'speculator'.

[35] *Dura Report of Excavation*, ix.3, 107ff. (Yale University, 1952).

[36] F. Cumont, *Fouilles de Doura-Europos*, Paris, 1926, 89ff. Pl. l. On the standard-bearer, M. Rostovtzeff, *JRS.*, xxxii, 1942, 93.

[37] M. Rostovtzeff, *Berytus*, viii, 1943, 58ff. Also, *Dura Report,* v, pl. xxxvi.3.

[38] *Dura*, vi, 430–1.

[39] Ibid., vi.410.

[40] Ibid., v.106–11. Aphlad was described on an inscription erected by the founder of the temple as 'god of the village of Anath', some 50 miles down river from Dura (Ibid., 112–13).

[41] M. Rostovtzeff, *Dura-Europos and its Art*, 46.

[42] *Dura*, vii–viii, (1939) 257ff. (Gad was the Palmyrene equivalent of the Greek τύχη).

[43] Ibid., 290ff.

[44] Ibid.

[45] Ibid., 64ff. and 124–6 (expense accounts of ritual meals eaten in the shrine).

[46] F. Cumont, *Fouilles*, p. 196.

[47] Herodian, v.5.9 for the reception in Rome of this sort of worship imported by Elagabalus; cf. also, Lampridius, *SHA.*, *Vita Antonini Heliogabali*, 7.3.

[48] M. Rostovtzeff, *Dura*, iv.207.

[49] Ibid., 105–19 and illustrations in text.

[50] *Excavation Report*; see H. F. Pearson, *Dura*, vi.309ff. *Discussion*: Ibid., 337ff. and bibliography to 1935 on p. 338 n. 1. Also. M. Rostovtzeff, *Dura-Europos and its Art*, ch. iv.

[51] H. F. Pearson, *Dura*, vi.309.

[52] H. F. Kraeling, *Dura*, vi.372ff. emphasizes the prominence of Babylonian Jewish influence in the choice of subjects for commemoration on the wall paintings.

[53] Ibid., 311.

[54] *Excavation Report*; G. Hopkins, *Dura*, v.238ff. Also, H. Lietzmann, *Gnomon*, xiii, 1937, 231.

[55] *Dura*, v.241.

[56] Ibid., v.240.

[57] Ps-Clem., *Recognitions*, x.71 (*P.G.*, 1.1453).

[58] See, for instance, J. Carcopino's excellent essay, 'Sur les Traces de l'Hermétisme africain', in *Aspects Mystiques de la Rome païenne*, Paris, 1942, especially 224ff.

[59] Churches in the province were burnt down in the persecution of 236. Origen, *Comment. in Matt.*, ch. 39.

[60] J. M. C. Toynbee, *Art in Roman Britain*, 133.

[61] See B. M. Apollonj's magnificent description of the Severan forum and basilica of Leptis, in *Monumenti Italiani*, Fasc. viii–ix, Rome, 1936.

[62] Y. Allais, *Djemila*, 1938, p. 22, and M. Leglay's comments on a dedication to 'cultui publicae religionis et honestamento dignae civitatis', dated 214/215 from Timgad, *Coll. Latomus*, 44, 1960, 487.

[63] M. P. Charlesworth, '*Providentia* and *Aeternitas*'. *HTR*, 29, 1936, 105ff.

[64] *CIL.*, viii.10570. M. P. Charlesworth, op. cit., 119. Note also, *CIL.*, viii.2585 (Lambaesis) a temple dedicated by Aesculepius and Salus, 'pro salute et incolumitate dominorum nostrum', and the formula 'devotis numini maiestatique eius' in common use, H. Gundel, *Epigraphia*, 15, 1953, 128ff.

[65] See M. P. Charlesworth, '*Pietas et Victoria*. The Emperor and the Citizen', *JRS.*, xxxiii, 1943, 1–10.

[66] For Commodus' designation of his reign as 'saeculum aureum', Lampridius, *Commodus*, 14.3.

[67] The silver denarius which had been debased 15 per cent under Trajan, and 25 per cent under Marcus Aurelius fell to 40 per cent silver content under Septimius Severus. The *antoninianus* struck by Caracalla in 215 was supposed to equal two denarii. In fact, it never

had a silver content of more than 1½ denarii. See H. Mattingly, *Roman Coins*, 1928, 125–6. For an incidental reference to the abounding wealth of the Empire in the Severan Age, Herodian, iii.13.4 (treasuries and temples 'overflowing with riches').

[68] *CIL.*, vii.142. The northern monumental arch at Verulamium also seems to be Severan. S. S. Frere, *Antiquaries Journal*, 1962, 148.

[69] *CIL.*, viii.8375. See, M. Platnauer, *The Life and Reign of Septimius Severus*, O.U.P., 1918, 210ff. For Djemila, see Y. Allais, op. cit., 20–24.

[70] Particularly in Mauretania Sitifensis. See *CIL.*, viii.8425 and 8426, 8702, 8777 and 8809.

[71] For those beyond the African *limes*, J. Baradez, *Fossatum Africae*, 139 (Castellum Dimmidi (Messad)), Built 198. Restoration of Hadrian's Wall by Severus, see Collingwood and Myres, *Roman Britain*, 158.

[72] 'Tantae urbes quantae non casae quondam. Iam nec insulae horrent, nec scopuli terrent, ubique domus, ubique populus, ubique respublica, ubique vita' (*CSEL.*, xx.350). For a contemporary witness to the size of the North African native population, Herodian, vii.4.14.

[73] For an outstanding example of public spirit at this period, note the story of the lawyer of Ephesus who between 209–217 served his city on embassies to the Emperor which carried him from Mesopotamia to Britain, to Rome and the Danube frontier. J. Keil, 'Ein ephesischer Anwalt des 3 Jahrhunderts durchreist das Imp. Rom'., *S.B. bayerischer Akad. der Wiss.*, 1956, Heft 3.

[74] M. Rostovtzeff, *Social and Economic History* (2nd ed., 1957), 323ff. and 682–3.

[75] *CIL.*, viii.1641 (1,300,000 HS. Sicca) in 175–180, or *IRT.*, 230 (1 million HS, Oea, for *sportulae* and *ludi* for decurions). Full list of African benefactions, R. Duncan-Jones, *P.B.S.R.*, 30, 1962, 92ff.

[76] *CIL.*, viii.11824.

[77] G. Charles-Picard, 102. To judge from the erection of public buildings, the prosperity lasted into the reign of Gordian iii (i.e. to 244). See R. Duncan-Jones, 'Costs, Outlays and Summae Honorariae from Roman Africa', loc. cit., 1962, 53

[78] Ulpian, *Digest*, 1.5.17 and P. Giessen, 40; cf. S. N. Miller, ch.1.5 'Caracalla' in *CAH.*, xii, 45–7, and A. H. M. Jones, 'Another Interpretation of the Constitutio Antoniniana', *JRS.*, xxvi.2.1936, 223–5. Also, J. Stroux, 'Die Constitutio Antoniniana', *Philogus*, 88, 1933, 272–95. For the view, however, that the *Constitutio* was evidence of a 'spirit of hostility towards the upper classes', M. Rostovtzeff, op. cit., 418–19 and 719–20, and for the suggestion that the date of the *Constitutio* could be 214 and its purpose mainly to raise money for the armies, F. Millar, *J.E.A.*, 48, 1962, 124–31.

[79] 'τοιγαροῦν | νομίζω οὕτω με | (γαλοπρεπῶς καὶ θεοσεβ)ῶς δύνασθαι τῇ μεγαλειότητι | αὐτῶν τὸ 'ικανὸν ποι | εῖν εἰ τοσάκις μυρίους ὁσάκις ἐὰν ὑπεισέλθωσιν εἰς | τοὺς 'εμοὺς 'ανθρώπους | (συνθύοντας)εἰς τὰ 'ιερὰ τῶν θεῶν συνεισενέγκοιμι', Stroux's text, op. cit., 294. The introduction of the cult of Jupiter to Arsinoe in 215 may be connected with the edict. U. Wilcken, *Grundzüge*, 116.

[80] Cf. Spartian, *SHA.*, Caracalla, 9.10. The Egyptian deities, Serapis and Isis, had appeared successively on the coins of the last year of Commodus' reign (Mattingly and Sydenham, *The Roman Imperial Coinage*, iii. p. 436, no. 614) and on the arch at Leptis Magna representing Severus and Julia Domna. The process was not to end until after the battle of Chrysopolis when Constantine placed the Empire under one divinity—the God of the Christians.

[81] J. Stroux, op. cit., 277–9. 'ein gleichartetes, Wunschbild seiner Herrscherphantasie', comparable to his colossal Baths at Rome.

[82] Thus Martianus, the *consularis*, to Acacius during the Decian persecution. 'Debes amare principes nostros, homo Romanis legibus vivens', *Acta Acacii* 1.2 (Knopf and Krüger, 57). Loyalty and love included sacrifice (ibid., 1.4).

83 Tertullian, *Ad Scapulam*, 2.8 (Buhlart, 11). 'Itaque et sacrificamus pro salute imperatoris, sed deo nostro et ipsius, sed quomodo praecepit deus, pura prece.' Also, *Apol.*, 31.3. Contrast, ibid., 32.2 where Tertullian regards the Genius as a fit subject for the exorcist. The title of 'kosmokrator' attributed to Caracalla would be especially distasteful to a Christian (cf. Eph. 6¹² and Tertullian, *De Res. Carnis*, 22, 'luctari habemus cum mundi potentibus'.)

84 Dating, P. Allard, *Les Persécutions*, 436, but doubted by P. Monceaux, *Histoire Littéraire de l'Afrique chrétienne*, i, 43 n.1, who points to the record of the martyr Namphamo on 5 December in the Martyrology of Jerome.

85 Tertullian, *Ad Scapulam* 3, 'primus hic gladium in nos egit'. Hence, the date 180 for the execution of Namphamo seems reasonable.

86 Namphamo was venerated as 'archimartyr', Maximus of Madaura to Augustine, in Augustine, *Ep.*, 16.2. His companions appear on a dozen Numidian inscriptions, and Miggin outstripped all in popularity (*ILCV.*, iii.111 and 112), P. Monceaux, *Histoire Littéraire*, iv.176 and A. Berthier, *Les Vestiges du christianisme*, 129 and 137.

87 The trial of the Scillitan martyrs took place 'Kartagine in secretario'. The text of the *Acta* is taken from Knopf and Krüger, 28–30, who cite the relevant literature to 1929. See in particular, J. A. Robinson, 'The Passion of S. Perpetua, with an Appendix on the Scillitan Martyrs', *Cambridge Texts and Studies*, 1.2. 1891, 112–16, and for recent criticism, F. Corzaro, 'Note sugli Acta martyrum Scillitanorum', *Nuovo Didascaleion*, 1956, 5–51. Dating: 'XVI Kalendas Augustas'.—not therefore 1 August 180 as proposed in *CAH.*, xii, 518. On the *numbers* of the victims, H. Karpp considers that only six were executed at 'the trial recorded in the *Acta*, but it does not seem very helpful to conclude the existence of eine zweite Gruppe von Märtyren, die vermutlich derselben Zeit und derselben Gegend entstammen, nachträglich aufgenommen wurde'. This 'second group' of Scillitans have yet to leave their mark on other sources—H. Karpp, 'Die Zahl der scillitanischen Märtyrer', *Vig. Christ.* xv, Sept. 1961, 165–72.

88 Acta Scill., 3. Saturninus, proconsul dixit 'Et nos religiosi sumus, et simplex est religio nostra, et iuramus per genium domini nostri imperatoris, et pro salute eius supplicamus, quod et vos quoque facere debetis'. The proconsul may have been going further than the Emperor himself, for tradition related that even Severus Alexander rejected the title of *dominus*. ('Dominum se appellari vetuit.' Lampridius, *Vita Alex. Sev.*, 4.1.)

89 Tertullian, *Apol.*, 24.1 and 28.2, and *Ad Scapulam*, 2.5; cf. M. Conrat, op. cit., pp. 57–8. It is interesting that Ulpian's codification of the seventh book *De Officio proconsulis*, seems to have placed penalties prescribed against the Christians under *lex maiestatis* rather than under *sacrilegia* (cf. P. Jörs, *P.W.*, s.v. Domitius(88)col. 1453). But the seventh book also included denunciations and penalties against Magi and Chaldaeans, indeed all disturbers of religious peace. (Riccobono, *FIRA.*, ii, 579–80).

90 Acta Scill., 6.

91 Ibid., 15.

92 Tertullian, *Ad Scapulam*, 4.

93 Ibid.

94 Eusebius, *H.E.*, v.16.19.

95 Eusebius, citing Apollonius, circa 210, *H.E.*, v.18.9.

96 Eusebius, *H.E.*, v.21; cf. R. Walzer, *Galen on Jews and Christians*, 10.

97 Dio Cassius, 73.18.1 (destruction of one hundred bears in a single day).

98 Dio Cassius, 73.15.2; cf. Spartian, *Pescennius Niger*, 6.9, and see M. Rostovtzeff, 'Commodus-Hercules in Britain', *JRS.*, xiii, 1923, 104–5.

99 Hippolytus, *Elenchos*, ix.11. Perhaps the lead-mines of Las Antas—an unhealthy place on an unhealthy island. The title of this work which had been ascribed traditionally to Origen is 'κατὰ πασῶν αἱρέσιων ἔλεγχος'. In the margin of MS. Ottobonianus 194, reads 'Ὠριγένους φιλοσοφουμένων'. I have used P. Wendland's ed. in GCS., *Hippolytus Werke*,

iii, Leipzig, 1916, and therefore have referred throughout to this work as *Elenchos* (=refutatio) (On the MS. tradition and earlier ed. see P. Wendland, op. cit., ix–xxiii.)

[100] *H.E.*, v.21.2; cf. Jerome, *De Viris Illust.*, 42 'a servo proditus'. Since Jerome's *De Viris Illustribus* was written in 392, and Rufinus' translation of Eusebius was not written until 395, Jerome could not merely have quoted from the latter, but was relying on an alternative tradition.

[101] *H.E.*, v.21.3; cf. *SHA.*, *Vita Pertinaci*, 9–10, 'eos qui calumniis adpetiti per servos fuerunt, damnatis servis delatoribus liberavit, in crucem sublatis talibus servis', cf. Herodian, v.2.2, a good piece of corroboration.

[102] One follows Th. Mommsen that the whole hearing took place before Perennis, and that so far as the accused himself was concerned, there were no closed proceedings before the Senate. Th. Mommsen, 'Der Process des Christen Apollonius unter Commodus', *SBAW.*, 1894, 497–503 at 499.

[103] Eusebius, *H.E.*, v.21.4.

[104] Eusebius, *H.E.*, v.21.4.

[105] 'Sancti Apollonii Romani acta graeca', *A.B.*, xiv, 1895, 286ff.

[106] A. Harnack, *Sitzungsber. der kgl. preuss. Akad. der Wiss*, 37, 1893, 721–46, publishing Buchardi's German translation of the Armenian *Acta*.

[107] R. Seeberg, 'Das Martyrium des Apollonius', *Neue kirchliche Zeitschrift*, 1893, 3, 836–72.

[108] E. G. Hardy, *Christianity and the Roman Government*, 200–8 (pp. 154–61 in 1894 ed.).

[109] A. Hilgenfeld, 'Apollonius von Rom', *Zeitsch. f. wissenschaftliche Theol.*, 37, 1894, 59–81.

[110] Th. Mommsen, art. cit.

[111] Th. Klette, 'Der Process und die Acta S. Apollonii', *T.U.*, xv.2, 1897. A very full account, with the Greek and a German translation of the Armenian text of the *Acta*.

[112] J. Geffcken. 'Die Acta Apollonii', *Nachrichten der kgl. Gesellschaft von Wissenschaften zu Göttingen*, 1904. 262–84. G. regarded the *Acta* as a pious fraud ('als frommer Trug', p. 283), and as apologetic literature of the same type as the 'decree of Tiberius' quoted by Tertullian (*Apol.*, 5.13) or the story of the Thundering Legion as recorded in Eusebius, *H.E.*, v.5.4. In this case the object of the Christians was to discourage denunciations by pointing to the fate of the slave who denounced Apollonius. (Cf. Eusebius, *H.E.*, v.21.3 'ὅτι μὴ ζῆν ἐξὸν ἦν κατὰ βασιλικὸν ὅρον τοὺς τῶν τοιῶνδε μηνυτάς'.)

[113] C. Callewaert, 'Questions de Droit concernant le procès du Martyr Apollonius', *Rev. des Questions Historiques*, 87, 1905, 353–96.

[114] J. Zeiller, 'Sur un passage de la passion du Martyr Apollonius', *Mélanges Lebreton* (= *RSR.*, xl, 1952), 153–7.

[115] For the discussion of the significant verbal differences between Eusebius and Jerome, Th. Klette, op. cit. 10–13.

[116] Klette, op. cit., 20ff., following Mommsen.

[117] Eusebius, *H.E.*, iv.15.20.

[118] *Acta S. Justini*, 5.

[119] See below, p. 410–11.

[120] Chs. 24–26, and 37ff.

[121] Ibid., 14–19; cf. Justin, *1 Apol.*, 24, *Ep ad Diognetum* 2.2, Tatian, *Oratio*, 19 for similar reproaches against paganism.

[122] Ibid., 36; cf. Justin, *1 Apol.*, 33 and 46.

[123] Ibid., 27–30 and 41ff; cf. Justin, *1 Apol.*, 5. The calm resignation before death betrays a very different spirit from that of Christians who provoked their doom.

[124] Ibid., 42.

[125] For instance, one cannot ignore verbal similarities between the *Acta Apollonii* and

Greek apologetic works and *Acta*, such as for example the *Acta Pionii*. Note for instance, 'τὸν θεὸν τὸν παντοκράτορα τὸν ποιήσαντα τὸν οὐρανὸν καὶ τὴν γῆν καὶ πάντα τὰ ἐν αὐτοῖς καὶ πάντας ἡμᾶς' (ch.8.3 of *Acta Pionii*) and ch. 2 of *Acta Apollonii*, 'τὸν θεὸν τὸν ποιήσαντα τὸν οὐρανὸν καὶ τὴν γῆν καὶ τὴν θάλασσαν καὶ πάντα τὰ ἐν αὐτοῖς . . . .' or Apollonius 'ἡδέως 3ῶ' (ch. 30) and Pionius', 'καγὼ λέγω ὅτι καλόν ἐστι τὸ 3ῆν (5.6). These may be mere commonplaces, or may indicate that the *Acta Apollonii* was a later apologetic work dependent on authentic Greek Acta including the *Acta Pionii*. The general argument of the *Acta Apollonii* indicates, however, a late second-century, rather than mid-third-century work. For other parallels with apologetic works of second/third century, J. Geffcken, art. cit., 267ff.

[126] J. Zeiller, art. cit., 155.

[127] Note Hardy's suggestion (op. cit., 160) that Perennis induced the Senate to resolve that the ordinary course of procedure regarding Christians should be followed, and that armed with this Perennis condemned Apollonius to death when he refused to recant.

[128] Hippolytus, *Elenchos*, ix.12.8–9.

[129] Dio Cassius, lxxiii.7, Hippolytus, *Elenchos*, ix.11–12.

[130] Hippolytus, *Elenchos*, ix.12.11.

[131] Hippolytus, *Elenchos*, ix.12.12–13.

[132] For his career, see *CIL.*, vi.8498 (= *ILCV.*, 3332a) and art. 'Proxenes' in *DACL*. He became successively, procurator vinorum, procurator numerum (overseer of gladiators), procurator patrimonii, procurator thesaurorum, and a cubiculo Augusti, dying in 217. He was 'receptus ad Deum'.

[133] G. la Piana, 'The Roman Church at the end of the second-century', 250ff., cf. J. Leipoldt, *Die Frau*, 169–70.

[134] Bricks used in constructing a stairway leading to a new level of tombs came from Imperial brick works (*figulae novae*) in the reigns of Marcus Aurelius and Commodus. J. B. de Rossi, *Roma sotteranea* ii.240–4, H. Leclercq, *DACL.*, ii.1695–6.

[135] Toynbee and Ward-Perkins, *The Shrine of St. Peter*, 174. The Valentinian catacomb on the Viale Manzoni would seem to have been built between 215–230, and subsequently enlarged. J. Carcopino, *De Pythagore aux Apôtres*, 87–9.

[136] Cited from R. Walzer, *Galen on Jews and Christians*, p. 15.

[137] Tertullian, *Ad Scapulam*, 2.5. 'Sic et circa maiestatem imperatoris infamamur, tamen numquam Albiniani nec Nigriani vel Casiani inveniri potuerunt Christiani.'

[138] *SHA.*, Spartianus, *Vita Severi*, 17.1. I cannot agree with A. A. T. Ehrhardt 'Christianity before the Apostles' Creed' (*HTR.*, lv, 1962) 98, n.20, that Spartianus' 'Idem et de Christianis sanxit' is 'no more than a shameless interpolation' on the part of the anti-Christian 'Spartianus'. The evidence both of Eusebius, *H.E.*, vi.2–3 and for the West, the *Passio Perpetuae*, show quite clearly that the weight of persecution fell not indeed on catechumens (as A. Ehrhard, *Die Kirche der Märtyrer*, 1932, 49) but on converts, however long ago converted.

[139] See M. Platnauer, *Septimius Severus*, 92.

[140] Spartianus, *Vita Pescenn. Nigri*, 7.9.

[141] Tertullian, *Ad Scapulam*, 3.5.

[142] Spartianus, *Vita Severi*, 9.5.

[143] *Digest*, l.2.3.3.

[144] The most recent scholar to examine Spartian's evidence, K. H. Schwarte 'Das angebliche Christengezetz des Septimius Severus', *Historia*, xii, 1963, 185–208, follows Ehrhardt, and considers (p. 207) that, 'Mit Sicherheit konnte festgestellt werden, dass Septimius Severus die Rechtslage der Christen nicht verändert hat. Was die Severusvita des "Spartians" hierüber zu berichten weiss, kann nicht als glaubhaft angesehen werden'. The victims of the outbreak would hardly thank Dr. Schwarte for telling them that the Severan decree against the Christians was an 'Erfindung'.

145 Hippolytus, *Comment. in Danielem* (ed. Bonwetsch), iv.18 (Syria), and ibid., 19 (Pontus).

146 Tertullian, *Adv. Marcionem*, iii.24—a separate incident from those cited above.

147 Hippolytus, *De Antichristo* (ed. Bonwetsch), 49 and 50, and *Comment. in Danielem*, ii.12; cf. Tertullian, *De Cultu Feminarum*, ii.13.6 (*CSEL.*, lxx. 95).

148 Tertullian addresses his *Apology* to the magistrates of Carthage in consequence of recent persecution (*Apol.*, 1.1). In the *De Spectaculis*, *circa* 200, he implies that persecution continued to be suffered. In the *Acta Perpetuae*, 13.3, Saturus saw many fellow-Christians whom he recognized in Paradise as martyrs.

149 See *Scorpiace*, 1, and *Ad Scapulam*, 1. The dating of the persecution in Alexandria is fixed by Eusebius' statement (*H.E.*, vi.3.3) that Origen grew up in the persecution under Aquila 'governor of Alexandria', and Subatianus Aquila succeeded Quintus Maccus Laetus as Prefect of Egypt early in 202.

150 J. G. Davies, 'Was the Devotion of Septimius Severus to Serapis the cause of the persecution of 202–203?', *JTS.*, N.S. v. 1954, 73–6.

151 *SHA.*, Spartian, *Ant. Caracallus*, 1.16 'ob Iudaicam religionem gravius verberatum'.

152 Eusebius, *H.E.*, vi.12.1. Serapion of Antioch tried evidently to re-convert him.

153 Dio Cassius, xxxvii.17.

154 This seems evident at least if one trusts Hippolytus, *Comment. in Danielem*, iv.51, 'πάντων πιστῶν πανταχοῦ ἀναιρουμένων καὶ κατὰ πᾶσαν πόλιν καὶ χώραν σφαζομένων', (ed. Bonwetsch, 318); cf. ibid., iv.50 (Jews and pagans against Christians).

155 Eusebius vi.5; cf. F. Augar, 'Die Frau im römischen Christenprocess', *T.U.*, N.F. xiii. 4, 1905, 17ff.

156 Eusebius, *H.E.*, vi.11.4.

157 *Acta Perpetuae*, iii.1 and v (ed. Knopf and Krüger. Note extensive bibliography, p. 44).

158 Ibid., vi.3.

159 *Stromata*, ii.20.125. Christians' endurance compared to the feats of fakirs recorded by Zeno, cf. ibid., ii.180.26, and ii.283.18.

160 Eusebius, *H.E.*, vi.2–3.

161 Ibid., 5.1–4; cf. Palladius, *Lausiac History* (ed. Lowther Clarke), lxv, citing Hippolytus. Potamiaena's death was remembered in Alexandria a century later.

162 Origen, *Homil. in Jerem.*, 4.3. (ed. Klostermann, 25–6).

163 Hippolytus, *In Danielem*, 1.23 (Bonwetsch, 35).

164 On St. Caecilia, see *D.C.B.*, art. and H. Delehaye, 'Etude sur le Legendrier romain', *Subsidia Hagiographica*, 23, 1936, 77–96. Her *Acta*, dating perhaps to the end of the fifth century, record how she converted her pagan husband Valerian and her brother, Tiburtinus, and all were martyred. The *Acta* place their deaths in the reign of Alexander Severus, which seems unlikely, and the possibility of confusion between the latter and Septimius Severus should not be ruled out. In which case 202/203 would be the obvious date.

165 Hippolytus, *In Danielem et Susannam*, 13 (Lagarde, 147). They agreed, 'ἐν ταῖς θεωρίαις καὶ ἐν παντὶ κοσμικῷ πράγματι'.

166 On the whole, one accepts the traditional view that Hippolytus was a Roman presbyter and rival to Callistus for the bishopric in 217, anti-pope and fellow exile with Pope Pontian 235–236 (see K. J. Neumann, *Hippolytus von Rom und seine Stellung zu Staat und Welt*, Berlin, 1902). The alternative view expounded by P. Nautin, that in fact 'Hippolytus' can be divided into three distinct people, a Jewish-Christian, Josephus who was the anti-pope, a loyal Roman presbyter, Hippolytus, and a firebrand Palestinian bishop of the same name, seems to cause more difficulties than it solves. Granted that it is not easy to associate the writer of the *Refutation of all the heresies* (the *Philosophoumena*) with the Hippolytan Syntagma *Against all the Heresies* or the *Commentary on Daniel*, it is

even more difficult to imagine an unknown Palestinian revolutionary so well informed about the Western world that he could relate in detail events in Corinth, who wrote a vast amount, including letters to the Empress Mammaea, had Origen as an admirer, and yet passed so completely out of history that Eusebius writing in Caesarea did not know where he had been bishop (see A. Harnack, *Chronologie*, ii.228, P. Nautin, 'La controverse sur l'auteur de l'Elenchos', *RHE.*, xlvii, 1952, 5–43, *Hippolyte et Josipe*, Paris, 1947, and chapters viii–x in *Lettres et Ecrivains*, reviewed by the author, *JTS.*, N.S. xiiii, 1963, p. 169).

[167] Hippolytus, *In Danielem*, iv.51 (Bonwetsch, 318–20). This would seem to have been written in the midst of the persecution, or when its memory was still vivid (i.e. 203–204).

[168] Ed. W. H. Lowther Clarke, ch. lxv, pp. 171–2.

[169] H. Mattingly, *Coins of the Roman Empire in the British Museum*, v, 1950, clxxi, and 326.

[170] *Ad Scapulam*, 4.6.

[171] Ibid. On the reputed friendliness of both Severus and Caracalla towards the Jews also, Jerome, *Comment. in Daniel* 11[34] (*P.L.*, 25, 570) 'Hebraeorum quidam haec de Severo et Antonino principibus intelligent, qui Judaeos plurimum dilexerunt'.

[172] Tertullian, *Ad Scapulam*, 4.7.

[173] Note for Carthage also, Tertullian, *Ad Uxorem*, ii.1 (Christian wives of pagan husbands).

[174] Hippolytus, *Elenchos*, ix.12–24. See, *Digest*, xxiii.2.16, 'Oratione divi Marci cavetur, ut si senatoris filia libertino sumpsisset, nec nuptiae essent', Paulus, *Sententiae*, ii.19.6. 'Inter servos et liberos matrimonium contrahi non potest; contubernium potest'; cf. *Digest*, 1.9.8 and 9 and xxiv.1.3.1.

[175] Eusebius, *H.E.*, vi.19.15 (before the riots in Alexandria of 215).

[176] Hippolytus, *Elenchos*, ix.12.14 (Wendland, p. 248), εἰς τὸ κοιμητήριον κατέστησαν'.

[177] See the important resumé of material by H. Leclercq, 'Calliste (Cimetière de)', *DACL.*, ii.1664–1754.

[178] Tertullian, *Ad Scapulam*, 3.1.

[179] Cf. *CIL.*, xiv.2112 (a *collegium* of Esculapius), ' . . . kaput ex S(enatus) C(onsulto) P(opuli) R(omani). | Quibus coire convenire collegiumque habere liceat. Qui stipem| menstruam conferre volent in funera, in it (*sic*) collegium|coeant neque sub specie eius collegi nisi semel in men|se coeant conferendi causa, unde defuncti sepeliantur. . . . '

[180] On this question, G. Bovini, *La Proprietà ecclesiastica e la Condizione giuridica della Chiesa in età preconstantiniana*, Milan, 1948, 95ff., and G. Krüger, *Die Rechtstellung der vorkonstantinischer Kirchen*, Stuttgart, 1935, 322, 'Die vorkonstantinischen Kirchen sind niemals als Begräbnisgemeinschaften organisiert gewesen'.

[181] Ignatius, *Polyc.*, 4.3. 'μὴ ἐράτωσαν ἀπὸ τοῦ κοινοῦ 'ἐλευθεροῦσθαι' (regarding freeing of slaves).

[182] Lucian, *De Morte Per.*, 12. 'τῶν χριστιανῶν στελλόντων ἀπὸ τοῦ κοινοῦ'. See G. Krüger, *Die Rechtstellung der vorkonstantinischer Kirchen*, 150–6, and 165–7 on these texts.

[183] G. Bovini, op. cit., pp. 114–25.

[184] See above, ch. V, p. 139.

[185] P. Monceaux, *Histoire littéraire*, 1.9. Note also the Christian use of the Jewish term *corban* to denote offerings in the Carthaginian Church, Cyprian, *De Opere et Eleemosynis*, 15.

[186] Inscriptions found in the cemetery near the site of the present San Ambrogii church at Milan, and note also Ambrose's claim that the bodies of the martyrs in the Great Persecution,Vitalis and Agricola were found in the Jewish cemetery in 393, *Exhort, Virgin.*, 1.7, and Paulinus, *Vita Ambrosii*, 29. It is interesting that at Salona the Christian cemetery was described as 'de lege christiana' in contrast to the rival (?) cemetery 'de lege judaica', see *CIL.*, iii.9508 and B. Gabričevič, 'Una nuova inscrizione Salonitana', *Atti dell' iii Congresso internazionale di Epigrafica greca e latina*, Rome, 1959, 79.

[187] For instance, at Edessa, Carthage, and Rome. See the detailed discussion in G. Krüger, op. cit., 147ff.

188 *Chronicle of Edessa* (ed. L. Hallier, *T.U.*, ix.1, 1892), *sub anno* 513 = 201, p. 86. It was obviously a prominent building.

189 G. Bovini, op. cit., p. 145ff.

190 Lampridius, *Alexander Severus*, 22. Origen's *Commentary on Matthew*, with its detailed information about the administration of Church property, written in Philip's reign, also had a wide circulation. Eusebius, *H.E.*, vi.36.2. In Antioch in the 260s immovable property was clearly vested in the hands of the bishop who was by then a public figure. It may have been the same elsewhere.

191 Eusebius, *H.E.*, v.28.14.

192 Lactantius, *Institutes* (ed. Brandt), v.11.19. In Book 7 of 'De Officio Proconsulis'.

193 See H. Mattingly's account in *Coins of the Roman Empire in the British Museum*, v (London, 1950), cxxxiii, and *CAH.*, xii.356–7 (cites references).

194 H. Mattingly, *Coins*, v.163–4 (Mint of Rome). 'Mater deum'.

195 See Alexandrian coins discussed by Abd el Mohsen el Khachab, ὁ καράκαλλος κοσμοκράτωρ', *J.E.A.*, 47, 1961, 119ff., and F. Cumont and L. Canet, 'Mithra ou Serapis ΚΟΣΜΟΚΡΑΤШΡ', *C.R.A.I.*, 1919, 313–28.

196 Philostratus, *Life*, 1.4.

197 Ibid., vi.43, 'τὰ πρὸς βασιλέας, οἱ ξύμβουλον αὐτὸν ἀρετῆς ἐποιοῦντο'.

198 P. de Labriolle, *La Réaction païenne*, 183.

199 Philostratus, *Life*, viii.11–12.

200 Ibid., viii.31.

201 P. de Labriolle, op. cit., 185; but see also O. Seeck, *Geschichte des Untergangs*, iii.182–3.

202 For instance, *Life*, v.30. Apollonius claimed, 'it was not permitted him by the religion of the Indians to proceed at mid-day in any other way than the Indians do themselves'; cf. iii.15.

203 For instance, *Life*, iii.1–16, v.30, vi.11, viii.7.4.

204 Scythianus, for instance, the Manichaean missionary was a rich merchant engaged in the trade between India and the Roman Empire, Epiphanius, *Panarion*, lxvi.1.

205 Hierocles, the governor of Bithynia's comparison between Apollonius and Jesus, Lactantius, *Institutes*, v.3, and Eusebius, *Contra Hieroclem Liber*, 1.1. (*P.G.* 22, 796ff.).

206 Eusebius, *H.E.*, vi.21 simply says that he lived as bishop five years, but tradition relates that he was scourged in a popular rising and eventually flung into a well; cf. R. Meiggs, *Roman Ostia*, 523 (concerning Asterius).

207 *SHA.*, Lampridius, *Ant. Heliogabalus*, 3.5. 'Dicebat praeterea Iudaeorum et Samaritanorum religiones et Christianam devotionem illuc (to the Palatine, where the Emperor was attempting to enforce the practice of his own exotic cult), transferendam, ut omnium culturarum secretum Heliogabali sacerdotium teneret'. The interest of this passage is that it shows that it was not outlandish to associate Christians, Jews and Samaritans together as different representatives of one type of cult.

208 *SHA.*, Lampridius, *Alex. Sev.*, 22, 29, 43, 45, 49 and 54.

209 K. Bihlmeyer, *Die 'Syrischen' Kaiser zu Rom* (211–35) *und das Christentum*, Rothenburg, 1916, 75. N. H. Baynes, *The Historia Augusta*, Oxford, 1926, ch. iii, and pp. 57ff. arguing for the date of the compilation under Julian.

210 J. B. Segal, 'Pagan Syriac Monuments in the Vilayet of Urfa', *Anatolian Studies*, iii, 1953, pp. 107–19. But, as P. Haase has pointed out neither Julius Africanus nor Epiphanius regarded Abhgar as Christian, though he was 'ἱερός ἀνήρ' to the one, and 'ὁσιώτατος καὶ λογιώτατος' to the other. He may have been a Jew and his kingdom Jewish at this date (P. Haase, *Altchristliche Kirchengeschichte*, Leipzig, 1925, 85). The story given in Eusebius, *H.E.*, 1.13 of Tobias acting as intermediary between the apostle Thaddaeus and Abhgar, perhaps conceals the historical fact that Christianity came to Edessa via Judaism.

211 See F. C. Burkitt's remarks, *CAH.*, xii, 496–8.

[212] W. Bauer, *Rechtgläubigkeit und Ketzerei*, 167, citing George Syncellos regarding Africanus' purchase of books of Egyptian magic while visiting the Catechetical School at Alexandria. Another instance of third-century syncretism of magic and Christianity is provided by the great Paris magical papyrus ll. 3019–20 where 'Jesus god of the Hebrews' is invoked together with unpronounceable demonic names, and on the Leiden Papyrus, Jesus is identified with Anubis. (ed. Ch. Wessely, *P. Or.*, iv.187–90).

[213] Lampridius, *Alex. Sev.*, 29. These references are fully discussed by Bihlmeyer, op. cit., pp. 103ff., and Baynes, op. cit., 134ff.

[214] Ibid., 45.

[215] Ibid., 49.

[216] *Dura Report*, v.248.

[217] *Pap. Oxy.* (ed. Grenfell and Hunt), iii, no. 412, lines 56ff.

[218] On this work, lost except for six small fragments in Syriac and two others quoted by Theodoret of Cyrrhus in *Eranistes*, see H. Achelis, 'Hippolytstudien', *T.U.*, N.F. 1.4, 1897, 189–94.

[219] 'εἰ καὶ τις ἄλλη θεοσεβαστάτη γυνή', Eusebius, *H.E.*, vi.21.3; cf. Lampridius, *Alex. Sev.*, 14,7, 'mulier sancta'.

[220] *H.E.*, vi.21.3.

[221] Bihlmeyer's suggestion, op. cit., 139–43.

[222] Gregory's *Address to Origen* (ed. and tr. W. Metcalfe), 5.

[223] *Ad Nationes*, 1.14. Written in 197; cf. *Apol.*, 37.4, and Tertullian's similar statement fifteen years later to the Proconsul Scapula—'Tanta hominum multitudo pars paene civitatis unius cuiusque'—*Ad Scapulam*, 2.

[224] Tertullian. *Apol.*, 18.4.

[225] Ibid., 18.3–4.

[226] Minucius Felix, *Octavius*, 8.4. Written probably *circa* 210.

[227] Minucius Felix, *Octavius*, 9.1.

[228] Ibid., 33.1; cf. 31.7.

[229] Eusebius, *H.E.*, vi.2.

[230] See below, p. 360.

[231] Tertullian, *Adv. Marcionem*, iii.20, 'Aspice universas nationes de voragine erroris humani exinde emergentes ad deum creatorem, ad deum Christum'.

[232] Minucius Felix, *Octavius*, 22.8.

[233] Tertullian, *Apol.*, 15.5–6.

[234] In an exceedingly valuable article, 'Pertinax et les prophètes de Caelestis', *R.H.R.*, 155, 1959, 41–62. I fully accept Charles-Picard's criticisms of the details of the argument found in my *Donatist Church*, p. 82 concerning the correlation of the romanization of the African Punic and Libyan cults and the spread of Christianity (art. cit. 56–8). It is also pleasant to find one's main thesis accepted, and the movement that led to the rapid change of religious allegiance pushed back to the middle of the second century. African Christianity in the second and third centuries was a religion of the 'petits gens'—just as Saturn-worship had been until then.

[235] Mme. C. Picard, *Catalogue des Collections puniques du Musée Alaoui*, and L. Leschi, *Etudes d'Epigraphie, d'Archéologie et d'Histoire africaines*, 117–23.

[236] For the survival of child sacrifice in the cult of Saturn/Caelestis at Carthage in the second century, C. Poinssot, *Karthago*, vi.1955, 36ff. Tertullian's father had been involved in the process of suppression, *Apol.*, 9.2 (ed. Waltzing). For a twentieth-century parallel, note the Kikuyu Nationalists' championship of female circumcision against the efforts by the Protestant missionaries and Kenya Government to suppress it as a cruel custom.

[237] J. Toutain, *Les Cultes païens*, i.3., 96–113. Other examples quoted in my *The Donatist Church*, 80–1.

[238] *SHA.*, *Vita Pertinaci*, 4.2.

239 *De Pallio*, 2.

240 See my 'Der Donatismus und die afrikanische Kirche', *Wiss. Zeitsch. der Martin-Luther Universität*, Halle, 1961, 55–6.

241 Dio Cassius, li.2. It is interesting that at Carthage in 203 the magistrates seem to have been worried lest Perpetua and her companions should be able to escape from prison by the use of magic spells and incantations—('ne subtraherentur de carcere incantationibus aliquibus magicis')—*Passio Perpetuae*, 16.2, and Tertullian, *Apol.*, 7, for the general belief in Christian black magic at this time.

242 Lampridius, *Vita Alex.*, Severi, 68.1 describes him as 'omnium vir sanctissimus'. As *praeses* of Pontus he was remembered by Firmilian as 'dirus et acerbus persecutor' (Cyprian *Ep.*, 75.10). Below, p. 391.

243 Tertullian, *Ad Scapulam*, 4.12. It may have been some violent local outbreak that allowed the future Alexander of Jerusalem to claim the title of 'confessor' (Eusebius, *H.E.*, vi.11.5.).

244 Tertullian, *Ad Scapulam*, 3.5, and for the influence of a Christian wife on the outlook of a pagan governor. Hippolytus, *In Danielem*, iv.18.

245 Clement, *Stromata*, ii.283.18. 'We are persecuted not because we have done anything wrong, but because our Christian profession is supposed to be a sin against life'.

246 Minucius Felix, *Octavius*, 8.4. Caecilius' object is to demonstrate the difference between Roman *religio* and Christian *superstitio* (*Octavius*, 1.5.) while the Christian seeks to prove his religion to be *religio* (cf. 38.6). See G. Lieberg, 'Die römische Religion bei Minucius Felix', *Rheinisches Museum*, 106, 1963, 62–79.

247 Hippolytus, *Comment. in Danielem*, iv.18.

248 Tertullian, *Apol.*, 21.3.

249 Tertullian, *Apol.*, 3.2.

250 Ibid., 35.4 'nec ulli magis depostulatores christianorum quam vulgus'.

251 Lampridius, *Commodus*, 18, 'delatores ad leonem', Tertullian, *De Spectaculis*, 21, 'homicida ad leonem', *De Resurrect. Carnis*, 22, 'Christianos ad leonem', and *Apol.*, 40.

252 Tertullian, *Apol.*, 40.2; cf. Augustine, *De Civitate Dei*, ii.3, citing a current proverb 'Pluvia desit, causa Christiani sunt'.

253 Tertullian, *Apol.*, 40, and *De Spectac.*, 27.

254 *Ad. Nationes*, i.14 ,'Quod enim aliud genus seminarium est infamiae nostrae'.

255 Ibid. For Rome, Hippolytus, *ad Danielem et Susannam*, 13 (Lagarde, 147).

256 *Adv. Judaeos*, 1.

257 Origen, *Homil. i, in Ps.* 36, P.G. xii.1321c. 'Etiam nunc Iudaei non moventur adversus Gentiles, adversus eos qui idola colunt et Deum blasphemant, et illos non oderunt, nec indignantur adversus eos; adversus Christianos vero insatiabili odio feruntur.' At the same time, he shows in *Ep. ad. Africanum* that he was on sufficiently friendly terms with local Jews to consult these on points of Scriptural interpretation.

258 *Ep. ad Africanum*, 9. Written *circa* 240.

259 *Vita*, 50.1 'tantus ac talis imperator domi et foris', 51.4 'summus imperator'; cf. 65.2 and 66.1. See Bihlmeyer, op. cit. 83ff.

260 *Select Papyri* (ed. A. S. Hunt and C. C. Edgar), ii.94.

261 Herodian, vi.1.10, cf. Lampridius, *Vita*, 14.7, 'fecit cuncta cum matre' and even *xii Sibyll*, 269, νηπίαχος καῖσαρ.

262 Lampridius, *Alex Severus*, lxiii.5–6.

263 Eusebius, *H E.*, vi.28; cf. Paulus Orosius, vii.19.2 'qui (Maximinus) maxime propter christianam Alexandri, cui successerat, et Mameae matri eius familiam persecutionem in sacerdotes et clericos, id est doctores, vel praecipue propter Origenem presbyterum miserat'.

264 Herodian, vi.9.4 and vii.1.4, and 3.4; cf. Capitolinus, *Maximinus*, 9.7.

CHAPTER TWELVE

The Great Divide: Alexandria, Carthage and Rome, 190–240

THE gradual but continuous increase in the numbers of Christians in the Severan epoch brought its own problems. By now, many were Christians more through family tradition than conversion, and though even in Alexandria the unlettered seem to have made up the majority of the congregations[1] there were those whose wealth and position stood in the way of overt acts which could compromise them with their neighbours. As the days of persecution were forgotten, militancy towards the Roman Empire began to recede and the confessor forfeited more and more of his influence within the Church. Besides this, a slow but decisive shift had been taking place in the East regarding the Christian's ultimate hope. Millennial expectations were fading, and those who held them were tending to despair of their fulfilment. Thus *circa* 200 a bishop of Pontus is said to have told his flock 'If this (the Parousia) does not happen, as I have said, believe the Scriptures no more but let each one of you do as he will'.[2]

Few Christians, however, accepted this advice. In Asia the first decades of the third century saw the intellectual defences of Montanism and its allies crumble. If there are grounds for believing that the Quintus story in the Acts of Polycarp is an insertion, this would be the period for it. For the contrast between Quintus' 'rash folly' and 'martyrdom according to the Gospel' was a living issue.[3] The bishop, however, was gradually assuming the right to define valid martyrdom in the name of the Church. Only rural Phrygia disagreed. The legacy of traditional apocalyptic was being reduced to acceptance of the *anno Domini* calendar[4] and the cult of saints and martyrs,[5] that is, the heroic past.

Even in Palestine, where the Severan persecution[6] had revived Millenarist thought, the situation was changing. Julius Africanus could argue in 221 that the world would last for 6000 years, and on this reckoning encouraged his readers to look forward to another 300 years before the onset of the millennial period, the 'Sabbath' of the world.[7] Thus, all over the East hopes of the Parousia went slowly underground, deeply embedded indeed in the consciousness of the mass of Christians but only emerging in times of crisis. In the reign of Alexander Severus crisis seemed remote.

Yet just when the East was substituting a metaphysical for an apocalyptic view of Christianity, Tertullian was opening his defence of the faith in Carthage with a vindication of the open profession of the Name and the goal of martyrdom. In Rome too, Hippolytus in his earlier years was obsessed by the conviction that all creation was moving rapidly and irrevocably towards its doom. East and West were coming to be separated by profound differences in eschatological belief, which were to have repercussions both on their respective attitudes towards the State and their understanding of the nature of the Trinity. Between 190 and 240 the main issues which were to divide East and West and, within the Western camp, Carthage from Rome, were becoming defined. In this chapter we shall be following this development so far as it concerns the theology of martyrdom.

First, however, a word must be said about the great offshoot of the Church in Asia, planted in southern Gaul, which in the decade 185–195 provided the Christian communities throughout the Mediterranean with intellectual and also a measure of ecclesiastical leadership. For all their trust in the Paraclete and hopes for immediate entry into Paradise hereafter, the martyrs of Lyons had abhorred schism.[8] So did the principal survivor of the holocaust, Irenaeus, who *circa* 178 succeeded Pothinus as bishop of the Gallic community.[9] Irenaeus was a disciple of Polycarp,[10] and his impassioned letter to Florinus, written *circa* 190, shows how deeply Polycarp influenced his thoughts.[11] Polycarp, however, had impressed him first and foremost as bishop, as the 'blessed presbyter' who upheld Apostolic tradition in teaching and practice.[12] Episcopacy was linked with authority, sanctioned by the example of the apostles and their followers. 'Obedience is due', he wrote, 'to those presbyters in the Church who, as we have shown, are in the succession after the Apostles, and who with their episcopal succession have received, according to the will of the Father, the sure charisma of truth' (*Adv. Haer.*, iv.26.2.).[13] All other forms of Church government were heretical.

If this had been his final word, then the epitaph of the prophet and 'spiritual man' within the Church would have been written. But, as often happens with Irenaeus, if one penetrates deeper, one finds a curious ambivalence of thought. Perhaps the fact of the persecution and the death of his friends and his predecessor as bishop, sustained as they had been by the blend of Johannine and Maccabean ideals, had made too great an impact. He was not described by the confessors as ἀδελφὸν ἡμῶν καὶ κοινωνὸν and 3ηλωτὴν ὄντα τῆς διαθήκης χριστοῦ for nothing.[14] He was deeply suspicious of secular learning. Plato, even, he discusses only as a source of the Valentinian system. Instead, eschatology lay at the heart of his theology. The *Adversus Haereses* looks forward to the Millennium and to the end of the world as the climax of all human history (v.28), the final overthrow of the powers of evil who had done their worst only a few years before. Irenaeus is perhaps less cautious than Julius Africanus in his estimate of the timing of the End. The 6000 years allowed for the education of mankind with the object of its reconciliation with God were nearly completed.[15] The end would be sudden. The Church's task was to prepare for the Rule of the Just in the Millennium.[16] This mission was undertaken under the guidance of the Holy Spirit, for 'Where the Spirit of God is, there is the Church and all grace'.[17] Moreover, the witness of the Church was being proclaimed through martyrs, and demonstrated by prophetic individuals possessed of spiritual gifts.[18] Martyrdom was the divine means of winnowing wheat from the chaff. Significantly, he cites the example of Ignatius (though without naming him). 'A certain man of ours said, when he was condemned to the wild beasts on account of his witness regarding God, "I am the wheat of Christ, and am ground by the teeth of the wild beasts, that I may be found the pure bread of God".'[19] The martyr, whatever his standing in the hierarchy of the Church, was he 'who tried to follow in Christ's footsteps'[20] and as the true friend of Christ would reign with Him hereafter.

How ultimately, could the authority inherent in these 'friends of Christ' be harmonized with that of the bishops and clergy?

Irenaeus does not say. Nor does he reconcile the deification of mankind in spiritual union with God with the material reign of the Saints hereafter. It was left to Tertullian to show where these thoughts might tend, and point out how in the eschatological setting which he assumed, the progressive education and illumination of mankind should be directed ultimately through the New Prophecy.[21] Irenaeus, however, went no further than to refrain from attacking the Montanists by name—alone among the countless deviationists who felt the lash of his criticism.[22] Tertullian does not claim him as a fellow spiritual man, but praises him as 'a most thorough investigator of all doctrines',[23] for him a compliment indeed.

Irenaeus' dilemma may also be traced in his attitude towards the State. On the one hand, he was the first theologian who appears consciously to have regarded the Church on earth as a political unit, and who sought to demonstrate the fact. The Church was oecumenical in character and its king was Christ. His *amici* could be compared to those of the Emperor, and his rule as both *rex et deus* was superior to that of the Emperor.[24] Yet Irenaeus admits that secular rule was also divine in character. Because men did not fear God, God imposed upon them the fear of man himself. Government was not a primitive condition, but it had become necessary through the vices and shortcomings of mankind.[25] Under the restraint of human law men could attain to a limited degree of justice. Irenaeus took Roms. 13[1ff.] in its literal sense and condemned attempts to allegorize it,[26] and though he denounced Pontius Pilate as the agent of a tyrannical power in ordering the Crucifixion, he rejoiced in the earthly peace which that same tyrannical power guaranteed.[27]

These ideas were to have great influence on the thought of the Church in the West. Indeed, Irenaeus must rank as one of the founders of Western mediaeval political thought. He develops the implications of the Pauline attitude to the State and associates government with the results of sin—Original Sin it was soon to be.[28] Its powers, therefore, were limited and could have no absolute validity. In Africa in the early fifth century, the Donatist bishop Gaudentius was also to remind the Imperial Tribune, Dulcitius, that the role of the secular ruler was restricted to a narrow sphere. He was to maintain religious freedom and civil peace[29]—this was not much more than mere absence of fighting.

The *Adversus Haereses* was known in Egypt,[30] but Irenaeus' legacy was to be to the Western Church. There the divergent and not truly reconcilable elements in his theology were to inspire both the Catholics and their rigorist opponents. Ultimately, he was lost to Asia, where his doctrine of the Holy Spirit, combined with his sound sense and conciliatory temper, so amply demonstrated in the Easter controversy, might have provided a necessary corrective to the Montanizing tendencies of the Christians in his own country and to the Logos-theologians of Alexandria. Under Irenaeus, Smyrna could have become a powerful force in the development of Christian doctrine. As it was, Polycarp had no great intellectual successors in his own see. The vacuum caused thereby, coinciding both with the failure of Montanism, and the decline of the Judaeo-Christian tradition in the Greek East, was filled in the first half of the third century by the school of Alexandria.

In *circa* 200 this would have seemed an obvious development. The Christian community in the Egyptian metropolis was long established, comparatively wealthy, and intellectually active.[31] It possessed its own churches, and more important, the most famous Christian catechetical school in the Hellenistic world. The two dominant schools of thought throughout the second century had been the Jewish-Christian, represented by writings such as the Epistle of Barnabas and the Gospel of Thomas, and the Gnostics represented by the great teachers, Valentinus, Basilides and Heracleon. The line between what passed for orthodoxy and Gnostic heresy was finely drawn,[32] and the tendency of the Gnostics was against open confession and martyrdom. But practical considerations rendered a purely negative attitude towards martyrdom impossible. The Church, like Judaism, was compelled to proselytize or perish. The answer was provided by the close co-operation between the Alexandrian bishop and his clergy with the orthodox catechetical school.

The main tasks of this latter, as they appeared to its head, Clement (150?–215),[33] were the defence of Christianity against philosophic attacks[34] and the charge of atheism,[35] and by carrying the battle into the enemy camp, the conversion of educated

Greeks to an ecclesiastical Gnosticism. Only one who feared God, argued Clement, could be a true Gnostic and approach towards communion with God.[36] Christianity represented the fulfilment of all that was best in current Greek philosophy. The bridge of Platonism which Philo had used 150 years before in the cause of Judaism was to serve the Alexandrian Christians as faithfully. Plato, 'the Attic Moses',[37] could also become a forerunner of Christ.

To attain these ends, a new approach to the problem of the Church and secular society, and thus to the problem of martyrdom, was necessary. Clement's Christian Gnosticism was pragmatic, partly the result of his own inclinations, and partly of dealing with actual situations in the Church of Alexandria. As presbyter and teacher he came to realize that it was hopeless to tell the well-educated catechumen that the Greek poets were inspired by the devil.[38] There must be a positive evaluation of Greek philosophy, and hence of the whole range of Classical civilization. 'The earth is the Lord's and the fulness thereof, and anyone who seeks to help catechumens, especially if they are Greeks, must not shrink from scholarly study' (Stromata, vi.89). He believed (like Justin before him)[39] that philosophy was of divine origin, inferior as a guide to truth to the teaching of the Hebrew prophets, but none the less the gift of the Logos (Strom., vii.6.4). It should be regarded as a sort of preparatory stage to the reception of truth by the Greeks, and their understanding of the Incarnation. 'Even if Greek philosophy', says Clement, 'does not comprehend the truth in its entirety, and, in addition, lacks the strength to fulfil the Lord's command, yet it at least prepares the way for the teaching that is royal in the highest sense of the word, by making men self-controlled, by moulding character and making them ready to receive the truth' (Stromata, i.80). It provided, he argued, the 'preliminary cleansing and training required for the foundation of the faith, on which foundation the truth builds up the edifice of knowledge' (ibid., vii.20).

Thus, Greek philosophy and Christianity were partners, not equal partners—Clement, following Philo, uses the analogy of the relation of Sarah with Hagar to define the relationship between theology and philosophy[40]—but certainly not opponents. The world was the 'universal school' which provided the Christian with the means of perfection.[41] The ultimate reconciliation of Church and Greco-Roman world was therefore possible, even if only on the Church's conditions. Clement provides the justification in Platonic terms for the standpoint which had already been expressed a generation previously by Justin and Melito of Sardes. Ultimately all reality could be understood as an interrelated whole above and beyond space, time, and all rational existence, as a vast and graduated hierarchy each saving and being saved, held together by Faith.[42] In the visible universe, the Divine Logos was the great educator of mankind,[43] moving different nations forward by different means, first towards cleansing from sin, and then gradually, through acceptance of the Christian message and baptism into the Church, to an apprehension of the truth.[44]

Salvation could not be won by short cuts, by the sudden illumination of Gnostic conversion or the confessor's desperate defiance of a pagan magistrate. It demanded long and hard schooling in self-mastery, through prayer and contemplation inspired by love of God.[45] Love towards God was the distinctive mark of the Christian Gnostic,[46] and this love must be expressed in outward form by loyal membership of the Church.[47] Understandably enough, Clement found himself forced to fight not only current pagan objections to his message, but also enemies within the Christian camp; both the Gnostics and 'simple Christians' opposed him. Much as he approached the point of view of some of the Gnostic teachers, notably Heracleon, Clement utterly rejected the dualism, fatalism and anti-social individualism on which the Gnostic systems were ultimately founded. At the same time, the 'multitude', as Clement calls them, of 'orthodoxists', Biblical Christians to whom Greek philosophy or anything of pagan origin was anathema, were equally an embarrassment to him.[48] Even in Alexandria, the primitive Jewish-Christian outlook retained some of its vigour and popular appeal. Its hopes still made martyrs.

Naturally, Clement's views about martyrdom aroused bitter hostility. In an important passage in the early part of *Stromata*, iv, he sets out the opposition standpoints. He writes:

Now some of the heretics who have misunderstood the Lord, love life in a manner which is at once impious and cowardly, saying that true martyrdom is knowledge of God (which we also confess), and

that a man who makes confession by death is a suicidist and braggart.
... But, we too, say that those who rush to their death (for there
are some, who are not ours, but merely share our name, who hasten
to give themselves up, athletes of death out of hatred for the Creator),
these we say depart from life not as martyrs (ἀμαρτύρως),[49] even
though they are punished publicly. For they do not preserve the
true mark of faithful martyrdom, because they do not know the real
God, giving themselves up to a futile death like Indian fakirs in a
senseless fire. (*Strom.*, iv. 4.17–18).[50]

This is the first explicit statement of two contrasting views of
martyrdom, both of which were henceforth to be at variance with
orthodoxy. Clement himself shared with his pagan contemporaries
a horror of the volunteer martyr, and the parallel with the Indian
fakirs is reminiscent of Lucian. But he also takes up the more
serious arguments of the Alexandrian Gnostics, and in so doing
reveals his own attitude. By now, a generation after their teachers'
deaths, the Alexandrian followers of Basilides and Valentinus had
evidently pushed into the background some of the sublimated
Jewish apocalyptic of the latter and emphasized the Platonic
elements in their teaching instead. Clement states expressly that
they were appealing continuously to passages in the Third Book
of the Republic as 'an authority against (bodily) generation',
but he countered with another passage that emphasized the
value of physical education as a means of training character and
thereby improving the soul. The true Gnostic progressed
'through life and health', not by exaggerated asceticism prescribed by his Gnostic opponents.[51] Perhaps these latter were
comparing themselves mentally with the Guardians whom Socrates was discussing. They were the Christian élite, and the
Socratic advice applied to them. At this period the influence of
Plato on Alexandrine Christianity was being represented in the
first place through the activity of Gnostic heretics.

A more profound statement of the anti-martyr point of view
had also been made by Clement's elder contemporary as a teacher
in Alexandria, Heracleon (*flor.* 150–180), 'the most distinguished
follower' of Valentinus.[52] His influence, however, was still
considerable a quarter of a century later. He did not deny the
value of the martyr's death, but argued that it was only of relative
importance. Even among the Apostles, Matthew, Thomas,

Philip and many others had never been obliged to confess the Lord with their lives. They had merited their title of Apostle through their manner of life.[53] The same held good for the Christian. It was of no avail to confess Christ with one's lips and deny him by one's conduct. Living a perfectly controlled life, the Gnostic could not deny Christ, however he might depart this life.[54]

To these arguments of the Gnostic teachers, was added the widespread feeling of revulsion felt by many Alexandrian Christians (and also Christians in Rome) against any idea that worship of God necessitated persecution and the martyrdom of worshippers.[55] These were apparently left unaided by God to the tender mercies of the judges—arguments which provide further evidence for a weakening of the urge to witness among members of a settled Christian community in the early third century.

Clement had his answer, though, unlike his great successor, Origen, he was not the man to offer himself up as a victim. In the persecution of 202/203 he left Alexandria, apparently never to return. He admitted that in some ways he agreed with Heracleon, 'To make a defence of our faith is not universally necessary'.[56] Martyrdom in his view, was a culminating act,[57] the rare climax of a life already directed solely by love towards God.[58] That love towards God would involve suffering, but it involved equally the understanding and keeping of His commands. The daily advance towards Freedom, 'the perpetual exertion of the intellect' and the emancipation of the self from bodily passions were the mark of the real Gnostic Christian.[59] 'Whoever', says Clement, 'follows out the commands of the Saviour, bears witness (μαρτύρει) in each of his acts, by doing what He wills, consistently naming the Lord's name, and being martyrs by deed to Him whom they trust, crucifying the flesh with its desires and passions.'[60] The Christian's life should become an increasingly perfect reflection of the Divine Love, until having purged his soul from all impurities, the 'truly reasonable spirit' would be prepared 'to give up his body to him who asks'. He would have no further use for it.[61]

This was Clement's real conviction: Martyrdom was a daily act involving word, life, conduct, the whole man.[62] The 'truly reasonable' man would find himself automatically outside the ordinary rules and requirements of society. They did not apply to him. Instead, he advanced by continuous moral progress 'until', says Clement, 'leaving behind all hindrances and scorning the distractions of matter, he cleaves the heaven by his wisdom, and having passed through the spiritual entities and every rule and authority, he lays hold of the throne that is on high, speaking to that alone, which alone he knows'.[63] In the East, however, this ideal was to be the foundation, not of martyrdom, but of its substitute, Christian asceticism. The 'perpetual imperturbability' of Clement's sage provided a basis for those who were to seek in solitude gradually to ascend a ladder of perfection towards God. He provides a link between the Jewish Therapeutae of Philo's time and the first Christian monks. He is the first Christian writer who placed the ascetic ideal on the same level as that of the martyr. Death, let alone violent death, was not the only way to achieve Christian Gnosis. He rejected the idea of seeking reward by death, or reacting to fear of future torment.[64] No wonder Clement's works were to be found in the libraries of the solitaries of the Thebaid.[65] The marriage between Platonism and Christianity had begun a revolution in the history of the Christian's relation to the world.

Clement, however, was also a presbyter in a Christian community sufficiently subject to persecution to prevent a purely theoretical approach being acceptable. It was little comfort to tell his flock that persecution 'could not happen without the foreknowledge of God', that it had been prophesied, and that God did not afflict but tested the endurance of Christians.[66] The injustice of the pagan magistrate was not a reflection of God's providence, but the act of a man who 'used his free-will wrongly'.[67] Such arguments were calculated only to swell the numbers of those who either rejected martyrdom altogether or in desperation rushed forward to their doom. It was Basilides' problem over again, and Clement had no real answer.

Clement tried to reconcile his convictions with traditional views of the Christian's battle against demonic powers,[68] and he willingly acknowledged the value of confession for the Name, citing the examples of faith found in i Clement in full, and the Lord's own precepts regarding suffering and persecution.[69] But it is noticeable that he considers them from the ethical point of view only. Like a Stoic philosopher he records these and other noble examples of endurance drawn from secular drama and history.[70] These also were aids in the ascent to perfection. Though he cites i John to teach the duty of love towards God,[71] the passages in the Fourth Gospel, insisting on 'witness unto the truth' and the role of the Paraclete 'convicting the world in respect of sin and of righteousness and judgment' are nowhere mentioned. There is no hatred of the judges, no rejoicing over the fate of the damned and no eschatology in Clement's concept of martyrdom, such as we find in Tertullian (De Spectaculis, 30). Even after death the flames were chastening flames, and God listened to the cry of the repentant sinner.[72] In view of the fact that Clement's opponent Heracleon had composed a great exegetical treatise precisely on the Fourth Gospel, these omissions may not be accidental. Instead, the Christian is urged to turn his attention to Heraclitus' and other pagan writers' glorification of those who fall in battle for a noble cause,[73] or to Plato's praise of the happiness of the just man even under torture.[74] Pagan poets therefore share with Christian evangelists the honour of providing the Christian Gnostic with the means of purifying his soul before he seeks release from the body. Characteristically, Clement ends the Fourth Book of Miscellanies with the words 'We know that the city of Plato is a copy (παράδειγμα) of that founded in heaven'.[75]

If Clement finds himself in some measure of agreement with the Alexandrian Gnostics, he has none with the simpler members of the 'great church'. Death indeed was to be despised, but not courted. There was nothing to be said for the fanatic who demanded extinction at the hands of the authorities.[76] Taking Mt. 10[23], 'When they persecute you in this city flee ye into another', he comments that it was clear that flight was advised, though not in order that the Christian should seek to avoid death or that persecution was a bad thing, but that we should not be the authors or abettors of evil, including evil to ourselves. 'If he who kills a man of God sins against God, he also who presents himself before the judgment-seat becomes guilty of his death.' The same was true of anyone who volunteered capture. Such a one was not a brave man but an accomplice of murder, and the same could be said of those whose acts provoked persecution. They were no better than gladiators, a prey to their own exhibitionism, blasphemers of the name.[77]

Recent students of Clement have underlined the traditional elements in his concept of martyrdom.[78] They have sought to link his emphasis on the martyr being the imitator of Christ with the ideas found in the *Acta Martyrum* of the second century, and even with Tertullian. It is quite true that, like his African contemporary, Clement regarded martyrdom as a means of bliss for the victim, by definition an act of repentance and a cleansing (ἀποκάθαρσις) from sin.[79] Both also emphasized the element of love towards God in the martyr's action.[80] But the differences between the outlooks of the two men were fundamental. Clement regarded the confessor's death as one among many means of salvation. Tertullian accepted it as the only sure means.[81] Only martyrs were seen in prophetic visions of Paradise.[82] Clement's Gnostic might undergo martyrdom as one incident in an existence continuously made more in the image of God. He died without heat or hate, God 'using up for good the wrongs which His adversaries have dared against Him'.[83] Tertullian's martyr died under the immediate inspiration of the Holy Spirit in the assurance that he would meet his adversaries in changed roles on the Last Day.

Ultimately, these contrasts rested on profound metaphysical differences. Clement's theology was really Binitarian, the Logos guiding, instructing and illuminating the human race in its onward progress towards imitation of a loving God, and combining in itself the attributes of Son and Holy Spirit. The Logos could indeed be identified with Jesus Christ as Word Incarnate, and though he mentions the Spirit as the agent of Faith in the believer there would appear to be little real place for Him in his system.[84] The single phrase 'and in the Holy Spirit', following the Christological paragraph in the Creed of Nicaea sums up the embarrassment of the Alexandrine school at the necessary existence of the Third Person. The Eastern theologians were never at ease in trying to reconcile the progressive education of humanity through the Logos with the Incarnation of Christ through the Holy Spirit.

In the West, however, the Holy Spirit was vital. He permeated the Christian's life from baptism to death, or as he might have expressed it from his baptism by water until his baptism of blood. The baptismal water was defined by Tertullian as 'the abode of the Holy Spirit';[85] it was poured out upon the convert, separating him from the world and saving him from involvement in its destruction. It hovered over the whole congregation whether large or small 'where three were gathered together in the name of the Trinity'.[86] It inspired the 'discipline' of the Church, meaning the entire range of Christian life outside the Rule of Faith. It urged the Christian to witness and to martyrdom, and it entered the prison with the confessors.[87] The reward of martyrdom was not condemnation as an unphilosophic exhibitionist but full pardon for all sins. Thus, Tertullian told the magistrates at Carthage 'all sins are forgiven to a death like this. That is why, on being sentenced by you, we give thanks to God'.[88] Conversely, where there was no Spirit there could be no Church. In words reminiscent of the Baptismal controversy of 255–6, 'the unclean could not cleanse, the lost liberate and the condemned acquit'.[89] Though Tertullian sometimes identifies Logos and Christ[90] the emphasis of his thought lay on the Spirit. It was the Platonizing Christian whom he named as an heretic.[91]

Clement's object was to harmonize the spiritual appeal of Gnosticism with the traditional teaching of the Church. The immense difficulties in the way of such an aim can be illustrated by his outlook towards the practical problem presented by a wealthy and educated congregation. There is no mistaking the significance of his tract, 'The Rich Man's Salvation', nor the answer which he gives to the question he raises. The problem was that of the wealthy would-be convert, and of rich Christians being treated with insolence by members of the Church who took the Scriptures literally.[92] Clement's method was to state the general proposition that it was not in the nature of God the giver of all good gifts to exclude from salvation those who enjoyed them and then to show that the parable of the Rich Young Man (Mk. 10[17-31]) was susceptible to meanings other than the obvious. The words in the story 'must not be understood literally, but with due inquiry and intelligence we must search out and master their hidden meaning'.[93] This enables Clement to assert that wealth could be a good thing ('We must not then fling away the riches that are of benefit to our neighbours as well as ourselves')[94] and put the whole issue as one of conduct. Outward things were a matter of indifference in themselves; what counted was their use. 'In this way then, the Lord admits the use of outward things, bidding us put away, not the means of living, but the things that use these badly.' Wealth rightly used 'to do some noble or divine deed', used in trust for others, made the possessor blessed.[95] Salvation depended not on material wealth or poverty, 'but with the character and disposition of the soul with regard to its obedience to God, and his ability to free himself from the desire for personal possessions'. Condemnation was determined conversely 'by transgression of commandments and accumulation of evil'. The rich young man had failed to understand the Master properly.[96] So perhaps had Clement.

Clement was using the same type of argument regarding riches that he had already used concerning martyrdom. In this too, he was paving the way for the monastic ethical ideal. No act of abnegation taken in isolation availed the Christian if his general conduct was evil. It was by daily abstinence and constant right use of free-will that the Christian attuned his soul to God. In this process wealth was neutral. It gave opportunity for use either for love of one's neighbour or for wasteful display.[97] The rich man, like any other Christian, could gain an eternal habitation.[98]

As Butterworth quite rightly points out, as the result of Clement's exegesis we are robbed of one of the most striking appeals to man's heroism that even the gospels contain.[99] Indeed, we find in Clement precisely those arguments in support of riches that Tertullian puts in the mouths of pagans and lax Christians who sought to defend the presence of Christians at pagan shows. 'It follows, they urge, that a thing cannot be counted foreign to God or hostile to Him that exists by His creation.'[100] This is what Clement was saying about wealth. Few issues show more clearly the rift between Eastern and Western thinking, between the concept of the universal Church assimilating the best of the surrounding world, and 'the Christian sect' in prayer awaiting the trumpet of the Angel.[101]

It is perhaps fortunate for the Church that Clement and Tertullian never met. If they had, or if the views of Clement and Origen had been propagated in Africa and Italy, the schism between East and West might have occurred in the third and not in the eleventh century. For if Tertullian could have found some fellow feeling with Origen, there was little in common between his views and Clement's. Though both theologians regarded the Gnostics as the most serious enemy of the Church, their own rebuttals of Gnostic teaching were poles apart. Clement recognized common ground with Heracleon, and only diverged from him because he regarded Gnosis without the continuous guiding power of the Logos through the Church as vain. With Tertullian, however, we find ourselves once more in the atmosphere of the past. It is an atmosphere of radical apocalypticism, of Maccabean inspiration, of siege conditions for the gathered community, of utter rejection of pagan society and pagan philosophy, of open disavowal of civic responsibilities and counsels of civil disobedience, of fear rather than love of God, of Judgment and hell-fire, of provocation of persecution and joyful voluntary martyrdom. To Clement the Christian Gnostic was the type of perfect Christian. To Tertullian it was the martyr.

Why this should be so remains for the moment a mystery. The origin of the African Church is one of the great 'missing links' in Church History. If we knew more about the beginnings of the Church there, we should be in a better position to say why Montanism was so successful in the West, and why the hard, rigorist, martyr-inspired code which it represented should find a permanent place in the Christianity of North Africa and hence in the Western Church as a whole.

It is not intended to repeat here what has already been said at length on this subject in other places.[102] Certain facts are, however, necessary to understand the part which martyrdom played in the thought of the North African Christians.

(a) Our knowledge of Christianity in North Africa begins with a story of martyrdom. There is an element of protest against the world in the African interpretation of the Christian message from the outset.

(b) The cult of Saturn which provided part of the background to the conversion of North African Christianity was itself a Semitic religion, with close parallels to those of Palestine and Phoenicia, and it contained a strong expiatory element. Even in the second century this had scarcely emerged from the requirement of human sacrifice.[103] Substitutionary offerings were made in the clear knowledge that these were in a real sense 'life for life', and 'blood for blood'.[104] The worshipper was literally the 'slave of the god'[105] and he continued so to be as a Christian. In such an environment, martyrdom, as indicating the individual's sacrifice of himself in order to appease an implacable Deity, becomes readily intelligible.

(c) There seems to have existed a strong Rabbinic Jewish element in Carthage,[106] and numerous Jewish communities among the African cities.[107] Evidence suggests that the first Christian communities were closely allied to the Jews, and not only used Jewish cemeteries, but also adopted some elements of the practices and organization of the synagogue.[108]

(d) The African Church was strongly influenced by the Roman Church[109] and also, to judge from Tertullian's use of Irenaeus' *Adversus Haereses* to controvert to African disciples of Valentinus, by the Church in southern Gaul. Its language, if originally Greek, like the rest of Mediterranean Christianity, had changed decisively to Latin by 200.[110]

The precise share each of these factors had in shaping the African Church is difficult to define. Coupled, however, with the lack of Greek philosophical influence, they must necessarily have resulted in African Christianity following different lines from those of its contemporary in Alexandria. Even without the genius of Tertullian the contrast would have been evident.

By 200 Christianity in Carthage was developing along lines which were to guide it during the next two hundred years. It was proud of its character of a 'sect' continually inspired by the Holy Spirit, a body, says Tertullian, 'united by a common apprehension of religion, common discipline and common bond of hope.[111] Its hope was derived from Scripture from which source, 'we feed our faith, lift up our life and confirm our confidence'.[112] Already their defiance of the world and belief in the power of martyrdom had made them members of 'a race ever ready for death',[113] and to outsiders fanatics to whom terms like 'faggot-fellows' and 'half-axle men' could be applied.[114] In the Ancient World only the most desperate and vindictive elements among the Jews harboured similar ideals. In this environment confessors and martyrs were held in the highest honour. Vigils outside their prisons, services in the *areae* in which they were buried,[115] the cult of their anniversaries (*natalicia*)[116] and powers of forgiveness universally ascribed to them, raised their status beyond that of the clergy.[117] Theirs was a full *militia Christi* whose 'storm troops' (*agonistici*) they formed in the fight against Satan.[118] Their deaths were the seed of the Church.

The evidence derived from Tertullian's *Ad Martyras* and elsewhere is confirmed by another remarkable contemporary document. The *Passio Perpetuae* could be based on the diary and records of Vibia Perpetua and the Carthaginian priest Saturus during their imprisonment in 202/203, and edited by a sympathizer (Tertullian) shortly after their deaths in the Carthage amphitheatre either on 2 February or 7 March 203.[119] It would be difficult to imagine anyone besides Perpetua herself writing the poignant and repetitive scenes between herself and her father, or her physical experiences in connection with the suckling of her infant. The longer Latin *Acta* are a precious, first-hand account of North African Christian thought at the turn of the third century.

Perpetua and her companions were still unbaptized catechumens at the moment of their arrest.[120] Thus, their beliefs and hopes as narrated by them in their dreams, may reflect current teaching to converts by the Church at Carthage. There is no doubt that the tendency of this teaching was strongly apocalyptic. The Similitudes of Enoch, Hermas, Revelation, and perhaps the lurid and horrible Apocalypse of Peter, all seem to have had a part in their formation as Christians. Perpetua also seems to have been inspired by the visions recorded in Genesis, Jacob's ladder (Gen. 28[12]),[121] for instance, but there are few sure references to the teaching of the Synoptics or the Pauline epistles in the autobiographical sections of the *Acta*. On the other hand, the description of the dragon of immense size,[122] but cowed by the steadfast believer could perhaps be derived partly from the Leviathan vision in Hermas, *Vis.*, iv, the description in Saturus' vision of Paradise[123] might be a reminiscence of i Enoch 32,[124] and the details of its inhabitants from Rev. 7[9ff.] and Daniel 7[9]. As in Hermas three-quarters of a century or so before, the hope of everlasting material bliss in such surroundings and the dreadful fate awaiting pagans and deniers

must have contributed to the defiance of the confessors to traditional and legal authority. The pleas of the Procurator were
brushed aside with the same abrupt decisiveness as those of
Perpetua's father. ' "Spare the white hairs of your father; spare your
child. Make sacrifice for the *salus* of the Emperors." "I shall not do
so." "Are you a Christian?" and I replied, "I am a Christian" '[125]—a
moving dialogue which illustrates the gulf between her adopted
culture and that which she was leaving.

Like Ignatius of Antioch, the martyrs at Lyons, and the
Donatist confessors of the fourth century, Perpetua and her
companions were set on one thing only, the imitation of their
Lord through martyrdom. In prison they felt themselves to be
under the direct inspiration of the Holy Spirit.[126] Their baptism
by water was simply the preliminary to the real baptism of
blood.[127] They were to request nothing of the Spirit in the
baptismal waters 'except the suffering of the flesh'.[128] Perpetua
herself was represented as being 'in great honour', acknowledged
as such even by her pagan father,[129] one who could demand a
vision, could converse with the Lord, and intercede effectively on
behalf of a pagan brother doomed otherwise to suffer indefinitely
the torment in which he died.[130] It is not surprising that fifty years
later the Carthaginian confessors should have made similar
claims to bind and loose, and have won so powerful a following
as the result.[131]

In contrast, the unrepentant and exulting pagan mob was
condemned to an unpleasant fate. On the way to the amphitheatre Saturus turned on the crowd that was following, 'Today
friends, tomorrow enemies. However, note our faces well, so that
you may recognize us in that day'.[132] The crowd retired in
confusion, and 'many believed'. In the arena he and his companions paused in front of Hilarianus' box for one final gibe.
'You (have condemned) us, but God (will condemn) you.'[133] The
beasts he was to fight represented the Devil himself, but beyond
the arena was Paradise and the everlasting 'refrigerium',[134] the
expectation of which was to inspire the final moments of multitudes of Christians in the West.

One final point should be mentioned, namely, the martyrs'
views about the status of the clergy. Their catechist Saturus was
himself a presbyter, but he had surrendered to the authorities

voluntarily, and so was a confessor in his own right. Of the others named in the *Acta*, such as the deacons, Tertius and Pomponius,[135] the presbyter Aspasius and the bishop Optatus, Perpetua undoubtedly regards them as her superiors. When the quarelling Aspasius and Optatus fall at her feet beseeching her to make peace between them, she is mildly deprecatory of her powers. Pomponius, too, even though he was only a deacon, is called 'Pater'.[136] Due respect was paid to Optatus and Aspasius,[137] but their office was regarded mainly as one of administration. They had disciplinary functions directed to keeping the congregation free from compromise with the surrounding pagan world. 'Correct thy people', was the Angels' command to the priest Aspasius in Saturus' vision; 'they assemble before thee as if returning from a Circus, rioting over the factions.' But theirs was an auxiliary role compared with that of the martyr, unless, like the priest Saturus, they accompanied their flock to their appointed end. Neither Aspasius nor Optatus entered Paradise even after they had settled their dispute. Perpetua saw only martyrs there, as Tertullian emphasized.[138] The way, indeed, from earth to Paradise led not through the priesthood but only by combat with the powers of evil in the amphitheatre.

Such was the Christianity of North Africa to which Perpetua and her friends had been converted. In contrast to Clement's religion, and the religion of his converts among the wealthy Alexandrians, this was an apocalyptic and prophetic faith, accepting as certain the approaching end of the world, the coming of the Day, and filling its adherents with such exaltation that no human convention or punishment would deter, and no earthly loyalty could shake. To some contemporaries this was treason inspired by demonology.[139] In others it awoke a latent spirit of revolt at the cruelties of the age, and a savage urge to join the martyrs in their protest. Such a convert was Tertullian,[140] who in the course of the next twenty years transformed this attitude from a disorganized popular approach to the preaching of the Word, to be the tradition of the African Church.

Tertullian[141] was first and foremost a superb political journalist. His most effective pieces such as the *De Corona Militis*, *De Fuga in Persecutione*, *Ad Scapulam*, or *De Pallio* are all 2000–4000-word articles, rebutting someone or something, topical to the day.

He takes up a particular problem or controversy, ruthlessly exposing the flabbiness and cowardice of his opponents and replaces their sophistries with an uncompromising and revolutionary Christianity. He was probably trained as a lawyer. He was profoundly influenced by Stoicism. He accepted a Judaistic interpretation of Christianity.[142] But essentially he was a man in lifelong revolt.[143] Revolt against the 'officers' mess' life of his father's household turned him into a pacifist, revolt against romanization made him a rebel against the outward forms of Roman civilization in favour of that of Carthage,[144] the sight of men and women prepared to die rather than accept the conventional form of loyalty to the Severan age led him to Christianity. As a Christian, revolt against worldly and complacent priests in Carthage and Rome drove him to Montanism,[145] and finally, revolt against Montanism led him into the sectarian wilderness to await the Parousia with his own 'Tertullianists'.[146] To each religious allegiance he brought the gifts of a trained debater. The snap and fire of the staccato sentences, full of scornful antitheses and daring neologisms, the splendid sarcasm of a chapter like De Spectaculis, 25, summed up the whole movement of protest which African Christianity was representing. The direction which Tertullian gave to the Church in the West has never been wholly lost. He was the father of Donatism, and ultimately, the ancestor of all puritan nonconformity. His was one of the formative minds of European civilization.

His first works, written between 197 and 200, or even his first drafts, leave no doubt as to the cast of his mind, and what Christianity meant to him. 'It is therefore against these things that our business lies, against the institutions of our elders, against the authority of traditions, the laws of the masters of this world, the arguments of lawyers, against the past, against custom and necessity, against the examples, prodigies and miracles that have fortified this bastard divinity.'[147] Clement of Alexandria had inveighed against 'custom' as a stumbling block to conversion,[148] but the spirit of his argument was very different from Tertullian's. This was a declaration of war against those very things for which the Roman administration stood,[149] 'the mos maiorum', the rule of secular law, and the binding authority of custom, which for centuries before and after Tertullian was to direct the lives of his fellow North-Africans. It was followed by the denial of the possibility of Christian emperors, 'because Caesars are necessary to the world' (*saeculum*)[150] and, by the equally formal statement that 'nothing is more foreign to us than the State. One state we know, of which we are all citizens—the universe'.[151] It seems that after a vain effort to show his readers that the Christians were loyal citizens, that they respected the person of the Emperor even if they did not worship him, and that the Empire was mankind's shield from chaos,[152] he suddenly allows himself to be carried away, and to say in a few short biting sentences what he really thought. 'What greater pleasure', he adds in *De Spectaculis* three years later, 'than contempt for pleasure than scorn for the activities of the world.'[153] Like his contemporary and fellow agitator, Hippolytus, he despised the Severan Golden Age as the Danielic 'age of iron'.[154]

Tertullian's rejection of the achievement of the Roman Empire was complete. He even denied that the greatness of Rome was due to scrupulous religious observance. It was 'after the establishment of the Empire that religion flourished in Rome'. 'The Romans', he adds, 'were not religious before they were great, and therefore they were not great because they were religious.'[155] Here, Tertullian anticipates the arguments of Orosius by two hundred years.[156] The Western tradition of hostility to the pagan state did not alter. Nor in his own lifetime did Tertullian stand alone. There is an interesting passage in Minucius Felix put into the mouth of Octavius. 'All that the Romans hold, occupy, and possess is the spoil of outrage; their temples are all of loot drawn from the ruin of cities, the plunder of gods and the slaughter of priests.'[157] The texts, taken together, suggest that this was more than formal polemic against idolatry. Latin Christianity appears on the stage of history as opposition to the values of pagan Rome.

Rejection of civil obligations involved also rejection of Rome's literary and philosophic heritage. Here too, there could hardly be a greater contrast between the Alexandrian presbyter, thanks to whom hundreds of otherwise lost quotations from the Classics have been preserved, and the Carthaginian presbyter, Tertullian, writing the *De Praescriptione* round about the year 200. Far from philosophy being a school by means of which educated pagans approached Christianity, Plato, Aristotle and Zeno were the 'patriarchs of the heretics'. Why not?

> Heretics and philosophers handle the same subject-matter; both treat of the same topics—Whence came evil? And why? Whence came man? And how? And a question lately posed by Valentinus—Whence came God? Answer: 'From *enthymesis* and *ectroma*'! Wretched Aristotle! who taught them dialectic, that art of building up and demolishing, so protean in statement, so far-fetched in conjecture, so unyielding in controversy, so productive of disputes; self-stultifying, since it is ever handling questions but never settling anything. . . . What is there in common between Athens and Jerusalem? What between the Academy and the Church? What between heretics and Christians? . . . Away with all projects for a 'Stoic', a 'Platonic' or a 'dialectic' Christianity! After Christ Jesus we desire no subtle theories, no acute inquiries after the gospel (*De Praescriptione* 7).[158]

Logically enough, Tertullian's attitude towards earthly wealth was in complete contrast to Clement.[159] Christianity required not only abstinence from luxury as a necessary preparation for martyrdom, but withdrawal from practically every gainful employment, on the grounds that these conflicted with the Gospel or were connected with idolatry.[160] Even to become a tailor was dangerous, for to transform God's sheep into costly raiment was the devil's work![161] The Christian must renounce riches. Their possession was not merely an additional test to be surmounted but sin.[162] Wealth belonged to the world and the things of the world belonged to Satan.[163] It is true that we do not find quite that identity between poverty and sanctity in Tertullian that we encounter among the Donatists, but the lead was there, and it was one of those which Cyprian was to take over from his 'master' in the stress of the Decian persecution.[164]

But the Christian had no need to take up arms against this civilization. Martyrdom was the means of victory, in itself an act of vengeance, as the presbyter Saturus showed. The command was already '*ad tubam angeli erigere, ad martyrum palmas gloriare*'.[165] And what of the unfortunate adherents to the 'customs of their ancestors'? Or those who were a little worried at the prospect of the Parousia?[166] The unhesitating answer comes also from one of Tertullian's early works—the grand finale of *De Spectaculis*, 30, for sheer dramatic power, splendour of imagery and defiance of the world the equal to Revelation.

But what a spectacle is already at hand—the return of the Lord, now no object of doubt, now exalted, now triumphant! What exultation will that be of the angels, what glory of the saints as they rise again! What the reign of the righteous thereafter! What a city, the New Jerusalem! Yes, and there are still to come other spectacles— that last, that eternal Day of Judgment, that Day which the Gentiles never believed would come, that Day they laughed at, when this old world and all its generations shall be consumed in one fire. How vast the spectacle that day, and how wide! What sight shall wake my wonder, what my laughter, my joy and exultation? as I see all those kings, those great kings, welcomed (we were told) in heaven, along with Jove, along with those who told of their ascent, groaning in the depths of darkness! And the magistrates who persecuted the name of Jesus, liquefying in fiercer flames than they kindled in their rage against the Christians! Those sages, too, the philosophers blushing before their disciples as they blaze together, the disciples whom they taught that God was concerned with nothing, that men have no souls at all, or that what souls they have shall never return to their former bodies! And, then, the poets trembling before the judgment-seat, not of Rhadamanthus, not of Minos, but of Christ whom they never looked to see! And then there will be the tragic actors to be heard, more vocal in their own tragedy; and the players to be seen, lither of limb by far in the fire; and then the charioteer to watch, red all over in the wheel of flame; and, next, the athletes to be gazed upon, not in their gymnasiums but hurled in the fire—unless it be that even then would I wish to see them, in my desire rather to turn an insatiable gaze on them who vented their rage and fury on the Lord. 'This is he,' I shall say, 'the son of the carpenter or the harlot, the Sabbath-breaker, the Samaritan, who had a devil. This is he whom you bought from Judas; this is he, who was struck with reed and fist, defiled with spittle, given gall and vinegar to drink. This is he whom the disciples secretly stole away, that it might be said he has risen—unless it was the gardener who removed him, lest his lettuces should be trampled by the throng of visitors!' Such sights, such exultation—what praetor, consul, queastor, priest, will ever give you of his bounty? And yet all these, in some sort, are ours, pictured through faith in the imagination of the spirit. But what are those things which eye hath not seen nor ear heard, nor ever entered into the heart of man? I believe, things of greater joy than circus, theatre or amphitheatre, or any stadium.[167]   (Tr. T. R. Glover)

These are all the product of Tertullian's early years as a Christian, and may therefore be accepted as the outlook of the Carthaginian Church as a whole, where he was presbyter. If we move on to his transition to Montanism from 205–208 we find martyrdom and Divine Judgment continuing to enter every aspect of his theology. Even when he was considering deeply metaphysical questions such as the reality of Christ's flesh and the truth of His bodily resurrection, divine judgment was in the forefront of his thought.[168] Man was a 'slave of God'[169]—a fatalistic concept which contributed perhaps to the African insistence on Predestination. The flesh was raised so that it could be judged, and therefore the body was given back to the soul so that it could be rewarded or punished.[170] While the Alexandrians held passionately to the hope expressed by Origen that after death, he as a Christian would 'come forth from the body and rest with Christ'[171] the Africans took their stand on the corporeal nature of the soul and on bodily resurrection.[172] Tertullian hated the Marcionites because of their denial of the reality of Christ's flesh. 'Away', they cry, 'with those census-rolls of Caesar, always tiresome, away with the cramped inns, the soiled rags, the hard stall, the wise men, and the offering of the Child in the temple.'[173] They 'had invented a God who doth not take offence, who neither groweth angry, nor taketh vengeance, a God in a hell wherein no flames bubble forth, and which hath no outer darkness, no terrors to make you tremble, no gnashings of teeth'.[174] All these were realities in Christian Africa.

It is clear as one reads these writings, that even at Carthage there must have been many Christians who would not willingly accept all the implications of their faith which Tertullian would have imposed on them. They were, after all, human. The occasional visit to the circus, the use of eye-tint, the purchase of a new dress could hardly suffice to condemn the believer to hell. Ecclesiastical penances were harsh enough without attempting to make them more rigorous. There were sufficient fast-days already without additional *stationes*. Basically, the problem was the same as that which was affecting the Alexandrine and Roman communities, namely how to maintain the highest standards of a religious sect, in the face of a growing influx of less heroic converts.[175] Tertullian's reaction was to abandon the Carthaginian community in disgust and go over to the Montanists.

How the New Prophecy had established itself in Africa is unknown. A reasonable assumption would be that the sect spread to Africa via Rome. It is known that Montanism was strong in the capital, but that just about at this time official opinion was hardening against it. Perhaps Tertullian's quarrel with the Roman presbyters which was believed to have finally caused his secession[176] concerned it. From 207 onwards laudatory references to the New Prophets begin to appear in his work. In the *De Resurrectione Carnis*, they 'dispelled all former ambiguities' by an 'open and clear preaching of the whole mystery'.[177] His was no sudden conversion, but a hardening of certain principles where he had previously left scope for concession. In *De Paenitentia*, written *circa* 203, he had allowed, like Hermas, that a grievous sinner could be absolved once through the Church,[178] in *De Pudicitia*, this was withdrawn and Hermas bitterly criticized.[179] The penitent could only move the brethren to intercede with God, from whom alone forgiveness must come.[180] In *ad Uxorem* he allowed flight in persecution.[181] In *De Fuga* he does not.[182] He had not always been an encratite on matters of sex,[183] and as a Catholic presbyter there was a time when even women prophetesses would not have been welcome in his church.[184]

Montanism, however, seemed to confirm both his puritan bent and his view of the progressive revelation of God in the Church through the Spirit. As he wrote in the *De Virginibus Velandis*, 'With the Devil continuously at work, are we to presume that the work of God has become passive? The Paraclete is sent to teach Discipline gradually to human beings incapable of grasping it all at once.'[185] In the *De Monogamia* he is more precise. 'Nothing is without its stages of growth. Righteousness has passed through the fervour of youth in the Gospel period; now, through the Paraclete is settling into maturity. Hardness of heart endured until Jesus Christ, infirmity of the flesh reigned until the coming of the Paraclete. The Gospel forbade adultery. The Paraclete forbade second marriage.'[186] The reasoning could have been Irenaeus' in the fourth book of the *Adv. Haereses*,[187] but Tertullian's conclusions might have surprised the bishop of Lyons.

Apart from progressive revelation, the Montanist prophets justified a continuously more hostile attitude towards contemporary society, a more feverish expectation of the Parousia, and a correspondingly more scathing contempt for laxer and more easygoing Christians. Tertullian's hatred for the Roman Empire seems to have grown over the years. In *De Idololatria* (*circa* 211) he does not trouble to affirm the formal loyalty which characterizes the *Apology* fourteen years before. 'The fact that Christ rejected an earthly kingdom, should be enough to convince you that all secular powers and dignitaries are not merely alien from, but hostile to God.' Accordingly, 'there can be no reconciliation between the oath of allegiance taken to God and that taken to man, between the standard of Christ and that of the devil, between the camp of light and that of darkness. The soul cannot serve two masters, God and Caesar'.[188] The rebel against his father's military career had appropriated the terminology of the camp in the service of pacifism. To him, as to his Montanist co-religionaries in Phrygia, the *militia Christi* was a reality,[189] with its own *sacramentum* to Christ, its own *castrum*, its *signa*, obeying its own *disciplina* and grasping at the envied *corona*—that of the martyr. The Christians were *milites*. The unbeliever was dismissed as a *paganus*, a mere civilian.[190]

The duties involved in this 'warfare' are discussed without reserve in Tertullian's later works. The duty of the Christian soldier, he tells his readers in the *De Corona*, was to abandon the service of the Devil. 'What was there in common between Christ and Belial?' he asks.[191] The crown was unworthy of God; it was worthy, however, of the Devil—and Mithras, he adds as a final taunt.[192] In the *Scorpiace* his attack on the Gnostics who counselled against martyrdom contained a full-scale assault on 'idolatry' in every form. 'Ye shall utterly destroy all the places wherein the nations which ye shall possess by inheritance served their gods (cf. Deut. 12²)', he declared.[193] With this are coupled expressions of hate and contempt of Roman history and tradition.[194] But even so, the Christian's weapon was his own death, martyrdom not merely to be suffered, but to be provoked and granted as a reward.[195] And though the martyrs, like the just in the Old Testament, only absolved themselves, they were 'the kinsmen of the Lord', those in whom 'Christ had his abode'.[196]

In all this there speaks the radical individualist. 'My only concern is myself, careful for nothing except that I should have no care.' 'I owe no obligation to the forum, assembly place or senate.'[197] Society and obligations to the community came second to the uninhibited search for and service of Truth.[198] And, if that service led to opposition to the established order and to death, no matter. 'I refuse to call the Emperor a god. If he is human, he should bow the knee to God.'[199] The Capitol was 'a temple of devils'. Government itself was part of the Devil's pomp.[200] Nothing could compel a Christian to say otherwise. True liberty lay in contempt for the world.[201] '*Sed nec religionis cogere religionem.*' Even the sacrificial animals had to be willing offerings. The State had only the right of prayer and payment of taxes from the Christian. Service to God was his own affair.

It would be difficult to deny that whatever policy the third-century emperors had adopted towards the Church, clashes on a grand scale were inevitable. In Tertullian there is not even a glimmer of future compromise between Church and State. The latter belongs to, indeed was representative of the *saeculum*, which though ultimately the creation of God, in fact was the field of the devil. The Two Cities theory, explicitly stated by Hermas in the previous century was revitalized and from now onwards it became part and parcel of Western theological thought. The emperors and their advisers were being compelled to face an implacable internal enemy resolved on the ultimate destruction of the civilization which they represented. The fanaticism of the Christian successors of the Maccabees extended throughout the western Mediterranean. The measures taken by Maximin, Decius and Valerian must be seen against the increasingly menacing situation on the borders and within the Roman world. In their own way, the Christians contributed to the transformation of the Empire into a vast besieged camp.

For the time being, however, Tertullian's political warfare against the pagan empire came to nothing. His last conflict was against the 'Psychics', the laxer, perhaps more percipient, members of the Christian Church. The wholly negative view of the Christian's duty towards his pagan neighbour, was leading him gradually to develop a sort of New Testament *halaka*, thus reversing the tendencies towards liberalization emerging in other parts of the Christian world. 'We have nothing to do with the Jews',[202] he wrote in the *Apology*, but the prescriptions contained in the *De Idololatria* are remarkably similar to those found in the Jewish *Aboda Zara* of the same date.[203] His criticism of Jewish abstinences were simply that they were conducted with too much formal display of grief, 'cultu et ornatu maeroris' (*De Jejunio adv. Psychicos*, 16). His desire was to 'exceed the righteousness of the scribes and Pharisees', to invent ever more severe Christian *sollemnia* to replace those abrogated by the Church.[204] His Christianity was rapidly becoming a baptized Judaism.[205]

Much in African Christianity was already tending in that direction. Some Christians were in the habit of keeping the Jewish Sabbath,[206] and the ritual abstinence from animal food whence the blood had not been drawn could also be interpreted as Judaistic.[207] So, too, was the tendency to attribute Levitical status to the priesthood. The curious institution of lay officials, *seniores*, in the African Church who had judicial and administrative functions points also to a direct link between Church and Synagogue.[208] Thus, when Callistus of Rome decided that the Church in his own person could forgive Christians who had committed the three cardinal sins of the Old Dispensation, namely apostacy, adultery and bloodshed, there was a blaze of opposition from Africa.[209]

Hitherto Rome had tended towards the rigorist camp. The strength of the tradition which taught that both Peter and Paul had been martyred in Rome ensured the existence of an active cult of these martyrs among the Roman Christians. The 'trophies' of the Apostles were among the best known features of the Church well before 200. In about that year Tertullian praised the Roman Church, as like the Carthaginian Church, 'she clothes with the Holy Spirit, feeds with the Eucharist and exhorts to martyrdom'.[209a] Moreover the prophetic tradition which Hermas had represented, apocalyptic in its attitude towards the non-Christian world and adoptionist in its Christology, continued to have support.[210] The language of the Roman followers of Theodotus in the first decades of the third century concerning the work of Christ, namely, that he was 'chosen and anointed by God because he turned us away from idols and showed us the way of Truth'[211] was very similar to that of Hermas a century before. Pope Soter (died 174) supported the rigorist Bishop Palmas against Dionysius of Corinth.[212] The Montanists received some consideration under his successor

Eleutherus (174–189), and probably at first from Victor also. Tertullian may have been justified in claiming that had it not been for the intervention of Praxeas, Rome might have continued to favour them.[213] In *circa* 200 there was still sufficient Montanist influence at Rome to rouse the presbyter Gaius to publish a violent diatribe against their leader, Proclus, and follow in the wake of the extreme anti-Montanists in Asia by reviving the legend of the Cerinthian origin of St. John's Gospel.[214]

There may also have been even more of the Jewish-Christian legacy remaining in the Roman Church than we can recognize now. It must be admitted that otherwise the outlook of Hippolytus (*circa* 160–236) is extremely difficult to understand. When every allowance has been made for the effect of the sudden outbreak of persecution in 202 on his mind, there remains much in his views as a young man which can only be accounted for by detailed knowledge of late-Jewish apocalyptic literature and interest in Jewish sect-life. Recently, Hippolytus has been recognized as one of the best-informed authorities on the Essenes,[215] his belief in a Messiah ben Levi appears to some critics to stem straight from the Testament of Levi, used by the Dead Sea sect.[216] The single page known as 49 Testimonia, which speaks of the priestly messiah drawn from the House of Levi also agrees with the sect's convictions.[217] Moreover, Hippolytus' descriptions of Church Order and Baptism also seem to hark back to Jewish models.[218] Like the Essenes two centuries before, Hippolytus combined his conservative Messianic and liturgical outlook with an unbridled hatred of idolatry which, as Tertullian, he associated with the Roman Empire and its rulers.

It has been pointed out that the *De Antichristo*, written *circa* 200 and the *Commentary on Daniel* (*circa* 204), contain statements more disloyal even than those of Tertullian.[219] To Hippolytus, the Empire coincided with the Pauline ἀνομια.[220] It ruled its subject peoples against their will. It derived its power from the Devil, its people were 'the new people of Satan',[221] soon doomed to destruction at the hands of rising 'popular' (δημοκρατίαι αἱ μέλλουσι γίγνεσθαι) forces.[222] The Roman Empire, like the statue of Nebuchadnezzar, had feet of clay, and he rejoiced over the approaching doom of an institution which he regarded at this time as both idolatrous and oppressive.[223] The Christians were the nation 'carrying in their hearts the dominating and new name'.[224] Though he does not advocate revolt, and doom is interpreted in supernatural and apocalyptic terms, his hatred for the Roman Empire and the privileged society of those who served it[225] was deep. Moreover, his appeal to 'democracy', and to the individuality of different peoples now forcibly suppressed by Rome, shows him as the representative of the element of political protest in Greek Christianity of the period. Like the Christian writer of viii Sibylline he looks forward to the day of liberation of all peoples from the Roman yoke.[226]

In this aspect of their thought Hippolytus and Tertullian were at one. Both were uncompromisingly against the 'leges dominantium'. But there is an important difference in their theology, which affected the force of their protest. Hippolytus was no Montanist, and though he believed in the approaching End, was no preacher of the witness of the Paraclete. He ridiculed Montanus, and was merciless towards the unfortunate women prophetesses whose Trinitarian theories he compared with those of Noetus.[227] To have appealed, like Tertullian, to the veracity of the utterances of Priscilla and Maximilla would have struck him as absurd. But for one whose ideas were otherwise uncompromisingly rigorist, outright rejection of the New Prophecy had its disadvantages. It confined his attack on his opponents to personal invective and unyielding defence of tradition, without positive alternatives to offer.

Hippolytus failed to develop a doctrine of the Holy Spirit. His opponents reproached him for 'ditheism', perhaps correctly.[228] In any event he thought of the Godhead in terms of God-Logos, rather than Father, Son and Holy Spirit. Thus, his theology of martyrdom lacked the boldness and logical consistency of Tertullian's. In this failure, he foreshadows the similar weakness of other rigorist and anti-Imperial theologians on the northern shores of the Mediterranean in the next century, such as Lucifer of Cagliari.[229] The martyr, indeed, leaves this world in glory. His sins are forgiven. He will not be judged, but will participate in Judgment.[230] Like the Maccabean brethren and the three Holy Children he will receive a heavenly crown.[231] But Hippolytus stops short, with the martyr as a living example of obedience to God. He does not, as the writer of the *Passio Perpetuae*, see in current martyrdoms evidence 'that the one and selfsame Holy Spirit is working to the present hour'.[232] Instead, he looks back to the past. The martyrs represented a continuance in the Church of the righteous examples of the Old Testament.[233] He does not go on from there to consider their acts as proof of the immanence of the Spirit in the Church. Tertullian, on the other hand, insists time and again on the agency of the Holy Spirit filling and inspiring the confessor in his active witness against the world. Hippolytus' was a conservative and individualistic protest. Tertullian saw the 'removal of ambiguities' through acceptance of the New Prophecy as the means of fusing rebellious puritanism into a comprehensive theology of the Church with which to challenge Callistus.

Perhaps one can even detect a change in Hippolytus' outlook towards the State and the governing classes as time goes on.[234] Twenty years after the Severan persecution, he addressed his work *On the Resurrection* to Julia Mammaea,[235] and another noble lady named Severina was among his correspondents.[236] He had mellowed considerably since his *Commentary on Daniel*. His pro-Judaism also faded and the Paschal Calendar which he devised *circa* 221, may be considered as a further step towards rendering the Christian Church independent of the Old Dispensation in the all-important dating of feasts. The bearded philosopher seated in dignity on the marble throne found on the Aventine in 1551 was no longer an enemy of the State.

It would not be unreasonable to attribute the change in part to the long years of peace which followed the Severan persecution. This peace contrasted with the perpetual religious unrest which prevailed in Africa and confronted Zephyrinus and Callistus with fundamental problems concerning the nature of the Church. How could the Church maintain its position as an exclusive *secta* or *didascaleion* with a three-year catechumenate and puritanical ethic in face of the ever-increasing numbers of willing but nominal members, people whose allegiance to Christ did not extend to sacrificing anything connected with their normal lives? We have already seen how Callistus declared legal in the eyes of the Church marriages contracted between freeborn Christian women and freedmen or slaves; the same unordered increase in numbers forced on him a drastic modification of the prevailing doctrine of the Church. He decided in effect to break with the

disciplinary legacy of Judaism. It had to be accepted that the
Church was a 'mixed body' containing unworthy as well as
worthy members. 'Let the tares grow along with the wheat'
(Mt. 13[30]), he is said to have quoted.[237] It was not to be the last
time that this text was used to buttress the anti-rigorist position. Callistus declared as a result, according to Hippolytus,
that no sin was too grave for absolution, and he welcomed
into the Church gross sinners whom even the Marcionites and
Gnostics had rejected.[238] The *tria capitula*, the traditional deadly
sins of adultery, apostasy and bloodshed could now be remitted
once (and once only) by the Church in the person of Callistus,
descendant of the Blessed Apostle Peter.[239]

Hippolytus had already quarrelled with Callistus during the
episcopacy of Zephyrinus, believing that he had influenced the
artless old bishop to tolerate the errors of Sabellius. On the death
of Zephyrinus the two men were apparently rival candidates for
the succession. Hippolytus claimed that he had been canonically
elected, but majority opinion favoured Callistus. Then came the
decision to modify the penitential system. This was intolerable to
any believer in the inviolable purity of the Church on earth.
Hippolytus laid bare the past of his adversary.[240] Tertullian wrote
the *De Pudicitia*. In this work, the theology of the gathered
community was given classic expression, buttressed with all the
author's powers of sarcasm and invective. It is a permanent
protest against institutional religion in favour of a religion of the
Spirit. The Church was 'bride of Christ', having 'neither spot nor
wrinkle',[241] the dwelling of the Holy Spirit,[242] the representative of
the martyrs. It could therefore not sustain the presence of the
impure, the adulterer and all other demon-inspired sinners—
particularly if they were clergy,[243] 'non communicandum operi-
bus tenebrarum'—the phrase echoes down African Church
history.[244] If theoretically, the Church might forgive deadly
offences, in practice she should not.[245] Power to forgive lay with
Him whom the sinner had offended.[246] The bishop might dispense godly discipline, the congregation might lend their prayers
to aid the sinner,[247] but his fate must await the Judgment of God.
The keys of St. Peter were in the hands of all faithful Christians,
and only if Callistus could exhibit his own apostolic gifts could
he lay claim to apostolic powers.[248]

The gage had been thrown down. Each side was defining its attitude and citing the texts which were to serve it for the next two centuries. In this conflict it is well to realize that Tertullian represented the hitherto prevalent outlook of the new Christianity of Gaul and Africa. In both Churches the confessors believed in their role as judges at the End, even in anticipation while still on earth, and that these claims were acceptable to the Christians in these areas as a whole. Similarly, on both sides of the Mediterranean the life-giving force of the Spirit had implications for the conduct of individual ministers. Irenaeus had denounced 'those who are believed to be presbyters by many', individuals, 'who served their own lusts', and 'worked evil deeds in secret'.[249] Such conduct could be added to heresy as disqualifying a man from priestly office. 'From such people let us keep aloof' he adds significantly.[249a] Callistus was now challenging these pre-suppositions. The establishment of the Church was substituted for the New Covenant. Spiritual gifts were to be canalized through the ordered ministry, held together by a sacramental communion stronger than the defects of individual members. These gifts were no longer the prerogative of the confessors, the prophets, and the visionaries. In Rome, Callistus had the majority opinion on his side. In Africa he did not. In the 220s, the Church in Gaul which might have acted as arbitrator was in eclipse.

On each side, however, the minorities were to prove influential. Hippolytus was to find a successor in Novatian, whose career as theologian and anti-pope was to be oddly similar to his own. In the Decian persecution some, but by no means all the Roman confessors were to rally to his support against Cornelius. But the presbyters and community remained loyal to the legitimate bishop. In Africa there was already a strong section of the Carthaginian Church that rejected Tertullian's puritanism. In the De Idololatria, the De Jejunio and the De Corona, he points a finger of scorn against those who were prepared to see the Church at peace with the State. Already his opponents were taking their cue from Callistus, and explaining that even the Ark contained clean and unclean beasts.[250] The 'long peace' of 38 years which was to last in Africa from 212–250 favoured the progress of these moderates within the Church.[251] Hippolytus and Tertullian seem to have become progressively more isolated. Both lived to extreme old age, Hippolytus to be arrested on Maximin's orders in 235 and to be sent with his rival, Pontianus, to Sardinia.[252] There according to tradition pope and anti-pope were reconciled, and Hippolytus became the first anti-pope saint of the Church. Tertullian was less fortunate. The persecution of Maximin evidently did not touch Africa. He may have survived also the revolution of 238. He died *circa* 240 the leader of his own minute sect of Tertullianists, more rigorous even than the Montanists,[253] perhaps of the same 'light fevers' he had so despised thirty years before.[254]

NOTES

[1] Clement, *Stromata* (ed. O. Stählin-L. Früchtel, Berlin, 1960), i.20.99.1.

[2] Hippolytus, *Comment. in Danielem* iv.18 and 19. For the significance of this failure of apocalyptic prediction on the development of doctrine, M. Werner, *The Formation of Christian Dogma* (Eng. tr. 1952), 41ff.

[3] Eusebius, *H.E.*, iv.15.8; cf. *Acta Polycarpi* 1.1. For similar views in Roman Africa in the decade 250–260, Cyprian, *Ep.*, 81.

[4] *Acta Polycarpi*, 21 (Knopf and Krüger, 7).

[5] The Feast of Polycarp was kept in 23 February on Smyrna in 250, *Acta Pionii*, 2 (Knopf and Krüger, 45), and for its immediate establishment there after Polycarp's death, Eusebius, *H.E.*, iv.15.44.

[6] Eusebius, *H.E.*, vi.7.

[7] *Africani Chronicon* 1.6 (ed. M. J. Routh, *Reliquiae Sacrae* ii.124–95, and notes on pp. 242–4). See F. C. Burkitt, *CAH.*, xii, 477–8.

[8] Eusebius, *H.E.*, v.2.7; cf. P. Nautin, *Lettres et Ecrivains*, 35ff.

[9] Eusebius, *H.E.*, v.23.4.

[10] Ibid., v.20.3; cf. iv.14.

[11] Ibid., v.20.4.

[12] Irenaeus, *Adv. Haer.*, iv.32.1 (*P.G.*, vii, 1070) Polycarp is never named in the *Adv. Haer.* in this connection, but the qualifications 'presbyter, disciple of the apostles' are applicable to him, and it is difficult to see anyone else in Asia whom Irenaeus knew personally and esteemed so highly.

[13] Also *Adv. Haer.*, iii.2.2, 'ad eam iterum traditionem quae est ab apostolis, quae per successiones presbyterorum in ecclesiis custoditur, provocamus eos . . . ' *Presbyteri* are here clearly 'bishops'.

[14] Eusebius, *H.E.*, v.4.2

[15] Irenaeus, *Adv. Haer.*, v.29 and 30.

[16] Ibid., v.31 and 33.2.

[17] Irenaeus, *Adv. Haer.*, iii.24.1, cf. iii.11.8, see N. Bonwetsch, *Die Theologie des heiligen Irenaeus*, 1925, 115, on the significance of these passages.

[18] Irenaeus, *Adv. Haer.*, ii.33.3–4 where he opposes Plato's arguments in favour of the transmigration of souls with those of visionaries and prophets who had glimpsed the world Beyond.

[19] Irenaeus, *Adv. Haer.*, v.28.4, citing Ignatius, *Rom.*, 4.

[20] Ibid., iii.18.5. (*P.G.*, vii, 936).

[21] Tertullian, *De Jejunio*, 11 (*CSEL.*, xx, 290); Cf. *De Monogamia* 2.2 (*CSEL.*, lxxvi, 45) and *Passio Perpetuae*, i.

[22] This can hardly have been accidental, for Irenaeus had actually been the bearer of the letter from the confessors at Lyons to Rome about Montanism. Eusebius, *H.E.*, v.4.1–2. See, P. de Labriolle's careful study, *La Crise Montaniste*, 238ff.

[23] Tertullian, *Adv. Valentinianos*, 5, 'Irenaeus, omnium doctrinarum curiosissimus explorator'.

[24] See A. A. T. Ehrhardt, *Politische Metaphysik*, ii. 105–12.

[25] *Adv. Haer.*, v.24.2.

[26] Ibid., 24.1.

[27] Ibid., iv.30.3.

[28] Tertullian, *De Anima*, 41, 'ex originis vitio antecedit' (*CSEL.*, xx.368), the first explicit mention of Adam's taint passing on to humanity.

[29] Augustine, *Contra Gaudentium*, 1.24.27 (*P.L.*, xliii, col. 722). 'Saeculi enim pax inter animos gentium dissidentes armis et belli exitu foederantur.'

[30] Pap. Oxy., 405.

[31] A. Fliche and V. Martin (eds.), *Histoire de l'Église*, ii.225–7; cf. Clement's *The Rich Man's Salvation*, 3 for wealthy church-members and *Paedogogos*, iii.5 for wealthy Christian ladies in public baths. Church-members with gold rings, ibid., iii.11.

[32] W. Bauer, *Rechtgläubigkeit und Ketzerei*, 49ff. Also, Ehrhardt's valuable remarks in *Christianity before the Apostle's Creed*, 95ff. Cf. Eusebius, *H.E.*, vi.2.14.

[33] See A. Fliche and V. Martin (eds.) op. cit., ii.228ff., and its list of relevant literature. Clement's own account of his early life—*Stromata* (ed. Stählin-Früchtel, 1.1.11).

[34] *Stromata*, ii.2. See especially the great study of Clement by Walther Völker, 'Der wahre Gnostiker nach Clemens Alexandrinus', *T.U.*, 57.2, Leipzig, 1952, pp. 6–8.

[35] *Strom.*, vii.54.3, cf. iii.84.1 and vii.15.89 (Jewish attacks also).

[36] Ibid., vii.1.1 and iii.3.27. See the 'Sayings and Extracts' of Clement assembled by R. B. Tollinton, *Clement of Alexandria*, London, 1914, vol. ii, 285ff.

[37] Numenius of Apamea, cited by Clement, *Stromata*, i.150.4 and ii.93.10, also Eusebius, *Praeparatio Evangelica*, xi.10.14.

[38] Contrast for instance, the multitude who 'feared Greek philosophy like children fear goblins'—*Strom.*, vi.10.80.5; 18.162.

[39] See, B. Seeberg, 'Die Geschichtstheologie Justins des Märtyrers', *Z. für K.G.*, 58, 1939, 53–7.

[40] *Stromata*, 1.5.30. The inferiority of Philosophy is, of course, emphasized in the *Protrepticus*, which after the first, fine, opening paragraph deteriorates into second-hand Jewish apologetic against Hellenism.

[41] *Rich Man's Salvation* (ed. Butterworth), 33.

[42] *Stromata*, vii.2.9. See C. Bigg, *The Christian Platonists of Alexandria* (ed. Oxford, 1913), 98–106.

[43] *Paedagogos*, i.7.54.2. '... καὶ ὡς ὁ κυβερνήτης οἰακίζει τὸ σκάφος σώζειν προαιρούμενους τοὺς ἐμπλέοντας, οὕτως καὶ ὁ παιδαγωγὸς ἄγει τοὺς παῖδας ἐπὶ τὴν σωτήριον δίαιταν τῆς ἡμῶν αὐτῶν ἕνεκεν κηδεμονίας. See E. Fascher's note 'Der Logos-Christus als göttlicher Lehrer bei Clemens von Alexandrien', *T.U.*, 77, 1961, 193ff.

[44] *Strom.*, vii.6.6 and iii.6.25. Völker, op. cit., 101–5.

[45] *Strom.*, iv.23.148.2; cf. 22.135–6.

[46] Ibid., 6.30; 18.111. See C. Bigg, *The Christian Platonists*, 126ff.

[47] *Paed.*, iii.12.99 and *Strom.*, vii.16.

[48] *Strom.*, i.80. 'ὡς δὲ ἄλλοι βούλονται. ἐκ τοῦ διαβόλου κίνησιν ἴσχει'; cf. 1.1.1., 1.1.18.2 and 1.9.43.1, also vii.14.84; Contrast Irenaeus, *Adv. Haer.*, ii.26.1 and see

J. Lebreton 'Le Désaccord de la foi populaire et de la théologie savante dans l'Eglise chrétienne du IIIe. siècle', *R.H.E.*, 19, 1923, pp. 481–506 and 20, 1924, 5–37 especially pp. 491–500, and his important chapter, in A. Fliche and V. Martin, *Histoire de l'Eglise*, ii, especially pp. 361–74.

⁴⁹ Literally, 'without witness'. See Arndt and Gingrich. op. cit., 43 quoting Hellenistic and third-century A.D. examples of this usage, and n.36 in *P.G.* viii, 1230.

⁵⁰ Not completely without a basis of truth, as the public suicide by fire of a Buddhist monk at Saigon has shown (reported in *The Times* of 12 June 1963 and followed by others in the summer and autumn of 1963). In the third century Buddhism was strong, if not predominant, in north India (see Mani, *Kephalaion*, 154), and had some influence in Alexandria.

⁵¹ *Strom.*, iv.18.1.

⁵² Ibid., iv.9.71.

⁵³ Ibid., iv.9.71.4 (Stählin-Früchtel, 280).

⁵⁴ Ibid., iv.9.72.4. See A. Orbe, *Los primeros herejes ante la persecucion*, v (*Analecta Gregoriana*, 83, 1956), 1ff. and von Campenhausen, *Die Idee des Martyriums*, 109–10.

⁵⁵ *Strom.*, iv.11.78, and see also Hippolytus, *in Danielem*, ii.35.1 (Bonwetsch, 108).

⁵⁶ *Strom.*, iv.9.73.

⁵⁷ Ibid., iv.14.3. 'τέλειον ἔργον ἀγάπης 'ενεδείξατο'.

⁵⁸ Ibid., iv.43.2; cf. 52.2–4. Völker, op. cit., 567–9.

⁵⁹ Ibid., ii.97.1. 'βασιλευων τῶν παθῶν', and iv.138.1. See Völker, op. cit., 187. His was the true 'imitation of God' like that of the martyr previously.

⁶⁰ *Strom.*, iv.7.43.4. (Stählin-Früchtel, 267). Cf. ibid. ii.20.104.

⁶¹ *Strom.*, iv.9.75.

⁶² Ibid., ii.104.1

⁶³ Ibid., vii.82 and 87; cf. ibid., ii.97.1. See H. E. W. Turner, *The Pattern of Christian Truth*, London, 1956, 398–9. Note the parallel ideal stated by Philo in *Quis Rerum Divinarum Heres.*, 70, 'For the mind, in this state of frenzy—no longer itself, but exalted and maddened by the heavenly love; led along by the One really Real; pulled towards Him, while Truth goes in advance and removes impediments that it (the mind) may travel along a plain road—behold this is the "inheritance".'

⁶⁴ Ibid., iv.14.1. cf. iv.41.1. Though he allows that 'beginners' who act thus are better than nominal Christians (iv.9.75.2).

⁶⁵ Palladius, *Lausiac History* (ed. Lowther Clarke), 60 (story of Collythus).

⁶⁶ *Strom.*, iv.11.78; see E. F. Osborn, *The Philosophy of Clement of Alexandria*, Cambridge, 1957, 70–3. For Hippolytus' views when confronted with the same problem, K. J. Neumann, *Hippolytus*, 96.

⁶⁷ *Strom.*, iv.11.79.

⁶⁸ Ibid., iv.47.2. The denier was a deserter to the Devil's army, iv.42.1; ii.267.4.

⁶⁹ *Strom.*, iv.17.105.

⁷⁰ Ibid., iv.7.48ff.

⁷¹ Ibid., iv.16.100. Jn. 4¹⁸ and 5³.

⁷² *Strom.*, vii.16.102 and 6.34, 'not the consuming fire of a furnace, but the reasonable fire that penetrates the soul that passes through the fire'.

⁷³ Ibid., iv.7.49–iv.8.63.

⁷⁴ Ibid., iv.7.52.

⁷⁵ Ibid., iv.26.172—an interesting version of the idea of the Two Cities as interpreted in Alexandria.

⁷⁶ Ibid., vii.11.66.

⁷⁷ *Strom.*, iv.10.76–7.

⁷⁸ Völker, op. cit., 560ff.

⁷⁹ *Strom.*, iv.74.3; cf. 73.3.

[80] Ibid., iv.72.1; cf. ii.483.7. Tertullian, *De Oratione*, 4 (*CSEL.*, xx.183). Völker, op. cit., 97.

[81] Tertullian, *Scorpiace*, 6, *De Res. Carnis* 43.

[82] Tertullian, *De Anima*, 55 (ed. J. H. Waszink, pp. 74 and 554–5). 'Quomodo Perpetua, fortissima martyr, sub die passionis in revelatione paradisi solos illic martyras vidit, nisi quia nullis romphaea paradisi ianitrix cedit nisi qui in Christo decesserint, non in Adam?'

[83] *Strom.*, iv.87; cf. ii.286.16.

[84] *Strom.*, vii.2.9.

[85] *De Baptismo*, 3, 'Divini spiritus sedes'.

[86] Ibid., 6.

[87] *Ad Martyras* 1, 'Nolite contristrare spiritum sancum qui vobiscum introiit carcerem'.

[88] *Apol.*, 50.16. *De Baptismo* 16, 'secundum lavacrum . . . sanguinis'.

[89] *De Baptismo*, 5.

[90] *Apol.*, 21.10ff.

[91] *De Praescript*, 7.

[92] *Rich Man's Salvation* (ed. G. W. Butterworth), 3.

[93] Ibid., 5. Contrast Tertullian, *De Carni Christi*, 9, on the importance of maintaining the literal view of the new Testament.

[94] Clement, 14, cf. *Paedag.*, iii.12.4, and Hermas, *Simil.*, 2.5–7, already discussed, p. 196. Note for a Jewish parallel to this teaching, Eccles, 8[15].

[95] *Rich Man's Salvation*, 31.

[96] Ibid., 5 and 20.

[97] Ibid., 16 and 19.

[98] Ibid., 20–1.

[99] G. W. Butterworth, *Clement of Alexandria*, 267.

[100] Tertullian, *De Spectaculis*, 2 (ed. Glover, p. 232), and 20.

[101] Tertullian, *De Oratione*, 29.

[102] See the author's *Donatist Church*, ch. vi. and art. *Donatismus, A.C.* (Lexikon), iv. 130–46.

[103] Tertullian's father had been one of the officials charged under the Proconsul Tiberius with rooting out this practice. Tertullian, *Apol.*, 9.2. I am accepting the amendment 'patri nostri' for 'patriae nostrae'. See, G. Ch. Picard, art. cit., *RHR.*, 155, 1959, p. 52, n.5.

[104] See J. Carcopino, *Aspects mystiques de la Rome païenne* (Paris, 1942), 39–48.

[105] Frend, *Donatist Church*, 79.

[106] M. Simon, 'Le Judaisme berbère dans l'Afrique ancienne', *Recherches d'Histoire Judéo-chrétienne*, Paris, 1962, p. 48.

[107] P. Monceaux, *Histoire littéraire*, i, ch. i, and M. Simon, 'Le Judaisme berbère dans l'Afrique ancienne', 30ff.

[108] Monceaux, op. cit., 9–10. Below, p. 374.

[109] Tertullian, *De Praecriptione*, 36 'Si autem Italiae adiaces, habes Romam, unde nobis quoque auctoritas praesto est' (*CSEL.*, lxx, 45).

[110] Tertullian wrote some of his works in Greek, as he says in *Adv. Praxean*, 3, 'Latini . . . Graeci. At ego si quid utriusque linguae praecerpsi . . . ' and in *De Corona*, 6 and *De Baptismo*, 15. See P. Monceaux, *Histoire littéraire*, i.187–8.

[111] *Apol.*, 39.1.

[112] Ibid.

[113] *De Spectaculis*, 1.

[114] *Apol.*, 50.3, 'licet nunc sarmenticos et semaxios appellatis'.

[115] *Ad Scapulam*, 3.1.

[116] *De Corona*, 3, 'Oblationes pro defunctis pro nataliciis annua die facimus'.

[117] *Ad Martyras*, 1.6, 'Quam pacem, quidam in ecclesia non habentes a martyribus in

carcere exorare consueverunt'. Also, *Ad Uxorem*, ii.4, 'Quis in carcerem ad osculanda vincula martyris reptare patietur'. For similar expectations among the Gallic Christians of this time, Eusebius, *H.E.*, v.2.5.

[118] The fight was literally against Satan (*Ad Martyras*, 3.3-4 and *Passio Perpetuae*, 10.7). For *agonistici* at this period see R. Reitzenstein's suggestions in 'Eine frühchristliche Schrift von der dreierlei Früchte des christlichen Lebens', *ZNTW.*, 15, 1914, 73.

[119] *Dating, and problems of authorship*: J. A. Robinson, *Cambridge Texts and Studies*, i.2, 1891, 47ff. The text used is ed. Knopf and Krüger, op. cit., pp. 35ff., and I have drawn on my comments in the *Donatist Church*, 116-18.

[120] *Passio*, 2.

[121] Ibid., iv.2. This seems the obvious explanation of the ladder vision, but remembering that Perpetua was an unbaptized catechumen, it is legitimate also to point to similar ladder symbolism in contemporary Mithraism (Origen, *Contra Celsum*, vi.22). See See J. Quasten, 'A Coptic counterpart of a Vision in the Acts of Perpetua and Felicitas', *Byzantion*, xv, 1940-41, 1ff. For martyrs being compared to 'stones of glistening whiteness' as in Hermas, *Simil.*, ix.29, see Tertullian, *Scorpiace*, 12.

[122] Ibid., iv.4.

[123] Ibid., xi-xii.

[124] Or perhaps *Apoc. Petri*, 15-17 (ed. A. Menzies, Ante-Nicene Christian Library, Additional volume, 1897). The debt of the *Passio* to the *Apocalypse* is also apparent in *Passio* xiii.8, 'Universi odore inerrabili alebamur, qui nos satiabat'. Compare with *Apoc.*, 16, 'The perfume (of the flowers and fruit of Paradise) was so great that it was borne thence even to us'.

[125] *Passio*, vi.2. For similar pleas by the authorities, Tertullian, *Scorpiace*, 11.

[126] Ibid., iii.3.

[127] Ibid., xviii.3 'lotura post partum baptismo secundo', and cf. xxi.2 'ut populus reverenti illi secundi baptismatis testimonium reclamaverit "Salvum lotum, salvum lotum" '. In the fourth-century church at Gonea near Castiglione the tomb of the martyr was placed symbolically perhaps, next to the baptismal font, cf. H. Grabar, *Martyrium*, i.446.

[128] Ibid., iii.3.

[129] *Passio*, iv.1, cf. v.2.

[130] Ibid., viii.

[131] Cyprian, *Epp.*, 20 and 22.

[132] *Passio*, 17. 'Hodie amici, cras inimici. Notate tamen vobis facies nostras diligenter, ut recognoscatis nos in die illo'; cf. Tertullian, *Apol.*, 49.6 on the attitude of the mob.

[133] *Passio*, 18.4 'Tu nos, inquiunt, te autem Deus'.

[134] A term used frequently in Carthaginian religious language, *Passio*, 3.3 and 4., 9.1 and 16.2 and Tertullian, *Apol.*, 49.2; see art. 'Refrigerum', *DACL.*, for the popularity of the term in the West in the third century and its connection with the cult of martyrs.

[135] *Passio*, 3.4.

[136] Ibid., 6.4.

[137] Ibid., 13.1.

[138] Tertullian, *De Anima*, 55, 'solos commartyres'. Cf. *Passio*, 13.3, 'et coepimus illic multos fratres cognoscere, sed et martyras'.

[139] *Passio*, 16.2.

[140] His conversion by the sight of the martyrs in the arena. *Apol.*, 50.16 and *Ad Scapulam*, 5. His previous delight at the cruel scenes he had watched there, *Apol.*, 15.5, and his scepticism, ibid., 18.4.

[141] See P. Monceaux's study, in *Hist. Litt. de l'Afrique chrétienne*, i.178ff., and in de Labriolle's *Latin Christianity* (Eng. tr. 1924) ch. ii; also, J. H. Waszink's masterly edition of *De Anima*, Amsterdam, 1947.

[142] See for instance, R. P. C. Hanson's note on Tertullian's methods of interpreting

Scripture, *JTS.*, N.S. xii.2, 1961, 273ff. and the refs. given by the author in his note on the '*Seniores laici* and the Origins of the Church in North Africa', ibid., 283.

[143] Note his own interesting self-revelation in *De Patientia*, 1. He describes himself as 'ever rich with the force of impulse, must needs long for and invoke and speak out all my thoughts about that healthy state of patience that I do not possess'.

[144] His admiration for Carthage, *Ad Martyras*, 4, *Ad Nationes*, 1.18 (both written in 197) and *De Pallio*, 1, written in 209; cf. P. Monceaux, op. cit. 179.

[145] The dating of this event is not easy. P. Monceaux, op. cit., 185, and E. Evans, *Adversus Praxean* (ed.), opt cautiously for 213. However, six years earlier in *circa* 207 Tertullian was already admitting the validity of the New Prophecy and the value of abstaining from second marriage (*De Resurrectione Carnis*, ed. E. Evans, 8, 11 and 63). See my review of Evans, *Tertullian's Treatise on the Resurrection*, London, 1960, *JTS.*, xi.2, 1961, 339.

[146] Augustine, *De Haeresibus ad Quodvultdeum*, 86 (*P.L.*, xlii, 46).

[147] *Adv. Nationes*, ii.1 (*CSEL.*, xx.94) 'Adversus haec igitur nobis negotium est, adversus institutiones maiorum, auctoritates receptorum, leges dominantium, argumentationes prudentium, adversus vetustatem, consuetudinem, necessitatem, adversus exempla prodigia miracula, quae omnia adulterinam istam divinitatem corroboaverunt'.

[148] Clement, *Protetrepticus*, x.89.

[149] See *De Spectaculis*, 29, 'Quae maior voluptas quam fastidium ipsius voluptatis, quam saeculi totius contemptus, quam vera libertas . . . '.

[150] Tertullian, *Apol.*, 21.24, 'Sed et Caesares credidissent super Christo, si aut Caesares non essent necessarii saeculo, aut si et christiani potuissent esse Caesares'.

[151] *Apol.*, 38.3.

[152] *Apol.*, 30.1–4, cf. 32.1 and 33.1–2. Cf. *De Res. Carnis*, 24.18.

[153] *De Spectaculis*, 15; cf. *Apol.*, 35.2 'Sicine exprimitur publicum gaudium per dedecus publicum'.

[154] *De Cultu Feminarum*, ii.13 (Kroymann, *CSEL.*, lxx. 95). Hippolytus, *In Danielem*, ii.12, (Bonwetsch, 68).

[155] *Apol.*, 25.12. Contrast, Cicero. *De Natura Deorum*, 3.8.

[156] *Historia adversus Paganos* (ed. W. Zangemeister, *CSEL.*, vii), vii. 1.

[157] Octavius, *Minucius Felix*, 25.5

[158] *De Praescriptione*, 7 and *Apol.*, 46 for similar sentiments; cf. *De Anima*, 6, 17, 18 and 23 directed against Plato. (Doleo bona fide Platonem omnium haereticorum condimentarium factum!) The point is commented upon by T. R. Glover, *Conflict of Religions*, 337–8. One is reminded of the answer of the equally puritan Caliph Omar when asked by his victorious general Amr what to do with the library at Alexandria: 'If these writings of the Greeks agree with the Book of God, they are useless and need not be preserved; if they disagree, they are harmful and should be destroyed.'

[159] Expressed mainly in the *De Cultu Feminarum*. For instance, 'I fear the neck, circled with pearl and emerald necklace, will have no room for the sword (ii.13)'. See discussion in J. P. Brisson, *Autonomisme et Christianisme*, 369ff.

[160] For the development of this view in his Montanist period, *De Idololatria*, passim.

[161] *De Cultu Feminarum*, ii.10. 'Quod nascitur, opus dei est. Ergo quod infringitur diaboli negotium est'—(ibid., ii.5)— the exact reverse of the Classical viewpoint!

[162] *De Cultu Feminarum*, ii.9. Also, *Adv. Marcionem*, 1.24. 'Blessed are the beggars'.

[163] *De Spectaculis*, 15, 'saeculum dei est, saecularia autem diaboli'.

[164] Cf. Cyprian, *De Eleemosynis*, 9 and *De Lapsis*, 6, 8 and 12.

[165] *De Spectaculis*, 29. Cf. *De Oratione*, 5.

[166] *De Oratione*, 5. 'How do some pray for the prolongation of the age (*saeculum*) while the kingdom of God which we pray may arrive will bring about its consummation? Our wish is that our reign be hastened, not that our slavery be protracted.'

[167] For a more amiable view of the happiness of the saints, *De Virginibus Velandis* (end).

[168] *De Res. Carnis*, 14 (ed. Evans, 36).

[169] *De Spectaculis*, i, 'servus Dei'. The way in which the relationship between God and man was envisaged seems to be a direct legacy of the national cult of Saturn. See, *The Donatist Church*, 79.

[170] *Apol.*, 18.3, 'ut qui producto aevo isto iudicaturus sit suos cultores in vitae aeternae retributionem, profanos in ignem aeque perpetem et iugem, suscitatis omnibus ab initio defunctis et reformatis et recensitis ad utriusque meriti dispunctionem'.

[171] Origen, *Discourse with Heracleides* (ed. and tr. Oulton and Chadwick), 167; contrast with Tertullian, *De Anima* (ed. Waszink), 9 and 35.

[172] *De Res. Carnis*, 6. In the Christian cemetery at Timgad, the bodies were laid for burial in wet plaster so that their outlines could be preserved indefinitely.

[173] Tertullian, *De Carne Christi*, 2.

[174] *Adv. Marcionem*, 1.27.

[175] The moral and religious situation which Tertullian was encountering in Carthage is excellently summarized in P. de Labriolle, *Latin Christianity*, 89ff.

[176] Jerome, *De Viris Illustribus*, 53.

[177] Tertullian, *De Res. Carnis*, 63, 'idcirco iam omnes retro ambiguitates et quantas volunt parabolas aperta et perspicua totius sacramenti praedicatione discussit per novam prophetiam de paracleto inundantem'.

[178] *De Paenitentia*, 9, but even here, the object of the *exomologesis* was to get the presbyters to reinforce the sinner's supplication to God Himself. In ch. 7 (7.14), however, Tertullian had written 'Offendisti sed reconciliari adhuc potes'.

[179] *De Pudicitia*, 20, 'illo apocrypho Pastore moechorum'.

[180] Ibid., 2.13 (*CSEL.*, xx.243–4); cf. c.14, 'ad quem lugerent? utique ad dominum'.

[181] *Ad Uxorem*, 1.3, 'etiam in persecutionibus melius est ex permissu fugere quam comprehensum et distortum negare'; cf. *De Patientia*, 13, 'Si fuga urgeret . . . '.

[182] *De Fuga*, 9 and 12, 'Infirmos sustineri iubet Paulus, utique enim non fugientes' (9.2).

[183] *Ad Uxorem*, I—marriage needed to propagate the human race, contrasted with *De Exhort. Castitatis*—folly of populating the world just before the End. Note too, the concession, 'Nam etsi non delinquas renubendo', *Ad Uxorem*, 1.7.

[184] *De Anima*, 9.4, contrasted with *De Praescriptione*, 41; cf. J. H. Waszink, op. cit., 167, and P. Guilloux' art. 'L'Evolution religieuse de Tertullien', *RHE.*, xix, 1923, 1–24 and 141–56 for a useful summary of differences between the pre- and post-Montanist periods.

[185] *De Virg. Vel.*, 1.6. 'Quale est enim, ut diabolo semper operante, et adiciente cottidie ad iniquitatis ingenia opus dei aut cessaverit aut proficere destiterit? Cum propterea paraclitum miserit dominus, ut, quoniam humana mediocritas omnia semel capere non poterat, paulatim dirigeretur et ordinaretur ad perfectum perduceretur disciplina ab illo vicario domini, spiritu sancto' (*CSEL.*, lxxvi.80).

[186] *De Monogamia*, 14.5 (*CSEL.*, lxxvi.73); cf. *De Virg. Vel.*, 1.8–9 (*CSEL.*, lxxvi.80).

[187] See *Adv. Haer.*, iv.38.

[188] *De Idololatria*, 19; cf. *De Corona*, 10.

[189] See in particular, *De Exhort. Cast.*, 12, 'non enim nos et milites sumus? eo quidem maioris disciplinae, quanto tanti imperatoris'. Also, *De Idololatria*, 18, and *Ad Martyras*, 3.

[190] *De Corona*, 11. For 'pagani' contrasted with 'milites', Callistratus, *Dig.*, 48.3.12. In general, E. Bichel, *Rheinisches Museum*, 97, 1954, 1–47 and E. Kornemann, art. 'Paganus', *P.W.*, 18.2, 2295–7. Christian usage: Orosius, *Historia adversus paganos*, prol. 1.9, and of course the title of the work. Also, B. Altaner, 'Paganus', *Z. f.K.G.*, 58, 1939, 130–41.

[191] *De Corona*, 10 (*CSEL.*, lxx.174).

[192] Ibid., 10 and 15.

[193] *Scorpiace*, 2 (*CSEL.*, xx.148).

[194] For instance, *Scorpiace*, 15.

[195] *De Fuga*, 9. *Ad Scapulam*, 5, 'nos haec non timere, sed ultro vocare'.

[196] *De Pudicitia*, 22; Lietzmann, *Geschichte*, ii.226.

[197] *De Pallio*, 5.4–55. See E. A. Isichei, *Political Thinking and Social Experience*, Christ-church, 1964, 36.

[198] *Apol.*, 1.1. The emphasis is on 'Truth'. Toleration was not extended to heretics. See *Scorpiace*, 2.

[199] *Apol.*, 33.3.

[200] *De Idololatria*, 17. The Christian must not 'sit in judgment . . . condemning or forecondemning (nec damnet neque praedamnet), binding and imprisoning'.

[201] *De Spectaculis*, 29, 'Quae maior voluptas quam fastidium ipsius voluptatis, quam saeculi totius contemptus, quam vera libertas, quam conscientia integra. . . .'

[202] *Apol.*, 21.3; cf. *De Pudicitia*, 8, 'Iudaei enim apostatae filii pronuntiantur'.

[203] W. A. L. Elmslie, 'The Mishna on Idolatry, Aboda Zara', *Cambridge Texts and Studies*, viii.2, 1911, xxiv.

[204] *De Jejunio adv. Psychicos*, 14 (*CSEL.*, xx.292). 'Quod si nova conditio in Christo, nova et sollemnia esse debebunt.'

[205] See the excellent comment by R. P. C. Hanson, 'Notes on Tertullian's Interpretation of Scripture', *JTS.*, N.S. xii.2, 1961, 278, 279.

[206] *De Jejunio adv. Psychicos*, 14 (*CSEL.*, xx.293). 'Quamquam vos (the Psychics) etiam sabbatum, si quando continuatis.' Also, 150 years later, as shown by Monnica's experience in Milan, 'Mater mea Mediolanum me consecuta invenit Ecclesiam sabbato non ieunare. Coeperat perturbari et fluctuari quid ageret'. Augustine, *Epist. ad inquisitiones Januarii*, liv.2.3, *CSEL.*, 34.2, 160.

[207] *Apol.*, 9.13. See also, C. W. Dugmore, *The Influence of the Synagogue on the Divine Office*, 29–36.

[208] See the author's 'The *Seniores Laici* and the Origins of the Church in North Africa', *JTS.*, N.S. xii.2, 1961, 280–4.

[209] See G. L. Prestige's essay on Callistus in *Fathers and Heretics*, London, 1954, 27ff.

[209a] Tertullian, *De Praescriptione*, 36.

[210] The Theodotians claimed that the 'truth of the preaching was preserved until the times of Victor', but that 'it was falsified from the days of his successor, Zephyrinus', Eusebius, *H.E.*, v.28.3.

[211] Epiphanius, *Panarion*, lv.8. See L. Duchesne, *Early History of the Church* (Eng. tr. i.219).

[212] Eusebius, *H.E.*, iv.23. See P. Nautin's comment, *Lettres et Ecrivains*, 30–1.

[213] Tertullian, *Adv. Praxean*, 1. 'Praxeas at Rome managed two pieces of the Devil's business: he drove out prophecy and introduced heresy. He put to flight the Paraclete and crucified the Father.'

[214] P. de Labriolle, *La Crise Montaniste*, 278ff.

[215] M. Black, 'The Account of the Essenes in Hippolytus and Josephus', *Studies in Honour of C. H. Dodd*, 172–5.

[216] Hippolytus, *Commentary on the Blessings of Jacob*, discussed by L. Mariès, 'Le Messie issu de Lévi chez Hippolyte de Rome', *RSR.*, xl. 1952 (*Mélanges Lebreton*), 381–96.

[217] J. M. Allegro, 'Further Messianic References in Qumran Literature', *JBL.*, 75, 1956, 174–87, Document iv: cf. B. Lindars, *New Testament Apologetic*, 280.

[218] See Dom G. Dix, 'The Apostolic Ministry in the Early Church' (ed. Kirk, *The Apostolic Ministry*), 217ff.

[219] Santo Mazzarino, '*La Democratizzazione della Cultura nel basso Impero*' (XIe Congres International des Sciences historiques, Stockholm, 1960, Rapports, ii, Antiquité, 37ff.);

cf. A. A. T. Ehrhardt, *Politische Metaphysik*, ii.130–2. *Dating*: I accept A. Harnack, *Chronologie*, ii.249–50 as against P. Nautin's theory of a later date and Palestinian origin. See also, G. Bardy's introduction to Hippolytus, 'Commentaire sur Daniel', *Sources chrétiennes*, 14, p. 17.

[220] *In Danielem*, iv.7.1 (ed. Bonwetsch); cf. ibid., iv.8 and 9.

[221] Ibid., iv.9.2–3.

[222] Ibid., ii.12 (Bonwetsch, 68)—a view reminiscent of Augustine's preference for small kingdoms as opposed to the Roman Empire, indicated in *De Civitate Dei*, iv and xix.

[223] *Comment. in Danielem*, ii.12 and iv.7.

[224] Ibid., iv.9.1.

[225] Ibid., iv.9.2.

[226] viii Sibyll. (ed. Geffcken), 353ff.

[227] Hippolytus, *Elenchos*, viii.19 (Wendland, 238). See, however, ibid., x.25, for a more favourable view of Montanus' orthodoxy.

[228] Ibid., ix.12.16.

[229] See below, p. 558.

[230] *In Danielem*, ii.37 (Bonwetsch, 112); cf. ii.36.6.

[231] Ibid., ii.35 and 38; cf. 1.17.8. See, K. H. Neumann, *Hippolytus*, 97.

[232] *Passio Perpetuae*, 1. See H. B. Swete, *The Holy Spirit in The Ancient Church*, 76.

[233] *In Danielem*, ii.18 (Three Holy Children) and ii.20 (Maccabees).

[234] A good deal too much for some critics. See, P. Nautin, *Hippolyte contre les Hérésies*, Paris, 1949.

[235] *De Resurrectione ad Mammaeam imperatricem* (fragments in H. Achelis, ed. *GCS.*, Hippolytus, i.252ff.)*Dating*: Harnack, *Chronologie*, ii.212.

[236] προτρεπτικὸς πρὸς Σεβερεῖναν,—the title is preserved on Hippolytus' statue.

[237] Hippolytus, *Elenchos*, ix.12.23; cf. G. L. Prestige's essay on Callistus in *Fathers and Heretics* (Bampton Lectures, 1940), London, S.P.C.K. 1954, 32–3.

[238] Hippolytus, *Elenchos*, ix.12.20–1.

[239] Ibid., ix.12.21. Tertullian, *De Pudicitia*, 1, refers to adulterers only.

[240] For the sequence of events, K. Müller, 'Kleine Beiträge zur Kirchengeschichte', *ZNTW.*, 1924, 231–4.

[241] *De Pudicitia*, 18, 'non habentem maculam aut rugam'; cf. Cyprian, *Ep.*, 69.2, and the Donatists in *Gesta Coll. Carth.*, iii.258.

[242] *De Pudicitia*, 21 (*CSEL.*, xx.271), 'Nam et ipsa ecclesia proprie et principaliter ipse et spiritus'.

[243] Tertullian's rejection of unworthy clergy, *De Monogamia*, 12.

[244] *De Pudicitia*, 21 (*CSEL.*, xx.269). So, of course, the Donatists to Caecilian.

[245] Ibid., 'potest ecclesia donare delictum, sed non faciam, ne et alia delinquant'.

[246] Ibid., 21. 'Quis enim dimittit delicta ni solus Deus.' Cf. Mk. 2⁷.

[247] *De Pudicitia*, 13.

[248] Ibid., 21.

[249] Irenaeus. *Adv. Haer.*, iv.26.3.

[249a] Ibid., 26.4

[250] *De Idololatria*, 24; Cf. Hippolytus, *Elenchos*, ix.12.23. (Wendland, 250.)

[251] Sulpicius Severus, *Chronicon*, ii.32.

[252] *Liber Pontificalis* (ed. L. Duchesne, 145) 'Eodem tempore Pontianus episcopus et Yppolitus presbyter in exilio sunt deportati in Sardinia, in insula nociva Severo et Quintiano consulibus.'

[253] Jerome, *De Viris Illust.*, 53 (*P.L.*, xxiii, 698) and Augustine, *De Haeres.*, 86 (*P.L.*, xlii, 46).

[254] Tertullian, *De Anima*, 55.5.

CHAPTER THIRTEEN

Decius

MAXIMIN was described by a contemporary as having a 'character in accordance with his nature and birth, that is to say, barbarian'.[1] He was an enemy alike of the Senate, the urban middle classes in the provinces, and the Christians.[2] A Thracian by birth, he was the first of the tough and efficient soldiers who rose through prowess in the ranks of the army, to a position of command, and then aspired to the government of the Empire. Such men were fitted to the needs of the day. For, the reign of the self-styled 'friend of manly and disciplined ways'[3] ushered in a period of anarchy, military disaster and civilian demoralization which was to last for the next thirty-five years.

We are not concerned with the detail of the military and economic upheavals which mark this watershed between the Ancient World and the European Middle Ages. At one time or another in the period 235–270, Rome lost the command of the Mediterranean to the Visigoths and Heruls, saw successively the Rhine, Danube and Euphrates frontiers overwhelmed, and the barbarians press into Gaul, Spain, Greece and Asia Minor, while her currency dissolved in an inflation more in keeping with the Modern than the Ancient World.[4] But the provincial administration remained intact and the higher administration of the Empire still included able men such as the lawyer Modestinus who survived into Gordian's reign and Taurus Volusianus who was Gallienus' chief adviser.[5] The barbarians, moreover, had neither the staying power nor the seige equipment to reduce large towns, while the countryside recovered relatively quickly from destruction which was neither planned nor systematic. By 268 the Roman command had adapted itself to the situation. Breaches in the frontier defences were closed, new tactics, based on the use of small but rapidly moving cavalry detachments were evolved, and a succession of able generals such as Claudius Gothicus (268–270), Aurelian (270–275) and Probus (276–282) threw back the Germanic barbarians.

The damage had, however, been done. The prosperity of the first decades of the third century ended. In the 240s, Origen was still living the life of a leisured and cultured citizen, and able to tell an assembly of bishops that the present life which was merely a shadow of the life to come, 'offers you so many good things'.[6] A decade later his words might not have been so well received. Even at this time, Cyprian wrote to his friend Donatus, shortly after his conversion to Christianity oppressed with pessimism,[7] and by 252 both he and his pagan opponent, the magistrate Demetrian, were agreed that the world 'was tottering towards its doom'.[8] The question was, who was to blame. In these years, plague, awe-inspiring and horrifying in its impact on a world ignorant of elementary physiology added to disillusion and despair.[9] Loyalty to the gods was shaken, and the ultimate gainer from the insecurity and bewilderment of the times was the Christian Church. The supreme crisis of the Decian persecution and its aftermath was overcome.

After its first surge of murderous activity, the persecution of Maximin amounted to little more than threat. The execution of the Christian members of Alexander Severus' court was, however, followed by the order that the 'leaders of the Church alone should be put to death as being responsible for the teaching of the Gospel'.[10] Though the tenor of this order is obscure, it seems as though Maximin wanted to restrict the expansion of Christianity, which he regarded as inimical to his policy by limiting the scope of its propaganda and singling out the leaders for punishment. The cult, however, does not seem to have been proscribed. He thus provided a precedent for Decius' similar drive against the Christian leaders in the first months of his reign, before the General Sacrifice. In 236, 'the leaders' in Rome included both Pontianus and his rival, Hippolytus. For each, permanent exile (*deportatio*) to an unhealthy climate replaced the sword as executioner.[11] Even in Rome, however, these measures do not seem to have been followed up. Pontianus resigned his position on 28 September 235, his successor, Anteros, was elected on 21 November, but died apparently a natural death (*dormit*) after a month's episcopacy, on 3 January 236.[12] Fabian who replaced him was not sent into exile, and was to enjoy a prosperous reign of fourteen years until it was ended by Decius.

In one province only, namely Cappadocia, did serious persecution break out. The example is instructive, as it shows once more the underlying agreement between the Roman aristocracy who hated the Christians as potential revolutionaries, and the provincial mob who feared them as atheists responsible for natural disasters. Pontus and Cappadocia had been devastated by earthquakes, and as in a similar situation in the province of Asia some eighty years before, these were regarded as signs of the anger of the gods. Scapegoats had to be found. The Christians lay to hand and some of them held views which lent colour to the pagan accusations. Two independent witnesses, Origen,[13] and Firmilian, bishop of Cappadocia writing, respectively, twelve and twenty years after,[14] have left vivid accounts of what happened. The persecution arose directly out of the earthquakes, i.e. not from any order by Maximin, and it came after a long period of peace. Old, half-forgotten hatreds were aroused and the Christians were set upon. 'Persecutions were suffered and churches were burnt', Origen states.[15] These measures were accepted and promoted by the governor of Cappadocia, Serenianus, 'a bitter and terrible persecutor',[16] as Firmilian describes him, and large numbers of Christians fled the province to safer areas beyond its borders.

Then a strange thing happened, indicative of the underlying force of the prophetic motive in Christianity in Asia, and foreshadowing probable reactions to more severe persecution later in the century. 'Suddenly a certain woman arose among us, who in a state of ecstasy announced that she was a prophetess, and acted as if filled with the Holy Ghost.' She went on to proclaim that she could actually cause earthquakes, maintained that she was in touch with sources of inspiration in Judaea and Jerusalem, and as if to prove her authenticity 'walked about barefoot over frozen snow during a hard winter'. She deceived many, adds Firmilian. These events left a profound impression on contemporaries, and Firmilian recorded them after an interval of more than twenty years. The Christian reaction to persecution was still likely to be renewed belief that the rule of Antichrist was at hand. In a crisis, prophetic rather than episcopal leadership would be the order of the day. Only in Africa were the two traditions to be fused—and then ultimately through Donatism.

Elsewhere, the persecution was either sporadic or non-existent.

In Caesarea, however, a presbyter named Prototectos, and Origen's patron, Ambrosius were both arrested, and this provoked Origen's flaming protest in the form of a long letter to Ambrose, entitled 'The Exhortation to Martyrdom'. The work provides one clue to the secret of Origen's power in the service of the Church. His life, indeed, marks the final transition of Christianity from sect to universal Church. When he was born, *circa* 185, in Alexandria, probably of mixed Greek and Egyptian parentage, Christianity was still on the defensive. When he died *circa* 254, the Decian persecution was over. For good or for bad Church and Empire would now be obliged to come to terms. The problem of how this was to be accomplished was to dominate European political thought for many centuries to come. Origen's contribution, however, lay in two conflicting directions. On the one hand, he was a zealot for martyrdom and a preacher of defiance against the established authorities, on the other, he was a mystic and philosopher, who continued the work of Clement of absorbing Platonism and Stoicism into Christian thought, and so preparing the way for the ultimate harmony of Church and Empire.

The *Exhortation to Martyrdom* represents Origen as the rebel. In words which echo Josephus, *Against Apion* (1.8.42), he claims that Christianity was true because people were prepared to die for it. 'The rest of mankind do not even make it appear that, if there is a persecution of religious people (εἰ ἔστι τὰ ἀνταγωνιζόμενα τοῖς εὐσεβέσι) they intend to die for religion and to prefer death rather than deny their religion and live.' The polytheists were the real atheists, those who failed to 'listen to God who says "Thou shalt have no other gods but me"'. Better honour God with one's lips if that included making open confession unto salvation than honouring him with the heart only.[17] Tertullian would have said no more. In the *Exhortation* one finds none of the Stoic and other examples of dauntless courage drawn from secular history that Clement uses. Instead, there is a catalogue of Old and New Testament heroism, designed to teach that martyrdom was both a symbol of the Christian's intimate love of Christ, of his gratitude for benefits received from Him, and an example to the heathen. Indeed, where in other works Origen does refer to the heroes of the pagan world such as Leonidas or Socrates, he does so only to point the superiority of Christian suffering.[18]

In the *Exhortation* the whole range of his immense knowledge of Scripture was brought into play in the exclusive service of Christ.[19] The Old Testament heroes, particularly the Maccabaean youths, whom Origen regarded as representing the Jewish equivalent of the Christian baptism by blood,[20] the example and exhortation of Jesus himself, all justified Christian passive resistance to illegal imperial demands.

This was the Origen who had encouraged his father to go to martyrdom, and who had to be restrained by his mother from rushing to a voluntary death, the mystic inspired by the ideals of Christian heroism, but also the intolerant hothead who could interrupt a lecture on the nature of the soul to pour out several minutes of impassioned invective at his audience for not hanging on every word he spoke.[21] It was also the unquiet, surging idealist who had taken Mt. 19[12] so literally as to preclude himself from a normal ecclesiastical career, whose hatred of Gnosticism was such as to provide the emotional impulse for his great *Commentary on John*,[22] who proclaimed that after martyrdom the most important fact in Christianity's claim to allegiance was the moral reform of the convert.[23] There might be many points in common between Greek philosophy and Christian teaching, but the effect of the latter on the mind of the individual was decisive.[24] Thus, he replies to Celsus' charge that Christians took advantage of human gullibility, to claim that the multitude of believers had renounced 'the great flood of evil in which they formerly used to wallow',[25] and that this consideration must support the view that a doctrine so beneficial to humanity could not come to mankind apart from divine providence. He never ceased to be prepared to defy the government if he thought that his defence of Christianity demanded it. In the opening chapter of the *Contra Celsum* he answers Celsus' charge of Christian illegality with the claim that 'it was not wrong to form associations against the laws for the sake of truth', and that Christians formed such associations 'against the devil, contrary to his law in order to persuade others whom they might be able to persuade'.[26] He rejoices that the efforts of 'the Roman Senate, the contemporary emperors, the army, the people and the relatives of believers' had not sufficed to defeat Christianity. Indeed, 'it has conquered the whole world that was conspiring against it'.[27] Later, in Book V, he points to the revolutionary and universalist character of Jesus' teaching,[28] and he ends his defence of Christianity with an explanation of why the Christians should not undertake the physical defence of the Empire or accept public office, as Celsus had demanded.[29]

But with all his turgid idealism Origen was not an Alexandrian Tertullian. There were deep differences between the theological outlooks of the two men. If Tertullian's hope lay in the resurrection of the body and its preservation from the physical torments of eternal damnation, Origen's lay in the liberation of the soul and in its progressive advance through its education by the Logos until it could rise towards Christ. Man moved, not into 'another body' but to a higher image of God.[30] To him individual predestination to Heaven or Hell did not exist,[31] as Man had within himself the means 'of laying hold of salvation'.[32] It is at this point that those who like Porphyry accused Origen of 'being a Christian contrary to the law' and then describing 'his devotion to philosophy',[33] were justified. He was strongly influenced by the middle Platonist school of Posidonius and Numenius. Through the language and text of Scripture there emerges always the Platonist concept of God and the Greek maxim for man, 'know thyself'. The human soul, communing with itself, comes to discover its true essence which is divine[34] and moves in accordance with that discovery. Thus in the *Commentary on Canticles* Origen wrote, 'If thou dost not know thyself O good or most beautiful among women, go out and seek after the flocks'.[35] This positive act of self-realization, rather than any passive acceptance of Grace marked the beginning of the individual's spiritual progress. Then, like his predecessors in the Alexandrine school he used the story of Exodus as an allegory of the progress of the human soul. The 'refrigeria' along the road through the wilderness were not types of the material benefits to be enjoyed by martyrs in Paradise, but 'the oases where the soul replenishes its powers to return to new tasks with greater vigour'.[36] So, to the ultimate objective, which was the contemplation and knowledge of the divine mysteries, the 'ὁμοίωσις θεῷ'.[37] In the long and painful ascent towards this goal Σοφία and γνῶσις were the highest of the Christian attributes.[38]

Therefore, in the last resort, martyrdom was only one of the roads leading to the Christian's goal. Curiously, Origen places it second after baptism among the means of winning remission of sins. After it, followed almsgiving, forgiveness of others, converting the sinner, manifestation of love, and finally, ecclesiastical penance.[39] The difference between the Eastern and Western eschatologies and consequent scale of moral values is clearly revealed even at this period. For Origen the relation of God to man is that of teacher to pupil, not master to slave, nor judge to criminal. Punishments had their educative purpose as befitting a soul which partook of the Logos.[40] One of his favourite metaphors is that of Christ as Healer and Physician, severe indeed to everything corrupt in the soul, but always cutting and cauterizing with a view to restoration, the recovery of what humanity had lost in the Fall.[41]

In that process, Jesus' victory over death, and the triumphant sacrifice of the righteous of the Old Israel and of the martyrs had their place, but one is also justified in asking, were they necessities? If the soul's perfection was a prolonged advance extending over many separate existences,[42] martyrdom could be only an adjunct, a sign of the possession of spiritual gifts. The long life of the Christian ascetic could be of equal importance, for instance as an expiation of sin,[43] or as an example to others.[44] And not for nothing is Origen accounted as one of the founding influences in Egyptian monasticism,[45] and even an upholder of desert solitude.[46] His 'philosophical' way of life, as described by Eusebius,[47] was that of an ascetic, frugal, without material comforts, sexless, free from all but the most necessary possessions, and we are told, he encouraged 'thousands' to do likewise for their own progress towards enlightenment.[48] His influence on the monks of Nitria was lasting.[49] For to Origen the theologian there was neither Judgment, nor material Paradise, nor the vision of a world dissolving into fiery chaos. All went forward gradually until souls were once more truly rational and God was again all in all.[50]

But the tension was sometimes too great. What he really felt about his own life may well be betrayed in a sudden but characteristic outburst in the middle of his speech to the council of bishops preserved in the *Dialogue with Heracleides*:

Bring wild beasts, bring crosses, bring fire, bring tortures. I know that as soon as I die, I come forth from the body, I rest with Christ. Therefore let us struggle, therefore let us wrestle, let us groan being in the body, not as if we shall again be in the tombs in the body,

because we shall be set free from it, and shall change our body to one
which is more spiritual. Destined as we are to be with Christ, how
we groan while we are in the body![51]

The philosopher and man of martyrdom were not easily reconcilable.

Defiance, however, was not the only attitude a Christian might
take up in face of pagan society. The Divine Logos was the guide
and instructor of the human race, leading mankind forward now
through Moses,[52] now through the prophets,[53] supremely through
Jesus,[54] and finally through the Apostles and martyrs.[55] If
defiance against individual laws at particular times was a necessity
that did not prevent the ultimate harmony between Church and
Empire from coming about. In the famous passage in *Contra
Celsum*, ii.30 Origen points out the importance of the unification
of the Empire under Augustus as providing the framework for
the spread of the Gospel. 'God was preparing the nations for his
teaching that they might be under one Roman emperor', undisturbed by wars 'caused by the existence of a large number of
kingdoms'. Polyarchy had given way to monarchy, the babel
of tongues to a uniformity of language, and as a result Jesus'
teaching had reached the ends of the world.[56] Origen looks forward at the end of his apology to the possibility of a world united
in the service of Christ. No wonder his disciple Eusebius of
Caesarea hailed the Constantinian monarchy as a further great
step along the same road.

Thus Origen was able to combine ideas which logically were
incompatible. The contemplation and the asceticism of a Christian philosopher demanded not sudden death, but a life as long
as some of Origen's disciples among the Egyptian monks were to
enjoy. But the force of his personality held both outlooks in
harness and drove them into the service of the Christian Church.
The Christian philosopher could now speak on level terms with
his pagan contemporary. The Church was lifted finally out of the
rut of Judaistic sectarianism, while its own triumph over its
Jewish rival was becoming increasingly complete. It would be
hardly too much to say that for the Greek-speaking intellectual
who was disturbed at the utter discredit into which current
philosophic systems were sinking,[57] Origen's vast, eclectic and
ultimately Christian system came as a vision of hope. The

family of Gregory Thaumaturgus ('the Wonderworker') was only
the first of those who remembered Origen as their master and inspiration.

The fourteen years which separated Maximin's persecution
from that of Decius were years of great progress for the Church.
The fact that there were those in the late third century who
thought the Emperor Philip (244-249) had been a Christian[58]
is evidence for the benevolent toleration the Church was now
enjoying. Certainly both the Emperor and his wife, Otacilia
Severa corresponded with Origen,[59] and Eusebius could emphasize that this reign was one in which 'the faith was increasing and
our doctrine was being proclaimed openly in the ears of all'.[60]

This statement is confirmed by all available evidence. In Africa no
less than ninety bishops had assembled at Lambaesis *circa* 245
to condemn its bishop, Privatus, of scandal and error.[61] The
first Christian buildings at Tipasa[62] and the cemetery at Henchir
Skihra in Byzacena[63] may date to this period. In Rome, catacombs
were extended and new *areae* built.[64] Origen in two striking
passages in *Contra Celsum* testifies to the astonishing increase in the
numbers of Christians. 'So great is the harvest of the people
gathered in and collected into the threshing floors of God, which
are the churches, that there are not the labourers to reap in the
harvest.'[65] Again in iii.9, he points to the impressive results
of the idealism of the Christian missionaries in the situation in
which he was living. There was no question any longer of Christianity being a narrow sect, which had evoked Celsus' gibe, 'If all
men wanted to be Christians, the Christians would no longer
want them'. No, says Origen, this is blatantly false. Christians
leave nothing undone to convert the world—and they are succeeding. Christians,

> in fact, have done the work of going round not only cities but even
> villages and country cottages to make others also pious towards God.
> One could not say that they did this for the sake of wealth, since
> sometimes they do not even accept money for the necessities of life,
> and if ever they are compelled to do so by want in this respect, they
> are content with what is necessary and no more, even if several
> people are willing to share with them and to give them more than
> they need. I admit that at the present time perhaps, when on account
> of the multitude of people coming to the faith even rich men and

persons in positions of honour, and ladies of refinement and high birth, favourably regard adherents of the faith, one might venture to say that some become leaders of the Christian teaching for the sake of a little prestige. Yet at the beginning when there was great risk attached particularly to teachers, no such suspicion could be reasonably entertained. Even now, however, the disgrace among the rest of society is greater than the supposed reputation among fellow-believers, and this does not exist in every case.[66]

(Tr. H. Chadwick)

This is an interesting picture of the new-style Church on the eve of the Decian persecution. Office in the Church could be openly sought as a means of winning respect within one's community. Origen tells of individuals entertaining and intriguing in order to become deacons, and then up the ladder of clerical success.[67] In the East, Christianity had become one of the principal religions of the Empire drawing its recruits from all classes of the population.

The tendency towards hierarchization was irresistible. The emergence of strong personalities within the episcopate, such as Alexander at Jerusalem, Babylas at Antioch, Cyprian at Carthage, Heraclas at Alexandria and Fabian at Rome was the counterpart of the frequent assembly of episcopal councils. There was no longer any hope for Tertullian's ideal of only a quarter of a century before of a 'Church of Spiritual Men' unless these were associated with the hierarchy. With these developments may be associated the development of the clerical career. To Fabian is credited the subdivision of ecclesiastical Rome into seven(?) regions designed to correspond with the seven deacons, and the establishment of seven sub-deacons, and seven notaries charged with the duty of drawing up complete lists of *Gesta Martyrum*.[68] And with the power to list went also the power to exclude and therefore control. The well-known description of the organization of the Church in Rome with its 46 presbyters, 7 deacons, 42 acolytes and 52 clerics of lesser degree given by Cornelius in a letter to Fabius of Antioch in 251 may be paralleled elsewhere.[69] Cyprian's first letter insists on the permanent and exclusive character of the Christian priesthood,[70] and we know from another letter that the clergy in Carthage enjoyed the security of a monthly stipend.[71] In this movement of ordered expansion the prophet and martyr were reduced to liturgical reminiscence and even in Carthage the Second Coming tended to fade into oblivion.

Among the congregations too, much was being taken for granted. Enthusiasm was on the wane. Services were being held, Origen complained, in an atmosphere of gossip and triviality.[72] In his *Commentary on Matthew* (*circa* 247–248) he urged older established Christians not to despise the efforts of the newly converted. 'Neither the recent date of their conversion', he argues, 'nor their heathen parents are obstacles to those who struggle vigorously to ascend through obedience to the commandments beyond those who have grown old in the faith.'[73] But there were others, even though they had become Christians who, 'spent their time boasting of their property, their houses and their wealth'.[74] In the West also, such people seem to have been conspicuous. Cyprian speaking on the outbreak of the persecution of 250 laments the fact that even bishops were taking up ordinary secular occupations, such as that of bailiff on an Imperial estate, and that wealth had clogged the spirit of martyrdom and self-sacrifice of many.[75] A generation before, Christians could argue that they stood for ordered change in opposition to the dead weight of custom. Now, the Church had too many of its own nominal adherents. The results showed themselves when the test came on the removal of the Emperor Philip in 249.

The experiences, however, of two important converts of this period demonstrate both why Christianity was making progress, and also the different message it was conveying to the Greek and Latin respectively. Gregory the Wonderworker and Cyprian express in their personal accounts of conversion two types of religious experience and standpoint. Gregory's address of gratitude to Origen was written on his departure from Caesarea to his native country after five years' stay and study with his master. How the two came into contact is one of those human stories which all too rarely light up the history of the Ancient World. Gregory and his brother Athenodorus had been destined by their widowed mother for the profession of public speaking, which involved a knowledge of Roman law. The brothers left their province of Pontus to study at the celebrated school of Roman law in Berytus *circa* 236. But they were not destined to arrive. Their sister had married a lawyer on the staff of the governor of

Palestine and her husband wanted her to join him. The two brothers suddenly found themselves confronted by a soldier armed with authority for them to use the public post, and instructions that they were to accompany their sister as part of an honourable escort to Caesarea. There they met Origen, and all thought of returning to Berytus evaporated. Gregory had for a long time felt drawn to Christianity. He dates his first 'conversion' to when he was fourteen, after his father' death, and gradually that interest grew.[76] Now, he gladly became Origen's pupil. For the next five years they were inseparable, and then finally, *circa* 242, Gregory left at long last to pay a brief visit to Berytus and then return to his native province. Within a year he had become a Christian bishop.

Gregory shows the immense personal influence which Origen exercised over his pupils, as well as the attraction which Christian Platonism was capable of exercising on receptive and educated Greek minds of the day. To cite his words regarding Origen himself,

> Like some spark kindled within my soul there was kindled and blazed forth my love both towards Him, most desirable of all for His beauty unspeakable, the Word holy and altogether lovely, and toward this man his friend and prophet. Deeply stricken by it, I was led to neglect all that seemed to concern me: affairs, studies, even my favourite law, home and kindred there, no less than those among whom I was sojourning. One thing only was dear and affected by me: philosophy and its teacher, this divine man.[77]

Certainly, Gregory came to regard heathenism as error, and Christianity as deliverance and escape from its bondage. But the process was one of education and advance. The sacred word must not be consigned to the soul 'not yet reasonable'.[78] 'Divine and human reason should work together in my soul, for its advancement towards understanding things divine',[79] he says. Indeed, Gregory learnt that Christianity was the true philosophy, that 'they only lived the life befitting to reasonable beings, who studied to live rightly . . . '[80] and that 'true religion was utterly impossible to one who did not philosophize'.[81] A proper study of all that was good in the current philosophic systems led step by step towards understanding the cause of all, but beyond that lay the Divine word contained in the Scriptures, to be understood truly only by those who were in communion with God's Spirit by whom the Prophets had been inspired. Such was conversion. 'In a word, this indeed was our paradise imitating that great Paradise of God, wherein we needed not to till the earth below, nor to minister to the body nor to grow gross, but only to increase the acquisitions of our souls, like some fair plants engrafting themselves, or rather engrafted in us by the Cause of all.'[82] To Gregory then, as to his master, Christianity was the highest form of education and thought for life which man could achieve. The road to Paradise led through normal secular study and then beyond that, via baptism towards true understanding of the word of God as contained in Scripture, achieved by control of body and mind alike. It was the ideal of the true ascetic to whom all the world was God's world.

From Gregory we turn to his contemporary Cyprian, an exact contemporary, who had gone further along the secular career of law and public speaking than he had. Cyprian had been on the anti-Christian side in Carthage, but had gradually been converted by the arguments and, one may perhaps presume, by the bearing of the Christians.[83] In *circa* 245 he was converted, and he wrote of his experience to his friend and fellow-convert Donatus. He had come into contact with Christian works (perhaps those of Tertullian) and realized from his reading that his own life had been one of 'darkness, ignorance of self and estrangement'. Then, to cite his own words:

> I seconded my own besetting vices, I despaired of improvement, I looked on my faults as natural and home-born. I even favoured them. But, as soon as the stain of my former life was wiped away by help of the birth-giving wave [of baptism], and a calm pure light from above flooded my purged breast, so soon as I drank of the spirit from Heaven and was restored to a new manhood by a second nativity, then marvellously doubts began to clear, secrets revealed themselves, the dark grew light, seeming difficulties gave way, supposed impossibilities vanished. I was able to recognize that what was born of flesh and lived under the rule of sin was of earth, earthy, while that which was animated by the Holy Spirit began to belong to God.[84]

For both converts, then, Christianity was a release from evil and a means of achieving the ideal of self-knowledge. Both men accepted high office in the Church. Both regarded Christianity as the essential means of human salvation But there the resemblances end. The emphasis in Cyprian is on sin, on the sinful even the diabolic nature of the world, and the Christian's duty of separation from it.[85] What was 'under the rule of sin was earth, earthy'. There is an element of sudden liberation through the fact of baptism[86] rather than the gradual growth of the 'reasonable soul'. There is the inspiration of the Holy Spirit rather than the educative guidance of the Logos. There is a background of personal insecurity rather than a desire to advance to better understanding of already accepted values, and the expression of disgust at the oppression and injustice that characterized his world.[87] Cyprian's conversion meant to some extent the abandonment of previous interests, rather than their deepening and transformation. One looks in vain for reference to secular works in his letters. But for the brief references in Lactantius and in Jerome's *De Viris Illustribus*, we could only guess at his previous career. The Church in the West was still an enclave of righteousness confronting a hostile society. In the East it was already absorbing and refining the ethical and philosophic legacies of the Ancient World.

There is another point of contrast. Cyprian developed into a great episcopal administrator, but once a member of the Christian Church his time seems to have been taken up entirely with its internal problems. From Lactantius half a century later we learn that Cyprian's influence on his pagan contemporaries was slight. Despite his eloquence, Lactantius says 'even he cannot please— further than his words—those who do not know the mystery'. He was ridiculed, called Koprian ('dung-head') and a purveyor of old wives' tales.[88] The fact is, that in Africa the language of Christianity was a specialized one, with its own jargon derived largely from the Old Latin Bible. It was in keeping with its narrow vision, and it has been compared, not unreasonably, to Quaker-English.[89] The attractive power of the Church even at this period accordingly was limited, until circumstances beyond its control played into its hands.

In Pontus, however, Gregory became a powerful missionary bishop, spending the remaining thirty years of his life spreading

Christianity into the furthest parts of the countryside. If it is not strictly true, as his biographer, Gregory of Nyssa[90] claimed a century later, that when he arrived there were seventeen Christians and when he died there were seventeen pagans, there is no doubt that he was responsible for a perceptible movement towards Christianity in Pontus and Cappadocia. His missionary methods were as intelligent as anything recorded about Christian proselytism in the Ancient World. He broke the power of the traditional local priests by revealing their oracles and cures as swindles, part of the 'irrational' world from which man could be emancipated by Christ, but he replaced the local festivals with those of the martyrs, celebrated also with a good deal of jollification.[91] We thus have an interesting example of the actual transition from the pagan cult of local divinities to the Christian cult of saints and martyrs accompanying the conversion of the inhabitants. This type of success involved the open discomfiture of the ruling priestly houses and aroused some latent opposition. The little incident related in the Acts of Pionius where a slave-girl, converted in the reign of Gordian, was driven out by her mistress and forced to take refuge in the mountains, shows that conversions were still not popular.[92] Origen saw that for all the apparent security which the Church was enjoying in the reign of Philip the danger signals were being hoisted the world over. The plague and disasters of the time were being laid at the door of Christians. The next persecution would not be 'partial as before, but general, everywhere'.[93] He had not long to wait.

It was in Alexandria, the nerve centre of religious tension, that the storm ultimately broke. Around the middle of 248 the populace, still apparently largely pagan, was stirred up by a priest to attack the Christians.[94] They did, and the result was a pogrom similar in scale and destructive fury to that which had befallen the Jews just over two centuries previously. Dionysius who had been elected bishop only a year before was an eye-witness and in a letter to his colleague Fabius of Antioch wrote in detail what happened. Individual Christians were seized and lynched. Others were dragged to the temples and forced to sacrifice, while the mob ran riot through the streets looting, burning and destroying Christian property. In one characteristic incident, we are told,

They seized then that marvellous aged virgin Apollonia, broke out all her teeth with blows on her jaws, and piling up a pyre before the city threatened to burn her alive, if she refused to recite along with them their blasphemous sayings. But she asked for a brief space, and, being released, without flinching she leaped into the fire and was consumed.[95]

Two fanaticisms were clashing. The rioters believed, like those in Lyons seventy years before, that they were fighting for their gods against a powerful enemy. Within a few months the whole Empire was to be engaged in the same struggle.

Things had been going badly for Philip. The combination of Persian aggression and Gothic invasion was proving too much. Heavy taxes had to be levied on the eastern provinces partly to pay the huge reparations (500,000 denarii) Philip had agreed to Sapor in 244, partly, it appears, to finance Rome's Millennium which fell on 21 April 248.[96] His pro-Christianity, shown by the high favour in which Pope Fabian evidently stood,[97] and his wife's correspondence with Origen,[98] and perhaps by his own reliance on the archers from the largely Christian kingdom of Osrhoene made him a target for animosities in both the capital and among the frontier armies. Religious tradition and military efficiency found their champion in the City Prefect of Rome, C. Quintus Messius Decius, an Illyrian who had married into a wealthy Etruscan family.

On 1 April 248, the Danube legions proclaimed their commander, Ti. Cl. Marinus Pacatianus, emperor, and shortly after, the burden of taxation levied by Philip's brother Ti. Julius Priscus as Praetorian Prefect produced a revolution in Syria.[99] The Germanic tribes who now found their subsidies cut off by Pacatian, went over to the offensive, crossed the Danube and besieged Marcianopolis. Philip considered abdication, was dissuaded by Decius, who promised him a successful campaign against the barbarians. His bold statement came true, but the troops elated at their victory proclaimed a somewhat unwilling Decius emperor. There followed an inconclusive period of negotiations and marches until at Verona in the autumn of 249 Philip's forces were defeated and he himself was killed.[100] A new and more sombre era had opened for the Church.

Decius' motives for launching the persecution are by no

means clear. Zonaras says that he appointed Valerian to assist him in the administration of the Empire, and that they egged one another on to persecute the Christians.[101] This seems unlikely, for Valerian when he became emperor in 253 was known to be personally favourable to the Christians during the first four years of his reign. Nor does it seem likely that the sole cause was the existence of widespread popular hostility to the Church, though this existed.[102] There would have been fewer nominal Christians to apostasize if the Church had seemed less secure in the reigns of Gordian III and Philip.

The explanation may lie in the same mixture of political and personal forces which had caused other rapid changes of religious policy since the accession of Maximin. Eusebius says that Decius 'on account of his enmity towards Philip raised a persecution against the churches' (*H.E.*, vi.39.1). This is also the view of the writer of xiii Sibylline, a reliable witness for the Roman East for the whole period 240–265.[103] But there may have been more than the personal hostility such as inspired Maximin fourteen years before. The tenor of Decius' reforms was the restoration of traditional Roman discipline. His revival of the office of Censor is paralleled by the restoration of discipline among the frontier armies, and an active offensive-defensive tactic against the Germanic barbarians on the Rhine and Dacian frontiers. His assumption of the appellation 'Trajan' shows him looking back to the heroic era of the *Optimus Princeps*. The striking of the *divi* series of *antoniniani* commemorating his predecessors who had been accorded divine honours also points in this direction. Like Diocletian after him, he sought to consolidate the Empire by a return to traditional virtues and *mores*. 'The Illyrian emperors stood for Rome.'[104] In popular estimation, the Christians did not. Moreover, their widespread organization and the power of their leaders had become something to be feared. 'I would far rather receive news of a rival to the throne, than another bishop in Rome', Decius is reported to have said after Pope Fabian's execution. He may well have been right.[105]

It would, however, be mistaken to think of Decius' measures as aimed negatively against the Christians. As Lietzmann has pointed out, 'the new Imperator was confronted with a task of unprecedented difficulty and wished to unite all the forces of the Empire for its achievement. He also called to his aid the hearts of his subjects by appointing a general sacrifice of homage and intercession before the images of the tutelary gods of the empire'.[106] As the important inscription from Aphrodisias shows, the provincials' 'sacrifices and prayers' were associated in Decius' mind with their solidarity 'with the Romans' (διὰ τὴν πρὸς Ῥωμαίους οἰκείοτητα) and the Emperor thanked the loyal inhabitants for their support 'of our empire', and their 'just sacrifices and prayers'.[107] One is reminded of Celsus' plea to the Christian' over seventy years before. 'What is dreadful in propitiating the powers on earth, both the others and the rulers and emperors among men, since not even they hold their position without the might of the daemons?'[108] Once Christians were prepared to 'pay formal acknowledgment'[109] to the gods of the empire, they could worship their private divinity 'the crucified one', as they chose.[110] And many did precisely this.

The contents of Decius' edict or edicts are not known. It would appear, however, that there were two main phases in the persecution with a certain amount of overlap between them. The first action must have taken place within weeks of Decius' entry into Rome late in 249.[111] It followed the precedent set by Maximin and resulted in the arrest of members of the higher clergy. At Rome the zealous and active Pope Fabian was seized, tried before the Emperor himself and executed on 20 or 21[112] January 250. In Antioch, Bishop Babylas was also martyred, perhaps on 24 January.[113] His colleague in Jerusalem, Alexander, who had survived one persecution in his youth, was brought before the provincial governor in Caesarea, imprisoned and died there.[114] In Caesarea, Origen was incarcerated and harshly treated so that he died as a result of his injuries three years later.[115] In Alexandria and Carthage respectively, Dionysius and Cyprian escaped the net, the former by a hair's breadth.[116] They went into hiding outside their capital cities and were not further molested. In Smyrna Bishop Euctemon hastened to apostasize,[117] leaving to others the honour of upholding Polycarp's name.

These measures were followed by a universal order to sacrifice, promulgated perhaps as early as February 250, and enforced in one province after another through the spring and summer of that year.[118] The exact form these measures took is not clear.

On the one hand, Alföldi has suggested a *dies Imperii* marked by a sacrifice in honour of the Emperor whose accession signified the inauguration of a new age of human happiness.[119] On the current coinage of this year the Emperor is in fact represented as saviour and bringer of peace. The types *Restitutor Orbis*, *Salus generis humani*, and *Saeculum novum* tell their own story of hopes for a restoration of prosperity and victory in the face of growing internal and external pressures. On the other hand, the long-drawn-out nature of the proceedings would argue against the naming of a single *dies Imperii*. In Theadelphia in the Arsinoite nome (Fayum), for instance, sacrifices continued from 12 June to 14 July 250. In Carthage and perhaps in Rome also, however, sacrifices seem to have been concentrated into the minimum time.

The requirement was for all free inhabitants of the Empire, men, women and children, to sacrifice to the gods of the Empire, pour a libation, and taste sacrificial meat.[120] The penalty for refusal was death (*Acta Pionii*, 7.4). Though these deities were not specified to the sacrificers we know from contemporary sources of offerings made to Jupiter, the Roman triad Jupiter, Juno and Minerva, to Dea Roma, to Apollo, Diana, Venus, Nemesis and to the genius of the Emperor himself. These were the gods 'who preserved the (emperors') kingdom'.[121] The aim seems to have been, therefore, a general declaration of adhesion to the state cults, in which the Christians also were given the chance to prove their loyalty. As Knipfing has stated, 'In requiring such an outward act and declaration of adhesion to the state cult, Decius was exploiting for military and political purposes the extensive grant of Roman citizenship made by the *Constitutio Antoniniana* in 212'.[122] The emphatic statements made for instance by the priestess of the crocodile god Petesouchos, 'the great, the mighty, the immortal', that she had 'sacrificed all her life', and held a number of offices in the cult shows that the order applied to all, including committed pagans. Their protestations indicate perhaps latent indignation against those who did not sacrifice habitually, namely the Christians.[123] If one may take the morale of the citizens of Arsinoe as typical of the times, there was every excuse for some such general measure of appeasement.[124]

The entire resources of the provincial administration were brought into play. We hear of commissions appointed to supervise

the sacrifices in Carthage,[125] Spain,[126] Alexandria[127] and many
other centres in Egypt. At Carthage the commission was
made up of five leading citizens who co-operated with the
magistrates, at Theadelphia a prytanis, one of the magistrates who
presided over the local council, was a member, and in the Greek
Acta of Trypho, where the scene is set in Rome, senior magistrates
are alleged to have taken part.[128] Moreover, census and tax rolls
provided by local officials in each district controlled the number
and identity of those who presented themselves to sacrifice. On
completion they received a certificate (*libellus*) signed by the
commission testifying that they had duly done sacrifice. No less
than forty-three of these certificates have been found on Egyptian
sites, thirty-four from Theadelphia in Arsinoe, two from
Oxyrhynchus, two from Arsinoe itself and one each from Narmouthis, Philadelphia and Alexandrou Nesos.[129] That from the
last-named village reads:

> 1st Hand. To the commission chosen to superintend the sacrifices
> at the village of Alexander's Isle. From Aurelius Diogenes, son of
> Satabous, of the village of Alexander's Isle, aged 72 years, with a
> scar on the right eyebrow. I have always sacrificed to the gods, and
> now in your presence in accordance with the edict I have made
> sacrifice, and poured a libation, and partaken of the sacred victims.
> I request you to certify this below. Farewell. I, Aurelius Diogenes,
> have presented this petition.
> 2nd Hand. I, Aurelius Syrus, saw you and your son sacrificing.
> 3rd Hand. . . . onos . . .
> 1st Hand. The year one of the Emperor Caesar Gaius Messius
> Quintus Trajanus Decius Pius Felix Augustus, Epeiph 2 (June 26,
> 250). (J. R. Knipfing, *Harvard Theological Review*, 16 (1923), p. 363,
> slightly altered.) (J. Stevenson, *A New Eusebius*, 228).

The description of the aged Diogenes, with his identification
marks, the attestation of the officials and the four full lines of
papyrus text taken up with Decius' titles and the date, demonstrated then and now the importance the authorities attached to
universal compliance on an occasion of more than usual solemnity.

The immediate effect of these tests must have satisfied the most
sanguine hopes of the Emperor and his advisers. There is no doubt
as to their immense initial success. The Church was a mainly
urban institution drawing a good deal of support from merchants

and artisans.[130] Its active membership was still specialized, while its centralized organization and hierarchy was particularly vulnerable to this sort of attack. The leaders were prominent enough to be known, but neither popular nor powerful enough to escape the consequences. Dionysius of Alexandria complains that Sabinus the prefect sent a *frumentarius* to arrest him, the 'self-same hour that Decius' edict arrived'.[131] The majority of the populace and the middle classes who filled the magistracies were still anti-Christian. The apparent exception, provided by Diony-sius of Alexandria's rescue by peasants of Mareotis from arrest seems to have been a simple act of defiance against the authori-ties by pagan villagers, regardless of whether Dionysius was a Christian or not.[132]

Contemporaries in Alexandria, Carthage, Smyrna and even in Rome, testify to the utter disorganization caused by the arrest or flight of the Christian leaders. Vast numbers lapsed forthwith. Many denied ever having been Christians.[133] The Church was only saved from ruin by the constancy of a few individuals, coupled with the authorities' lack of organization and means to press home their initial advantage. In each of the main areas there are first-hand accounts of what took place. For Alexandria, Dionysius writing to his colleague Fabius of Antioch who had succeeded the martyred Babylas says:

> And what is more, when the edict arrived, and it was almost like that which was predicted by Our Lord, wellnigh the most terrible of all so as if possible to cause to stumble even the elect. How-soever that be, all cowered with fear. And of many of the more eminent persons, some came forward immediately through fear, others in public positions were compelled to do so by their business, and others were dragged by those around them. Called by name they approached the impure and unholy sacrifices, some pale and trembling, as if they were not for sacrificing but rather to be them-selves the sacrifices and victims to the idols, so that the large crowd that stood around heaped mockery upon them, and it was evident that they were by nature cowards in everything, cowards both to die and to sacrifice. But others ran eagerly towards the altars, affirming by their forwardness that they had not been Christians even formerly; concerning whom the Lord very truly predicted that they shall hardly be saved. Of the rest, some followed one or other of these, others fled; some were captured, and of these some

went as far as bonds and imprisonment, and certain, when they had been shut up for many days, then forswore themselves even before coming into court, while others, who remained firm for a certain time under tortures, subsequently gave in. (*H.E.*, vi.40.10–12. Trans. J. E. L. Oulton, *Eusebius*, ii, 103–05).

The effective staff of this already important see was reduced to four priests who were in hiding and 'secretly visited the brethren'. Two others, Faustinus and Aquila 'who are better known in the world, are wandering about in Egypt'.[134]

In Africa matters were, if anything, worse. Cyprian admits (*Letter*, 11.1) that the great majority of his flock had lapsed; few of his clergy stayed at their posts. The treatise *On the Lapsed*, written in 251, recounts in awe-inspiring terms the extent of the disaster. Here, the system seems to have been that one particular day was set apart for sacrifice to Jupiter,[135] for we find that the magistrates at Carthage were so busy that they begged would-be sacrificers to return on the morrow (*De Lapsis*, 8). This opened the way, however, for a good deal of prevarication and avoidance, even though those who fled risked confiscation of property.[136] Some Christians bribed friends to get a *libellus* for them, or purchased one themselves,[137] and these *libellatici*, as they were called, were to set the African Church a serious problem when the question of their readmission to Communion came to be considered. Others just lay low, to emerge as *stantes*, almost on the level of confessors, at the end of the crisis. But even this amount of courage was usually lacking. In the provincial towns where it was almost impossible to conceal one's views, whole congregations apostasized, in one case led by the bishop himself (*Letter*, 59.10). Nor are we dependent on the word of a single bishop whose own role had not been a heroic one. The whole problem of the *libelli pacis*, that is the pardons given out by surviving confessors to their friends and relatives at the end of the persecution, arose only because of the enormous numbers of lapsed.

In Asia Minor, the hitherto triumphant mission of Gregory in Cappadocia came to an abrupt halt. Gregory himself seems to have accepted the fact that most of his new converts would give way under the threat of persecution, and he himself fled.[138] In Smyrna, the bishop and other leading Christians sacrificed.[139] Here, perhaps for the last time, the Jews in Asia were able to exploit the situa-

tion, telling the Christians that Jesus was executed as a criminal
(ὡς βιοθανής), and inviting them to take the sensible course and
join the synagogue.[140] The pagan magistrates also felt confident of
their intellectual superiority. They knew that the Christians
'worship the crucified one', and openly laughed at the idea.[141]
They also knew that the Church was riddled with sects. Pionius
was asked at his trial to which one he belonged[142] and he was
regarded as a sort of local fanatic.[143] In Pisidian Antioch, even the
Montanists, for the moment quite respectable as 'the ancient sect
of Cataphrygians', were apostasizing.[144] This in itself indicates the
extent of the crisis.

In Rome, though the picturesque details are lacking, the situation seems to have resembled that of Carthage. For many days on
end Christians were sacrificing to the Roman gods in the
Capitol.[145] The Church was described as 'laid waste' (vastata).[146]
There were numbers of libellatici who prided themselves on their
cunning and their escapes.[147] Those presbyters who remained at
their posts felt righteous indignation against those who had fled.
The lash of their invective was visited on Cyprian himself. 'We
have learnt', they wrote, 'from Crementius the subdeacon that the
blessed pope Cyprian has retired, and that indeed he did rightly
being an eminent person . . . '. In Rome, 'eminent persons' had
been among the lapsed. A good shepherd guarded his flock.
The hireling saw the wolf coming, and fled.[148] Their indignation
provided the background to the disputes concerning the re-
admission of the lapsed which were to beset Carthage and Rome
alike in the next few months.

The majority of the confessors of whom any record has survived
seem to have been far from eminent. Lucianus their leader at
Carthage 'was little instructed in holy scripture',[149] and his Latin
suggests the same comment in the art of composition. Others,
like Aurelius, were illiterate.[150] In Egypt, of the seventeen martyrs
named, six were described by Bishop Dionysius as 'native
Egyptians' or 'Libyans'; there were also four soldiers, four women,
including Mercuria, Dionysia and Ammonarion, a youth who
survived, named Dioscorus, and three other aged Christians.[151]
Apparently the confessors included the sort of people who might
be suspected of consorting with bandits,[152] a point not without
interest in view of the special measures being taken by the

authorities to curb brigandage at this time in Egypt.[153] In Asia Minor, also, Pionius and his friends seem to have been artisans or of servile origin. Under stress, it was the apocalyptic and anti-imperial outlook that prevailed among them. Pionius saw in the volcanic eruptions which he had either seen or heard about, the promise that the world would be destroyed by fire,[154] and like Papylas and Carpus before him 'hastens to the stadium' and his death.[155] To the writer of the *Acta* he was a 'noble athlete' as in the Maccabean tradition. Neither he, nor Bishop Acacius were prepared to obey laws which clashed with their beliefs.

In Rome and Africa the confessors, humble enough in secular life, were prepared to defy to the end the commands of the pro-consul of Africa or the legal representatives of an emperor whom they regarded as a serpent, the 'forerunner of antichrist'.[156] As their predecessors in the second century, they trusted in the fact that they were 'friends, yes, and witnesses of Christ',[157] and would be crowned with glory hereafter. With Celerinus of Carthage, though an emigrant to Rome, we find a pattern of martyrdom running through three generations, and reaching its climax in his own defiant career. His grandmother, Celerina, had been martyred in some earlier persecution, so had her son and son-in-law, both soldiers in the Roman army, who had taken the same stand as the *speculator* in Tertullian's *De Corona Militis*.[158] Their names were all celebrated in the Carthaginian roll of martyrs.[159] Theirs is a curious example of militancy alternating for and against the Roman Empire. Whatever might be the ideas of the Christian intellectuals in times of prosperity, the Macca-bean tradition represented by these almost professional con-fessors would prevail in the Church whenever persecution threatened. This was true even at Alexandria.[160]

No one can tell what would have happened if Decius' long duel with the Gothic king Kniva had not ended in the Emperor's death in the marshes of Abrittus in the Dobrudja (end of June 251). True, the persecution had begun to flag, but with the Emperor back in Rome, victorious, it could easily have been re-vived. At this moment, Church and Empire appear to be equally balanced. The initial success of the authorities is undeniable. The Church throughout the Empire was disorganized, dispersed and momentarily discredited. Able leaders had lapsed, others had fled. The mixture of severity and comparative mildness employed towards recusants had been the product of strength. But, as Origen had already foreseen, the very diffusion of the Christian Churches was a measure of protection. Given the lack of administrative skill and co-ordination in the Ancient World, no persecution could strike everywhere at the same time. After the initial fury it was usually possible, if one wanted, to escape the net. Origen's belief that even a general persecution would suffer the fate that befell the enemies of Israel in Joshua's day was largely fulfilled.[161] Within a year of Decius' death the Christian message was being proclaimed openly once more in Carthage.[162]

How many victims were there? Porphyry believed that 'thousands' had died in the persecution of Decius and Valerian.[163] The writers of the Ancient World, however, had only their personal experience and rumours to rely upon. Accurate statistics are the product of the needs of modern government. Dionysius of Alexandria states that 'very many' were killed in Egyptian towns and villages,[164] but he only names seventeen victims. In Palestine and Syria the deaths only of Bishops Alexander and Babylas are recorded, though Origen was imprisoned. In Asia Minor hardly a dozen deaths are known, though others, like the famous Seven Sleepers of Ephesus said to have been immured in a cave outside the city, survived in legend. Rome could boast of its Bishop Fabian, and the Presbyter Moses.[165] In Africa, where Cyprian's letters and other writings give a remarkably complete picture of the situation in Carthage in Decius' reign, eighteen martyrs who died in various ways are recorded by name, and another seventeen as confessors.[166] The numbers of the victims may have been considerably higher, however, for there is no knowing how many 'companions' accompanied their leaders, nor indeed, how many died in prison and were accepted by Cyprian as martyrs.[167] Deaths over the whole Empire may probably be numbered in hundreds rather than thousands, but they were enough to vindicate the martyr-spirit at the moment when it was in danger of foundering amid the outward prosperity of the Church.

Meantime, other events were nullifying the successes of the authorities. The confusion which followed the deaths of Decius

and his son hundreds of miles from Rome left the central government without direction. Trebonianus Gallus, on whom Decius'
mantle fell, did not last very long.[168] Though much remained to
be done on the Danube frontier, Gallus hastened to Rome to
make good his title to the Empire, and there he stayed. Persecution was recommenced, sufficiently for a mob in Carthage to
demand 'Cyprian to the lion',[169] and for Cornelius to be suddenly
banished to Centumcellae (Civita Vecchia) where he died in
June 253.[170] But more important matters even than the Christians were clamouring for attention. In 252 a devastating plague
broke out, which was to rage on and off for the next fifteen years
with frightful effect on the lives of the provincials and the morale
of their anti-Christian leaders. Decius' son Hostilianus perished;
Gallus set to work at least to promote a decent burial for the poor
in Rome who were being carried off in scores. Then his neglect of
the barbarian peril overtook him. Aemilian, the governor of the
Danube province of Lower Moesia beat the Goths, imposed a
peace on them and immediately marched against his master. He
was successful. Gallus' troops surrendered in Umbria, and the
Emperor was murdered (mid-253). Aemilian himself survived a
bare two months, his supplanter being Decius' former censor,
Valerian,[171] but for the moment persecution was not renewed.[172]

In Carthage, the plague had been having awesome effects.
Lapsed Christians confronted with the immediate prospect of a
frightful death clamoured for readmittance to the Church.
Rumours of persecution spurred others on in the same direction.
Many feared that they would lose the chance of expunging their
sins through martyrdom. This time, Cyprian was in command of
the situation. In a speech (recorded in *De Mortalitate*) which his
deacon, Pontius, years later, wished could have been heard by
all, he urged Christians to work and pray for fellow-believers and
ex-persecutors alike. He reminded them of the constancy of the
martyrs—'respondere natalibus nostris', and to remember their
duty of facing death at all times.[173] The instructions were obeyed
and next year, when the country was threatened with disaster once
more, this time by the Kabyle revolt, no less than 100,000 sesterces
were sent by the Church in Carthage for the ransom of prisoners.[174] Converts began to stream in once more.

A similar course of events was taking place elsewhere. In

Alexandria, the plague struck the survivors of the persecution severely,[175] but here also Christians stayed at their posts as they were to do ten years later during a far greater disaster. As *Apollo Salutaris* failed, the Christian God triumphed.[176] But even so, the aftermath of the persecution was serious. Hitherto, the Church had been able to deal with defections by way of a stringent penitential system. Now, the issue had to be faced what was to be done about the hordes of repentant lapsed. It raised the problem of the very nature of the Church, and whereas in the East, more interested in metaphysical than in disciplinary matters, it could be solved pragmatically by a shrewd mixture of lenience and severity,[177] in the West it could not.[178] The issues raised by the quarrel between Callistus and Tertullian emerged in a new and more acute form. Rigorist and laxist parties sprang to life in both Rome and Carthage. As in the previous generation victory went to the rigorists in Carthage, but in Rome to their opponents. In the few years that followed the end of the persecution each side took up irrevocable positions.

The story of this vital phase in the history of the Church in the West may be followed in detail in Cyprian's correspondence and treatises. Here, however, only the salient points, arising directly out of the persecution can be noticed. In Carthage, the autumn of 250 saw Cyprian's stock low. He had led his army gallantly from the rear, praising the constancy of the confessors from the safety of his hide-out, and at the same time attempting to instil unpopular measures of discipline designed to dampen the enthusiasm of the would-be volunteer for martyrdom.[179] The result was, that in the reaction which followed the relaxation of tension towards the end of the year, lapsed but penitent Christians sought help from those whom they knew and trusted, namely the confessors.[180] These latter, for the most part ordinary, brave and good-hearted men, were ready to do their best for their friends and relatives. After all, as 'lords who had been crowned', they had amassed a treasury of merit through their sufferings; why should they not spend it as they wished?

Cyprian was in a difficulty. He admitted that the martyrs were 'friends of the Lord' and 'would sit in judgment with him',[181] and hence he could not deny without qualification, the confessors' right to forgive sins. What he did was to claim first, that the martyr's glory in reality belonged to the bishop, the representative of God in the Christian community,[182] and secondly, that he himself had acted on direct Divine command in order to safeguard the interests of the Church.[183] Then he took to task those who 'boasted of their powers as confessors', and reminded them of the condign punishment awaiting such behaviour at the Judgment.[184]

The medicine worked. Lucian and his fellow confessors overplayed their hand, granting recommendations for indulgence wholesale (gregatim)[185] and urging Cyprian himself to have 'peace with the holy martyrs'.[186] Had they been more intelligent and more moderate, and known how to combine with the rigorist element in Rome, a form of 'Donatism' might have started there and then. Intrinsically, there were the same problems confronting the African Church as arose after the Great Persecution, but with two all-important exceptions. First, Numidian Christianity had not yet developed an identity and interest of its own, and secondly, Cyprian was not the former arch-deacon Caecilian.

By the spring of 251, Cyprian had returned to Carthage. He had already warned his clergy that each case of lapse must be examined on its merits by them.[187] Lapsed clergy were to be deprived permanently of their office, but in articulo mortis even they were to be readmitted to the Church (though not to Orders). Then, after Easter (perhaps June 251), he summoned a Council of bishops in Carthage. This decided that no one should be totally excluded from penance. Libellatici were to be readmitted to communion after periods varying in proportion to the amount of pressure to which they had been subjected. Sacrificati might be readmitted only in articulo mortis. The confessors were told that the right of readmission lay with the bishop.[188] Next year, the threat of further persecution allowed some lessening of the stringency of these orders.[189]

Cyprian had won. An extremely important principle of Church order had been established, namely that the Church was empowered to remit even the deadly sin of apostasy. The ultimate effect on the Western doctrine of the Church was to be immense, and so too, on the penitential system as a whole.[190] Moreover, final authority lay with the bishops in council, each responsible for his thoughts and actions before God alone, each trusting in the inspiration of the Holy Spirit. From now on, however, there might 'seem to be tares in the Church', 'vessels of dishonour' as well as of honour.[191] Such was the price of unity centred on the bishop.[192] The majority of the confessors grumbled and submitted. Some were promoted to Orders,[193] another sign of the changed relationship of cleric to confessor. The few irreconcilables who joined the Novatianists were never strong enough to threaten Cyprian's position. Moreover, his own views were rigorist enough to satisfy most critics. The evil of wealth,[194] the vanity of worldly success, the merits of suffering and martyrdom in anticipation of 'the setting of the present age', and 'the coming of Antichrist',[195] were ideas which inspired the majority of active Christians in Africa. In his letter to the people of Thibaris (*Letter*, 58), Cyprian showed that the African Church had made the Maccabean spirit its own.[196] 'Left of centre' was even then the most effective position for the leader of a minority reforming movement to occupy.

In Rome, meanwhile, similar pressures had been building up. Though it is not certain exactly when the ground on which the Memoria on the Appian Way dedicated to Peter and Paul as martyrs, passed into Christian hands,[197] there is no question about the growth of the cult in the 250s onwards. The shrine provides the earliest concrete example, and one of the most fervent, of the growth of the cult of martyrs in the West,[198] and as in Carthage, devotion to the martyrs could go hand in hand with a rigorous attitude towards Church discipline.[199] Moreover, the circumstances in which Pope Fabian had been seized, tried and executed were also calculated to favour rigorism. Meantime, Cyprian's personal enemies arrived in Rome with the object of preventing the election of a bishop favourable to Cyprian. In the event, however, the Roman puritans lacked an adequate champion. Novatian, excellent theologian though he was, was not of the stuff of which martyrs are made. The choice fell on the mediocre Cornelius (4 June 251), and he was elected and consecrated canonically.[200] Novatian's supporters were strong enough, however, to form a rival community and to announce their choice to the other great bishoprics. In Antioch, smarting under the execution of Babylas, the Novatianist emissaries were at first well received.[201]

Cyprian supported Cornelius. It is well to remember that the *De Unitate Ecclesiae* with its disputed chapters 4 and 5 was written mainly as a pamphlet against the Novatianists, not as a formal theological treatise.[202] Even so, in this work and in the *De Lapsis* which he had written earlier in the year, Cyprian was already beginning to proclaim views which were to cause disruption between Rome and Carthage. In *De Lapsis* he had made clear that the apostate was in a state of ritual sin which was liable to affect all those with whom he came into contact. 'Flee from the pestilential cancer of these men. Their speech is an infection', he wrote, 'their conversation a contagion, their persuasion more deadly and more poisonous than the persecution itself'.[203] The same advice was repeated towards the end of the *De Unitate*, 'We must withdraw, indeed we must flee, from those who fall away, but while anyone is associated with those who walk wickedly, and goes on in ways of error and of sin, he himself wandering away from the path and the true road should also be implicated in guilt. God is one, Christ is one, and His Church is one, and the faith is one, and the people is joined together in a unity of substance by the cement of concord'.[204] Oneness, however, depended on purity. The New Israel like the Old might have to suffer backsliders among the laity, but apostates among the clergy were unthinkable. Nor could the means of salvation be given by those whose conduct had put them outside the Church.

It was not until the early summer of 254, however, that the implications of these views were put to the test. The relations between Cyprian and Cornelius and with his successor Lucius remained cordial, but the latter died early in March 254,[205] and on 12 May, Stephen became bishop. Problems at once arose. First, there was a dispute over Marcianus, bishop of Arles, who had turned Novatian. 'Many brethren had died at Arles without being restored to communion in these past years.'[206] Cyprian urged Stephen to write to the Gallic bishops and depose him, but Stephen was reluctant, perhaps because he had to contend with a large Novatianist faction in Rome. What eventually happened is unknown. More important, was the appeal to Cyprian by the Spanish Christians of Leon and Merida against the reinstatement of their apostate bishops at Stephen's instance. On this issue the rival views held by the two men on the nature of the Church, clashed.[207]

The evidence provided by the affair shows that the Decian persecution had been as severe in Spain as elsewhere. Both Basilides of Leon and Martial of Merida had become *libellatici*, and indeed, Martial's conversion to paganism seems to have been temporarily complete. He had become a member of a pagan *collegium*, and buried a member of his family in the ordinary pagan cemetery. Basilides had repented, confessed and gratefully accepted the position of a layman; his see and that of Martial had been filled by firmer Christians. Basilides, however, had second thoughts. He paid a visit to Rome, and accompanied by Martial obtained by one means or another a declaration from Stephen that it was still lawful for them to hold their sees. Stephen was evidently following Callistus' precedent in granting pardon even to clergy who had repented of deadly sin.

The Spanish congregations turned to Cyprian, and the Council of thirty-seven bishops that assembled in the autumn of 254 reversed the Roman decision. The letter in which Cyprian informed them of this contained a remarkable defence of the right of a congregation to separate itself from a cleric in deadly sin, for whom no restoration was possible. What might be remitted to a penitent layman could not be to the descendant of the Levite. It reads,

> Let not the people flatter themselves as if they can be free from the contagion of the offence, when communicating with a priest who is a sinner, and lending their consent to the unrighteous and unlawful episcopate of their prelate, since the divine censure threatens by the prophet Hosea, and says, Their sacrifices shall be as the bread of mourning; all that eat thereof shall be polluted: plainly teaching and shewing that all are altogether bound by sin, who have been polluted by the sacrifices of a profane and unrighteous priest.
>
> . . . Wherefore a people, which obeys the precepts of the Lord, and fears God, ought to separate itself from a prelate who is a sinner, nor mingle itself up with the sacrifices of a sacrilegious priest, especially since it has itself the power either of choosing worthy priests or rejecting the unworthy.'[208]

Here, too, we can see the continuation of an African theological tradition which emphasized that sin could be passed on from generation to generation as something eternally contagious.[209] Not for nothing did the Donatists include this letter in their dossier as justification for their separation from Caecilian half a century later.[210] Stephen's comment is not extant.

The Baptismal controversy which followed almost immediately demonstrated even more clearly the nature of the rift which was opening between Rome and Carthage as the result of the persecution. The immediate question, the validity of Novatianist baptism, was one which affected both sees. In Africa, unlike in Asia Minor, the Novatianist success had been short-lived. The claims of Novatian's emissaries to be 'assertores evangelii et Christi',[211] and that the Church was not empowered to forgive the deadly sin of apostasy were gladly heard. But the African puritans who opposed Cyprian lacked what their friends in Asia Minor possessed, namely the foundation of a rigorist Christian movement on a provincial basis. Cyprian's power also extended over the entire Christian Church in Africa, including the communities in Numidia and Mauretania,[212] and his own vigorous puritan temper was reinforced by a logically coherent doctrine of Church order depending on a universally accepted doctrine of God. The uniqueness of God, of His Church, and of His Ministry and His Baptism, followed on one from the other. The true Gospel, Cyprian claimed, could not be preached except by His Ministry within the narrow confines of His Church. The figure of Noah's Ark tossed about on the waves of an evil world came easily to the minds of North African Christians.[213] They were already the Elect without the need of Novatian. Schism was the worst of crimes. The fate of Dathan, Kore and Abiram was a perpetual warning to schismatics and their sacraments.[214] Soon those baptised by Novatianist emissaries began to think again.[215]

What was to happen? Were those who had received Novatianist baptism to be admitted to the Church by a laying on of hands or was their baptism invalid and needed to be done anew? Behind the question of the rite lay the question of the Church. For Cyprian and his colleagues, baptism was the moment of conversion, when the pagan past was renounced and the rule of the Elect accepted. The convert was litterally 'born again in the Spirit'.[216] From now on the Bible must take the place of secular literature and hope in the approaching end supplant hopes of worldly advancement.[217] Outside the gathered community of the Church there was no salvation, and it followed that he who was outside had no Grace to dispense. Thus, every baptism and indeed every sacrament must be renewed on conversion to the Church. The African view of Baptism was part and parcel of its doctrine of the Holy Spirit. It formed the link which bound the teaching of Tertullian to that of Donatus and his followers. For Cyprian there could be no surrender.

Stephen took a different view, and he too appealed to the tradition of his Church.[218] Baptism indeed marked entry into the body of the Church, but reception of the Spirit was reserved for the laying on of hands.[219] Stephen was thinking in terms of the needs of a world-wide Church, where good and bad must mingle, and Christ preached 'in every way, whether in pretence or in truth' (Phil. 1[18]).[220] Cyprian, even though he grudgingly admitted the penitent lapsed as members, held fast to the ideal that the Church was 'Bride of Christ', 'without spot or wrinkle',[221] and accepted the view of the Christian priesthood that was modelled on the sacramental purity of the Levites.[222] The baptism of Novatianists, being outside the Church, was as damning as that of the Spanish apostates.

Not all the African clergy supported Cyprian's thesis,[223] but in three Councils held in 255 and 256 the rigorist position prevailed. The Novatianists were taught that puritanism without organization was of no avail, and Stephen was left in no doubt that the tradition of the African Church was now irrevocably that of the Elect opposing the world and its allies. Cyprian too, gained support from the East, enthusiastically from Firmilian who was faced with the same problems of Montanists and Novatianists in Cappadocia,[224] and more judiciously and warily from Dionysius of Alexandria. The latter's correspondence with Popes Xystus and Dionysius on the subject display graphically the learning and statesmanship which was now passing from paganism to the Church.[225]

Events, however, prevented final conflict between Rome and Carthage. Stephen died in the summer of 257, and his successor Xystus did not renew the challenge. Cordial relations with Rome were resumed,[226] and in the same year Imperial policy changed once more.

The persecution of Valerian was yet another sudden turn in the Church's fortunes, and in some ways the most difficult to understand.[227] Eusebius and other sources give some clue to what lay behind Maximin's and Decius' measures, but none for Valerian's. The latter had been Decius' censor or perhaps *legatus* (deputy)[228] in Rome, but having assumed power after Gallus' death he did not revert to his master's policy. Indeed, the Church enjoyed four years of undisturbed peace and prosperity. Recalling this interval in a letter to Hermammon in the spring of 262, Dionysius of Alexandria could write that at the outset,

> Valerian was mild and friendly to the men of God. For not a single one of the emperors before him was so kindly and favourably disposed towards them, not even those who were said to have been openly Christians, as he manifestly was, when he received them at the beginning in the most intimate and friendly manner; indeed, all his house had been filled with godly persons, and was a church of God.[229]

This is an exaggeration, for Dionysius wanted to flatter Gallienus,[230] and so attempted to put the blame for what now took place on Macrianus, Valerian's finance minister (*curator summarum rationum*), rather than on the Emperor himself. Even so, Eusebius speaks of the Churches of the East being united and at peace in this period,[231] while in Carthage the baptismal controversy could not have arisen without converts to be baptized, and Cyprian's three councils of the years 255-256 could not have met except in a time of comparative security.

The combination of a demand to 'acknowledge the saving deities'[232] of the Empire, with the explicit interest in the Church's property may provide one reason for Valerian's measures. The decade which followed Decius' defeat by the Goths was one of the most disastrous ever experienced by the Empire. In the west, the Alemanni reached Milan, Dacia was harrassed by the Carpi, the Goths threatened Greece; in the east, Dura-Europos fell probably in 256, and Sapor found the lower classes of Antioch ready to support a pro-Persian usurper.[233] It was 'the uprising of the peoples', as Zonaras was to describe it.[234] The economy already grievously strained, collapsed. In the space of nine years, between 251-260, the *antoninianus* which had become the main unit of exchange declined from 40 per cent silver under Decius to 2 per cent in *circa* 260.[235] The imperial coinage became worthless trash, and in Oxyrhynchus, the bankers refused to accept it.[236] In this appalling crisis, the Church was relatively prosperous and stable, the one obvious refuge for persons and wealth in a disintegrating world. It did not need Egyptian magicians to convince a financial administrator in Egypt where help for the failing treasury might be found.[237]

In addition, at least in one important area Christians had been openly disloyal. When in 255 the Goths invaded Pontus the Christians had either acquiesced or rallied to them. Gregory Thaumaturgus records that some had acted as spies and guides to the invaders, had shared their loot, had helped them to attack houses and property, and had even hunted down those who had escaped from barbarian captivity.[238] It is tempting to connect this fanaticism with the situation in rural Asia Minor revealed by the petition of the Aragueni to the Emperor Philip only a decade before.[239] Were the African Circumcellions anticipated a century before by the Christian peasants in Pontus and Cappadocia? One cannot say, but it is evident that here Christianity was expressing deep-felt social bitterness, and to some Roman authorities it must have appeared that the Christians could not be relied upon in the crisis.

The actual texts of Valerian's edicts have perished, but their tenor can be gathered from Cyprian's final letters, perhaps the opening comments of the proconsul at his trial in 257, and also by Dionysius' account of the events in Alexandria. The first edict, probably August 257, seems to have concerned only the Christian clergy. It was comparatively mild, and appears merely to have required that those who did not observe the Roman religion should none the less give some token of recognition or veneration to Roman ceremonies.[240] It was what every patriotic provincial had demanded from the time of Celsus.[241] Its aim was to oblige the Christians to co-operate with other citizens in regaining the favour of 'the gods' at a moment of peril for the Empire as a whole. In the same way, to ward off contrary influences, no Christian services were to be held, nor were there to be gatherings in the cemeteries. This measure against corporate Christian life was immediately applied. Both Cyprian and Dionysius[242] were summoned before the proconsul of Africa, and prefect of Egypt respectively. Cyprian's answer to Aspasius Paternus' request for some formal acknowledgment of the gods was met by the memorable words 'Christianus sum et episcopus. Nullos alios deos novi, nisi unum verum Deum…huic Deo nos Christiani deservimus; hunc deprecamur diebus et noctibus…et pro incolumitate ipsorum imperatorum'.[243] Cyprian replied as Origen had to Celsus at the end of *Contra Celsum*. On the one hand, the Christian *Deus* could not be worshipped in combination with 'the gods' but, on the other, the assertion of loyalty, in that the Christians prayed for the well-being of the emperors to their own more powerful God may not have been intended as a gesture only. Christians did claim that their prayers had in fact been instrumental in saving Roman armies from disaster.[244] But in this and other cases where the Christians claimed the privileges long accorded to the Jews, they were refused. The Empire was not yet prepared to accept two exclusive and rival monotheisms.

Cyprian, despite his defiance, was only exiled (*deportari*) to comparatively comfortable surroundings at Curubis (Kurba) on the Gulf of Hammamat. In Numidia, however, the legate condemned many bishops and other clergy to the mines.[245] In Alexandria, also, the measures were severe. Dionysius with a priest, three deacons and Marcellus, probably a Roman priest, were deported to Cephro (the oasis of Kufra) and he describes graphically in the course of his long letter to Hermammon his encounter with the prefect of Egypt, Aemilianus.

> *Aemilianus, the deputy-prefect*, said, ' … And verbally I discoursed with you concerning the kindness that our lords have displayed on your behalf. For they gave you the opportunity of safety if ye were willing to turn to that which is according to nature and worship the gods which preserve their Empire, and forget those gods which are contrary to nature. What, therefore, say ye to these things? For I do not expect that ye will be ungrateful for their kindness, forasmuch as they urge you on to the better course.'
>
> *Dionysius replied:* 'Not all men worship all gods, but each one certain whom he regards as such. We therefore both worship and adore the one God and Maker of all things, who also committed the Empire to the Augusti, most highly favoured of God, Valerian and Gallienus; and to Him we unceasingly pray for their Empire, that it may remain unshaken.'
>
> *Aemilianus, the deputy-prefect*, said to them: 'And who prevents you from worshipping this god also, if he be a god, along with the natural gods? For ye were bidden to worship gods, and gods whom all know.'

Dionysius replied: 'We worship no other God.'

Aemilianus, the deputy-prefect, said to them: 'I see that ye are at once ungrateful and insensible of the clemency of our Augusti. Wherefore ye shall not be in this city, but ye shall betake yourselves to the parts of Libya and [remain] in a place called Cephro. For this is the place I chose in accordance with the command of our Augusti. And it shall in no wise be permitted either to you or to any others either to hold assemblies or to enter the cemeteries, as they are called. If anyone be proved not to have gone to the place that I commanded, or be found at any assembly, he will bring the peril upon himself, for there shall be no lack of the necessary observation. Be gone therefore whither ye were bidden.'[246]

Meantime, Cyprian remained at Curubis. Here he received news of colleagues who had been harshly beaten and sent to the mines of Sigus in Numidia. The four letters in Cyprian's collection dealing with this episode show that the progress made in the previous few years by the Church in Africa had been real. Though the horrible conditions in which the prisoners worked are described and bitterly lamented by Cyprian,[247] the letters breathe a different spirit from his writings of the Decian period. In contrast to the utter dejection of the *De Lapsis* there is assurance and optimism. 'This earthly and brief suffering will be exchanged for the reward of a bright and eternal honour', and he cites Roms. 12^2 in support. 'Be not conformed to this world (*saeculum*), but be transformed by the renewing of your mind that ye prove what is that good, and acceptable and perfect will of God'.[248] He goes on to tell them of the effect of their example on the Christian people who now refused to be separated from their clergy 'neither by the prison nor by the mines'.[249] He himself is sure of ultimate victory.[250] The memory of the great councils of the previous years, when they had stood firm against 'haereticorum iniurias et pressuras gentilium simul' united them still.[251] The answers he received were equally stirring. His own example was being cited as one of bravery and inspiration. He was no longer the hireling who had deserted his flock, but the prophetic leader, 'filled with the Holy Spirit' whose words had inspired these simple and hardly literate clergy with a certainty that their sufferings were nothing in comparison with the rewards which the crown of martyrdom would bring.[252] In the previous decade the atmosphere had changed entirely. African Christians now wrote with the enthusiasm of victory. The bloodless persecution failed, and as in 303, more stringent measures were attempted.

The second edict was published in the summer of 258, and was addressed by Valerian to the Senate with instructions for the provincial governors. It was harsher than its predecessor, including not only clergy, but laymen in influential positions. In the analysis found in Cyprian's penultimate letter, 'bishops, presbyters and deacons should be punished immediately, that senators, *viri egregii*, and knights should lose their dignities and be deprived of their property. If they still persisted in their Christianity, they would be executed. *Matronae* would lose their property and be banished. The *Caesariani* (civil servants) would be reduced to slavery and sent in chains to work on the Imperial estates'.[253]

The same messengers brought information about the edict's enforcement. When they left Rome, Xystus and four of his deacons had been seized in the catacombs and executed on 6 August.[254] The City Prefects were actively participating in the persecution and urging the seizure of Christians and claiming their property for the State.[255] Among their victims are said to have been the three other deacons, Agapetus, Felicissimus and Laurentius.[256] A century later, Ambrose of Milan preserved the memory of aristocratic women who had been executed.[257] Cyprian's last letter shows him hourly awaiting the return of the proconsul to Carthage with his orders.[258] Even so, he instructs there must be no tumult or voluntary martyrdom. This was contrary to 'ecclesiastical discipline'.

On 13 September 258, Cyprian was visited by two senior officials of the staff of the new proconsul Galerius Maximus. They took him by chariot to the Villa of Sextus where the proconsul was resting, and next day as a great crowd collected, he was brought before the rapidly failing administrator.

Galerius. Are you Thascius Cyprianus?
Cyprian. I am.
Galerius. The most sacred Emperors have commanded you to conform to the Roman rites.
Cyprian. I refuse.

Galerius. Take heed for yourself.

Cyprian. Do as you are bid; in so clear a case I may not take heed.

Galerius, after briefly conferring with his judicial council, with much reluctance pronounced the following sentence: 'You have long lived an irreligious life, and have drawn together a number of men bound by an unlawful association, and professed yourself an open enemy to the gods and the religion of Rome; and the pious, most sacred and august Emperors, Valerian and Gallienus, and the most noble Caesar Valerian, have endeavoured in vain to bring you back to conformity with their religious observances;—whereas, therefore you have been apprehended as principal and ringleader in these infamous crimes, you shall be made an example to those whom you have wickedly associated with you; the authority of law shall be ratified in your blood.' He then read the sentence of the court from a written tablet: 'It is the sentence of this court that Thascius Cyprianus be executed with the sword.'

Cyprian. Thanks be to God.[259]

The sentence throws into the clearest possible relief the issue between the Christian and the Roman Empire. The Christian was a member of a 'nefaria conspiratio'; his was a 'mens sacrilega'. He was 'diis Romanis et religionibus sacris inimicus'. Cyprian had been given time to reconsider his position—and he had failed to use it—therefore he deserved the prescribed penalty. The official mind had not moved far from the Bacchanals, but now the threat to the age-old Roman *disciplina* by the *disciplina* of the Church was final and deadly.

This time, too, the Christian community demonstrated their anger at the sentence, demanding to share their bishop's fate.[260] Hardly as he died Cyprian was acclaimed a martyr and his blood and clothing became the source of relics.[261] Other bishops may have been similarly treated. Augustine preserves the memory of Bishop Theogenes of Hippo, executed perhaps on 26 January 259.[262] On 30 April two other bishops, Agapius and Secondinus, succumbed. For the whole of 259 the persecution continued unabated, and the terror of those days was long remembered in Africa and the West. The deacon Jacobus and the reader Marianus with three others were beheaded at Lambaesis on 6 May after being tried and tortured in Cirta,[263] Lucius and Montanus died at Carthage on 23 May,[264] and legend recorded a holocaust of three hundred Christians in August 259 at the Massa Candida near

Utica, who were thrown into quicklime.[265] Where the populace is mentioned, it is still hostile to the Christians.[266] In Spain the interrogation of Fructuosus, bishop of Tarragona, on 21 January 259 and two of his deacons ends thus,

> *Proconsul.* Are you the bishop?
> *Fructuosus.* I am.
> *Proconsul.* You were.[267]

He was hurried off with his clergy to be burnt alive.

In Palestine the persecution struck Marcionite and Catholic alike, and here, Eusebius preserves the record of three Christians making a long journey to Caesarea in order to confess their Christianity before the governor. The tradition of voluntary martyrdom had been renewed, and was to blaze again forty years later.[268]

Dionysius of Alexandria, however, survived, and he was to be the recipient of an historic document which amounted to an acknowledgment of the failure of the policy of repression and the grant of legal status to the Church. At Cephro he had not been inactive. Supervision of the Christians was apparently so lax that they were able to carry out missionary work among the inhabitants, and after initial opposition convert a number of them to Christianity.[269] Meantime, utter disaster had befallen the Roman world. In the campaign of 259/260 against the Persians, Valerian was defeated in Mesopotamia, shut up in Edessa and finally lured into captivity in late June 260. His son, Gallienus, broke with his father's policy, and broke too with the persecution. He 'acted with more prudence', Eusebius says, 'and immediately by means of edicts (διὰ προγραμμάτων) put an end to the persecution against us'.[270] Perhaps he had no option, for already on 20 July 260, the moment the capture of Valerian was known in Rome, the Christians elected a new bishop, Dionysius. The resilience of the Church was obvious, and in Egypt, as Macrianus attempted to establish himself as rival emperor, supported perhaps by the prefect Aemilian,[271] Gallienus made a bid for public opinion, and it was to the powerful Bishop Dionysius that he turned. The Greek text of his rescript to the bishops in Egypt has survived.

The Emperor Caesar Publius Licinius Gallienus Pius Felix Augustus to Dionysius and Pinnas and Demetrius and the other bishops. I have given my order that the benefit of my bounty should be published throughout all the world, to the intent that they should depart from the places of worship, and therefore ye also may use the ordinance contained in my rescript, so that none may molest you. And this thing which it is within your power to accomplish has long since been conceded by me; and therefore Aurelius Quirinius, who is in charge of the Exchequer, will observe the ordinance given by me[272] (tr. J. E. L. Oulton).

The facts of the situation were accepted. For the previous two centuries the Church had held its property through what would appear to have been the silent toleration of the authorities both in Rome and in the provinces. Now, this situation was explicitly accepted. But it still did not make Christianity *religio licita*. A soldier who refused to sacrifice to the gods on the grounds of Christianity could still be executed, as the case of Marinus at Caesarea was to show.[273] None the less, the Church had achieved a great advance. It was an acknowledged factor in the political situation within the Empire. Gallienus' action set him among those emperors who favoured the Church, and perhaps more important, it provided a precedent for Constantine's immediate action of restoring Church property after his victory at the Milvian Bridge. The downfall of Valerian marked the beginning of the end of Greco-Roman paganism.

NOTES

[1] Herodian, vii.1.2; cf. Lampridius, *Alex. Sev.*, lxiii.2. 'asperitas atque rusticitas Maximini'. For a more favourable estimate. W. Ensslin, *CAH.*, xii.72–5.

[2] The tradition preserved in Capitolinus, *Maximini Duo* 9.6–8 sums up his brutality towards the traditional ruling classes. 'Nobilem circa se neminem passus est, prorsus ut Spartaci aut Athenionis exemplo imperabat. Praeterea omnes Alexandri ministros variis modis interemit. Dispositionibus eius invidit. Et dum suspectos habet amicos ac ministros eius, crudelior factus est.'

[3] Herodian, vii.8.7.

[4] Mattingly and Sydenham, *Roman Imperial Coinage*, v.i., 1927, 5–8.

[5] J. A. Crook, *Concilium Principis*, 93–5.

[6] *Dial. with Heracleides* (ed. and tr. Oulton and Chadwick, *Alexandrian Christianity*), p. 454. Attention is drawn to the *editio princeps* of Jean Scherer, *Entretien d'Origène avec Héraclide* (Publications de la Société Fouad I de Papyrologie, Textes et Documents, ix, Cairo, 1949).

[7] Especially *Ad Donatum*, 13 and 14. It is clear from Cyprian's 'una igitur placida fides et tranquillitas, una solida et firma securitas si quis ab his inquietantis saeculi turbinibus extractus salutari portus statione fundetur', that fear and insecurity contributed to his conversion.

[8] *Ad Demetrianum*, 4, 'Christianis inputas quod minuantur singula mundo senescente'.

[9] Ibid., 2, 'Sed enim cum dicas plurimos conqueri et quod bella crebrius surgant, quod lues, quod fames saeviant, quodque imbros et pluvia serena longa suspendant nobis imputari . . . '. Cf. ibid., 3, with its details of collapse of the economy and of morale.

[10] Eusebius, *H.E.*, vi.28. For a concise account of Maximin's persecution, see B. Aubé, *Les chrétiens*, 459ff.

[11] The merciful intent behind this measure need not be exaggerated. It was combined with confiscation of goods, loss of citizen status, and was intended to be permanent. Cf. Modestinus, *Lib. Diff.*, 2, 'Deportatis vero haec solent insulae assignari, quae sunt asperrimae, quaeque sunt paulo minus summo supplicio comparandae'; and Pomponius, *Digest*, xlviii.22.17 'Deportatio autem non fit ad tempus'. See Kleinfeller, art. 'Deportatio', *PW.*, v.1.231–3.

[12] *Catalogus Liberianus*, 'Antheros m. uno d.x. Dormit iii. non Jan. Maximo et Africano cons.' Cited from L. Duchesne, ed. *Liber Pontificalis*, p. 147 n.1.

[13] Origen, *Comment. in Matthaeum*, 39 (ed. E. Klostermann, *GCS.*, *Origenes Werke*, xi).

[14] Firmilian, *ap.* Cyprian, *Ep.*, 75.10.

[15] Origen, loc. cit., 'Ut qui erant impii extra fide causam terrae motus dicerent christianos, propter quod et persecutiones passae sunt ecclesiae et incensae sunt.'

[16] Firmilian, loc. cit., 'acerbus et dirus persecutor'.

[17] *Exhortation*, 5 (Koetschau, 6–7). Also, *Contra Celsum* ii.45. The New Testament 'surpassing many stories told by the Greeks about the courage and bravery of the philosophers'.

[18] Ibid., ii.17, and ii.41. Even to Gregory the Wonderworker, Origen's final advice is 'diligently apply yourself to the reading of Scripture', and warns him that study of Greek philosophy was only a preparation for Christianity. (*Letter to Gregory* 1 and 3.) The same point is made in the *Commentary on Canticles* ii. (Baehrens, 148). The 'flocks' to be fed represented 'diversas scilicet sectas philosophorum'.

[19] For this aspect of Origen's idealism, see J. Lebreton, 'La Source et la caractère de la mystique d'Origène'. *A.B.*, 67, 1949, 55–62.

[20] Also. *Comment. in Rom.*, iv.10. *P.G.*, 14, 998–9.

[21] Origen, *Dialogue with Heracleides*, pp. 446–9.

[22] *Comment. in Ioannem.* (ed. E. Preuschen, p. 105), 5.8, the peroration of his sermon: 'Today under pretext of Gnosis, heretics rise against the Church of Christ. They pile on their books of commentaries. They claim to interpret the Gospels and Apostolic texts. If we are silent, if we do not oppose them with true teaching, famished souls will be fed by their abominations'.

[23] *Contra Celsum*, 1.26.

[24] Ibid., cf. Clement, *Stromata*, vi.18.167, 3–5 (the climax of the argument of this book).

[25] Origen, *Contra Celsum*, 1.9 and 27. Note the similar argument in Eusebius. *Theophania*, v.49. Below, p. 544.

[26] Ibid., 1.1

[27] Origen, *Contra Celsum*, 1.3; cf. ii.79.

[28] Ibid., v.33. On this aspect of the *Contra Celsum*, see A. Miura-Stange, *Celsus und Origenes*, *ZNTW.*, Beiheft 4, 1926, pp. 1–4.

29 Ibid., viii.72–5.

30 Ibid., iv.17 and 18.

31 As E. de Faye, *Origène*, iii.230, points out, Origen's soteriology was 'comme une sorte d'annexe de sa doctrine générale'; cf. H. Koch, *Pronoia und Paideusis*, 90.

32 *Dialogue with Heracleides*, p. 454.

33 Eusebius, *H.E.*, vi.19.3. Origen's Platonic concept of God, *Contra Celsum*, iv.14, 18, vi.1, vii.32, 38 and 46.

34 Compare, Plotinus, *Enneads*, 1.6.5 and 6 (Eng. tr. S. MacKenna, London, 1917–30, pp. 60–1).

35 Origen, *Comment. in Cant.* ii (Baehrens, 141ff.), cf. Gregory Thaumaturgus, *Address to Origen* (ed. W. Metcalfe), 6 and 11. See, J. Daniélou, *Origène*, p. 287ff., to whom I am indebted for this estimate of Origen's spirituality.

36 *Homil. xxvii in Numeros*, 11 (Baehrens, 271); cf. Philo, *Quaest. in Exod.*, 2.40 (Marcus, 82–93).

37 *Comment. in Rom.*, iv.5. See H. Koch, *Pronoia und Paideusis*, Berlin, 1932, 77ff.

38 *Comment. in Ioannem.*, xiii.28, 355–7 (Preuschen, 474), cf. *Contra Celsum*, iii.46 and iv.13.

39 Origen, *Homil. in Levit.*, 2.4 (Baehrens, 245–6). 'Audi nunc quantae sint remissiones peccatorum in evangeliis. Est ista prima, qua baptizamur in remissione peccatorum. Secunda remissio est in passione martyrii. Tertia est, quae per eleemosynam datur. . . . '

40 *De Principiis*, ii.10.4–7 (Koetschau, 177–83).

41 *Contra Celsum*, ii.24, iv.19, vi.56, viii.72. Gregory Thaumaturgus, *Address*, 17. See H. Koch, op. cit., pp. 74–5.

42 *Comment. in Ep. ad Rom.*, viii.12, 'propter hoc, quod perfectio omnium non intra unum saeculum concluditur, sed in multa protenditur et vix aliquando adimplenda speratur'. Each new world would be 'pro correptione et emendatione eorum qui talibus indigent'. Also, *De Principiis*, ii.8.3.

43 *Homil. in Num.*, xxiv.1 (Baehrens, 225–7) (*pace* Basileides!).

44 *Homil. in Num.*, x.2; *Exhort.*, 36; *Contra Celsum*, iii.8.

45 Origen's influence on the monastic movement, see W. Völker, *Das Vollkommenheitsideal des Origenes*, Tübingen, 1931, 84ff. and W. Seston, 'Remarques sur le Rôle de la pensée d'Origène dans les origines du monachisme', *R.H.R.*, 108, 1933, 197–213.

46 Thus in *Homil. xi in Lucam* (ed. M. Rauer, Berlin, 1959, 69) (John the Baptist) 'fugiens tumultum urbium, populi frequentiam, vitia civitatum, et absit in deserta, ubi purior aer est et caelum apertius et familiarior Deus . . . '.

47 Eusebius, *H.E.*, vi.2–3.

48 Ibid., vi.2.7.

49 See for instance, *Lausiac History*, 11.4 (Ammon), 37.12 (Serapion).

50 *De Principiis*, 1.6.3.

51 *Dialogue*, p. 453, perhaps even echoing Ignatius of Antioch. Note, however, the strongly anti-Millenarist sentiment expressed even in a moment of exaltation. Origen does not expect the resurrection of the body but that he will 'come out of the body' and 'be with Christ at once'. See Dom B. Capelle's comments in 'L'Entretien d'Origène avec Héraclide', *J.E.H.*, ii, 1951, pp. 143–57.

52 *Contra Celsum*, 1.18. Moses' superiority to philosophers in his role as Lawgiver to the world.

53 *Contra Celsum*, vii.10.

54 Ibid., vi.67–8.

55 Ibid., 1.31.

56 Compare, for instance, with Eusebius, *Demonstratio Evangelica*, vii.2. Below, ch. XVI, p. 545.

57 Gregory Thaumaturgus, *Address to Origen* (ed. W. Metcalfe), 11. Previously professed

teachers 'had made philosophy consist of mere phrases'. Note Clement's opinion of the philosophers of his day, 'worn out shoes except for their tongues' (*Strom.*, 1.3.22) uttering 'random rivers of words' (ibid.).

58 Eusebius, *H.E.*, vi.34.

59 Ibid., vi.36.3.

60 Ibid., vi.36.1; cf. Origen, *Contra Celsum*, 1.43.

61 Cyprian, *Ep.*, 59.10.

62 L. Leschi, *Tipasa*, Algies, 1950, 40ff,

63 Moh. Fendri, 'Basiliques chrétiennes de la Skhira', *Bibl. de l'Université de Tunis*, Faculté des Lettres. 1e Ser. archéologie, histoire, vol. viii, 1961, Cemetery A, p. 17. At Knossos the earliest graves in the Christian (?) cemetery beneath the Byzantine basilica appeared to be third century. See the author's 'The Christian Basilica at Knossos', *BSA.*, 1962, 211.

64 So I take the meaning of the description of Pope Fabian's activities, 'et multas fabricas per cymeteria fieri praecipit' (*Liber Pontif.*, Duchesne, 148–9).

65 *Contra Celsum*, 1.43.

66 *Contra Celsum*, iii.9.

67 *Comment. in Matth.* (Series) 12, P.G., 13, 1616 B and C. 'novae gloriae amatores'.

68 *Liber Pontif.* (Duchesne, p. 148).

69 Eusebius, *H.E.*, vi.43.11.

70 Cyprian, *Ep.*, 1.

71 Ibid., 34.6.

72 Origen, *Hom. in Exod.*, xiii.3 (Baehrens, 272); cf. *Hom. in Genesim*, x.1 (Baehrens, 93). See J. Daniélou, *Origène*, Paris, 1948, p. 52ff., for an excellent description of Christian communities in the East at this time, derived from Origen's Commentaries.

73 *Comment in Matth.*, xv.26. (Klostermann, 426).

74 *Homil. in Jerem.*, xii.8. (Klostermann, 94).

75 Cyprian, *De Lapsis*, 6.

76 Gregory Thaumaturgus, *Address to Origen* (ed. W. Metcalfe), 5.

77 Ibid., 6.

78 Ibid., 5.

79 Ibid.

80 Ibid., 6

81 Ibid., 6.

82 Ibid., 15.

83 Jerome, *De Viris Illust.*, 67; cf. Lactantius, *Institutes*, v.1.24, and Cyprian, *Ad Donatum*, 2 and 3.

84 *Ad Donatum*, 4.

85 Note for instance, Cyprian's comment on Decius' order to sacrifice—such sacrifices were 'sacrilega obsequia' (*Ep.*, 6.1.).

86 *Ad Donatum*, 4 'Postquam caelitus Spiritu hausto in novum me hominem nativitas secunda reparavit'.

87 Ibid., 10–12.

88 *Institutes*, v.1.27.

89 See the enlightening art. by A. A. T. Ehrhardt, 'Quäker-Latein', in 'Soziale Fragen in der alten Kirche', *Exitenz und Ordnung*, 167–71.

90 Gregory of Nyssa, *De Vita Gregorii Thaumaturgi*; P.G., 46, col. 909 C. and 954 D.

91 Ibid., col. 954 B and C. See A. Harnack, *Die Mission und Ausbreitung des Christentums* (Leipzig, 1902), 476. Eusebius, *H.E.*, vi.30 makes Gregory bishop of Pontus.

92 *Acts of Pionius*, 9.4.

93 Origen, *In Matth.*, 24.9. Sermo 39 (Lommatsch, iv.270). 'Cum haec ergo contigerint mundo, consequens est quasi derelinquentibus deorum culturam, ut propter multitudi-

nem christianorum dicant fieri bella et fames et pestilentia . . . Ut tunc fiant persecutiones iam non ex parte sicut ante, sed generaliter ubique.' Also, *Contra Celsum*, ii.79, iii. 15.

[94] Eusebius, *H.E.*, vi.41.1.

[95] Ibid., 7.

[96] Zosimus, 1.20–21, Zonaras, xii.19. See the valuable art. by A. T. Olmstead, 'The Mid-3rd century of the Christian Era', *CP.*, 37, 1942, 241–62 and 389–420, especially 250–62, for Philip's difficulties. Also, B. C. Macdermot, 'Roman Emperors in Sassanian Reliefs'. *JRS.*, xliv, 1954, 76–80.

[97] Suggested by the ceremony with which Fabian brought back the remains of Pontian and Hippolytus to Rome, *Liber Pontif.* (Duchesne, 145) 'cum clero per navem', etc.

[98] Eusebius, *H.E.*, vi.36.3.

[99] Zosimus, 1.20.1. Iotapian who was proclaimed emperor was related to the Syrian dynasty of Alexander Severus; or so it would appear from Aurelius Victor, *De Caesaribus*, 29.2. I find it difficult, however, to discover a reference to Alexander the Great in, 'Alexandri tumens stirpe'. (See F. Altheim, *Die Soldatenkaiser*, Frankfurt, 1939, 241, n. 2).

[100] For the chronology of this period, based largely on interpretation of accounts of events given by Zosimus and Zonaras, M. Besnier, *L'Empire romain*, 154–5, and F. S. Salisbury and H. Mattingly, 'The Reign of Trajan Decius', *JRS.*, xiv, 1924, and Wittig, art. 'Messius', in *P.W.*, xv, 1932, 1244–84. Important for our purpose is that the earliest mention of Decius as emperor in Egypt is 27 Nov. 249 (Grenfell and Hunt, *Pap. Oxy.*, xii, 1636).

[101] Zonaras, xii.20. Note the three separate accounts of the Decian persecution to be found in *CAH.*, xii (A. Alföldi, 166ff., 193, 202ff.). H. Lietzmann, 521ff. and N. Baynes, 656–8) discussed by H. Last in *AJP.*, 61, 1940, 88ff. The most important contribution remains A. Alföldi, 'Zu den Christenverfolgungen in der Mitte des 3 Jahrhunderts', *Klio*, 31, 1938, 323–48, and for the General Sacrifice and Egyptian *libelli*, J. R. Knipfing, *HTR.*, 16, 1923, 345ff. See also F. Krebs's detailed résumé of evidence in the light of the Alexandrou Nesos *libellus*. *ABAW.*, 1897. Phil. Hist. Kl., 1007–14.

[102] A. Alföldi, *CAH.*, xii.203, and art. cit., 325ff.

[103] A. T. Olmstead, art. cit. 398–420 and A. Kurfess, 'Zu den Oracula Sibyllina'. *Texte und Arbeiten*, Abt. i, Beiheft ii. (Festschrift Alban Dold) Beuron, 1952, 75–83. The last event 'prophesied' (ll. 164–71) praises 'Odenathus who shall rule the Romans' *circa* 265.

[104] H. Last, art. cit., *AJP.*, 1940, 88.

[105] Cyprian, *Ep.*, 55.9, 'cum multo patientius et tolerabilius audiret levari adversus se aemulum principem quam constitui Romae Dei sacerdotem'. Cf. Edward Gibbon, *Decline and Fall* (ed. O. Smeaton, 1933 edition) ch. xvi. p. 43.

[106] H. Lietzmann, ch. xv, 'The Christian Church in the West', *CAH.*, xii.521.

[107] *M.A.M.A.*, viii.424, Oct.–Nov. 250.

[108] Celsus, ap. Origen, *Contra Celsum*, viii.63.

[109] Ibid., viii.61.

[110] For instance in the *Acts of Konon*, the judge tells Konon, 'If you acknowledge Christ, acknowledge also our gods' *Acta* 4.4 (Knopf and Krüger, 65). The judge assured him that all that was required was 'μόνον δὲ λάβε λίβανον βραχὺν καὶ οἶνον καὶ θαλλόν, καὶ εἰπέ. Δίε πανύψιστε, σῶζε τὸ πλῆθος τοῦτο'. Not even sacrifice was required (ibid., 4.4).

[111] In *Ep.*, 37.2 which he seems to have written in Dec. 250, Cyprian says that persecution had been going on for a year, but it is idle to read too much accuracy into the rather lyrical description of the changing seasons!

[112] *Liber Pontif.* (Duchesne, 148); cf. *Chron. Paschale*, i, p. 503, and *Depositio Episcoporum* (ed. H. Lietzmann, 3).

[113] Eusebius, *H.E.*, vi.39.4. Dating: *Syrian Martyrology* (ed. Lietzmann, p. 8).

[114] Ibid., vi.39.2.

[115] Eusebius, *H.E.*, vi.39.2.

[116] Ibid., vi.40.2ff.

[117] *Acta Pionii*, 15.2.

[118] Pionius and his companions were arrested allegedly on the anniversary of Polycarp's death, 23 February, and executed on 12 March.

[119] A. Alföldi, art. cit., p. 333. The order seems almost certainly to have been in the form of a general edict. Cyprian, *Ep.*, 43.3. refers to an 'edictum', Dionysius to a 'πρόσταγμα' (*H.E.*, vi. 41.10).

[120] Egyptian *libelli* contain phrases such as, 'κατὰ τὰ προσταχθέντα ἔθυσα καὶ ἔσπεισα' or 'κατὰ τὰ κελευσθέντα ἔσπεισα καὶ ἔθυσα' and 'γενέσθαι τῶν 'ιερῶν'.

[121] Eusebius, *H.E.*, vii.11.7 'θεοὺς τοὺς σώζοντας αὐτῶν τὴν βασιλείαν' (Aemilian in A.D. 257); cf. *Acta Acacii*, ii.2. Also *Acta Pionii*, 18.14, Bishop Euctemon of Smyrna swore by the Genius of the Emperor and Nemesis that 'he was not a Christian'.

[122] J. R. Knipfing, art. cit., 357.

[123] In Alexandria some swore that 'they had never been Christians', Eusebius, *H.E.*, vi.41.12.

[124] Note the remarkable trial held before Appius Sabinus, Prefect of Egypt, in 250, in which the parties were the citizens of Arsinoe and villagers of the surrounding *nome*, the latter contesting an imposition of liturgies by the town. Counsel for the senate of Arsinoe claims that 'the citizens of Arsinoe, formerly a numerous body, but now going to ruin (?) if they hold office for two days only . . .'. He implies that the ruin began after the prefecture of Honoratianus, i.e. after 236. See T. C. Skeat and E. P. Wegener, 'Trial before the Prefect of Egypt Appius Sabinus', *JEA.*, 21, 1935, 224–47, especially notes on pp. 239–40.

[125] Cyprian, *Ep.*, 43.3, 'quinque primores illi qui edicto nuper magistratibus fuerant copulati'. See F. Krebs, art. cit., 1010–11.

[126] Cyprian, *Ep.*, 67.4. Bishop Martialis performed his sacrifice before the procurator.

[127] Eusebius, *H.E.*, vi.42.1, 'ἄλλοι δὲ πλεῖστοι κατὰ πόλεις καὶ κατὰ κώμας ὑπὸ τῶν ἐθνῶν διεσπάσθησαν'. In the villages the *strategos* and his assistants formed the commission.

[128] *Acta S. Tryphonis* (ed. P. Franchi di Cavalieri, *S.T.*, xix, 1908), ch. 5.

[129] See the discussion of the literature available to 1950 in H. Grégoire's 'Les Persécutions dans l'Empire romain', *Mémoires de l'Académie Royale de Belgique*, xlvi, fasc. 1 1951, 113–14. This is an excellent study for the period 212 onwards, but of less value for the earlier persecutions.

[130] In Carthage, for instance, Paula the mat-maker and Soliasus the mule-keeper seem to have been quite prominent members of the Church (Cyprian, *Ep.*, 42). On the influence of foreign merchants in spreading Christianity in the West, and the advantages and disadvantages of this mission, my article in *Mullus, Festschrift Theodore Klauser*, Bonn, 1964, pp. 125–30.

[131] Eusebius, *H.E.*, vi.40.2.

[132] Ibid., 40.4–9.

[133] Ibid., 41.12; cf. Cyprian, *De Lapsis*, 7 and 8.

[134] Eusebius, *H.E.*, vii.11.24.

[135] Cyprian, *De Lapsis*, 25, 'apud idoleum quo populos confluebat'.

[136] Cyprian, *Ep.*, 24: 'reliquerunt possessiones quas fiscus tenet'; cf. *De Lapsis*, 10 and *Ep.*, 66.4 for the confiscation of Cyprian's own property.

[137] Ibid., *Ep.*, 55.14: 'dare me ob hoc praemium, ne quod non licet faciam'. Also *De Lapsis*, 27. The habit was not new in Africa. Tertullian comments scornfully on Christians taking out this form of 'insurance', *De Fuga*, 12 and 13, 'massaliter totae ecclesiae tributum sibi irrogaverunt'.

[138] Gregory of Nyssa, *Life*, P.G., 46, col. 945D.

[139] *Acta Sancti Pionii*, 15.2, 16.1 and 18.4.

140 Ibid., 13.1–4.

141 Ibid., 16.5.

142 Ibid., 19.5.

143 Ibid., 10.2. The ironical 'πῶς ἀεὶ χλωρὸς ὢν νυν πυρρὸν ʾεχει τὸ πρόσωπον'.

144 *Acta Sancti Acacii*, 4.8. For discussion of these *Acta*, H. Delehaye, *Les Passions des Martyrs*, 344ff.

145 *Acta Tryphonis*, 4. Celerinus' sister was one of the lapsed in Rome.

146 Celerinus, ap. Cyprian, *Ep.*, 21.2 'in hac vastatione'.

147 Cyprian, *Ep.*, 30.3 (the Roman presbyters to Cyprian).

148 Cyprian, *Ep.*, 8.2, 'quidam terrore ipso compulsi, sive quod essent insignes personae sive adprehensi timore hominum, ruerunt'. A passage in the Greek *Acta* of Trypho (ch. 4) gives the same picture, 'Ἱερέων τε καὶ τῶν 'ἐπαρχομένων οὐκ ὀλίγοι 'ἠρνήσαντο τὸ ὄνομα τοῦ χριστοῦ'. On the possible authenticity of this passage, P. Franchi di Cavalieri, 'Hagiographica', *S.T.*, xix, 1908, 29ff. To the present writer the situation described in chs. 4–5 appears authentic when compared with other contemporary documents (e.g. Cyprian's Letters), but the interrogation of Trypho, including ch. 9, which di Cavalieri accepted, seems more fanciful.

149 Cyprian, *Ep.*, 27.1 (Lucianus) 'virtute robustus sed bene nimis dominica lectione fundatus'.

150 Ibid., 'litteras ille non nosset'.

151 Eusebius, *H.E.*, vi.41.14–42.4.

152 Ibid., vi.41.21.

153 P. *Oxy.* 80 (Gordian), and U. Wilcken, *Grundzüge*, 472 from Soknopaiou Nesos in the Fayum. See M. Rostovtzeff, *Social and Economic History*, 488.

154 *Acta Pionii*, 4.21–24: for similar expectations at this time, *Orac. Sibyll.*, xii.290.

155 Ibid. 21.1. 'μετὰ σπουδῆς εἰς τὸ στάδιον.' Cf. above, ch. X, n. 146.

156 Cyprian, *Ep.*, 22.1. Decius described by Lucian as 'ipsum anguem maiorem, metatorem antichristi'; cf. *Ep.*, 55.9.

157 Ibid., 21.3, 'quoniam estis amici sed et testes Christi'.

158 Cyprian, *Ep.*, 39.3.

159 Ibid.

160 Under stress, Bishop Dionysius was to hark back to the literal words of the Apocalypse for inspiration (Eusebius, *H.E.*, vii.10.2). In calmer moments he appears to have had a less high regard for its apostolic authority (ibid., vii.24). Like Cyprian he spoke of the martyrs as 'assessors of Christ', who 'share His kingdom and take part in His decisions and judge with him' (ibid., vi.42.5).

161 Origen, *In Jesu Nave, Homil.* ix.10. (Baehrens, 356–7).

162 Cyprian, *Ad Demetrianum*, 13, 'in foro ipso, magistratibus et praesidibus audientibus'.

163 Porphyry, Frag. 36 (ed. A. Harnack) *ABAW.*, 1916, 63 (citing Macarius Magnes, iv.4) 'μύριοι τούτοις 'ὁμόδοξοι οἱ μὲν 'ἐκαύθησαν, οἱ δʾἄλλοι τιμωρίαν ἢ λώβην δεξάμενοι διεφθάρησαν'. The context suggests gross exaggeration!

164 *H.E.*, vi.42.1. See for a summary of the available evidence, Albert Ehrhard, *Die Kirche der Märtyrer*, München, 1932, 66–8.

165 *Liber Pontif.*, xxi (Duchesne, 148). Also mentions Maximus the presbyter and Nicostratus, a deacon, who were imprisoned.

166 Cyprian, *Ep.*, 22.2–3 (*CSEL.*, iii.1, 534–5).

167 Ibid., *Ep.*, 12.1.

168 About two years. For the chronological problems of the period 251–253, see the discussion between A. Stein and H. Mattingly, 'Observations on the Chronology of the Roman Emperors in the second half of the Third Century', *J.E.A.*, 14, 1928, 16–19.

169 Ibid., *Ep.*, 59.8.

170 Ibid., *Ep.*, 61.3. 'repentina persecutio . . . saecularis potestas subito prorupit'.

[171] For the facts, A. Alföldi, 'The Crisis of the Empire', in *CAH.*, xii.167–9.

[172] A new bishop, Lucius, was elected in Rome soon after but died early in March 254 (Benson, op. cit., 304–5).

[173] Pontius, *Vita Cypriani*, 9; cf. *De Mortalitate*, 16.

[174] Cyprian, *Ep.*, 62.4 (*CSEL.*, iii.2, p. 700).

[175] Eusebius, *H.E.*, vii.11.24. I am accepting an emendation of νόσος for νῆσος which would mean that four Alexandrine deacons died in the plague. I would not rule out the reverse type APOLL. SALUTARI on Gallus' coinage as referring to the plague (*A Catalogue of Roman Coins*, compiled by G. Askew for Seaby's, 1948, p. 89, R. 2131).

[176] For the extent of the Church's recovery in Africa by the end of 251, see Cyprian's defiant 'quamvis nimius et copiosus noster populus ulciscitur' to Demetrian (*Ad. Dem.*, 17). For Apollo's saving powers against plague and famine, *Acta Acacii*, ii.2.

[177] Eusebius, *H.E.*, vi.42.5 and vi.44 on Dionysius' solution at Alexandria, when faced by precisely the same problem as Cyprian. There was no Novatianist element in Alexandria, and Dionysius appears to have had no difficulty in supporting Cornelius.

[178] See also E. W. Benson's still valuable *Cyprian, His Life, His Times, His Work*, 134ff., and the present author's *The Donatist Church*, ch. x.

[179] *Ep.*, 5.2. Clergy in Carthage to discourage mass demonstrations outside the prisons. See also, *Ep.*, 14.2 and 3. Benson, op. cit., 103.

[180] *Epp.*, 21.2 and 3, and 35.

[181] *Ep.*, 18.1. 'praerogativa eorum adjuvari apud Deum possunt'. Also. *Ep.*, 19.2. For the confessors' own view, Celerinus to Lucian, *Ep.*, 21.3, 'estis amici sed et testes Christi', and ibid. 2. 'auxilium domini . . . per eos dominos meos qui coronati fuerint'.

[182] *Ep.*, 13.1, 'nam cum gaudere in hoc [honor confessionis] omnes fratres oportet, tunc in gaudio communi maior est episcopi portio. Ecclesiae enim gloria praeposiˀi gloria est'

[183] *Ep.*, 20.1. Also *Epp.*, 11.5 and 16.4.

[184] *Ep.*, 11.1. 'tumida et inverecunda iactatio' (*CSEL.*, iii.2.496).

[185] *Ep.*, 27.1; cf. 20.3.

[186] *Ep.*, 23. 'Optamus te cum sanctis martyribus pacem habere'.

[187] *Ep.*, 17.2. (*CSEL.*, iii.2.522).

[188] Ibid., 55.6–7. Benson, op. cit., 156–9.

[189] Ibid., 55.13. Benson, op. cit., 222ff.

[190] See, W. Telfer, *Forgiveness of Sins*, SCM Press, 1960, 69ff.

[191] Cyprian, *Ep.*, 54.3; cf. 55.21 for previous resistance by some bishops to the peace of the Church being granted to adulterers.

[192] Ibid., 54.4 'sed et catholicae ecclesiae unitatem quantum potuit expressit nostra mediocritas'.

[193] For instance, Celerinus and Numidicus, Cyprian, *Epp.*, 39.1 and 40.

[194] For instance, in the *De Opere et Eleemosynis*, 10 and 11.

[195] *Ep.*, 58.2. Also, *Ad Fortunatum, passim*, written probably in 257, where Cyprian shows clearly that he holds the traditional Western equation of approach of Antichrist, persecution, Christian confession, and crown of martyrdom. Martyrdom was in his view, as in Tertullian's, the Second Baptism.

[196] Cf. *Ad Fortunatum*, 11 (*CSEL.*, iii.1. 337–43) and *Ep.*, 58.5–6, and for the presence of the same spirit in the years after the Valerianic persecution, *Passio Mariani et Jacobi*, 13.

[197] As H. Chadwick points out '238 is the earliest possible date for the tomb, of the years preceding the Memoria, with its inscription in Greek lettering . . . recording the names of members of the imperial household who had taken as *cognomina* the names of their imperial masters Pupienus and Balbinus' ('St. Peter and St. Paul in Rome', *JTS.*, N.S. viii.1, 1957, 33, n. 1). Also, the discussion between A. von Gerkan and Th. Klauser in *J.A.C.*, v., 1962, 23–42, and the critical Bibliography by A. de Marco, *The Tomb of St. Peter*, Leiden, 1964, Part ii.

[198] Cyprian in *Ep.*, 12.1 refers specifically to the cult of martyrs being celebrated in Africa in 250. That distinctions were made between those who were executed and those who died in prison, ibid., paras. 1–3.

[199] H. Grégoire for instance, believes that the cult of the Apostles celebrated on the Appian Way was celebrated on the initiative of the Novatianists and that the date given for the *Depositio Martyrum*, for Peter and Paul, in the Calendar of Philocalus of 354 (iii. Kal. Iul. Petri in Catacumbas et Pauli Ostense Tusco et Basso consulibus') marks in reality the date of Novatian's own martyrdom. *Nouvelle Clio*, 1953, 53.

[200] Cyprian, *Ep.*, 55.8, 'Factus est enim Cornelius episcopus de Dei et Christi eius judicio, de clericorum paene omnium testimonio, de plebis quae tunc adfuit suffragio.'

[201] Eusebius, *H.E.*, vi.44.1.

[202] See, *inter alia*, M. Bévenot, 'St. Cyprian's *De Unitate*', *Analecta Gregoriana*, xi, Rome, 1938, and T. G. Jalland *The Church and the Papacy*, 161–6. For the present author's views, *Modern Churchman*, 1958, 196–9.

[203] *De Lapsis*, 34.

[204] *De Unitate*, 23.

[205] *Dating*: Benson, op. cit., 304–5.

[206] Cyprian, *Ep.*, 68.3. Benson, op. cit., 316ff.

[207] *Ep.*, 67. Benson, 311ff.

[208] *Ep.*, 67.3 (tr. J. Stevenson, *A New Eusebius*, pp. 248–9).

[209] Tertullian, *De Anima*, 41.

[210] R. Reitzenstein, 'Ein donatistisches Corpus cyprianischer Schriften', *Nachrichten von der kgl. Ges. zu Göttingen*, Phil. Hist. Kl., 1914.4, 85–92.

[211] *Ep.*, 44.3.

[212] Ibid., 48.3.

[213] Ibid., 74.11. Cf. Tertullian, *De Baptismo*, 12.

[214] *Ep.*, 69.8.

[215] Ibid., 73.3, 'exinde in hodiernum tot milia haereticorum in provinciis nostris ad ecclesiam conversi. . . . '

[216] Cyprian, *Ep.*, 63.8, 'Per baptisma autem Spiritus accipitur, et sic baptizatis et Spiritum sanctum consecutis ad bibendum calicem Domini pervenitur'.

[217] Well expressed in the Donatist *Passio Marculi* (*circa* 350) (*P.L.*, viii, 760) but evident also in Cyprian's own career. See, in general, G. W. H. Lampe, *The Seal of the Spirit*, London, 1951, p. 171ff.

[218] As shown in Cyprian, *Ep.*, 73.13, 'consuetudinem nobis opponunt'.

[219] Cyprian took the opposite view. *Ep.*, 72.1, 'eo quod parum sit eis (haereticis) manum imponere ad accipiendum spiritum sanctum, nisi accipiant et ecclesiae baptismum'. Also 74.7.

[220] *Ep.*, 75.20.

[221] Ibid., 74.7 and 11.

[222] Note Cyprian's quote of Lev. 21.21 in his letter to Stephen. *Ep.*, 72.2.

[223] For open opposition to Cyprian's standpoint, Anon, *De Rebaptismate* (*CSEL.*, iii.3, 69ff.). Cyprian's *Letters* 69, 70, 71, 73 and 74 were written to convince friendly, but worried, African critics.

[224] Cyprian, *Ep.*, 75.

[225] Eusebius, *H.E.*, vii.5.3–4 and vii.7–9, extracts from a long and protracted correspondence extending into the pontificate of Dionysius (260–69). See K. Müller, 'Kleine Beiträge zur alten Kirchengeschichte No. 9', *ZNTW.*, 23, 1924. Dionysius was far more concerned with heretical than with schismatic baptism, and prepared to accept the baptism of those baptized in the name of the Trinity, but other formulae were unacceptable.

[226] Cyprian's appreciation of Xystus, 'bono et pacifico sacerdote'. Pontius, *Vita*, 14.

[227] For the events, see Manaresi, *Il cristianismo*, p. 387ff. and for thorough discussion of

relevant literature, J. Moreau, Lactance, *De la Mort des Persécuteurs*, Sources chrétiennes, 39.ii, 1954, pp. 217–25, and H. Grégoire, *Les Persécutions*, 149–52.

[228] M. Besnier's view expressed in 'La Censure de Valérien', *Mél. Glotz*, Paris, 1932, 185–92.

[229] Eusebius, *H.E.*, vii.10.3.

[230] Ibid., vii.23.3.

[231] Ibid., 15.1.

[232] Ibid., 11.7. 'θεοὺς τοὺς σώζοντας αὐτῶν τὴν βασιλείαν.'

[233] See A. Alföldi, *CAH.*, xii, ch. v, for details of the barbarian invasions of this period and the analysis of Persian and Greco-Roman sources for the extent of the Persian threat, by Wm. Ensslin, 'Zu den Kriegen des Sassinaden Schapur', *S.B. der bayerischen Akad. der Wiss.*, Phil. Hist. Kl., 1947, Heft 5.

[234] Zonaras xii.23, 'εθνῶν οὖν καὶ 'επὶ τούτου γενομένης ἐπαναστάσεως.

[235] The early coinage of Postumus, whose reign in Gaul begins in December (?) 259 contains up to 15 per cent silver, but follows the coinage of Gallienus into its catastrophic decline later. It is questionable whether, if the debasement had already taken place in 259, Postumus would have bothered to mint good coinage at all.

[236] *Pap. Oxy.*, 1411 (A.D. 260).

[237] As Dionysius suggested. Eusebius, *H.E.*, vii.10.4.

[238] Gregory Thaumaturgus, *Canonical Epistle* (ed. A. Roberts and J. Donaldson, Ante-Nicene Christian Library, xx, 30–5).

[239] *CIL.*, iii.14191. See M. Besnier, *L'empire romain*, 195–6.

[240] *Acta Proconsularia*, 1. 'Sacratissimi imperatores Valerianus et Gallienus litteras ad me dari dignati sunt, quibus praeceperunt eos, qui Romanam religonem non colunt, debere Romanas caerimonias recognoscere.' This sounds like the actual text of a letter.

[241] *Contra Celsum*, viii.67.

[242] Eusebius, *H.E.*, vii.11–12.

[243] *Acta Proc.*, 1.

[244] Eusebius, *H.E.*, v.5; Tertullian, *Apol.*, 5.6.

[245] Cyprian, *Epp.*, 77–80. For this punishment, see J. G. Davies, 'Condemnation to the Mines. A neglected chapter in the history of the Persecutions', *University of Birmingham Historial Journal*, vi.2, 1958, 99–107. The legate in question may have been C. Macrinius Decianus (E. Birley, *JRS.*, xl, 1950, 65).

[246] Eusebius, *H.E.*, vii.11.9–11 (trans. J. E. L. Oulton).

[247] *Ep.*, 76.2.

[248] Ibid., 76.3.

[249] Ibid., 76.6.

[250] Ibid., 76.5. 'Ipsius enim esse quod vincimus et quod ad maximi certaminis palmam subacto adversario pervenimus declarat et docet Dominus.'

[251] Ibid., 76.7.

[252] *Epp.*, 77–9.

[253] *Ep.*, 80.1.

[254] *Depositio Martyrum* (ed. H. Lietzmann), p. 3.

[255] Cyprian, *Ep.*, 80.1. See J. Moreau's bibliographical note in *Lactance, De la Mort des Persécuteurs* (Sources chrétiennes, 39), ii.220.

[256] *Ep.*, 81. Cf. *Vita*, 15.

[257] *De Officiis*, 1.41. and ii.48.

[258] *Ep.* 81. The same fate, namely exile followed by recall for trial and execution, was suffered by two Numidian bishops Agapius and Secundinus (of Cedias?) probably also towards the end of 258. *Passio Mariani et Jacobi*, 3.

[259] *Acta Proconsularia*, 3–4. Trans. J. Stevenson, *A New Eusebius*, no. 227, pp. 260–3.

[260] *Acta Proconsularia*, 5.

[261] Ibid.

[262] Augustine, *Sermo*, 273–7, but not included in *Martyrol. Carth.*

[263] *Acta Mariani et Jacobi* (ed. Knopf and Krüger, 67–73), I regard the *Acta* as reporting genuine occurrences. See H. Delehaye, *Les Passions*, 78–82, and P. Franchi de Cavalieri, *S.T.*, iii, 1900, 15–26. Dating: *Martyrol. Carth.* (ed. Lietzmann), 5, ii. Non. Mai.

[264] *Passio Montani et Lucii* (ed. Knopf and Krüger, 74–82); cf. H. Delehaye, *Les Passions des Martyrs*, 72–8. For a view of the *Acta* as a genuine, but rhetorical account of events, by a disciple of Cyprian, inspired by the *Passio Perpetuae*, P. Franchi di Cavalieri, *S.T.*, iii, 1900, 1–15. I would agree that there seems to be a genuine core to the *Passio*, but the incidents in prison and the visions appear to be unimaginative copying of the *Passio Perpetuae*. Dating: *Martyrol. Carth.*, X Kal. Jun . . .

[265] Augustine, *Sermo*, 306 and 311.10; see P. Monceaux, *Histoire Littéraire*, ii.141, and P. Franchi di Cavalieri, *S.T.*, ix, 1902, 39–51.

[266] Cf. *Acta Mariani et Jacobi*, 2.2. At Cirta, 'in qua tunc maxime civitate gentilium caeco furore et officiis militaribus persecutionis impetus quasi fluctus saeculi tumescebant', and *Passio Montani et Lucii*, 2.

[267] *Acta Fructuosi*, 2 (ed. Knopf and Krüger, 93). 'Aemilianus praeses Fructuoso episcopo dixit "Episcopus es? Fructuosus episcopus dixit, Sum. Aemilianus dixit, Fuisti, et iussit eos sua sententia vivos ardere".' *Dating* of these *Acta* must be pre-360 because Augustine cites it in *Sermo*, 213.2 and 273.3 and Prudentius in *Peristephanon*, 6. Detailed discussion, P. Franchi di Cavalieri, *S.T.*, 65, 1935, 129–81.

[268] Eusebius, *H.E.*, vii.12.

[269] Ibid., vii.11.13.

[270] Ibid., vii.13. One of the edicts must have been published in Rome before 9 August 260, because the cult centre of Peter and Paul on the Appian Way was flourishing at that time, and a graffito giving this date has been discovered. See R. Marichal, 'La Date des Graffiti de la Basilique de Saint-Sébastien à Rome', *Nouv. Clio*, v, 1953, 119.

[271] A. Alfoldi, *CAH.*, xii.173–4. In 257 he had been Deputy-Prefect. Above, n. 246.

[272] Eusebius, *H.E.*, vii.13.

[273] Ibid., vii.15.

CHAPTER FOURTEEN

The Triumph of Christianity, 260–303

THE forty years of peace which followed the Valerianic persecution was a significant period in the life of the early Church. Over much of the southern and eastern part of the Mediterranean the balance between paganism and Christianity was shifting in favour of the latter. Christianity was now spreading rapidly into the countryside, ousting the traditional native gods from popular favour. If one were to look at a map of the Roman Empire on the eve of the Great Persecution, and indicate the degree of Christianization by darker or lighter colouring according to density, western Asia Minor, Syria, the Nile valley and Cyrenaica, Roman North Africa and the city of Rome would show up as the most christianized areas, with proportionately lighter shades for southern Spain and southern Gaul, and almost white for the Celtic north-western and Danube frontier provinces. Christianity was winning wherever its way had been prepared by a strong Jewish Dispersion, or where, as in North Africa or on the Euphrates frontier the national cults had a strongly Semitic tincture. But elsewhere, particularly in Illyricum, the Danubian and western provinces of the Empire, it was still largely the religion of the immigrant merchant and settler from the east.[1] In those parts it had not moved far off the main lines of communication.

The unevenness of the Christian mission was to have its effect on the development of its relations with the Empire at this critical juncture. The soldier-emperors who were restoring the fortunes of the Empire came from Illyricum, among the least christianized areas. They could hardly be expected to sympathize with the rise of the new cult. When the frontiers were at last secured, Christianity would be judged according to whether it was regarded as a unifying or a disrupting element in the Empire. Yet in the key provinces for provisioning Rome and defending the eastern frontiers it was immensely strong. There, it could neither be ignored nor brushed aside, and this was decisive. By 300 the question had become on what terms Church and Empire could co-operate, and whether a settlement would come peacefully, or after one final, bloody encounter.

The evidence from which to reconstruct the events which led up to this situation is incomplete and scattered. There are no equivalents to Cyprian's letters for the decade 248-258 in Africa, nor for Eusebius' and Lactantius' accounts of the Great Persecution. But from the jig-saw fragments of literature and archaeology one can detect a quickening in the pace of the Christian mission and detect also non-theological, social and economic factors contributing to this movement. Finally, one must consider the impact of these new converts, mainly from the countryside, on what had become the ordered hierarchical government of the Church.

In the period of civil war, confusion and reconstruction which followed Valerian's capture, the policy of persecution collapsed. In Egypt, where the struggle with the supporters of Macrianus and Quietus went on into 262, Gallienus bade for and won Christian support.[2] In Alexandria itself it is interesting that the rebel Prefect Aemilian held the Greek quarters of the city where most of the important pagan buildings were situated.[3] The Christians were firmly on the other side, if for no other reason than that it had been the same Aemilian who had sent Dionysius and his colleagues into exile four years before. In 261 Dionysius was back, and in the last three years of his episcopacy was a powerful public figure in Egypt. Each year, the Festal Letter of the Church of Alexandria, written nominally to announce the date of Easter, enabled him to make his voice heard on a larger number of matters, and to weld the Christians throughout Egypt into unity. In this he was the forerunner of Athanasius. Persecution was no longer a major concern. Instead, he found himself occupied with a long-drawn-out correspondence with his namesake in Rome over the alleged Sabellian views of some of the bishops in Cyrenaica,[4] and by the more serious conflict over the anti-Origenistic Christology of Paul of Samosata, now bishop of Antioch. Three Councils at Antioch held in 264, 265 and 268, were necessary before the latter could be sentenced for heresy and misconduct. The controversies of the reign of Gallienus were a warning that the dawn of peace was not necessarily to be the dawn of concord.

It would be mistaken, however, to regard Gallienus as positively favourable to Christianity. His own predilections lay elsewhere, with the Neo-Platonists, quietist perhaps in political outlook but becoming increasingly hostile to the Church. Plotinus found a ready welcome at Gallienus' court, especially from the Empress Salonina,[5] and received the Emperor's support for his plan for his ideal city of Platonopolis in Campania.[6] Christians were still kept at arm's length. Eusebius records the curious story of the martyrdom of Marinus at Caesarea in Palestine as having taken place in Gallienus' reign.[7] Marinus, an *optio*, was about to be promoted to the rank of centurion when a disappointed rival stepped forward before the governor's tribunal asserting that 'in accordance with the ancient laws' Marinus could not 'share in the rank that belonged to Romans since he was a Christian and did not sacrifice to the emperors', and he claimed the office for himself.[8] The governor, Achaeus, accepted the complaint, gave Marinus 3 hours to reconsider his position. Marinus met the bishop of Caesarea, Theotecnus, was persuaded by him to choose the Gospels rather than the centurion's vine-switch and went to his death. The story, even if embroidered in its details, was apparently circulating in Caesarea and perhaps owes its preservation to Eusebius being bishop. The denunciation and the short respite for reconsideration granted by the judge have a ring of truth. If the account is accepted, Gallienus' benevolence towards the Christians must be seen largely as a political act designed to meet threatening local situations in Rome and Alexandria. The legal situation of the Christians remained as it had been in the second century.[9]

The brief reign of Claudius II was almost wholly occupied in continuing the work of Gallienus' last years hunting down and destroying invaders, this time a vast Gothic inroad into Illyricum. He gained a decisive victory at Naissus in 269, but early in 270 fell victim to plague. Neither he nor his brother Quintillus, who succeeded him for three months, seem to have had any firm policy towards the Christians.[10]

With Aurelian (April 270–August (?) 275) who ousted Quintillus, the situation changed once more. The new emperor was, as he claimed to be on his coinage, 'restitutor saeculi'.[11] In just over five years he restored the Roman Empire to order, and gave it the boundaries which it was to retain until the barbarian onslaught at the turn of the fifth century. First the Goths, and then in quick succession, the Vandals, Sarmatians and Iazygi were expelled from the Danube provinces. The Juthungi were eliminated from Italy and a beginning was made on the great walls which surround Rome to this day. In 271 Aurelian had the courage and foresight to evacuate the increasingly untenable Dacian salient and make the Danube the Roman frontier. Then it was the turn of the Palmyrene kingdom, too powerful to be used any more as a makeweight between Rome and Ctesiphon. By the end of 272, Zenobia was gracing Aurelian's triumph and her motley ministry of expert advisers who included the Neo-Platonist Longinus and the Christian bishop Paul of Samosata imprisoned, executed or scattered to the winds. Next year came the downfall of the Gallic empire, and here too, Aurelian timed his intervention to the moment. Tetricus, harassed by renewed threats from across the Rhine and peasant revolt (the Bagaudae) in Gaul itself, preferred the life of a minor provincial governor—he became *corrector* of Lucania—to the doubtful triumphs of Gallic power. By 274 the Roman world was reunited under a single outstanding military leader.[12]

Twice in his reign Aurelian had dealings with the Christians. The first was in 272 when he captured Antioch from Queen Zenobia. There he had to decide the fate of Bishop Paul who was also Zenobia's chief financial minister (procurator with the rank of *ducenarius*) in the city. Secondly, in 275, when according to Eusebius, 'he was moved by certain counsels to stir up persecution against us'.[13] In the first situation, Aurelian showed considerable diplomatic skill. Zenobia's Palmyrene empire had no bias against Christianity. The queen herself may plausibly be regarded as having leant towards a monotheism akin to Judaism,[14] and she had supported Paul of Samosata despite all abuse and condemnations by his enemies. Aurelian, too, needed the support of the Christian population of Syria, and though Paul's Adoptionist theology may have shocked the Origenists, it is clear from the almost contemporary *Acts of Archelaus* that it coincided with an outlook widely held in Syria.[15] There seems to have been no popular demand for his expulsion from the bishop's house whither he had withdrawn after his final condemnation in 268. Aurelian had therefore to tread warily. The decrees of the

Origenist councils were ignored, and instead, the decision whether Paul or his rival Domnus was entitled to the bishop's house was left for 'the bishops of the doctrine in Italy and Rome' to award.[16] Honour was satisfied. The Emperor had shown himself no less benevolent to the Christians than Zenobia had been, and the wisdom of distant neutrals who might appear to the Emperor to be in no way involved in the issue, invoked.[17] There was no 'appeal to Rome',[18] but arbitration in a civil dispute between two rival parties in a powerful sect. A precedent, however, had been set for Constantine's action when confronted by the Donatist rejection of Caecilian forty years later.

The fighting against Zenobia's generals was severe. Whether or not in 272 Aurelian believed that his final victory had been aided by a divine helper, the Sun-god of Emesa, is problematical. One reform, however, he undertook on his return to Rome in 274 was the erection of a magnificent temple to the Sun-god, the establishment of a new college of senators entitled 'pontifices dei Solis', and the striking of coins bearing the inscriptions, 'Sol Dominus Imperii Romani', and 'Aurelianus Augustus consecravit' in the deity's honour.[19] As in the time of Elagabalus, the Syrian sun-god was to be the centre of the religion of the Roman world, and Aurelian his representative on earth. Even so, the Emperor was also known to later tradition as a faithful observer of the prescribed demands of the official State gods,[20] and the Iovi Conservatori issues on which the Emperor is shown receiving the orb from Jupiter could also foreshadow the 'Jovian' policy of Diocletian.[21]

Both Eusebius and Lactantius record Aurelian's intention to try conclusions with the Church.[22] Lactantius in fact goes further than Eusebius in stating that 'his bloody edicts had not yet reached the most distant provinces' when their perpetrator received his deserts at the hand of his own immediate staff (ab amicis suis interemptus). Neither author, however, says that persecution had actually commenced when Aurelian was murdered (perhaps end-August 275).[23] None the less, a number of martyrdoms scattered from Italy, Gaul and Asia Minor are attributed to this reign.[24] On the basis of there 'never being smoke without fire', it is possible that some of these Acta might conceal a grain of historical truth. But as Homo points out, the persecution could only have taken place in the summer of 275, and the *natales* of the victims are dated the year round. The argument is not quite conclusive, as occasionally the dates recorded in genuine *Acta* do not correspond with a *natalis* subsequently chosen by the Church.[25] But in this case, it adds weight to those who refuse to accept martyrs for the reign of Aurelian. It is difficult to credit Sabinianus and his companions in Gaul with reality.[26]

Almost equal obscurity shrouds the policy of Probus (276–282) towards the Christians, following the senatorial interregnum (275–276). The historian is confronted by the *Acta Sancti Trophimi* of Synnada in Phrygia, and embarrassed by the discovery of a reliquary dedicated to the saint in the museum at Bursa. Moreover, the dedication is couched in the crypto-Christian formula usual in the late third century in Asia Minor, 'Here are the bones of the martyr Trophimus. He who displaces them from this box let him render his account to God'.[27] The association of the saint with a Montanist κοινωνός on an inscription from near Sebaste dated to *circa* A.D. 500, suggests the possibility of an isolated Montanist devotee who provoked his own death.[28] One is justified in concluding, with Henri Grégoire, that here we may have trace of some local pogrom in Synnada.

Probus was murdered in 282, and the reigns of Carus and his sons Carinus and Numerian (282–285) were spent mainly in the struggle with Persia. Carus died on a successful campaign in September 282 and thereafter his sons had little thought beyond preserving their lives. By the spring of 285, Carinus had been laid low, and the Empire passed to yet another successful Illyrian general. Diocletian, however, was to stay, the only Roman emperor to abdicate, after 21 years' rule. How and why his policy towards the Christians was to change from benevolence to the Great Persecution must be reserved until the next chapter.

The preoccupation of successive emperors with the task of restoration left them little time for the Christians, and the Church profited thereby. To quote Eusebius who was growing up in Caesarea in Palestine in this period,

> It is beyond our powers to describe in a worthy manner the measure and nature of that honour as well as freedom which was accorded by all men, both Greeks and barbarians, before the persecution in our day, to that word of piety towards the God of the universe

which had been proclaimed through Christ to the world. Yet proofs might be forthcoming in the favours granted by the rulers to our people; to whom they would even entrust the government of the provinces, freeing them from agony of mind as regards sacrificing, because of the great friendliness that they used to enter-tain for their doctrine.[29]

There is abundant evidence to show that he was not exaggerating.

First, Church leaders were beginning to emerge as real leaders of the provinces in which the great sees had been established. The organization of the metropolitan dioceses accepted at Nicaea in 325 refers to a situation already coming into being half a century earlier.[30] Dionysius of Alexandria shows that in his day Egypt and Cyrenaica formed an ecclesiastical entity under his own control. In Africa, the role played by Cyprian and by suc-ceeding bishops of Carthage is well known. In Antioch, the synodical letter of the Council of 268 shows that Paul not only combined his episcopal duties with those of a senior minister, but lived like a lord, and had a willing following among the bishops and clergy of Syria.[31] In Rome, also, in the same period 260–300 may be placed the organization of the *tituli* or parishes within the city boundaries. This resulted in an increase in the authority of the bishop in the area of the city, as the *tituli* were financed from the latter's central fund and served by his clergy.[32] The influence of the see of Peter was being felt even in distant Cappadocia, where an embassy was sent by Dionysius (259–268) to negotiate the ransom of prisoners taken by the Goths. It brought gifts to the local Churches on the scale which was remembered in the time of Basil of Caesarea over a century later.[33]

The Church's power of organization and freedom of action was reflected in the position which prominent Christians were gaining for themselves in the general life of the Empire. Paul of Samo-sata apart, Eusebius cites the instance of Anatolius who succeeded his fellow Alexandrine Eusebius, as bishop of Laodicea in 269.[34] This man had already founded a school of Aristotelian philosophy in Alexandria—no mean achievement in itself in the city of Philo, Clement and Origen, and had played a prominent part in the civil war of 261–262. Though a Christian living in the part of the city held by Aemilian, he had taken the initiative to convene a representative gathering of Alexandrians, which decided to open negotiations with Gallienus' general for the evacuation of non-combatants. In view of the intensity of the fighting it is surprising that he succeeded and his personal success may be a measure of the extent of the Christian recovery from the debâcle of only a dozen years before.[35] A few years later, between 264–282, an interesting letter written by a Christian corn-dealer in Arsinoe shows that his link with his agent in Rome was no other than Dionysius' successor, Bishop Maximus of Alexandria, and he would be sharing any profit from the transaction. The letter sheds an interesting light on the ramifications of Alexandrian ecclesiastical interests even at this period.[36]

Christians were also prominent in the Imperial service. We hear of Adauctus who was *magister rei privatae* and *rationalis summarum* at Diocletian's court, i.e. a senior administrative and financial officer.[37] Eusebius also mentions Dorotheus, a eunuch and a learned presbyter of Antioch, who was the friend of the Emperor (Diocletian?) and was appointed by him to superintend the imperial dye-works at Tyre.[38] He also records Philoromus later a martyr, 'who had been appointed to no mean office in the royal administration of Alexandria, and daily administered justice, attended by soldiers according to his Roman dignity and Roman rank.'[39] At Nicomedia there were Christians among the Emperor's senior personal officials, as there had been under the Severi. We hear of two of these, Dorotheus and Gorgonius, both of whom were martyred there in 303.[40] There were Christian officers like M. Iulius Eugenius serving in Pisidia and elsewhere.[41]

In Spain and Africa also, both literary and archaeological evidence point to the penetration of Christianity ever more deeply into educated provincial society. In Africa the example of Arnobius and later his pupil Lactantius was being followed by many others. The change of climate in favour of Christianity is well reflected in the former's statement that many members of the liberal professions who once despised the Word, now believed.[42] When the Great Persecution broke, 'patres familias', i.e. heads of families of some standing, were among the victims.[43] In southern Spain, the Council of Elvira (perhaps 15 May 309 during Maxentius' rule[44]) illustrates very well the problems of an era of rapid conversion. Could Christians continue to hold nominal priesthoods which formed part of the recognized hierarchy of municipal

government?[45] What about 'mixed marriages' in a society where
Christian women outnumbered the menfolk?[46] Or, Christians
who lent clothes for use in circus processions,[47] or looked on at
pagan sacrifices?[48] These were real problems in a mixed pagan-
Christian society, where Christianity was, however, clearly
emerging as the predominant force.[49] In north Italy, excavations
at Aquileia have revealed a basilica and Christian buildings paved
with fine mosaics built perhaps in the last years of the third
century,[50] and within a stone's throw of an equally ornate Jewish
synagogue.[51]

Finally, in Rome, there is clear evidence for the prosperity and
expansion of the Christian community. It was still a community where, to judge from its inscriptions, a wealthy element
among the Roman *plebs* predominated.[52] But money and resources
were flowing in. Existing catacombs were enlarged and new ones
excavated, such as those of Maximus, Pamphilius and Thrason
on the Via Salaria.[53] There may have been as many as twenty
Christian churches in the city and the same number of cemeteries.[54]
In the pontificate of Gaius (283–296) Christians are recorded as
buying *arcosolia* in the cemetery of Callistus near martyrs' tombs.[55]
One can begin to speak too, of the great renewal which took place
in Christian art, when the symbolism of the earlier age gives way
to explicitly Christian figures, such as the cycle of St. Peter, or
scenes from Jesus' life.[56] The intensity of the Christian devotion to
the martyr-apostles was being vividly demonstrated by the
crowded graffiti invoking their aid and memory on the walls of
the shrine on the Via Appia under the Church of St. Sebastian.
Near the shrine of St. Peter, Christians were already being buried
in the Vatican cemetery and also leaving their marks of reverence
among the graffiti on the wall built to support and repair the
famous Red Wall in about A.D. 250.[57] It was concerning Rome
too, that Porphyry wrote *circa* 270 that it was no wonder that
disease had been raging for so long, since neither Aesculapius nor
any other god could take up its abode in the city. Since Jesus was
honoured no one had experienced any public benefit from the
gods[58]—sour grapes perhaps, but none the less indicative of the
advance of Christianity in the capital.

All this points to an acceleration of tendencies at work since the
early years of the third century. The penetration of Christianity

into Greco-Roman society in its old mission field in Asia Minor had probably resulted in whole towns, such as Eumeneia[59] and Cotiaeum[60] in Phrygia becoming Christian. In these parts, Christianity seems to have worked upwards through the various social strata towards the top. An interesting example of this process is to be found in Sozomen's account of Cyzicus in the province of Asia in Julian's reign. In 362, the town council sent an official delegation to the Emperor requesting the restoration of the temples. Bishop Eleusis, however, who had been responsible for closing them, and converting numerous pagans was supported in his opposition by workers in a local clothing manufactory and in the imperial mint.[61]

A similar pattern can, however, be discerned in other parts of the Empire. In Egypt, Hellenism (paganism) survived in the towns long after the countryside had become Christian. There were sufficient rich Hellenes for Schenute of Atripe to curse in the fifth century.[62] At Timgad, the North African Donatist stronghold in the fourth and fifth centuries, a considerable proportion of the city's magistracy were to remain pagan,[63] though the extent of the Christian cemetery consisting of row upon row of simple penthouse tile graves provides evidence for the size and humble character of the Christian population. For Africa too, Lactantius, who could see the rapidly approaching triumph of Christianity,[64] warns the unwary against accepting the conversion of some educated provincials as meaning that the faith was finding wide support among them. He cites Cyprian's as an example of a brilliant convert who, however, 'failed to find much popularity'.[65] The stridency of Arnobius' *Adv. Nationes* also indicates the strength of the opposition among educated Africans which confronted him in the 290s.[66] When they had a fleeting chance under Julian the members of the pagan city councils demonstrated their feelings.[67] Even at Salona, soon to be one of the most prosperous Christian centres in the Balkans, the first bishops and their adherents seem to have been immigrants from Nisibis on the Euphrates frontier in the last decade of the third century.[68] In the Celtic lands generally, religion still meant the Romano-Celtic temple as late as the reign of Valentinian I.[69]

In the East, however, Christianity had begun to spread beyond the frontiers of the Empire. Though obscurity surrounds the exact progress of the missions, it is clear that there were numerous Christians in Persia and that Armenia was a Christian kingdom by the end of the century. In 250–251, Dionysius of Alexandria referred to Armenian Christians in Alexandria and to an Armenian bishop named Meruzanes.[70] Twenty years later it appears that King Tiridates was converted and by his action raised Christianity to the level of an international problem. Persecution could jeopardize the delicate balance of Rome's relationships on her eastern frontier. In 312/313 the Armenians showed that they were prepared to defend their adopted faith by force against Maximin.[71]

The spread of the Christian mission in the towns and among the educated generally was important, but not decisive for the victory of the Church in the Great Persecution. The experiences of Decius and Valerian had shown that the Roman authorities could inflict considerable damage on the Church so long as it was concentrated among the poorer townsfolk and their leaders. Once it spread, however, to the mass of cultivators who provided the food, transport and recruits for the Roman state, the situation for a persecuting government would become more difficult. By fleeing his land, as he was prepared to do in Egypt for the sake of his Christianity, the peasant had effective means of escaping both his religious and economic liabilities to the State.

What evidence is there for large-scale religious changes in the countryside of some of the key provinces in the Empire, and why did these changes take place now?[72] The course of events is often difficult to establish but on the whole is intelligible. In Egypt, North Africa and parts of Asia Minor and Syria we find evidence for a decline in the popularity of the hitherto all-powerful native cults, coupled with positive indications for the extension of Christianity. We find too, that Christianity takes a form which expresses the needs and outlook of the rural population as distinct from the townsfolk, such as monasticism did in Egypt and Syria. For Egypt, Idris Bell has remarked that, 'as we advance into the Roman period, we get the impression that even the traditional temple worship of Egypt was losing some of its vitality'.[73] Outwardly, all was the same. Sacrifices were still offered with due formality. The festivals were observed, the animal deities, such as Petsouchos the Crocodile-god still recruited their priests. But a certain formalism and lifelessness was becoming apparent. Mum-

mies were often embalmed in a perfunctory fashion, the symbolism on the mummy-cases shows that the original religious meaning of the signs was becoming lost. Hieroglyphic inscriptions
degenerated. Decius' is the last emperor's name that occurs in
hieroglyphic writing on the walls of an Egyptian temple, that of
the god Khnum at Esna. The last known hieroglyphic stele
represents Diocletian making an offering to the bull Buchis at
Erement in 295.[74] It is not perhaps surprising that one reads of
tombs and deserted temples of Serapis, hitherto the object of great
popular devotion,[75] affording shelter to monastic saints in the
fourth century. Finally, whereas in the 170s popular opposition to
Rome was still led by priests, a century later it was represented by
the monks.[76]

In Asia Minor too, the third century sees a decline in the popular
religion of the countryside. Ramsay believed that the old Phrygian
religion had degenerated into a superstition before the century
was out, and that educated men and women were therefore
prepared to listen to the new Christian preaching.[77] Certainly,
the oracle of Apollo at Didyma seems to have been demoralized
by the power of Christian influence when the emissary of Diocletian and Galerius visited his tripods in 302/303;[78] Lactantius also,
suggests that the ferocity of the persecution which he witnessed
in Bithynia in 303–305 was due to pagan fears that 'as justice
grows strong from day to day, they (the pagans) should be
deserted altogether with their decaying (cariosis) gods'.[79] However, cult organizations such as the Tekmoreian brotherhood
flourished on the Imperial estates around Pisidian Antioch in the
late third century,[80] and one shrine at least, that of Mén at
Colonia Caesarea near the same city retained its worshippers until
early in the next century.[81] Indeed, the more obvious signs of
collapse, such as the wholesale abandonment of temples, the
transfer of temple lands to the Church, and the absorption of
priestly families into Christianity, did not come about until the
second quarter of the fourth century.[82] Julian watched the
process as a despairing eye-witness (Letter 89, ed. Bidez).

In Africa, the erstwhile national deity of both Carthaginians
and Berbers, Saturn (Baal-Hammon), seems to have forfeited
most of his popularity sometime before the more Romanized
cults which flourished in the cities lost theirs.[83] No dedication

to him has been found dated later than A.D. 272, and though in itself this might not be very significant, the next dated religious inscriptions in the same area (Sillègue in Mauretania, A.D. 299 and 324) are Christian and continue to be so from then onwards.[84] There was no revival of interest in Saturn under the Tetrarchy, such as the Roman gods experienced in some of the North African towns. At Cuicul also in Mauretania, dedications in Saturn's honour were even being used as paving stones in the fourth century.[85] The cult had died out. Arnobius too, gives some interesting information as to the low ebb to which pagan religious observance had fallen. Pagans even were blaming themselves for the neglect of their own cults and the consequent advance of Christian propaganda. Despite all the efforts of the Tetrarchy, observers could see that 'the ancient ceremonies were being held in derision'.[86] When Constantine wrote to Miltiades of Rome in 314 concerning the Donatist schism, he appears to treat Africa as Christian, but divided between the Catholics and their opponents.[87] Paganism had lost contact with the people.

Quite apart from the evidence for the decline in the popularity of the main pagan cults, some facts point to the actual conversion of the rural areas to Christianity. For Egypt the testimony of Eusebius is impressive. He was an eye-witness of the final ferocious stages of Maximin's persecution in 311–312. He stresses that Christians formed the majority of the population, and that while the evil spirit of idolatry was striving to keep the Egyptians in a ferment, 'thousands' were deserting 'hereditary superstition'— 'and anyone who is not wholly lacking in vision can see that'.[88] Fifty years before, Dionysius of Alexandria had stated that though Christianity had made some progress in the countryside there were still places near Alexandria which had not heard the name of Christ.[89] Eusebius, however, claimed circa 313, 'His altars were now in every town and village', and this had 'happened in our time'.[90] Later, in the 330s the scandal of the broken chalice shows that there were both Catholic and Meletian parishes in the villages of Mareotis.[91]

That this represents a real movement in native Egyptian opinion seems clear from events in the Great Persecution where, as in rural North Africa, the repression of Christianity inspired amazing feats of courage and endurance. For the Thebaid (Upper

Egypt) Eusebius says, 'sometimes more than ten, at other times above twenty persons were put to death: and at other times above thirty, now nearer sixty, and again at other times a hundred men would be slain in a single day along with quite young children and women, being condemned to manifold punishments which followed one on the other'.[92] Yet there were always volunteers for martyrdom. That Egyptian confessors were numerous is shown by the fact that in 308 parties of more than 100 each were being sent up north to work in the mines of Palestine and Cilicia, as though there were sufficient in those of the Thebaid.[93] All efforts to crush the Church proved vain, and in the mind of the Copt, the 'era of the martyrs' replaced the official 'era of Diocletian', a symbol of national resistance.

In Egypt we find two religious movements, both non-Greco-Roman in character, gaining ground in the countryside at the same time, namely monasticism and Manichaeism. Though their adherents hated each other, they had much in common, and drew support from the same groups of self-consciously Coptic Egyptians.[94] We may place Antony's flight from his ancestral village in the *nome* of Heracleopolis Magna in Upper Egypt into the desert in about 270, and he was not the only hermit of the time. Fifteen years later he forsook even the company of local hermits for the Arabian mountains where he remained until the Great Persecution twenty years later. This part of Egypt was particularly suitable for withdrawal, since the eastern desert was crossed here by caravan routes leading to the Red Sea ports. The hermit could avoid contact with normal life while leaving himself means for supplying his basic needs.[95] Similar conditions applied in the other cradles of monasticism, Palestine and eastern Syria[96]— but not in North Africa.

Meantime, Mani's disciples Papus and Thomas had penetrated as far as Upper Egypt and were presenting a message of the strictest asceticism and cosmological dualism coupled with Docetic Christology in rivalry to the Christian mission.[97] These Manichaean missionaries were successful enough to draw a searing denunciation from Theonas (?) bishop of Alexandria in an encyclical letter towards the end of the century,[98] and the unsympathetic attention of the Neo-Platonist, Alexander of Lycopolis (Assiut) at the same period.[99] How closely, however, the Manichees were impinging on Christianity and swaying the minds of individual Coptic Christians is evident from the career of Hieracas. Though Epiphanius places him in a category of heresy of his own next to Manichaeism, he stood sufficiently near to the parent sect to be included among those teachers whose works the convert from Manichaeism had to renounce before reception into the Church. He was a Copt from Leontopolis, more at home in his own language than in Greek, and at the time when Antony was living in the desert, he was teaching the ascetic groups he founded the typical encratite precepts of abstinence from marriage, wine and animal food, together with a denial of the resurrection of the body.[100] It was evidently on ground well prepared by the acceptance of encratism leading to the hoped-for liberation of the soul (not the resurrection of the body) that the Manichees won their hold in rural Egypt. The presence of their communities was to form an important element in the background of the Arian controversy. In the fourth century what every Egyptian Christian leader feared most was the denunciation of 'Manichaeism'.

In North Africa also there is little doubt regarding the extension of Christianity in the countryside between 260–303. Already, in Cyprian's time, there were bishoprics in the rural areas of Numidia and Mauretania. For instance, at the great Council of 256, there was a bishop from Octava, a *locus* or village in southern Numidia which, less than a century later, was to be a centre of Circumcellion activity.[101] During the next forty years the Christian message was carried further abroad. Christian inscriptions of the period 265–275 have come from near Sitifis[102] and Satafi[103] in Mauretania, and from the garrison centre of Numerus Syrorum[104] in the far west of the province. We know of a number of rural or semi-rural bishoprics in 300, which do not appear to have existed in 256. These include Tigisis, a prosperous overgrown village north-west of Constantine, and the see of Secundus, primate of Numidia in 303, Limata, Garba, Casae Nigrae on the edge of the Sahara, Legisvolumen, and Rotaria probably in central Numidia.[105] If one estimates the number of bishoprics in Africa as about 110 in Cyprian's time, and takes into account that 270 bishops attended Donatus' Council at Carthage in 336, one would agree with Harnack that the number of sees may have doubled between 260–303,[106] and further, that the greatest gains were made in the countryside.

North African opinion was changing gradually but irrevocably in favour of the Church. As late as 259, for instance, Cirta (Constantine) and the countryside surrounding had not been safe for Christians.[107] An hostile mob had hounded the confessors Marianus and Jacobus before the city magistrates.[108] In the succeeding half-century all this had changed. Even before the Persecution ended, the same city of Cirta was the scene of formidable Christian demonstrations. From the countryside there streamed in a variegated army of labourers and quarrymen who joined with the lower orders and the women of the town to force the sub-deacon Silvanus on to the reluctant burghers as their bishop.[109] Assured of such support, the presbyterate was a post worth having and Victor the fuller was ready to pay 20 *folles* there and then for his election.[110] Farther south, the strength of the cult of martyrs was to reach phenomenal proportions. Swarms of churches dedicated to the saints were to spring up in the Numidian villages during the fourth century.[111] The *Praeses*, Valerius Florus, governor of Numidia during the Great Persecution, played the part of the persecuting villain in a century of Numidian folk-legend.[112] But the countryside north of the Timgad–Mascula road must already have been Christian in 303 for this legend to come into being.

Similar developments were taking place in Asia Minor. In the north, in western Pontus, Gregory's mission was resumed after the decade of persecution and Gothic invasion, apparently with complete success. By his death in 272 it seems that paganism was broken in much of the province. He had shown Christianity as an active force for the good of ordinary people.[113] Farther south in Phrygia, the remarkable series of inscriptions, some of which are dated between 249–279 show a rural population on some of the Imperial estates, especially north of Dorylaeum, openly proclaiming their Christian faith. The call 'from Christians to Christians' on nine out of fifteen early Christian epitaphs is unrestrained and clear.[114] They are mostly large inscriptions and the favourite designs on them are of everyday objects, such as a weaving comb, a plough, or a sickle, illustrative perhaps of the society from which these Christians were drawn. On some of these inscriptions also the Latin Cross has been included prominently in the design. One of these may be dated to about A.D. 275.[115] Two others indicate that the deceased was probably a convert.[116]

Finally, on the Empire's eastern frontier Christianity had also been making progress. As early as the 240s Mani had compared Christianity in these parts with Buddhism in north India as the predominant religion.[117] The martyrdom, probably under Decius, of Sharbil, high priest of Bel and Nebo but converted to Christianity by Bishop Barzyma, may be taken as a symptom of a movement towards the new religion.[118] In the next half-century the traditional astral deities which Sharbil had represented were increasingly ousted from popular favour, and in the Great Persecution the official worship of the emperors and 'this Zeus', were regarded as foreign cults which the mass of the people had rejected in favour either of Christ or, as in rural Egypt, Mani.[119]

What had caused these changes? People do not forsake ancestral deities who have guarded their tribe for generations without profound and searching reasons. The abandonment of the age-old sanctuary of Saturn outside the Numidian village or that of Cybele in rural Phrygia, or the astral deities in Edessa, must have been a momentous step in the lives of the inhabitants. Religious syncretism was certainly one cause. Both in Africa and Asia Minor local gods tended to be absorbed into an amorphous, Romanized pantheon, and thus to lose their particular loyalties and associations. Aurelius Antoninus styled on an Eumeneia inscription 'ἱερεύς τῶν τε θεῶν πάντων' (priest of all the gods) could easily degenerate into priest of none.[120] The same fate awaited a priest of Saturn at Idicra near Cirta whose allegiance was divided with Silvanus, Mercury, Fortuna, Victoria and the *Dii Mauri*.[121] Arnobius, significantly enough, pours scorn on such diffuseness, and he may have reflected contemporary opinion.[122] The craving for a redemptive religion was real. It could not be satisfied by these rootless and compromise deities.

Another clue is that given by the Emperor Julian in a letter to Theodorus, High Priest of Asia in 362. He observes that, 'It was the sight of their undeserved misery that led the people to despise the gods'. It was not, however, 'the gods who were responsible for their poverty but rather our own insatiable greed. It was that which gave men a false idea of the gods, and in addition, was an unjust reproach against them'.[123] But even so, people could not expect the rains sent by the gods to fall as gold among them. In contrast, Julian points out to Arsacius, Theodorus' colleague in Galatia, how Christian social and ascetic ideals had attracted the mass of the provincials to the faith. 'Why do we not observe', he says, 'that it is their benevolence to strangers, their care for the graves of the dead, and the pretended holiness of their lives that have done most to increase atheism (Christianity).[124] Julian, as we know from his critic Gregory of Nazianze.[125] took his role as a social reformer very seriously, and he implies that the Anatolians failed to secure earthly σωτηρία from the traditional gods and turned to Christianity instead. The movement, however, had started earlier. An interesting inscription dated by Anderson to the early years of the fourth century describes the Phrygian presbyter Aquila as 'minister of God's service, beloved by the angels, a leader of the people (λαοῦ προστάμενον) wont to entertain just thoughts'.[126] How these 'just thoughts' could be interpreted might be shown by another, late fourth-century memorial to a Lycaonian presbyter which records that his fair dealing, simplicity, open-heartedness and good family life were the qualities expected of a parish priest and led to the bearer rising to high influence in the service of his community.[127] The tradition of social action inherited from Judaism and displayed on numberless occasions throughout the first three centuries was now contributing powerfully to the victory of the Church. The Christian presbyter was displacing the traditional priest-ruler as leader of the people.[128]

Moreover, from the middle of the third century onwards the code of conduct implied in Tertullian's 'Look how they love one another' had become increasingly relevant.[129] Changes in the social and economic situation in the Empire had been profound and affected the lives of the provincials in very many ways. First and most obviously, was the reversal of living standards compared with those prevailing earlier in the century. The overheads of city administration, such as fountains, paved streets, public water closets, organized markets and even public order could only be maintained in an era of continuous prosperity. Long-term credit facilities were lacking. One year's debts had to be paid out of one year's income. By 250, the public services were running down and the result was plague, bankruptcy and

demoralization.[130] It may not be entirely true that when the
Tetrarchy took over government towns in the west were 'overgrown with bushes and the haunt of wild boars',[131] but sufficient
inscriptions have been found in North Africa alone which point
to a period of urban neglect and decay in the decades before Diocletian.[132] Elsewhere, even at Athens, the barbarian invasions
had left their mark in permanently declining standards of urban
life, and squalor.[133] In Alexandria even, a large part of the population had left the city on account of the civil war of 260–262.[134]
Diocletian's restoration of the cities as fiscal and administrative
centres was an expensive attempt to put the clock back, and it
added to the cost of his other reforms.

There was also the effect of barbarian invasion. Both Upper
Egypt and the plains of Mauretania Sitifensis and Numidia were
sufferers. No one can estimate exactly the misery and desperation
caused by the attacks of the Blemmyes, but from 250 onwards
these savage and destructive barbarians who had once been
vassals of the Meroitic kings were raiding far into Upper Egypt
and for a time occupied Coptos and Ptolemais.[135] To judge from
the royal tombs found at Q'astal and Ballana, near the modern
Sudanese border, their ruthlessness was equalled only by their
appetite for loot.[136] The Romans regarded them with horror, and
with good reason.[137] In Africa the Quinquegentani played the same
part as the Blemmyes as agents of destruction. Their containment
and ultimate overthrow in a series of campaigns by the Emperor
Maximian 289–297, however, added greatly to the burdens of the
provincials.[138]

Nearly all these charges were borne ultimately by the peasants,
who not only had to provide the bulk of the quota of taxes demanded from the city territoria, but also must supply the annona
for the 'honourable soldiers'[139] settled in the province, as well as
providing the army with its recruits, maintaining the cursus publicus
and the provincial road system.[140] Prices too, were moving against
them. To quote the examples given by A. Segrè for Egypt,[141] the
price of a she-ass, always the essential beast of burden in the countryside in the whole of the Mediterranean area, had risen in
nominal value about twenty times between the Antonine period
and that of Probus (276–282). In 277 it cost no less than 3800
drachmae.[142] An artaba of wheat which cost 16 drachmae (old

currency) in 255–264, cost 120 drachmae in 277 and in 301, $1333\frac{1}{2}$ drachmae.[143] In a society where barter reinforced by copper coinage of various degrees of antiquity and nominal value would be the general rule, these changes might not have been so disastrous as they appear. But it can hardly be an accident that the late third century provides evidence for violent outbreaks of peasant discontent in provinces as far apart as Gaul and Egypt. The Gallic Bagaudae first come into history in 269 and rebelled again in 286, and in Egypt the revolt of Achilleus in 296/297 received strong rural support.

As one would expect, Egypt provides evidence of how these changes were affecting the relations between various groups in society. When probably some time in the reign of Diocletian, the senate at Oxyrhynchus met to elect a substitute for a public banker who had been unsatisfactory, there were no takers for the office. The president (prytanis) tried to persuade Ptolemaeus who was already a chief priest to accept. Ptolemaeus protested, 'I entreat you, I cannot serve. I am a man of moderate means. I live in my father's house . . . the office is beyond my powers'. None the less, he was elected 'on account of his good faith'.[144] No refusal was accepted. He could only decamp, as the officials in charge of the collection of wine, and of barley had already done shortly before. The second papyrus, dated 251, indicates the repercussions of the progressive impoverishment of the towns on the villagers. This papyrus records a law suit instituted by villagers in the nome of Arsinoe justifying their refusal to undertake a costly charge imposed on them by the town, on the grounds that they had been immune from such burdens under the terms of an edict of Septimius Severus. The following revealing dialogue took place:

> *Serenus* (counsel for the senate of Arsinoe) 'To the law of Severus, I will say, Severus ordained the law in Egypt while the cities were still prosperous.'
> *The Prefect* 'The argument from prosperity, or rather, the decline from prosperity, is equal both for the villages and the cities.'[145]

To this blissful ignorance of elementary economics were added the cumulative effects of the military, administrative and financial reforms carried out by the Tetrarchy. Many of the reforms were intelligent reactions to a situation which was already in being; others, such as the increase in the number of provincial units from 47 to 87, measures of self-protection against the revival of the military pronunciamentos of the previous thirty years.[146] But all made for heavier taxation.[147] When in the 290s an empire-wide census was carried out to assess human and property values on a new and perhaps more equitable and rational scale, it seems to have often been administered with a cruelty and venality which shocked contemporaries.[148] On 16 March 297 during the final stages of the revolt of Achilleus, the Prefect of Egypt, Aristius Optatus issued an edict, in connection with the introduction of *iugatio* and *capitatio*, and admitted that 'fiscal burdens had been levied in such a manner as to let some taxpayers off lightly while overcharging others'.[149] As A. H. M. Jones points out,[150] the level of taxes was not exorbitant as the result of the reforms. In fact, in the reign of Constantius II, the level was regarded as '*modestia tolerabilis*' contrasted with the '*pernicies*' then prevailing,[151] but distribution could be regarded as unfair as between area and area and man and man. The assessment varied greatly in exactitude in the different dioceses of the Empire. In Oriens (Syria and Palestine) for example, there was an elaborate system of land classification according to its use as pasture, arable, vines or olives, and land was graded in quality within these classes. But in Asiana (south-west Asia Minor) Italy, North Africa and Egypt, the system was much more rough and ready. Land was assessed by area, making little or no allowance for use or quality. Moreover, landowners were often forced to take up poor land which was then included in their assessment.[152] Thus, burdens which could be accepted as equitable in areas of good or average land, might well absorb the whole rent of less fortunate areas. In such areas the tenants either had to flee their holdings or sink ever deeper into debt. In Egypt and North Africa, the reaction was revolt expressed primarily in religious terms.

Already some discontent was finding its way into various forms of religious propaganda. Another papyrus of the late third century preserves the text of a long oracle depicting woes befalling Egypt and rejoicing in the humiliation of the 'city by the sea' (Alexandria) 'ἡ τε παραθαλάσσιος πόλις.' As the commentators suggest, it may be interpreted as 'an anti-Greek production by the "poor white" class of Greeks and Greco-Egyptians who did not belong to the Greek cities and πολιτεύματα'. It shows that by now little conscious bond existed between the wealthier Hellene class represented by the Greeks in Alexandria and the rest of the population, regardless whether they spoke Greek or Coptic. To such people the Roman administration would seem even more remote and malevolent,[153] and to the Roman governing class of the next century an Egyptian was often synonymous with a revolutionary.[154] In Asia Minor too, evidence is provided by Lactantius for a revival of anti-Roman and pro-Persian oracle literature of the type which had been widespread among Jews and Christians in the first and second centuries.[155] It indicates the presence there of similar widespread discontent as in Egypt, and that this also was searching for an outlet in the guise of anti-Greco-Roman religion.

It was at this point that the appeal of Christianity became relevant. Its social message did not indeed make the Gallic Bagaudae Christian. Elsewhere, however, where it had already demonstrated its power of survival and was advancing for other reasons this became important. To some extent it had always attracted people who had felt a grievance against society and the traditional religions that protected society's institutions. Now it began to give coherence and direction to those who saw in the reforms of the Tetrarchy nothing more than a system of unlimited extortion and oppression. Lactantius' *De Mortibus Persecutorum* provides some evidence for this development. The unrestrained torrent of protest against the Tetrarchy and its reforms comes curiously from this African emigrant to Bithynia who was far from the Cyprianic, let alone the Tertullianist tradition, who believed in *Romanitas* and in aristocratic government as completely as some of his opponents, and who was familiar with the ways of Diocletian's capital. Lactantius was no Commodian, yet he describes in flaming anger and biting sarcasm the inhumanities that resulted from the compilation of the census. 'Only beggars from whom nothing could be exacted', escaped the measures of 'this pious man' (Diocletian). 'Neither age nor infirmity was accepted as an excuse. Old men and the sick were forced to appear. The age of each was estimated, years being added on to that of children and deducted from that of the aged', i.e. there was large-scale administrative chicane by officials, the 'multiplicity of whose bureaux crushed every province and nearly every city'.[156] Lactantius was a convert, he had a passion for the abstract idea of justice and there is no doubt that he linked the social injustices of the Tetrarchs with their paganism. Other Africans seem to have done likewise, including those whose inability to pay their debts to the Treasury was to lead them to defy the authorities in 303 and offer themselves for martyrdom.[157] Looking further on in the fourth century, the African martyr's *agon* against the persecuting powers became avowedly extended to fighting the results of debt and extortion in the countryside. Fasir and Axido, the Numidian *'duces sanctorum'* in the 340s demonstrated the connection between the forces of religious and social discontent in the countryside at this period.[158]

In Egypt, we have already seen that the Copts suffered harshly from increased taxes and extortions by local officials and soldiers. Apart from outright rebellion, the traditional form of rural protest, to flee one's holding and village increased. 'Shall I take to flight?', 'Am I to become a member of a municipal council?', 'Shall my flight end?'—such were among the questions addressed to an oracle at Oxyrhynchus in the late third century.[159] As Athanasius pointed out in the *Life of Antony*,[160] flight from the world included flight from the tax-gatherers and unjust judges. The same term, *anachoresis*, was used in Egypt to describe flight in face of debt and flight to fulfil a religious vocation. Devils and tax-collectors were sometimes combined in composite representations of evil.[161] In the first half of the fourth century the great monasteries that grew up under the Pachomian rule were economic units producing some essential goods cheaply[162] as well as centres of prayer and ascetism. We may perhaps agree with K. Heussi that 'the very success of the monasteries denoted widespread misery in the countryside whence these recruits were drawn'.[163]

It would be a mistake, however, to think of the rural populations in these provinces as utterly impoverished and hopeless. The abandonment of the old outworn gods and acceptance of Christianity coincides with important cultural and artistic developments. During the third century, the native in Syria, Egypt and Phrygia seems to have turned from copying Greco-Roman sculpture and even speech to reviving his own traditions drawn from the pre-classical or even prehistoric past, and these were then developed as the means of expressing a new religious allegiance. Coptic, the lineal descendant of Pharaonic Egyptian probably first used on magical papyri became the script and language of native Christian Egypt.[164] Africa and perhaps Isauria produced vigorous movements of native Christian art.[165] As Gauckler commented long ago regarding Africa, 'in the domain of art as well as that of politics the triumph of the Church assures the victory of the native over the foreign'.[166] The victory of Christianity in the Mediterranean lands of the Roman Empire was not an isolated event. It accompanied other tendencies which amounted to a rejection of Classicism and a renewal of native, pre-Roman ways of life, which the decline of the city as the unit of culture and administration had allowed to emerge. In Africa and Syria the economic basis for this Christianized native civilization was to be provided by the expansion of olive oil production which was centred in the villages. As so often in revolutionary movements, the Christian protest spread among populations which were prosperous and articulate enough to feel a sense of grievance and were prepared to break with their immediate past in order to express it.[167]

This great movement of Christian expansion was to ensure the defeat of the Great Persecution. At the same time, however, it was to complicate vastly the disciplinary and doctrinal problems which were already dividing the Church. The influx of rural Christians, inspired by strong motives of rejection of Greco-Roman culture, took place just at the moment when the Church represented by its urban congregations was coming to terms with that culture. In all the provinces which we have been discussing there was latent tension between the ideas of the new rural Christians and those of the settled and long-established congregations. In Africa the views of the latter were being expressed within a few years of Cyprian's death in Pontius' *Vita Cypriani* and the *Acta Martyrum* relating to the persecution under Valerian. In these works, one can detect a bias against the prevailing glorification of low-born and lay martyrs, and instead, Christians were recommended the virtues of sacerdotal meekness.[168] After complaining that it was hard to tolerate so much honour having been paid in the past to plebeians and catechumens,[169] Pontius claimed that Cyprian's 'opera et merita' would have gained him his reward in their own right even if he had not been martyred,[170] and further, that flight from the world, sale goods to the poor, and estrangement from one's earthly city provided an alternative road to perfection to martyrdom.[171]

Moreover, the continuous elaboration of ecclesiastical administration which had taken place in Cyprian's time, involving liaison over great distances with only poor communications, resulted in a further increase in the power of the diaconate[172] and the emergence of an *archidiaconus* as the bishop's right-hand man and heir presumptive.[173] This might have led to better understanding between town and country, or between Numidia and Carthage. In the event it did not, for in the person of Caecilian, the *archidiaconus* busied himself in damping down irregular enthusiasms in the Carthaginian congregation, and in seeing that the Cyprianic quality 'temperies'[174] led to order, stability and peace with the world.

This was not the object of a large number of the new Christians. Typical perhaps is the story of the confessor Victoria and her two companions who deliberately left Carthage early in the Great Persecution for the township of Abitina 150 miles up country, where they evidently had heard that there were 'brethren who kept the precepts of God'.[175] These brethren were numerous enough in Numidia and farther west in Mauretania. Even Secundus of Tigisis, vacillating and irresolute in face of danger though he was, accepted the Maccabees as the example for a Christian to follow[176] and boasted himself a follower of Eleazar the priest. Many regarded Scripture as the literal 'word of God', the 'verbum Dei' of John 1¹,[177] and their anger would know no bounds when they heard that complacent priests in Carthage and Rome had betrayed it to idolators. The anti-worldly asceticism and anti-militarism too, of young Christians such as Victoria and Maximilian, the latter presumably a villager from somewhere near Theveste, shows that the old puritan tradition of the African Church was by no means dead. Anti-militarism had divided African Christians in Tertullian's time,[178] and was to continue to do so for another twenty years after Maximilian's execution in 295.[179] Farther away in the west, the dedication of Euelpius of Caesarea, though not securely dated, sums up on one inscription the aspirations of these African Christians. The Christians he knew were 'cultores Verbi' (worshippers of the Word), an 'ecclesia fratruum'—as in Tertullian's day, and the centre of their religious life was the *cella* or shrine set in the midst of the Christian *area*.[180] Separation from the world remained complete.

In parts of Asia Minor similar tendencies were at work. Here puritan schism in the countryside was already more than a century old. In the 250s it had been powerfully reinforced by Novatian's missionaries who soon gained a hearing and converts throughout western Asia Minor.[181] The χριστιανοί-χριστιανοῖς inscriptions of the Tembris Valley and elsewhere may reasonably be attributed to this tradition.[182] As Calder has pointed out, 'the open profession' formula reflects a very different school of thought from the adaptation, even with biblical reminiscences, of a pagan formula consigning tomb-robbers to the wrath of heaven. The 'Eumeneian' 'he shall have to reckon with (the living) God' was not needlessly provocative to pagans. Those who used it in the towns of central and eastern Phrygia in the latter half of the third century were to all intents good citizens, including magistrates and leaders of their communities.[183] The 'Christians to Christians' dedicators on the other hand, were ready to boast their faith and claim the virtues of militancy and asceticism.[184] As in Africa these were virtues which appealed to the young and ardent, men like Apphianus of Lycia who abandoned his home and his wealthy parents to become an ascetic and later to challenge paganism in Palestine,[185] and Ammia who was ready to 'offer her virginity to Christ', and who seems to have found the Novatians as most expressive of the Christian ideal,[186] and Novatianist she remained despite the opposition of her family.[187] Here too, the old bottles of stable Christian order were being threatened by irrepressible ferments characteristic of the new generation of Christians.

In Egypt and in parts of Syria, the 'forty years of peace' also saw native Christianity develop along its own regional lines. Antony was a born philistine, in his early years despising education[188] and, later on, any religion based on dialectic arguments. He considered the Bible 'sufficient for instruction' as a means of routing demons.[189] There were twenty years of his career, between 285 and 305, when he could not have partaken of a

Eucharist administered by a priest.[190] Considerations of hierarchy, public worship and an ordered liturgy played only a
subordinate part in his thought. The religion which he and his
disciples were practising was not anti-hierarchical, however; it
was non-hierarchical involving complete rejection of the world
and its institutions, including Christian institutions. So far were
some of Antony's contemporaries, converts among the Egyptian
confessors, to carry this ideal during the Great Persecution that
when they were asked their names by the Governor of Palestine at
Caesarea, while en route to the Cilician mines, they refused to give
them since they recalled the names of idols.[191] Instead, they
assigned themselves Old Testament names such as Elijah, Jeremiah, Isaiah, Samuel and Daniel. Like the African Donatists, the
early Egyptian ascetics lived in the Bible alone.

Here was an outlook quite different from the reigning Logos-
theology of Alexandria. In the 260s Dionysius of Alexandria had
controverted Bishop Nepos of Arsinoe's millenarist interpretation
of Revelation and rejected his protest against the allegorization of
Scripture.[192] In a work of critical scholarship equal to anything
prior to the modern historical school he had demolished the view
that the Apocalypse could be the work of the writer of the Fourth
Gospel.[193] He had no hesitation in associating material apocalyptic
hopes with Scriptural interpretation 'after a Jewish fashion'. A
generation later Eusebius of Caesarea was to be only a little more
tolerant of Papias.[194] But Nepos was speaking for the rural
Christians with whom he was working in the Arsinoitenome, and
who were prepared to go into schism rather than accept Dionysius'
interpretations of Scripture.[195] The Bible, together perhaps with
reminiscences from the Book of the Dead, inspired them too with
hopes of material betterment hereafter in compensation for the
evils of their present life. How the predominant Logos-theology
of the Greek Christian intellectual in Alexandria and Caesarea
was to be reconciled with the Spirit-inspired hopes of the converted Copt was an open question. To have grappled with it
successfully is one of Athanasius' claims to genius.

On the eve of the Great Persecution, therefore, all over the
Mediterranean world, the gap between the *ecclesia episcoporum*
and the Greco-Roman State was closing. Whether one reads the
canons of Elvira with their catalogue of vices and shortcomings

of well-to-do Christians and their clergy,[196] whether the testimony of the prudent believers of Eumeneia, or of the commercial activities of Bishop Maximus of Alexandria, the story is the same. Church and world were about to come to terms. The Great Persecution was a catastrophe which only delayed this development and with Constantine's conversion the tide of events flowed evenly once more. In the countryside, however, a profound religious reformation was taking place. Anger against extortion, fiscal injustices and oppression of all kinds were rekindling the flames of millenarist and apocalyptic hopes. The rural Christian presbyter who acted as spokesman for his people did not necessarily speak the same secular or ecclesiastical language as his urban contemporary. Church unity would have been hard to maintain even without the shock of persecution. Religion was being caught up with emergent social problems within each province and with inter-regional rivalries. If Athanasius had conceded an *iota* to Arius, Coptic Egypt might have gone Meletian just as Africa went Donatist. All the time, the doctrinal and personal rancours that had marked Church history in the third century slumbered, and festered. Eusebius describes the situation in which he had grown up.

> But when, as the result of greater freedom, a change to pride and sloth came over our affairs, we fell to envy and fierce railing against one another, warring upon ourselves, so to speak, as occasion offered, with weapons and spears formed of words; and rulers attacked rulers and laity formed factions against laity, while unspeakable hypocrisy and pretence pursued their evil course to the furthest end.[197]

He was describing a world ripe for religious change, but not for religious peace.

NOTES

[1] See the present author's art. 'A note on the influence of Greek merchants on the Spread of Christianity in the West', *Mullus* (= *Festschrift Theodor Klauser*), *J.A.C.* (Ergänzungsband, 1, 1964) 125–30.

[2] Eusebius, *H.E.*, vii.23.3. (Dionysius' loyalism in the cause of Gallienus).

[3] *H.E.*, vii.32–6.

4 Details, J. F. Bethune-Baker, *Early History of Christian Doctrine* (9th ed. 1951), ch. viii, and K. Müller, 'Kleine Beiträge zur alten Kirchengeschichte 10, Dionys von Alexandrien im Kampf mit den libyschen Sabellianern', *ZNTW.*, 24, 1925, 278-85. Müller makes clear that the controversy had gone on throughout the period of persecution, a factor suggesting that this was less disruptive of inter-Church relations in Egypt and Cyrenaica than a reading of Eusebius alone would lead us to imagine.

5 Porphyry, *Vita Plotini* (ed. and tr. S. MacKenna), 1.12.

6 The project failed, however, owing to alleged intrigues at court. Prophyry, loc. cit.

7 Eusebius, *H.E.*, vii.15. There is no reason to put the event in the interlude of Macrianus' and Quietus' reign (260–261). It was a simple question of discipline. Marinus' offence was similar to that of the *optio* whom Tertullian records in the *De Corona* or of the other African military martyrs in the period 295–300. The fact was, that the centurion as the officer in command of a detachment of troops would have to perform religious functions on ceremonial occasions, such as the anniversary of the Emperor's accession, and this Marinus as a Christian would not do. Other Christian officers less scrupulous, would find ways round the dilemma at this period. See W. M. Calder's remarks. *Expositor*, 7th Series, vi. 1908, 396–400.

8 Implied in the words, 'αὐτῷ δὲ ἐπιβάλλεν τὸν κλῆρον'.

9 Note Eusebius' complaint that the incident took place in a period of 'universal peace for the Churches', 'εἰρήνης ἀπανταχοῦ τῶν ἐκκλησιῶν οὔσης', *H.E.*, vii.15.1.

10 Unless, as Harnack suggests, Porphyry, writing his κατὰ χριστιανῶν *circa* 270, might have regarded himself as an interpreter of Claudius' ideas, *ABAW.*, 1916, Phil. Hist. Kl., p. 1.

11 Mattingly and Sydenham, op. cit., v, 1, 290, no. 235; cf. 'restitutor orbis' on a North African milestone, *CIL.*, viii, 10217 and Mattingly and Sydenham, op. cit., v, 1, pp. 264, and 299, no. 305ff.

12 The best account of Aurelian's reign is still that of L. Homo, 'Essai sur le règne de l'Empereur Aurélien', Paris, 1904 (= Fasc. 89 of *Bibl. des Ecoles françaises d'Athènes et de Rome*). Also H. Mattingly, 'The Imperial Recovery', in *CAH.*, xii, ch. ix.

13 Eusebius, *H.E.*, vii.30.20. Eusebius' view that Aurelian changed his mind as his reign advanced and became hostile towards Christianity seems to be corroborated.

14 H. Grégoire, *Les Persécutions*, 60; cf. F. Cumont, *Les Religions Orientales*, 367.

15 See *Acta Archelai* (ed. Beeson, *GCS.*, 1906), 56 and 60.

16 Eusebius, *H.E.*, vii.30.19.

17 He was, of course, wrong, as the synodical letter of 268 had been addressed jointly to Rome and Alexandria, *H.E.*, vii.30.1.

18 The text reads, 'οἷς ἂν οἱ κατὰ τὴν Ἰταλίαν καὶ τὴν Ῥωμαίων πόλιν ἐπίσκοποι τοῦ δόγματος ἐπιστέλλοιεν' (*H.E.*, vii.30.19). There is no reason to see with G. Bardy, *Paul de Samosate*, 363, any recognition of 'the unique place that the Church of Rome held in the eyes of Christians'—unless one includes the 'bishops in Italy' as well!

19 L. Homo, *Essai sur le Règne de l'Empereur Aurélien*, Paris, 1904, ch. v, and see also N. H. Baynes' trenchant note in *JRS.*, xxv, 1935, 83–4.

20 *SHA.*, Vopiscus, *Vita Aureliani*, 18.5 and 21.4.

21 On the significance of the orb handed by the gods to the Caesars as 'masters of the κόσμος', see A. Strong, *JRS.*, vi, 1916, 35ff.

22 This would not be unexpected, for there could not be two authorities in the world claiming to be 'deus et dominus'. Phrases that occur regularly on third-century inscriptions, such as 'devoti numini eius', or 'devotus numini maiestatique eius', were not lacking in religious significance either to the emperors or the provincials. Had Aurelian lived, the Great Persecution might have been anticipated by a quarter of a century. Eusebius, *H.E.*, vii.32.6. Lactantius, *De Mortibus Persecutorum*, 6. See, for references and comments, J. Moreau's ed. (Sources chrétiennes, 39), 226–31, and W. Ensslin, *CAH.*, xii, 358–9.

23 For an earlier date for Aurelian's murder (April 275) based on numismatic evidence, H. Mattingly, *CAH.*, xii, pp. 309–10.

24 Listed and discussed by L. Homo, op. cit., 375–7.

25 H. Delehaye, *Les Passions des Martyrs*, 81.

26 These *Acta*, are discussed in detail by J. van der Straeten, 'Actes des Martyrs d'Aurélien en Gaule', *A.B.*, lxxxx, 1962, p. 117ff. If the earlier date for Aurelian's death is accepted, it would be easier to reconcile the martyrs' *natales* from January to May with their death in persecution.

27 H. Grégoire, *Académie royale de Bruxelles* (Bull. de la Cl. des Lettres) 38, 1952, 163ff. Below, n. 183.

28 W. M. Calder, 'Early Christian epitaphs from Phrygia', *Anatolian Studies*, v, 1955, 37–8.

29 Eusebius, *H.E.*, viii.1.1.

30 Canon 6. See Wm. Bright's valuable note, *Notes on the Canons of the First Four General Councils*, Oxford, 1882, 17ff.

31 Eusebius, *H.E.*, vii.30.8ff.

32 L. Duchesne, 'Note sur la topographie de Rome au moyen age. II. Les Titres presbytéraux et les diaconies', *Mélanges*, vii, 1887, 218–20, differentiating these from the deaconaries founded by Pope Fabian. For the suggested organization of *tituli* by Pope Marcellus after the end of the Persecution, below, p. 534, n. 277. For the status of the *tituli* A. H. M. Jones, *The Later Roman Empire*, 284–602, Oxford, 1964, 900.

33 Basil, *Ep.* 70.

34 See short art. by E. Venables *D.C.B.*, i.111.

35 Why eventually he had to make his career in Laodicea is a mystery. The explanation, however, may be the simple one, that his actions during the civil war were controversial, well though they may have turned out.

36 A. Diessmann, *Light from the Ancient East*, pp. 192–201.

37 Eusebius, *H.E.*, viii.11.

38 Eusebius, *H.E.*, vii.32.4.

39 Eusebius, *H.E.*, vii.9.7. For some other examples, C. J. Cadoux, *The Early Church and the World*, 560.

40 Eusebius, *H.E.*, viii.6.1. and 5. See, B. de Gaiffier, 'Palatins et Eunuques dans quelques Documents hagiographiques', *A.B.*, lxxv, 1957, 17–46.

41 W. M. Calder, 'A Fourth Century Lycaonian Bishop', *Expositor*, vi (7th Ser.), 1908, 392ff.

42 *Adv. Nationes* (ed. Reifferscheid), ii.5; cf. ibid., 1.57.

43 Augustine, *Breviculus Collationis cum Donatistis*, iii.13.25.

44 The dating accepted is that of H. Grégoire, op. cit., 128–30 following up the hint in Mansi, *Collectio* ii.3, that it was held when the church was at peace 'in the time of Constantius Chlorus rather than Constantine'. An earlier date would be necessary if it were known that Valerius of Saragossa, one of the nineteen bishops present, had died in the Great Persecution; but the *Acta S. Vincentii* state merely that he was exiled (Ruinart, ii.343). Hosius of Cordova was himself a *confessor*, who survived the persecution and presides at the council. In addition, the council's immediate concern, as shown by canons 1 and 25, was lapse presumably during persecution. The penalties are very severe, yet the canons lack the vindictive edge which one would expect if the persecution had been as ferocious as it had been in Africa. All in all, the situation fits Spain after the abdication of Maximian, and if the Council were held on a Sunday, the date 15 May A.D. 309, during the rule of Maxentius, has very serious claims for consideration.

45 Canons 2 and 3, 55 and 56.

46 Ibid., 15 and 17. Note also, the text of Porphyry cited by Jerome (*Comment. in Isaiah*, 3.2) '. . . ne iuxta impium Porphyrium matronae et mulieres sint noster senatus,

quae dominantur in ecclesiis, et de sacerdotalis gradu favor iudicet feminarum'. A shrewd touch, true of Roman Christianity in both the third and fourth centuries.

[47] Ibid., 57.

[48] Ibid., 59.

[49] Conversions to Christianity are assumed in Canons 4, 10, 39, 42, 44 and 62.

[50] G. B. Brusin and L. P. Zovatto, *Monumenti paleocristiani de Aquileia e Grado*, Udine, 1957, p. 21ff.

[51] L. P. Zovatto, 'Le antiche Sinagoghe di Aquileia e di Ostia', *Mem. storicha forogioliese*, 44, 1960–61, 54ff.

[52] See J. Suolahti's survey of information derived from Christian inscriptions in the Vatican Museum, *Acta Instituti Romani Finlandiae*, 1.2, pp. 167–77, Helsinki, 1963. There was also a strong Jewish-Christian element, to judge from the frequency with which names like Sabbatius occur in Christian Rome, see I. Kajanto, ibid., ii.1, 107.

[53] See J. Lebreton and J. Zeiller, *Hist. de l'Eglise*, ii, 447–8.

[54] G. Bovini, *La Propietà ecclesiastica*, 38, J. P. Kirsch, *Die römische Titelkirchen in Altertum*, Paderborn, 1918.

[55] *ICLV.*, 2132.

[56] L. De Bruyne, 'Initiation chrétienne et Art paléochrétien', *Rev. des Sciences religieuses*, 36.3, 1962, 48.

[57] M. Guarducci, *The Tomb of St. Peter* (Eng. tr. J. McClellan), 1960, p. 95–6.

[58] Theodoret of Cyrrhus, *De curatione Graec. affect.*, xii (end), *P.G.*, 83, 1150–1.

[59] For the gradual Christianization of Eumeneia perceptible through the formulae used on third-century funerary inscriptions, see W. M. Calder, 'The Eumeneian Formula', *Anatolian Studies presented to W. H. Buckler*, 15–26 and *M.A.M.A.*, vii, p. xxxvii. Eumeneia may have been the unnamed Phrygian town which both Eusebius and Lactantius describe as having been wiped out in the Diocletianic persecution since all its inhabitants, including the magistrates, were Christians. Eusebius, *H.E.*, viii.11.1, Lactantius, *Institutes*, v.8.11. W. M. Ramsay, *Cities and Bishoprics*, 496ff. Below, p. 496.

[60] In 325 Cotiaeum petitioned Constantine for promotion to *civitas* status, among other reasons, 'since everyone was Christian'. Inscription republished with amendments by W. M. Calder, *M.A.M.A.*, vii.305. The situation, as Calder points out, p. xxxviii, 'did not come about in a day'.

[61] Sozomen, *H.E.*, v.15. This and the following sections contain interesting information on the spread of Christianity.

[62] J. Leipoldt, 'Schenute von Atripe', *T.U.*, 25, 1904, 26ff.

[63] L. Leschi, *Revue des Etudes anciennes*, l, 1948, 71ff. For a pagan magistracy at Calama as late as 400, Augustine, *Epp.*, 90 and 91.

[64] *Institutes*, v.13.1. 'But since our number is continuously increased from the worshippers of gods, but is never lessened not even in persecution itself. . . .' Dating: *circa* 311. See N. H. Baynes, *JRS.*, xxxiv, 1944, 137; also J. Moreau, op. cit., 1.16ff. (full discussion of evidence).

[65] Lactantius, *Institutes*, v.1.24.

[66] See P. Courcelle's discussion of Arnobius' significance in ch. vii of A. Momigliano' (ed.), *The Conflict between Paganism and Christianity in the Fourth Century*, Oxford, 1963, 151ff.

[67] For instance, by honouring the Emperor Julian, *CIL.*, viii.4226 and 4771.

[68] See R. Egger, *Römische Antike und frühes Christentum*, i, Klagenfurt, 1962, 186–8. In this case, the Christian immigrants seem to have come from Nisibis on the Euphrates frontier.

[69] For the Danube lands: R. Egger, 'Der Tempelbezirk des Latobius in Lavanttale (Kärnten)', *Römische Antike*, 98ff. 'In den Alpenländen haben die Städte früh im 4 Jahrhundert die neue Lehre empfangen, am flachen Lande dauerten die alten Kulte fort'

(p. 109). *For Roman Britain,* see the author's 'Religion in Roman Britain in the Fourth Century', *JBAA.,* xviii, 1955, 1–19. The Silchester church would seem to be later than A.D. 350 (coin evidence)—information from Professor I. A. Richmond (to be published).

[70] Eusebius, *H.E.,* vi.46.2. See also, P. N. Akinian, 'Die Reihenfolge der Bischöfe Armeniens des 3 und 4 Jahrhunderts', *A.B.,* 67, 1949, 74–86.

[71] N. H. Baynes, *CAH.,* xii.688.

[72] In general, see W. Eltester, 'Die Krisis der alten Welt und das Christentum', *ZNTW.,* 42, 1949, 1–19, and the present author's 'The Failure of the Persecutions in the Roman Empire', *Past and Present,* 16, November 1959, 10–30.

[73] H. I. Bell, *Cults and Creeds in Greco-Roman Egypt,* Liverpool 1957, 64. See also, J. Geffcken, *Der Ausgang des griechschrömischen Heidentums,* Heidelberg, 1929, 21, for the decline of the Egyptian national religion from the middle of the third century onwards.

[74] J. Cerny, *Ancient Egyptian Religion,* 149.

[75] 'I gave thanks to the lord Serapis that when I was in peril at sea he saved me at once'— a typical example, Hunt and Edgar, *Select Papyri,* i.112. Other references, Bell, op. cit., 66–9.

[76] See J. G. Milne's art., 'Egyptian Nationalism under Greco-Roman Rule, *JEA.,* 14, 1928, 226–34.

[77] W. M. Ramsay, *Cities and Bishoprics,* 137.

[78] Lactantius, *De Mortibus Persec.* 11, and Eusebius, *Vita Constantini,* ii.49–50. See H. Grégoire, 'Les chrétiens et l'Oracle de Didymes', *Mél. Holleaux,* 1913, 81–91.

[79] *Institutes,* v.12.

[80] W. M. Ramsay, 'The Tekmoreian Guest-friends, an anti-Christian Society on the Imperial estates at Pisidian Antioch', *Studies in the Eastern Roman Provinces,* 1906, 305–77.

[81] W. M. Ramsay, 'Studies in the Roman province of Galatia', *JRS.,* viii, 1918, 107–45.

[82] Julian (ed. Bidez) *Letter* 84 to Arsacius, High-Priest of Galatia, and Sozomen, *H.E.,* v.16.

[83] It is interesting to note that in contrast, Caelestis seems to have retained her popularity in Carthage until the end of the fourth century, J. Toutain, *Cultes païens,* ii.99, and 104, n. 4.

[84] P. Massiera, 'Inscriptions chrétiennes de Maurétanie Sitifienne', *Revue Africaine,* C, 1956, 325. See the author's *The Donatist Church,* 84ff. for other examples.

[85] M. Leglay, 'Les Stèles à Saturne de Djemila-Cuicul', *Libyca,* i. 1953, 76. Also *CIL.,* viii.6960, a dedication obliterated by the sign of the Cross.

[86] Arnobius, *Adv. Nationes,* 1.24. 'Neglegentur dii clamitant, atque in templis iam raritas summa est, iacent antiquae derisui caerimoniae et sacrorum quondam veterrimi ritus religionum novarum superstitionibus occiderunt'—a significant description of the decline spirit which once had animated African paganism.

[87] Eusebius, *H.E.,* x.6.

[88] Eusebius, *Demonstratio Evangelica* (Eng. tr. W. J. Ferrar), ix.2.4; and also, vi.20.9.

[89] ap. Eusebius, *H.E.,* vii.11.15.

[90] Eusebius, *Demonstr, Evangelica,* viii.5; cf. N. H. Baynes, *CAH.,* xii.675, and C. Schmidt, 'Die Urschrift der Pistis Sophia', *ZNTW.,* 24, 1925, 218–40. For a church in the village of Chenoboskion in the Thebaid, *circa* 314. *Vita Pacomii* 5, (*P.L.,* 73, 233A).

[91] Athanasius, *Apol. contra Arianos,* 75; cf. 63–4. For other information showing how Christianity was beginning to spread among the Copts during the early part of the third century. H. I. Bell, *Cults and Creeds,* 88–9.

[92] Eusebius, *H.E.,* viii, 9.3.

[93] Eusebius, *Mart. Pal.,* 8.13. See below, p. 508.

[94] Antony's parents were comparatively wealthy, but apparently Coptic-speaking, and Antony was never at home with Greek. One, Cronius, claimed to have acted as his interpreter, *Lausiac History,* (ed. Lowther Clarke) 21.15. In the mid-fourth century at

Tabennesi, Duchesne points out, 'the people of the great towns were like foreigners there ... Their first care if they wished to join the community was to learn the Coptic of Thebes (Sahidic). *The Early History of the Church* (Eng. tr. ii.398).

⁹⁵ E. R. Hardy, *Christian Egypt: Church and People*, O.U.P., 1952, 36–7.

⁹⁶ For regular bands of ascetics in Palestine *circa* 300, see Eusebius, *Mar. Pal.*, 11.22 (career of Seleucus). By 315 the career of Hilarion was beginning in Palestine and Syria. It would, however, be an exaggeration to believe as Jerome apparently did (*Vita Sancti Hilarionis*), that by 330, Palestine and Syria were filled with populous colonies of hermits. See Grützmacher, art. 'Hilarion', Hauck, *Realenzyklopädie*, 8, 54–6.

⁹⁷ F. Cumont, 'La Propagation du Manichéisme dans l'Empire romain', *R.H.L.R.*, Nouv. sér., i, 1910, 31–43.

⁹⁸ See A. Adam, *Texte zum Manichäismus* (= Kleine Texte, 175), Berlin, 1954, no. 35, pp. 52–4.

⁹⁹ Ibid., no. 36, pp. 54–6, for the relevant extracts of Alexander's work.

¹⁰⁰ Epiphanius, *Panarion*, 67. See also Carl Schmidt, 'Die Urschrift der Pistis Sophia', especially the last part of the article. Hieracas is described by Epiphanius as 'πάνυ τὴν τῶν Ἀιγυπτίων ἐπιστάμενος γλῶσσαν, ἄλλα καὶ τῇ τῶν Ἑλλήνων τετρανωμένος οὐ μικρῶς, ὀξὺς κατὰ πάντα τρόπον''. In 320, the formula 'light from light' was objected to by Arius, on the ground that it was taught by Hieracas. Arius placed him on the same level of heresy as Valentinus, Sabellius and Mani. (*Letter to Alexander* cited by Athanasius, On the Synods of Ariminum and Seleucia, and Epiphanius, *Haer*. 69.7, Eng. tr. J. Stevenson, *A New Eusebius*, pp. 346–7).

¹⁰¹ No. 78 in H. von Soden's ed. (*Nachrichten der K. Ges. der Wiss. zu Göttingen*, Ph. Hist. Kl., 1909, p. 275). As a centre of Circumcellion activity, Optatus of Milevis, *De Schismate* iii.4.

¹⁰² *ILCV.*, 3665a.

¹⁰³ Ibid., 4038.

¹⁰⁴ Ibid., 406 and 3682.

¹⁰⁵ A. Harnack, *Mission*, 526.

¹⁰⁶ Ibid., 519–20. P. Monceaux, *Histoire Littéraire*, iii, 5ff.

¹⁰⁷ *Passio Mariani et Jacobi*, 2.2.

¹⁰⁸ *Passio Lucii et Montani*, 2. P. Franchi de Cavalieri, *S.T.*, iii, 1900, 14–15, on dating the *Acta* before the persecution of Diocletian.

¹⁰⁹ *Gesta apud Zenophilum* (ed. C. Ziwsa, App. to *CSEL.*, 26, 194–6).

¹¹⁰ Ibid., 195.

¹¹¹ The best account of these is to be found in A. Berthier (with F. Logeart and M. Martin), *Les Vestiges du Christianisme antique dans la Numidie centrale*, Algiers, 1942.

¹¹² Optatus, *De Schismate*, iii.8; *CIL.*, viii.6700 = 19353.

¹¹³ Socrates, *H.E.*, iv.27 on the conversion of pagans 'by his acts as well as by his discourses'.

¹¹⁴ W. M. Calder, *Philadelphia and Montanism*, 319ff. and 337ff. and *M.A.M.A.*, vii. no. 296b. Also, J. G. C. Anderson, 'Paganism and Christianity in the Upper Tembris Valley', *Studies in the Eastern Roman Provinces*, 1906, 199ff. At the same time, rural paganism persisted in parts of Bithynia until the early fifth century (Callinicus, *Vita Hypatii*, 103, 124–5) and even in the reign of Justinian (527–565) John of Ephesus carried out a prolonged missionary campaign in Asia, Caria, Lydia and Phrygia, all heavily Christianized provinces, and found 80,000 peasants to baptize! (John of Ephesus, *H.E.*, 36, *Lives of the Saints* 43, 47). See A. H. M. Jones's valuable essay, 'The Social Background of the Struggle between Paganism and Christianity' (ch. ii, in ed. A. Momigliano, *The Conflict between Paganism and Christianity in the Fourth Century*, p. 19). For an island of paganism near Alexandria in the seventh century, John the Almsgiver, *Life* (ed. N. H. Baynes, *Three Byzantine Saints*, ch. 8, p. 203).

[115] W. M. Calder, *Early Christian Epitaphs*, p. 35 and pl. ii, no. 3.

[116] W. M. Calder, *Philadelphia and Montanism*, 9 and 10 of offprint, referring probably to the deceased's baptism.

[117] *Kephalaion*, 154, published by C. Schmidt in *SBAW.*, 1933, 60 and commented on H. C. Puech, *Le Manichéisme*, 62 and 146.

[118] *Acts of Sharbil* (printed in A-N.C.L., xx.ii, Syriac Documents, 56-80. See F. C. Burkitt's comments in *CAH.*, xii, 499-500.

[119] *Acts of Habib* (A-N.C.L., xx.ii.96). Habib said, 'But this Zeus is an idol, the work of men . . .'. For Christians in the majority in the villages around Edessa, ibid., 91.

[120] Cited from W. M. Ramsay, *Cities and Bishoprics*, 375.

[121] *CIL.*, viii, 8246.

[122] Arnobius, *Adv. Nationes*, iii.6. 'Saturnus inquit et Janus est, Minerva, Juno, Apollo, Venus, Triptolemus, Hercules et alii ceteri.'

[123] *Ep.*, 89b (ed. Bidez, 157).

[124] *Ep.*, 84. See, Sozomen, *H.E.*, v.16, and for Christian ascetics in Palestine active in social works, Eusebius, *Mart. Pal.*, 11.22. Pachomius, demobilized soldier from Licinius' army in 314 is a good example from Egypt of a conversion due to the charity and example of the Christians whom he had met. (*Vita Pachomii*, 4, PL. 73, 232). For the church in Cirta as a sort of social welfare and clothing centre in 303, *Gesta apud Zenophilum*, Ziwsa, 187.

[125] Gregory of Nazianzus, *Oratio*, v.21 (*P.G.*, 35, 689).

[126] J. G. C. Anderson, *Paganism and Christianity in the Upper Tembris Valley*, 201. I see no reason, however, to connect Aquila's death with the Great Persecution.

[127] From Dinek Serai, see W. H. Buckler, W. M. Calder and C. W. M. Cox, 'Asia Minor 1924, i, Monuments from Iconium, Lycaonia and Isauria', *JRS.*, xiv, 1924, no. 57, p. 57.

[128] See W. M. Ramsay's remarks, *Expositor*, 7th Ser., vi, 1908, 298.

[129] *Apol.*, 39.7.

[130] Note Zosimus' account of the disastrous effects which the plague in the reign of Gallienus had on urban life. This rather than the barbarian attacks rendered the towns uninhabitable, 1.37. Also, 1.26, 45 and 46.

[131] Eumenius, *Pro Instaurendis Scholis*, 18.1 (ed. Baehrens, *Paneg. Latini*, pp. 259-60). Also, Aurelius Victor, *De Caesaribus*, 39.45, for Diocletian's restoration of Rome, Carthage, Milan and Nicomedia; cf. C. E. van Sickle, 'Diocletian and the Decline of the Roman Municipalities', *JRS.*, xxviii, 1938, 9ff.

[132] For instance, *CIL.*, viii, 2480-1 (Ad Maiores), 2572 (Lambaesis) and 18328 (Macomades). Discussion by C. E. van Sickle, 'Public Works in Africa in the Reign of Diocletian', *CP.*, 1930, 173ff., and in my 'The Donatist Church', 61.

[133] H. A. Thompson, 'Athenian Twilight 267-600', *JRS.*, xlix, 1959, 61-72.

[134] Eusebius, *H.E.*, vii.22, van Sickle, art. cit., *JRS.*, xxviii, 11.

[135] *SHA.*, Trebellius Pollio, *Tyranni XXX*, 22.6. For the best account of the Blemmyes see W. B. Emery and L. Kirwan, 'The Royal Tombs of Ballana and Qustal' (Mission archéologique en Nubie, 1929-1934), Cairo, 1938, 5-17.

[136] Ibid.

[137] *SHA.*, Vopiscus, *Vita Probi*, 17.3. Excavations by Professor J. M. Plumley and the author at Q'asr Ibrim in 1963/4 suggest that, to judge from their homes, the mysterious X-Group people and the Blemmyes were one and the same, and that their ancestry to the Nubians is probable.

[138] *Passio Tipasii*, 1 (ed. *A.B.*, ix, 1890, 116-23), *CIL.*, viii.8836, and Wm. Seston, *Dioclétien*, 117ff. It is noticeable that after the victorious conclusion of the campaign the provincials had to set about building and no doubt furnishing military depots (*horrea*) in the pacified area.

[139] *P. Oxy*, 1543 (A.D. 299) πρὸς διάδοσιν τοῖς διαδεύουσιν γεννεοτάτοις στρατιώταις. In view of the Blemmyic menace there were plenty in the province.

[140] See my article on the organization *angareia* in third-century Phrygia, in *JRS.*, xlvi, 1956, 46–56.

[141] A. Segrè, 'Inflation and its Implication in early Byzantine Times', *Byzantion*, xv, 1940–41, 249–79.

[142] A Segrè, art. cit., 259. Even so, the requisite 950 debased copper tetradrachmae then in circulation could not have represented a very large sum. For the same reason one takes the alleged rise in prices by 1000 per cent between 256–280 in Gaul *cum grano salis* (C. Jullian, *Histoire de la Gaule*, viii.214–30 and P. Lambrechts, 'Les Thèses de Henri Pirenne', *Byzantion*, xiv, 1939, 517–18).

[143] A. Segrè, art cit., 260. Based on Pap. PS, 8021 from Narmouthis in Arsinoite nome. It is hardly safe to base conclusions on these scattered figures, especially in view of the confusion of currency which reigned in Egypt until 296, but one can hardly disagree with Segrè's general conclusion (p. 261). 'We see that the end of the third century and the first half of the fourth century are characterized by a very low purchasing power of gold, which, connected with the bad harvest, bad conditions of agriculture, wars, high taxes, etc., made of this period one of the worst in the economic and political history of the world. The preamble of Diocletian's edict *De Pretiis rerum Venalium* of 301 took a pessimistic view of the situation ('cottidie in peiora praecipites et in publicum nefas quadam animorum caecitate vergentes . . . ').

[144] *P. Oxy*, 1415 (Grenfell and Hunt, xii, 52–59). Also, ibid., 1416, lines 11–17. In general, M. Rostovtzeff, *Social and Economic History*, ch. xi, and notes on pp. 743–5.

[145] T. C. Skeat and E. P. Wegener, art. cit. *JEA.*, 21, 1935, 236–7. Also, the interesting letter dated to *circa* A.D. 318 from a *centurio princeps* to his brother Heras, asking him to obtain the release of one of his tenants who had been appointed to the office of 'collector of tunics and cloaks'. This was regarded as a means of doing him injury by other villagers. (*P. Oxy*, 1424).

[146] Wm. Seston, *Dioclétien et la Tétrarchie* (vol. i, *Guerres et Réformes*), Paris, 1946, pp. 322ff.

[147] Note the comment by Paianios, the translator of Eutropius, concerning the situation in Egypt 296–297 (Diocletian) τοὺς μὲν κατασφάξας τῶν Ἀιγυπτίων, τοῖςδὲ λοιποῖς φόρους τάξας ὡς μάλιστα βαρυτάτους ἐκ ταύτης δὲ τῆς αἰτίας καὶ πάσης τῆς βασιλευομένης τὰς εἰσφορας ἐπέθηκε διαμετρησάμενος τὴν γὴν καὶ εἰς ἐπιγραφὴν ἀναγαγῶν ἃ πάντα εἰς τόδε ἐκράτησεν. It is interesting that the author sees the crippling nature of the taxation and open revolt in Egypt as the immediate pretext for the great census. See Wm. Ensslin, 'Zur Ostpolitik der Kaisers Diokletians'. *Sitzb. der bayer. Akad. der Wiss.*, 1942, 31ff.

[148] Lactantius, *De Mortibus Persecutorum* 7. The census was not completed in Gaul until 311.

[149] Wm. Seston, op. cit. 283. Also A. E. R. Boak 'Early Byzantine Papyri from the Cairo Museum' in *Etudes de Papyrologie*, ii.1, 1933, 1ff.

[150] A. H. M. Jones, 'Overtaxation and the Roman Empire', *Antiquity*, 33, 1959, 39–43, and *The Later Roman Empire*, 61–67.

[151] Aurelius Victor, *De Caesaribus*, 39.32.

[152] The well-known system of ἐπιβολή. Rostovtzeff, op. cit., 481, and 742, note 32.

[153] The Oracle of the Potter = Pap. Oxy. 2332 (ed. Lobel and Roberts, vol. xxii, p. 93); cf. U. Wilcken, *Hermes*, xc, 1905, 544ff., and R. Reitzenstein, 'Ein Stück hellenistischer Kleinliteratur', *Göttingen Nachrichten*, 1904, 309–32, on previous discoveries of fragments of this oracle dating to the late second and third century A.D.

[154] For instance, *SHA.*, Vopiscus, *Vita Saturnini*, 8.5, and Trebellius Pollio, *Tyranni Triginita*, 22.1ff.

155 Lactantius, *Institutes*, vii.15 and 18.

156 Lactantius, *De Morte Pers.*, 23; cf. ibid., 7 (criticism of Diocletian's building programme) and *Institutes*, v.8 on the social aspects of Christian justice, and ibid., v.15 for the social injustice of pagan states. For Cyprian's similar anger against the injustice of prevailing social and economic conditions in Africa *circa* 245, *Ad Donatum*, 10–12.

157 Augustine, *Breviculus cum Donatistis*, iii.13.25 (*P.L.*, 43, 638); cf. *Passio Sancti Theodoreti*, ('audivi te esse fisci debitorem . . . . .')

158 Optatus, *De Schismate*, iii.4.

159 *Pap. Oxy.*, 1477.

160 *Vita Antonii*, 44.

161 John the Almoner believed he 'would be met on his way to heaven by devils as fierce and pitiless as tax-collectors', cited from N. H. Baynes, *Three Byzantine Saints*, p. 248. John was also renowned for his practical charity, including building maternity hospitals in Alexandria (ibid., ch. 7, Baynes, 202–3).

162 Note the description of the Pachomian monasteries in the *Lausiac History* (ed. and tr. W. K. Lowther Clarke) 32.7, with more than 1000 monks including 'tailors, smiths, camel-drivers, carpenters and fullers'.

163 K. Heussi, *Der Ursprung des Mönchtums*, Tübingen, 1936, 114–5.

164 See C. Schmidt, 'Die Urschrift der Pistis Sophia', *ZNTW.*, 24, 1925, 218–40. H. I. Bell, op. cit., 72.

165 See the author's 'The Revival of Berber Art', *Antiquity*, 1942, 342–52, and for Isauria, Miss Ramsay in *Studies in the Eastern Roman Provinces*, 3–92. (Summary, p. 91.)

166 P. Gauckler, 'Mosaiques tombales d'une chapelle des Martyres à Thabraca', *Monuments Piot*, xiii, 1906, 225. See also my 'Revival of Berber Art', *Antiquity*, loc. cit.

167 Note de Tocqueville's remarks on the situation in France in 1789. 'A mesure que se développe en France la prospérité que je viens de décrire, les esprits paraissent cependant plus mal assis et plus inquiets; le mécontentement public s'aigrit; la haine contre toutes les institutions anciennes va croissant. La nation marche visiblement vers une révolution'. He goes on to show how the wealthy Isle de France was far more affected by revolutionary ideas than the more backward Provence and Britanny (*L'Ancien Régime*, ed. G. W. Headlam, Oxford, 1925, p. 281).

168 e.g. *Acta Mariani et Jacobi* 1.3, 'non quod in terris vellent coronae suae gloriam per jactantiam praedicari . . . ' and *Acta Montani et Lucii*, 11.6, with reference to Cyprian's appearance in Montanus' version, 'qua de re, fratres dilectissimi concordiam, pacem, unanimitatem omni virtute teneamus'. The writers of both *Acta* are conspicuously loyal to Cyprian's memory.

169 Pontius, *Vita*, 1 'certe durum erat, ut cum maiores nostri plebeiis et catechumenis martyrium consecratis tantum honoris pro martyrio ipsum veneratione tribuerint'— probably a reference to the popularity of the *Acta Perpetuae* at this time.

170 *Vita*, 1, 'qui et sine martyrio habuit quae docerat', and note also Pontius' defence of Cyprian's conduct in the Decian persecution (*Vita*, 7).

171 Pontius, *Vita*, 2.

172 E.g. *Ep.*, 52.1 (administering trust funds for widows and orphans).

 Ep., 75.1 (liaison with Firmilian).

 Ep., 78.1 (liaison with Numidian confessors. In this case the sub-deacon (hypodiaconus) was accompanied by three acolytes).

173 Optatus, *De Schismate*, 1.16–17. The archdeacon clearly overshadowed the Carthaginian presbyters at this time.

174 Pontius, *Vita*, 6. Cyprian, 'admixta utrimque temperies'.

175 *Acta Saturnini*, 6 and 14 (*P.L.*, viii, 693 B and C and 698 D).

176 Augustine, *Breviculus Collationis*, iii.13.25.

177 Pseudo-Cyprian, *Ep.*, 3 (*C.S.E.L.*, iii.3, p. 274).

[178] Tertullian, *De Corona*, 1, 'Exinde, sententiae super illo, nescio an Christianorum, non aliae enim ethnicorum—ut de abrupto et praecipitat novi cupido. . . .'

[179] *Acta Maximiliani* (Knopf and Krüger, 86–7); cf. P. Monceaux, *Histoire littéraire*, iii. 114–21. Canons of the Council of Arles (ed. Hefele-Leclercq), 3.

[180] *CIL.*, viii.9585 (20958) = *ILCV.*, 1583.

[181] For Novatianism's early success in Asia Minor, Socrates, *H.E.*, iv.28 and v.21; Sozomen, *H.E.*, ii.32.

[182] W. M. Calder, *Philadelphia and Montanism*, pp. 10–11, and 28 ff. of off-print, and 'Early Christian Epitaphs from Phrygia', *Anatolian Studies*, 5, 1955, 27–31, H. Grégoire, *Byzantion*, 1, 1924, 703, and *Les Persécutions*, 18 (answered by Calder's art. in *Anatolian Studies*).

[183] W. M. Calder, 'Early Christian Epitaphs', 29, and *M.A.M.A.*, vii, p. xxxvii. The ' Ἔσται αὐτῷ πρὸς τὸν (3ῶντα) θεόν' formula was in use to A.D. 273 in central Phrygia, and between 270–300 in eastern Phrygia.

[184] W. M. Calder, *Philadelphia and Montanism*, 343–5. Domnus described as 'μέγαν 'ιστρατιώτην Ιτὸν πάσης ἀρετῆς (lines 1 and 2). This attitude was equated to just observance of (Christian) law and excellence of character.

[185] Eusebius, *Mart. Pal.*, 4. Note Eusebius' reference (4.5L) to his 'inability to consort with his relatives on account of dissimilar habits' and the shorter recension's statement that 'he fled secretly from his family'.

[186] Inscription from Kurd Köi in the Tembris valley, published by Buckler–Calder–Cox in *JRS.*, 1927, 49–58; comments by W. M. Calder in *Bull. of J. Rylands Library*, 13, 1929, and corrections in emphasis, H. Grégoire, 'Notes épigraphiques', *Byzantion*, 8, 1933, 61–5.

[187] Buckler–Calder–Cox, loc. cit., 53. The inscription 'introduces us to four generations of a rustic Phrygian family, probably passing from paganism to Christianity, certainly passing from the age of persecution to the peace of the Church'—a priceless document for the period we are discussing.

[188] Athanasius, *Vita Antonii*, 1.

[189] Ibid., 16.

[190] L. Duchesne, *Early History of the Church*, ii.390.

[191] Eusebius, *Mart. Pal.*, 8.1. It is interesting that Coptic monastic names, such as Pachomius, Serapion or Pambo, still continued to contain the names of the old Egyptian gods. These are seldom, if ever, mentioned in the legends of the Coptic saints, though Greco-Roman gods, such as Apollo and their priests provide the demons over which the saints triumphed.

[192] Eusebius, *H.E.*, vii.24.

[193] Ibid., vii.25. Cf. iii.28.3–5.

[194] Ibid., iii.39.12.

[195] Ibid., vii.24.6. Note also, the circulation of apocalyptic material and Judaeo-Christian works, like the Gospel of Thomas in up-country Egypt in this period and later.

[196] Canons (ed. Hefele-Leclercq) 19 and 20 (trading and usury) 45 (slack church-going by catechumens), 65 (adulterous wives of clergy), 73–6 (backbiting by clergy and laity).

[197] *H.E.*, viii.1.7. (tr. Oulton, p. 253).

CHAPTER FIFTEEN

The Great Persecution, 303–312

Exactly why, on 23 February 303, Diocletian signed an edict aimed at outlawing the Christian Church may perhaps never be known.[1] For nineteen years now his government had been engaged in the long uphill task of restoring the army, the administration, and the economy of the Empire. Germanic and Persian enemies had been defeated. In the last decade a vast apparatus of state bureaucracy had been engaged in attempting to enforce complicated systems of tax assessment and price-regulation which would have strained the resources of a modern state. If the provinces were quiet, there were none the less deep undercurrents of discontent. The Bagaudae in Gaul, the army of Allectus in Britain, the supporters of Achilleus in Egypt and the Kabyles in Mauretania had been defeated or repressed but not in all cases destroyed. If ever the Empire needed the QUIES AUGG. proclaimed on some of the later mintings of the new *folles* issued by the Tetrarchy in 294,[2] it was now. Why risk the whole achievement of the reign by declaring war on the Christians?

Some such question has been asked from that day to this. Eusebius could find no rational explanation, except that God's chastisement was necessary for the Church which had grossly abused the long period of toleration.[3] Nor apparently could Constantine, whom Eusebius records as saying that 'the pagan emperors, my predecessors stirred up civil wars at a moment when affairs, human and divine, were enjoying peace'.[4] Lactantius, who was perhaps on the spot in Nicomedia, gives a convincing account of the events leading up to the publication of the edict,[5] but he is far from penetrating to the deeper causes. Only by looking back into the character of the reforms of the Tetrarchy and the spirit that animated its directors may the Great Persecution be seen as something more than a gigantic aberration and a vast and unnecessary waste of life.

Diocletian, despite Lactantius' opinion to the contrary, was no

477

revolutionary. This shrewd, statesmanlike but superstitious ruler, as he appeared both to contemporaries and later historians, had no stomach for reform for reform's sake, nor for romantic gestures at odds with the past.[6] 'It is the greatest crime', he declared in his edict concerning the suppression of Manichaeism in 297, 'to wish to undo what once has been fixed and established by antiquity, and holds to its course and is possessed of proper status.'[7] The voice could have been that of Cicero in the *De Legibus* or even of Cato. In 285, however, he had found himself sole ruler over an empire which in the previous thirty years had come to resemble a vast besieged camp, beset by the Persian and barbarian armies without, and faced with demoralization, discontent and bankruptcy within. His countermeasures were those of an efficient military administrator.[8] The hereditary principle of government had manifestly failed in the persons of Carinus and Numerian, and an alternative marked by loyalty and efficiency was needed. Almost at once Diocletian turned to a born second-in-command, another Illyrian officer, Maximian, to fill the role first of Caesar, and then on 1 April 286 of joint-Augustus. The subsequent delegation of powers to the Caesars, Galerius and Constantius could also be justified on the basis of military and administrative need. Then, the cities, the lynch-pin of the economy and administration of the Empire must be restored, the army the guardian of the frontiers increased and re-deployed, the provinces reorganized, and finally, the divine favour of the immortal guardians of the Roman people must be regained. The revolutionary element in Diocletian's measures, such as the establishment of a large administrative caste, independent both of the senatorial aristocracy and the provincial *curiales*, and eventually more powerful than either, was the by-product and not the motive power of his reign.[9]

Restoration then, not innovation was the hall-mark of the whole period that preceded the Great Persecution. Diocletian's assumption of the title *Jovius* was aimed in all probability at demonstrating that the Emperor was more than the successful general and slayer of the over-mighty Aper, but that he ruled 'by consent of the gods', indeed was the incarnation of the father of the Roman gods, Jupiter, and the father of the Roman people.[10] It was also a title redolent of high antiquity. Nearly two centuries before, Trajan had been depicted on the arch of Beneventum receiving the thunderbolt from Jupiter, and on Aurelian's earlier coinage Jupiter had been shown handing the orb to the soldier emperor.[11] Diocletian took up this tradition as personifying the Roman virtues and the 'Roman majesty' he intended to express, and the Roman state whose glory his aim was to increase.[12] As Hercules was Jupiter's son and lieutenant, so were the *Herculii* represented by Maximian and his Caesar Constantius his juniors and lieutenants. As he was the mind, so Maximian was the strong arm of the Roman world.[13]

At the end of the fourth century Libanius could state that Diocletian wished the gods of the emperors to govern the world,[14] but he also accepted from the recent past all that exalted the status of the Emperor himself. His long reign provided the court ceremonial with a permanency it might otherwise have lacked. The ceremony of the *adoratio*,[15] the triple adoration of the suppliant or official in the imperial presence, the reiteration of the term 'sacer' in connection with anything pertaining to the Emperor and his government, and the possible selection of Mithras as patron of the Empire provided the Tetrarchy with a supernatural aura.[16] This was designed to heighten its prestige among the provincials,[17] protect itself against usurpers—Carausius was neither *Jovius* nor *Herculius*—and guard against other internal enemies of the Roman people.

The Tetrarchy like the other Illyrian emperors stood for the traditional values of Rome. This was the message which Diocletian and Maximian attempted to impress on the minds of their subjects in both east and west alike. Two examples may be given.

First, the clauses of the long edict, *De Nuptiis* (A.D. 295), designed primarily against marriage of close kinsfolk, returns time and again to the theme of Roman antiquity and religious uniformity.[18] Incest was displeasing to the immortal gods. The Roman people had prospered thanks to their respect for traditional morality.[19] The favour of the gods must not be lost because some of the inhabitants of the Empire, whether through ignorance or 'through the prescription of some barbarian savagery', were guilty of contracting illicit unions. The 'discipline of our times' the emperors claimed, compelled them to intervene,[20] and they urged in conclusion 'our laws protect nothing that is not holy and venerable, and thus Roman majesty has attained to so great a plenitude by the favour of all the divine powers'.[21] The appeal was directed to antiquity and religious uniformity: barbarian superstition was to be rejected. But mercy was to be shown to unwitting offenders,[22] and in this also the edict foreshadows Diocletian's dealings with other offenders against the honour of the Roman name.

A second aspect of the same policy may perhaps be detected in the reform of the currency in 294. The multitude of Virtues and divinities which had cluttered the coinage of the last half century was eliminated, and Diocletian and his advisers chose a few simple ideas whose representation on the reverse types of the new coinage would demonstrate their aims to the widest ranges of the population.[23] On the new *aureus* stood the Roman gods, the supreme guardians of the State. On silver, there were the military virtues and the sacrificial cult, the means by which honour and duty to those gods were to be performed. On the hundreds of thousands of the new, and larger *folles* which replaced the wretched billon of the previous thirty years, there was one type, 'Genio Populi Romani' ('to the genius of the Roman people'). This, as Sutherland has claimed, 'was essentially "the people's coin"—mass produced for world-wide use', and the people's guiding spirit was Rome. There in simple pictorial form was the stability and eternity of Rome which the emperors intended their government to uphold. The few later reverse types such as 'Providentia Deorum, quies augustorum' also emphasized how peace and prosperity depended on popular reverence for the traditional gods of Rome.

When one considers how strongly traditional was the religious basis of the Tetrarchy, it is even difficult to understand why Diocletian took nineteen years to make up his mind that Christians were beyond the pale and must forcibly be brought back. For, in addition to the visible panoply of restored paganism shown by rebuilt temples in the provincial cities and the coinage in general circulation, the last decades of the third century were witnessing the final effort of the thinking pagan to meet the intellectual challenge of Christianity on equal terms. Paganism in all its forms was in decline; so much is certain from the evidence discussed in the last chapter, but for the great majority of the educated population of the Roman Empire, Christianity was not yet unmistakably the answer. The traditional gods were still the forces which preserved the universe and the Empire,[24] and those who openly repudiated them could be regarded as enemies. Christianity had not yet entirely lived down its novelty nor the taint of atheism. So much is clear from the beginning of Eusebius' *Praeparatio Evangelica* in which he records accusations against Christianity he had encountered in his own day.[25]

Moreover, pride in and veneration for the traditions of the past, allied to an educational system which relied heavily on pagan mythological subjects and themes drawn from secular Greco-Roman history, inured the individual against acceptance of the new religion. In the west also, this demanded renunciation of those values in which he had grown up, and even of the secular literature and language of his day.[26] Not everyone felt as pessimistic as Arnobius or as angry as Lactantius. In the east even, where Clement and his successors had been bridging the gaps between Greek and Hebrew thought for the past century, the hold of custom and ancestral observances was still immensely strong.[27] It took a conscious effort, often induced by some far-reaching personal experience, for an educated man to accept Christianity. The historian Sozomen, for instance, relates how his grandfather was converted with his whole family *circa* 330 when one of his relatives in the village in Palestine where they lived was cured from demonic possession by the monk Hilarion, after Jews and other physicians had failed.[28] But even then these had been the first conversions to Christianity in the village, and such occurrences could not have been very frequent.

Thus, despite neglect of observances and the demoralization tinged with envy which Arnobius describes,[29] the educated pagan could still be counted upon to rally to a defence of his religion against Christianity, if given a lead. When the persecution came there is no recorded case of defection among the authorities required to carry it out.[30]

As in the previous century the intellectual leadership of paganism fell to the Neo-Platonists.[31] In the 260s Plotinus was in Rome, and he encountered Gnostics at his lectures there. Though part of his exposition of the Oneness and Goodness of the Creator Principle of the universe in Book ii of the *Enneads* was directed against Gnostic dualism, it seems clear that sometimes he had more orthodox Christians in mind.[32] Thus, the attack on 'people who do not hesitate to call the most worthless of individuals brothers, but refuse to give this name to the sun, to the stars of heaven and even to the soul of the world',[33] is reminiscent of Celsus' attack on the sectarian and anthropocentric Christianity of his day. So also is Plotinus' reproach against 'fools who are found to accept such teaching at the mere sound of the words, "You yourself are to be nobler than all else, nobler than men, nobler than even gods", and others who previously modest, ordinary folk were carried away by the assertions "You, you are a son of God: those men whom you used to admire, none of these are His children. Without lifting a hand you are nobler than the heavens themselves"—and others take up the cry.'[34] On the contrary, the powers of nature required respect; they added to the beauty and harmony of the universe, where all species had their place. The Gnostic hatred of the body was due to a simple misunderstanding of Plato.[35] Much of this could be paralleled from Celsus cited in Origen's *Contra Celsum*, Book iv. Indeed, in Rome at any rate, little seems to have changed in the argument between Christian and Platonist from the previous century. Whether they called themselves Gnostics or Christians, Plotinus' opponents in Rome still seem to be expressing a somewhat rustic theology left far behind by the Christian philosophy prevailing in the east.[36]

Apart from the significant reminder that 'every evildoer began by despising the gods',[37] no question of active measures against the sectaries was being raised. The courteous and even conciliatory tone towards Christians was at first maintained by Plotinus' disciples. Thus Porphyry's friend, Amelius' treatise is cited approvingly by Eusebius in the *Praeparatio Evangelica*.[38] Amelius saw value in the Christian explanation of the Logos in the Fourth Gospel, despite his prejudice against the 'barbarian origin' of its author. An Incarnation manifesting God's majesty, and representing in some way the perpetual and universal incarnation of the Heavenly Reason that penetrated and enlightened every creature in the universe, was acceptable to him.[39] A fairly positive appreciation of Christianity was also accepted by Porphyry in the *De Regressu Animae* written *circa* 262 when he was about 30. As the title suggests, this work was concerned largely with the immortality of the soul and the argument '*ut beata sit anima, corpus omne fugiendum*'—words which Augustine echoes like a refrain liberating him from the anti-Christian prejudices of Manichaeism.[40] This, however, would hardly have been Porphyry's intention.[41] If he conceded the exemplary character of Christ's life,[42] he also allowed the justice of the sentence passed on him by the Jews,[43] the absurdity of the Christian belief in the resurrection of the body[44] and the mendacity and malevolence of the apostles, especially of St. Peter.[45] Above all, he castigated the Christians for their arrogance, their credulity and their deceit,[46] their sour dislike of their fellow beings, their hopes for the end of the world and for their attitude of non-co-operation. To all this he, like his older contemporary, Demetrianus of Carthage, ascribed the disasters from which the Empire was suffering.[47] In this the pagan charge never wavered; and the fall of Rome to Alaric in 410 seemed to justify it completely.[48]

A change to a more hostile outlook was therefore not unexpected. Porphyry's κατὰ χριστιανῶν, written perhaps *circa* 270, suggests a mounting Neo-Platonist attack on the Christians.[49] It occupies an important place in the background of the Great Persecution because it seems to have influenced some of Diocletian's senior advisers, and it gave direction to anti-Christian propaganda when the persecution broke out. As Arnobius shows, it was already playing its part in the Christian-pagan debate in North Africa during the previous decade.[50] The effectiveness of the fifteen books may be judged from the fact that from the time of Constantine to Valentinian III, Christian emperors ordered their destruction,[51] that Apollinaris of Laodicea devoted thirty books to the task of refuting him,[52] that Augustine both admired and hated their author,[53] and that Theodoret of Cyrrhus (*circa* 450) used Porphyry's reluctant admission of the success of Christianity in Rome as the climax of twelve books of rebutting paganism.[54] To him Porphyry was the commander-in-chief of the anti-Christian forces.[55]

The destruction of the great work has had its effect, but something of the power and calculated hostility of the writer may still be gauged from the fragments. Porphyry of Tyre (*circa 232–circa 305*) may have at one time been a catechumen turned away from Christianity by personal insult and injury received from Christians,[56] and his hostility towards them increased with age. He always seems to have retained a certain veneration for the life of

Jesus though he criticized many of his acts and his pusillanimous bearing towards Pilate,[57] but the apostles and evangelists he despised as deceivers and false witnesses. His attack on the truth and consistency of Scripture was as old as Marcion's, but Porphyry brought to it the literary acumen and method of Origen, combined with profound lack of sympathy towards his subject. He showed intelligent Greek-speaking Christians and pagans what could be done if current methods of literary criticism were used to destroy rather than to uphold the veracity of Scripture. He exploited the ground already to some extent prepared by the Christians themselves.

The Alexandrian school of theologians had steadily relegated acceptance of the literal word of Scripture to second place, in favour of a truer significance of texts to be discovered through analogy and allegory based on an understanding of Scripture as a whole. Origen had stated that some of the incidents narrated in the Gospels could not be literally true.[58] For instance, the story of the cleansing of the Temple was 'improbable' (ἀπίθανος), if only because it was uncharacteristic of the Son to use a scourge of cords.[59] The account of the entry into Jerusalem had to be treated similarly, for not even the Son could ride an ass and a colt at the same time,[60] while the Synoptic accounts of many of the main incidents in Jesus' ministry and passion contradicted one another. Origen, however, had tried to reconcile the difficulties through his own idealistic interpretation of Christianity. He defended the Evangelists against Celsus' critique on the grounds of their general credibility, even if some details were inaccurate.[61] In the hands of an enemy, however, this line of criticism could be damaging. Porphyry had made a more exhaustive study of Scripture than had Celsus and had a deeper knowledge of both secular history and the art of textual criticism; he was correspondingly more formidable. He would compare in detail two accounts of the same incident, such as the death of Judas, and point out how Mt. 27[5] could not be reconciled with Acts 1[18].[62] One of the two was false. Or, why did Jesus send freshly exorcised demons into a herd of defenceless swine,[63] and were His miracles any more impressive than those of Apuleius or Apollonius?[64] Elsewhere, he would appeal to known facts of geography, for instance, that Lake Tiberias was no sea (θάλασσα) but a stretch of water easily traversible by a man in a small boat in two hours and therefore not subject to a storm such as Mk. 4[37ff.] described.[65]

Gradually, the picture was built up of the Evangelists as romancers and fantasists retailing stories not worth the hearing. Some of the criticism of Scripture was, moreover, perfectly true. Porphyry evidently devoted the whole of his Book 12 to a discussion of the Book of Daniel, and from the long extracts preserved in Jerome's embarrassed commentary, it is clear that he perceived that it was recent work dating from the Maccabean wars, and could only be explained by reference to that period.[66] Hence, it had no merit as prophecy, and Christian arguments derived from it consequently were valueless. Finally, he was able to point out notable weaknesses in the characters of both Peter and Paul,[67] and draw attention to the importance of the quarrel between them, which Christians had tended to gloss over.[68] If one refused the Christians the use of allegory[69] for Scriptural interpretation, was not their faith based on falsehood and fable?

In the last resort, however, Porphyry was not interested in the refutation of Christianity as an academic pursuit. Like Celsus, his real charge against the Christians was their lack of civic sense, their unscrupulous wooing of the underprivileged, especially the women,[70] and their hostility towards the state. He can speak about the punishment of the Christians for impious disobedience to the common law[71] and remark complacently on the 'thousands' destroyed during the recent persecutions.[72] To him, 'the greatest fruit of virtue was to honour the Divine according to traditional usage (κατὰ τὰ πάτρια).[73] In contrast, Christianity represented 'barbarian adventure', the embodiment of a threat to those institutions.[74] Like Celsus, he knew on which side the Platonist must stand. So did those who read his works, such as Hierocles, the able administrator who in 302 found himself *consularis* of Bithynia. Porphyry had become the prophet of the Great Persecution.

When it came, however, the persecution was more the outcome of the needs of military discipline than the result of intellectual conflict. Despite the *adoratio*, Diocletian's court at Nicomedia was no centre for anti-Christian agitation. The Emperor's wife and daughter and his personal attendants seem to have been pro-Christian.[75] There were plenty of Christian civil servants both at court and in the provinces, and plenty of Christians serving in the armies.[76] Whatever the theoretical possibilities of conflict, personal factors weighed strongly on the side of compromise and delay. One can point to the bare possibility of one incident only in the first decade of Diocletian's reign and this, significantly, one which affected the army. The so-called massacre of the Theban Legion on Maximian's orders in 286, has been discussed in two important monographs.[77] When in that year the newly appointed Emperor set out on his first campaign of pacification in the west, directed against the Bagaudae, did his army contain a detachment of Christian troops from the Thebaid? Did the Emperor, having crossed the Great St. Bernard pass into the valley of the Rhone and reaching the easier country east of Lake Geneva, command sacrifice to the gods, and did the Thebans first take evasive action by marching on another twelve miles beyond where the rest of the army was halted, and then refuse point-blank to comply? Did they persist in their refusal despite parleys, and did they then suffer the military penalties for disobedience in the field, first decimation and then massacre?

Is there an element of truth behind the account sent by Eucher of Lyons to Bishop Salvius *circa* 450? As D. van Berchem has shown, and L. Dupraz has not been able to rebut beyond doubt, all the 'proofs' of the historicity are suspect. It is impossible to fit any legionary detachment from the Thebaid[78] into the context of Maximian's operations, and the details preserved in the accounts of the martyrdoms concerning the personnel of the 'legion' are impossible. Whereas the term 'legio' presupposes an infantry formation, some of the ranks mentioned, *primicerius* and *senator* in the Acta are those of cavalry and well known even among civilians like Jerome to be so.[79] One would conclude with van Berchem that here is an example of the conflation of the legend of an eastern martyr named Maurice of Apamea and local traditions about the campaign against the Bagaudae. This may have been the work of the immigrant eastern bishop. Theodore, who set about Christianizing the upper valley of the Rhone from his see at Octodurus (Valais) in the second half of the fourth century. The 'massacre' of the Theban legion cannot be invoked as a precursor of the Great Persecution.

We may, however, be on firmer ground when we turn to the military saints who are said to have perished in North Africa between 295 and 300.[80] On 12 March 295 a prospective conscript for the Roman army named Maximilian was led by his father before a commission at Theveste presided over by the proconsul Dion Cassius. Maximilian, however, refused categorically to serve on the grounds that he was a Christian. 'Non facio, non possum militare', he declared. To his credit, the proconsul refused to lose patience, but pointed out that there were Christian soldiers active in the service of the emperors. Was to serve to do evil? As Maximilian persisted, the order to execute him was given, not on the ground that he was a Christian, but that he had refused to take the oath of service. In the remarks attributed to the proconsul, it is quite clear that the fact of Christianity was now accepted, so long as it did not involve refusal of the legitimate demands of the State. The centurion Marcellus of Tingis who on 21 July 298 (?) threw down his belt of rank in the middle of a ceremonial parade in honour of the anniversary of Maximian's assumption of the title of Herculius,[81] and of Fabius the standard-bearer who acted similarly on a ceremonial occasion at Caesarea the provincial capital of Mauritania Caesariensis, probably in 299, were also punished for gross military offences.[82] These and perhaps other similar events in Rome[83] indicated that if a major war broke out, taxing the full strength of the Roman army, accounts might have to be settled once and for all with the Christians. A vast organization which countenanced conscientious objectors and worse, and silently opposed the ideals on which the Tetrarchy was based could not be tolerated when the Empire was fighting for its life.

The renewal of the Persian war in the summer of 296 marked the beginning of this development. In the early stages it went badly for the Romans. The Persian general, Narses, invaded Syria, taking advantage of troubles there and the revolt of Achilleus in Egypt which had broken out the same year. Galerius forced him to retire, but was ambushed and heavily defeated near the Euphrates at Callinicum. He returned, to be publicly humiliated by Diocletian.[84] Meantime, as we have seen in the last chapter, Manichaeism had been spreading across the Persian frontier into Arabia and Egypt, and by 296/297 had found support in Carthage. The

edict which Diocletian sent from Alexandria to Julianus, proconsul of Africa, at the height of the Persian war[85] on 31 March
297, demonstrated the religious beliefs by which the Tetrarchy
was guided, and the Emperor's determination to crush a proselytizing creed which he regarded as enemy propaganda hostile to the
interests of the State.

The edict is an exceptionally interesting document, showing
once again how little the official outlook towards religion had
changed from the time of the Republic down to Diocletian's
day. 'The wickedness of attempting to undo past tradition'
required the emperors to act with great zeal 'to punish the
obstinacy of the perverted mentality of these most evil men'. The
Manichaeans were therefore to be punished as innovators and
indeed as enemy agents working for Persia. Their leaders and
their books were to be seized and burnt;[86] other adherents of the
sect to be put to death by more normal means. The lives of any
honestiores among them were to be spared, but their goods were to
be confiscated and they were to be sent to the mines. The edict,
with its references to the duty of protecting old religious belief
against the novel, and the definition of the latter as 'prava', looks
back to the past, but some of the penalties were to be applied
against the Christians six years later. Though it was not blue-
print for the first edict of persecution, as the objective was the
defeat of enemy assault under the colour of religion[87] it leaves no
doubt that the restoration of the Roman people was to be restoration under the Roman gods. There would be a restricted place for
Judaism,[88] but none for an assertive Christianity.

The gods were kind. By the end of 297 Galerius had won a
complete victory over the Persians, captured the harem of Narses
and pushed on from Armenia to take Ctesiphon with enormous
booty. The exploitation of the victory caused a momentary but
significant rift between Diocletian and his Caesar. Galerius
wanted to establish a new Roman province out of the occupied
territory. Diocletian was more prudent, realizing the true strength
of Persia and opted for a moderate settlement.[89] In the end, the
terms brought satisfaction to each. The Persians surrendered five
small provinces astride the Tigris and the Roman protectorate
over Armenia was acknowledged. Thus, Rome had scored her
greatest triumph for a century or more and her eastern frontier

was secured for forty years. In May 298 (?) the *Circensis Adiabi-censis victis* were celebrated in Rome. An arch was erected at Thessalonica to commemorate the victory. Galerius boasted him-self a son of Mars. His star was now in the ascendant.

Gradually, the situation began to worsen for the Christians. Eusebius states[90] that pressure was first applied to soldiers in the army of the east (where Galerius' influence was strongest), and that it mounted gradually. At this stage, however, soldiers who refused to sacrifice were apparently allowed to resign and after corporal punishment, to retire into civil life. By 301, however, the measures which Veturius, Galerius' *magister militum*, was taking against Christians were amounting to persecution, and from then on, Eusebius adds, 'little by little persecution against us began'.[91]

Lactantius adds how meantime an incident, probably at Antioch, had confirmed any suspicions Diocletian may have had about the loyalty of the Christians. At a public sacrifice performed in the presence of both emperors the *magister haruspicum*, Tagis, reported that the gods refused to make their will known because contrary influences, namely Christians, were present at the rites.[92] This touched the superstitious side of the Emperor's nature. He was furious, ordered all at court to sacrifice, and sent instructions to magistrates to oblige soldiers to do likewise. Any who failed to obey would be dismissed from the army. The affair, however, died down. Lactantius says no further measures were taken. Neither the Emperor's chamberlains nor Lactantius appear to have been molested.

We have now reached the last months of the year 302. How one describes the events immediately preceding the persecution depends on the credence one places on Lactantius. The latter held the post of professor of Latin at Diocletian's court at the time, and he claims to know what passed between Diocletian and Galerius there.[93] In their long discussions about the Christians, Galerius, urged on by his avowedly pagan mother, demanded their suppression by force, but Diocletian argued that to upset the peace of the world by bloodshed could do nothing but harm. The Christians in any event, would go voluntarily to their deaths. It was enough to purge the administration and army of them. High officials who were consulted gave different opinions. Some, prominent among whom was Hierocles, thought that the enemies of the gods and public religion should be destroyed, and others though less certain, were prepared to offer similar advice. Before deciding finally, however, Diocletian sent a senior augur to the famous oracle of the Milesian Apollo at Didyma in the Maeander valley, and when the latter replied in a hostile spirit to the divine religion (Respondit ille ut divinae religionis inimicus')[94] he needed no further prompting. The repression of Christianity had become a necessity.

Lactantius' story deserves credit. The contrast between Diocletian's caution and Galerius' impetuosity was not new, nor the subtle but real difference between the Emperor's loyalty to religious tradition and his Caesar's fanaticism for paganism. We see Diocletian reacting to the impotence of the oracle in the same way as he had reacted to the absence of livers in the sacrificial animals a few years before. The Christians were to blame. His devotion to this oracle of Apollo is further suggested by dedications to Zeus and Leto found in the sanctuary and erected in his name and Maximian's between 286 and 293.[95] It is difficult too, to dismiss Grégoire's brilliant reconstruction of the much-mutilated commemorative inscription enumerating the virtues of the shrine's prophets, which dates to this period. The mention of the 'βασιλεῖς' must refer to Diocletian and Galerius, and the readings χρηστιανῶν and θεός are clear. Even if Grégoire's embroideries are unjustified, the inscription indicates that the two emperors consulted the god on the subject of Christians and thus provides striking confirmation of Lactantius' accuracy.[96] Finally, the tradition preserved in Constantine's manifesto after the battle of Chrysopolis in October 324 appears to amplify Lactantius' enigmatic statement about the oracle's reply.[97] Constantine stated that the oracle lamented its impotence, on the grounds that 'the just upon earth stand in the way of his speaking the truth, and for this reason lies issued from his tripods'.[98] A priest in Diocletian's entourage was quick to point out that 'the just' in this context meant 'Christians', and the Emperor thereupon made his decision to persecute. On the whole, it must be conceded that if Lactantius was not hiding behind the curtains of the council chamber, he had a very good idea of what was about to happen.[99]

There remained only to fix a propitious day. Action was to be taken that same winter; the feast of Terminalia, 23 February, was settled upon, 'ut quasi terminus imponeretur huic religioni', adds Lactantius.[100] To the very end, however, Diocletian with his concern for public order and the welfare of the Empire as a whole, insisted that there must be no bloodshed. The object was to recall Christians to their duty of honouring the gods. The edict was prepared according to his wishes. At first light on 23 February, soldiers and Guardians of the Peace (irenarchs) accompanied by the pretorian prefect and other high officers went to the church at Nicomedia, situated in full view of the Imperial palace, and demolished it. The sacred books were burnt, and anything else found in the church given over to the mob.[101] The next day, the edict was published. It commanded that throughout the whole Empire churches were to be destroyed, and sacred books handed over to be burnt. Christians in the public service were to be removed from their offices: in civil life the *honestiores* were to lose their important privileges of birth and status, and no Christian might act as accuser in cases of personal injury, adultery and theft. Christian slaves might no longer be freed. Only the lives of the sectaries were spared; otherwise they were to be outlaws.[102] The precedents of Maximin and Valerian, striking principally at the Christian leadership, had been invoked; and as in these previous repressions the wealth of the Church was a primary target also.

The same day as the edict was posted up in the forum of Nicomedia it was torn down by a Christian, with the acid comment 'More victories over Goths and Sarmatians'. He was seized and roasted alive.[103] There followed other incidents. A mysterious fire broke out in the imperial palace, and this 'Reichstag Fire' sixteen centuries before time gave Galerius a chance to urge his thesis, namely that Christians should be treated as 'hostes publicae'. Once more, Diocletian hesitated. Exemplary punishment was meted out on Christians in the Imperial household who might conceivably have had a hand in the affair, but measures were confined to them. It was evidently a purge like that which had taken place in the army in 298-299 but this time involving the civil servants and slaves in the immediate service of the Emperor.[104]

A fortnight or so later, however, there was yet another fire, and this time Diocletian showed no mercy. From Lactantius we hear that several of 'the most powerful eunuchs' were executed, and from Eusebius it seems clear that this was the occasion when Peter, Gorgonius and Dorotheus were martyred.[105] The Empress Prisca and her daughter Valeria were compelled to sacrifice,[106] and in the capital the presbyters (though possibly not Bishop Anthimus himself) deacons and members of the Christian community were arrested and executed. The Calendar of Martyrs of the Church of Nicomedia records the priests Eusebius and Charalampus with no less than 268 martyrs on 28 April, a date chronologically possible for this incident.[107] Eusebius also speaks of 'heaps' of those done to death.[108] And as if to emphasize the uselessness of attempting an entirely bloodless repression, the next few weeks brought news of revolts in Syria and Melitene, both strongly Christian areas, and the Christians were said to be the instigators.[109] These were ruthlessly suppressed.

The next steps, however, still stopped short of general persecution against all Christians. The series of instructions to provincial governors sent out during the summer of 303 ordered the arrest of the heads of the Christian Churches,[110] and next, that they should be forced to sacrifice on pain of imprisonment, 'be compelled', says Eusebius, 'by every kind of device'.[111] Those who did so were to be set at liberty.

Meantime, Diocletian's western colleagues had been informed of what was afoot, but apart from Rome itself, North Africa, perhaps Baetica and some of the larger towns in the prefecture of the Gauls, Christianity was not an urgent problem in the western world. Maximian who controlled Italy and Africa enforced the First Edict, but not apparently the supplementary provisions contained in the Second and Third.[112] His Caesar, Constantius, took measures against Christian buildings in the prefecture of the Gauls, but did little else.[113]

In the autumn of 303, Diocletian left Nicomedia for Rome to celebrate his *Vicennalia* which fell on 20 November.[114] On this festival the customary amnesty was given to criminals, and the most determined efforts were made to force unwilling Christian leaders to sacrifice and so qualify for release. To cite Eusebius again, concerning events in Palestine,

Thus, in the case of one man, others held him fast by both hands, brought him to the altar, and let fall on it out of his right hand the polluted and accursed sacrifice: then he was dismissed as if he had been sacrificed. . . . When yet another cried out and testified that he was not yielding, he was struck on the mouth and silenced by a large body of persons appointed for that purpose, and forcibly driven away even though he had not sacrificed. So much store did they set on seeming by any means to have accomplished their purpose. (*Martyrs of Palestine*, 1.4.[S], tr. Lawlor and Oulton.)

In fact, during 303, the measures of the authorities did not appear to Eusebius as futile. Some leaders did lapse, 'shamefully hiding themselves here and there', or were produced as objects of public mockery.[115] His description of the crowds besieging the temples at Caesarea, perhaps in Diocletian's presence, shows that the Emperor's orders were not being treated lightly. For a brief moment it was the turn of Christians to feel desperate, and the deacon Romanus paid for his act of fanaticism with his life.[116]

Diocletian did not enjoy his stay in Rome. Like Constantine and Constantius II after him he found the hearty turbulence of the Roman people too much.[117] He economized on the Games, and by mid-December he and the populace were glad to see the last of each other. He left on 20 December, and like his fifth-century successors made for Ravenna, but the mid-winter journey laid him open to a lingering infection, which incapacitated him at this vital moment in the struggle against the Christians. The spring and summer were spent in the Danube provinces, and when some time before 28 August[118] he re-entered Nicomedia his health deteriorated seriously. He was confined to his palace through the winter. in December there were rumours of his death, but by February 305 he was recovering, just sufficiently to make one ghastly public appearance on 1 March 305 at which he was scarcely recognizable.[119] Meantime, Galerius had been in control. The Fourth Edict ordering a general sacrifice by all Christians had been promulgated. The 'dies thurificationis' was enforced first in Galerius' own provinces, then in the summer by Maximian in the west, and finally, so it appears, by Diocletian himself in February-March 305.[120]

If this chronology is correct, it may be possible to reconcile the account given by Lactantius of Galerius' pressure in the winter

304/305 on the feeble Diocletian to abdicate, with Aurelius Victor's verdict that the Emperor 'imminentium scrutator',[121] chose this course to escape 'impending internal disasters'. The tardy acceptance of Galerius' edict could be seen as the reluctant admission of defeat, and the abdication as the logical conclusion. On 1 May 305, a great parade of troops were held at Nicomedia. Diocletian addressed them for the last time, claimed in a moving speech that he has saved the civilized world (the οἰκουμένη) and then stepped down from the rostrum a private citizen.[122] At Milan, Maximian performed the same act less willingly. Diocletian was still only in his late 50s and had eight (or perhaps eleven) years of retirement before him,[123] but he had finished, and the great palace at Spalato beckoned.

Then came a surprise. For the last few years Constantine, Constantius' son, had been at Diocletian's court, supposedly being trained to take over a share in the government. But the two new Caesars introduced for acclamation were Galerius' nephew Maximin Daza and another rough but efficient Illyrian officer named Severus.[124] Possibly youth and inexperience, but possibly also on account of his birth out of wedlock had decided against Constantine; but for whatever reasons, he and Maxentius, Maximian's son who had also been passed over, would be wary of the new rulers. The Second Tetrarchy had begun by disinheriting the heirs-apparent of the First. It remained to be seen whether they would be able to continue the war against the Christians in face of the opposition of these princes. For, if that policy succeeded the latter would stay disinherited.

We must now turn to the application of the edicts in the provinces. The information comes from four main areas, in the west, North Africa, and in the east, Palestine, Egypt and Bithynia with Nicomedia. For North Africa, the accounts of the official investigations at Cirta and Apthungi are supplemented by authentic *Acta Martyrum*, and other contemporary documents. These were sedulously kept by Donatists and Catholics in the fourth century for the purpose of vindicating their respective roles in the Great Persecution. Outside North Africa, including Rome, we are very badly informed. For Baetica (southern Spain) the canons of the Council of Elvira may be relevant, and are treated as such here. Rome, largely thanks to its involvement in the Donatist controversy, provides some documentation strongly suggestive of its bishop, Marcellinus (296–304), having sacrificed to the gods. Sicily provides the *Acta* of the deacon Euplus.[125] Gaul and Britain may have escaped the effects of the persecution almost entirely. In Britain, however, the tradition of St. Alban's martyrdom at Verulamium is a consistent one attested by two independent sources, and his shrine on the hill east of the city formed the major link between the Roman and mediaeval occupations.[126] St. Ursula of Colonia (Köln), on the other hand, seems to be legendary.[127]

In the east, to the probable eye-witness accounts of events in Nicomedia-Bithynia by Lactantius 303–305 and of Palestine from 303–311 and Egypt 311–312 by Eusebius, may be added as contemporary sources the canons of the Council of Ancyra in 314 and of Peter of Alexandria in 306 and two important papyri, the account of Peter's visit to Oxyrhynchus soon after the persecution had begun,[128] and the Letter of Psenosiris.[129] The extent, however, to which the multifarious *Acta Martyrum* of the period can be used must remain largely a matter of subjective judgment.[130] For the Danubian provinces, however, the *Acta* of Dasius,[131] of Agape, Eirène, Chioné and companions from Thessalonica,[132] of Philippus of Heraclea,[133] probably for Egypt under Maximin, those of Phileas and Philoromus[134] and in Edessa *circa* 310, the *Acta of Habib*,[135] all seem to contain authentic contemporary material. The *Acta* of Tarachus and his companions,[136] of Theodotus of Ancyra[137] and the Forty Martyrs of Sebaste (for Licinius' repression)[138] are perhaps among those which provide the historian with something more solid than pious legend. None the less, reliance on the two principal witnesses remains heavy.[139]

The persecution took slightly different forms in east and west respectively. In the west, the question was still one of enforcing the law, law directed as much against Church property as against persons. Even in North Africa the authorities showed themselves masters of the situation, and appear from extant records to have carried out their duties without fuss or panic. In less than two years all, from their point of view, had been completed. Buildings had been destroyed, Scriptures handed over, the organization of the Church severely shaken, and a goodly number of clergy and laity coerced into sacrificing. In the east, however, one feels a deeper sense of urgency. The persecution was part of a long-drawn-out battle for the minds of the provincials, the final, bloody act of a great tragedy. There was propaganda and counter-propaganda, acts of judicial cruelty balanced by acts of anti-pagan fanaticism; repression on the one hand, and rebellion on the other. It was real 'war' as Eusebius described it.[140] In Egypt it was in the end civil war.[141] By 311, however, it was clear that Christianity could not be crushed. Licinius had already realized the fact. Constantine's victory at the Milvian Bridge the next year set the seal on the Christian victory.

It is unfortunate that neither Eusebius (*Hist. Eccl.*) nor Lactantius have set down the events they describe in precise chronological order. Lactantius, for instance, would appear to relate the general sacrifice ordered by Galerius in 304 to the period immediately after the second fire in the Imperial palace at Nicomedia in the previous year. It was then, he appears to say, that the magistrates 'dispersed through all the temples forced everyone to sacrifice' (*De Mortibus*, 15.4) and altars were set up in the halls of civil basilicas and in front of magistrates' tribunals so that litigants should be forced to do sacrifice or cast incense before pleading their cases (*De Mortibus*, 15.5).[142] From other sources it seems quite clear, however, that the measures in 303 were directed mainly at the clergy and public organization of the Church.[142a] Similarly, it is not possible to date all the various outrages against the Christians which Eusebius describes province by province in *H.E.*, viii.7–13 to specific phases in the persecution. While those relating to Palestine (viii.7) and the Thebaid (viii.9) where Eusebius writes as an eyewitness can be determined by reference to the chronology established in the *Palestinian Martyrs* or by known facts about his movements, this cannot be done for some of the other provinces, such as Arabia and Cappadocia. On the other hand, as both Eusebius and Lactantius describe the destruction of the Christian township in Phrygia and the massacre of its inhabitants, one is inclined to place this event early in the persecution before Lactantius left for Gaul. The horrors, however, which Eusebius records in Pontus (*H.E.*, viii. 12.6–7) may have occurred after Hierocles' governorship, i.e. after the abdication of Diocletian, and the scenes at Antioch (*H.E.*, viii.12.3–6) fit the first half of Maximin's reign, before the latter modified the death penalty to torture and forced labour.[143]

Much obscurity remains. What is clear, however, is that so long as Diocletian was in control the emphasis lay on propaganda and measures aimed at forcing Christians either to submit or to co-operate in prayer and service to the gods of the Empire. The policy of Diocletian follows in the same tradition as Trajan's and Decius'. This remains true despite the Emperor's ferocious reaction to the second outbreak of fire in his palace at Nicomedia and the massacre in Phrygia. Hierocles, whom Lactantius names as the 'author and counsellor of the persecution against us',[144] and his fellow magistrates in Bithynia concentrated on winning the intellectual battle of persuading Christians that sacrifice was not harmful, and they put tremendous effort into it.[145] Their object was to show that as matters stood, the Christian religion was not only incompatible with loyalty to the Tetrarchy and its achievement, but was self-contradictory and woven around an individual who on close investigation turned out to be merely a minor rebel chieftain in Palestine. It was a religion unworthy of a sane individual's credence.

Lactantius preserves evidence of two of these propaganda tracts.[146] The first, that of Hierocles entitled 'Philalethes' or 'The Lover of Truth to the Christians', was the subject of a lengthy refutation by Eusebius, which proves its circulation beyond Bithynia and perhaps indicates its comparative effectiveness.[147] Hierocles seems to have extracted material from Porphyry's massive κατὰ χριστιανῶν assembling in two books aspects of his mentor's work which he thought best calculated to appeal to a literate and conservative-minded provincial audience.[148] The majesty of God was contrasted with the inadequacy of Jesus and the futility of his pretensions. Hierocles upbraided people who believed in Jesus on account of his miracles, which in fact were no more remarkable than the deeds of Aristeas of Proconnesos, Pythagoras, and above all, of Apollonius of Tyana, to whom he subjected Jesus to a detailed comparison.[149] Compared, too, with Apollonius' biographer, Damis, Jesus' disciples, including Peter and Paul, were crude and unlettered individuals whose accounts of their hero's life were romances which did not tally with each other. Finally, Jesus' pretensions as a magician covered social-revolutionary aims justly ended when he and his band of 900 followers were routed by his own people, the Jews.[150] The moral behind this diatribe was that those who continued to put their trust in such a person and refused honour to the immortal gods of the Empire could not complain if they were punished.

The second work was slighter.[151] Lactantius speaks of an unnamed philosopher who 'vomited forth three books against the Christian religion and name', which in fact was an exhortation to Christians to give up defiance and exhibitionism and return to the worship of the gods, for whom he provided a reasoned defence. This was the sort of tract, upholding and explaining the value of traditional rites and ceremonies, which paganism had needed for the previous two centuries, but now it was outdated, and many, Lactantius adds, thought it untimely.[152]

These efforts did not go wholly unrewarded. Indeed, at this stage, the best hope for paganism lay in applying constant pressure to the Christian leaders, combined with adroit anti-Christian propaganda for the benefit of an audience to whom charges of disloyalty and magic were credible.[153] Both Eusebius and Lactantius admit that considerable numbers of Christians yielded, some willingly, others worn down after standing firm for some time. Canon 3 of the Council of Ancyra shows that some Christians even became government agents and persuaded others to lapse with them. Another canon refers to those who put on their best clothes to offer their submission to the gods (Canon 4), a genuine return to ancestral usages. In Egypt, Peter of Alexandria fled, an action which was to have grave consequences for Christianity there in the next decades. Braver men, such as Meletius, bishop of Lycopolis in Upper Egypt resented this chicken-heartedness and they were supported by many of the monks and clergy imprisoned with them. Apart from rare instances, however, such as at Gaza in Palestine there was no great popular enthusiasm for the persecutions.[154] Times had changed radically since Decius.

The Fourth Edict, however, changed the emphasis of the persecution from forcible persuasion to outright repression, and with this development the zeal of the authorities came into conflict with the desperate resolution of members of the Christian laity. In this trial of strength the Christian tradition of martyrdom was perhaps of decisive importance.

In the eastern provinces there was little need for the death penalty at the outset. For instance, in Palestine the 'first year' of the persecution, which in Eusebius' view evidently lasted from the arrival of the First Edict on 2 April 303 until 1 January 305 only three Christians lost their lives, and these provoked their fate.[155] In the remainder of Diocletian's dominions Gordius (a voluntary martyr),[156] Tarachus and his companions at Anazarbus in Cilicia,[157] and Calliopus at Pompeiopolis in Lycia on 7 April 304 perhaps complete the tale of victims for 303–304.[158] With the publication of the Fourth Edict however, and the execution of eight Christians at Caesarea on 24 March 305 one begins to detect a new spirit.[159] Each side was coming to realize that this was the decisive battle.

The pagan forces were now commanded by Galerius, a man in whose affections, even if we discount much of Lactantius' description, neither Rome nor her culture had much place, and who also burned with a fanatical hatred for the new religion.[160] But even in Galerius' Danubian and Thracian provinces, the period before the Fourth Edict produced relatively few victims. At Durostorum, Dasius was executed on 20 November 303 as much for military insubordination as for Christianity.[161] At Heraclea in Thrace, the provincial governor, Bassus, whose wife was a Christian, merely locked and sealed the church. Only later when he saw the bishop holding a service outside it, he had him arrested with his deacon and brought to trial on 6 January 304. Still, though the Scriptures and sacred vessels of the church were burnt, the death penalty was not exacted. Both clerics were committed to prison until 22 October when Bassus' successor Justinus, who was a keener pagan than he, ordered them to be burnt alive as an example to others.[162] Meantime, three sisters, Agape, Chioné and Eirene and their friends who refused to sacrifice and admitted to hiding large numbers of copies of the Scriptures were martyred at Thessalonica on 1 April 304.[163] Later that same month Bishop Irenaeus was executed at Sirmium on the orders of Probus, the governor of Pannonia,[164] and Domnio the immigrant bishop of Salona died on 11 April a martyr.[165] But that was seemingly all. The wild beast in Galerius was still held in check.

In the West the attitude of the authorities was not notably different. The city magistrates often knew and liked the Christian leaders, but were determined to administer the law. In modern police terminology, they were 'correct'. The first edict arrived in North Africa by mid-April and was immediately acted upon. Christian clergy were required to hand over their Scriptures, and in some (but apparently not all) cases do sacrifice as well. Churches were destroyed, church property confiscated, and Christian services were forbidden. In Proconsular Africa the relations between pagans and Christians do not seem to have been bad, for it was from his Christian acquaintances that the *Duumvir* of Apthungi, Alfius Caecilianus first heard of the arrival of the edict, though the destruction of the churches at Furni and Zama had shown him something was afoot.[166] He at once carried out its provisions in Apthungi, and in accordance with proconsular instructions, ordered public sacrifices to be made as well.[167] At this stage there was a good measure of compliance among the Christian clergy. The bishops of Furni, Zama and Abitina are among those who openly co-operated with the authorities and surrendered their Scriptures, thus earning for themselves the ill-omened name of 'traditor'. Even at Carthage, Bishop Mensurius salved his conscience by handing over scriptures of 'the new heretics' (Manichaeans?) to satisfy the authorities.[168] Few ecclesiastics followed Felix, bishop of Thibiuca and accepted martyrdom rather than surrender (15 July 303).[169]

In Numidia, the news of the persecution caused initial panic. At Cirta, the capital, the Christians fled disconsolately into the Chettaba (Mons Bellona), a mountainous wilderness some five miles south of the city. On 19 May the *curator* (mayor) of the city 'came to the house where the Christians used to meet', and the following scene took place.

> The mayor to Paul the bishop: 'Bring out the writings of the law and anything else that you have here, according to the order, so that you may obey the command.'
> *The Bishop:* 'The readers have the Scriptures, but we will give what we have here.'
> *The Mayor:* 'Point out the readers or send for them.'
> *The Bishop:* 'You all know them.'
> *The Mayor:* 'We do not know them.'
> *The Bishop:* 'The municipal office knows them, that is the clerks, Edusius and Junius.'

The Mayor: 'Leaving over the matter of the readers whom the office will point out, produce what you have.'
(*Gesta apud Zenophilum, CSEL.,* 26, pp. 186–7. Cited from J. Stevenson, *A New Eusebius,* pp. 287–8.)

The bishop complied and there was brought out church plate and other property, including a large amount of men and women's clothes and shoes. All this was produced in front of the clergy who included three priests, two deacons, and four sub-deacons, and a number of 'diggers'. The mayor then continued his examination in order to get hold of the Scriptures. Successively the sub-deacons and readers were questioned. There was a certain amount of argument and prevarication, as each tried to shield the other, but in the end the mayor got his way. The copies of the Scriptures were quietly given up and so too was the movable wealth of the church at Cirta. Among those who took part was the sub-deacon Silvanus, and he was not allowed to forget his share in the surrender.

Nothing further seems to have befallen the bishop who died not long afterwards. His case was not exceptional. At a synod of twelve Numidian bishops who met on 5 March 305 to elect his successor, no less than four admitted to having handed over the Scriptures to the authorities and a fifth only escaped doing so by feigning blindness. The Primate, Secundus of Tigisis, was far from being above suspicion. At this stage, the authorities were clearly on top, and to some extent they remained so as long as they held the initiative—and so long as the death penalty was merely hinted at. When on 5 December 304 the Proconsul Anulinus interrogated the confessor Crispina at Theveste (Tebessa) he could say with some justification, 'All Africa had sacrificed',[170] so why should not she?

On the other hand, the compliant conduct of many of the clergy was not universally accepted. Another near-contemporary document tells how towards the end of 303 the congregation of the small settlement of Abitina in the upper valley of the Mejerda river had continued to hold services under the leadership of a presbyter after their bishop had given way to the authorities. News of their stand had apparently reached Carthage, for, as we have seen, they were being joined by ardent Christians from the capital. Not surprisingly their activities became known to the authorities, and one day all forty-seven members of the congregation were

arrested and sent for judgment to Carthage.[171] While in prison
these confessors met in solemn conclave and condemned *traditor*
clergy in angry terms.[172] If even to alter a single letter of Scripture
was a crime, then to hand over the whole Bible for destruction by
pagan magistrates merited eternal damnation. Whoever, therefore, they declared, maintained communion with *traditores*
would not participate with them in the joys of Paradise. Thus they
claimed the same rights of binding and loosing which the confessors of the Decian and earlier persecutions had claimed, and the
language of the martyrologist specifically recalls that of the
bishops at Cyprian's great Council on Baptism.[173] Here was an
attack on the existing hierarchical system in Carthage, and the
behaviour of Mensurius' archdeacon Caecilian did not make the
position easier. Caecilian was said to have prevented the confessors
being brought food by well-wishers and to have assisted their
ultimate death by starvation. [174]

From an independent contemporary source it is possible to
gather that Caecilian was hostile to the veneration which the
confessors aroused. In an exchange of letters between Mensurius
and Secundus of Tigisis shortly after the end of the persecution,
Mensurius describes how in Carthage many rushed forward in
enthusiasm, pretending they possessed Scriptures which they
refused to give up. Others found prison and the reputation of
being a confessor a convenient way of evading debts to the
treasury.[175] Such action Mensurius deplored and the archdeacon
was there to give his views effect. Mensurius, to be just, was
merely following the other aspect of Cyprianic teaching which
forbade voluntary martyrdom[176]—but he lacked the courage and
conviction which Cyprian inspired, and which the confessors
had in full measure.

The issue of the *traditor* clergy would in any case have disrupted
the African Church. The year 304, however, by adding a large
number of individual martyrs, especially from Numidia, to the
roll,[177] introduced a new element of bitterness which was to
render that disruption permanent. That the Fourth Edict was
enforced in Africa seems evident despite the many difficulties in
interpreting the evidence.[178] First, the victims in 304 were layfolk,
such as the women arrested on the Saltus Cephalitanus in proconsular Africa and executed on 30 July,[179] and perhaps all the

thirty-four martyrs recorded at Haidra (Ammaedara),[180] in contrast to the clerics or organized congregations arrested in the previous year. Secundus of Tigisis speaks of 'patres familiae' who had been killed, as though he had first-hand evidence.[181] Secondly, Eusebius compares specifically the persecution in Africa with the horrific scenes he witnessed in Egypt.[182] Neither this, nor the statement in *Mart. Pal.* (13.12) that the persecution in the west lasted 'not fully two years'[182a] would make sense if the persecution had ended effectively in the spring of 304, i.e. before Eusebius' first 'persecution year' was complete, especially when Maximian was known to have been more anti-Christian than Diocletian. Thirdly, the *Acta Crispinae* refer to December 304, and the confessor was required to sacrifice (and not hand over Scriptures). This seems to be based on an authentic incident.[183] In addition, Valerius Florus' *dies thurificationis* and the martyrs of Milevis who died as a result have been recorded on an inscription from Mastar (Castellum Elephantum).[183a] Though this has been discounted on the grounds that by November 303 he had already ceased to be governor of Numidia Militana, he is now shown by an inscription from Aqua Viva to have been governor of Numidia as a whole (not only Numidia Militana) in 303.[184] It is not certain that he had been relieved of this position by the end of the year. Finally, if the dating of the Council of Elvira to 15 May 309 is correct, the case against the Fourth Edict becomes even more difficult to uphold. These canons clearly have apostasy by sacrifice rather than surrender of the Scriptures in mind,[185] and Spain formed part of Maximian's dominions.

In Rome the chief recorded incidents refer to the requirement that the bishop and his clergy should sacrifice and surrender Scriptures (i.e. Edicts 1 and 2). The question whether Marcellinus did or did not lapse has been debated for over two centuries. Tillemont[186] rejected the suggestion with horror, but more recent writers have been less sure.[187] The case against Marcellinus is derived from two quite different sets of documents. In the first place, the Donatists possessed two separate accounts of the affair. One was probably an ecclesiastical document relating to the return of Church property to Pope Miltiades by Maxentius in 311, in which the deacons Strato and Cassian were mentioned. It implied that these had in some way participated in acts of sacrifice (perhaps when the property was handed over) during the Persecution 'under the third bishop before Miltiades', which could only be Marcellinus.[188] The second was used by Petilian of Constantine on two occasions and was probably also a protocol recording that Marcellinus and his presbyters, Marcellus, Miltiades and Silvester sacrificed. As Röttges points out, we cannot assume that the Donatists forged both documents.[189] In particular, the reference to Marcellus suggests authenticity. The latter, whether 'acting bishop' or true successor to Marcellinus, had passed from the scene some years before the Donatist conflict broke out, and left a reputation as a stern enforcer of penitential discipline towards the lapsed.[190] A Donatist forger, even if he had heard of him, would hardly have associated him with Miltiades and Silvester. At the Conference of Carthage between the Donatists and the Catholics in 411, the latter did not accuse their opponents of forgery but asserted simply that the prolix *Gesta* which the Donatists produced did not prove what they wanted, namely that Marcellinus himself had been a *traditor*.

To these documents may be added others less immediately concerned with Marcellinus himself. The *Liber Pontificalis* (circa 530) records that Marcellinus was led to sacrifice 'in order that he might throw incense, which he did . . . ', and bitter was his regret. Secondly, the Acts of the Council of Sinuessa also describe Marcellinus as sacrificing and as admitting to casting incense on a brazier on top of live coals (*super prunas*).[191] The *Acta* are now generally agreed to be an early sixth-century forgery derived from the challenge to the validity of Pope Symmachus' election in 500, but none the less they would appear to incorporate traditions circulating in Rome at the time. There was a long-standing Novatianist movement in Rome, active in one form or another down to the first half of the fifth century,[192] and this may have been responsible for perpetuating Marcellinus' ill fame. If one adds finally, that as early as 314 the Donatists showed their suspicions of Miltiades, Marcellinus' presbyter, by regarding the Roman see as 'vacant' and appointing their own 'intervenor' there,[193] the case against Marcellinus would appear to be a strong one. As Röttges suggests, the probability is that an act of *traditio* did take place in Rome.[194] It seems hardly possible that the bishop was not in some way concerned in it.

In the remainder of the west there were scattered martyrdoms as the result of the edicts. In Spain, Hosius of Cordova could claim 40 years later to have been a confessor,[195] and his colleague Valerius of Saragossa is said to have been exiled, though the latter's arch-deacon, Vincentius, was killed.[196] At Merida, Eulalia the virgin provoked her end by declaring that the gods and Maximian were 'nothing', spitting at the praetor and overthrowing his altar.[197] In Sicily the deacon Euplus also courted martyrdom by acts of defiance, telling the *consularis* Calvisianus that he had long wanted to die for the name of Christ, and refusing either to give up the Scriptures or sacrifice to Mars.[198] The magistrate thought him mad. In Gaul, the consensus of contemporary opinion was that Constantius did not continue the persecution beyond token acts, and therefore Gallic bishops were suitable arbitrators in the dispute between Caecilian of Carthage and his opponents in 313.[199]

Altogether in the west, the persecution hardly deserves the title of 'Great'. Outside of the province of Numidia there were relatively few victims. Church life was disrupted, and ecclesiastics discredited but the laity as a whole were little affected. Even before the abdication of Diocletian persecution in North Africa was ending. Just as under Decius the authorities seemed to have been satisfied once the Imperial orders had been given formal obedience. In the first months of 305 the Christians in Numidia were raising their heads again, and the popular tumult which carried the sub-deacon Silvanus to the vacant bishopric of Cirta foreshadowed what was in store once external pressure was released, and confessor and *traditor* confronted one another.

The Final Conflict 306-313

In the east there were to be six more years of misery. Eusebius speaks of the violent contrast which now developed in the politics of the eastern and western parts of the Roman world with regard to the Christians.[200] In his nephew, Maximin, Galerius had found an ideal lieutenant. In many ways the most intelligent of the persecuting emperors, he was also served by able adminis-trators such as Hierocles, promoted 306/307 (?) to be prefect of Egypt,[201] Picentius, three times consul, who headed his finances, Culcianus who had preceded Hierocles as prefect of Egypt[202] and the Neo-Platonist, and perhaps a convert from Christianity,[203] Theotecnus, *curator* of Antioch. These were the men who planned and executed the final assault against the Christians. The Emperor himself can hardly be dismissed as the lewd parasite and 'monster of iniquity' as Eusebius and Lactantius paint him.[204] His few surviving letters show him to be an able man who saw the problem of Christianity as a whole, in both its theological and political aspects, and acted accordingly. In his rescript to the citizens of Tyre in answer to their petition for the removal of Christians from their midst, written in late spring of 312, he makes an idealistic plea for religious unity centred on the immortal gods of Rome. The harmony of the physical universe which kept the forces of chaos at bay and made human life and happiness possible depended on the benevolent care of the gods for mankind. Human prosperity shown in 'the waving ears of corn already ripening in the broad plains', was the answer given by the gods to the return of numerous Christians to their ancestral faith.[205] The appeal to public opinion in the cities when nearly all seemed lost after the palinode of Galerius was a bold move in keeping with the character of its author. The appeal too, to religious harmony and unity under divine guidance was in tune with the aspirations of the provincials, as Constantine was to find within a decade.

Moreover, except perhaps in Egypt where persecution degenerated into brutality and civil war, the repression of Christianity was accompanied by energetic and intelligent measures to reform and reorganize paganism. Temples which had fallen into disuse were restored and sacred groves re-planted.[206] Perhaps in conscious imitation of the Church, each city was to have its local hierarchy of priests closely allied to the city magistrates. The priests themselves were drawn from amongst those who had shown themselves zealous in the service of paganism.[207] In turn, they were to be responsible to high priests serving the provincial capitals, chosen also for the same qualities. All the time too, the reconversion of Christians was being pressed forward. Maximin was the only emperor before Julian who seems to have considered this a serious possibility. Others had either followed the passive hopelessness expressed by the Sibyl,[208] or had been content to accept symbolic loyalty to the pagan past. The circulation (and perhaps fabrication) of the *Acts of Pilate*, and their teaching to school-children suggests that Maximin had longer-term views.[209] Like his great rival in the west, Constantine, he aimed at the unification of his dominions through the common bond of religion. He was true to the ideals of the Tetrarchy; but for paganism, his efforts came fifty years too late.

The actual repression of the Church during his government, both as Caesar (305-309) and Augustus (309-313) was as intermittent as before. If Eusebius' *Palestinian Martyrs* is representative, the periods of acute persecution were confined to the spring of 306 and the autumn and winter of 309/310, and even then many of the martyrdoms were provoked. On the other hand, prominent Christians and the great libraries of Caesarea and Jerusalem escaped harm. But Christian services were banned, arrested confessors were not released and a sense of brooding insecurity hung over all. It is clear that throughout the period 306-311 Christians never knew when their turn might come. Even so, the spirit of the pagans was flagging. Persecution was no longer a popular policy and, as Athanasius was to say, many pagans now sympathized with the Christians.[210]

After nearly a year of suspense and confusion,[211] Maximin issued an edict around Easter 306[212] calling on everyone regardless of age and sex to sacrifice at the temples under the supervision of the magistrates.[213] The planning had been thorough. In addition to heralds calling everyone to the temples, army officers were equipped with census lists from which to call out individuals to sacrifice. In Caesarea, Eusebius relates how Apphianus, a youthful and zealous convert from one of the noble houses in Lycia, seized the governor Urbanus by the right hand to prevent him sacrificing. He was atrociously tortured and executed on 2 April 306.[214] The same day another Christian was done to death at Tyre as if he was a parricide, i.e. shut up in a sack of raw ox-hide with a dog and poisonous snake and thrown into the sea. However, Eusebius records no further victims in Palestine following these measures. In the summer persecution died down, and when Maximin arrived in Caesarea in November to celebrate the games there on 20 November, there was only one Christian to be thrown to the impressive array of beasts which had been brought together for the occasion, and he had been arrested under Diocletian.[215]

Next year, 307, Maximin changed his tactics. For the death penalty he substituted savage mutilation and consignment to hard labour in the mines and quarries.[216] This situation lasted from the spring of 307 until the autumn of 308. In Caesarea, some well-known Christians were arrested, including Pamphilus the leading Christian scholar in Palestine, the disciple, defender and biographer of Origen. Not even fifteen months in prison broke his spirit and finally he was executed even as he wrote his *Defence of Origen*, 16 February 310.[217] Meantime, the Egyptian quarries were becoming overpopulated by Christian convicts, and Egyptian confessors, many of whom had been terribly mutilated, began to be transferred to the copper mines of Phaeno in southern Palestine. They brought with them a new spirit of resolution and resistance. The last chapters of the *Palestinian Martyrs* are dominated by tales of their defiance. Their 'invincible constancy' and fanatical zeal in face of every form of torment impressed pagan, Jew and Christian alike.[218] Their activity is further evidence for the grimness of the situation in Egypt itself. None the less, some executions continued in Palestine during 308. Christians holding services in secret near Gaza were tortured and sent to the mines. One of them, a woman, who made a seditious remark was cruelly executed, together with a bystander who protested against this treatment.[219] On 25 July there was another execution,[220] and soon after the provincials could witness the world wide character of the conflict, as another convoy of 130 Egyptians was moved through Palestine on its way to the mines in Cilicia.[221]

By the autumn of 308 tension had been relaxed once more.[222] Two reasons may be suggested. First, the sudden fall from favour of the governor of Palestine, Urbanus, and secondly, Maximin's attention was diverted to the conference at Carnuntum held in November. The recognition there of his rival Licinius as Augustus was believed by Christians to have been the cause of what proved to be the last order for a general sacrifice.[223] It is difficult, however, to see any direct connection between these two events, though Maximin was exceedingly angry at being passed over. Licinius himself had been a loyal comrade-in-arms of Galerius, and though from 311–314 he was to trim his sails before the wind of victorious Christianity he was at heart no enemy of the traditional worship.[224] In any event, the following year, when he struck again, Maximin's measures were thorough. Eusebius speaks of an 'edict', designed both to strike at Christianity and restore paganism. It must be dated some time in the middle of 309, before 13 November, the date of martyrdoms as the result of it. Food on sale in the markets was sprinkled with libations and the blood of sacrifices. As in Antiochus' day, people were compelled to taste the sacrifices.[225] The *curator* and *duoviri* of each city, and the *tabularius* who kept the census records were instructed to enforce the edict and soldiers stood on duty at public baths to compel bathers to conform. This period too, saw steps taken to rebuild ruined temples and reorganize the cult. It was the decisive moment, but it was the pagans' will that began to give way. Eusebius noted that even the 'unbelieving heathen' thought the edict harsh and even absurd,[226] even though public opinion was still prepared to see it carried out. The reaction of the Christians also was strong. Three young men attempted to prevent the new governor, Firmilian, from sacrificing, and they, together with a woman named Ennathas, were beheaded on 13 November 309.[227] Before the end of the year three more Egyptians, carrying comforts to their imprisoned compatriots, were apprehended and put to death.[228]

In the first months of 310 persecution continued, but after February which witnessed the execution of Pamphilus and his pupils it tended to become more desultory. Eusebius records Eubulus, as the last of the Palestinian martyrdoms, 7 March 310.[229] At Phaeno Christians contrived to organize themselves and build rudimentary house-churches,[230] and when the superintendent of the copper mines wished to take action against them, he felt it necessary to apply to Maximin first before making any move. Once more the wrath fell on the Egyptians, and the ringleaders, who were executed, comprised two bishops, Meletius' friend Peleus, and Nilus, a presbyter, and a well-known confessor, Patermuthius.[231] Shortly after, however, the brittle nature of the pagan revival began to be unmasked. Galerius had presumably been carrying out persecuting measures in his own dominions, and is perhaps fortunate in having no Eusebius to record them as an eye-witness.[232] In the spring of 311 he was struck down by a fatal disease which the Christians gleefully described in horrific detail.[233] It was a lingering malady, and the Emperor had time to

meditate over its causes.[234] Was this the vengeance of the Christian God? If so, what amends could he make? In April 311 Licinius
was at Serdica, and perhaps at his instance, the Emperor drafted
the famous edict which has gone down to history as the Palinode
of Galerius.

Among other steps which we are always taking for the profit and
advantage of the State we had formerly sought to set all things right
according to the ancient laws and public order (*disciplinam*) of the
Romans and further to provide that the Christians too who had
abandoned the way of life (*sectam*) of their own fathers should
return to sound reason (*ad bonas mentes*). For the said Christians had
somehow become possessed by such obstinacy (read [*mala*] *voluntas*)
and folly that, instead of following those institutions of the ancients
which perchance their own ancestors had first established, they were
at their own will and pleasure making laws for themselves and
acting upon them and were assembling in different places people of
different nationalities. After we had decreed that they should
return to the institutions of the ancients, many were subjected to
danger, many too were completely overthrown; and when very
many (or 'most'—*plurimi*) persisted in their determination and we saw
that they neither gave worship and due reverence to the gods nor
practised the worship (*observare*) of the god of the Christians, considering our most gentle clemency and our immemorial custom by
which we are wont to grant indulgence to all men, we have thought
it right in their case too to extend the speediest indulgence to the
effect that they may once more be free to live (*sint*) as Christians
and may re-form their churches (*conventicula componant*) always
provided that they do nothing contrary to (public) order (*disciplinam*). Further by another letter we shall inform provincial governors
(*iudicibus*) what conditions the Christians must observe. Wherefore
in accordance with this our indulgence they will be bound to entreat
their god for our well-being and for that of the State and for their
own so that on every side the State may be preserved unharmed and
that they themselves may live in their homes in security. (Tr. N. H.
Baynes, *CAH.*, xii, 672).

The problem of text need not be discussed here.[235] The
meaning is clear enough.[236] The measures against the Christians
had been aimed (as in the past)[237] at upholding the traditions which
had made the Roman commonwealth great, and of correcting
aberrant folly (*stultitia*) of the Christians. The words in the
opening sentence '*iuxta leges veteres et publicam disciplinam*

Romanorum cuncta corrigere, atque id providere, ut etiam christiani qui parentum suorum reliquerant sectam, ad bonas mentes redirent', portray the spirit of the legislation of the Tetrarchy on other matters. 'Publicam disciplinam Romanorum' had been invoked by Diocletian against both Manichees and those living in unlawful wedlock.[238] But the Christians had remained obdurate. They had refused to return to the worship of the gods but did not worship their own god.[239] This had now had dire effects. The Christian God had shown that he required placating. So, let there be Christians again (*denvo sint christiani et conventicula sua componant*) as long as public order was not offended. Anything was better than a large group in the Empire with no god at all! This meant a return to the situation pre-303. It was an amnesty. Prisons were to be opened and confessors freed.[240] In a second rescript the Christians were requested to pray to Him 'for our safety and that of the commonwealth'. The edict and rescript were published on 30 April. The Christian God was not appeased. On 5 May Galerius was dead. The edict had been promulgated in the names of Galerius, Constantine, Licinius and Maximin.

Meantime, events in the west had already ensured that persecution could never again be renewed effectively. Constantine, we remember, had been passed over at the ceremony at Nicomedia on 1 May 305. For some months he remained at Galerius' court, then early in 306 he received the Emperor's permission to visit his father in Britain, who was seriously ill. Immediately afterwards, however, Galerius thought better of it, and tried to stop him. Constantine got clean away, arrived in Britain and when Constantius died at York on 25 July 306 the legions proclaimed him not Caesar, but Augustus. He was then about 25 years old. He had won the first of many triumphs.

Galerius was too prudent to defy the legions from the distance of Nicomedia. Constantine was recognized as Caesar and this he accepted. Meantime, however, the other 'disinherited', Maxentius, had been active. Severus' rule in Italy was unpopular, and when he attempted to institute a census for Rome and Italy preparatory to raising taxes, the people of Rome rebelled. On 26 October 306 Maxentius assumed the title of 'princeps invictus' and held the city with south Italy and Africa. When Severus attempted to assert his authority early in 307 the legions faithful to Maxentius' father defeated him. Severus was taken prisoner and later killed. An expedition led by Galerius himself merely confirmed that Italy was loyal to the house of Maximian (summer 307).

It is not necessary for us to follow in detail the complicated pattern of events in the next four years.[241] Important only is that at each turn of the wheel Constantine emerged in a more favourable position than before, and that neither he nor Maxentius advocated the recommencement of the persecution in the west. The emergence of Maximian from retirement in 306 to champion his son's cause, resulted in Constantine supporting the 'Herculian' side of the Tetrarchy and marrying Maximian's daughter, Fausta. After the conference of Carnuntum in November 308, Maximian was forced into retirement, Constantine was recognized by Galerius as *filius Augusti*, while Galerius' old friend and brother-in-arms, Licinius, was substituted for Severus as Augustus.[242] Constantine's position was legalized whereas that of Maxentius was not. In the first half of 310 he rid himself of the old Maximian, and the same year Spain transferred its allegance from Maxentius to him. He was now supreme ruler of the vast and wealthy western territories of the Empire, all that his father held at his death. Even at this time, his court panegyrist suggests that he was thinking of further advancement. He was the true 'filius Augusti', and his nebulous claim to be descended from the great Illyrian soldier-emperor Claudius Gothicus[243] might be interpreted as a reply to those who a bare five years before had impugned his legitimacy. The Tetrarchs were the upstarts, and the subtle but significant change on the reverse of his *folles* from '*Genio Populi Romani*' to '*Soli Invicto Comiti*' points also in the direction of outspoken independence towards Galerius and his followers.

In the same year, 310, occurred the mysterious episode of the pagan vision. After Maximian's death at Arles, Constantine was recalled to the Rhine frontier once more on account of a revolt there. The news that he was on his way caused consternation among the rebels and the rebellion collapsed. Constantine turned aside to the temple of Apollo at Autun to pay the vows he had made to the gods for victory. Then adds the panegyrist, 'O Constantine, you saw I believe your protector Apollo in company with Victory, offering you laurel crowns each of which bear the presage of thirty years'. He goes on, 'But why indeed do I say "I believe"? You really saw the god and recognized yourself in the appearance of one to whom the prophecies of poets have declared that the rule of the whole world should belong'.[244] This was the prophecy of long life, victory and perhaps world dominion. The three crowns each carried an X symbolizing a *votum* of ten years' rule (as on the coinage of the House of Constantine). There is no hint of Christian influence. When next year, Constantine defeated the Franks and threw their kings to the beasts in the amphitheatre at Trier, he must have meditated on the power of the saving gods of the Empire.[244a] In any event, the patronage of Apollo and Victory was not to be dispensed with lightly.

Meantime in Pannonia, Licinius had also discontinued the persecution, perhaps because there were few Christians there, and perhaps because of his personal rivalry with Maximin. In the spring of 311 he was at Serdica where Galerius lay dying, and the latter committed the care of his family to him.[245] At this stage, Licinius and not Constantine would appear to have been the most outspoken champion of a settlement with the Christians. Faced with this crisis Maximin displayed energy and resource. First, there was the question of Galerius' dominions. The Emperor dead, the prize of Asia Minor and the pro-capital of Nicomedia awaited him who got there first. Maximin was at Tarsus, Licinius at Serdica, but it was Maximin who, by mobilizing the elaborate transportation system prevailing in Asia Minor, pushed his army across the breadth of Phrygia and Asia and anticipated Licinius at Chalcedon on the Asiatic side of the Straits.[246] Lactantius may be right in attributing to him the abolition of the tax in money payable by artisans as a means of winning favour, and in this he succeeded.[247]

He was now senior Augustus,[248] senior both to Constantine and Licinius. What was more important, he had won a respite to solve his second problem, that of the Christians after Galerius' edict. He played the only card he could.

Galerius' edict had allowed the Christians 'to exist'; it had made no mention of the restoration of Church property, and even the permission to hold services again was not explicit.[249] Moreover, supposing the Christians did commit acts contrary to public order, or if pagans believed they did, what then? Should not the new ruler protect his loyal subjects against even the threat of disturbance? Maximin under some pressure from Constantine appears to have informed his provincial governors of the strict letter of Galerius' order,[250] and waited. Meantime, the reorganization of the pagan cult was being vigorously pursued. The inscription from Otourak in Phrygia in honour of the High Priest of Pisidian Antioch, Athanatos Epitynchanos, showed the effort Maximin was making to harness the traditional forces of provincial loyalty in the service of renewed paganism. The reference on the same stone to the priestess Ispatolé claiming to save numerous individuals from 'evil afflictions' may refer to active measures of reconversion,[251] and these 'afflictions' as the epitaph of Bishop Eugenius shows, extended to the army as well as the provincials. Life was made unpleasant for the Christian officer, but in contrast to the rules in force under Diocletian, he was not allowed to resign.[252]

Then, perhaps in the early autumn 311, pagan public opinion in Asia, Syria and Palestine was galvanized into action for the last time. There was to be a 'plebiscite' against the Christians. The oracle of Zeus Philios at Antioch found its voice again,[253] so did that old enemy of the Christians, the oracle at Miletus. They asked for the banishment of their tormentors. The city councils were encouraged to take up the tune and petition the Emperor that Christians might be expelled from their midst.[254] The example of Antioch was followed by Nicomedia and Tyre and by the end of 311 even by so comparatively small a centre as Aricanda in Lycia.[255] The Aricanda inscription shows that the petition was sent in the name of the peoples (ἔθνη) of Lycia and Pamphylia.[256] In his replies Maximin drew attention to the prosperity that resulted from individuals turning once more to the gods. Even the weather was better, and the converted Christians themselves were to be compared with men and women, 'as if they were delivered from an unexpected hurricane or severe illness and were reaping life's sweet enjoyment for the future'.[257] Others, such as the Council of Tyre and the Lycians and Pamphylians, were informed that in return for their devotion to the gods the Emperor would grant them any concession they liked to ask.[258] It was desperate work. Eusebius concedes that there had never been such measures before,[259] and they were accompanied by an intensification of anti-Christian propaganda. At Damascus, the military commander forced prostitutes to confess that they had been Christians and had witnessed disgraceful scenes in Christian churches.[260] These were published. So, too, the *Acts of Pilate* were given widest vogue and Theotecnus the *curator* of the city of Antioch and now Maximin's right-hand man instituted a reign of terror.[261] Without promulgating a formal edict, executions of prominent Christians began again. Silvanus of Emesa was thrown to the beasts in the late autumn, Peter of Alexandria executed on 25 November 311 and 'many other Egyptian bishops with him', also the bishop and author Methodius of Olympus in Lycia,[262] and the theologian, Lucian, presbyter of Antioch at Nicomedia on 7 January 312.[263] The final savage outburst lasting from November 311 to January 312[264] deprived the Christians of some of their ablest leaders who had hitherto escaped molestation.

It was in Egypt that these last years saw the worst. There, the persecution had gradually risen to a crescendo of violence. Matters had started quietly. In 303, at the moment when Peter of Alexandria was fleeing his metropolitan see, the Christians of Oxyrhynchus were going about their business more interested in the election of a new bishop than the distant rumblings of danger.[265] But by 304-305, this had changed. Persecution against clergy and laity had become more severe, as Peter of Alexandria's Canons show. Peter himself was evidently in prison for part of this time.[266] At this stage it was like the Decian persecution over again, with some standing firm, but many more apparently finding means of either conforming or pretending to conform.[267] Then, on the abdication of Diocletian there was a long pause, sufficiently long for Peter to publish his encyclical letter containing fourteen canons on the treatment of those who had lapsed at Easter 306.[268] Soon after, the storm struck. The simmering fanaticisms between pagan and Christian to which Eusebius refers in the *Demonstratio*[269] blazed into the open. Town, village and family were divided against each other, and with Hierocles now promoted to be prefect of Egypt every artifice was used by the authorities to break the will of the Christian population.

Eusebius gives two glimpses of events. First, the report of Phileas on the situation in Alexandria to the Christians of Thmuis in the Delta where he was bishop, perhaps late in 306,

> What account would suffice to reckon up their bravery and courage under each torture? For when all who wished were given a free hand to insult them, some smote them with cudgels, others with

rods, others with scourges; others, again, with straps, and others with ropes. And the spectacle of their tortures was a varied one with no lack of wickedness therein. Some with both hands bound behind them were suspended upon the gibbet, and with the aid of certain machines stretched out in every limb; then, as they lay in this plight, the torturers acting on orders began to lay on over their whole body, not only, as in the case of murderers, punishing their sides with the instruments of torture, but also their belly, legs and cheeks. Others were suspended from the porch by one hand and raised aloft; and in the tension of their joints and limbs experienced unequalled agony. Others were bound with their face towards pillars, their feet not touching the ground, and thus their bonds were drawn tight by the pressure upon them of the weight of the body.[270]

To this account Eusebius added his own as eye-witness of events in the Thebaid for the year 311–312.

And we ourselves also beheld, when we were at these places, many all at once in a single day, some of whom suffered decapitation, others the punishment of fire; so that the murderous axe was dulled and, worn out, was broken in pieces, while the executioners themselves grew utterly weary and took it in turns to succeed one another. It was then that we observed a most marvellous eagerness and a truly divine power and zeal in those who had placed their faith in the Christ of God. Thus, as soon as sentence was given against the first, some from one quarter and others from another would leap up to the tribunal before the judge and confess themselves Christians; paying no heed when faced with terrors and the varied forms of tortures, but undismayedly and boldly speaking of the piety towards the God of the universe, and with joy and laughter and gladness receiving the final sentence of death; so that they sang and sent up hymns and thanksgivings to the God of the universe even to the very last breath.[271]

It is a terrible picture, confirmed from other sources,[272] of desperation encountering fanaticism. Nothing reveals more clearly the change of morale among the Egyptian Christians which had taken place since Decius' time. Then the Christians were cowed, now they scented victory. This was a revolution on the point of success.

All this time the sands were running out for Maximin. His successful seizure of Asia Minor had thrown Licinius into Con-

stantine's arms. His own efforts to form a belated alliance with
Maxentius in Rome only speeded the latter's downfall.[273] In 311
Constantine won a decisive victory over the Franks and was free
to turn to accomplish his greater ambitions. Maxentius was a
bastard he declared,[274] and thus could not be legitimate ruler—
the same reproach that only six years before had been levelled at
him with the same object in mind. In the spring of 312 his forces
invaded Italy, but Maximian's old soldiers fought well. Advance
was slow, and casualties not light.[275] By mid-October, however,
Constantine was on the Via Flaminia north of Rome. Would
Maxentius trust to the walls of the city and force his adversary to
conduct a winter siege, or would he come out and fight? As all
the world knows, he chose the latter course and at the Milvian
Bridge on 28 October he lost his army, his claim to be emperor
and his life. Maximin had been his ally. His turn could not be
long delayed.

Though Maxentius had consulted the Sibylline books before
making his momentous decision, this was not a battle of paganism
versus Christianity. In circumstances far more testing than those
which had confronted Constantine so far, he had maintained a
policy of benevolence towards the Church in Rome.[276] In the
brief interregnum under Severus the persecution had not been
renewed. For the ensuing six years Maxentius' policy was to let
matters be and intervene only when public order demanded. In
this he foreshadowed the ideas of other fourth-century rulers of
Rome, notably Eugenius 392–394, who improved their weak
position by adopting a prudent and neutral attitude towards the
Church. He needed patience to deal with the situation that was
developing among the Christians themselves, but the exiling of
the rival claimants to the Roman see in 307/308 and 311 is not to be
interpreted as renewing persecution. In 366 Valentinian I was to
take similar action in the struggle between Damasus and Ursinus,
by exiling Ursinus, and later summoning Damasus to stand his
trial before a secular court. Indeed, Christianity flourished in the
city, and the numbers of Christians increased.[277] The same policy
was extended to Africa, where Optatus of Milevis says categorically that the churches were given back to the Christians by
Maxentius.[278] When Bishop Mensurius was summoned to Rome
he was not asked to explain his Christianity, but the conduct of

one of his priests who had sided too openly with Maxentius' rebellious prefect, Alexander, between 308–311.[279]

Constantine had, however, been accompanied by Bishop Hosius of Cordova. How and why he had arrived at Constantine's court remains a mystery, but if one looks back into the latter's purely pagan outlook hitherto, and his willingness to attribute success to the gods, one must grant to Hosius some credit for Constantine's ultimate conversion. There is no reason to doubt the fact of the phenomenon which led him to place his destiny at the Milvian Bridge in the hands of the Christian God. He won, as contemporaries recognized, against the odds.[280] The debt must now be repaid, this time to the Christian God. When Africa fell without a blow, thus guaranteeing Rome's corn supplies through the first critical winter of 312–313 nothing could be too good for His worshippers. What Maximin was performing for the benefit of the adherents of the gods, Constantine now did for those of the Christian God. The Senate had rapidly declared him senior Augustus. In the winter of 312 he used his legislative authority to dismantle the remains of the persecution.[281] There followed, probably in February 313, the meeting with Licinius at Milan and the famous statement embodied in Licinius' edict promulgated at Nicomedia on 13 June 313.[282] N. H. Baynes' translation is given.

> Since we saw that freedom of worship ought not to be denied, but that to each man's judgment and will the right should be given to care for sacred things according to each man's free choice, we have already some time ago bidden the Christians to maintain the faith of their own sect and worship. But since in that edict by which such right was granted to the aforesaid Christians many and varied conditions (αἱρέσεις) clearly appeared to have been added, it may well perchance have come about that after a short time many were repelled from practising their religion. Thus when I, Constantine Augustus, and I, Licinius Augustus, had met at Mediolanum (Milan) and were discussing all those matters which relate to the advantage and security of the State, amongst the other things which we saw would benefit the majority of men we were convinced that first of all those conditions by which reverence for the Divinity is secured should be put in order by us to the end that we might give to the Christians and to all men the right to follow freely whatever religion each had wished, so that thereby whatever of Divinity there be in the heavenly seat may be favourable and propitious to us and

to all those who are placed under our authority. And so by a salutary and most fitting line of reasoning we came to the conclusion that we should adopt this policy—namely our view should be that to no one whatsoever should we deny liberty to follow either the religion of the Christians or any other cult which of his own free choice he has thought to be best adapted for himself, in order that the supreme Divinity, to whose service we render our free obedience, may bestow upon us in all things his wonted favour and benevolence. Wherefore we would that your Devotion should know that it is our will that all those conditions should be altogether removed which were contained in our former letters addressed to you concerning the Christians [and which seemed to be entirely perverse and alien from our clemency]—these should be removed and now in freedom and without restriction let all those who desire to follow the aforesaid religion of the Christians hasten to follow the same without any molestation or interference. We have felt that the fullest information should be furnished on this matter to your Carefulness that you might be assured that we have given to the aforesaid Christians complete and unrestricted liberty to follow their religion. Further, when you see that this indulgence has been granted by us to the aforesaid Christians, your Devotion will understand that to others also a similar free and unhindered liberty of religion and cult has been granted, for such a grant is befitting to the peace of our times, so that it may be open to every man to worship as he will. This has been done by us so that we should not seem to have done dishonour to any religion. (*CAH.*, xii. 689–90.)

There followed detailed instructions for the complete restoration of Church property, *bona fide* purchasers having the right, however, to indemnity from the Imperial Treasury. Then came the statement of the Emperors' purpose 'that the divine favour which we have experienced in a crisis of our fortunes may for all times prosper our undertakings and serve the public weal'. As Lactantius pointed out (*De Mortibus*, 49.13) between 'the ruin and the restoration of the Church' just ten years and four months had elapsed.

As though the alliance between Constantine and Licinius was not enough, further misfortune befell Maximin. How he became involved in a disastrous conflict with the client kingdom of Armenia (autumn 312) is not known, but his failure demonstrated that coercion of Christianity could not be extended beyond the

Roman frontier.[283] Simultaneously, the crops failed, and disease followed famine. Once more the Christians showed that only they knew the real meaning of self-sacrifice and charity in the face of disaster.[284] Reformed paganism failed at its first test. It was however, the old quarrel with Licinius that ultimately doomed Maximin. The Milvian Bridge had cost him his rank of senior Augustus, but he was to share the consulship with Constantine for 313.[285] Meantime, Constantine had informed him of his measures in favour of the Christians, and Maximin had grudgingly instructed Sabinus that 'if some (Christians) desire to follow their own worship, you should leave it in their own power'. The reason he gave for the change of policy was that his previous orders had given rise to 'insults and extortions'. Even at this, the 12th hour, his aim still remained, 'to recall our provincials to the worship of the gods rather by exhortations and persuasive words'.[286]

The final reckoning with Licinius followed, but it did not turn out as Maximin hoped. Bold to the last, and trusting in the numerical superiority of his forces, he crossed the Bosphorus into his enemy's territory. But Licinius had not been Galerius' lieutenant for nothing. A monotheistic prayer raised the morale of his troops, and on 30 April he won a complete victory over his enemy at Campus Serenus near Heraclea.[287] On 13 June he entered Nicomedia in triumph, and ordered the governor of Bithynia to observe the edict of toleration which he promulgated in the capital. Maximin had escaped with his life and retreated to Tarsus. He survived long enough to issue a final decree, this time restoring lands and property to their Christian owners, and guaranteeing complete toleration.[288] He died (August 313 ?) in the realization that the policy of 'the most divine Diocletian and Maximian, our fathers' had failed utterly. Paganism as an effective political and religious force died with him. Most of his henchmen perished in revolutionary outbreaks that followed his fall. When, in his turn, Licinius tried to rekindle the flame of persecution (322–323) in preparation for his decisive struggle with Constantine, the response was negligible. By this time there were 'more persecuted than persecutors',[289] not only in Edessa.

Persecution had failed as a policy. When one looks for the immediate causes of the Christian triumph one need only consult Lactantius. The pagan world had had enough, enough of blood-

shed, enough of the butchers' shop in service to the gods, enough
of the deaths of men known (like Pamphilus) to be upright,
learned and brave.[290] As the killing went on, so more turned to
Christ. Persecution even quickened the pace of conversions.[291]
Indeed, as Lactantius declared, it was a means through which the
Divine Providence won pagans to His service, for pagans wanted
to know more about this belief which men were prepared to
defend to the death, and having learnt, accepted it themselves.[292]
Finally, it was clear that the Christian message contained much,
perhaps nearly all, that the pagans had been groping towards.
It was no longer a 'strange, new religion'. In the Vatican cemetery,
a mosaic dated to this period shows Christ resplendent with
halo, whose rays of light form a cross, driving a little chariot of the
sun.[293] So it was in this Christian's mind. Sol Invictus and Christus
Victor could be assimilated, but the victor was Christ and it was
thus that Constantine was interpreting the vision of the Milvian
Bridge.

NOTES

[1] The best general account of the Great Persecution (despite H. Grégoire's trenchant
criticism in *Byzantion*, xiv, 1939, 318–21) remains N. H. Baynes's, ch. 19 in *CAH.*, xii,
and the valuable bibliography attached, pp. 789–95. Also A. Manaresi, op. cit., 423–79, H.
Achelis, *Das Christentum*, ii.291–334, G. E. M. de Ste Croix, 'Aspects of the "Great
Persecution" ', *HTR.*, 47.2, April 1954, 76–113, and J. Moreau's commentary on Lactantius *De Mortibus Persecutorum* (Sources chrétiennes, 39), an indispensible study.

[2] *Dating:* C. H. V. Sutherland, 'Diocletian's Reform of the Coinage: A Chronological
Note', *JRS.*, xlv, 1955, 116ff. For the date 296, Mattingly and Sydenham, *The Roman
Imperial Coinage*, v.i.1, and H. Mattingly, *Roman Coins*, 217.

[3] Eusebius, *H.E.*, viii.1.6.

[4] Eusebius (ed. Heikel) *Vita Constantini*, ii. 49. I am accepting (with A. H. M. Jones,
Roman Empire, 77) this panegyric as being written by Eusebius *circa* 337 despite the
objections of Grégoire, loc. cit. and G. Pasquali 'Die Komposition der *Vita Constantini* des
Eusebius', *Hermes*, xlv, 1910, 369–86. On the authenticity of some of the documents cited,
see A. H. M. Jones, 'Notes on the genuineness of the Constantinian Documents in Eusebius's
Life of Constantine', *J.E.H.*, v, 1954, 196–200.

[5] *De Mortibus*, 11.

[6] Note the verdict of the fourth-century historian, 'Vir reipublicae necessarius', *SHA.*,
Vita Cari, 10.

[7] 'Maximi enim criminis est retractare quae semel ab antiquis statuta et definita suum
statum et cursum tenent ac possident.' *Codex Gregorianus*, bk. vii, *De Maleficiis et Mani-*

chaeis, cited from S. Riccobono, *FIRA.*, ii.580. Note Aurelius Victor (*De Caes.* 39.45) 'Veterrimae religiones castissime curatae. . . .'

⁸ Even the *De Pretiis rerum Venalium* of 301 seems to have had the aim of providing a basis for the calculation of public expenditure, especially the *annona militaris*. A Segrè, 'Annona Civica and Annona Militaris', *Byzantion*, xvi, 1942–43, 394.

⁹ N. H. Baynes, *JRS.*, xxix, 1939, 116–18. 'His changes are not so much innovations as the open recognition of what had in fact resulted in the administrative practice of the Empire from the crisis of the third century.'

¹⁰ *SHA.*, *Vita Numeriani*, 13, 'Diocletianum omnes divino consensu, cui multa jam signa facta dicebantur imperii, Augustum appellaverunt'. I follow W. Seston, *Dioclétien et la Tétrarchie*, 211ff. The paternalistic phrasing of Diocletian's edicts is very marked.

¹¹ Mattingly and Sydenham, *Roman Imperial Coinage*, v.i, 270, no. 48 (Mint of Rome).

¹² *CIL.*, iii, 12326, 'Diis auctoribus ad reipublicae amplificandae gloriam procreato pio nostro Jovio maximo', Seston, loc. cit., 214.

¹³ Mamertinus, *Pan. Lat.*, x (ii), 11 (ed. Baehrens, 272), 'Diocletianus facem, tu (Maximianus) tribuis effectum'. Again, ibid., 'Iove rectore caeli et Hercule pacatore terrarum'. On Aurelian's coinage Hercules is equated to Virtus, see Mattingly and Sydenham, op. cit., 271, no. 57.

¹⁴ Libanius, *Oratio*, iv (ed. Förster, 331), 'βασιλέων θεοὺς ἡγεμόνας ποιούμενος'.

¹⁵ See E. Ch. Babut, 'L'Adoration des empéreurs et les Origines de la Persecution de Dioclétien', *Rev. Historique*, 123, 1916, 225–52. In this valuable detailed study Babut perhaps overemphasizes the importance of this element of court ceremonial in unleashing the persecution. After all, there were many Christian officials at Diocletian's court in 303 (Eusebius, *H.E.*, viii, 2).

¹⁶ *ILS.*, 659 (*CIL.*, iii, 4413), but see N. H. Baynes's (*JRS.*, xxxviii, 1948, 111–12) criticism of Seston's over-emphasis of the role which Mithraism played in Diocletian's religious policy. It certainly did not obscure the veneration for the 'immortal gods of Rome' which was the hall-mark of the regime.

¹⁷ Diocletian, 'se primus omnium Caligulam post Domitianumque dominum palam dici passus et adorari se appellarique uti deum' (Aurelius Victor, *De Caes.*, 39.4). Not entirely true, as Aurelian's use of the term 'Deo et Domino nato Aureliano Aug.' on some of his coins (Serdica mint) shows. (Mattingly and Sydenham, op. cit., 299, nos. 305–6). An interesting dedication from Virunum shows the two emperors represented as Jupiter and Hercules looking like friendly supermen guarding the interests of the provincials, R. Egger, *Römische Antike*, i. 123–5.

¹⁸ *Codex Gregorianus*, v (= Mosaicarum et Romanarum Legum Collectio vi.4) ed. C. Riccobono, *FIRA.*, ii.558–60.

¹⁹ 'Ita enim et ipsos immortales deos Romano nomine, ut semper fuerunt, faventes atque placatos futuros esse non dubium est, si cunctos sub imperio nostro agentes piam religiosamaque et quietam et castam in omnibus mere colere perspexerimus vitam' (p. 559). Religious and moral uniformity under the guidance of the immortal gods of Rome is surely the key to the religious policy of the Tetrarchy.

²⁰ 'insurgere nos disciplina nostrorum temporum cohortatur'. *Disciplina* generally denoting 'public order' is a favourite word under the Tetrarchy, contrasting with the more open-handed and optimistic *liberalitas* of the Antonine era.

²¹ 'Nihil enim nisi sanctum ac venerabile nostra iura custodiunt et ita ad tantam magnitudinem Romana maiestas cunctorum numinum favore pervenit.' (Ibid., 560).

²² Note M. Besnier's comment on Diocletian, op cit., 302, 'Quant au fond, toute cette législation a un caractère à la fois conservateur et humain', and, one might add, intended to be universal in application, like the First Edict against the Christians.

²³ See C. H. V. Sutherland, 'Flexibility in the "reformed" Coinage of Diocletian', *Roman Coinage* (Essays presented to Harold Mattingly) London, 1956, 179. I also owe the

description of Diocletian's gold and silver coinage to Dr. Sutherland. For examples, Cohen, *Médailles impériales*, vi.

24 The connection is vividly stressed by Maximin in his letter to the citizens of Tyre, written in 312, Eusebius, *H.E.*, ix.7.

25 Probably written *circa* 311–312. *Praepar. Evang.*, 1.2 (*P.G.*, 21, 28–9).

26 On the problem which pagan education presented to the Christians see H. I. Marrou, *A History of Education in Antiquity* (Eng. tr. G. R. Lamb, 1956), ch. ix.

27 Lactantius, *Institutes*, v.20.1. 'And if you ask them (educated pagans) the ground for their persuasion, they can assign none, but have recourse to the judgment of their ancestors, saying that they were wise, that they approved them, and that they knew what was best'— a bitter criticism of the spirit of the Tetrarchy. (Eng. tr., *A.N.C.L.*)

28 Sozomen, *H.E.*, v.15.14 (ed. J. Bidez/G. C. Hansen, Berlin, 1960, p. 215).

29 *Adv. Nationes*, 1.27 and iii.24. See P. Courcelle's essay 'Anti-Christian Arguments and Christian Platonism' in *The Conflict between Paganism and Christianity* (ed. A. Momigliano), 151ff.

30 I am accepting the 'martyrdom' of Saturius Arrianus in Egypt as myth.

31 The cause and effect was clear enough to Augustine, *Ep.*, 118.5.33 (*CSEL.*, 34.2.697). 'Cum iam Christi nomen terrenis regnis admirantibus perturbatisque crebesceret, emergere coeperant ad proferendum atque aperiendum, quid Plato sensisset. Tunc Plotini schola Romae floruit habuitque condiscipulos multos acutissimos et sollertissimos viros, sed aliqui eorum magicarum artium curiositate depravati sunt. . . .'

32 *Enneads*, ii.9 (ed. Henry and Schwyzer, Eng. tr. Stephen Mackenna). See Porphyry, *Vita Plotini* 16; C. Schmidt, 'Plotinus Stellung zum Gnosticismus und kirchlichen Christentum', *T.U.*, N.F. v.4, 1900, and J. Lebreton, 'L'Opposition païenne', in *Histoire de l'Église* (ed. A. Fliche and V. Martin) vol. ii, ch. viii.

33 *Enn.*, ii.9.18; cf. Celsus, ap. Origen, *Contra Celsum* iv.23, 74–5, and 99.

34 *Enn.*, ii.9.9; cf. Celsus, iv.23, 88 and 99.

35 *Enn.*, ii.9.18.

36 For the general rusticity of the theology of the accepted leaders of the Roman Church in the period 250–300, see H. J. Carpenter, 'Popular Christianity and the Theologians', *JTS.*, N.S. xiv. 2, 1963, 307.

37 *Enn.*, ii.9.16. Porphyry's publication of the *Enneads circa* 304 suggests that he himself regarded his master's work as valuable in the battle against Christianity.

38 Eusebius, *Praeparatio Evangelica* (*P.G.*, 21, cols. 900–1) xi.19. A less favourable estimate of Amelius' interest in pointing the analogy between the Logos of Heraclitus and that of John, see P. Courcelle, *Les Confessions de Saint Augustin dans la tradition littéraire*, Paris, 1963, 73.

39 Eusebius, ibid.

40 Augustine, *De Civ. Dei*, xxii.26.1. See J. O'Meara's study of *Porphyry's Philosophy from Oracles in Augustine*, Etudes Augustiniennes, Paris, 1959, ch. iii.

41 Augustine, *De Consensu Evangel.*, 1.23 was well aware of Porphyry's friends' hostility to Christianity. His comment 'vani Christi laudatores et Christianae religionis obliqui obtrectatores'.

42 Augustine, *De Civ. Dei*, xix.23, citing the oracle of Hecate quoted by Porphyry in his ἐκ λογίων φιλοσοφίας, 'Piissimum igitur virum, inquit, eum dixit et eius animam sicut et aliorum piorum, post obitum immortalitate dignatam et hanc colere Christianos ignorantes'. Similar statement quoted by Eusebius, *Demonst. Evang.*, iii.7.1.

43 Porphyry, cited by Augustine, *De Civ. Dei*, x.29, 'Christus est humilis, vos superbi', and *De Consensu Evangel.*, 1.23 and *De Civ. Dei.*, xix.23 for Jesus' just condemnation. It is interesting that Porphyry here rates the Jews and their religion far higher than the Christians 'Iudaei suscipiunt Deum magis quam isti (Christiani)'; cf. xx.24 'pietatam laudet Hebraeorum'. By 260 the Jews had ceased to be worth worrying about as a political danger.

44 *De Civitate Dei* x.29. O'Meara, op. cit., 24–7.

45 Ibid., xviii.53. 'Petrum autem maleficia fecisse subjugunt' and 'de Petri apostoli locutione, quem vehementer oderunt, ibid., xx.24.

46 *De Civitate Dei*, xix.23. O'Meara, op. cit., 51–4.

47 Augustine, *Ep.*, 102.8 and 16.

48 Cyprian, *Ad Demetrianum*, 2: cf. Arnobius, *Adv. Nationes*, 1.1 (for North Africa in the 290s) and Augustine, *De Civitate Dei*, 1.1.

49 The surviving fragments of the κατὰ χριστιανῶν have been collected by A. Harnack in 'Porphyrius, *Gegen die Christen*, 15 Bücher, Zeugnisse, Fragmente und Referate', *Abh. der kgl. Preuss. Akad. der Wiss.*, 1916, 1–115. (This accepts the anti-Christian fragments in Macarius Magnes as Porphyry's.) See also, the excellent commentary in P. de Labriolle's *La réaction païenne*, p. 242ff., and also H. Muller, *Christians and Pagans from Constantine to Augustine*, part ii, Pretoria, 1948, chs. 1 and 2.

50 See P. Courcelle's comments in his chapter 'Anti-Christian Arguments and Christian Platonism: Arnobius to St. Ambrose', *The Conflict between Paganism and Christianity in the Fourth Century* (ed. A. Momigliano, Oxford, 1963),151–93.

51 Socrates, *Hist. Eccl.*, 1.9 (Constantine), *Cod. Just.*, 1.1.3 and 1.5.6. *Cod. Theod.*, xvi.6.66 (Valentinian III and Theodosius II).

52 Cited from Jerome, *De Viris Illust.*, 104; cf. Harnack, op. cit., 33–6.

53 *De Civitate Dei*, xix.22 '(Porphyrius) philosophus nobilis, magnus gentilium philosophus, doctissimus philosophorum, quamvis Christianorum acerrimus inimicus'. Also, ibid., xxii.4 and *Ep.*, 118.5.33.

54 Theodoret, *De Curatione Graecorum affect.*, xii (end), *P.G.*, 83, 1151.

55 Ibid., x.12. 'Πορφύριος ὁ ἄσπονδος ἡμῖν ἐχθιστος': cf. ii.44 'ὁς τῆς ἀσεβείας γενόμενος πρόμαχος κατὰ τοῦ θεοῦ'.

56 Socrates, *Hist. Eccl.*, iii.23. The story of Porphyry being bullied by Christian youths and thence, turning away from Christianity is not fantastic. Many extremist leaders have looked back to one such incident as crucial in their lives.

57 Fragment, 63.

58 See R. M. Grant, *The Earliest Lives of Jesus*, S.P.C.K., London 1961, 54ff.

59 *Comment. in Joann.*, x.22 (ed. E. Preuschen, 194). R. M. Grant, op. cit., 64.

60 Ibid., x.26. Other examples drawn from the Old Testament, *De Principiis*, iv.3.1.

61 *Contra Celsum*, 1.42., Grant, op. cit., 70ff.

62 Frag. 17.

63 Frag. 49.

64 Frag. 4. The comparison was not even with the semi–divine Hercules but with mere mortals!

65 Frag. 55. In this assumption Porphyry was wrong.

66 Frag. 43. Harnack, op. cit., 67–73 (a useful collection of extracts illustrating Porphyry's methods).

67 e.g. Peter's 'murder of Ananias and Sapphira', frag. 25. Cf. Jerome, *Ep.* 130.14.

68 Frags. 21 and 22, especially the latter.

69 Frag. 45.

70 Frag. 97.

71 Frag. 64. 'μὴ δόγματι κοινῷ καταψηφίσωνται θάνατον ὡς ἀσεβῶν τῶν πειθομένων αὐτῷ'.

72 Frag. 36. Above, p. 413.

73 'οὗτος γὰρ μέγιστος καρπὸς εὐσεβείας τιμᾶν τὸ θεῖον κατὰ τὰ πάτρια'. *Letter to Marcella* 18; cf. J. Bidez, *La Vie de Porphyre*, Gand, 1913, p. 76, n.4, and U. von Wilamowitz-Möllendorf, 'Ein Bruchstück aus der Schrift des Porphyrius gegen die Christen', *ZNTW.*, 1 (1900), 101ff. See also, Julian; criticism, Christianity was 'newfangled', *EP.* 47.

74 Eusebius, *H.E.*, vi.19.2, concerning Origen's 'defection to Christianity'.

[75] Lactantius, *De Mortibus Pers.*, 15, Eusebius, *H.E.*, viii.1.3.

[76] Dion Cassius in *Acta Maximiliani*, 'In sacro comitatu dominorum nostrorum Diocletiani et Maximiani, Constantii et Maximi, milites Christiani sunt et militant'. Also, Eusebius, *Demonstr. Evangel.*, 1.8 (Christian officers and magistrates). Phileas and Philoromus are examples for Egypt (Eusebius, *H.E.*, viii.12).

[77] D. van Berchem, 'Le Martyre de la légion thébaine, Essai sur la formation d'une legende', *Schweizerische Beiträge zur Altertumswissenschaft*, fasc. 8, Basle, 1956. L. Dupraz, 'Les Passions de S. Maurice d'Agaune', *Studia Friburgensia*, N.S. 27, 1961. See the writer's review of Dupraz in *JEH.*, xiv., 1963, pp. 85–6. For the possibility of other local Gallic martyrs in the early years of Maximian's reign, C. Jullian, *Histoire de la Gaule*, vii, 67–72, and N. H. Baynes, *CAH.*, xii, 663, n.i.

[78] The Thebaid was not made into a separate province until 295, ten years after the massacre is supposed to have taken place.

[79] D. van Berchem, op. cit., pp. 32–3. Draws attention to a cavalry 'order of battle' given by Jerome in *Contra Iohann. Hierosol.*, 19, *P.L.* xxxiii, 386.

[80] See P. Monceaux, *Histoire littéraire*, iii, 114–18. Text, Knopf and Krüger, op. cit., 86–7.

[81] Ed. Knopf and Krüger, 87–8. H. Delehaye, 'Les Actes de S. Marcel le Centurion', *A.B.*, 41, 1923, 257–87, and B. de Gaiffier, *A.B.*, 61, 1943, 116. Ch. iv, recording the surprised indignation of the *praeses* Agricolanus at a centurion's insubordination is striking, and strongly suggestive of what actually happened. ('*Quo furore accensus es, ut proiceres sacramenta et talia loqueris*'). Also Wm. Seston, 'Apropos du Passio Marcelli centurionis', *Mélanges Goguel*, Neuchâtel/Paris, 1950, 239–46 for the occasion of the incident.

[82] Ed. Knopf and Krüger, 89–90. P. Monceaux, *Hist. litt.*, iii, 122 and H. Delehaye, *A.B.*, 54, 1936, 300–2. Marcellus was executed, not as a Christian, but, 'qui centurio ordinarius militabat, qui abiecto publice sacramento pollui se dixit, et insuper apud acta praesidialia verba furoris plena deposuit, gladio animadverti placet' (v.1). The same may be true of the more legendary story of the veteran Tipasius of Tigava in the Cheliff valley, and the scene of operations against the Baquates at this period. (P. Monceaux, op. cit., 126–31, dating the extant *Acta* to the early fifth century.)

[83] Note the lines written by Pope Damasus concerning the soldiers Achilleus and Nereus, supposedly martyrs under Diocletian,

'. . . subito posuere furorem
Conversi fugiunt, ducis impia castra relinquunt,
Proiciunt clipeos faleras telaq(ue) cruenta,
Confessi gaudent Christi portare triumfos
Credite per Damasum, possit quid gloria Christi.' (*ILCV.*, 1981).

It is interesting that despite the Councils of Arles and Elvira, this attitude was still being honoured in Rome in the 380s.

[84] Eusebius, *Chronicon* (ad. ann. 301), Helm, 227. Ammianus Marcellinus, xiv.11.10, 'et in Syria Augusti vehiculum irascentis, per spatium mille passuum fere pedes antegressus est Galerius purpuratus'. Discussion, see N. H. Baynes, *JRS.*, xxxviii, 1948, 109.

[85] *Dating:* Wm. Seston, *Mélanges Ernout* (Paris), 1940, 345ff.

[86] This aspect of Diocletian's edict seems to have been well remembered by the Manichees themselves. In 405 Augustine's Manichaean opponent offered in public debate to be burnt along with his books if he were proved wrong. *Gesta cum Felice*, 1.12, *P.L.*, 42, col. 526.

[87] Text from C. Riccobono, *FIRA.*, 580–1. For instance, para. 3, 'hi enim, qui novellas et inauditas sectas veterioribus religionibus obponunt, ut pro arbitrio suo pravo excludant quae divinitus concessa sunt quondam nobis'.

[88] The comparative favour enjoyed by the Jews in Diocletian's reign, M. Simon, *Verus Israel*, 135.

[89] Aurelius Victor, *De Caesaribus*, 39.36. See, W. Ensslin's account in his masterly, 'Zur Ostpolitik des Kaisers Diocletian'. *Sitzungsber. der bayer. Akad. der Wiss.*, 1943, 40–5.

[90] Eusebius, *H.E.*, viii.4.3. Punishment, see *Mart. Pal.*, 11.22 concerning Seleucus.

[91] Eusebius, *Chron.*, ad ann. 301 'paulatim ex illo iam tempore persecutione adversum nos incipiente'.

[92] Lactantius, *De Mortibus.*, 10. A striking example of the Christians being regarded even in this period as being in touch with occult, harmful powers, as at the time of the great fire in 64.

[93] Lactantius, *De Mortibus*, 11.

[94] Ibid., 11.7. Also, *Div. Inst.*, iv.27.4. What seems to be intended is a 'defectus oraculi'. the oracle being overcome by stronger (and more truly 'religious') influences was silent. In Julian's time the oracle of Apollo at Daphne had been reduced to silence by the presence of·the bones of the bishop–martyr Babylas in the neighbourhood (Sozomen, *H.E.*, v.19). As a boy, Pachomius reduced a local oracle to silence, *Vita*, 3.

[95] A. Rehm, 'Kaiser Diokletian und das Heiligtum von Didyma', *Philologus*, 93, 1938 (= *Festgabe E. Schwartz*) pp. 74–84, and Ad. Wilhelm, 'Zwei Inschriften aus Didyma', *JÖAI.*, 35, 1943, 154–89.

[96] *CIG.* ii, 2883ᵈ, H. Grégoire, 'Les Chrétiens et l'Oracle de Didymès', *Mélanges Holleaux*, Paris, 1913, 81–91; revised in 'Les pierres qui crient', i, *Byzantion*, xiv, 1939, 320.

[97] Eusebius, *Vita Constantini*, ii.50. (ed. Heikel, p. 62).

[98] 'ὡς ἄρα οἱ ἐπὶ τῆς γῆς δίκαιοι ἐμπόδιον εἶεν τοῦ ἀληθεύειν αὐτόν, καὶ διὰ τοῦτο ψευδεῖς τῶν τριπόδων τὰς μαντείας ποιεῖσθαι'.

[99] Note Moreau's verdict on Lactantius' general reliability (op. cit., 287), 'Les récits de Lactance et d'Eusèbe se complètent parfaitement. Si l'un ne fournit pas les mêmes détails que l'autre, ils ne se contredisent pas et permettent de reconstruire avec quasi–certitude le déroulement de la persécution'.

[100] *De Mortibus*, 12.1.

[101] Ibid., 12.

[102] Ibid., 13; cf. Eusebius, *H.E.*, viii.2.4–5. These deprivations of civil rights suggest that the Christians were to be treated as 'infames', as being guilty of a crime under public law (*Dig.*, 48.1.7, Infamem non ex omni crimine sententia facit, sed ex eo, quod iudicii publici causam habuit'). See M. Kaser, 'Infamia und Ignominia in den römischen Rechts-quellen', *Ztschr. der Savigny. Stiftung f. Rechtsgeschichte*, 73.2, 1956, 254ff.

[103] Lactantius, *De Mortibus*, 13.2, 'irridens diceret victorias Gothorum et Sarmatorum propositas'. According to the Syrian Martyrology, his name was Evethius (ed F. Nau, *Pat. Or.*, x, p. 13).

[104] Ibid., 14.1. Perhaps this purge is referred to in the enigmatic l. 9 'ἀπεώσθησαν στρατίας' on the inscription of the Milesian Apollo discussed by Grégoire (*Mélanges Holleaux*, p. 90).

[105] Eusebius, *H.E.*, viii.6.5, and the Roman Martyrology under 2 October, cited by J. Moreau, *Lactance*, 288, for the death of a 'soldier and martyr' with 'innumerable companions', arising out of the accusation of incendiarism. In general, B. de Gaiffier, 'Palatins et Eunuques', *A.B.*, 75, 1957, 20ff.

[106] Lactantius, *De Mortibus*, 15.1.

[107] Included in the Syrian Martyrology. (*Pat. Or.*, x, 15). The doubt concerning Bishop Anthimus is due to the *Chronicon Paschale* stating that Lucian of Antioch who was not executed until January 312, refers to Anthimus' death as though it was recent news in a letter to his flock (*Chron. Pasc.*, ad ann., 303), see Routh, *Rel. Sacr.* iii.285.

[108] *H.E.*, viii.6.6.

[109] Ibid., 6.8. The Syrian Martyrology records Helpidius and Hermogenes as martyred in Melitene on 3 May.

[110] Eusebius, *Mart. Pal.*, Praefatio, and *H.E.*, viii.6.8.

[111] *Mart. Pal.*, 1.1.

[112] There is no evidence for the wholesale imprisonment of bishops and clergy in North Africa or elsewhere in the west.

[113] Lactantius, *De Mortibus*, 15.7, 'conventicula id est parietes, qui restitui poterant dirui passus est'. The scattered martyrdoms recorded for 304 in the prefecture of the Gauls suggests, however, something more than token measures the next year.

[114] The chronology is difficult, and comes down to a choice between the *Chronicon Paschale* which fixes 17 September 284 as Diocletian's accession date, associating it with his entry into Nicomedia as emperor, and Lactantius who is equally definite in favour of 20 November. See K. C. Guinagh, 'The *Vicennalia* in Lactantius', *Classical Journal*, 28, 1933, 449, and Moreau's able summary of the evidence, op. cit., 297-305.

[115] *H.E.*, viii.2.1.

[116] Eusebius, *Mart. Pal.*, 2.2. Romanus deemed the sight of the destroyed churches and the multitudes sacrificing 'intolerable', and upbraided them.

[117] Lactantius, *De Mortibus*, 17.5. 'Cum libertatem populi Romani ferre non poterat'. Constantine's impatience during his visit to Rome in 326, Zosimus, ii.30, and Constantius' impassive 'godlike' bearing on a similar occasion in 357, Ammianus Marcellinus, xvi. 10.10.

[118] *C.J.*, iii.28.26.

[119] Lactantius, op. cit., 17.8. Lactantius states that Diocletian's illness had lasted nearly a whole year.

[120] I am accepting the chronology worked out by N. H. Baynes, 'Two Notes on the Great Persecution', *CQ.*, xviii, 1924, 189-93. Also G. W. Richardson, 'The Chronology of Eusebius', *CQ.*, xix, 1925, 96-100.

[121] *De Caesaribus*, 39.48, 'ubi fato intestinas clades et quasi fragorem quendam impendere comperit status Romani'.

[122] Lactantius, op. cit., 19.3, Zosimus ii.7, Aurelius Victor *De Caesaribus*, 39.48 and Eutropius, ix, 27-8. In fact, Diocletian and Maximian retained their imperial titles.

[123] On the two traditions, one placing Diocletian's death in 313 and the other in 316, see Moreau, op. cit., 420-3.

[124] Lactantius emphasizes the stupefaction that these appointments caused, *De Mortibus*, 19.4.

[125] Possibly dating 303-305. Authenticity suggested, *inter alia*, by the title of *Consularis* given to the governor, Calvisianus. In 314, Constantine's letter to Chrestus, bishop of Syracuse, shows that by that time, the governor of Sicily, Latronianus, was a *corrector* with the rank of *vir clarissimus* (Eusebius, *H.E.*, x.5.23). The presumption is that the *Acta* were written at least before the former régime had been forgotten.

[126] The cult of St. Alban can be traced back to A.D. 429 when St. Germanus is said to have visited his tomb. Constantius, *Vita Sancti Germani*, 16 and 18 (*M.G.H.*, vii.262 and 265) and Gildas, *De Excidio*, 10 perserve the tradition of his martyrdom. Not before Bede, *Hist. Eccl.*, 1.7 was the event placed in the Great Persecution. One tradition, preserved in the Turin MS. and forming the basis of the account preserved in the *Vita Sancti Germani* and Bede is so accurate in its geographical detail of Verulamium that it must go back into the Roman period, but according to this tradition Alban was a victim of Severus' reign, condemned by Geta when he was governing southern Britain while his father and brother were absent on campaigns. Here also, the accurate presentation of circumstantial detail must be taken into account. To quote correspondence from Dr. John Morris, University College, London, 'I think you have here a fragment of a fourth-century *passio* written by someone who knew fourth-century Verulamium, taken over by the MSS.' It would be difficult to deny the reality of Alban's martyrdom, but rash to attempt to choose between Severus, Decius or Diocletian as the emperor concerned. It is very hard, however, to reconcile the martyrdom of Alban in the early or even mid third century with the complete

absence of evidence for Christianity in Verulamium until the first quarter of the fifth. See, Wm. Meyer, 'Die Legende des Albanus, des protomartyr Angliae in Texten vor Beda', *Abhand. Göttingen*, 1904, 1ff., Wm. Levison, 'St Alban and St Albans', *Antiquity*, 1942, 337ff., and C. E. Stevens, 'Gildas Sapiens', *EHR.*, 1941, 373.

[127] See *D.C.B.*, art. 'Ursula'.

[128] Ed. C. Schmidt, 'Fragmente einer Schrift des Märtyrerbischofs Petrus von Alexandrien', *T.U.*, N.F. Vb., 1901.

[129] See A. Deissmann, *Light from the Ancient East*, p. 201.

[130] For brief but precise discussions of the usefulness of the various *Acta Martyrum* of this period, A. Harnack, *Chronologie* ii, 463–82, N. H. Baynes, *CAH.*, xii, 790–3. See also, A. Manaresi, *L'Imperio romano*, 463–66, notes, and Lawlor and Oulton's notes on Books 8 and 9 of Eusebius's *H.E.* (*Eusebius*, vol. ii, 266ff.). Tillemont, *Mémoires*, v. is also valuable.

[131] The text of the *Acta* is, of course, post-Nicene as the credal statement put into Dasius' mouth confessing the Trinity 'in three Names and hypostases' (*Acta*, 8.2) shows. The incident, however, detailing the celebration of Saturnalia in the Roman army on the Danube seems genuine enough, as also do the refusal of Dasius to participate, and the attempts of his superior officer to persuade him. See F. Cumont's note, 'Le Tombeau de S. Dasius de Durostorum', *A.B.*, 27 (1908), 369–73 (bibliography, 369 n. 1), and H. Delehaye, 'Saints de Thrace et de Mésie', *A.B.*, 31 (1912) 265–8. Text, Knopf and Krüger, 91–5.

[132] Ed. Knopf and Krüger, with bibliography, op. cit., 95–100.

[133] Ed. Ruinart, 440–8.

[134] Eusebius, *H.E.*, viii.9.7 and 10.1–10, and Latin *Acta*, ed. Knopf and Krüger, 113–16. I agree with Duchesne's view that the Acta 'peut avoir été retouchée çà et là d'après Rufin, mais elle contient des bonnes parties' (*Histoire ancienne de l'Eglise*, ii (4 ed., Paris, 1910) 46 n. 3). See J. R. Knipfing, 'The Date of the Acts of Phileas and Philoromus', *HTR.*, 16 (1923), 198–203, and Lawlor and Oulton, *Eusebius*, ii, 276–7. Both accept 307 as the date of the martyrdoms.

[135] Published (Eng. tr. Roberts and Donaldson) *Ante-Nicene Fathers*, xx, 91–105. *Dating:* F. C. Burkitt, *CAH.*, xii, p. 500.

[136] Ed. Ruinart, 451–76.

[137] H. Delehaye, 'La Passion de S. Théodote d'Ancyre', *A.B.*, 22, 1903, 320–8.

[138] Ed. Knopf and Krüger, op. cit., 116–19.

[139] Attention is drawn to H. J. Lawlor's two essays. 'The Chronology of Eusebius's *Martyrs of Palestine*' and 'The Chronology of the ninth book of the *Ecclesiastical History*', *Eusebiana*, Oxford, 1912, 179–236; on the chronology of Lactantius' works. Moreau, op. cit., 1. 16ff. (*Institutes* written 305–313 and *De Mortibus* written 318–321), and N. H. Baynes's remarks in *JRS.*, xxxiv, 1944, 136ff. (*Institutes* written in Gaul before 311).

[140] Eusebius, *H.E.*, viii.13.9.

[141] *Demonstratio Evangelica*, vi.20.

[142] My attention has been drawn by G. E. M. de Ste Croix and E. G. Turner to an unpublished papyrus in which an Egyptian Christian describes how he employed a rhetor to conduct his case for him so as to avoid performing any idolatrous act in the court room.

[142a] See, *Mart. Pal.*, preface (S), and 3.1(c).

[143] Eusebius, *H.E.*, viii.12.8 and *Mart. Pal.*, 7.3.

[144] *De Mortibus*, 16.4 'deinde in Hieroclem ex vicario praesidem, qui auctor et consiliarius ad faciendam persecutionem fuit'. The promotion is surely significant as to Diocletian's aims.

[145] See Lactantius' well-known description of how he 'saw in Bithynia the prefect (Hierocles?) wonderfully elated with joy as though he had subdued some nation of barbarians, because one who had resisted for two years with great spirit appeared at

length to yield' (*Institutes*, v.11.15; cf. his friend Donatus' experiences, *De Mortibus*, 16.3–6.) Culcianus, prefect of Egypt in the first phase of the persecution is also shown by Eusebius and by martyrologists as an official who tried to argue with and persuade Christians, only sentencing them when his efforts proved futile (Eusebius, *H.E.*, viii.10.8, and *Passio S. Dioscori*, ed. H. Quentin, *A.B.*, 24, 1905, 321–42).

[146] Lactantius, *Div. Inst.*, v.2–3.

[147] *Liber Contra Hieroclem* (*P.G.*, 22, 797ff.).

[148] Eusebius does not mention Porphyry as a source, but suggests instead that Hierocles used Celsus, *Liber* 1.

[149] Eusebius, *Liber* 2. For similar arguments, Julian, *Against the Galileans*, (ed. Wright, 376).

[150] Lactantius, *Div. Inst.*, v.3.4.

[151] Ibid., v.2.4.

[152] Ibid., 2.10.

[153] For the longevity and force in the charge of magic, see the old, but still valuable, arts. by M. le Blant, 'Recherches sur l'accusation de Magie dirigée contre les premiers chrétiens', *Mém. de la Soc. des Antiquaires de France*, 31, 1864, and *Mémoires de l'Acad. des Inscr. et Belles-Lettres*, 30.2, 1883, 155ff.

[154] *Mart. Pal.*, 3.1. (L).

[155] For Eusebius' 'persecution years', see H. J. Lawlor, *Eusebiana*, Oxford, 1912, 179ff. Diocletian and Maximian's abdications are given by Eusebius as 'secundo anno persecutionis' (*Chron. ad. an.*, 305, Helm, 228) when by reckoning from 23 Feb.–23 Feb. as a year it should be 'the third year'.

[156] Gordius, *Panegyric* by St. Basil, *P.G.*, 31, col. 489–507.

[157] As B. J. Kidd, *A History of the Church to 461*, 1.520, points out, they were executed more for treason than Christianity. The length of the Acts (Ruinart, 451–76) may be due to accretions rather than the claim that the Christians bribed an official to make a transcript of the proceedings (*Acta*, Preface).

[158] P. Allard, *La Persécution sous Dioclétien*, i.305. Manaresi, op. cit., 464, adds the youths Claudius, Asterius and Neon, as well as two women, Theonilla and Domnina, as victims of the governor of Lycia.

[159] *Mart. Pal.*, 3.3–4.

[160] *De Mortibus*, 23.5.

[161] *Acta Dasii*, 12.

[162] Ed. Ruinart, 440–8. It is interesting that Hermes the deacon receives no adverse comment from the biographer for acquiescing in the seizure of the Scriptures and vessels (1.4–5). B. J. Kidd, *History of the Church*, i.519.

[163] Ed. Knopf and Krüger, pp. 95–100.

[164] Ed. Knopf and Krüger, pp. 103–5. Not a contemporary document, but based on fairly accurate tradition. Interesting for the slow spread of Christianity in the Danube lands is the fact the Irenaeus was still a young man though bishop, and all his relatives were pagans. His is typical of the psychology of rejection shown by many Christian converts in the west.

[165] See H. Delehaye, 'L'Hagiographie de Salone d'après des dernières découvertes archéologiques', *A.B.*, 23 (1904), 1–10 and *DACL.*, art. 'Salone'.

[166] *Acta Purgationis Felicis* (ed. Ziwsa, *CSEL.*, 26) 199, 'mittunt ad me (Alfius Caecilianus) in praetorio ipsi christiani ut dicerent, sacrum praeceptum ad te pervenit? ego dixi, non, sed vidi iam exempla et Zama et Furnis dirui basilicas et uri scripturas vidi'.

[167] Ibid., p. 198, 'et quoniam eius temporis officium incumbebat, ut ex iussione proconsulari omnes sacrificarent et si quas scripturas haberent, offerrent secundum sacram legem. . . . ' An interesting example of local zeal on the part of the authorities. General sacrifice had not been ordered in April 303 anywhere else.

[168] Augustine, *Breviculus cum Donatistis*, iii.13.25.

[169] *Acta Felicis* (ed. Knopf and Krüger, 90–1). 'Habeo, sed non do' (c. 4). See H. Delehaye, 'La Passion de S. Félix de Thibiuca', *A.B.*, 39, 1921, 241ff. *Dating* and acceptance as an authentic record, 263–268.

[170] *Acta Crispinae*, 7 (ed. Knopf and Krüger, 109–11) 'Quod et omnis Africa sacrificia fecit nec tibi dubium est'.

[171] *Acta Saturnini* (*P.L.*, viii, 695ff.) See Franchi di Cavalieri *S.T.*, 65, 1935, p. 1ff., and the author's *Donatist Church*, pp. 8–10.

[172] Ibid., 18.

[173] For instance, compare *Acta Saturnini*, 19 (*P.L.*, viii, 702 C) 'cum erigat altare sacrilegus, celebrat sacramenta profanus, baptizat reus, curat vulneratus, veneratur martyres persecutor . . .' and the utterance of Caecilius of Bilta at Cyprian's council in 256 (ed. von Soden, *Göttingen Nachrichten*, 1909, 249–50), 'fidem dat infidelis, veniam delictorum tribuit secleratus et in nomine Christi tingit antichristus, benedicit a deo maledictus, vitam pollicetur mortuus, pacem dat inpacificus, deum invocat blasphemus, sacerdotium administrat profanus, ponit altare sacrilegus'.

[174] *Acta Saturnini*, 17 (*P.L.*, viii, 700 D).

[175] Augustine, *Brev. Coll. cum Donatistis*, iii.13.25. (*P.L.*, xliii, 637–8).

[176] *Acta Proconsularia*, 1, and *Ep.*, 81.

[177] For details of inscriptions in honour of Numidian martyrs, P. Monceaux, *Histoire littéraire*, iii.177–8, and A. Berthier, and associates, *Les Vestiges du Christianisme antique dans la Numidie centrale*, Algiers, 1942, 210ff.

[178] Ably set out by G. E. M. Ste Croix, 'Aspects of the "Great Persecution" ', *HTR.*, 47, 1954, 84ff. See my 'Note on the Great Persecution in the West', *Studies in Church History*, ii, 1965.

[179] *Acta*, probably Donatist, have survived as well as an orthodox recension. See P. de Smedt, *A.B.*, 9, 1890, 110 and H. Delehaye, ibid., 54, 1936, 296.

[180] 'Qui persecutionem Diocletiani et Maximiani divinis legibus passi sunt', *Bull. Arch. du Comité des Travaux historiques*, 1934, 69. See also H. Delehaye, *A.B.*, 54, 1936, 313–16.

[181] Augustine, *Brev. Coll. cum Donatistis* iii.15.27 (*P.L.*, xliii , 640).

[182] For discussion of martyrdoms in Numidia, see my *Donatist Church*, pp. 7–8. *H.E.*, viii.6.10.

[182a] For the same phrase used in connection with Diocletian's abdication in 305, Eusebius, *H.E.*, viii, App.

[183] See Introduction, p. xii.

[183a] *CIL.*, 6700 = 19353; Optatus, op. cit., iii.8.

[184] On this important discovery, L. Leschi, 'Le *Centenarium* d'Aqua Viva', *Revue Africaine*, 87, 1943, 5–22. Valerius Florus was 'vir perfectissimus', and 'praeses Numidiae', Valerius Ingenuus was *praefectus limitis* and Valerius Alexander (perhaps the future opponent of Maxentius in Africa) 'v[ir] perfectissimus vices praefecto praetorio'.

[185] Canons 1–4.

[186] *Mémoires*, Paris (1702), vol. v, 30 and 63, and 613–16.

[187] The most recent summary of the evidence has been made by E. H. Röttges, s.j., 'Marcellinus-Marcellus zur Papstgeschichte der diokletianischen Verfolgungszeit', *Zeitschr. f. kath. Theol.*, 78, 1956, 385–420, and A. Amore, 'Il preteso "Lapsus" di papa Marcellino', *Antonianum*, 32, 1955, 411–26. Also *Revue des Études Augustiniennes*, vi 1960, 191–2.

[188] *Gesta Collationis Carthaginensis*, iii, 489–514 (*P.L.*, xi, 1255–6); cf. Augustine, *Breviculus Coll. cum Don.*, iii.18.34 (*P.L.*, xliii, 645). 'In prosecutione autem sua dixerunt Melchiadem tertium episcopum fuisse ab illo, qui tunc cum traditio illa facta esset.' This would lead back from Eusebius and Marcellus to Marcellinus. The Catholics did not challenge the authenticity of the Donatist *Gesta* at the Conference.

[189] E. H. Röttges, art cit., 395, 'Eine Fälschung dieser beiden Quellen ist nicht anzunehmen'.

190 *ILCV.*, 962, A. Ferrua, *Epigrammata Damasiana*, Roma, 1942, 181.

191 Mansi, *Collectio Concil.*, 1.1250. Tillemont, op. cit., 613–16.

192 Socrates, *H.E.*, vii.9, says that Innocent (401–417) was the first to take action against the Novatianists in Rome, and 'deprived them of many churches'. The persecution was continued by Celestine, 422–432 (ibid., vii.11) and apparently up to that time they were very numerous.

193 Augustine, *De Unico Baptismo*, 16.28, *P.L.*, xliii, 610.

194 art. cit., 395. For the contrary view, A. Amore, art. cit., 425–6.

195 Athanasius, *Historia Arianorum*, 44 (Hosius' letter to Constantius in 355), *P.G.*, xxv, 744D.

196 *Passio Sancti Vincenti* (ed. Ruinart, 400–6), 5ff. A typical fourth-century epic *Acta*.

197 On the authority of Prudentius, *Peristephanon*, iii.25ff. (*P.L.*, lx, 350).

198 *Acta Eupli* (ed. Knopf and Krüger, 100–2) ii.4 and 5. Euplius dixit 'Adoro Christum, detestor daemonia, fac quod vis. Christianus sum. Haec (i.e. torture) diu optavi'. He was executed as 'inimicus deorum et imperatorum' (iii. 2) See G. E. M. Ste Croix, *Why were the early Christians persecuted?*, p. 22.

199 Augustine, *Ep.*, 88.2 (*CSEL.*, 34, 408), Optatus 1.22.

200 Eusebius, *H.E.*, viii.13.11.

201 *Dating: Mart. Pal.* 5.3(L) See H. Delehaye, 'Les Martyrs d'Egypte', *A.B.*, 40, 1922, 28.

202 I cannot reconcile Eusebius' evidence with the obvious problem it raises in connection with Culcianus' career. It is difficult, however, to dismiss Eusebius who was an eye-witness of events in the Thebaid. He must have known who was the governor. It is interesting, too, that Epiphanius' informants about the origins of the Meletian controversy *circa* 370 also placed Culcianus in the Thebaid, though in the time of Diocletian. This is not possible, but one cannot rule out the chance that Culcianus was sent to the Thebaid later as part of Maximin's desperate gamble against the Christians. The details of his career had become hazy by 370, though it is quite evident that his association with the Thebaid had somehow or other passed into folk-memory (*Panarion*, 68.1). Much the same had happened to Florus' association with Numidia. See also, below, n.270.

203 *Acta Sancti Theodoti*, 4.

204 Eusebius, *H.E.*, viii.14.11ff. and ix.9a.12. Lactantius, *De Mortibus*, 38.

205 Quoted by Eusebius, *H.E.*, ix.7.3–14.

206 Ibid., viii.14.9; *Mart. Pal.*, 9.2 (A.D. 309).

207 *De Mortibus*, 36.4. Lactantius dates these measures to the period after Galerius' palinode. They would seem, however, to belong to the restoration of the urban temples.

208 Porphyry cited by Augustine, *De Civ. Dei*, xix.23. See above, p. 299, n.110.

209 Eusebius, *H.E.*, ix.7.1.

210 *Historia Arianorum*, 64.

211 Eusebius' description, *Mart. Pal.*, 4.2.

212 Probably towards the end of March. It could not have reached Egypt until a little later since Peter of Alexandria had time to issue his fourteen canons regulating the re-admission of the lapsed, after Easter 306, i.e. 18 April.

213 *Mart. Pal.*, 4.8.

214 Ibid., 4.8–15. One would date the martyrdom of his brother Aedesius by command of Hierocles, prefect of Egypt to 307 (*Mart. Pal.*, 5.3), rather longer than the 'σμικρὸν τῷ χρόνῳ ὕστερον allowed by Eusebius. See Knipfing, art. cit., 202, and Lawlor and Oulton, op. cit., 325.

215 *Mart. Pal.*, 6.

216 Eusebius, *H.E.*, viii.12.10, viii.12.8–13, *Mart. Pal.*, vii.2. (*Dating:* Lawlor, spring 308, Delehaye, *Les Martyrs d'Egypte*, 29, spring 307).

217 Eusebius, *Mart. Pal.*, 11.5 puts his death in the seventh year of the persecution, i.e. 310; and his imprisonment dated from 5 Nov. 308.

[218] *Mart. Pal.*, 8.1. There were ninety-seven in the first convoy consisting of men, women and children. See also 11.6ff. and Lawlor and Oulton's exhaustive note, *Eusebius*, ii.328.

[219] *Mart. Pal.*, 8.5–8.

[220] Ibid., 8.9–12.

[221] Ibid., 8.13.

[222] Ibid., 9.1. A short respite indicated in both versions of *Mart. Pal.* 'But the fire of persecution lessened a little towards us' (in L.) and 'we were just about to regain a breath of pure air . . .' (in S.).

[223] Ibid., 9.1. For Maximin's annoyance at Licinius' promotion, Eusebius, *H.E.*, viii.13.14 and Lactantius, *De Mortibus*, 36.2.

[224] Note Aurelius Victor's description of his character (*Epitome de Caes.*, 41.8–10) which after castigating his avarice, illiteracy and tendency towards debauchery adds, 'satis utilis ac militiae custos ad veterum instituta severissimus', not a verdict one would associate with a philo-Christian.

[225] Ibid., 9.2–3. An interesting revelation that *idolothytia* remained a real issue among Christians as late as the turn of the fourth century.

[226] Ibid., 9.3.

[227] Ibid., 9.4ff.

[228] Ibid., 10.1.

[229] Ibid., 11.30.

[230] Ibid., 13.1.

[231] Ibid., 13.2.

[232] The only reminiscence of this period in Asia seems to be embedded in the *Acta Sancti Theodoti* (ed. Franchi di Cavalieri, *S.T.*, vi, 1901; critique by H. Delehaye, *A.B.*, 22, 1903, 320–8).

[233] Lactantius, *De Mortibus*, 33. Eusebius, *H.E.*, viii.16.3. Compare Josephus' description of the last days of Herod, *Antiquities*, xvii, 169, and ii Macc. 9.9 for those of Antiochus IV.

[234] According to Orosius, *Hist. adv. Paganos*, vii.28, one doctor informed Galerius that the sickness had been sent by God.

[235] On the edict see J. R. Knipfing 'The Edict of Galerius, 311 A.D. reconsidered', *Revue Belge de Philologie et d'Hist.*, I, 1922, 695ff., and for more recent discussion, J. Moreau, op. cit., 388–95. Also, a useful summary in P. Batiffol, *La Paix Constantinienne*, 180–6.

[236] See the commentaries in E. Schwartz 'Zur Geschichte des Athanasius', IV, *Göttingen Nachrichten*, 1904, 527, n. 1 and 2. J. Moreau, op. cit.

[237] Compare the proconsul's statement in the *Acta Scillitanorum*, 'oblata sibi facultate ad Romanorum morem reddi obstinanter perseveraverunt'.

[238] See above, n. 20.

[239] 'nec diis eosdem cultum ac religionem debitam exhibere nec deum christianorum observare'.

[240] This is evident enough from Lactantius, *De Mortibus*, 35.2. 'Tunc apertis carceribus, Donate carissime, cum ceteris confessoribus custodia liberatus es, cum tibi carcer sex annis pro domicilio fuerit.' Also, Eusebius, *H.E.*, ix.1.7.

[241] For the narrative, A. H. M. Jones, *Constantine and the Conversion of Europe*, ch. v and E. Schwartz, *Zur Geschichte des Athanasius*, iv, 520–7, and H. Mattingly, *CAH.*, xii, 344ff.

[242] On Licinius' relationship to Galerius, Zosimus, ii.11.

[243] *Paneg. Lat.*, vii.2. 'Ab illo enim divo Claudio manat in te avita cognatio, qui Romani imperii solutam et perditam disciplinam primus reformavit'—Constantine would do the same! Written shortly after 25 July 310, the date of Constantine's *dies imperii*.

[244] *Paneg. Latini*, vii.21, with acknowledgments for the translation to J. Stevenson, *A New Eusebius*, pp. 297–8. See H. Grégoire, 'La Statue de Constantin et le Signe de la Croix', *Antiquité Classique*, i, 1932, 135ff.

[244a] *Paneg. Lat.*, ix.23.

245 Lactantius, *De Mortibus*, 35.2. His wards, however, judged Licinius rightly and took refuge with Maximin.

246 Lactantius, *De Mortibus*, 36.1. It must, however, have taken him to the end of July 311 before he had consolidated his hold on the Asiatic provinces (H. J. Lawlor, *Eusebiana*, 211 and 235). Licinius was unaccountably slothful.

247 Lactantius, ibid. For discussion, O. Seeck, *Untergang*, i⁴, 114, J. Moreau, op. cit., 398-400, who considers that the measure was a temporary one and concerned only Bithynia or Nicomedia itself, and H. J. Lawlor, *Eusebiana*, 215ff.

248 E. Schwartz, op. cit., 524-5.

249 Eusebius, *H.E.*, ix.2.1. (Christians not permitted to assemble in *areae*.)

250 Ibid., ix.1.3–6 (the rescript to the Prefect, Sabinus). Lactantius, op. cit., 36 and 37.1.

251 Dated 313–314 (i.e. after Maximin's defeat), 'ἐλυτρώσατο πολλούς ἐκ κακῶν βασάνων'. The idea of 'ransom' (ἐλυτρώσατο) suggests re-conversion, especially as Maximin was fond of describing his own measures as those of rescue (Eusebius, *H.E.*, ix.7.11). See, however, H. Grégoire, 'Notes épigraphiques', *Byzantion*, 8, 1933, 49–56. Epitynchanos was obviously one of Maximin's municipal ἀρχιερεῖς, but his service in honour of Apollo, Hecate and Manes Daos, might suggest simply the union of Roman and provincial gods without necessarily a reference to the gods of Dacia as well (pp. 55–6). Epitynchanos belonged to a priestly family, his grandfather, Aurelius Epitynchanos was also a 'εἰροφάντης' (ibid).

252 W. M. Calder, *Expositor*, 1908, 385–408, and *Bull. of John Rylands Library*, viii, 1924, 354.

253 Eusebius, *H.E.*, ix.3 and *Praep. Evangel.*, iv.2.10–13.

254 Eusebius, *H.E.*, ix.2–4 and ix.9a.4. Petition by citizens of Nicomedia 'bringing images of the gods' and asking, 'ἵνα παντὶ τρόπῳ τὸ τοιοῦτον ἔθνος (i.e. the Christians) μηδαμῶς ἐπιτρέποιτο ἐν τῇ αὐτῶν πατρίδι οἰκεῖν'.

255 *CIL.*, iii.12132, *ILCV*, ia and b. The Christians were still denounced as ἄθεοι and it was demanded that they be made to sacrifice, i.e. persecution to be re-started—an interesting example of support for Maximin in the smaller towns.

256 The Pamphylians are mentioned (ll.3–4 of the Greek text), but Aricanda itself is in Lycia and therefore the Lycians must have joined in the petition. See Th. Mommsen's 'Zweisprachige Inschrift aus Arykanda', *Gesammelte Schriften*, vi. 555–65.

257 Eusebius, *H.E.*, ix.7.10–11.

258 Ibid., 7.13; cf. *ILCV*, 1a (Latin text of Maximin's reply to the Lyco-Pamphylian petition).

259 Ibid., 7.1.

260 Ibid., 5.2.

261 Ibid., 4.

262 Jerome, *De Viris Illust.*, 83. (*P.L.* xxiii, 691A) 'ad extremum novissimae persecutionis'.

263 Ibid., 6.1–3. Other martyrdoms at this period, such as Julian of Emesa, Tillemont, *Mémoires*, v.108–12, and W. M. Calder, op. cit., 358–60 (Bishop Severus and Presbyter Gennadius).

264 November seems indicated as the start of this final phase, from Eusebius' statement that the Church enjoyed 'not six whole months of peace' after the publication of Galerius' edict (*H.E.*, ix.2.1).

265 C. Schmidt, *Petrus v. Alexandrien*, 9 and 36.

266 This must be the case if one accepts Epiphanius' account of the origins of the Meletian controversy as being accurate (*Panarion*, 68.1). Meantime, however, Meletius of Lycopolis had been taking the law into his hands.

267 Eusebius, *H.E.*, viii.2.1. Peter of Alexandria, Canons 5, 6, 7 and 14. A reminiscence of this period may be contained in the Passio S. Dioscori. Dioscorus son of a *lector* is

reported by the *curator civitatis* of Cynopolis, '*tanquam christianum nolentem complere praecepto imperatoris*'. The case is heard in Alexandria by the 'praeses' Culcianus, i.e. for *contumacia* as well as Christianity. Dioscorus refuses either to reveal his father's hiding-place or to sacrifice and is ordered to be beheaded. As in his interrogation of Phileas and Philoromus (Eusebius, *H.E.*, viii.9.8 and in the *Acts of Phileas and Philoromus*, ed. Knopf and Krüger, 113–16) Culcianus is shown as an official who was prepared to try to convince Christians of their folly before passing to extreme measures. ('Passio Sancti Dioscori', ed. H. Quentin, *A.B.*, 24, 1905, 321–42). See above, n. 145. Another record may be the exiling of Politika to the Great Oasis referred to in the Letter of Psenosiris.

²⁶⁸ Text, Routh, *Reliquiae Sacrae*, iii.321–43.

²⁶⁹ Eusebius, *Demonst.*, vi.20 and ix.2.

²⁷⁰ Eusebius, *H.E.*, viii.10. 4–5. The dating, like most of the events in Egypt at this period, is uncertain. The *Acta* of Phileas record his long cross-examination by Culcianus in Alexandria, and therefore should be placed between 303–305. But Eusebius puts his letter to the people of Thmuis in the context of Maximin's rule, and it must be admitted that the account of the tortures and general violence of the persecution fits the period 306–312 better than the earlier phase. The deaths of Phileas and Philoromus are commemorated on 4 Feb. in the Martyrology of Jerome, and, on the whole, one is inclined to accept as the most probable date for both martyrdoms, 4 Feb. 307 (Lawlor and Oulton, *Eusebius*, ii. 276–7). The possibility remains (Knipfing, op. cit., 202–3) that Hierocles did not take over from Culcianus until early in 307. Cf. above, note 202.

²⁷¹ Eusebius, *H.E.*, viii.9.4–5.

²⁷² In the *Mart. Pal.*, 11.1, Eusebius refers to 'mere boys' being among the Egyptian prisoners whom he encountered in Palestine in 310.

²⁷³ Lactantius, *De Mort. Pers.*, 43.3.

²⁷⁴ *Pan. Lat.*, ix.4.

²⁷⁵ Note the death near Spoleto of a 'vir ducenarius protector ex ordine leg(ionis) Divite(ensium)', on Constantine's side, *CIL.*, xi, 4787.

²⁷⁶ Cf. Eusebius, *H.E.*, viii.14.1.

²⁷⁷ *Liber Pontificalis* (Duchesne, 1.164) gives a circumstantial account of Pope Marcellus being responsible for both the Coemeterium Novellae and the organization of Rome into 25 *tituli* or parishes 'on account of' (*propter*) the baptism and penance of numerous heathen who were converted at this time. The *tituli* may have come into being, however, before the persecution. See above, ch. XIV, n. 32.

²⁷⁸ Optatus, *De Schismate*, 1.16–17.

²⁷⁹ For the Donatist accusation *circa* 380 that he had been condemned by a Spanish Council for some unspecified offence, Augustine, *Contra Epist. Parmeniani*, 1.4.7.

²⁸⁰ *ILCV.*, 2a (Inscription on the arch of Constantine at Rome) and Anon, *Lat. Panegyr.* ix.2, recited in 313/314. 'Habes profecto aliquod cum illa mente divina, Constantine, secretum, quae, delegata nostri diis minoribus cura, uni se tibi dignatur ostendere.' Note also the discovery of the graffito in the Vatican cemetery, dating before 322. 'In oc signo'. This could be a vindication of the account which Eusebius claims that Constantine gave him of the incident. *Vita Constantini*. 1.28. See M. Guarducci, *I graffiti sotto la confessione di San Pietro in Vaticano*, Vatican City, 1958, ii.2 and 27. (See P. M. Fraser's discussion *JRS.*, lii, 1962, 217).

²⁸¹ The instructions to Anulinus proconsul of Africa and to Patritius, the deputy prefect, reproduced in Eusebius, *H.E.*, x.5 and 6.

²⁸² That there was an actual Edict of Milan has been rightly doubted since Seeck's article in *Zeitschrift f. Kirchengeschichte*, xii 1891, 381ff. The sequence of events seems to have been as follows. After Constantine's victory at the Milvian Bridge, the Senate declared him senior Augustus (the rank previously held by Maximin). In virtue of the legislative authority which he now possessed, Constantine promulgated an edict of toleration

and restoration, a copy of which was sent to Maximin, which the latter then included in his long instruction to the prefect, Sabinus, end-312 (Eusebius, *H.E.*, ix.9a, 1ff.). The exact text of Constantine's edict is not known, though its tenor can be reconstructed perhaps from the instructions sent to Anulinus, proconsul of Africa (*H.E.* x.6), to Maximin, and in Licinius' edict, promulgated at Nicomedia June 13, 313. In February, Constantine met Licinius at Milan and there Licinius married Constantia, Constantine's sister, and pledged his agreement to the pro-Christian policy of the senior Augustus. There was discussion of religious policy, but no new edict. After his victory over Maximin, however, Licinius proceeded to publish his own edict which incorporated much of Constantine's edict of the previous year; hence, the double preamble and repetitions in the surviving text. Like Maximin, Licinius was determined to maintain some vestige of independence. What has survived is his executive instruction to the governor of Bithynia in June 313. See H. Nesselhauf's study of the evidence, 'Das Toleranzedikt des Licinius', *Histor. Jahrbuch*, 78, 1955, 33–61. The slight variations in the text of Licinius' edict in Lactantius' and Eusebius' versions may be due both to drafting variations in Nicomedia and Caesarea in Palestine respectively, but also some second thoughts on the part of Licinius (cf. Lact., 48.3, and Eusebius, x.5.5. 'ὅπως ἡμῖν 'εδυνηθῆ τὸ θεῖον 'εν πᾶσι τὴν ἔθιμον σπουδὴν καὶ καλοκάγαθίαν παρέχειν'. Nesselhauf, art. cit., 55). For Constantine's career and movements 311–313, see also J. R. Palanque, 'A propos du prétendu édit de Milan', *Byzantion*, x, 1935, 612.

[283] Eusebius, *H.E.*, ix.8.2.
[284] Ibid., 3–15.
[285] *Chron. Minora*, iii.397.
[286] Eusebius, *H.E.*, ix.9a (dating probably Dec. 312–Jan. 313).
[287] Lactantius, *De Mortibus*, 46.
[288] Eusebius, *H.E.*, ix.10.7ff.
[289] *Acta Habibi*, p. 91.
[290] *Div. Inst.*, v.13.11; cf. ibid., 19, and 22.19–24.
[291] Ibid., v.22.18, 'Est et alia causa cur adversus nos persecutiones fieri sinat, ut dei populus augeatur'—and he goes on to show why.
[292] *Div. Inst.*, v.22.22. Compare, of course, Tertullian's similar statement in *Apol.*, 50.15.
[293] See J. M. C. Toynbee and J. Ward-Perkins, *The Shrine of St. Peter*, Pl. 32 and pp. 116–17.

CHAPTER SIXTEEN

What has the Emperor to do with the Church? 312–361

THE wreckage of the persecution remained. In human terms its toll had been heavy. We shall never know the exact number of martyrs and confessors, nor of those who perished in the reprisals that followed the victories of Constantine and Licinius. As Henri Grégoire has pointed out,[1] the only figures which can claim accuracy for the period as a whole came from two provinces of *Palestina I* and *II*. Counting a Palestinian executed at Antioch, and another at Alexandria and three Egyptians martyred at Ascalon, the total deaths numbered 44 from the spring of 303 until Galerius' edict in 311. In addition forty-two Palestinians who had been deported died in captivity. Thus, after eight years' intermittent repression there were 86 victims of whom the presbyter Pamphilus was the only outstanding individual martyr, while many of the bolder spirits provoked their own deaths.[2] In contrast, determined Christians such as Eusebius himself survived, and only one of the Palestinian bishops, Silvanus of Gaza,[3] was martyred. Indeed, of the senior bishops who eventually perished in the east most fell victim of the final desperate effort by Maximin during the autumn of 311. The moral seems to be that as in the Decian persecution prudence generally guaranteed safety.

In Egypt, there was violence and bloodshed but precise details are lacking. Eusebius tells us that Culcianus gloried in the 'deaths of thousands of Christians in Egypt',[4] but he regards Culcianus as governor of the Thebaid,[5] and whether right or wrong in this, the allegation that he caused 'thousands of deaths' does not help the historian statistically. Nor does Eusebius' other statement, that 10 or 20 and 'sometimes 30, sometimes 60, and sometimes 100 were executed in a day' in the Thebaid.[6] The language of the Parable of the Sower conveys the horror of the events, but not the precise number of the martyrs. More to the point is his report of the two convoys containing 97 and 130 Egyptians respectively which passed through Palestine on the way to the Cilician mines in 307/308[7] and the execution of 39 Egyptians who perished together with Bishop Silvanus of Gaza at Phaeno on 4 May 311.[8] These indicate the scale of the repression. So, too, perhaps does the list of martyrs preserved in the Coptic Synaxarium. Of 381 named (excluding multiple batches of 50 or more) 149 are stated definitely to have suffered under Diocletian or his governors. In nearly all these cases the governor was Satrius Arrianus whose province included Arsinoë in the Fayum, but the Thebaid hardly figures in this record.[9] Assuming that the executions there were indeed on a large scale, martyrdoms in Egypt could easily have run into four figures; and if one includes victims in other eastern provinces, together with acts of exemplary punishment such as meted out to the Christians of Nicomedia in March–April 303, or the Christian Phrygian township probably in the same year, one might arrive at the figure for the east alone suggested by Grégoire for the whole Empire of 2500–3000.[10]

In the west, only two precise records giving numbers of confessors have survived, namely the 47 Abitinians arrested late in 303,[11] and a list of 34 martyrs preserved on the mosaic of a fifth-century church at Haidra (Ammaedara).[12] Any figure for Africa beyond this is speculation, for most of the martyrs whose names are preserved on inscriptions from Numidian churches were accompanied by an unknown number of 'comites'. An addition of 500 perhaps, for the whole of the west in the two years 303–305 might be justified, bringing a grand total of 3000–3500 victims.

More important, however, than the numbers of victims was the aftermath of persecution. The Christians had won, but the attitude of the survivors reflected the bitterness of the struggle. Latent tensions, doctrinal, disciplinary and personal, now came out into the open. The Church was never to know harmony again. Among the direct results of the persecution may be included the two major schisms of African Donatism and Egyptian Meletianism, and among the indirect results the permanence of the dualistic concept of Church-State relations in the west, and the origins of the Arian controversy in the east. The theology both of Athanasius and Augustine form part of the ultimate legacy of these times.

In 312 two important questions confronted each Christian

community. First, on what terms were penitent lapsed to be re-admitted to Christian fellowship, and secondly, what was to be the attitude of Christians towards an unmistakably pro-Christian emperor. What had the Emperor to do with the Church? The repercussions arising from the first question were already being felt by the time Constantine entered Rome. Where the persecution had been sporadic or tolerable, it still proved possible to find solutions for the lapsed within the framework of ecclesiastical discipline. Where for one reason or another passions had run high, this was no longer the case. In Spain, the Council of Elvira punished with lifelong excommunication adult baptized Christians who had sacrificed,[13] and was equally severe on those Christians who held formal pagan priesthoods and who would have been more or less compelled to attend spectacles or sacrifices during the Persecution.[14] It was only a little more lenient towards catechumens and those who, without sacrificing had given games and in other ways conformed to the needs of the time.[15] Lapse, however, had been of measurable proportions, for though it was an important problem it was by no means the only one with which the Council dealt, and most of the canons are concerned with disciplinary matters and morals.

In Asia Minor the Christian leaders were more tolerant. The synod of Ancyra in Galatia (probably 314) permitted clergy who having first lapsed 'resumed the combat not only in appearance but in reality', to keep the honours of their office but not to celebrate, and those who had been compelled by force to sacrifice were to be reinstated in their offices.[16] The remainder of the fallen were to be readmitted after going through one or more of the various orders of penitent for a period of three to five years, and even the real traitors who 'had become enemies of the brethren' and denounced their fellow Christians to the authorities might be rehabilitated after ten years' probation.[17] In the East, outside Egypt, the wounds were to be healed within a measurable time.

Where, however, high ecclesiastics had failed and there had been cowardice and worse in contrast to the steadfastness of the martyrs, a heavier price had to be paid. Eusebius alludes to 'rash and unlawful ordinations, and the schisms among the confessors themselves', and innovations devised by 'young agitators' during Maximin's régime in the east.[18] As early as the end of 305 the atmosphere of schism, or schism itself, hung over Rome, Egypt and North Africa.

In Rome the damage was not permanent. The obscure events which surround the names of the 'bishops' Marcellus, Eusebius and Heraclius seem to be connected with violent disputes regarding the discipline to be imposed on the lapsed, as now one side and now the other gained the upper hand.[19] But as in the crisis after the Decian persecution the rigorists, though formidable in influence, were not strong enough to prevail. On 2 July 311 the bishopric came into the hands of a moderate, an African named Miltiades, who had been one of Marcellinus' presbyters. The successful negotiations for the return of Church property which he appears to have concluded with Maxentius may have strengthened his position.[20] Discontent, however, remained below the surface, and when in 313/314 the Donatists challenged his credentials and acted first as though the Roman see was vacant and then appointed Victor, bishop of Garba, as his rival,[21] support for their moves was not lacking.

It was characteristic of the latent strength of the Novatianist tradition in Rome, that not only did Victor and his successors maintain themselves for another century without any sort of official backing, but that the two great fourth-century records of Roman bishops and confessors, the *Depositio Episcoporum* and the *Depositio Martyrum*, both seem to stem from non-orthodox, rigorist sources.[22]

In Egypt and Africa the struggle was not so quickly over, and in the African provinces victory eventually went to the puritan rebels. For Egypt we have the dramatic description of the origins of the Meletian schism told by Epiphanius from information he had received from the Egyptian bishops exiled to Palestine by the Emperor Valens.[23] We see a number of Egyptian clergy in prison including Peter of Alexandria and Meletius of Lycopolis (Assiut) in Upper Egypt. Discussion turned on the treatment to be accorded to the lapsed. Peter recommended a mild policy, for fear lest the lapsed might otherwise apostasize altogether. Meletius was for more severity, and he was supported by the majority of clergy and monks in the prison. The dispute waxed bitter. Eventually the two sides ceased to be on speaking terms. Peter hung a curtain up separating him from Meletius and his supporters. More fuel was added to this pettiness during the lull which followed Diocletians' abdication. Peter's encyclical letter, setting out conditions under which various degrees of lapse could be restored was more lenient than many confessors believed right. Those who had lapsed under severe pressure could resume communion after 40 days fasting and meditation (Canon 1). Indeed, all who confessed their offence were to be reintegrated within three years; they were allowed to begin their restoration as 'penitents' (ὑποπίπτοντες) without going through the two meanest grades of ecclesiastical penance.[24] It implied too, that clergy were to have the chance of eventual rehabilitation provided they first did penance as laymen.[25] In addition, Peter strongly reproved those who offered themselves for martyrdom, and as in Carthage the ecclesiastical authorities showed themselves suspicious of the awakened enthusiasm of the laity.[26] Meletius and his friends were not opposed to the eventual restoration of the lapsed, but insisted that this could not take place during the persecution, and also, that lapsed clergy must be replaced.[27] In the confused years 306–310 Meletius, though opposed by prominent and wealthy clerics like Phileas of Thmuis,[28] found support among the confessors in the mines, and he continued to perform his own consecrations and ordinations.[29] By the time of Peter's martyrdom the Church in Egypt was split asunder. Coptic Upper Egypt was threatening the authority of Greek Alexandria.

Eventually, by circa 325 the Meletians had their bishops in every second or third city in Middle and Upper Egypt, compared with only one out of every six or seven cities in the Delta. There was an extensive network of Meletian monasteries.[30] But despite their claim to be 'the Church of the Martyrs' and their strength in Coptic Egypt they were not destined to prevail. Apart from the all-important personality of Athanasius, the reasons may be sought in the Egyptian disciplinary and intellectual tradition of the previous century. Egypt, as we know, had not supported Novatianism. There was therefore a lack of a long-standing rigorist tradition to which Meletius could appeal, the lack also of a strong and coherent school teaching the literal interpretation of the Bible favourable to Millenarism and witness through martyrdom. Nepos of Arsinoe had failed against Dionysius of Alexandria and Antony's Biblicism was his alone.[31] The issue too, between Meletius and his opponents was a narrow one, and the latter when challenged had also gone cheerfully to martyrdom. The effect of their conduct was not lost on high-minded intellectual Christians in Alexandria, men such as Arius, who first supported Meletius and then had made their peace with Peter. Such turncoats were not to be forgiven, especially when their Christology differed from the prophetic Modalism of the Church of the Martyrs. In 318, Meletius still had sufficient power to hint to Bishop Alexander that unpleasant consequences might await him if he took no cognisance of Arius' views.[32] He did; and thus the chain of events which started the Arian controversy was set in motion.

The Meletians took their revenge on Arius, but otherwise they derived little benefit. Between 328-332 Athanasius allied the patriarchate with Anthony's desert monks. The Meletians were henceforth outbid for ascetic support. In Egypt, despite the immense and lasting veneration for the martyrs, and the vogue enjoyed even by the African *Acta Perpetuae*, the Church of the Martyrs failed.[33] Once the majority of the monks had rallied to Athanasius, Christianity in Egypt became the Christianity of the martyr's substitute, his 'brother' and sometimes his rival, the ascetic.

In Africa, however, the opposite development took place as the result of much the same situation. Opposition to the official leadership of the Church from Carthage, sprang up on the desert fringes of Numidia. Here also, the issue was the rehabilitation of lapsed clergy. Like Meletius, between 305-311, the leader of the movement, Donatus of Casae Nigrae performed irregular ordinations.[34] Contrary to general belief, it seems evident that Donatus and his colleagues were prepared to see the lapsed received back after penance, as laymen, though not restored to the priesthood. In this respect their policy followed on that of Cyprian fifty years before. In Africa too, the issue went much deeper than in Egypt. The problem was not forced or formal acts of apostasy committed by Christians under duress, but the surrender of the Scriptures to pagan magistrates. The Bible was not regarded as 'a vast treasury of mysterious meanings'[35] to be compared with Homeric and Platonic writings but as we have already seen, the literal Word of God, the word of Jn. 1¹, which had existed from all time; and it was referred to as such in a Donatist encyclical letter to the people of Carthage.[36] Witness and denial could not be allegorized away, and this left little scope for lenience to those who fell. The confessors of Abitina had spoken for much of African Christianity. The followers of the martyrs could not communicate with the *traditores*.[37] For the rest, the character of Caecilian, the cohesion of the Numidian episcopate and the leadership of Donatus ensured that by the middle of 312, altar would be set against altar in Carthage and Constantine would be faced with the scandal of schism among 'the ministers of the Supreme Divinity' in Africa. It was this situation which confronted Constantine in the winter of 312/313.

Constantine's personal religion and his religious policy, are relevant only in so far as these moulded the attitudes of eastern and western Christians towards the Emperor as representative of the secular power.[38] It is doubtful whether one can speak of the Emperor's 'conversion' as the result of the phenomena which he saw on the eve of the battle of the Milvian Bridge.[39] It seems evident, however, that he accepted a Christian interpretation of the vision put to him perhaps by Hosius of Cordova. Just as after the overthrow of Maximian in 310 he had felt himself under obligation to the Sun-god, so now he felt himself under an obligation to the God of the Christians for the victory he had achieved. The debt must be paid. Thus, Constantine proceeded to the complete and rapid dismantling of the visible evidence of the persecutions during the winter of 312/313, as shown by his letters to Patritius the vice-prefect of Africa, Anulinus the proconsul and Caecilian himself. Divine favour must be retained; and if we remember how only the previous year Maximin had pointed to the prosperity of his dominions being directly due to the favour of the gods resulting from the return of Christians to their worship, so Constantine also gave thanks to his new-found protector. As he told Anulinus, the prayers of Christian clergy 'seem to confer incalculable benefit on the affairs of State'.[40] Yet for the next twelve years, so far as the general public and even the authorities were concerned, the emperors were merely 'deigning to show favour to the Christians'.[41] The real agent of the 'liberation of the world' which Constantine proclaimed in 313[42] was still 'the unconquered sun, my companion'.

The sense of obligation for benefits received explains much of

Constantine's subsequent favour to the Church down to Nicaea in 325. To the Church of Rome he gave an imperial palace (the Basilica Constantina in the Lateran) and lands worth some 15,000 solidi annually.[43] He prohibited branding and crucifixion as punishments,[44] he freed clergy from expensive obligations towards individual cities[45] and he granted complete freedom of bequest to the Church.[46] He bitterly assailed the traditional enemies of the Christians, the Jews, renewing the prohibition on proselytism decreed by Septimius Severus in 202, on pain of death.[47] At the same time he demanded that the Christian ministers should be united among themselves. The reason he gives in the postscript of a letter to the Christian official Aelafius explaining why he was summoning the Council of Arles in 314 is interesting.

> Since I am informed that you too are a worshipper of the Highest God, I will confess to your gravity that I consider it absolutely contrary to the divine law that we should overlook such quarrels and contentions whereby the Highest Divinity may perhaps be moved to wrath not only against the human race, but also against me, to whose care He has by his celestial will committed the government of all earthly things, and that He may be so far moved as to take some untoward step. For I shall really fully be able to feel secure and always to hope for prosperity and happiness from the ready kindness of the most mighty God, only when I see all venerating the most Holy God in the proper cult of the catholic religion with harmonious brotherhood of worship.[48]

The Emperor's turgid and ill-educated style speaks for itself. As his predecessors, he senses religion as part of a bargain. One condition of this was that the Supreme Deity required unity among his chosen servants. It was the duty of the Emperor to whom He had committed supreme power to impose and maintain this unity.

The flaw in this ideal lay in the fact that no more than his immediate predecessors did Constantine possess the power to impose religious unity on the Empire. Moreover, even if he had, like Theodosius between 388–391, obtained the nominal assent of all to a comprehensive formula of 'Catholic truth', the differences of interpretation would have been so great between east and west as to have rendered his success meaningless. In the fourth century, as in the third, the Church's understanding of its own nature and its outlook towards the State diverged on geographical lines.

In the east the progress of the Constantinian programme between 312–324 was followed with unconcealed joy. When he wrote the vast *Praeparatio Evangelica* in 311–312 (?) (i.e. perhaps even before the final defeat of Maximin) Eusebius was already prepared for victory. The Word of God invited all, 'Greeks and barbarians alike, men and at the same time women and children, poor and rich, wise and foolish—even slaves'; all had a service to perform in honour of Christ. He was writing, as he explains, for those who did not know Christianity yet, 'but as Greeks, Jews and aught else, were making an honest inquiry into the Christian way of life'.[49] It was intended as an elementary guide 'to our recent converts from the heathen',[50] and the companion *Demonstratio* was designed for their advanced instruction.

In both these huge and learned works, originally fifteen books of the one and twenty of the other, and in the five books of the *Theophania*, the inquirer was confronted by the fact of Christianity as a great, a blessed and a growing power, and above all, a power designed to exist in peace and harmony with the Roman Empire. Thus, towards the end of the *Theophania* he writes:

> Nevertheless, when again I view its [the preaching of the Apostles] power and the result of its doings, how the many myriads have given their assent to it, and how churches of tens of thousands of men have been brought together by these deficient and rustic persons—nor that these were built in obscure places, nor in those which are unknown, but rather in the greatest cities, I say in the Imperial city of Rome itself, in Alexandria, in Antioch, in all Egypt, in Libya, in Europe, in Asia, both in the villages and (other) places and among all nations —I am again compelled to recur to the question of (its) cause and to confess, that they could not otherwise have undertaken this enterprise than by a Divine power which exceeds that of man, and by the assistance of Him who said to them: Go and make disciples of all nations in my name (*Theophania*, v.49).

The answer which he himself gave was 'that the teaching of Christ is not new or strange, but if one may speak truthfully, is primitive, unique and true'.[51] The victory of that teaching which Origen had foreseen he had actually witnessed. He is full of optimism for the future of the human race led by Constantine and his sons.

Eusebius represents the final stage in a long history, first of Hellenistic Jewish and then of Christian political thought.[52] Like Melito of Sardes, and like Origen he points in the first book of the *Praeparatio* to the association of the salvation brought to the secular world by Augustus and the salvation brought to mankind by Christ.[53] The people of God were to be reconciled with the people of the Empire. The constant internecine conflicts between rival cities and rival gods were a sign of the oppression of humanity by demons, and the demons represented to Eusebius, as they had to Justin, the forces of chaos and irrationality in the universe. Christ 'freed mankind at one stroke both from the polytheism of the influence of the demons and from the polyarchy of different nations'.[54] Then in words reminiscent of Philo's praise of the work of Augustus in the *Legatio ad Gaium* (144) he writes how,

> of old there existed among the nations a multitude of kings and local rulers who bore sway in different cities and countries; some of the cities and countries were democratically governed, some tyrannically and some by a mixture of governments; there were, as was natural, wars of all sorts in consequence; nations clashed with nations and continually attacked their neighbours; they ravaged and were ravaged; they fought and besieged one another's cities, with the result that the inhabitants of cities and the labourers in the countryside were one and all trained to war from their childhood upward, and always carried arms on the roads and in their villages and fields. But when Christ came, of whom it was said of old by the prophets, 'There shall arise in His days righteousness and fullness of peace, and they shall beat their swords into ploughshares . . .', there followed upon His coming works according to what they foretold; all the polyarchy in the Roman world was ended, and Augustus became the sole ruler at the same moment that our Saviour was manifested.[55] (Tr. Ernest Barker, *Alexander to Constantine*, 474–5.)

What Augustus had begun Constantine (and Licinius at this stage!) were called upon by Providence to complete.

For anyone who claimed to be a disciple of Origen, Constantine's reign, moving from one triumphant climax to another must have represented the miraculous fulfilment of lifelong hopes. Already by 314, Eusebius points to the obliteration of the visible traces of the persecution as new and better churches were being built on the site of the old.[56] A decade later, Constantine's victory at Chrysopolis allowed him to end the tenth book of the *Ecclesiastical History* on a note of unrestrained praise. There was 'singing and dancing' in honour of God and of Constantine. The ordinances of the victorious Emperor were 'full of love for humanity', 'munificence and true piety'[57]—the grand finale of a work which had taken its starting point as the birth of Christ, and faithfully chronicled the disasters of persecution and heresy in the intervening three centuries.

As for Constantine, once he had decided to make Byzantium the capital of the Roman Empire, he seems readily to have accepted the role of universal bishop and earthly manifestation of the Divine Logos which the eastern bishops pressed on him.[58] The transformation from Roman *Pontifex Maximus* to the Equal of the Apostles was smooth. Indeed, if one regards the Emperor as now ruling by something like the grace of God, there was no break between Aurelian and Diocletian on the one hand, and Constantine on the other. To let Eusebius speak again, this time in 336 near the end of both his and his master's lives, at the celebration of Constantine's thirtieth anniversary of his assumption of Imperial power,[59] 'He it is—the Word of God proceeding above all things, and through all things, and in all things, both visible and invisible —who is the Lord of all the Universe; from whom and through whom the king (*basileus*), the beloved of God, receives and bears the image of His Supreme Kingship, and so steers and directs, in imitation of his Superior, the helm of all the affairs of this world.' 'As there was one God, so there was one King', Constantine, whose power was supreme in matters both secular and religious. Apart from Athanasius this was a position the eastern bishops were prepared to accept.[60]

The 'godly monarchy', the ideal of Philo and his school had been fulfilled by Constantine. And, just as he accepted from his predecessors the aim of humanity as the reflection of the Divine Logos, so Eusebius appropriated from them the means. The religious life, combining active obedience to God's law in daily works and the contemplation of the ascetic, had long been eulogized by the Alexandrian theologians. The debt to Philo 'sublime and elevated in his views' was generously acknowledged, and the Therapeutae emerge as the prototypes of the true Christian.[61] Their abstinence from food and drink as hindrances to 'their search for the knowledge swelling in them', corresponded to Eusebius' view of the Christian vocation. He himself believed that the 'prophetic' or 'philosophic' life, meaning that of the ascetic, was the 'true citizenship of heaven according to the Gospel'.[62] This was the lesson he would have his readers draw from his account of Origen's life, and similarly, he holds it up to the 'advanced Christians' who were to profit from the Demonstratio.[63] In contrast, apocalyptic whether of Papias or of Nepos received scant respect.[64]

He had the wit to understand that the ascetic ideal was not one to be confined to the rich and cultivated. The monks of his day he praised as 'the first order of those pre-eminent in Christ', but he adds perhaps with reference to Palestine alone, 'they were few'.[65] In this estimate he was, of course, wrong, but he had seen how the ultimately optimistic view of humanity which he held, and the alliance between Church and State could be combined with religious enthusiasm, and that the ideal of the confessor was also that of the ascetic. Thanks to the Alexandrian tradition Egyptian monasticism was to be kept within the political and cultural framework of the Empire for another three centuries. Constantine's tact towards the surviving Egyptian confessors,[66] and his mixture of goodwill and firmness towards Antony and Athanasius ensured that at this critical juncture, in the full tide of victory, popular Christianity in Egypt became a reforming rather than a revolutionary influence.

In popular estimate the age of martyrs became the heroic age, venerated in legend, unrepeatable in fact. As Mennas, Pantaleon, George, Mercurius, and a host of other sufferers were relegated to the tapestries and liturgical homilies of the Coptic Church, their place was taken by the monks. The point is made very clearly in the seventh-century romance entitled Barlaam and Joasaph. 'Monasticism', we are told, 'arose from men's desire to become martyrs in will, that they might not miss the glory of them who were made perfect by blood'.[67] The monk, like the martyr, was the 'athlete' and 'soldier of Christ'.[68] Each fought the demons in his own way, the martyr as witness to Christ, the ascetic in his struggle to maintain his spiritual ascent to Christ. This was the challenge of the desert where the demons had their abode. The extremes of mortification and self-torture to which the monk subjected himself might be compared to the pangs endured by the martyr, and the punishment even of being eaten by wild beasts was simulated by some of the more venturesome spirits. In the daily struggle against the demons of idolatry, heresy, sex, boredom and gluttony, the monk became the man of the Spirit, armed by Him with the same weapons as had served the martyr. His rewards too were the same, the gift of prophecy even against emperors,[69] of visions of the world beyond, of contact with the heavenly powers, and the assurance of salvation from the terrors of the Judgment.[70]

Already during the Great Persecution the way was being prepared for the monk to take up the mantle of the martyr. Many of the Egyptian and Palestinian martyrs combined the qualities of both.[71] In these years, Christians were beginning to share Antony's solitude, while Antony himself went down from Pispir to Alexandria to encourage the confessors in their defiance of Maximin's officials.[72] Evidently Antony had kept just within bounds of moderation, for he was not condemned to death but merely ordered out of the city. The gradual ascent to holiness 'to become like God'[73] did not demand offering oneself to martyrdom. Athanasius, however, does not hesitate to compare Antony 'daily a martyr to his own conscience' to the great Peter of Alexandria who died the martyr's death in 311.[74] With the ending of persecution the substitution of ascetic for martyr as the highest of the Christian's goals became complete.

Two other yearnings were satisfied by the monastic movement. Protest against social oppression and unrelenting war against the gods who had failed were both causes espoused by the monks. Demons were fought by absolute poverty as well as absolute continence. The Coptic monastery became a refuge against the tax-collector and often a vast economic unit of its own. Tens of thousands of *fellahin* found security and work in the Pachomian settlements in the fourth and fifth centuries.[75] They had the chance of defying their erstwhile oppressors through constant attacks against the remains of Greco-Roman paganism. The story can be repeated throughout the east, wherever monasticism was strong. Thus, Libanius in his plea 'On behalf of the Temples' castigates 'the men dressed in black who eat more than elephants' and over-throw the shrines and temples in the countryside.[76] The remark made by the *magister militum* Timasius in 386 when he heard of the destruction wrought against Jews and Valentinian sectaries by the monks of Callinicum, 'the monks commit many crimes', may have been an understatement.[77] Social evils, cruelty and oppression however, they did fight, and in 387 the city of Antioch owed its reprieve from a sentence of destruction largely to the earnest and repeated prayers to the commissioners of the Emperor Theodosius of the local monks.[78] John Chrysostom tells how these came down 'like angels of heaven' to the aid of the city trembling at the prospect of doom. Their action, however, though insistent and peremptory, remained within the bounds of ultimate loyalty to the Empire. Even under Schenute of Atripe the monks of the White Monastery did not behave like Circumcellions, and Byzantine Egypt was to become the classic land of great estates.

The Eusebian ideal seems to have corresponded to the prevailing mood among Christians in the east as a whole. Among the educated, the ascetic and 'philosophic' life was already by the first half of the fourth century proving attractive independently of Origen's influence. From Eusebius of Emesa (*circa* 350) one gathers that in the larger towns it was quite usual for wealthy families to establish private 'nunneries' for their daughters.[79] One is reminded of the 'partheneia' among the Copts of Upper Egypt to which Anthony could consign his sister when he resolved to adopt a solitary life.[80] In Asia Minor the inscriptions commemorating two members of the wealthy family of Collega Macedo show that Christianity had come to be regarded as a sort of philosophic culmination to a career which included the practice of medicine and the study of Plato and Socrates. Thus equipped, the spirit transferred to heaven 'in the convoy of the holy angels'.[81] The Christian Platonist ideal has been accepted en bloc. Socrates, to the educated Greek-speaking Christian always the prototype of martyrdom, becomes the prototype also of Christian philosophy.[81a] To Gregory of Nazianzus, the ascetic 'philosophy' of the monk might be superior to that of Homer and Euripides, as he tells Julian, but philosophy it still was.[82]

Among these noble, Christianized landowners the career of Basil of Caesarea involving study at the still pagan university of Athens, retreat to the beautiful solitude of the Iris valley, episcopal Orders, and the formulation of a Rule for ascetics was exceptional only in that it was fuller and busier than that of most of his contemporaries. Basil's Rule brought the monk into society through making him the agent of necessary good works, such as looking after the sick and needy, and educating the children, as well as being a man of prayer and contemplation. He simply emphasized the collective validity of ideals already being preached by the individual pastor.[83] By the end of the century the traveller Etheria could speak of bishops she had met in the East as 'monks and confessors'.[83a] Finally, among the rigorist sects of Asia Minor monasticism was regarded as fulfilling the aim of the Christian life previously expressed through Millennial hopes. The story Socrates tells of Eutychian the Novatianist who was also famous as a monk, may not stand alone.[84] From top to bottom much of the Greek-speaking world was being absorbed into the Christianity of Origen and his disciples. It was to leave its mark on the Byzantine world and its Balkan and Russian successors from that day to this.

When one asks why no similar development was taking place in the west at this time, one has to give full weight to religious and other factors which in the third century had combined to make Christianity the religion of a 'gathered community', absorbed in defending itself against the world, its culture and its philosophy. The theology of the Two Cities, Jerusalem and Babylon, was never to die out completely in western Christian thought. It was not merely that the west lacked its Plato or its Philo to make Plato acceptable, but western theologians had always stressed the legal relationship which they believed to exist between Christ and His Church. Christ repaid a debt owed by sinful mankind to the Devil, but redemption itself involved merit to be earned so that the Judge's sentence might be avoided. As we have noticed in discussing Tertullian, the Christian *halaka* differed little in its legalism from its Rabbinic counterpart. Not surprisingly, western apologists had consistently associated philosophy with heresy, had emphasized the differences between the philosophical schools and Christianity, and had spurned the possibility of rapprochement between the two, 'Away with all projects for a "Stoic or Platonic" or a "dialectic" Christianity'. Tertullian's cry had been taken up by others, and only a few years before the Great Persecution, Arnobius had once more castigated Plato and 'the new men', his latter-day disciples, who were mounting their subtle attacks on Christianity.[85] Unfortunately, rejection of philosophy deprived an emergent ascetic movement in the west of a powerful argument and means of attraction, namely that this movement represented 'true philosophy' as well as the teaching of the New Testament. Though in Tertullian's De Habitu Virginum, in Pontius' Vita Cypriani and the anonymous De Singularitate Clericorum asceticism is praised, its organized practice remained in the background. The confessor and martyr had no monastic rival. Not until the arrival in the west of Athanasius accompanied by two monks in his second exile in 341, did monasticism begin to gain acceptance, and even then it was a vogue, a diversion for the daughters of the great, rather than a popular movement as it was in the east.

Rejection of pagan society characteristic of the west did not easily fade. Quite the contrary, Lactantius in his Ciceronian prose could appeal to human reason as the basis of his criticism of the outworn pagan past, but the purpose of conversion was as much the avoidance of God's anger as the attainment of justice. The historical theory of the De Mortibus is based on the existence of manifest proofs that God takes vengeance on the persecutors of Christians. The background, as Baynes points out, is Apocalypse, and in the Great Persecution apocalyptic was re-born, if in the west it ever died.[86] Divine ultio combining vengeance and correction, inherited from the historiography of the writers of Maccabees and from Josephus, found lasting place among the Christian historians of the west. In this political theory no respect needed to be shown to rulers if they were persecutors or heretics. Decius was described simply as 'execrabile animal qui vexaret Ecclesiam'.[87] Lactantius' expression would find its imitators among the western clergy, but now directed at the House of Constantine. And would Lactantius encourage Christians to participate in political life and in the army as the victory of Christianity approached? The answer was not encouraging. 'The just and wise man does not long for any power or honour, lest he inflict injury on anyone.'[88] He 'despises riches, honour, powers and kingdoms'.[89] Certainly he does not fight their wars.[90] It is always unlawful to put to death a man whom God willed to be a sacred animal.[91] Tertullian's *De Corona* spoke for him.

Moreover, the acceptance of principles which would make co-operation, let alone alliance, with the Empire problematical was not confined to Christians in Africa. In other parts of the west the equation of Rome/Babylon versus the Church/Jerusalem was as vigorous if not as vocal. The surviving fragments of Victorinus of Pettau (Poetovio) *circa* 300 look forward with uninhibited glee to the 'ruin of the great Babylon, that is of the city of Rome' (ruina Babylonis, id est civitatis Romanae).[92] Elsewhere, Victorinus while admitting the military strength and the sway exercised by the Empire, compared it to the proud Assyrian described by Ezekiel (Ezek. 31) 'whom strangers cut off and destroyed', or the beast arising out of the abyss, and the Emperor himself to 'the Wicked One', the mystery of iniquity already at work (ii Thess. 2[7]).[93] It was not encouraging for the peace-makers.

In 312, therefore, Constantine's victory confronted the western Christians with the necessity of re-thinking their traditional standpoint towards secular society. How were they to respond to the 'repudiation of errors and the restoration of Justice' to which Lactantius alludes in his address to Constantine, perhaps as early as 312?[94] There was to be no easy transition as there had been in the east. In addition, the situation was exacerbated by the outbreak of the Donatist movement in Africa. At the Council of Arles in August 314 we already find a 'moderate' or 'Catholic' view beginning to emerge in opposition to that of the rigorists.

This was the accepance of co-operation with the Empire on a *de facto* basis, the continuance with greater assurance and security of the situation which had been developing before the Great Persecution. Christian soldiers were not to throw down arms in times of peace under pain of excommunication,[95] and Church ordinances were adjusted so that a Christian could take on imperial or municipal office without being obliged to abstain in all circumstances from church services.[96] Meantime, the privileges accorded to the Caecilianists in Africa were accepted gratefully, as were the gifts showered on the Roman community by Constantine. Moreover, the steady pressure of Donatist success in the next two decades forced the Caecilianists to lean more and more on the secular power in order to maintain themselves, until they became out-right defenders of an alliance with the State in which the Church occupied the subordinate position. Thus, to quote Optatus of Milevis' well-known passage in the *De Schismate Donatistarum*, written *circa* 365 in answer to Donatist arguments denying the State's right of intervention in ecclesiastical affairs, 'The state (*respublica*) is not in the Church, but the Church is in the State, that is, the Roman Empire which Christ in the Song of Songs calls Lebanon, where there is holy priesthood, and chastity and virgin-ity which do not exist among the barbarian nations, or if they do, do not exist in safety'.[97] Lebanon no longer represented the strength of an oppressive power as it did in Victorinus' exegesis. The Roman Empire was regarded as the protector of the Church and its clergy, and had the right to service and obedience.

Optatus accepted the Church and the Empire as representing two independent powers. *Ecclesia* and *respublica* could still be contrasted. There is no idea of a cohesion between them under the inspired guidance of the Emperor as we find in the thought of Eusebius and in the outlook of Constantius II.[98] It was a question who was to be senior partner, and not many westerners accepted Optatus' exegesis. When pressed, Hosius, Liberius, Hilary and the others would be giving an answer more akin to that of Optatus' opponents.

In 312/313 the Donatists were prepared to accept the Emperor's arbitration, much in the same way as the Antiochene Christians had accepted Aurelian's decision forty years before in their conflict with Paul of Samosata. The issue at this stage was largely a civil matter, a question of possession of Church property, buildings, and revenues on the one hand, and privileges on the other. The Emperor as ruler of the secular world had the duty of maintaining peace, order and freedom of religion. Hence, he could be requested to appoint suitable ecclesiastical judges. Thus there was nothing extraordinary about the Donatist appeal. It followed Biblical precept and practice. The rejection, however, of the Donatist charges against Caecilian by Constantine in November 316 and the persecution which followed in May 317 convinced them that after all with Constantine nothing had changed. The 'royal favour' accorded to the Caecilianists was a sign of their service to the Devil. The latter having failed to break the servants of God through persecution had now turned to guile to achieve his aim.[99] The plea that 'Christ was a lover of unity' was flung back at the Devil who made it.[100]

The crisis of 346/347 evoked anger and defiance as strongly expressed as anything found in Tertullian. Contemporary pamphlets, such as the *Passio Maximiani et Isaaci* and the *Passio Marculi* were written in the spirit of the unending struggle of the saints against the Devil acting through the Roman authorities. The descriptions of the confessors' visions, tortures and triumphant martyrdoms recalled those of the *Acta Martyrum* of the previous century. Constans was stigmatized as a 'tyrant'[101] (like the Donatist view of Maxentius[102]) and a 'forerunner of Antichrist', as Decius had been a century previously.[103] The authorities were 'maddened butchers',[104] the Catholics the treacherous wolves belonging to the anti-Church of the *traditores*, the Donatists 'soldiers of Christ' and 'glorious martyrs'. The struggle was between 'a soldier of Christ' and 'the soldiers of the Devil'. It was the spirit of Tertullian and of the Great Persecution over again.[105] For Donatus and his followers the Empire was still Babylon and the Emperor had no call to meddle in Church affairs.

More than half a century later, this was still the Donatist outlook. The names of the emperors might change; they only swelled the roll of persecutors. They were 'the kings of this world from whom Christianity has never found anything except envy against her'.[106] Then there follows the great panorama of persecution and suffering. The Donatist, Petilian of Constantine, related the persecution of the Maccabees by Antiochus, of John the Baptist by Herod, the Crucifixion of Jesus by the Jews and Pontius Pilate to the persecution of the Christians. He makes no distinction between pre-Constantinian and post-Constantinian times. Attacks by Nero, Trajan, Geta, Valerian and Diocletian merely preceded those of Ursacius and the persecutions by Constans' emissaries, Paul and Macarius against the saints. He drew the same moral as Lactantius drew, namely that God avenged the righteous by the hideous deaths of the persecutors themselves.[107]

More lay behind this outburst than invective. In all these fourth-century Donatist writings one finds the theme of actual suffering linked with the theoretical duty of the righteous to renounce contemporary society and suffer persecution at its hands. The theme which we have followed through Judaism and the first two generations of the primitive Church continued to inspire the majority of the African Christians. Thus, a Donatist sermon preached on the Feast of the Holy Innocents, claimed that the righteous always suffered, that this had gone on from the time of Abel to that of the victims of Herod and now continued in his own day. The Donatists remained a 'fraternitas' as their predecessors had described themselves a century before. The opening words of the Donatist memorandum presented at the Council of Carthage in 411 read, 'Januarius and the other bishops of the catholic truth that suffers persecution but does not persecute'.[108] In the absence of physical persecution the guidance of the Spirit directed the believer towards a life of penance and attuning the will towards God, not, however, by leaving the world, but by guiding and reforming it. The Donatist was no monk.

In this theology, the Holy Spirit and Biblical inspiration remained all-important. On conversion the Donatist Christian put away both his secular career and his secular books. He had the Bible on his lips and martyrdom in his soul.[109] Throughout the fourth century this outlook does not change. In the years after the Great Persecution, the Donatist writer of the *Acta Saturnini* could claim that, 'in our Church the virtues of the people are multiplied in the presence of the Spirit. The joy of the Spirit is to conquer in the confessors and triumph in the martyrs'.[110] At the end of the century, Petilian included a similar statement in his encyclical to his clergy in Constantine.

> Therefore I say, He ordained that we should undergo death for the faith, which each man should do for the communion of the Church. For Christianity makes progress by the deaths of its followers. For if death were feared by the faithful, no man would be found to live with perfect faith. For the Lord Jesus says, 'Except a corn of wheat fall into the ground and die, it abideth alone, but if it die it bringeth forth much fruit'(Jn. 12[24]).[111]

The words of Tertullian at the end of the *Apology* were being faithfully echoed by African Christians two hundred years later in the reign of Theodosius' successors.

Martyrdom therefore was still the goal of a Christian's life; but towards the end of his long tirade Petilian makes a significant extension of its scope. He links righteous suffering with poverty. 'So too', he tells the Catholics, 'you do not cease to murder us who are just and poor',[112] and he went on to warn those Donatists who gave way to pressure, 'out of love for their worldly goods' of the consequences of their act.[113] Both Tertullian's *Ad Uxorem*[114] and Cyprian's *De Lapsis*[115] had drawn attention to the danger of personal wealth as a hindrance to carrying out the duty of martyrdom. Petilian, however, stresses the positive value of poverty. During the previous half-century, if not before, the martyr's struggle had become extended to the overthrow of Antichrist represented by injustice as well as by paganism. We have already found indications of this tendency in Lactantius' equation of the oppression of the Tetrarchy's rule with the Tetrarchy's paganism.[116] Both were equally lacking in Justice. Now these ideas penetrated far down the social scale. By the 340s, the Numidian Donatists regarded the landowners as well as the authorities as the Devil's representatives. The result was the Circumcellions.

This movement, partly agrarian and partly religious, has been discussed many times before.[117] It suffices to say here that though by Augustine's time they had become so notorious as to be regarded as forming an *Ordo* of their own, there is no reason to believe that they originally drew their strength from any one group of rural society. Mancian *coloni*, day-labourers, slaves, all who had to work 'curvato dorso',[118] and who believed that the Millennium would reverse this situation, joined the movement. They were the 'circumcelliones agonistici', pursuing the martyr's crown through the *agon* against the visible powers of evil. Fasir and Axido, the 'duces sanctorum'[119] were the prototype of every agrarian revolt inspired by the teaching of the Bible down to John Ball and the German Peasant Revolt of 1523–24. Looking back one sees the Jewish *sicarii* as a parallel movement in the Old Israel, whose members were also alternatively courted and reprobated by the official hierarchy of the Saints.[120]

Were the Donatists, however, a residual movement, conservative fanatics, whom the tide of events was leaving behind?[121] By the end of the fourth century this was almost certainly becoming true, but fifty years before they still represented albeit in an exaggerated form something of the mind of western Christianity. This is clear when one looks at the tracts written by the western leaders during the crisis of 355-361, caused by Constantius' attempt to force a non-Nicene Trinitarian formula on the west. In these years there were repeated on a lesser scale the tensions among western Christians which had characterized the period immediately after the Great Persecution and had resulted in the Donatist schism. The reply of Lucifer of Cagliari and Hilary of Poitiers to the defection of powerful bishops (such as Saturninus of Arles and Epictetus of Centumcellae[122]), was similar in form and ferocity to the Donatist reaction to Caecilian and his supporters. These men were regarded as apostates. They were deserters to a religion which was not Christianity, but resembled the paganism of the persecutors fifty years before, and was sponsored by the Emperor. Not only was the attack as unrelenting, but many of the ideas expressed by Constantius' opponents in the west were the same as those of the Donatists fifty years before. That the schism led by Lucifer of Cagliari, probably in opposition to Athanasius' policy of reconciling Old and New Nicenes after the Council of Alexandria in 362, did not become an Italian and Gallic Donatism, was due largely to the fact that the underlying doctrine of the Church and of Church-State relations in those provinces was still as exclusive and uncompromising as it had been in the previous century.

The Luciferians were Donatists in embryo. The same problems of the nature of the Church and its place in a hostile world which gripped Donatists and Catholics in Africa agitated them also. For the Luciferian and Orthodox spokesmen whom Jerome wrote up in his *Dialogus contra Luciferianos*, *circa* 378, much turns on the question of admission to the Church. Was Arian baptism valid? The Luciferian begins, like his Donatist contemporary, with the assertion that 'the entire universe belongs to the devil', and that 'the Church has become a brothel',[123] Heretics (in this case, the Catholics) were the equivalent of pagans, their meeting-places were 'camps of the devil'[124] and in consequence, their clergy could not be accepted without being reduced to penitent lay status and their laymen would be re-baptized.[125] These phrases and actions both remind one strongly of North Africa. So too, does the exclusive view of the Church, in strict logic reduced to the real salt of the earth, namely Lucifer and his followers. The Catholics are blamed here also, for 'opening the camp to the enemy'.[126]

Lucifer's surviving writings, compiled before his breach with his colleagues, also show a remarkably similar theological approach to his environment to that which prevailed on the other side of the Mediterranean. He also represented the Roman Empire as part of the *saeculum*. Constantius himself was identified variously with the precursor of Antichrist, an idolator and an apocalyptic beast,[127] just as his brother had been identified by the writer of the Donatist *Passio Marculi* some ten years before.[128] Naturally, his intervention into ecclesiastical affairs must be resisted, and like the Donatists, Lucifer was never tired of citing as justification for his attitude the parallel of the Maccabean rebellion against Antiochus.[129] The latter was regarded as a 'persecutor nostrae religionis'[130] and his times, like those of Constantius, were under the direct sway of Antichrist.[131] Lucifer clearly considered the Christian Church of his day as the lineal descendant of the persecuted Jews in the Seleucid era.[132] Though he lacks the pungency of Donatus' attack, he leaves no doubt that he regarded the Church's duty of obedience to the laws of the Empire as limited, that Constantius was no 'bishop of bishops',[133] that on the analogy of the Old Testament prophets which, like the Donatists, he uses constantly, the bishops of the living God had the right and positive duty of command over the Roman Emperor.[134] If need be, they must defy him, together with the strength of the Roman Empire.[135] If they failed to get their way, then martyrdom was the only course. However, from the quotations from i Maccabees which Lucifer cites (especially i Macc., 2^{11}, etc.)[136] it is clear that he was prepared to go a good deal farther along the path of open rebellion than were the Donatist leaders. What would have happened to Constantius if, he asks, he had fallen into the hands of Mattathias or Phineas?[137] In any event, Constantius was doomed as a blasphemer and apostate to divine vengeance.

Neither Donatus nor Lucifer advocated physical rebellion against the Emperor. Martyrdom leading to vindication hereafter was their aim. It is interesting to notice, however, how lacking in theological depth were the arguments of Lucifer and his colleagues when compared with those of their Donatist contemporaries. In Lucifer, there is none of the deeply considered relationship that we find among the Donatists between persecution and the Christian's call to a life guided by the Holy Spirit, that was being preached by Tyconius and even by Petilian. There is no theory of martyrdom in Lucifer, only the lengthy assertion of its necessity in face of an impious tyrant. Implicitly, he stands for the same principles as the Donatists, but he prefers personal invective to theology. Only when his followers take the step of breaking with the majority do we find the glimmerings of a system, and that system follows the same lines as Donatus', namely opposition to the contemporary world, and rejection of an 'apostate Church' which had sold the pass to the enemy.

The crisis of 355–361 showed that Donatism was no mere African aberration. The west had not yet reconciled itself to Christian emperors. When faced with the situation caused by Constantius' determination to foist a non-Nicene creed on them, backed by an assertion that he could do this by right, even moderate men such as Hosius and Pope Liberius resisted.[138] Constantius found himself confronted by an entirely different set of ideas from those to which he had been used in the east. The western bishops believed like Athanasius that the essence of the Christian message was the salvation of man from sin, the conquest of the sinful world and not its ultimate refinement into the likeness of God. The Emperor was not the reflection of the Logos, but the type of the Israelite ruler, righteous or sinful according to whether he heeded the word of his prophet, or in Christian times, his bishop.[139] Politically as well as theologically Athanasius and the westerners found themselves on the same side.

It is interesting to see how both Athanasius and Hilary of Poitiers move gradually through protest and expostulation to outright defiance of Constantius. Athanasius, indeed, starts with the Eusebian theory of the Christian emperor. Even in 357 he quails before the prospect of resisting authority; he would not resist so much as a local city treasurer,[140] and finally only nerves himself to defy Constantius by claiming that the Emperor was a heretic and therefore no true Christian ruler. Hilary exiled as a 'trouble-maker' though he was, observed a reasonably respectful tone to the Emperor as late as 359 and shows this in his request for an audience contained in the *Liber ad Constantium Augustum*. The mask only falls towards the end of the following year when he set down the *Liber contra Constantium Imperatorem*. It is directed 'against' and not merely 'to' a Roman emperor and it reads exactly like a Donatist pamphlet. Not only does Hilary abuse his sovereign as 'Antichrist', but denounces his rule as a direct continuation of the age of persecution. Constantius was the heir of Nero, Decius and Maximian,[141] and if that was not sufficient echo of current Donatist writing, there follows the claim that the Devil having failed to destroy Christians by force was turning to treachery instead. No wonder Hilary's writings were to be found in the libraries of Donatist bishops in the early fifth century,[142] but the moral is, that faced with similar circumstances, western Christian leaders on both sides of the Mediterranean reacted in the same way. It is not so surprising perhaps that when he was in exile Donatus was able to find a non-African cleric, Parmenian, to succeed him as bishop of Carthage. The latter fully shared his master's views.

This analysis shows that as late as the middle of the fourth century the attitude of Latin Christians on both sides of the Mediterranean towards the Empire remained in broad agreement. Whereas in the east a Christian empire brought joy, in the west it brought crisis. The heirs to the theology of Tertullian and Cyprian could accept co-belligerence between well-intentioned rulers and the Church,[143] but hardly permanent alliance. Sooner or later the Devil would re-assert his sway over the *saeculum* and its kings. Persecution would start again. But as in Tertullian's time, the non-African rigorists lacked a consistent doctrine of the Holy Spirit and a philosophy of history dependent on it which were necessary to sustain prolonged resistance. The Donatists in the fourth and fifth centuries expected persecution whether from Constans, Honorius, or Gaiseric[144] as a matter of course. The Italians and Gauls confronted by Constantius' demands responded to an instinct of resistance, but they never seem to have thought out the theological implication of resistance. The difference between Tertullian and Hippolytus was reproduced once more in the difference between Donatus and his disciples and Lucifer of Cagliari. In the end, the moderating influence of neo-Platonism was welcomed with relief, and the typological dualism of Church-

State relations expressed by Ambrose and Augustine was accepted in the west as a whole.[145]

Finally, direct action against social oppression under the inspiration of the apocalyptic message also was not confined to African extremists. In their different ways Commodian and Salvian of Marseille reflected this same mood. Whether Commodian is placed in the late third or in the early fifth century, he expresses what may well be described as 'l'impatience populaire' of the oppressed classes in the western provinces of the later Roman period.[146] He was not a Donatist; there are no 'traditores' in his requisitory, though Gennadius included Tertullian and Cyprian together (and more appropriately) with Papias in his pedigree. But Commodian, like the Donatists, regarded the Christians as the *sancti*,[147] saw them as suffering and defying a succession of seven persecutions, and looking forward beyond these to the Millennium. Human fortunes and human miseries would be reversed in apocalyptic fire. Much of Commodian's work was devoted to a defence of the poor against the rich, and though he denies that he finds fault with wealth itself, his invective against the rich was as sustained as anything written by his African contemporaries. To gather wealth 'to fill one's belly'[148] was an act of the Devil and an insult to God. Wealth, injustice and immorality were synonymous terms. As Brisson remarks, it is very difficult to dissociate this embittered propaganda from the facts of economic and social oppression in the western provinces of the later Roman Empire.[149]

In the better defined situation of southern Gaul during the barbarian settlement, *circa* 439, Salvian's denunciation of the Roman world was also based on the visible evidence of growing corruption and oppression.[150] He was aware how serfdom had developed under the pressure of crushing taxation and of patronage and he paints a grim picture of the extortions practised by the *curiales* and officials against the provincial population. 'Yet what else is the life of all business men but fraud and perjury of the curials but injustice, of the petty officials but slander, of all soldiers but rapine?'[151] In such circumstances, the rule of the barbarian invaders was to be preferred to that of Rome. The difference between southern Gaul and Spain on the one hand and Africa on the other, was again a question of integration. In

Gaul and Spain denunciation of ecclesiastical abuses and the assertion of the independence of the Church were not specifically
linked to the forces of popular revolt. The Bagaudae were not
Circumcellions. In North Africa the forces directed against
the old order, both religious and secular, were united. The
inspiration was that of the martyr, drawing on a 500-year-old
tradition through late Judaism into the story of martyrdom and
persecution in the early Church. In this respect, Donatus was the
true successor of Judas Maccabaeus.

NOTES

[1] H. Grégoire, Les Persécutions, 161–3.

[2] At Edessa also there were apparently only three confessors of whom one, Habib the
deacon, proclaimed himself a Christian and came voluntarily from his village to appear
before the governor. His bishop, Konna, was not molested and as early as 312/313 began
to build a great church in Edessa.

[3] H.E., viii.13.5, probably 311. See Mart. Pal., 13.10.

[4] H.E., ix.11.4.

[5] Above, p. 531, n.202.

[6] H.E., viii.9.3.

[7] Mart. Pal., 8.1 and 13.

[8] Ibid., 13.11, and H.E., viii.13.5.

[9] H. Delehaye, 'Les Martyrs d'Egypte', 91–113. The existence of Arrianus is proved by
a papyrus dated 307, published by B. P. Grenfell, Greek Papyri, ii.78. Also, L. Cantarelli,
Atti della R. Accad. dei Lincei, xiv, 1909, 328.

[10] H. Grégoire, op. cit., 162.

[11] Acta Saturnini, I.

[12] Bull. Arch. du Comité des Travaux historiques, 1934, 69.

[13] Canon I.

[14] Canon 2, 'placuit eos nec in finem accipere communionem'.

[15] Canons 3 and 4. The canons show how in southern Spain as in Africa, the Talmudic
crimes of apostasy, bloodshed and immorality remain those for which no pardon could
be granted to full members of the Church.

[16] Canon I; for actual discouragement of clergy who had lapsed taking up the fight
again, see Peter of Alexandria's Canon 10 (Routh, iii, 333). He considered it was better
for even a lapsed cleric to remain with his flock.

[17] Council of Ancyra, Canon 9.

[18] Mart. Pal., 12.

[19] E. H. Röttges, 'Marcellinus-Marcellus'. The real problem seems to be whether one
accepts the statement of the Chronograph of 354 (ed. Th. Mommsen, MGH., ix, Chron. Min.,
75) which claims that after Marcellinus' death, there was a vacancy in the Roman see for
7 years, 6 months and 25 days, or whether one accepts the later Catalogus Liberianus
which gives Marcellus a pontificate of 1 year, 6 months and 20 days between 308 and 309.
There are obviously many alternatives. Marcellus might have been dropped on purpose
on the grounds that he was suspected of being pro-Novatianist, or there may have been a

copyist's mistake due to the similarity of the two names and the dates. Marcellus certainly seems to have existed, whether he was bishop or merely managed the see during a lengthy vacancy. Heraclius and Eusebius led the rigorist and anti-rigorist factions respectively (*Lib. Pontif.*, 167).

[20] A protocol recording negotiations for the return of property would seem to fit the document which the Donatists produced at the conference of Carthage in 411.

[21] Optatus, *De Schismate*, ii.4.

[22] L. K. Mohlberg, 'Historich-kritische Bemerkungen zum Ursprung der sogenannten "Memoria Apostolorum" an der Appischen Strasse', *Texte und Arbeiten* (Colligere Fragmenta = Festschrift Alban Dold), Beuron, 1952, 58ff. Further evidence, above, p. 530, n. 186.

[23] *Panarion*, 68.3. E. Schwartz, *Zur Geschichte des Athanasius*, v.165; and B. J. Kidd, *A History of the Church*, i.531–3.

[24] Canons 3 and 7; Schwartz, op. cit., 172.

[25] Canon 3.

[26] Canons 9 and 10; cf. Mensurius' instructions, Augustine, *Brevic. cum Donatistis*, iii. 13.25.

[27] Schwartz, op. cit., 173.

[28] See text in Routh, *Rel. Sacr.* iii, 381–3 of the letter of the four Egyptian bishops to Meletius protesting against his ordination outside his own diocese. (Eng. tr., J. Stevenson, *A New Eusebius*, pp. 290–2).

[29] Epiphanius, *Panarion*, 68.3.

[30] E. R. Hardy's estimate, *Christian Egypt*, 52–3. Meletian monasteries in the 330s, see H. I. Bell, *Jews and Christians in Egypt*, 38ff. and K. Holl, *Gesammelte Aufsätze*, ii.2, Der Osten, 292–7.

[31] Note, however, the comparatively numerous papyri of apocalyptic extra-canonical works (such as the *Apocalypse of Peter*, and of *Baruch*), together with Judaeo-Christian works such as the Oxyrhynchus *Logia* and Gospel of the Hebrews, suggesting the existence in the fourth and fifth centuries of a strong undercurrent of Millenarism outside Alexandria.

[32] Socrates, *Hist. Eccl.*, 1.6, says that Meletius 'entered into a conspiracy' against the bishop (Alexander) during the opening phase of the Arian controversy. In view of his hostility towards Arius, the nature of his threat would seem to be plain. See W. Telfer, 'St. Peter of Alexandria and Arius', *A.B.*, 67, 1949, 117–30.

[33] On the influence of the *Acta Perpetuae* on Coptic *Acta Martyrum* such as the *Martyrium Theodori Orientalis*, J. Quasten, *Byzantion*, xv, 1940/41, 1–9.

[34] See the author's *The Donatist Church*, ch. I, for details.

[35] Rashdall's phrase, *Atonement*, 264. For the high standing of both Homer and Plato in Methodius of Olympius' work even in the Great Persecution, see V. Bucheit, 'Homer bei Methodius von Olympios', *Rheinisches Museum*, 99, 1956, 17–36.

[36] Pseudo-Cyprian, *Ep.*, 3 (CSEL., iii.3.273–4). This is an extremely interesting document, to which attention was first drawn by G. Mercati in 1899 ('Un falso donatistico nelle opere di S. Cypriano', in *Rendic. degli Institut, Lombardo di Sci. e Letter.*, Ser. ii, 32, 1899, 986–97, and revised by the author in *S.T.*, 77, 1937, pp. 268–78). It is just possible that this encyclical could be the work of Mensurius. The Council was held immediately after the restoration of churches, and the tendency was moderate. *Traditores* would be investigated by category and lay communion would not be denied to penitents. The reference too, to *antecessores nostri* (p. 274) could indicate Mensurius. At the same time, the appeal to '*sententiam fixam sanctis et amicis Dei*', strongly suggests the sentence of the Abitinian confessors towards whom Mensurius had no friendly feelings. He would also have found himself criticized among those who had even pretended to hand over copies of the Scriptures (*qui utique finget tradere supplebit traditionem*). On the whole, one is inclined to suggest an encyclical by Donatus perhaps as early as summer 313.

37 *Acta Saturnini* 18 (*P.L.*, viii, 701 C). 'Exinde Ecclesia sancta sequitur martyres, et detestatur execratae perfidiae traditores.'

38 See N. H. Baynes, 'Constantine the Great and the Christian Church' (*Proc. British Academy*, xv, 1929), and A. Alföldi, *The Conversion of Constantine and Pagan Rome* (tr. H. Mattingly, Oxford, 1948), for the development of the Emperor's religious views and policy.

39 For the contrary view, J. R. Palanque, 'Apropos du prétendu édit de Milan', *Byzantion*, x, 1935, 607–14, 'Mais quel que soit le sens qui on donne à ce mot (conversion), je crois qu'il faut parler d'une conversion de Constantin à l'automne 312, et y voir l'origine des mesures revolutionnaires, concertées à Milan par les deux empéreurs au debut de l'année suivante'.

40 Eusebius, *H.E.*, x.7.2.

41 *Acta Purgationis Felicis* (Ziwsa, 203, lines 5–8). 'Aelianus proconsul dixit: [Constantinus] maximus et Licinius Caesares ita pietatem christianis exhibere dignantur, ut disciplinam corrumpi nolint, sed potius observari religionem istam et coli velint. Noli itaque tibi blandiri quod cum mihi dicas dei cultorem to esse, [ac] propterea non possis torqueri'— a nice indication of popular opinion in the period after the 'Edict of Milan'.

42 LIBERATOR ORBIS—Cohen, *Medailles impériales*, vii, no. 317.

43 *Liber Pontificalis* (ed. Duchesne), 170–87 for the full list of magnificent gifts of lands and goods. See A. H. M. Jones, *Constantine and the Conversion of Europe*, 99, and *The Later Roman Empire*, 90 and 900.

44 *Cod. Theod.*, ix.40.2. For 'the horrible cruelty' of some of the alternative punishments ordered by Constantine. A. Alföldi, *The Conversion of Constantine and Pagan Rome* (Eng. tr. H. Mattingly, Oxford, 1948, 128–9).

45 *Cod. Theod.*, xvi.2.2, Augustine, *Ep.*, 88.

46 *Cod. Theod.*, xvi.2.4.

47 *Cod. Theod.*, xvi.8.1 (18 Oct. 315). Also, Jones, *Constantine*, 220, and J. M. Parkes's essay 'Jews and Christians in the Constantinian Epoch', Parkes Library publications, 1964.

48 *Constantinus Augustus Aelafio* (Ziwsa, p. 206).

49 Eusebius, *Praeparatio Evangel.*, i.1. (*P.G.*, 21, 28 A–B).

50 Ibid.

51 *H.E.*, 1.4.15.

52 See the account of Eusebius' ideas in K. M. Setton, 'The Christian attitude towards the Emperor in the fourth Century', New York, 1941, pp. 46–56.

53 Eusebius, *Praeparatio Evangel.*, 1.4. (*P.G.*, 21, 37c).

54 Ibid, 1.4.

55 Ibid., 1.4 (col. 37 C–D). See also, *Demonstr. Evangel.*, iii.2, iii.7, and vii.2 for the same theme, quoted by Barker, op. cit., 475–7. Contrast Augustine's emphasis in *De Civitate Dei*, iii.30, on Augustus' involvement in numerous civil wars. 'Nam ipse Augustus cum multis gessit bella civilia et in eis etiam multi clarissimi vivi perierunt, inter quos et Cicero'. —a typical difference of outlook between east and west.

56 *H.E.*, x.3. Including Marcionite churches'. *O.G.I.*, 608, *A.D.* 318/319.

57 Ibid., 9.7.

58 Thus Eusebius, *Vita Constantini*, i.44 and iv.8, and Constantine's reported speech to the bishops at Nicaea. Socrates, *H.E.*, 1.9. See A. Alföldi, op. cit., 34–5, and S. L. Greenslade, *Church and State from Constantine to Theodosius* (S.C.M., London, 1953), ch. i.

59 *De Laudibus Constantini*, 1.6 (cited from Barker, loc. cit.).

60 Even John Chrysostom could state that 'the emperor is without peer upon earth, for he is the head and crown of everything in the world'. *Homil. de Statuis*, ii.2. See F. Homes Dudden, *St. Ambrose, His Life and Times*, O.U.P., 1935, 369–70.

61 *H.E.*, ii.17–18.

62 Ibid., vii.32.30.

63 *Demonstr. Evang.*, 1.8. and bk. v (proemium).

64 *H.E.*, iii.39. 12–13 and vii.24.

65 *Comment. in Ps. 67*; cf. *Comment in Ps. 83* and *Mart. Pal.*, 5.2.

66 Socrates, *H.E.*, 1.11. (Paphnutius).

67 *Barlaam and Ioasaph* (ed. Woodward and Mattingly), xii.103.

68 Particularly among the Meletian monks. See K. Holl, op. cit., 295.

69 Isaac the monk foretold the death of Valens, Sozomen, *H.E.*, vi.40.

70 For the many examples of this spirit, see *Lausiac History*, Sozomen, *H.E.*, vi.28–34 and discussion in L. Duchesne, *The Early History of the Church* (Eng. tr. ii.392ff.). For a bibliography of monasticism, see P. de Labriolle's chapter in Fliche and Martin, *Histoire de l'Eglise*, iii, 299–301.

71 e.g. *Mart. Pal.*, 4.4–5 (Apphianus) and 11.21 (Seleucus).

72 *Vite Antonii*, 46.

73 Antony's ideal (ibid., 15) and the ideal of all future generations of monks. (See Holl's essay, op. cit., 270–82).

74 *Vita Antonii*, 47.

75 *Lausiac History* 32; J. Leipoldt. 'Schenute von Atripe', 125. The Egyptian monks were far from being 'idle mouths'. cf. A.H.M. Jones. op. cit., 933.

76 Libanius, *Pro Templis* (ed. R. van Loy, 'Le pro Templis de Libanius', *Byzantion*, viii, 1933, 7–39), ch. 8.

77 Ambrose, *Ep.*, 41.27 (*P.L.*, xvi, 1120); cf. *Cod. Theod.*, xii.1.63 (Valens).

78 John Chrysostom, *Homil. de Statuis*, xiii.1.2, and Theodoret, *H.E.*, v.20, speech and successful intervention of the monk Macedonius, 'totally ignorant of all learning'. Their undisciplined redress of any and every wrong was probably instrumental in their being banned from the towns by Theodosius, *Cod. Theod.*, xvi.3.1 of 2 Sept. 390, revoked two years later (*Cod. Theod.*, xvi.3.2). See Homes Dudden, *Saint Ambrose, His life and times*, Oxford, 1935, 1.364–5.

79 See D. Amand de Mendieta's study, 'La Virginité chez Eusèbe d'Emèse et l'ascéticisme familial dans la première moitié du IVe siècle'. *RHE.*, l, 1955, 777–820.

80 *Vita Antonii*, 3.

81 W. M. Ramsay, 'A Noble Anatolian Family of the Fourth Century', *CR.*, 33, 1919, 1–9.

81a Cf. *Acta Apollonii*, 40, and *Acta Phileas* (ed. Knopf and Krüger 2).

82 *Oratio contra Julianum*, iv.73, *P.G.*, xxxv, 598.

83 For these aspects of the rule of St. Basil, E. Amand de Mendieta (D. Amand), *L'Ascése monastique de Saint Basile*, Brussels, 1950, 118ff. Note Ramsay's comments on clergy in Lycaonia in the fourth century as revealed on their epitaphs. 'We have the Church of the people, creator of charitable and hospitable institutions, the Church as it was in the mind and aspirations of Basil'. 'The Orthodox Church in the Byzantine Empire', *Expositor*, 1908, 289–305.

83a *Pilgrimage of Etheria*, ed. McClure and Feltoe, xiii.

84 Socrates, *H.E.*, 1.13.

85 *Adv. Nationes*, ii.13. See P. Courcelle's 'Antichristian Arguments and Christian Platonism, from Arnobius to St. Ambrose', in ed., A. Momigliano, *The Conflict between Paganism and Christianity*, 153–5.

86 N. H. Baynes, *JRS.*, XXXIV, 1944, 136–40.

87 *De Mortibus*, 4.1.

88 *Institutes*, vi.20. Cf. 6.19–20 (against patriotism).

89 Ibid., vi.17.10.

90 Ibid., 20.16 'Ita neque militare iusto licebit'.

91 Ibid., 17 'quem deus sacrosanctum animal esse voluit'.

92 Victorinus of Pettau (ed. J. Haussleiter, *CSEL*, 39) viii. 2 (p. 86).

[93] Victorinus, xi.4.

[94] *Institutes*, 1.1. Dating: Baynes, loc. cit, 138.

[95] Canon 3.

[96] Canon 7.

[97] Optatus, *De Schismate* iii.3 (Ziwsa, 74). See, Setton, op. cit., 54–6, and Frend, *The Donatist Church*, 325–6. Contrast Victorinus, op. cit., xi.4.

[98] Note Constantius' views expressed in his letter to the Princes of Axum when demanding the extradition of Frumentius, *circa* 357. 'It is altogether a matter of the greatest care and concern to us to extend knowledge of the supreme God. And I think that the whole race of mankind claims from us equal regard in this respect. In order that they may pass their lives in hope, being brought to a proper knowledge of God and having no differences with each other in their enquiries concerning justice and truth. Desiring to show equal regard for your welfare as for that of the Romans, we command that the same doctrine be professed in your churches as in theirs' (Athanasius, *Defence before Constantius*, Eng. tr. A. Robertson, 31).

[99] *Passio SS. Donati et Advocati*, 2, (*P.L.*, viii, 753 B.) 'Primo et enim ut inveterato draconi mos est insitus, quasi non ipse jamdudum persecutione manifesta christiani nominis impugnator exstiterit, eos quos aperta persecutione superare non potuit, callida fraude circumvenire molitus est. . . . '

[100] Ibid., 3. (*P.L.*, viii, 754 A) 'Christus, inquit (Diabolus) amator unitatis est'.

[101] *Passio Marculi* (*P.L.*, viii, 761 A) 'de Constantis regis tyrannica domo et de palatii arce pollutum Macarianae persecutionis murmur increpuit'.

[102] *Passio Donati et Advocati* 2. See Frend, *The Donatist Church*, 159–61.

[103] *Passio Marculi*, col. 761 D. For Decius. Cyprian, *Ep.*22.1, Lactantius. *De Mortibus*, 3.4.

[104] *Passio Maximiani et Isaaci* (*P.L.*, viii, 767–74) especially 769. 'Proconsul furibundus', etc. . . .

[105] *Passio Maximiani et Isaaci*, col. 769 C, 'inter militem Christi et milites Diaboli'.

[106] Petilian of Constantine cited by Augustine. *Contra Litteras Petiliani*, ii.92–202 (*P.L.*, xliii, 323–4).

[107] Ibid. For Paul and Macarius, see my *Donatist Church*, 177ff.

[108] *Gesta Collationis Carthaginensis*, iii, 258. *P.L.*, xi, 1408.

[109] *Passio Marculi* (760 D) 'Ille (Marculus) namque olim praeelectus et praedestinatus a Domino, mox ubi primum beatae fidei rudimenta suscepit, statim mundanas litteras respuens, forense exercitium et falsam saecularis scientiae dignitatem suspensa ad coelum mente calcavit'—a career similar to that of Cyprian, and a good example also of the connection between Grace and martyrdom in the African Church. Both are activities of the Holy Spirit.

[110] *Acta Saturnini*, 20 (*P.L.*, viii, 703 A) 'et gaudet Spiritus sanctus in confessoribus victor, in martyribus triumphator'.

[111] *Contra Litteras Petiliani*, ii.85, 196.

[112] Ibid., ii.92, 202.

[113] Ibid, ii.98, 225.

[114] *Ad Uxorem*, ii.8.

[115] *De Lapsis*, 6 and 12. cf. *De Opere et Eleem.*, 10, 12 and 13. See J. P. Brisson, *Autononisme et Christianisme*, 370–1.

[116] See above, p. 461.

[117] In particular by the present author in *The Donatist Church*, 171–5 and by H. J. Diesner in a series of papers collected in *Kirche und Staat im spätromischen Reich*, Berlin, 1963.

[118] Optatus, *De Schismate*, v.7, the day labourer 'qui curvato dorso et desudatis lateribus sinus terrae faciat' (Ziwsa, 135–6).

[119] Optatus, iii.4 (Ziwsa, 82).

[120] For the inheritance of the Circumcellion movement in the European Middle Ages, see Th. Büttner and E. Werner, *Circumcellionen und Adamiten*, Berlin, 1959 (stereotyped Marxist account, but some useful insights).

[121] From this point on I have borrowed heavily from my art., 'The Roman Empire in the Eyes of the Western Schismatics'. *Miscellanea Historiae Ecclesiasticae* (= *Bibl. de le Revue d'Histoire ecclésiastique*, Fasc. 38, Louvain, 1961, 9–22).

[122] Lucifer, *De non conveniendo cum Haereticis* (*P.L.*, xiii, 777 C).

[123] Jerome, *Dialogus contra Luciferianos* 1 (*P.L.*, xxiii, 155): 'Asserebat quippe universum mundi esse diaboli, et ut jam familiare est eis dicere, factum de Ecclesia lupanar'.

[124] *Dialogue* 3 (*P.L.*, xxiii, 157 A).

[125] Ibid., 4: 'Recipimus laicos, quoniam nemo convertetur, si se scieret rebaptizandum' (col. 158 B).

[126] Ibid., 10: 'Vos hosti castra traditis', col. 165 D.

[127] Lucifer, *De non conveniendo cum haereticis*, *Pro Sancto Athanasio* and *Moriendo esse pro Dei filio*. *P.L.*, xiii, 781, 783, 911, 1018.

[128] *Passio Marculi* (*P.L.*, viii, 761 D).

[129] e.g. in *De non Parcendo in Deum delinquentibus*, col. 964–7.

[130] *De non Parcendo*, 958 B.

[131] For the survival of this view in the west until the end of the century, see Q. Julius Hilarianus, *De Mundi Duratione Libellus*, xvii (*P.L.*, xiii, 1105 B).

[132] *De non Parcendo in Deum delinquentibus*, col. 963 and 1006. Constantius hardly acted like Antiochus, contenting himself with surprised protests against Lucifer's insults, and pointing out that he had, after all, survived a goodly time!

[133] *Moriendum esse pro Dei Filio*, col. 1032 C.

[134] *De non Parcendo*, col. 957 B: 'Quae hic tibi injuria fit a nobis? quae ingeritur Imperatori Romano contumelia ab antistitibus Dei vivi'.

[135] Ibid., 963 B. Also, *Moriendum esse pro Dei filio*, 1037 A.

[136] *De non Parcendo*, col. 960–1.

[137] Ibid., col. 962.

[138] Excellently demonstrated by S. L. Greenslade, *Church and State from Constantine to Theodosius*, London, 1954, 39–46.

[139] See E. Petersen, *Der Monotheismus als politisches Problem*, 94ff. for the connection between Nicene theology and opposition to Constantinian absolutism.

[140] *Defence to Constantius*, 19 *P.G.*, xxv.620; cf. ibid. 10, 32 and 35. (See S. L. Greenslade, op. cit., 47–8).

[141] Hilary, *Contra Constantium Imperatorem*, 5, 8 and 9. *P.L.*, x, 585–6.

[142] Augustine, *Ep.*, 93.6.21.

[143] Note Petilian's concession, that 'the kings of this world might desire to be Christians'; but the fact remained that they continued to persecute the servants of Christ. (Augustine, *Contra Litt. Petil.*, ii.92.202).

[144] For Gaiseric, see the *Liber Genealogus*, 618 and 628 (ed. *MGH.*, ix, 195). The final edition of this Donatist Chronicle must date to the Vandal occupation. Contrast the eastern position at this period. Socrates, *H.E.*, vii.15, 'And surely nothing can be further from the spirit of Christianity than massacres, fights and deeds of that sort'.

[145] K. M. Setton, op. cit., 109ff. Also, N. H. Baynes's pamphlet, 'The Political Ideas of St. Augustine's *De Civitate Dei*', Historical Assoc. Pamphlet No. 104, 1936, 2nd ed., 1949, and reproduced in *Byzantine Studies and other Essays*, London, 1955, 288–306.

[146] J. P. Brisson, *Autononisme et Christianisme*, 379ff. (Bibliography, 379, n. 1). Late third century—H. Grégoire, 'Note sur la survivance chrétienne des Esséniens et des sectes apparentées', *Nouv. Clio*, ii, 1950, 354–60, and J. Vogt, *La Parola del Passato*, ix, 1954, 5–15.

Early fifth century—P. Courcelle, 'Commodien et les Invasions du 5e siècle', *Revue des Etudes latines*, 24, 1946, 227–46.

[147] *Instructiones* (ed. B. Dombart, *CSEL.*, xv) I.xxiii.13. 'Tu modo profanus modo sanctus esse videris'; and *Carmen*, 812, 'qui persecutionem dissipet sanctorum in armis'; compare with the terminology of Donatist inscriptions and the memorandum presented at the council of Carthage '... ceterosque exsecutores quos in sanctorum necem a principibus saeculi meruerunt' (*Gesta Coll. Carth.*, iii. 258, *P.L.*, xi, 1413 C). The coincidence of thought between Commodian and the Donatists is remarkable. Other references, see J. P. Brisson, op. cit., 392, n. 1.

[148] *Instr.* I.xxiii,1, 'Dum ventri servis, innocentem esse te dicis/et quasi communis facis te ubique paratum'. Cf. ibid., I.xxxi.8.

[149] J. P. Brisson, op. cit., 396, 'Et il y a lieu de se demander si nous ne saisirions pas chez lui un exemple de ce glissement de l'économique au religieux qui valut au donatisme la clientèle des circoncellions révoltés'.

[150] *De Gubernatione Dei.*, Eng. tr. ed. E. M. Sanford (Columbia University Records of Civilization, New York, 1930).

[151] Salvian, *De Gubernatione Dei*, iv.4.

Conclusion

THE ultimate legacy of the persecutions was the lasting division of Christendom into its eastern and western parts. In the east, apocalyptic hopes were fading by the turn of the third century, their place taken by a more optimistic view of the destiny of man and his relations with his Maker; and this in turn affected for good the Church's relations with the rulers of the Empire. From then on, persecution, if severe, became too sporadic to reverse this development and once the Great Persecution was over, the Emperor was accepted as the earthly manifestation of that Divine Reason which guided, instructed, chastened but would finally save the human race. Thus the Byzantine sovereigns were to continue. Those of the later centuries regarded themselves as the direct successors of Constantine and his heirs—and a Patriarch of Constantinople in opposition could be deposed and exiled just as Constantine had exiled Athanasius.

In the west, on the other hand, apocalyptic continued to dominate the hopes of most Christians through the third and fourth centuries. While persecution in the east faded into pious memory even in Constantine's reign, it continued to stir passions among their Latin-speaking brethren for another century. Indeed, the dilemma of the dualistic relations between Church and State was never satisfactorily to be solved. If Augustine substituted a Neo-Platonist typology for the literal acceptance of the teaching of the Book of Revelation, the State was always reminded that its existence was due to Original Sin, and its representatives told that their happiness was bound up with the status of handmaids of the Church.[1] Jerusalem and Babylon still existed, even if in the persons of Gratian, Theodosius and their successors Babylon was now tamed. Christian historiography drew much of its inspiration from the victorious suffering of Christian martyrs at the hands of the pagan emperors. Little wonder then, that the Council of Serdica 342/343 was to prove a landmark in the story of eastern

569

and western Christendom, and Mount Soucis, 'dividing the nation of the Thracians from that of the Illyrians' a symbol of their disunity.[2]

We have seen, however, how these developments can be traced to their ultimate origin behind the Christian period. The appreciation of Christian history can perhaps be started profitably with the Maccabean wars. Out of the heat and tensions which they engendered emerged distinctive Jewish outlooks towards the pagan power, in Palestine looking to its destruction, elsewhere and in the freer atmosphere of the Dispersion to its conversion. Much as he admired the Essenes, the figure of Philo stands in direct contrast to their aspirations. The life and example of Jesus, moreover, while it provided mankind with a vision of self-sacrifice and martyrdom which was to serve as an alternative to armed rising, did not deter his fellow countrymen from three futile rebellions against Rome and the non-Jewish provincials. The Jews rivalled the other great Semitic power, Carthage, in providing an example of desperation akin to racial suicide in the Ancient World. Indeed, to the historian, one of the tragedies of the Crucifixion lies in the fact that Jesus' sacrifice appeared to have not the slightest effect on the attitudes of the major interested parties in Palestine. Within a few years of 33, Romans and Jews were set on collision course. Though after 70 the rebels' heroism saved Palestine for the Jewish nation, elsewhere the field was left open to the Christians. Among these latter, however, rivalries similar to those which had divided the Jews were never completely dormant. With the conversion of North Africa to the religion of a gathered Church, and the emergence of the school of Clement and Origen at Alexandria Christian unity became a mirage.

The Roman Empire at first successfully contained the new threat. In the first place, the enthusiasm with which Classical civilization had been accepted both as material culture and as religion was proof against the threats and the attractions of this 'strange new sect'. Moreover, so long as Christian apologetic retained millenarism as an aspiration and anthropocentricity as an attitude of mind its exponents could easily be discomfited by the broader and more mature arguments of the Platonists and Stoics. Even so, the example of martyrdom and an extraordinarily compact organization gave Christianity a defensive power already by 200 regarded as formidable. With Origen the balance also began to shift in favour of the Christians. Even so, the Decian persecution was the gravest setback the Church ever suffered.

Victory came eventually from a combination of circumstances. The catastrophic events of the 250s and 260s seem to have shaken the faith of many in the saving power of the 'immortal gods'. The city aristocracies, the traditional enemies of the Christians and indeed of all revolutionary sects, declined in wealth and power. As Christianity gained ground in the countryside so the chances of suppressing it diminished. Now, the very extravagance of some of the Christian hopes and demands proved an advantage. Their tradition of charitable works and brotherly self-help may have been decisive, for neither the African Circumcellions nor the desert monks can be understood outside the misery and frustration of rural conditions of the time. Both illustrate the link between religious and social protest in the fourth century. These new Christians found in the Church a refuge which the old gods could not give. The Church had become a great popular movement. But though refusing to admit that the State had an absolute claim on their loyalties, the Christians had become deeply involved in its destinies. The conversion of Constantine raised as many problems as it solved. Thus, the story of persecution and martyrdom, extending through five hundred years of the history of the Ancient World, cannot be isolated from the general history of the time. It is a story which still has its lessons today.

NOTES

1 For instance, Augustine, *De Civitate Dei*, v.26.
2 Socrates, *H.E.*, ii.22.

Bibliography

THE study of persecution and martyrdom touches practically every aspect of early Church history. The construction of an adequate bibliography designed to include also the Jewish, Greco-Roman and New Testament background is a formidable task and the result could easily run into four figures. It is questionable, however, whether such a list would be of real value to the student. Here, a system has been chosen whereby first the sources together with some translations and important critical discussion of the texts have been given, followed by a short list of really important works, which a student must know if he is to master this subject. A bibliography of more general works is succeeded by specialized books and articles arranged according to subject. It should be noted that all the standard text-books on early Church history, namely Carrington, Duchesne, Kidd, Lietzmann, and Fliche and Martin contain valuable discussions on the persecutions and their causes, and have not been included in the bibliographies.

An English translation of some of the *Acta Martyrum* and other important texts have been included by my colleague, Mr. J. Stevenson, Fellow of Downing, in his *A New Eusebius* (London, 1957).

SOURCES AND TRANSLATIONS

Acta Martyrum
  (1) Dom Th. Ruinart, *Acta Sincera*, Paris, 1689, and later eds. to Ratisbon, 1859.
  (2) R. Knopf and G. Krüger, *Ausgewählte Märtyrerakten*, Tübingen, 1929. (An essential source-book for *Acta Martyrum* down to the Great Persecution. Includes full bibliography of studies to 1928. Supersedes R. Knopf, *Ausgewählte Märtyrerakten*, Tübingen and Leipzig, 1901.)
  (3) Eng. tr. E. C. E. Owen, *Some Authentic Acts of the Early Martyrs*.

Other *Acta*

Acta Habib and *Acta Sharbil*, ed. and tr. A. Roberts and J. Donaldson. Ante-Nicene Christian Library, xx.

Acta Saturnini, *P.L.*, viii, 689–715.

Passio Marculi, *P.L.*, viii, 758–766.

Passio Maximiani et *Isaaci*, *P.L.*, viii, 767–774.

(Other Donatist *Acta* are listed in my *Donatist Church*, p. 337.)

Apocalypse of Abraham, ed. and tr. G. H. Box, London, 1918.

Apocalypse of Baruch, ed. and tr. R. H. Charles, London, 1917.

Apocalypse of Peter, ed. E. Hennecke—W. Schneemelcher, *Neutestamentliche Apokryphen*, 3rd ed., Tübingen, 1964, vol. ii. (Eng. tr. M. R. James, *The Apocryphal New Testament*, Oxford, 1925.)

Aelius Aristides, *Orationes* (ed. S. Jebb, Oxford, 1726–30). Only vol. ii of B. Keil's ed., Berlin, 1898, has been available to me.

Arnobius, *Adversus Nationes*, ed. A. Reifferscheid, *CSEL.*, iv.

Ascension of Isaiah, ed. E. Hennecke–W. Schneemelcher, *Neutestamentliche Apokryphen*. (Also ed. and tr. R. H. Charles.)

Assumption of Moses, ed. and tr. R. H. Charles, London, 1897. Also C. Clemen (*Kleine Texte*, ed. H. Lietzmann, 1904).

Athanasius, *Vita Sancti Antonii*, *P.G.*, xxvi, 837–976.

Athenagoras, *Legatio*, ed. E. Schwartz, *T.U.*, iv. 2, 1891. (Eng. tr. C. C. Richardson, *Early Christian Fathers*, Library of Christian Classics, i.)

Aurelius Victor, *de Caesaribus*, ed. F. Pichlmayr, Teubner, Leipzig, 1911.

Christian Inscriptions, *Inscriptiones Latinae Christianae Veteres*, ed. E. Diehl–J. Moreau, Berlin, 1961.

Church Councils

    a. J. D. Mansi, *Sacrorum Conciliorum Collectio nova et amplissa*, Florence, 1759.

    b. C. J. Hefele–H. Leclercq, *Histoire des Conciles*, Paris, 1907 (Eng. tr. of C. J. Hefele, *Conziliengeschichte*, by W. R. Clark, Edinburgh, 1871).

Chronicon Paschale, *P.G.*, xcii.

Clement of Alexandria

    Stromata, i–vi, ed. O. Stählin and L. Früchtel, *GCS.*, Berlin, 1960.

    Stromata, vii, ed. O. Stählin, *GCS.*, Leipzig, 1909.

Codex Theodosianus, ed. Th. Mommsen and Wm. Meyer, Berlin, 1905.

Coins, H. Mattingly and E. A. Sydenham (and successors), *The Roman Imperial Coinage*, London, 1923–; H. Mattingly (and successors), *Coins of the Roman Empire in the British Museum*, vols. i–vi, London, 1923–62.

Commodian, *Instructiones* and *Carmen apologeticum*, ed. B. Dombart, *CSEL.*, xv.

Corpus Iuris Civilis, vol. i, *Institutiones et Digesta*, ed. Th. Mommsen and P. Krueger, Berlin, 1901.

Cyprian, *Opera omnia*, ed. W. Hartel, *CSEL.*, iii.

Dio Cassius, text and Eng. tr. of Books li–lxxx, E. Cary, Loeb library.

i Enoch, ed. and tr. R. H. Charles, Oxford, 1912.

ii Enoch (the *Book of the Secrets of Enoch*) ed. and tr. F. W. Morfill and R. H. Charles, London, 1896.

Eusebius

Historia Ecclesiastica (Books i–v, text and tr. Kirsopp Lake, vi–x, J. E. L. Oulton). (For Eng. tr., Introduction and Notes, H. J. Lawlor and J.E. L. Oulton, *Eusebius, Bishop of Caesarea, The Ecclesiastical History and Martyrs of Palestine*, 2 vols., London, 1928, reprinted 1954.)

Vita Constantini (ed. I. A. Heikel, *Eusebius Werke*, i, *GCS.*, Leipzig, 1902).

Demonstratio Evangelica (ed. I. A. Heikel, *Eusebius Werke*, 6, *GCS.*, Leipzig, 1913). (Eng. tr. W. J. Ferrer, London, 1920.)

Praeparatio Evangelica (ed. K. Mras, *Eusebius Werke*, 8, Berlin, 1954–56).

Liber contra Hieroclem, *P.G.*, xxii, 797 (text and Eng. tr. F. C. Conybeare, as annex to ed. of Philostratus, *Life of Apollonius of Tyana*).

Chronicon (ed. R. Helm, *GCS.*, *Eusebius Werke*, 7, 1913–26).

Fontes Iuris Romani anteiustiniani, ed. S. Riccobono and others, Florence, 1940–43 (3 vols.)

Gregory of Nyssa, *Vita Gregorii Thaumaturgi*, *P.G.*, xlvi.

Gregory the Wonderworker, *Address to Origen* (Eng. tr. W. Metcalfe, London, 1920). *Epistola Canonica* (ed. M. J. Routh, *Reliquiae Sacrae*, Oxford, 1815, ii, 437–60).

Hermas, *Similitudes, Visions and Mandates* (text and tr. Kirsopp Lake, *Apostolic Fathers*, ii, Loeb Library).

Hilary of Poitiers, *Contra Constantium Imperatorem*, *P.L.*, x.

Hippolytus

De Antichristo and *In Danielem commentarius*, ed. N. Bonwetsch, *GCS.*, *Hippolytus Werke*, i, Leipzig, 1897.

Elenchus (Philophosumena) ed. P.Wendland, *GCS.*, *Hippolytus Werke*, iii, Leipzig, 1916.

Ignatius of Antioch, *Letters* (text and tr. Kirsopp Lake, *Apostolic Fathers*, i, Loeb Library.)

Inscriptions (pagan and general)

Corpus Inscriptionum Latinarum.

Corpus Inscriptionum Graecarum.

Sylloge Inscriptionum Graecarum, ed. W. Dittenberger, Leipzig, 1900.

Orientis Graecae Inscriptiones Selectae, ed. W. Dittenberger, Leipzig, 1903.

Inscriptiones Latinae Selectae, ed. H. Dessau, Berlin, 1892–1916.
Monumenta antiqua Asiae Minoris, i-viii (especially vols. vii and viii), Manchester, 1928–62.
Supplementum Epigraphicum graecum, Leiden, 1923–.
Irenaeus, *Adversus Haereses*, Libri v, *P.G.*, vii. (Eng. tr. J. Roberts and W. Donaldson, Edinburgh, 1868. Fr. ed. and tr. of Book iii, P. Sagnard, *Sources chrétiennes*, 34, Paris, 1952).
(In this work Massuet's pagination and chapter divisions, reproduced in Migne, *P.G.*, have been followed.)
Jerome, *De Viris Illustribus*, *P.L.*, xxiii.
Jewish Apocrypha (ed. and tr. R. H. Charles, *Apocrypha and Pseudepigrapha of the Old Testament*, 2 vols., Oxford, 1913).
Jewish Inscriptions, Corpus Inscriptionum Judaicarum, ed. J. B. de Frey, Rome, 1936–52.
Josephus, *Antiquitates judaicae, Bellum judaicum*, and *Contra Apionem*, ed. B. Niese, Berlin, 1887.
(Eng. text and tr. H. St. Thackeray, Ralph Marcus and A. Wikgren (Loeb Library).
Also *The Works of Josephus*, by W. Whiston, London, 1890.
Julian the Apostate, *Librorum contra Christianos quae supersunt*, ed. K. J. Neumann, Leipzig, 1880.
Justin Martyr *Apologiae Duo*, *P.G.*, vi. (Eng. tr. i. Apology, C. C. Richardson, Library of Christian Classics, i, 1953. ii. Apology, tr. Roberts and Donaldson, Edinburgh, 1867.)
Dialogus cum Tryphone, *P.G.*, vi. (Eng. tr. A. L. Williams, London, 1930.)
Lactantius
Institutiones Divinae, ed. S. Brandt, *CSEL.*, xix.
De Mortibus Persecutorum (ed. and Fr. tr. J. Moreau, *Sources chrétiennes*, 39, 2 vols. Paris, 1954. A fundamental work for the study of the Great Persecution).
Liber Pontificalis, ed. L. Duchesne, Paris, 1886–92.
Lucian of Samosata, *De Morte Peregrini* (text and Eng. tr. A. M. Harmon. Loeb Library, *Lucian*, v).
Lucifer of Cagliari, *Opera*, *P.L.*, xiii.
Macarius Magnes, *Apocritus* (Eng. tr. T. W. Crafer, London, 1919).
iii Maccabees, ed. M. Hadas, New York, 1953.
iv Maccabees, ed. M. Hadas, New York, 1953.
Martyrologies
Depositiones of the chronographer of 354, the *Martyrology of Carthage* and *Syrian Martyrology* (ed. H. Lietzmann, Kleine Texte 2, Bonn, 1911).
(Also F. Nau, *Patrologia Orientalis*, iv, for the Syrian Martyrology.)

Martyrologium Hieronymianum, ed. L. Duchesne and J. B. de Rossi (*Acta Sanctorum*), Brussels, 1894.
(See H. Achelis, discussion 'Martyrologien', *Abh. der Heidelberger Akad. der Wissenschaften*, 1900.)

Minucius Felix, *Octavius* (text and tr. G. H. Rendall, Loeb Library).

Montanism, 'Texte zur Geschichte des Montanismus', ed. N. Bonwetsch =H. Lietzmann, *Kleine Texte*, 129, Bonn, 1914.

New Testament Apocrypha, ed. and tr. M. R. James, *The New Testament Apocrypha*, Oxford, 1925, also ed. Hennecke-W. Schneemelcher, op. cit.

Optatus of Milevis, *De Schismate Donatistarum*, ed. C. Ziwsa, *CSEL.*, xxvi.

Oracula Sibyllina, ed. J. Geffcken, *GCS.*, Leipzig, 1902. Also Hennecke-Schneemelcher, op. cit. ii, 498–528, and includes extensive bibliography.

Origen
  Commentarius in Matthaeum (ed. E. Klostermann, *GCS.*, Leipzig, 1937).
  Contra Celsum (ed. P. Koetschau, *GCS.*, Leipzig, 1899. (Eng. tr. and notes H. Chadwick, Cambridge, 1953).
  Exhortatio ad Martyrum, ibid., ed. Koetschau (Eng. tr. J. E. L. Oulton and H. Chadwick, *Alexandrian Christianity* = vol. ii, Library of Christian Classics.) Also ed. J. O'Meara, *Ancient Christian Writers*, No. 19, London, 1955.

Pachomius, *Vita* (ed. F. Nau, *Patrologia Orientalis*, iv, 5ff.). Also *P.G.*, lxxii.

Palladius, *Historia Lausiaca*, *P.G.*, lxv. *Lausiac History* (critical study, E. C. Butler, Cambridge Texts and Studies, vi. 1, 1898).

Papyri
  Corpus Papyrorum Judaicarum, ed. V. A. Tcherikover and A. Fuks, Harvard, 1957–.
  Oxyrhynchus Papyri, ed. Grenfell and Hunt (and others), London, 1898–.

Peter of Alexandria, Canons, ed. M. J. Routh, *Reliquiae Sacrae*, iii, 321–43.

Philo
  In Flaccum (text and tr. F. H. Colson, Loeb ed., *Philo*, ix).
  Legatio ad Gaium (ed. and tr. E. M. Smallwood, Leiden, 1961).

Pliny, *Epistolae* (text and tr. William Melmoth). (Also critical ed., E. G. Hardy, Oxford, 1889.)

Pontius, *Vita Cypriani* (ed. Hartel, *CSEL.*, iii. 3).

Porphyry of Gaza, κατὰ χριστιανῶν (ed. A. Harnack, *Abh. der Berliner Akademie der Wissenschaften*, 1916, 1–115).

Scriptores Historiae Augustae, (ed. E. Hohl, Teubner, Leipzig, 1927, 2 vols.). (Critical study, N. H. Baynes, *The Historia Augusta. Its Date and Purpose*, Oxford, 1926.)

Socrates, *Historia Ecclesiastica*, *P.G.*, lxvii. (Eng. tr. *The Greek Ecclesiastical Historians*, iii, Oxford, 1844.)

Sozomen, *Historia Ecclesiastica*, ed. J. Bidez-G.C. Hansen, *GCS.*, Berlin, 1960. (Eng. tr. E. Walford, Bohn series, London, 1855.)

Suetonius, *Vita Caesarum* (text and Eng. tr. J. C. Rolfe, Loeb series).

Sulpicius Severus, *Chronicon*, ed. C. Helm. *CSEL.*, i.

Tacitus

Annales, text and tr. J. Jackson (Loeb series).

Historiae, ed. G. H. Moore and J. Jackson (Loeb series).

Talmud, Babylonian Talmud, ed. I. Epstein and collaborators, Soncino Press, London, 1935–55.

Tatian, ed. E. Schwartz, *T.U.*, iv. i, Leipzig, 1888.

Tertullian *Apologeticus* and *De Spectaculis* (text and tr. T. R. Glover, Loeb series).

De Anima, ed. and tr. J. H. Waszink, Amsterdam, 1947.

De Baptismo, ed. and tr. E. Evans, London, 1964.

De Resurrectione Carnis, ed. and tr. E. Evans, London, 1960.

Other works, A. Reifferscheid, *CSEL.*, xx, V. Buhlart, *CSEL.*, lxxvi (Montanist works) and E. Kroymann, *CSEL.*, lxx.

Theophilus of Antioch, *Ad Autolycum*, *P.G.*, vi.

Victorinus of Pettau, ed. J. Haussleiter, *CSEL.*, xxxix.

Zonaras, *Annales*, ed. M. Pinder, Bonn, 1844.

Zosimus, *Historia Nova*, ed. L. Mendelssohn, 1887.

GENERAL BIBLIOGRAPHY

I

BAYNES, N. H., 'The Great Persecution', ch. xix in *CAH.*, xii, 646–77 and 789–95. (Includes a critical survey of sources relating to the Great Persecution to 1938.)

——'Constantine the Great and the Christian Church', *Proceedings of the British Academy*, xv, 1929.

CAMPENHAUSEN, H. VON, *Die Idee des Martyriums in der alten Kirche*, Göttingen, 1936.

CANFIELD, L. H., 'The Early Persecutions of the Christians', *Columbia Univ. Studies in History, Economics and Public Law*, 55, 1913. (Contains a full bibliography of the earlier works on the persecutions.)

DE STE CROIX, G. E. M., 'Why were the Early Christians Persecuted?', *Past and Present*, 26, Nov. 1963, 6–38.

DELEHAYE, H. *Les Passions des Martyrs et les Genres littéraires*, Brussels, 1921.

GIBBON, E., *Decline and Fall of the Roman Empire* (ed. J. B. Bury), ch. xvi.

GRÉGOIRE, H., 'Les persécutions dans l'empire romain', *Mémoires de l'Académie royale de Belgique*, xlvi. i, 1951.

HARDY, E. G., *Christianity and the Roman Government. A Study in Imperial Administration*, 1st ed., 1894; 2nd ed. with supplementary material under the title *Studies in Roman History*, 1906 (reprinted, 1925).

HARNACK, A., *The Expansion of Christianity in the First Three Centuries* (Eng. tr. J. Moffatt, London and New York, 1904–05).

——'Der Vorwurf des Atheismus in den ersten drei Jahrhunderten', *Texte und Untersuchungen*, xxviii, N.F. xiii. 4, 1905.

JUSTER, J., *Les Juifs dans l'Empire romain*, Paris, 1914, 2 vols.

MANARESI, A. *L'Impero romano e il Cristianesimo*, Turin, 1914.

MOMMSEN, TH., 'Der Religionsfrevel nach römischen Recht', *Historische Zeitschrift*, lxiv, 1890, 390–429 (= *Gesammelte Schriften*, Berlin, 1907, iii, 389).

PERLER, O., 'Das vierte Makkabäerbuch, Ignatius von Antiochien und die ältesten Märtyrerberichte', *Riv. di archeologia cristiana*, xxv, 1949, 47–72.

RAMSAY, W. M., *The Church in the Roman Empire before 170*, London, 1906.

SHERWIN-WHITE, A. N., *Roman Society and Roman Law in the New Testament* (The Sarum Lectures, 1960–61), Oxford, 1963.

——'The Early Persecutions and Roman Law Again', *Journal of Theological Studies*, N.S. iii, 1952, 199–213.

VOGT, J., 'Zur Religiosität der Christenverfolger im römischen Reich', *Sitzb. Akad. Heidelberg. Phil.-hist. Kl.*, 1962.

VOGT, J. and LAST, H., 'Christenverfolgungen', i. Historisch (J. Vogt), ii. Juristisch (H. Last), *Reallexikon für Antike und Christentum*, ii, Stuttgart, 1954, cols. 1159 and 1208.

II

ALLARD, P., *Histoire des Persécutions pendant les deux premiers siècles*, 3rd ed., Paris, 1903.

——*Histoire des Persécutions pendant la première moitié du troisième siècle*, 2nd ed., Paris, 1894.

——*Les dernières persécutions du troisième siècle*, 2nd ed., Paris, 1898.
(These are all somewhat uncritical works. The reader would be advised to refer to Allard's *Le Christianisme et l'Empire romain de Néron à Théodose*, Paris, 1925, for a summary of this author's views.)

——*Ten Lectures on the Martyrs* (Eng. tr., London, 1907).

ALLO-ISICHEI, E., *Political Thinking and Social Experience*, Christchurch, 1964.

ANDRESEN, C., 'Logos und Nomos', *Arbeiten zur Kirchengeschichte*, vol. 30, Berlin, 1955.

AUBÉ, B., *Histoire des persécutions de l'Eglise*, 3 vols., Paris, 1875–85.

AUBREY, E. E., 'The Holy Spirit in Relation to the Religious Community', *JTS.*, xl, 1940, 1ff.

BARDY, G., *La Conversion au Christianisme durant les premiers siècles*, Lyon, 1949.

BARKER, E., *From Alexander to Constantine*, Oxford, 1956.

BATIFFOL, P., *L'Eglise naissante et le Catholicisme*, Paris, 1914.

BELL, H. I., *Cults and Creeds of Roman Egypt*, Liverpool, 1956.

——*Jews and Christians in Alexandria*, Oxford, 1924.

BENZ, E., 'Christus und Sokrates in der alten Kirche', *ZNTW.*, 43, 1950/51, 195–223.

BOUCHÉ-LECLERCQ, A., *L'Intolerance religieuse et la Politique*, Paris, 1924.

BOUSSET, W., *Der Antichrist*, Göttingen, 1895.

BREZZI, P., *Cristianesimo e Impero Romano*, 2nd ed., Rome, 1944.

BUONAIUTI, E., *Geschichte des Christentums* (German tr., Berne, 1948).

CADOUX, C. J., *The Early Church and the World*, Edinburgh, 1925. (Contains a great deal of useful source material.)

CALDER, W. M., 'Early Christian Epitaphs from Phrygia', *Anatolian Studies*, 5, 1955, 27–38.

CAMPENHAUSEN, H. VON, *Aus der Frühzeit des Christentums*, Tübingen, 1963.

CHADWICK, H., 'St Peter and Paul in Rome', *Journal of Theol. Studies*, N.S. viii. 1, 1957, 31.

COCHRANE, C. N., *Christianity and Classical Culture. A Study in Thought and Action from Augustus to Augustine*, Oxford, 1944.

COHN, N., *The Pursuit of the Millennium*, London, 1957.

COSTA, G., *Religione e politica nell' impero romano*, Turin, 1923.

CUMONT, F., *Les Religions orientales dans le paganisme romain*, Paris, 1908.

——'La fin du Monde selon les mages occidentaux', *Revue de l'Histoire des Religions*, 103, 1931, 29 (See also p. 586).

——*Lux perpetua*, Paris, 1949.

DAVIES, J. G., 'Condemnation to the Mines. A neglected Chapter in the History of the Persecutions', *University of Birmingham Historical Journal*, vi. 2, 1958, 99–107.

DAVIES, W. D. and DAUBE, D. (ed.), 'The Background of the New Testament and its Eschatology', *Studies in Honour of C. H. Dodd*, Cambridge, 1956.

DEISSMANN, A., *Light from the Ancient East* (Eng. tr. C. R. M. Strachan, London, 1910; 2nd ed. 1926.)

DELEHAYE, H., *Sanctus. Essai sur le Culte de saintes dans l'antiquité*, Brussels, 1927.

DILL, S., *Roman Society from Nero to Marcus Aurelius*, London, 1905.

DODD, C. H., *The Bible and the Greeks*, London, 1935 (2nd impression, 1954).

DÖLGER, F. J., 'Sacramentum Infanticidii', *Antike und Christentum*, iv, 1934, 188–228.

——'Das Martyrium als Kampf mit dem Teufel', *Antike und Christentum*, iii, 1933, 177–188.

DOWNING, J., 'Jesus and Martyrdom', art. *JTS.*, N.S. xiv. 2, 1963, 279–93.

DUFOURCQ, A., *Le Christianisme et l'Empire (200–700)*, Paris, 1930.

EASTON, S. B., *Early Christianity*, London, 1955.

EGGER, R., *Römische Antike und frühes Christentum*, i. Klagenfurt, 1962. (Includes some interesting papers relating to the spread of Christianity.)

EHRHARD, A., *Die Kirche der Märtyrer*, Munich, 1932.

EHRHARDT, A. A. T., *Politische Metaphysik von Solon bis Augustin* (2 vols. published, Tübingen, 1959).

——'Christianity before the Apostles' Creed', *HTR.*, 55, 2, 1962, 74–119.

ENSSLIN, W., 'Gottkaiser und Kaiser von Gottes Gnaden', *Sitzungsber. der bayerischen Akad. der Wissenschaften*, 1943, 6.

FOAKES JACKSON, F. J. and KIRSOPP LAKE, *The Beginnings of Christianity*, London, 1922, vol. i.

FREND, W. H. C., 'The Persecutions: Some Links between Judaism and the Early Church', *Journal of Ecclesiastical History*, ix, 1958, 141–58.

FUCHS, H., *Der geistige Widerstand gegen Rom*, Leipzig, 1938.

GAIFFIER, B. DE, 'Reflexions sur l'Origine du Culte des Martyrs', *Maison Dieu*, 32, 1959, 19.

GEFFCKEN, J., 'Komposition und Entstehungszeit der Oracula Sibyllina', *T.U.*, N.F. viii, 1902.

——'Die christlichen Martyrien', *Hermes*, xlv, 1910, 481–505.

GLOVER, T. R., *The Conflict of Religions in the Early Roman Empire*, London, 1909.

GOODENOUGH, E. R., 'Catacomb Art', *Journal of Biblical Literature*, lxxxi, 1962, 113–42.

GRABAR, A., *Martyrium, Recherches sur le culte des reliques et l'art chrétien antique*, Paris, 1946, 2 vols.

GRANT, R. M., *The Sword and the Cross*, New York, 1955.

GREENSLADE, S. F., *Schism in the Early Church*, London, 1952.

——*Church and State from Constantine to Theodosius*, London, 1954.

GRIFFE, E., *La Gaule chrétienne à l'époque romaine*, Paris, 1947.

GUARDUCCI, M., *The Tomb of St. Peter* (Eng. tr., 1959).

HAASE, P., *Altchristliche Kirchengeschichte*, Leipzig, 1925.

HALLIDAY, W. R., *The Pagan Background of Early Christianity*, Liverpool, 1925.

HANSON, A. T., *The Wrath of the Lamb*, London, 1957.

HARDY, E. R., *Christian Egypt: Church and People*, Oxford/New York, 1952.

HARNACK, A., *Geschichte der altchristlichen Litteratur bis Eusebius*. 1. Die Überlieferung. 2. Die Chronologie. Leipzig, 1893-1904. (See especially vol. ii for dating the martyrdom of Polycarp and evaluating the *Acta Martyrum* of the Great Persecution.)

——'Der Geist der morgen ländischen Kirche', *Sitzungsber. der kgl. preuss. Akad. der Wissenschaften*, 1913. (important study).

——*Militia Christi*, Die christliche Religion und der Soldatenstand in den ersten drei Jahrhunderten, Tübingen, 1905.

HATCH, E., *The Influence of Greek Ideas and Usages upon the Christian Church*, London, 1907.

HERTLING, L. and KIRSCHBAUM, E., *Die römischen Katakomben und ihre Märtyrer*, Vienna, 1950.

HOMO, L., *Les empereurs romains et le christianisme*, Paris, 1931.

HYDE, W. W., *Paganism to Christianity in the Roman Empire*, Philadelphia, 1946.

JACOBY, A., 'Der angebliche Eselskult der Juden und Christen', *Archiv.f. Religionswissenschaft*, 25, 1927, 265-82.

JONES, A. H. M., *The Later Roman Empire, 284-604*, Oxford, 1964.

JULLIAN, C., *Histoire de la Gaule*, vols. iv-vii, Paris, 1913-.

KATTENBUSCH, F., 'Der Märtyrertitel', *Zeitschr. f. neutest. Wiss.*, iv, 1903, 111-27.

KLAUSER, TH., 'Studien zur Entstehungsgeschichte der christlichen Kunst', articles in *Jahrbuch für Antike und Christentum*, 1960-63.

LABRIOLLE, P. DE, *La Crise Montaniste*, Paris, 1913.

——*Latin Christianity* (Eng. tr., London, 1924).

LAMPE, G. W. H., *The Seal of the Spirit*, London, 1951.

LEBRETON, J., 'Le désaccord de la foi populaire et de la théologie savante dans l'Eglise chrétienne du IIIe siècle', *RHE.*, 19, 1923, 481-506, and 20, 1924, 5-37.

LECLERCQ, H., arts., 'Persécutions', *DACL.*, xiv. 1. 1939, cols. 523-94; 'Oracle', ibid., xii. 2. 22.

LEIPOLDT, J., *Die Frau in der antiken Welt und im Urchristentum*, Leipzig, 1955.

LIETZMANN, H., art. 'Martys', *Pauly-Wissowa, Reallexikon*, Suppl. xiv, 1930, 2044.

LINSENMAYER, A., *Die Bekämpfung des Christentums durch den römischen Staat*, Munich, 1905.

LOEWE, H., *Render unto Caesar*, Cambridge, 1938.

LOHMEYER, E., 'Die`Idee des Märtyrers in Judentum und Urchristentum', *Zeitschr. f. systematische Theologie*, v, 1927, 222–49.

LOHSE, E., *Märtyrer und Gottesknecht*, Göttingen, 1955. (Forschungen zur Religion und Literatur des A.T. und N.T., Neue Folge, 46.)

MARCO, A. A. DE, *The Tomb of St. Peter* (a bibliographical catalogue of work on the theme of St. Peter in Rome), Leiden, 1964.

MARUCCHI, O., *Le Catacombe romane*, Rome, 1903.

MATTINGLY, H., *Roman Imperial Civilization*, London, 1957.

——*Christianity in the Roman Empire*, Otago, 1955.

MAYNARD SMITH, H., *Atonement*, London, 1925.

MERRILL, E. T., *Essays in Early Christian History*, London, 1924.

MEYER, E., *Ursprung und Anfänge des Christentums*, 3 vols., Stuttgart and Berlin, 1921 (especially vol. iii).

MONCEAUX, P., *Histoire littéraire de l'Afrique chrétienne* (vols. i–iii are concerned with the period down to and including the Great Persecution; vol. iv outlines the history of the Donatist movement and the salient Donatist texts), Paris, 1901–20.

MOREAU, J., *La Persécution du Christianisme dans l'Empire romain*, Paris, 1956.

MÜLLER, K., *Kleine Beiträge zur alten Kirchengeschichte*, ZNTW., xxiii, 1924, and xxiv, 1925.

NAUTIN, P., *Lettres et Ecrivains chrétiens des IIe et IIIe Siècles*, Paris, 1961.

NEUMANN, K. J., *Der römische Staat und die allgemeine Kirche bis auf Diocletian*, Leipzig, 1890.

NOCK, A. D., 'Early Gentile Christianity' (*Essays on the Trinity and the Incarnation*, ed. A. E. J. Rawlinson, London, 1927).

——*Conversion*, Oxford, 1933.

PARIBENI, R., Christianesimo e impero, *Rendiconti della reale academia dei Lincei*, iii.13, 1927, 684–97.

PARKER, T. M., *Christianity and the State in the Light of History* (Bampton Lectures for 1953), London, 1955.

PARKES, J., *The Conflict of the Church and the Synagogue*, London, 1934.

PELLEGRINO, M., 'Le Sens ecclésial du martyre', *Rev. des Sciences religieuses*, 35, 1961, 152–75.

PETERSON, E., *Der Monotheismus als politisches Problem*, Leipzig, 1935.

PFAFF, art. 'Superstitio' *PW.*, ii.7 (1931), 937–9.

PINCHERLE, A., 'Impero Romano e Christianesimo', *Rivista Storica Italiana*, 1933.

PUECH, A., *Histoire de la littérature grecque chrétienne*, 2 vols., Paris, 1928.

RAMSAY, W. M., *Cities and Bishoprics of Phrygia*, 2 vols., Oxford, 1883 (especially chs. xv and xvi).

RIDDLE, D. W., *The Martyrs*, Chicago, 1931.

SCHOENAICH, G., *Die Kämpfe zwischen Römertum und Christentum in ihrer geschichtlichen Entwicklung von Nero bis auf Konstantin den Grossen*, Breslau, 1927.

SETTON, K. M., *The Christian Attitude Towards the Emperor in the Fourth Century*, New York, 1941. (See N. H. Baynes's review, *JRS.*, xxxiv, 1944, 135–40.)

SIMON, M., 'La polémique antijuive de Saint Chrysostome et le mouvement judaisant d'Antioche', *Mélanges Franz Cumont* (= *Annuaire de l'Institut de Philologie et d'histoire orientales et slaves*, iv, 1936, 403–21).

——'Christianisme antique et pensée paienne', *Bull. de la Faculté des Lettres à Strasbourg*, 38, 1960, 314.

——*Recherches d'Histoire Judéo-Chrétienne*, Paris/The Hague, 1962. (A very useful collection of essays.)

STAUFFER, E., 'Märtyrertheologie und Täuferbewegung', *Zeitschr. für Kirchengeschichte*, iii, Folge 3, 1933, 545–609.

——*Christ and the Caesars* (Eng. tr., London, 1955).

STRATHMANN, H., art. μάρτυς, μαρτυρία, Kittel's *Wörterbuch*, iv, 477–519.

STRAUB, J., 'Vom Herrscherideal in der Spätantike', *Forschungen zur Kirchen- und Geistesgeschichte*, 18, Stuttgart, 1939.

STYGER, P., *Die römischen Katakomben*, Berlin, 1935.

SURKAU, H. W., 'Martyrien in jüdischer und frühchristlicher Zeit' (Forschungen zur Religion und Literatur des Alten u Neuen Test., N.F. 36), Göttingen, 1938.

SWETE, H. B., *The Holy Spirit in the Ancient Church*, London, 1912.

TOYNBEE, J. M. C. and WARD-PERKINS, J. B., *The Shrine of St. Peter and the Vatican Excavations*, London, 1956.

TRAVERS HERFORD, W., *Christianity in Talmud and Midrash*, London, 1903.

TURNER, H. E. W., *The Pattern of Christian Truth*, London, 1956.

WILLIAMS, A. LUKYN, *Adversus Judaeos*, London, 1935.

WINDISCH, H., *Taufe und Sünde im ältesten Christentum bis auf Origenes*, Tübingen, 1908.

WISCHNITZER, R., *The Messianic Theme in the Paintings of Dura-Europos*, Chicago, 1948.

WORKMAN, H. B., *Persecution in the Early Church*, 4th ed., London, 1926.

ZEILLER, J., *L'empire romain et l'Eglise*, Paris, 1928.

——'Nouvelles remarques sur les persécutions contre les chrétiens', *Miscellanea Giovanni Mercati* v (= *ST.*, 125, 1946, 5).

SPECIAL THEMES

I. JEWISH BACKGROUND

ABEL, F. M., *Le livre des Maccabées*, Paris, 1949.

BARON, S. W., *A Social and Religious History of the Jews*, New York, 1952 (especially vol. i).

BEVAN, E., *Jerusalem under the High Priests*, London, 1952.

BICKERMANN, E., *Der Gott der Makkabäer*, Berlin, 1937.

BLANK, S. H., 'The Death of Zechariah in Rabbinic Literature', *Hebrew Union College Annual*, xii–xiii, 1937–38, 327–46.

BONSIRVAN, J., *Le judäisme palestinien au temps du Jésus-Christ*, 2 vols., Paris, 1935.

BOUSSET, W. and GRESSMANN, H., *Die Religion des Judentums im späthellenistischen Zeitalter*, Tübingen, 1926.

BURROWS, F. MILLAR, *The Dead Sea Scrolls*, London, 1956.

——*More Light on the Dead Sea Scrolls*, London, 1958.

CROSS, F. M., *The Ancient Library at Q'mran and Modern Biblical Studies*, London, 1958.

CUMONT, F., 'A propos de Sabazius et le Judaisme', *CRAI.*, 1906, 63.

DAVIES, W. D., *Paul and Rabbinic Judaism*, London, 1948.

FARMER, W. R., *Maccabees, Zealots and Josephus*, Columbia University Press, 1956.

FISCHEL, A., 'Prophet and Martyr', *Jewish Quarterly Review*, 37 (1946–47), 265–80 and 363–86.

FREY, I. B., 'Les communautés juives à Rome aux premiers temps de l'Eglise', *Recherches de science religieuse*, xx, 1930.

GOODENOUGH, E. R., *An Introduction to Philo Judaeus*, New Haven, 1940. (See also A. Momigliano's comments, *JRS.*, xxxiv, 1944, 164.)

GREENSTONE, J. H., art. Martyrdom (restriction of), *Jewish Encyclopaedia*, viii.

GUIGNEBERT, CH., *The Jewish World in the Time of Jesus* (Eng. tr. S. H. Hooke, London, 1939).

HEINEMANN, I., art. 'Antisemitismus', *PW.*, Suppl.v. 28.

HENGEL, R., *Die Zeloten*, Leiden/Köln, 1961.

JONES, A. H. M., *The Herods of Judea*, Oxford, 1938.

KATZ, J., 'Exclusiveness and Tolerance', *Scripta Judaica*, iii, Oxford, 1961.

KITZINGER, E., 'A Survey of the Town of Stobi', *Dumbarton Oaks Papers*, iii, 1946, 141. (Description of Polycharmus' synagogue.)

LEANEY, A. R. C., 'The Eschatological Significance of Suffering in the O.T. and the Dead Sea Scrolls', *Scottish Journal of Theology*, 16, 1963, 286–96.

LECLERCQ, H., art. 'Oracle', *DACL.*, xii. 2, 2225.

Leon, H. J., *The Jews of Ancient Rome*, Philadelphia, 1960.

Licht, J., 'Taxo, or the Apocalyptic Doctrine of Vengeance', *Journal of Jewish Studies*, xii, 3 and 4, 1961, 95–105.

Monceaux, P., 'Les colonies juives dans l'Afrique romaine', *Revue des Etudes juives*, 44, 1902, 1ff.

Montefiore, G. C. and Loewe, H., *A Rabbinic Anthology*, London, 1938.

Moore, G. F., *Judaism in the First Centuries of the Christian Era*, 3 vols., Cambridge, 1930.

Noth, M., *Gesammelte Studien zum Alten Testament*, Munich, 1957. (See, in particular, 'Das Geschichtsverständnis der alttestamentlichen Apokalyptik', 248–73.)

Osterley, W. O. E. and Robinson, T. H., *Jews and Judaism during the Greek Period*, London, 1941.

Perowne, S., *The Life and Times of Herod the Great*, London, 1956.

Pfeiffer, R. H., *History of New Testament Times*, New York, 1949.

Rowley, H. H., *The Relevance of Apocalyptic*, 2nd ed., London, 1947.

——*Darius the Mede and the Four World Empires in the Book of Daniel*, Cardiff, 1935.

——*Jewish Apocalyptic and the Dead Sea Scrolls*, London, 1957.

Russell, D. S., *Between the Testaments*, London, 1960.

Schürer, E., *Geschichte des jüdischen Volkes im Zeitalter Jesu Christi*, 3 vols., 4th ed., Leipzig, 1901.

Simon, M., *Verus Israel*, Paris, 1948.

Smallwood, E. M. 'The Chronology of Gaius' Attempt to Desecrate the Temple', *Latomus*, xvi, 1957, 3–17.

Squarciapino, M. F., 'La sinagoga recentemente scoperta ad Ostia', *Rendiconti di Pontif. Acad. romana di Archäologia*, 35, 1961–62, 128.

Stauffer, E., *New Testament Theology* (Eng. tr. J. Marsh, London, 1955). (Appendix i contains useful list of references to martyrdom in Late-Jewish literature.)

Stuart Jones, H., 'Claudius and the Jewish Question at Alexandria', *JRS.*, xvi, 1926, 17–35.

Tcherikover, V., *Hellenistic Civilization and the Jews* (tr. from Hebrew by S. Appelbaum, Philadelphia, 1959).

de Vaux, Père R., *L'archéologie et les Manuscrits de la Mer morte* (Schweich Lectures, 1959), London, 1961.

Wilcken, U., 'Zum alexandrinischen Antisemitismus', *Abhandlungen d. Kön. Sächs. Gesellschaft der Wissenschaften*, lvii, 1909, 783–839.

2. GRECO-ROMAN RELIGIOUS BACKGROUND

Altheim, F., *History of Roman Religion* (Eng. tr. H. Mattingly, London, 1939).

Beaujeu, J., *La religion romaine à l'apogée de l'empire*, Paris, 1955.

BIDEZ, J. and CUMONT, F., *Les Mages hellénisés*, Paris, 1938.

BOWRA, C. M., 'Melinno's Hymn to Rome', *Journal of Roman Studies*, xlvii, 1957, 21.

CARCOPINO, J., *De Pythagore aux Apôtres, Etudes sur la conversion du Monde Romain*, Paris, 1956.

——*Aspects mystiques de la Rome païenne*, Paris, 1942.

CHARLESWORTH, M. P., 'Providentia et Aeternitas', *HTR.*, 29, 1936, 105.

——'Pietas et Victoria. The Emperor as Citizen', *JRS.*, xxxiii, 1943, 1–10.

——'Some observations on the Ruler-Cult, especially in Rome', *HTR.*, 28, 1935, 32.

CUMONT, F., 'La Fin du Monde selon les mages occidentaux', *Revue de l'Histoire des Religions*, 103, 1931, 29–96.

DRACHMANN, A. B., *Atheism in Pagan Antiquity*, Copenhagen, 1922.

ENSSLIN, WM., 'Gottkaiser und Kaiser von Gottes Gnaden', *Sitzungsber. der bayerischen Akad. der Wissenschaften* (Ph. Hist. Kl.), 1943, fasc. 6.

FRANKEL, E., 'Senatus Consultum de Bacchanalibus', *Hermes*, 67, 1932, 367–96.

GRANT, M., *From Imperium to Auctoritas*, Cambridge, 1946.

GREEN, P., 'The First Sicilian War', *Past and Present*, 22, 1961, 10–30.

GUTERMAN, S. C., *Religious Toleration and Persecution in Ancient Rome*, London, 1951.

HERRMANN, L., 'Le Miracle de Gnatia', *La nouvelle Clio*, v, 1953, 59–64.

IMMISCH, O., 'Zum antiken Herrscherkult', *Aus Roms Zeitwende*, 1931.

EL KHACHAB, ABD EL-MOHSEN, "ὁκαρακαλλος' κοσμοκρατωρ' *Journal of Egypt. Archaeology*, 47, 1961, 119ff.

KORNEMANN, H., 'Zur Geschichte der antiken Herrschenkulte', *Klio*, i, 1902, 52–143.

LAMBRECHTS, P., 'La politique appollinienne d'Auguste et le culte impérial', *La nouvelle Clio*, v, 1953, 63–81.

LAST, H., 'Rome and the Druids: A Note', *JRS.*, xxxix, 1949, 1–5.

——'The Study of the "Persecutions"', *Journal of Roman Studies*, xxvii, 1937, 80–92.

LATTE, K., *Römische Religionsgeschichte*, 2nd ed., Munich, 1960.

MUSURILLO, H., *The Acts of the Pagan Martyrs*, Oxford, 1954.

NILSSON, M. P., 'Bacchic Mysteries of the Roman Age', *Harvard Theological Review*, 46, 1953, 175.

NOCK, A. D., 'The Roman Army and the Roman Religious Year', *Harvard Theological Review*, 45, 1952, 187–245.

——'The Augustan Restoration', *Classical Review*, 39, 1925, 60–7.

——'Severi et Augustales' *Mélanges Bidez*, 627–38, (= Ann. de l'Institut de Philologie et d'histoire orientales 2, Brussels, 1934).

——'The Emperor's Divine "Comes" ', *JRS.*, xxxvii, 1947, 102–16.

OESTERLEY, W. O. E., 'The Cult of Sabazios', *The Labyrinth*, 1935, 115–58.

LA PIANA, G., 'Foreign Groups in Rome during the First Centuries of the Empire', *Harvard Theological Review*, 20, 1927, 183–403.

ROBERTS, C. H., SKEAT, T. C. and NOCK, A. D., 'The Gild of Zeus Hypsistos', *Harvard Theological Review*, 29, 1936, 39.

ROSTOVTZEFF, M., 'Commodus-Hercules in Britain', *Journal of Roman Studies*, xiii, 1923.

SCHNIEWIND, J., *Evangelion*, 3 vols, Berlin, 1931.

SIMON, M., *Hercule et le Christianisme*, Strassbourg, 1955.

SWAIN, J. W., 'The Theory of the Four Monarchies: Opposition History under the Roman Empire, *Classical Philology*, 35, 1940, 1–21.

TARDITI, G., 'La Questione dei Baccanali a Roma nel 186 A.C.', *La Parola del Passato*, ix, 1954, 265–87.

TAYLOR, L. R., *The Divinity of the Roman Emperor* (American Philological Assoc. Monographs, i), Middletown, Connecticut, 1931.

TOUTAIN, J., *Les Cultes païens dans l'Empire romain*, 3 vols, Paris, 1907–20.

TOYNBEE, J. M. C. and WARD-PERKINS, J. B., *The Shrine of St. Peter and the Vatican Excavations*, London, 1956.

WARDE FOWLER, W., *The Religious Experience of the Roman People*, London, 1911.

WEINSTOCK, S., 'Pax and the "Ara Pacis" ', *Journal of Roman Studies*, 1960, 44–58.

3. NEW TESTAMENT AND MARTYRDOM

BARRETT, C. K., 'The Holy Spirit in the New Testament', *JTS.*, N.S. i, 1950, 1–15.

——*St. John* (*Commentary and Notes on the Greek Text*), London, 1955.

——'The Background of Mark 10^{45}, *New Testament Essays, Studies in Memory of T. W. Manson* (ed. A. J. B. Higgins, 1959) 12–15.

BOUSSET, W., *Die Offenbarung Iohannis*, Göttingen, 1906.

BROX, N., *Zeuge und Märtyrer*, Munich, 1961.

BURKILL, T. A., 'The Trial of Jesus', *Vigiliae Christianae*, xii, 1958, 1ff.

CHARLES, R. H., *Revelation*: International Critical Commentary, 2 vols, London, 1920.

CROSS, F. L., *1 Peter, a Paschal Liturgy*, London, 1954.

CULLMANN, O., *The State in the New Testament*, London, 1957. *Christus und die Zeit*, Zürich, 1946.

DODD, C. H., 'The fall of Jerusalem and the Abomination of Desolation', *Journal of Roman Studies*, xxxvii, 1947, 47.

EASTON, S. B. and GRANT, F. C., *Early Christianity; The Purpose of Acts*, London, 1955.

ELLIOT BINNS, L. E., *Galilean Christianity*, London, 1956.

FARMER, W. R., 'The Palm Branches in Jn. 12^{13}', *Journal of Theological Studies*, N. S. iii. 1, 1952, 62–6.

GOGUEL, M., *La naissance du Christianisme*, Paris, 1946.

GRANT, F. C., *Roman Hellenism and the New Testament*, Edinburgh and London, 1962.

KNOX, W. L., 'Church and State in the New Testament', *Journal of Roman Studies*, xxxix, 1949, 23–30.

LIGHTFOOT, R. H., *The Gospel Message of St. Mark*, Oxford, 1950.

MANSON, T. W., 'Martyrs and Martyrdom', *Bull. of John Rylands Library*, 39, 1957, 463–84.

——*Jesus the Messiah* (Cunningham Lectures), London, 1945.

——*The Servant Messiah; A Study of the Public Ministry of Jesus*, Cambridge, 1953.

MONTEFIORE, H. W., 'Revolt in the Desert (Mk. 6$^{38ff.}$)', *NTS.*, 8, 1961–62, 135–41.

MORRISON, C. D., 'The Powers that Be: Earthly Rulers of Demonic Powers' (*Studies in Biblical Theology*, 37) London, 1960.

RIDDLE, D. W., 'Die Verfolgungslogien in formgeschichtlicher und sozioligischer Beleuchtung', *ZNTW.*, 33, 1934, 271–88.

ROBINSON, J. A. T., *Twelve New Testament Studies*, London, 1962. (Important contributions on the connections between the Covenanters and the primitive Christian community at Jerusalem.)

RYDER SMITH, C., *The Bible Doctrine of the Hereafter*, London, 1958.

SCHÜTZ, O., *Die Offenbarung des Johannes*, Berlin, 1933.

TAYLOR, V., *Jesus and His Sacrifice*, London, 1937.

WINTER, P., 'On the Trial of Jesus', *Studia Judaica*, i, Berlin, 1961.

——*The Trial of Jesus* (Friends of the Kibbutz, London, 1964).

4. PRIMITIVE CHURCH TO THE FALL OF JERUSALEM

BAMMEL, E., 'Ein Beitrag zur paulinischen Staatsanschauung', *Theol. Literaturzeitung*, 1960, 838–40.

——'Judenverfolgung und Naherwartung. Zur Eschatologie des Ersten Thessalonicherbriefes', *Zeitschrift f. Theologie und Kirche*, 56, 1959.

BAUER, J. B., 'Tacitus und die Christen', *Gymnasium*, 64, 1957.

BEAUJEU, J., 'L'incendie de Rome en 64 et les chrétiens', *Coll. Latomus*, xlix, Brussels, 1960.

BRANDON, S. G. F., *The Fall of Jerusalem and the Christian Church*, London, 1951.

CAIRD, G. B., *The Apostolic Age*, London, 1955.

CLAYTON, F. W., 'Tacitus and Nero's Persecution of the Christians, *Class. Quarterly*, xli, 1947, 81–5.

DEISSMANN, A., *St. Paul, a Study in Social and Religious History* (Eng. tr. L. R. M. Strachan, London, 1912).

DIBELIUS, M., 'Rom und die Christen im ersten Jahrhundert', *Sitzungsber. der Heidelberger Akad. der Wissenschaften, Phil. Hist. Kl.*, xi.2, 1941/42, 1ff.

FUCHS, H., 'Tacitus über die Christen', *Vigiliae Christianae*, 1, 1950, 65–93.

HERRMANN, L., 'Quels chrétiens ont incendié Rome?' *Revue Belge de Philologie*, 27.2, 1949, 637.

JANNE, H., 'Impulsore Christo', *Annuaire de l'Institut de philos. et d'hist. orientales*, Brussels, 1934.

JUDGE, E. A., *The Social Patterns of the Christian Groups in the First Century*, London, 1959.

KNOX, W. L., *St. Paul and the Church of the Gentiles*, Cambridge, 1938.

LIETZMANN, H., *Petrus und Paulus in Rom*, Berlin, 1927.

MOMIGLIANO, A., 'Nero' (= ch. xxi and notes, in *Cambridge Ancient History*, vol. x).

NESTLE, W., 'Odium generis humani (zu Tacitus, Ann. xv. 44)', *Klio*, 21, 1927, 92.

NOCK, A. D., *St. Paul*, Home University Library, 1948 ed.

RAMSAY, W. M., *St. Paul, the Traveller and the Roman Citizen*, London, 1896.

——*Pauline and Other Studies*, London, 1906.

SCHOEPS, H. J., *Paul, the Theology of the Apostle in the light of Jewish Religious History* (Eng. tr. H. Marsh, 1961).

SESTON, W., 'L'empereur Claude et les chrétiens', *Rev. d'histoire et de philos. religieuses*, xi, 1931.

SIDEBOTTOM, E. M., *The Christ of the Fourth Gospel in the Light of First Century Thought*, London, 1961.

5. JEWS AND CHRISTIANS, 70–135

ALLEN, E. L., 'The Jewish Christian Church in the Fourth Gospel", *Journal of Biblical Literature*, 74, 1955, 88–92.

AUDET, J. P., *La Didaché. Instructions des Apôtres* (Etudes Bibliques), Paris, 1958.

——'Affinités littéraires et doctrinales du Manuel de Discipline', *Revue Biblique*, 60, 1953, 41–82.

AUERBACH, M., 'Zur politischen Geschichte der Juden unter Kaiser Hadrian', *Festschrift zum 50 jähr. Bestehen des Rabbinerseminars zu Berlin*, Berlin, 1924, 1–40.

BARNARD, L. W., 'Clement of Rome and the Persecution of Domitian', *New Testament Studies*, 10, 1964, 251–60.

BAUER, W., art. 'Chiliasmus', *Antike und Christentum*, ii, 1073–8.

BERNAYS, J., 'Die Gottesfürchtigen bei Juvenal', *Commentarii philologii in honorem Th. Mommsen*, Berlin, 1877.

BORNKAMM, G., 'Enderwartung und Kirche in Matthäusevangelium', *Studies in Honour of C. H. Dodd*, Cambridge, 1956, 222–60.

CALLEWAERT, C., 'Le rescrit d'Hadrien à Minucius Fundanus', *Revue d'histoire et de Littérature religieuse*, viii, 1903.

CHARLESWORTH, M. P., 'Nero. Some Aspects', *Journal Roman Studies*, xl, 1950, 69.

DANIÉLOU, J., *Théologie du Judéo-Christianisme*, Paris, 1958.

EHRHARDT, A. A. T., 'The Birth of the Synagogue and Rabbi Akiba', *Studia Theologica*, ix.2, 1955, 96.

FINKELSTEIN, L., *Akiba. Scholar, Saint and Martyr*, New York, 1936.

FRASER, P. M. and APPELBAUM, S. P., 'Hadrian and Cyrene', *Journ. Roman Studies*, xl, 1950, 83.

FUKS, A., 'Aspects of the Jewish Revolt of 115–117', *Journal of Roman Studies*, li, 1961, 98–104.

GINSBERG, M., 'Fiscus Judaicus', *JQR.*, 1930, 218ff.

GRANT, R. M., 'Hermeneutics and Tradition in Ignatius of Antioch', *Archivo di Filosofia*, 1–2, 1963, 183–201.

HART, H. ST. J., 'Judaea and Rome. The Official Commentary', *Journal of Theological Studies*, N.S. iii, 1952, 172–98.

HOSPERS JANSEN, A. M. A., *Tacitus over de Joden*, Gröningen, 1949.

JOUSSUARD, G., 'Aux origines du Culte des martyrs dans le Christianisme', *Rev. des Sciences religieuses*, 39, 1952, 362.

KNOX, J., 'Pliny and 1 Peter. A note on 1 Peter 4$^{14-16}$ and 3^{15}', *Journal of Biblical Literature*, 72, 1953, 187–9.

KRAEMER, C. J., 'Pliny and the Early Christian Service', *Classical Philology*, 29, 1934, 293–300.

KURFESS, A., 'Zum V. Buch der Oracula Sibyllina', *Rheinisches Museum*, 99, 1956, 225–41.

LAST, H., 'The Rotas-Sator Square. Present Position and Future Prospects', *Journ. Theol. Studies*, N.S. iii, 1952, 92–7.

LECLERCQ, H., art. 'Aristocratiques (classes)', *DACL.*, i.2, 2845–86.

——arts. 'Domitien' and 'Domitilla' (Cimitière de) *DACL.*, x.

——art. 'Millénarisme', *DACL.*, xi.1.

LIGHTFOOT, J. B., *The Apostolic Fathers*, London, 1889.

LOEWE, R., 'A Jewish Counterpart to the Acts of the Alexandrians', *Journal of Jewish Studies*, 12, 1961, 105–22.

MERILL, E. T., 'Tertullian on Pliny's Persecution of the Christians', *Am. Journ. of Theology*, xxii, 1918, 124–35.

MILBURN, R. L. P., 'The Persecution of Domitan', *Church Quarterly Review*, 1945, 154–64.

MILDENBERG, L., 'The Eleazar Coinage of the Bar Kochba Rebellion', *Historica Judaica*, xi, 1949, 77.

MONTEFIORE, H. W., 'Sulpicius Severus and Titus' Council of War,' *Historia*, xi, 1962, 156.

MOREAU, J., 'A propos de la Persécution de Domitien', *La Nouvelle Clio*, v, 1953, 121–9.

RAMSAY, W. M., *The Letters to the Seven Churches*, London, 1906.

——'The Letter to the Church in Thyateira', *Expositor*, 1906, 45.

RONCONI, A., 'Tacito, Plino e i Cristiani', *Studi in onore di U.E. Paoli*, Florence, 1956, 615.

SCHLATTER, P., *Die Kirche Jerusalems, 70–130*, Gütersloh, 1915.

SCHMID, W., 'The Christian Reinterpretation of the Rescript of Hadrian', *Maia*, vii, 1955, 5–13.

SCOTT, K., *The Imperial Cult under the Flavians*, Stuttgart, 1936.

SIMON, M., 'Retour du Christ et reconstruction du Temple dans la pensée chrétienne primitive', *Mélanges Goguel*, Neuchâtel, 1950, 247–57.

SMALLWOOD, E. M., 'The Legislation of Hadrian and Antoninus Pius against Circumcision', *Latomus*, 18, 1959, 334–47.

STYGER, P., *Juden und Christen im alten Rom*, Berlin, 1934.

SUKENIK, E. L., 'The Earliest Records of Christianity', *Am. Journ. Archaeology*, 51, 1947, 364.

TOUILLEUX, P., *L'Apocalypse et les Cultes de Domitien et de Cybèle*, Paris, 1935.

WEBER, W., 'Bemerkungen zum Briefwechsel des Plinius und Trajan über die Christen', *Festgabe K. Müller*, Tübingen, 1922, 24–45.

WILSON, W. J., 'The Career of the Prophet Hermas', *Harvard Theological Review*, 20, 1927, 95–120.

YADIN, Y., 'New Archives of the Revolt of Bar-Kochba', *Illustrated London News*, Archaeological Section, 4 and 11 November 1961.

6. SECOND CENTURY

BARNIKOL, E., 'Celsus und Origenes', *T.U.*, 77, 1961.

BETZ, H. D., 'Lukian von Samosata und das Neue Testament', *Texte und Untersuchungen*, 76, 1961.

CALDER, W. M., 'Philadelphia and Montanism', *Bull. of John Rylands Library*, vii, 1923, 309–54.

CHADWICK, H., 'Justin Martyr on Church and State' (Fourth International Conference on Patristic Studies, 1963, to be published in *Texte und Untersuchungen*).

CHARLES-PICARD, G., 'Pertinax et les prophètes de Caelestis', *Revue de l'histoire des religions*, 155, 1959, 41–62.

DIEU, L., 'La persécution au 11e siècle. Une loi fantôme', *Revue d'hist. ecclesiastique*, xxxviii, 1942, 5–30. (Reply by J. Zeiller, *Studi e Testi*, 125, 1946, 1–6.)

DORESSE, J., 'Les apocalypses de Zoroastre, Zostrien et de Dosithée', *Studies Presented in Honour of W. E. Crum*, Boston, 1950, 255.

EHRHARDT, A. A. T., 'Justin Martyr's Two Apologies', *Journ. Eccl. History*, iv.i. 1953, 1–12.

ELZE, M., *Tatian und seine Theologie*, Göttingen, 1960.

EPP, E. J., Dissert. 'Theological Tendency in the Textual Variants of Codex Bezae Cantabrigensis' (Anti-Judaic tendencies in Acts). Noted in *Harvard Theol. Rev.*, 54.4, 1961, 299.

FARQUHARSON, A. S. L., *Marcus Aurelius, His Life and World* (ed. Rees), Oxford, 1952.

FLICHE, A., 'A propos des origines chrétiennes de la Gaule', *Mélanges Jules Lebreton* (= *Recherches des Sciences religieuses*, xl, 1951–52, 1–16).

FREND, W. H. C., 'The Gnostic Sects and the Roman Empire', *Journ. Eccl. History*, v, 1954, 25–37.

GRANT, R. M., *Second-century Christianity* (Translations of Christian Literature, Ser. 6), London, 1946.

——'The Chronology of the Greek Apologists', *Vigiliae Christianae*, ix.1, 1955, 25–33.

——*Gnosticism and Early Christianity*, Oxford, 1959.

GRÉGOIRE, H., 'Les Inscriptions hérétiques d'Asie Mineure', *Byzantion*, 1924, i, 695–710.

GRÉGOIRE, H. and ORGELS, P., 'Le véritable date du martyre de Saint Polycarpe', *A.B.*, lxix, 1951, 1–38.

HAMMOND, MASON, *The Antonine Monarchy* (Papers and Monographs of the American Academy in Rome, xix, 1959).

HARNACK, A., 'Das Edict des Antoninus Pius', *Texte und Untersuchungen*, xiii.4, 1895.

HÜTTL, W., *Antoninus Pius*, Prague, 1936.

La PIANA, G., 'The Roman Church at the End of the Second Century', *Harvard Theological Review*, 18, 1923, 201–277.

LECLERCQ, H.. art. 'Lyon', *DACL.*, x.1, 1–81.

——art. 'Vienne', *DACL.*, xv.2, 3047–9.

——art. 'Ane', *DACL.*, i.2, 2043–4.

OLIVER, J. J. and PALMER, R. E. A., 'Minutes of an Act of the Roman Senate', *Hesperia*, 24, 1955, 320–49. (An important article on the background to the pogrom at Lyons.)

ORBÉ, A., 'Los primeros herejes ante la persecucion. Estudios Valentinianos V', *Analecta Gregoriana*, 83, 1956.

PRÉAUX, J., 'Deus cristianorum Oenocoetes', *Coll. Latomus* 44, 1960, 639–54.

PUECH, A., *Les apologistes grecs du 11e siècle*, Paris, 1912.

PUECH, H. C., 'Les nouveaux écrits gnostiques découverts en Haute-Egypte', *Coptic Studies in Honour of Walter Ewing Crum*, Boston, 1950, 106ff.

SALVATORELLI, L., 'Il pensiero del cristianesimo antico intorno allo Stato dagli apologisti ad Origene', *Bilychnis*, viii, 1920.

SCHEPELERN, W., *Der Montanismus und die phrygischen Kulte*, Tübingen, 1929.

SORDI, M., 'I "nouvi decreti" di Marco Aurelio contro i cristiani', *Studi Romani*, 9, 1962, 365.

TONETTI, L., 'Il "Peregrinus" di Luciano e i cristiani del suo tempo', *Miscell. di storia e cultura ecclesisatica*, iii, 1904.

WALZER, R., *Galen on Jews and Christians*, Oxford, 1949.

WALTZING, J. P., 'Le crime rituel reproché aux chrétiens du 11e siècle', *Bull. de l'Académie royale de Belgique*, Cl. des Lettres, 1925, 205–39.

7. THE THIRD CENTURY

D'ALÈS, A., *L'édit de Calliste. Etude sur les origines de la pénitence chrétienne*, Paris, 1924.

ALFÖLDI, A., 'Zur den Christenverfolgungen in der Mitte des 3. Jahrhunderts', *Klio*, xxxi, 1938, 323–48, and *Cambridge Ancient History*, xii, 166ff.

ANDREOTTI, R., 'Religione ufficiale e culto dell'imperatore nei "Libelli" di Decio', *Studi in onore di A. Calderini e R. Paribeni*, i, Milan, 1956, 369–76.

BENSON, E. W., *Cyprian: His Life, his Times, his Work*, London, 1897.

BIGG, C., *The Christian Platonists of Alexandria* (2nd ed.), Oxford, 1913.

BIHLMEYER, K., *Die 'syrischen' Kaiser zu Rom und das Christentum*, Rothenburg, 1916.

——'Die syrischen Kaiser Karacalla, Elagabal, Severus Alexander und das Christentum', *Theol. Quartalschrift*, 97, 1915, 71–91.

BESNIER, M. *L'Empire romain de l'avènement des Sevères au Concile de Nicée*, Paris, 1937.

CARCOPINO, J., *Aspects mystiques de la Rome païenne*, Paris, 1942. (Valuable essays on religion in North Africa at this period.)

CAVALLERA, F., 'La Doctrine d'Origène sur les rapports du christianisme et de la société civile', *Bull. de littérature ecclésiastique*, 38, 1937,

CHADWICK, H., 'St. Peter and St. Paul in Rome: The Problem of the

Memoria Apostolorum ad Catacumbas', *JTS.*, N.S. viii.1, 1957, 30–52.

DAVIES, J. G., 'Was the Devotion of Septimius Severus to Serapis the Cause of the Persecution of 202–203?', *JTS.*, N.S. v, 1954, 73–6.

FINK, R. O., HOEY, A. S. and SNYDER, W. F., 'The Feriale Duranum', *Yale Classical Studies*, vii, 1940.

FREND, W. H. C., 'The Failure of the Persecutions in the Roman Empire', *Past and Present*, 16, Nov. 1959. 10–30.

GREGG, J. A., *The Decian Persecution*, London, 1897.

GRÉGOIRE, H., 'Note sur l'édit de tolérance de l'empereur Gallien', *Byzantion*, x, 1935, 587–8.

GUIGNEBERT, CH., *Tertullien, Etude sur ses sentiments à l'égard de l'Empire et de la société civile*, Paris, 1901,

HARNACK, A., 'Greek and Christian Piety at the end of the Third Century', *Hibbert Journal*, Oct. 1911, 65–82.

HEALY, P. J., *The Valerian Persecution*, London, 1905.

HOMO, L., 'Essai sur le règne de l'empereur Aurélien' (= Fasc. 89 of the Bibliothèque des Ecoles françaises d'Athènes et de Rome), Paris, 1904.

KNIPFING, J. H., 'The *Libelli* of the Decian Persecution', *Harvard Theological Review*, 16, 1923, 345–90.

KOCH, H., *Cyprianische Untersuchungen*, Bonn, 1926.

LIEBERG, G., 'Die römische Religion bei Minucius Felix', *Rheinisches Museum*, 106, 1963, 62–79.

LIETZMANN, H., 'The Christian Church in the West' = ch. xv in *Cambridge Ancient History*, xii. (See H. Last's comments in *Amer. Journ. of Philosophy*, 61, 1940, 88ff.)

MIURA-STANGE, A., *Celsus und Origenes. Das Gemeinsame ihrer Weltanschauung* (Beiheft z. Zeitschrift f. N.T. Wissenschaft 4), Giessen, 1926.

NEUMANN, K. J., *Hippolytus von Rom in seiner Stellung zu Staat und Welt*, Leipzig, 1902.

OLMSTEAD, A. T., 'The Mid-3rd-century of the Christian Era', *Classical Philosophy*, 37, 1942, 241–62 and 398–420.

PLATNAUER, M., *The Life and Reign of Septimius Severus*, Oxford, 1918.

DE REGIBUS, L., *Problemi d'impero nella storia romana del iii secolo*, Turin, 1936.

REITZENSTEIN, R., 'Die Nachrichten über den Tod Cyprians', *Sitzber. der Heidelberger Akad. der Wissenschaften, Phil. Hist. Kl.*, 1913.

RICHMOND, I. A. and GILLAM, J. P., *The Temple of Mithras at Carrawburgh*, Newcastle on Tyne, 1951.

ROSTOVTZEFF, M., (ed.), *The Excavations at Dura-Europos, Conducted by*

Yale University and the French Academy of Inscriptions and Letters (Preliminary Reports of Season's work), Yale, 1929–38.

(See, in particular, H. F. Pearson's report of the excavation of the Jewish synagogue, *Report*, vi, 309, and G. Hopkins's description of the church, ibid., v, 238. Final Report on the Synagogue. Yale, 1956.

SALISBURY, F. S. and MATTINGLY, H., 'The Reign of Trajan Decius', *Journal of Roman Studies*, xiv, 1924, 1–23.

SCHMIDT, C., 'Plotinus Stellung zum Gnosticismus und kirchlichen Christentum', *T.U.*, N.F. v.4, 1900.

——'Die Urschrift der Pistis Sophia', *Zeitschr. f. N.T. Wissenschaft*, xxiv, 1925, 218–40.

SCHWARTE, K. H., 'Das angebliche Christengesetz des Septimius Severus', *Historia*, xii, 1963, 185–208.

ZEILLER, J., *Les Origines chrétiennes dans les provinces danubiennes de l'empire romain*, Paris, 1918.

8. THE GREAT PERSECUTION

ACHELIS, H., *Das Christentum in den ersten drei Jahrhunderten*, 2 vols., Leipzig, 1912 (especially vol. ii, 291–334 and notes).

ALLARD, P., *La Persécution de Dioclétien et le Triomphe de l'Eglise*, 2 vols., Paris, 1908.

AMORE, A., 'Il preteso "lapsus" di Papa Marcellin', *Antionianum*, 32, 1955, 411–26.

BABUT, E., L'adoration des empereurs et l'origine de la persécution de Dioclétien', *Rev. Historique*, 123, 1916, 222.

BARINI, I., 'La politica religiosa di Massimino Daia', *Historia*, iv, 1928, 716–30.

BAYNES, N. H., 'Two Notes on the Great Persecution', *Class. Quart.*, 18, 1924, 189.

BIHLMEYER, K., 'Das Toleranzedikt des Galerius von 311', *Theol. Quartalschrift*, xciv, 1912, 311–427 and 527–89.

CALDER, W. M., 'A Fourth Century Lycaonian Bishop', *Expositor*, 7th ser., vi, 1908, 385–408, and 'Studies in Early Christian Epigraphy', *Journal of Roman Studies*, x, 1920, 42–59.

——'Some Monuments of the Great Persecution', *Bull. of John Rylands Library*, viii, 1924, 345.

DELEHAYE, H., 'La persécution dans l'armée sous Dioclétien', *Acad. Royale de Belgique, Bull de la Classe des Lettres*, 1921, 150–66.

——'Les Martyrs d'Egypte', *Analecta Bollandiana*, xl, 1922, 5–154 and 299–364.

ENSSLIN, W., 'Zur Ostpolitik des Kaisers Diokletian', *Sitzber. der bayerischen Akad. der Wissenschaften*, 1942. 1.

FREND, W. H. C., 'Two Notes on the Great Persecution', *Studies in Church History*, ii, 1965.

GAIFFIER, B. DE, 'Palatins et Eunuques dans quelques documents hagiographiques', *Analecta Bollandiana*, lxxv, 1957, 17–46.

GELZER, M., 'Der Urheber der Christenverfolgung von 303', Festsch. f. Eberhard Vischer (*Vom Wesen und Wandel der Kirche*), Basel, 1935, 35–44.

GÖRRES, F., 'Die Religionspolitik des Kaisers Licinius', *Philologus*, lxxii, 1913.

GRÉGOIRE, H., 'Les chrétiens et l'oracle de Didymes', *Mélanges Holleaux*, Paris, 1913, 81–91.

——'Notes épigraphiques', *Byzantion*, viii, 1933, 49–88.

——'About Licinius' Fiscal and Religious Policy', ibid., xiii, 1938, 551–60.

——'Les Pierres qui crient', ibid., xiv, 1939, 317–21.

GSELL, S., 'Les Martyrs d'Ammaedara', *Bulletin archéologique du Comité des Travaux historiques*, 1934, 69–82.

GUINAGH, C. C., 'The *Vicennalia* in Lactantius', *Classical Journal*, xxviii, 1933, 449.

HARNACK, A., 'Porphyrius gegen die Christen, 15 Bücher, Zeugnisse, Fragmente und Referate', *Abhandlungen der Berliner Akad. der Wissenschaften*, 1916, 1–115.

HERTLING, L., 'Die Zahl der Christen zu Beginn des iv. Jahrhunderts', *Zeitschrift f. katholische Religion*, 58, 1934.

——'Die Zahl der Martyrer bis 313', *Gregorianum*, xxv, 1944, 103–29.

HULEN, A. B., 'Porphyry's Work against the Christians. An Interpretation', *Yale Studies in Religion*, i, 1933.

KNIPFING, J. R., 'The Edict of Galerius (311 A.D.) Reconsidered', *Revue belge de philologie et d'histoire*, i, 1922, 693–705.

LACY, O'LEARY DE, *Coptic Martyrs*, London (Church Historical Society), 1937.

LALLEMAND, J., 'Les préfets d'Egypte pendant la persécution de Dioclétien, *Mélanges H. Grégoire* (= *Annuaire de l'Institut oriental de l'Université de Bruxelles*, xi, 1951, 185–93).

LAWLOR, H. J., *Eusebiana*, Oxford, 1912.

LAWLOR, H. J., BAYNES, N. H. and RICHARDSON, G. W., 'The Chronology of Eusebius', *Class. Quart.*, 19, 1925, 94.

MASON, A. J., *The Persecution of Diocletian*, London, 1876.

MOMMSEN, TH., 'Die zweisprachige Inschrift aus Arykanda', *Gesammelte Schriften*, vi, 555–65.

MOREAU, J. (ed.), *Lactance de la Mort des Persécuteurs*, 2 vols. (Sources chrétiennes, 39).

NESSELHAUF, H., 'Das Toleranzedikt des Licinius', *Historische Jahr-buch*, 78, 1955, 44–61.

NESTLE, W., 'Legenden vom Tod der Gottesverächter', *Griechische Studien*, Stuttgart, 1948, 567.

O'MEARA, J., *Porphyry's Philosophy from Oracles in Augustine* (Etudes Augustiniennes, Paris, 1959).

ORGELS, P., 'La première vision de Constantin (310) et le temple d'Apollon à Nîmes', *Bull. de l'Acad. royale de Belgique*, xxiv, 1948, 176–208.

PALANQUE, J. R., 'A propos du prétendu édit de Milan', *Byzantion*, x, 1935, 607–14. (Reply by H. Grégoire, ibid., 616–19).

PINCHERLE, A., 'La politica ecclesiastica di Massenzio', *Studi italiani di filologia classica*, vi, 1928, 716. and vii, 1929, 131–43.

RAMSAY, W. M., '*The Tekmoreian Guest Friends, in Studies in the History and Art of the Eastern Roman Provinces*, London, 1906.

REHM, A., 'Kaiser Diocletian und das Heiligtum von Didyma', *Festgabe E. Schwartz* (= *Philologus*, 93, 1938, 74–84).

RÖTTGES, E. H., 'Marcellinus-Marcellus. Zur Papstgeschichte der diokletianischen Verfolgungszeit', *Zeitschr. f. kathol. Theologie*, 78, 1956, 385–420.

DE STE CROIX, G. E. M., 'Aspects of the "Great" Persecution', *Harvard Theol. Rev.*, 47, 1954, 75–113.

SCHMIDT, C., 'Fragmente einer Schrift des Märtyrerbischofs Petrus von Alexandrien', *Texte und Untersuchungen*, N.F. v, 1901.

——'Ein neues Originaldokument aus der diokletianischen Christenverfolgung', *Theolog. Literaturzeitung*, lv, 1930, 227.

SCHOENEBECK, H. VON, 'Beiträge zur Religionspolitik des Maxentius und Constantin', *Klio*, Beiheft xxx, 1939.

SCHWARTZ, E., 'Zur Geschichte des Athanasius', *Göttingen Nachrichten*, 1904, Heft 4 and 5; 1905, Heft 2 and 3; and 1911, Heft 4. (Very important for the understanding of the Meletian Schism.)

SEECK, O., 'Hierocles', art. *PW.*, viii, 1477.

——'Licinius', *PW.*, xiii.1, 222–31.

SESTON, WM., L'Edit de Diocletion coutre les Manichéens', *Mélanges A. Ernout*, Paris, 1940, 345–54.

——*Dioclétien et al Tétrarchie*, vol. i, Guerres et réformes, Paris, 1946. (Useful for the background of Diocletian's religious policy.)

——'L'amnistie des Vicnnalia de Dioclétien d'après P. Oxy. 2187', *Chronique d'Egypte*, 44, 1947, 250–64.

——'A propos de la Passio Marcelli centurionis', *Mélanges Goguel*, Neuchâtel, 1950, 240–6.

STADE, K., *Der Politiker Diokletian und die letzte grosse Christenverfolgung*, Dissertation, Frankfurt am Main, Wiesbaden, 1926.

TILLEMONT, LE NAIN DE, *Mémoires pour servir à l'histoire ecclésiastique des six premiers siècles*, Paris, 1690–1712.

9. DECLINE OF GRECO-ROMAN PAGANISM

AKINIAN P. N., 'Die Reinhenfolge der Bischofe Armeniens des 3. und 4. Jahrhunderts', *A.B.*, 67, 1949, 74–86.

ANDERSON, J. G. C., 'Paganism and Christianity in the Upper Tembris Valley', *Studies in the Eastern Roman Provinces*, London, 1906.

BIDEZ, J., *La Vie de Porphyre*, Ghent, 1913.

BOISSIER, G., *Fin du paganisme*, Paris, 1891.

CALDER, W. M., 'The Eumeneian Formula' in *Studies Presented to W. H. Buckler*, Manchester, 1926.

ELTESTER, W., 'Die Krisis der alten Welt und das Christentum', *Zeitschr. f. N.T. Wissenschaft*, xlii, 1949, 1–19.

FREND, W. H. C., 'The Revival of Berber Art', *Antiquity*, xv, 1942, 342–52.

GEFFCKEN, J., *Der Ausgang des griechisch-römischen Heidentums*, Heidelberg, 1920.

DE LABRIOLLE, P., *La réaction païenne*, Paris, 1934.

LEBRETON, J., L'Opposition païenne', = ch. viii in J. Lebreton and V. Martin (eds.) *L'Histoire de L'Eglise*, ii.

LIETZMANN, H., 'Das Problem der Spätantike', *Sitzungsber. der preussischen Akademie der Wiss.*, Phil. Hist. Kl. 1927.

MOMIGLIANO, A. (ed.), *The Conflict Between Paganism and Christianity in the Fourth Century*, Oxford, 1963. (Important essays on this theme.)

MULLER, H., *Christians and Pagans from Constantine to Augustine*, 2 vols., Pretoria, 1946–48.

SCHULTZE, V., *Geschichte des Untergangs des gr.-röm. Heidentums*, Jena, 1887.

SCHÜSSEL, O., *Das Ende des Platonismus im Altertum*, Fulda, 1929.

VAN SICKLE, C. E., 'Diocletian and the Decline of the Roman Municipalities', *Journal of Roman Studies*, xxviii, 1938, 9–18.

10. CONSTANTINE AND THE CHRISTIANS

ALFÖLDI, A., *The Conversion of Constantine and Pagan Rome* (Eng. tr. H. Mattingly, Oxford, 1948).

——'The Helmet of Constantine with the Christian Monogram', *JRS.*, xxii, 1932, 9.

BATIFFOL, P., *La Paix constantinienne et le Catholicisme*, Paris, 1914.

DÖRRIES, H., *Constantine and Religious Liberty* (Eng. tr. R. H. Bainton, Yale, 1960).

GRÉGOIRE, H., 'L'authenticité et l'historicité de la Vita Constantini attribuée à Eusèbe de Césarée', *Bull. de l'Académie royale de Belgique*, 39, 1953, 466–83.

——'La "conversion" de Constantin', *Revue de l'Université de Bruxelles*, 36, 1931.

——'La statue de Constantin et le signe de la Croix', *Antiquité classique*, I, 1932, 134–43.

LIETZMANN, H., 'Der Glaube Konstantins des Grossen', *Sitzungsber. der Akad. der Wissen. zu Berlin*, 29, 1937, 263–5.

——'Die Anfänge des Problems Kirche und Staat', ibid., xxxvii–xlvi.

KNIPFING, J. R., 'Religious Tolerance during the Early Part of the Reign of Constantine the Great, 306–313', *Catholic Historical Review*, N.S. iv, 1925, 483–503.

JONES, A. H. M., *Constantine and the Conversion of Europe*, London, 1948.

MAURICE, J., 'Les origines religieuses de Constantin le Grand', *Bull. d'ancienne littérature et d'archéologie chrétienne*, 1914, 37–45.

——'La politique religieuse de Constantin le Grand', *CRAI.*, 1919, 282–92.

PIGANIOL, A., *L'Empereur Constantin*, Paris, 1932.

SCHWARTZ, E., *Kaiser Konstantin und die christliche Kirche*, 2nd ed., Leipzig and Berlin, 1936.

SEECK, O., 'Das sogenannte Edikt von Mailand', *Zeitschrift für Kirchengeschichte*, xi, 1891.

II. CHRISTIANITY AS PROTEST IN THE FOURTH CENTURY

BRISSON, J. P., *Autonomisme et Christianisme dans L'Afrique romaine*, Paris, 1958.

BÜTTNER, TH. and WERNER, E., *Circumcellionen und Adamiten*, Berlin, 1959.

DIESNER, H. J., *Kirche und Staat im spätrömischen Reich*, Berlin, 1963. (Useful collection of studies on the Circumcellions in Africa.)

FREND, W. H. C., *The Donatist Church, a Movement of Protest in Roman North Africa*, Oxford, 1952.

——art. 'Donatismus', *Antike und Christentum*, iv, 121–48.

——'The Roman Empire in the Eyes of the Western Schismatics', *Miscellanea Historiae Ecclesiasticae* (= Bibliothèque de la Revue d'Histoire ecclésiastique, Fasc. 38, Louvain, 1961, 9–22).

HEUSSI, K., *Der Ursprung des Mönchtums*, Tübingen, 1936.

HOLL, K., 'Das Fortleben der Volkssprachen in Kleinasien in nach christlicher Zeit', *Hermes*, xliii, 1908, 240–54.

LADNER, G. B., *The Idea of Reform*, Cambridge, Mass., 1959.

LEIPOLDT, J., 'Schenute von Atripe', *Texte und Untersuchungen*, xxv, 1904.

MARTROYE, F., 'La repression du donatisme et la politique religieuse de Constantin et ses successeurs en Afrique', *Mémoires de la Soc. nationale des Antiquaires de France*, 1913.

MILNE, J. G., 'Egyptian Nationalism under Greco-Roman Rule', *JEA.*, 14, 1928, 226–34.

MOHLBERG, L. K., 'Historisch-kritische Bemerkungen zum Ursprung der sogenannten "Memoria Apostolorum" an der Appischen Strasse', *Texte und Arbeiten, Festschrift Alban Dold*, Beuron, 1952, 58.

VON SODEN, H., 'Urkunden zur Entstehungsgeschichte des Donatismus', *Kleine Texte*, Bonn, 1913.

WOODWARD, E. L., *Christianity and Nationalism in the Later Roman Empire*, London, 1916.

12. MARTYRDOM AND ASCETICISM

HARNACK, A., 'Die Askese, eine Skizze', *S.B.A.W.*, 1916.

HOLL, K., 'Die Bedeutung der neuveröffentlichten melitianischen Urkunden für die Kirchengeschichte', *Gesammelte Aufsätze*: Der Osten, Halbband ii, Tübingen, 1928, 283–97.

——'Über das griechische Mönchtum', ibid., 270–82.

KOCH, HAL, *Pronoia und Paideusis*, Berlin, 1932.

LABRIOLLE, P. DE, Chapter, 'Les Débuts du Monachisme' in A. Fliche and V. Martin's *Histoire de l'Eglise*, iii, Paris, 1949. (Contains excellent bibliography, pp. 299–301.)

LIETZMANN, H., Chapter, 'Das Mönchtum' (vol. iv, *Geschichte der alten Kirche*, Berlin, 1944).

LOWTHER CLARKE, W. K., *St. Basil the Great, a Study in Monasticism*, Cambridge, 1913.

MENDIETA, E. A. AMAND DE, 'La Virginité chez Eusèbe d'Emèse et l'ascétisme familial dans la première moitié du IVe Siècle', *Revue d'Histoire ecclésiastique*, l, 1955, 777–820.

RAMSAY, W. M., 'The Orthodox Church in the Byzantine Empire', *Expositor*, 1908, 289–305.

SCOTT-MONCRIEFF, P. D., *Paganism and Christianity in Egypt*, Cambridge, 1913.

SESTON, W., 'Remarques sur l'Influence d'Origène sur les origines du monarchisme', *Revue de l'Histoire des religions*, 108, 1933, 197–213.

VÖLKER, W., *Das Volkommenheitsideal des Origenes*, Tübingen, 1931.

——'Der wahre Gnostiker nach Clemens Alexandrinus', *T.U.*, 57.2, Leipzig, 1952.

WYTZES, J., 'Paideia and Pronoia in the Works of Clemens Alexandrinus', *Vigil. Christianae*, x, 1956, 148ff.

13. CHRISTIANS AND ROMAN LAW

AUGAR, F., 'Die Frau im römischen Christenprocess', *T.U.*, xxviii. 4, 1905.

BORLEFFS, J. W. P., 'Institutum Neronianum', *Vigil. Christ.*, vi, 1952, 129–45.

BOVINI, G., *La Proprietà ecclesiastica e la condizione giuridica della chiesa in età preconstantiniana*, Milan, 1940.

CALLEWAERT, C., 'Les premiers Chrétiens furent-ils persecutés par édits généraux ou par mesures de police?' *Revue d'histoire ecclés.*, ii, 1901, 771; iii, 1902, 5, 324 and 601. Also ibid. xii, 1911, 5 and 633.

——'Les premiers chrétiens et l'accusation de lèse-majesté', *Rev. des questions historiques*, lxxv, 1904.

CÉZARD, L. *Histoire juridique des persécutions contre les chrétiens de Néron à Septime-Sevère*, Paris, 1911.

CONRAT, M., *Die Christenverfolgungen im römischen Reiche vom Standpunkte des Juristen*, Leipzig, 1897.

CUQ, E., 'De la nature des crimes imputé aux chrétiens d'après Tacite', *Mélanges d'archéol. et d'histoire de l'Ecole française à Rome*, vi, 1886.

GUÉRIN, L., 'Etude sur le fondement juridique des persécutions dirigées contre les chrétiens pendant les deux premiers siècles de notre ère', *Nouv. Revue historique du droit français et étranger*, xix, 1895, 601 and 714.

HARNACK, A., 'Der Process des Christen Apollonius', *Sitzungsber. der kgl. preuss. Akad. der Wiss.*, 1893, 728.

HÜBNER, art. 'Collegia', *PW.*, iv.1, 396.

KRÜGER, G., *Die Rechtsstellung der vorkonstantinischen Kirchen*, Stuttgart, 1935.

KUEBLER, art. 'Maiestas', *PW.*, xiv, 542–59.

LE BLANT, E., 'Sur les bases des poursuites dirigés contre les chrétiens', *Mémoires de l'Académie des Inscriptions et Belles-Lettres*, 1886.

LECLERCQ, H., 'Droit persécuteur', art. in *Dict. arch, chrét. et de liturgie*, iv,2, 1921, 1565–1648. (Contains valuable bibliography of earlier works on the persecutions.)

MOMMSEN, TH., *Römisches Strafrecht*, Berlin, 1899, 760ff., especially 'Der Process des Christen Apollonius unter Commodus', *SBAW.*, 1894, 497–503.

PFAFF. art. 'Sacrilegium', *PW.*, zweite Reine, IA, 1678–81.

ROBERTIS, F. M. DE, *Il diritto associativo romano*, Bari, 1938.

SHERWIN-WHITE, A. N., 'Why were the Christians Persecuted?—An Amendment', *Past and Present*, 27, April 1964, 22–7 (and G. E. M. de Ste Croix's 'Why were the Early Christians Persecuted?—A Rejoinder', ibid. 28–33).

VISSCHER, F. DE 'Le régime juridique des plus anciens cimitières chrétiens de Rome', *A.B.*, lxix, 1951, 39.

WENGER, L., 'Erste Berührungen des Christentums mit dem römischen Rechte'. *S.T.*, 125, 1946 (Miscellanea, G. Mercati), 584–93.

WLOSOK, A., 'Die Rechtsgrundlagen der Christenverfolgungen der ersten zwei Jahrhunderten', *Gymnasium*, lxvi, 1959, 14–32.

ZEILLER, J., 'Nouvelles observations sur l'origine juridique des persécutions contre les chrétiens aux deux premiers siècles', *Rev. d'Hist. Eccles.*, 1952, 521–33.

——'Institutum neronianum', ibid., 1955, 393–400.

14. ACTA MARTYRUM

ACHELIS, H., 'Die Martyrologien. Ihre Geschichte und ihr Wert', *Abhandlungen der kön. Gesellschaft zu Göttingen*, Ph. Hist. Kl., N.F. iii, 1900 (Berlin, 1901).

BAXTER, J. H., 'The Martyrs of Madaura', *Journal Theological Studies*, xxvi, 1924, 21.

BERCHEM, D. VAN, 'Le Martyre de la légion thébaine. Essai sur al formation d'une légende', *Schweizerische Beiträge zur Altertumswissenschaft*, fasc. 8, Basel, 1956.

BURKITT, F. C., 'The Oldest MS of Justin's Martyrdom', *Journal of Theological Studies*, xi, 1910, 61–6.

CAMPENHAUSEN, H. VON, 'Bearbeitungen und Interpolationen des Polykarpmartyrimus', *Sitzungsber. der Heidelberger Akad. der Wissenschaften*, Ph. Hist. Kl., 1957, 3, Abh. 1–48.

CAVALIERI, FRANCHI DI, 'Acta Sancti Theodoti', *Studi e Testi*, vi, 1901.

——'Hagiographica', ibid., xix, 1908.

——'Nuove Note agiographiche', ibid., ix, 1902. (Editions of Acta of St. Crispina; Agape, Eirene and Chione, and the martyrs of the Massa Candida.)

——'Osservazioni sopra alcuni Atti di martiri da Settimio Severo a Massimo Daza,' *Nuovo Bull. di arch. crit.*, x, 1904, 5.

——'La Passio dei martiri Abitinensi', *Studi e Testi*, 65, 1935, 3–49.

——'S. Fabio vessilifero', ibid., 101–16.

——'Gli Atti di S. Fruttuoso di Tarragona', ibid., 129–99.

CORSARO, F., 'Note sugli Acta martyrum Scillitanorum', *Nouvo Didascaleion*, 1956, 5–51.

CUMONT, F., 'Le Tombeau de S. Darius de Durostorum', *A.B.*, xxvii, 1908, 369–73.

DELEHAYE, H., 'L'Hagiographie de Salone d'après des dernières découverts archéologiques', *Analecta Bollandiana*, xxiii, 1904, 1–10.

——art. 'Salone', *DACL*.

——'Martyr et Confesseur', *Analecta Bollandiana*, xxxix, 1921.

——'Les Actes de S. Marcel le Centurion', ibid., xli, 1923, 257–87.

——'La Passion de S. Felix de Thibiuca—Thibiuca', ibid., xxxix, 1921, 241–69.

——'Saints de Thrace et de Mésie', ibid., xxxi, 1912, 265–8.

——'Les Actes des Martyrs de Pergame', ibid., lviii, 1940, 142–76.

——'La Passion de S. Théodote d'Ancyre', ibid., xxii, 1903, 320–8.

——*Les Origines du Culte des Martyrs*, 2nd ed., Brussels, 1933.

——*Les légendes hagiographiques*, 3rd ed., Brussels, 1927.

——'Le Témoignage des martyrologes', *Anal. Bolland.*, xxvi, 1907, 78.

——'Contributions récentes à l'hagiographie de Rome et d'Afrique', ibid., liv, 265.

DUPRAZ, L., 'Les Passions de S. Maurice d'Agaune', *Studia Friburgensia*, N.S. 27, 1961.

EGLI, EMIL, *Martyrien und Martyrologien ältester Zeit* (Altchristliche Studien), Zürich, 1887.

GAIFFIER, B. DE, 'S. Marcel de Tanger ou de Léon?', *Analecta Bollandiana*, lxi, 1943, 116.

GRÉGOIRE, H., 'La Passion de Saint Théodote d'Ancyre, œuvre du pseudo-Nil, et son noyau montaniste', Festschrift J. Dölger = *Byzantinische Zeitschrift*, xliv, 1951, 165–84.

——'La véritable date du martyre de S. Polycarpe [23 février 177], et le Corpus Polycarpianum', *Analecta Bollandiana*, lxix, 1951, 1–38.

GRIFFE, E., 'A propos de la date du martyre de Saint Polycarpe', *Bulletin de littérature eccles. de Toulouse*, 1951, 170–7.

——'Les actes du martyr Apollonius', *Bulletin de littérature ecclésiastique*, 53, 1952, 65–76.

HALKIN, F., 'Une nouvelle passion des martyrs de Pergame', *Mullus* (Festschr. Th. Klauser), Münster, 1964, 150–4.

HARRIS, R. and ROBINSON, J. A. (eds.), 'Apology of Aristides', *Cambridge Texts and Studies*, 1, 1891.

HOLL, K., 'Die Vorstellung von Märtyrerakten', *Gesammelte Aufsätze*, Der Osten, Halbband 1, Leipzig, 1926.

KARPP, H., 'Die Zahl der scillitanischen Märtyrer', *Vigiliae Christianae*, xv, 1961, 165–72.

KLETTE, TH., 'Der Process und die Acta S. Apollonii', *Texte und Untersuchungen*, xv.2, 1897.

KNIPFING, J. R., 'The Date of the Acts of Phileas and Philoromus', *Harvard Theological Review*, 16, 1923, 189–203.

LEVISON, W., 'St. Alban and St. Albans', *Antiquity*, xv, 1942, 337.

MARROU, H. I., 'La Date du Martyre de S. Polycarpe', *Analecta Bollandiana*, lxxi, 19, 5–20.

MEYER, W., 'Die Legende des Albanus des Protomartyr Angliae in Texten vor Beda', *Abhandlungen der kgl. Gesellschaft der Wissenschaften zu Göttingen*, Ph. Hist. Kl., 1904, 1.

MONCEAUX, P., 'Les Actes de Ste. Crispine', *Mélanges G. Boissier*, 1903, 386.

QUASTEN, J., 'A Coptic Counterpart of a Vision in the Acts of Perpetua and Felicitas', *Byzantion*, 15, 1940/41, 1–9.

QUENTIN, H., 'Passio Sancti Dioscori', *Analecta Bollandiana*, xxiv, 1905, 321–42.

——*Les Martyrologes historiques du Moyen Age. Etude sur la formation du Martyrologe romain*, Paris, 1908.

——'La liste des martyrs de Lyon de l'an 177', *Analecta Bollandiana*, xxxix, 1921.

RAMSAY, W. M., 'The Date of St. Polycarp's Martyrdom', *Jahresheft des oesterr. arch. Instituts*, 27, 1932, 249.

REGIBUS, L. DE, 'Storia e diritto romano negli Acta Martyrum', *Didarkaleion*, N.S. iv, 1926, fasc. 2, 127.

ROBINSON, J. A., 'The Passio of St. Perpetua, with an Appendix on the Scillitan Martyrs', *Cambridge Texts and Studies*, 1, 1891.

STEVENS, C. E., 'Gildas Sapiens', *English Hist, Rev.*, lvi, 1941, 373.

STRAETEN, J. VAN DER, 'Actes des Martyrs d'Aurélien en Gaule', *Analecta Bollandiana*, lxxx, 1962, 117.

TELFER, W., 'The Date of the Martyrdom of Polycarp', *Journal of Theological Studies*, N.S. iii, 1952.

ZEILLER, J., 'Sur un passage de la Passion du Martyr Apollonius', *Recherches des Sciences religieuses*, xl, 1952, 153–7.

Index

Abel, 57, 82, 555
Abhgar IX, ruler of Osrhoene, 329
Abitina, 464, 500–1, 537
  sentence of martyrs, 502, 542
Abraham, 157, 250
  Apocalypse of, 86, 212
Achaeus, governor of Palestine, 442
Achilleus, Egyptian rebel, 459, 477, 487
Acilius Glabrio, 113, 214–15
Acta Martyrum,
  reliability of, xi–xii, 494–5, 528 (n. 131)
  Donatist, 554–5
  Eusebius' collection, 295 (n. 121), 315
Acta Saturnini, 45, 555
  other *Acta*, *see* names of individual martyrs
Actium, battle of, 116, 128
Acts of the Pagan Martyrs, 66, 211
Acts of Pilate, 505–6, 515
Ado, Martyrology of, 2, 24 (n. 39)
Adonai, 305, 307
Adoratio, 479, 485
Aelafius, Christian official, 543
Aelius Aristides, rhetorician of Smyrna, 256, 269, 275
Aelius Serenianus, *praeses* of Cappadocia, 333, 391
Aemilianus, emperor, 414
Aemilianus, prefect of Egypt, 424–5, 428, 441, 446
Aemilius Frontinus, proconsul of Asia, 314
Africa, prosperity of, 311
  origins of Church in, 361–2
  language of Church, 362
  expansion of Church, 330ff., 425, 454–5
  Decian persecution, 410ff.
  Valerian persecution, 424, 425–8
  Great Persecution, 495, 499–503
  'Fourth Edict' in, 503
  Donatism in, 553–6
  Paganism, 309–10, 451–2
  Jews in, 334, 373–4

Agabus, prophet, 291
Agape, 222
Agape and companions, martyrs of Thessalonica, 495, 499
Agapetus, martyr, 426
Agapius, martyr, 427
Agathonike, martyr, 198, 270
Age (to come), 46, 182
  end of, 79, 86, 156, 185
  'Golden Age', 310, 323, 337 (n. 66)
Agonistici, 363, 384 (n. 118), 462
Agricola, governor of Britain, 215
Agrippa, *see* Herod Agrippa
Ahura Mazda, 34
Akiba, rabbi, 56, 57, 179, 185, 226, 227
Alaric, 483
Alaxamenos, 252
Alban, martyr, 495, 527 (n. 126)
Alcibiades, martyr, 3, 17, 18
Alemanni, 335, 422
Alexander, martyr of Lyons, 9, 15
Alexander, martyr of Eumeneia, 287
Alexander, bishop of Jerusalem, confessor, 284, 398, 406, 413
Alexander the Great, 36–7, 114, 128, 286, 312
Alexander of Abonouteichos, 260
Alexander, Tiberius Claudius, 188
Alexander of Lycopolis, philosopher, 453
Alexander Severus, emperor (222–235), 117, 329, 333, 335, 339 (n. 88), 348, 390
  policy towards Christians, 329–30
Alexandria, 40, 50–1, 63, 66, 114, 119, 130, 133, 137, 181, 189, 223, 241, 458, 466
  anti-Semitism in, 36, 135, 143–6, 211
  Gnosticism in, 245–6, 351ff.
  Christian Platonism in, 251, 351ff.
  Catechetical School, 322, 351
  persecutions in, 322, 335, 403–4
  civil war in, 441–2, 446–7
  Aristotelianism in, 446
  see also Clement of Alexandria, Dionysius, and Origen

Lightning Source UK Ltd.
Milton Keynes UK
UKOW050748271212

204109UK00002B/21/P